*For all the cats, dogs, horses, ponies, and the rabbit
who enriched my life*

BRIEF CONTENTS

CONTENTS

An Introduction to Institutions, Management, & Investments

TENTH EDITION

HERBERT B. MAYO

The College of New Jersey

SOUTH-WESTERN
CENGAGE L

Australia • Brazil gdom • United States

077004

SOUTH-WESTERN
CENGAGE Learning™

An Introduction to
Institutions, Management,
& Investments, Tenth Edition
Herbert B. Mayo

Publisher/Editor-in-Chief: Joe Sabatino

Executive Editor: Mike Reynolds

Developmental Editor: Clara Goosman

Editorial Assistant: Adele Scholtz

Marketing Manager: Nathan Anderson

Senior Art Director: Michelle Kunkler

Senior Marketing Communications Manager:
Jim Overly

Senior Media Editor: Scott Fidler

Frontlist Buyer, Manufacturing: Amy Rogers

Production Manager: Jennifer Ziegler

Content Project Management:
PreMediaGlobal

Permissions Acquisition Manager/Photo:
Deanna Ettinger

Permissions Acquisition Manager/Text:
Deanna Ettinger

Cover Designer: Patti Hudepohl

Internal Designers: PreMediaGlobal

Cover Photo Credits:
B/W Image: Ryan McVay/Getty Images
Color Image: Shutterstock Images/Stasys
Eidieju

Compositor: PreMediaGlobal

Library of Congress Control Number: 2011924341

International Edition:

ISBN-13: 978-1-111-82064-0

ISBN-10: 1-111-82064-3

Cengage Learning International Offices

Asia
www.cengageasia.com
tel: (65) 6410 1200

Australia/New Zealand
www.cengage.com.au
tel: (61) 3 9685 4111

Brazil
www.cengage.com.br
tel: (55) 11 3665 9900

India
www.cengage.co.in
tel: (91) 11 4364 1111

Latin America
www.cengage.com.mx
tel: (52) 55 1500 6000

UK/Europe/Middle East/Africa
www.cengage.co.uk
tel: (44) 0 1264 332 424

**Represented in Canada by
Nelson Education, Ltd.**
tel: (416) 752 9100/(800) 668 0671
www.nelson.com

Cengage Learning is a leading provider of customized learning solutions with office locations around the globe, including Singapore, the United Kingdom, Australia, Mexico, Brazil, and Japan. Locate your local office at: **www.cengage.com/global**

For product information: **www.cengage.com/international**
Visit your local office: **www.cengage.com/global**
Visit our corporate website: **www.cengage.com**

Printed in Canada
1 2 3 4 5 6 7 15 14 13 12 11

Chapter 9   **Analysis of Financial Statements**   **168**

Chapter 13 Cost of Capital   260

Chapter 14 Capital Budgeting   288

Chapter 24   Preferred Stock   537

Chapter 25   Convertible Securities   548

"Finance" is a broad discipline. From an individual's perspective, finance encompasses financial institutions and investments. Virtually every day I have some contact with a financial institution. I write and receive checks, review my bank balance on-line, and use my credit cards. Other members of my family do the same. Your contact with financial institutions is probably just as frequent.

I make investment decisions that often meet a specific purpose, such as a stock purchase in my retirement account or my grandchildren's college fund accounts. I may sell a stock that I believe is overvalued or buy one that I think is undervalued. Many people periodically make investment decisions. They may not even be conscious of these decisions: Having funds withheld from your paycheck and invested in your employer's 401(k) retirement plan is an investment decision, even if you don't select the specific assets to include in the plan. And the same applies when you leave funds in a mutual fund or continue to hold a stock. Maintaining those positions are also investment decisions.

Business owners and managers make financial decisions, so the third facet of finance is often referred to as business finance or corporate finance. The employees of governments and nonprofit institutions also make similar financial decisions. Since expected future cash inflows and outflows affect current financial decisions, many tools used for making business decisions also apply to nonbusiness financial decisions.

Of course, financial institutions, investments, and business finance do not operate independently. Some courses in finance are called "Managerial Finance," while others have titles such as "Financial Management." You might infer from such names that Financial Management is the same as Managerial Finance, but such an inference is probably incorrect. The focus in managerial finance is business financial decision making. Financial management is generally broader and combines financial institutions, investments, and business finance, although the emphasis is usually on their application to business decision making.

This text introduces you to the three areas of the finance discipline. It provides you with breadth (but not depth) of knowledge of finance and is a foundation on which you may build. I realize that many students will take only one course in a specific discipline. Finance majors generally do not take additional courses in marketing; marketing majors may take only this one course in finance. Since you may have only this exposure to the areas of finance, this text gives you a working knowledge of the terms, environment, and mechanics of financial decision making.

Besides introducing you to the broad field of finance, *An Introduction to Institutions, Management, & Investments* also aims to encourage all students to do additional work in the field. I am, of course, biased, but survey courses and introductory texts do offer instructors excellent opportunities to encourage (do I dare say "lobby"?) students to do additional work in their areas. To do this additional work, you need basic background. By exposing you to all facets of finance, this textbook lays a foundation that will encourage and facilitate your taking additional courses in finance.

The Conceptual Change from the Previous Edition

The initial concept for *An Introduction to Institutions, Management, & Investments* was a book with many short chapters. The first edition had 27 chapters, and most were less than 20 pages. Each chapter was essentially a self-contained unit, with one important exception, the chapter on the time value of money. Many topics in finance require knowledge of compounding and discounting. Hence coverage of the time value of money is required for you to comprehend much of the material in subsequent chapters.

Over time I reduced the number of chapters and combined topics. For example, I combined preferred stock and long-term bonds. One result of consolidation was that chapters became much longer. If instructors did not want to cover all of the material in a particular chapter, they could pick their way through it. I have decided to return to the initial concept and separate the various topics into individual chapters or modules. With the exceptions of the time value of money and the analysis of financial statements, each chapter is relatively short and can be covered in a single class period. For chapters with a large number of problems, one class can be devoted to the explanations and the next class to the problems.

Possible Organizations for a Basic Finance Course

The book is divided into five parts: financial institutions, financial tools, corporate finance, investments, and derivatives. Few instructors will complete all the chapters. One advantage of short chapters is their adaptability to several approaches. If the course is meant to survey the field of finance, the instructor may select chapters throughout the text and place less emphasis on numerical problems. An alternative strategy is to approach finance through investments. Many students have an inherent interest in investments, especially since they can easily have their own on-line brokerage accounts. The course can be constructed to build upon this interest and expand topics into other areas of finance.

If the course emphasizes corporate finance, Part 3 is especially important, in conjunction with additional selected chapters (e.g., time value of money, risk measurement, initial public offerings, and the descriptions of stocks and bonds). The self-contained chapters should facilitate converting the book into a text that is readily used in a traditional corporate finance course.

Pedagogical Features

All textbooks feature a variety of pedagogical tools designed to improve learning. Anecdotal evidence suggests varying degrees of success. Definitions are placed in boldface in the margins. Over the years, several students have commented on the benefits of the marginal definitions. Time value illustrations permeate this text. Their solutions using a financial calculator are also placed in the margins. This approach avoids breaking the flow of the text material. Since different financial calculators use different formats, the marginal presentation is generic. It lists the known variables and their values, and identifies the unknown. The solution for the unknown is given separately.

In previous editions every chapter began with learning objectives. One day I walked into class and casually asked, "Who reads the learning objectives at the beginning of the chapter?" By the looks on their faces I could tell I needed to add, "I want an honest answer. Don't tell me Yes if you think that is what I want to hear." A couple of students said they did read the learning objectives. I then asked, "Who reads the questions at the end of the chapter?" One student said, "Only if you assign them!"

I should not have been surprised, because as an undergraduate, I would not have read them. In this text, I have placed the learning objectives at the end of each chapter, retitled them "review objectives," and identified where the material is covered in the chapter. The instructor may convert these review objectives into questions and use them in class to efficiently help students review the material.

Where appropriate, the chapters have numerical problems with which to review the material. These problems primarily replicate the text illustrations or present straightforward variations on the text examples. Selected answers are provided in Appendix F.

A new pedagogical feature in this edition is a section at the end of many chapters entitled "Additional Problems with Answers." These problems are similar to the other problems and illustrations in the chapters. However, unlike the selected answers to the chapters' problems provided in Appendix F, the "Additional Problems with Answers" provide the steps necessary to determine the solution. The expectation is that the individual student will work through each problem and then consult the answers. Such an approach should increase the student's ability to work through and solve the problems.

This edition also has a new feature entitled "Relationships." Relationships play an important role in finance. Changing one variable or factor often causes something else to change. For example, lower interest rates increase bond prices. Many of the chapters have a self-test in which the student is asked to determine how a change in one thing affects something else. There are three possible answers: increases, decreases, or has no impact (no change). Realizing that there may be no effect can be just as important as perceiving the direction of change! The answers to these fill-in-the blank relationships are provided at the end of the assignment.

Acknowledgments

A textbook author uses the input and assistance of many individuals. Over the years, I have received many thoughtful reviews and comments from individuals who sincerely offered suggestions. Unfortunately, suggestions may be contradictory. Since I cannot please all of the people all the time, I trust that those who offered advice that was not taken will not be offended.

At this point in the Preface, it is traditional for the author to thank members of the editorial and production staffs for their help in bringing the book to fruition. These individuals are geographically dispersed, and it never ceases to amaze me how this far-flung group somehow manages to pull the pieces together. For this edition, I would like to thank Mike Reynolds, executive editor, for his continued support over the years; Clara Goosman, developmental editor; Prashanth Kamavarapu, project manager; and Nate Anderson, marketing manager.

Anne Piotrowski created the PowerPoint slides. Her willingness to work through various styles and possible presentations greatly enhanced the final product.

I also must extend a huge thank-you to Suzanne Davidson and Margaret Trejo for copy editing and proofreading the text. Their attention to detail caught minute errors that I would never perceive. And, of course, special thanks must be extended to Margaret's two dogs, Ella and Simon, who always greeted me with licks and barks, even if I forgot to bring them a treat!

An Introduction to Basic Finance

"Princes come and princes go." This quote from the musical *Kismet* is exceptionally apropos of finance. Yesterday's success may be today's failure. Bear Stearns, WorldCom, and Enron were major success stories, but thanks to questionable accounting and even illegal acts, they reported huge losses and filed for bankruptcy. Today, eBay and Google are major success stories. Will they experience the same fate as WorldCom and Enron?

Finance studies money and its management. Like economics, it explores the allocation of resources. The process of resource allocation occurs over time. Firms invest in inventory, plant, and equipment, but the returns are earned in the future. An investor constructs a portfolio of assets, but the return is earned in the future. A commercial bank grants a loan in anticipation of earning interest and having the principal repaid. In each case the financial decision is made in the present but the return is in the future.

Because the future is unknown, finance studies the allocation of resources in a world of uncertainty. Of course, future events are anticipated, but they are not certain. Not every possible outcome that may affect returns can be anticipated. Unexpected events infuse financial decisions with uncertainty and the potential risk of loss. Investors, portfolio managers, and corporate financial managers may take actions to help manage risk, but risk still exists and is a major component in the study of finance.

The Divisions of Finance

Finance as a discipline is generally divided into three areas: financial institutions, investments, and business finance. The divisions are somewhat arbitrary, and they certainly overlap. Investment decisions and corporate financing decisions are made within the current financial environment and its institutions. And business finance is not independent of investments. For a firm to be able to issue and sell new securities, there must be individuals who are willing to invest in and buy the new securities.

The study of financial institutions, as the name implies, is concerned with the institutional aspects of the discipline, which encompass the creation of financial assets, the markets for trading securities (for example, the New York Stock Exchange), and the regulation of financial markets. Financial assets are created through investment bankers and financial intermediaries, such as commercial banks, savings and loan associations, and life insurance companies. Each of these financial firms transfers the savings of individuals to firms needing funds, and this transfer produces financial assets. Once these financial assets are created, many may subsequently be bought and sold in the secondary markets. These securities markets transfer billions of dollars of financial assets among investors ranging from individuals with small amounts to invest to large mutual funds and trust departments in commercial banks and insurance companies.

The study of investments is primarily concerned with the analysis of individual assets and the construction of well-diversified portfolios. It encompasses financial planning, specifying the investor's financial goals, analyzing various securities that the individual may acquire, and constructing diversified portfolios. Of course, investment decisions are not made in a vacuum, and the financial environment plays a role in the investment decision process. Certainly taxation, the monetary policy of the Federal Reserve, and the flow of information that publicly held firms are required to provide stockholders can and do affect the decision to buy or sell specific assets.

The study of corporate or business finance emphasizes the role of the financial manager. The financial manager must make certain that the firm can meet its obligations as they come due, determine which are the best sources of financing for the firm, and allocate the firm's resources among competing investment alternatives. The financial manager has a large and demanding job; in a large corporation, this job is performed by a staff that reports to the chief financial officer (CFO). Of course, the management of a small business must also make many of the same decisions, but these individuals have fewer resources to devote to financial management.

Financial managers and investors make similar decisions, although on a different scale. While the individual may have a few thousand dollars to invest, the corporate treasurer may have millions to allocate among competing assets. The financial manager may also make more decisions involving real assets (plant and equipment) than the individual investor, who is primarily concerned with financial assets. Both, however, are affected by the financial environment. The Federal Reserve's monetary policy, the federal government's fiscal policy, the legal requirements for the dissemination of information, and fiduciary responsibilities to creditors and stockholders affect financial decision making. Neither the firm's financial manager nor the individual investor can ignore the potential impact of the financial and legal environment.

While individual investors may work alone for their personal benefit, a firm's financial manager must work within the framework of the business. Marketing and managing decisions can have important implications for the firm's financial well-being. Virtually every business decision has a financial implication, and financial resources are often a major constraint on the firm's nonfinancial personnel. It is certainly desirable for individuals in marketing, human resources, information systems, and planning to understand the basic concepts of finance and the role of the financial manager. Such understanding may lead to better communication, the creation of better data for decision making, and better integration of the various components of the business.

Key Financial Concepts

Several crucial concepts appear throughout this text. The first is the sources of funds used by a firm. Firms can acquire assets only if someone puts up the funds. For every dollar the firm invests, someone must invest that dollar in the firm. The second concept centers around risk and return. Individuals and firms make investments to earn a return, but that return is not certain. All investments involve risk. The third concept is financial leverage, which is an important source of risk. The last concept is valuation, or what an asset is worth. Because the return earned by an investment occurs in the future, the anticipated cash flow to be generated by the asset must be expressed in the present. That is, the asset must be valued in today's dollars in order to determine whether to make the investment. Because the goal of financial management is often specified as the maximization of the value of the firm, the valuation of assets is probably the most crucial individual concept covered in this text.

Balance sheet

Financial statement that enumerates (as of a point in time) what an economic unit owns and owes and its net worth

Assets

Items or property owned by a firm, household, or government and valued in monetary terms

Liabilities

What an economic unit owes expressed in monetary terms

Equity

Owners' investment in a firm; a firm's book value or net worth

Sources of Finance

Finance is concerned with the management of assets, especially financial assets, and the sources of finance used to acquire the assets. These sources and the assets that a firm owns are often summarized in a financial statement called a balance sheet. (Notice that important terms are in boldface and the definitions appear in the margin to facilitate learning. The terms and their definitions that appear in this chapter illustrate the presentation. Each reappears in its proper place in the text.) A balance sheet enumerates at a moment in time what an economic unit, such as a firm, owns, its assets; what it owes, its liabilities; and the owners' contributions to the firm, the equity.

Other economic units, such as a household or a government, may also have a balance sheet that lists what is owned (assets) and what is owed (liabilities).

However, since there are no owners, the equity section may be given a different name. For example, the difference between the assets and the liabilities might be referred to as the individual's "net worth," or estate.

Although the construction of financial statements is explained more fully in Chapter 9, the following balance sheet provides an introduction.

Corporation X Balance Sheet as of December 31, 20XX			
Assets		Liabilities and Equity	
Total assets	$100	Liabilities	$ 40
		Equity	60
	$100		$100

Notice that the economic unit, Corporation X, has $100 in assets. It could not have acquired these assets unless someone (or some other firm) put up the funds. In this example, $40 was lent to the corporation, and the lenders have a legal claim. The equity ($60) represents the funds invested by the owners, who also have a claim on the corporation. The nature of the owners' claim, however, is different because the corporation does not owe them anything. Instead, the owners receive the benefits and bear the risks associated with controlling the corporation.

Both the creditors who have lent funds and the individuals who own the corporation are investors. Both groups are sources of the capital that will subsequently be invested in the corporation's assets. It is important to realize that creditors as well as owners are investors; the difference lies in the nature of their respective claims. The creditors have a legal claim that the borrower must meet; the owners do not have such a claim. The creditors and the owners, however, are both willing to make their respective investments in anticipation of earning a return, and both bear the risk associated with their investments.

A large part of this text is devoted to the sources of finance and their subsequent investment by the firm's financial managers. For example, Chapters 14 and 17 are devoted to the management of current and long-term assets, while Chapters 18, 20, 22, and 24 consider various sources of finance. It is important to understand the interdependence between the firm that uses the funds and the investors who supply the funds. Bonds, for example, are a major source of long-term funds for many corporations, but it should be remembered that investors buy the bonds that a corporation (or government) issues. The sale of the bonds is a source of finance to the corporation, while the purchase of the bonds is a use of investors' funds. The basic features of the bonds, however, are the same for both the issuer and the buyer.

Return

What is earned on an investment; the sum of income and capital gains generated by an investment

Risk and Return

All investments are made because the individual or management anticipates earning a return. Without the expectation of a return, an asset would not be acquired. While assets may generate this return in different ways, the sources of return are the income generated and/or price appreciation. For example, you may buy stock in anticipation of dividend income and/or capital gains (price appreciation). Another investor may place funds in a savings account because he or she expects to earn interest income. The financial manager of a firm may invest in equipment in anticipation that the equipment will generate cash flow and profits. A real estate investor may acquire land to develop it and sell the properties at an anticipated higher price. And the financial manager of a nonprofit institution may acquire short-term securities issued by the federal government in anticipation of the interest earned.

In each case, the investment is made in anticipation of a return in the future. However, the expected return may not be attained. That is the element of risk. Risk is the *uncertainty that an expected return may not be achieved.* All investments involve some element of risk. Even the funds deposited in a federally insured savings account are at risk if the rate of inflation exceeds the interest rate earned. In that case, the investor sustains a loss of purchasing power. The individual certainly would not have made that investment if such a loss had been anticipated; instead, an alternative course of action would have been selected.

Because financial decisions are made in the present but the results occur in the future, risk permeates financial decision making. The future is not certain; it is only expected. However, possible sources of risk can be identified, and, to some extent, risk can be managed. One way to manage risk is to construct a portfolio consisting of a variety of assets. When the portfolio is diversified, events that reduce the return on a particular asset may increase the return on another. For example, higher oil prices may benefit oil drilling operations but may hurt users of petroleum products. By combining both in the portfolio, the investor reduces the risk associated with investing in either the oil producer or the oil consumer.

Because risk is an integral part of financial decision making, it appears throughout this text. All investors and financial managers want to earn a return that is commensurate with the amount of risk taken. An investor may be able to achieve a modest return and bear virtually no risk. A federally insured savings account with a commercial bank that pays 2.5 percent is virtually risk free and will be referred to in subsequent chapters as risk-free investment. But to earn a higher return, the individual investor or the firm's management will have to accept additional risk.

Risk

Possibility of loss; the uncertainty that the anticipated return will not be achieved

Financial Leverage

One major source of risk that permeates financial decision making is the choice between equity and debt financing. You may acquire an asset by using your own funds or by borrowing them. The same choices are available to firms and governments. A corporation may retain earnings or sell new stock and use the funds to acquire assets. Or the firm may borrow the money. Governments use tax revenues and receipts to buy assets and provide services, but governments also may borrow funds. In each case, the borrower is using financial leverage. Financial leverage occurs when you borrow funds in return for agreeing to

Financial leverage

Use of borrowed funds in return for agreeing to pay a fixed return; use of debt financing pay fixed payments such as interest and repay the principal after a period of time. If you can earn a higher return than you have agreed to pay, the difference accrues to you, the borrower, and magnifies the return on your investment. Notice, however, that if you earn a lower return, you have to make up the difference, which magnifies your loss. You cannot have it both ways. To increase the potential return, you also increase the potential loss. This trade-off between magnifying returns versus magnifying potential losses occurs frequently in the chapters that follow.

Valuation

Assets are acquired in the present, but their returns accrue in the future. No individual or firm would purchase an asset unless there was an expected return to compensate for the risk. Since the return is earned in the uncertain future, there has to be a way to express the future in terms of the present. The process of determining what an asset is currently worth is called valuation. An asset's value is the present value of the future benefits. For example, the current value of a federal government bond is the sum of the present value of the expected interest payments and the expected repayment of the principal. The current value of equipment is the present value of the expected cash flows it will generate.

Valuation

Process of determining what an asset is currently worth

The determination of present value is one of the most important topics developed in this text. It requires estimates of future cash flows and measurements of what the funds invested in the asset could earn in alternative, competitive investments. The mechanics of determining present value (as well as determining future value) are covered in Chapter 7. Understanding this material is crucial to understanding much of the material covered in this text.

A firm is a combination of many assets and, therefore, its value must be related to the value of the assets it owns. The value of these assets, in turn, depends on the returns they will generate in the future. In finance, the goal of the financial manager is to *maximize the value of the firm*. Schering-Plough even titled one of its annual reports "Maximizing Shareholder Value." All financial decisions are judged by their impact on the value of the firm. Did the decision increase or reduce the present value of the firm?

This value may be readily measured if the firm has shares of ownership (stock) held by the general public. The market price of the stock is indicative of the value of the company. Because the value of the firm is the sum of the value of its shares, the market value of a share of stock times the number of shares gives the value of the company. For example, as of 2010, Capital One Financial had 456,530,000 shares outstanding. At a price of $44 a share, that made the value of the firm's equity $20,087,000,000.

Although security prices are subject to fluctuations, firms that have consistently grown and prospered have seen the price of the stock, and hence the value of the company, increase. In 1996, the value of Capital One Financial was $2,319,600,000; the value of Capital One thus rose $18 billion from 1996 to 2010. This suggests that management made decisions that increased the value of the company. Over time, the price of a company's stock is indicative of management performance.

Smaller firms or firms whose stock is not owned by the general public—by far the largest number of firms in existence—do not have market prices for their stock. Hence, owners and managers may not be able to ascertain the value of the firm. In these cases, the value is determined only when the firm is liquidated or sold (at that time, the value of the firm is the liquidation value or sale price). Since such liquidation or sale generally occurs only once, the owners and managers do not know the true value of the firm. They may use the value of the firm's equity as shown on the accounting statements as some indication of the firm's worth, but management cannot be certain of the firm's true value.

Finance and Other Business Disciplines

Although finance is a separate academic discipline, its roots are in accounting and economics. Several years ago, the first finance courses tended to emphasize the analysis of financial statements and legal topics, such as the order of legal claims. Although this emphasis has diminished, accounting principles and financial statements continue to be a major source of information, and the analysis of financial statements is an integral component in the value approach to the selection of securities.

With the development of theories of portfolio behavior and asset valuation, economics began to play a more important role in finance. Theories based on economic principles encompassing corporate financial structure, the importance (or unimportance) of dividends, and option valuation became the backbone of finance and, in many cases, supplanted accounting's role. The development of empirical tools further augmented financial analysis, as statistics became a means to verify economic theory as it applies to finance. The ability to test economic and financial hypotheses further enriched the field of finance.

Although finance uses economic theory and accounting principles and financial statements, it has developed its own body of material. Finance courses, however, are generally offered as part of a program in business. Other academic disciplines within business may include information systems, human resource management, and marketing as well as accounting and economics. Finance, however, differs from these areas in one exceedingly important way. It can be studied from two perspectives: that of the users or that of the suppliers of funds.

This ability to approach finance from more than one perspective is important. Consider human resource management or marketing. In both of these disciplines (and in accounting or information systems or strategic planning), the emphasis is on the business. The individual area may have many subdivisions, but the emphasis is how each division fits into the business and its operations. The emphasis is not from an individual's perspective.

Finance may also be studied from a business perspective, which is exactly what occurs in corporate finance or financial management courses. Finance, however, may be studied from the investor's perspective. While corporate finance emphasizes raising funds and their subsequent allocation, investments emphasizes the construction of diversified portfolios and the allocation of wealth among competing securities. Of course, these two perspectives are often opposite sides of the same coin. The firm issues securities (for example, bonds or stock) to raise funds. Investors buy these securities to earn a return and diversify their portfolios. In either case, it is the same security.

The tools of analysis used in corporate finance and investments are also the same. A firm's financial statements are employed by both management and investors to analyze the firm's financial condition. Methods used to value and evaluate an investment in plant and equipment are conceptually the same as those used to value stocks and bonds. The calculations of returns on investments in stocks and bonds are the same as the calculations used to determine the returns on investments in plant, equipment, and other real (tangible) assets. The tax and legal environments and the financial institutions in which securities are initially sold and subsequently traded apply both to businesses and to individuals.

Although finance can have more than one perspective, the material as presented in an introductory finance course often emphasizes one side. Many traditional introductory finance courses stress corporate finance or financial management with a corporate emphasis. This approach makes the course more consistent with other classes taught in a business program. It also facilitates tying together marketing, human resource management, information management, and the various other areas of a business education.

Plan of the Text

This text is a basic introduction to the three areas of finance: financial institutions, investments, and business finance. Part 1 is devoted to financial institutions and the process by which savings are transferred into investments. Chapter 1 introduces this process and Chapter 2 covers financial markets and intermediaries. Chapter 3 considers the direct transfer, that is, the creation and initial sale of securities to the general public through investment bankers. The next chapter (Chapter 4) covers the subsequent trading in stocks and bonds in the securities markets. Chapters 5 and 6 add the impact of the Federal Reserve on the money supply and credit markets (Chapter 5), and international flows of funds (Chapter 6).

Part 2 is devoted to three important tools used in investment decision making and corporate finance. Most financial decisions involve time. An investment is made in the present but the return is earned in the future. Standardizing for time is achieved by expressing the present in terms of the future or the future in terms of the present. Every student using this text needs to read carefully and understand the material in Chapter 7, "The Time Value of Money." If you do not comprehend the time value of money, much of the remaining text will have little meaning.

All investments involve risk. Chapter 8 examines the sources of risk, the measurement of risk, and the importance of diversification. As with the time value of money, the measurement of risk and risk management are difficult topics. While Chapter 8 is primarily descriptive, it does cover statistical measures of risk. Even if your background in statistics is weak, simple illustrations are provided so that you should be able to grasp the concepts. The last chapter in Part 2 covers the analysis of financial statements. Chapter 9 is a long chapter because it reviews financial statements and then illustrates the calculation of various ratios used to analyze financial statements. If you already know the analysis of financial statements, you may move forward to Part 4.

Part 3 is devoted to business finance with emphasis on corporate finance. Chapter 10 reviews the forms of business and corporate taxation, and Chapter 11 describes two simple techniques used to make investment decisions: breakeven analysis and the payback period. Chapter 12 explains leverage as it applies to business: the leverage associated with the nature of the firm's operations and the leverage associated with management's financing decisions. Financing decisions raise the question of the firm's optimal combination of debt and equity financing or optimal capital structure (Chapter 13). The cost of capital associated with the optimal capital structure is then used in Chapter 14 on capital budgeting, which is the process of selecting long-term investments in plant and equipment. Chapters 13 and 14 (the determination of a firm's optimal capital structure and its use in capital budgeting) are among the most important in this text.

Chapters 15 and 16 consider forecasting techniques. Chapter 15 is devoted to the percent of sales and the use of regression analysis to forecast a firm's need for funding, and Chapter 16 covers the cash budget, which helps determine when the firm will need external finance. Chapters 17 and 18 treat the firm's working capital and the management of its current assets and current liabilities. The last chapter (Chapter 19) of Part 3 adds intermediate-term debt financing and leasing to the financial manager's choices of external funding.

Part 4 is devoted to specific financial assets. Chapters 20 and 21 cover common stock. The first is descriptive and the second applies valuation techniques. This order is repeated in Chapters 22 and 23, which are devoted to bonds and their valuation. Chapters 24 and 25 explain preferred stock and convertible bonds, which are hybrid securities that include features of equity and debt. Chapter 26 illustrates the calculation of returns and provides historical returns that have been earned on various securities. After completing Chapters 20 through 26, you may decide to delegate investment decisions to someone else. Chapter 27 covers the variety of investment companies that relieve you of having to select specific securities. However, it remains your responsibility to select specific investment companies.

The text ends (Part 5) with an introduction to derivatives: options to buy and sell securities (Chapter 28) followed by swap agreements and futures contracts for the future delivery of commodities and financial assets (Chapter 29). Derivatives are used to speculate on anticipated price changes or to hedge to reduce the risk of loss from fluctuations in prices and interest rates. You may find derivatives the most interesting and exciting topic covered in this introduction to basic finance. They are, however, complex, so these two chapters can only scratch the surface, but they can lay a foundation on which you may build. If you continue to study finance, you will quickly realize that the use of derivatives permeates finance.

Relationships

Relationships play an important role in finance. For example, a change in interest rates affects bond prices or a change in risk affects the required return on an investment.

It is important for you to perceive these relationships. To help you test your understanding, many of the chapters have a self-test called "Relationships." In each case, one thing is changed, and you are asked to determine the impact on something else. For example, "With the passage of time life expectancy _____." There are three possible answers: increases, decreases, or no change (no impact). In this example, the answer is "decreases." Another illustration is "If a firm collects its accounts receivable, total assets _____." In this illustration, the answer is "are not affected (no change)."

There are, however, situations in which an answer cannot be determined. An increase (or decrease) in sales may increase, decrease, or not affect earnings. To determine the impact on earnings, you need to know the impact on BOTH revenues and costs. Just as it is important to perceive changes, it is also important to realize that there may be NO change or that the impact cannot be determined.

The possible answers to "relationship" self-tests will be increase (or increases depending on the word usage), decrease (decreases), or no change (have no impact). Care has been taken to avoid situations in which an answer cannot be determined. The answers to each of these fill-in-the-blanks is provided at the end of the assignment.

Financial Institutions

My bank has assets in excess of $10 billion. My checking account may have $1,000 in it. I account for about 0.00001 percent of my bank's sources of funds. Just think how many depositors my bank must have in order to generate the money it has lent.

I own 500 shares of VF Corporation. At $70 a share, that is $35,000. Although $35,000 is sufficient to buy any of a number of consumer goods, it is a very small fraction of the total value of all VF Corporation shares. The firm has 110,100,000 shares outstanding for a total value of $7,707,000,000. My holdings are obviously a minute portion of the total.

Recently my family vacationed in Canada. We spent over $3,000 outside the United States, which added to the nation's deficit in its merchandise balance of trade. The amount we spent was small, however, when compared to the federal government's foreign aid programs or military spending abroad, which also contributed to the deficit in the balance of trade.

Hardly a day goes by that I do not have contact with a financial institution. The same is true for most individuals. They write and receive checks, make deposits and withdrawals from depository institutions, buy and sell shares of stock in corporations and mutual funds, make contributions to pension plans, pay taxes, buy imported goods, and borrow funds from a variety of sources. Each of these acts involves contact with a financial institution.

The first part of this text discusses the financial environment and institutions with which we have so much contact. Some of these financial institutions facilitate the transfer of funds from lenders to borrowers (such as commercial banks), while others facilitate the exchange of securities from sellers to buyers (for example, the stock exchanges). Other financial institutions affect the level of income and the stability of consumer prices (such as the Federal Reserve), and yet another financial institution, the market for foreign currency, makes possible the exchange of foreign goods and services. The participants in these markets for financial products and services range from the large corporate giants and the federal government to the small corner store and the individual saver. Everyone reading this text is touched by these financial institutions, and increasing your knowledge of them by learning the material in Part 1 can help you to better function in today's financial environment.

The Role of Financial Markets and Financial Intermediaries

I n *Hamlet*, Polonius gave Laertes the advice to "neither a borrower nor a lender be." Participants in financial markets and financial intermediaries violate both parts of that advice. Financial intermediaries borrow from one group and lend to another, a process that channels resources into productive investments. Consider how firms would be constrained if they could not borrow funds to purchase plant and equipment or how individuals would be prevented from purchasing homes by borrowing funds through mortgage loans. This transfer of savings through financial intermediaries—from individuals with funds to firms, governments, and other individuals who need funds—is one crucial component of the financial system.

Financial markets perform two exceedingly important functions. Like financial intermediaries, financial markets facilitate the transfer of funds from savers to firms, governments, and individuals who use the funds. Financial markets, however, also facilitate the transfer of existing securities from sellers to buyers. You and I are willing to make investments because we know these investments may be subsequently sold through the financial markets.

This chapter sets the framework for the remaining chapters in this text. It begins with the roles of money and interest rates. This is followed by transfer of savings to investments and the purpose of financial intermediaries through which these savings are channeled to the ultimate users of the funds. (The process of transferring funds through investment banking and the "secondary" markets in existing securities is covered in the next two chapters.) In terms of the amount of outstanding loans, commercial banks are the most important financial intermediary. Commercial banks, however, must compete with other intermediaries such as thrift institutions, life insurance companies, and money market mutual funds for the funds of savers. Attracting these savings is obviously important, since the individual intermediary can only lend what savers have lent it.

The bulk of this chapter provides a basic introduction to financial intermediaries. Emphasis is placed on commercial banks, their sources of funds, the types of loans they make, and regulation of the banking system. The subsequent sections consider life insurance companies and pension plans. And the chapter ends with money market mutual funds and money market instruments. Money market mutual funds offer individuals an alternative to the checking accounts, savings accounts, and savings certificates issued by banks and thrift institutions.

By acquiring shares in money market mutual funds, individuals are able to invest indirectly in a variety of short-term securities. Since these securities are usually issued in large denominations, most investors have insufficient funds to purchase them. By selling shares in small units, money market mutual funds permit individuals to participate in the market for money market securities. Since money market mutual funds tend to offer marginally higher yields than traditional savings accounts, shares in these funds have become a major competitor with other financial intermediaries for individuals' savings.

The Role of Money

Money

Anything that is generally accepted as a means of payment

Money is anything that is generally accepted in payment for goods and services or for the retirement of debt. This definition has several important words, especially *anything* and *generally accepted*. Anything may perform the role of money, and many different items, including shells, stones, and metals, have served as money. During the history of this country, a variety of coins and paper moneys have been used. The other important words are *generally accepted*. What serves as money in one place may not be money elsewhere. This fact is readily understood by anyone who travels abroad and must convert one currency to another. The paper that serves as money in Great Britain, called pounds, is not used as money in Paris, where European euros are used. A British traveler must convert pounds into euros to buy goods in Paris.

Money may also be used to transfer purchasing power to the future. In this second role, money acts as a store of value from one time period to another. Money, however, is only one of many assets that may be used as a store of value. Stocks, bonds, savings accounts, savings bonds, real estate, gold, and collectibles are some of the various assets that you may use to store value.

Liquidity

Ease of converting an asset into cash without loss; the depth of a financial market

While you may store value in these nonmonetary assets, you cannot buy goods and services with them. To do that, you must convert the assets into money. The ease with which an asset may be converted into money is its liquidity.

Unfortunately, the word *liquidity* is ambiguous. In some contexts it means ease of converting an asset into cash without loss. A savings account with a commercial bank is liquid, but shares of IBM would not be liquid, since you could sustain a loss. In other contexts, liquidity means ability to sell an asset without affecting its price. In that context, liquidity refers to the depth of the market for the asset. You may be able to buy or sell thousands of shares of IBM stock without affecting its price, in which case the stock is liquid. The context in which the word is used often indicates the specific meaning.

The power to create money is given by the Constitution to the federal government. Congress established a central bank, the Federal Reserve System, and gave it power to control the supply of money and to oversee the commercial banking system. Initially it was not the intent of Congress to create a central bank, for the Federal Reserve Act of 1913 established 12 district banks. The Federal Reserve was reorganized by the Banking Acts of 1933 and 1935 to become the central bank known today. Although the Federal Reserve has control over the supply of money, most of the money supply is produced through the creation of loans by the banking system. (The Federal Reserve and the process of loan creation are explained in Chapter 5.)

Measures of the Supply of Money

Money supply

Total amount of money in circulation

M-1

Sum of coins, currency, and demand deposits

M-2

Sum of coins, currency, demand deposits, savings accounts, and small certificates of deposit

There are several measures of the composition of the money supply. The traditional measure (commonly referred to as M-1) is the sum of coins and currency in circulation outside of banks plus demand deposits (including interest-bearing checking accounts and travelers' checks) held by the general public in all depository institutions. A broader definition of the supply of money (commonly referred to as M-2) includes not only demand deposits, coins, and currency but also regular savings accounts and small certificates of deposit (less than $100,000). The actual amount of money outstanding depends on which definition is used. As of January 2010, the Federal Reserve reported that M-1 and M-2 were:

	M-1	M-2
Coin and currency	$ 861.2	$ 861.2
Demand deposits	438.1	438.1
Other checkable deposits (e.g., NOW accounts)*	376.4	376.4
Travelers' checks	5.1	5.1
Savings accounts and time deposits	–	4,855.9
	$1,680.8	$6,536.7

*NOW stands for "negotiable order of withdrawal."

Source: Summary monetary statistics are available in the Federal Reserve Bulletin. Detailed data is available at the Federal Reserve's Web site **http://www.federalreserve.gov**.

As may be seen in the preceding data, savings accounts constitute about 74 percent of the money supply when the broader definition (M-2) is used. This broader definition of the money supply is preferred by those economists and financial analysts who stress the ease with which individuals may transfer funds among the components of M-2. Individuals may transfer funds from a savings account or time deposit into a checking account. Such a movement increases M-1, because demand deposits have risen, but the transaction has no impact on M-2, because the increase in demand deposits is offset by the decline in the other account.

In summary, money is crucial to an advanced economy, for it facilitates the transfer of goods and resources. An advanced economy could not exist without something to perform the role of money. Since a large proportion of the money supply consists of deposits in various depository institutions, the student of finance should understand financial markets, the banking system, and their regulation.

The Role of Interest Rates

The words *money* and *interest* are often used together, but their meanings differ and they perform different roles. Money is a medium of exchange; its value is related to what it will purchase. Interest is the cost of credit; it is the price paid for the use of someone else's money.

The cost of credit is often expressed as a percentage, that is, the *rate* of interest. Interest rates help allocate scarce credit among competing uses for the funds. Higher interest rates increase the cost of credit and should discourage borrowing, so that the scarce credit is directed toward its best usage.

As is discussed throughout this text, there are many types of loans (such as mortgage loans, trade credit, and bonds). In addition to many debt instruments, there are also many interest rates that reflect the amount borrowed, the length of time the borrower will have the use of the funds, and the creditworthiness of the borrower. Generally, the longer the term of the debt and the riskier (or less creditworthy) the debt instrument, the higher will be the rate of interest.

Debt, and hence interest rates, is often classified as short or long term. The time period is arbitrarily established at one year. *Short-term* refers to a year or less. *Long-term* refers to greater than a year. (Debt that matures in one to ten years is sometimes referred to as intermediate term.) Of course, with the passage of time, long-term debt instruments become short-term when they mature within a year.

Financial markets have an analogous classification. The "money market" refers to the market for low-risk, large-denomination debt instruments that mature within a year. The "capital market" refers to securities with a longer-term horizon. In the case of a bond or mortgage loan, the term may be 10, 20, or more years. In some cases, such as common stock, the time dimension is indefinite. A corporation may exist for centuries. Many of the nation's banks, such as Citicorp, were started in the 1700s or early 1800s. Industrial firms such as AT&T, Coca-Cola, and ExxonMobil commenced operations in the 1800s.

Term structure of interest rates

Relationship between yields and the time to maturity for debt with a given level of risk

Yield curve

Graph relating interest rates and the term to maturity

The Term Structure of Interest Rates

The relationship between interest rates (the cost of credit) and the length of time to maturity (the term) for debt in a given risk class is referred to as the term structure of interest rates. This structure is illustrated by a yield curve, which relates the yield on debt instruments with different terms to maturity. Such a yield curve is illustrated in Figure 2.1, which plots the yield on various U.S. government securities as of June 2005. This figure shows that the bonds with the longest term to maturity have the highest interest rates. For example, short-term securities with three months to maturity had yields of 2.99 percent, five-year bonds paid 3.63 percent, and bonds that matured after 20 years paid 4.31 percent.

Although the positive relationship between time and interest rates illustrated in Figure 2.1 does usually exist, there have been periods when the opposite occurred. During 1981, short-term rates exceeded long-term rates; the yield curve became inverted and had a negative slope. This is illustrated in Figure 2.2. Securities maturing in less than a year had yields exceeding 14 percent, while long-term debt that matured after ten years yielded 13 percent.

Such a yield curve can be explained by inflation and the action of the Federal Reserve to curb rising prices. As is explained in Chapter 5, the Federal Reserve fights inflation by selling short-term federal government debt securities. Such sales absorb credit by reducing the supply of money and the capacity of banks to lend because paying the Federal Reserve for the securities pulls money out of the banking system.

The sales depress securities prices and increase their yields. While the yields on all debt instruments respond to changes in the supply of credit, the Federal Reserve's selling of short-term securities has the most impact on short-term rates.

FIGURE 2.1
Positively Sloped Yield Curve (June 1, 2005)

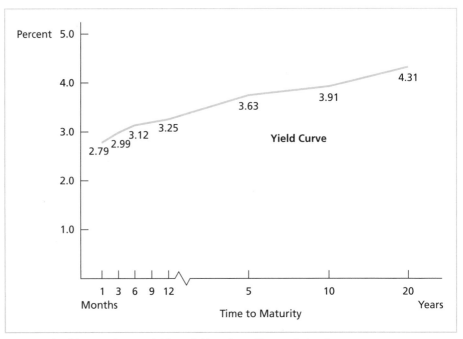

Source: Federal Reserve data on yields available at **http://www.federalreserve.gov**.

F I G U R E 2.2
Yield Curves (Yields on
Federal Government
Securities)

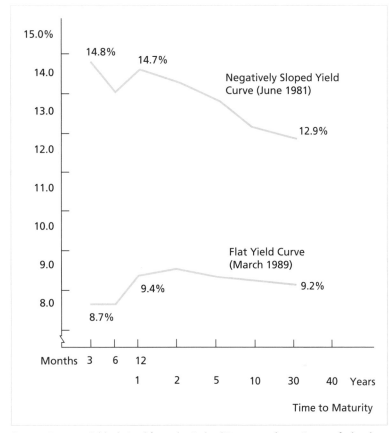

Source: Data on yields derived from the Federal Reserve at **http://www.federalreserve.gov**.

In the illustration in Figure 2.2, short-term yields rose above long-term rates, resulting in an "inverted" yield curve. When the rate of inflation abated, the yield curve returned to the positive slope that it has maintained during most periods.

There have also been periods when the yield curve was relatively flat. Such a structure is also illustrated in Figure 2.2 by the yield curve for March 1989. The yield on short-term debt with three to six months to maturity was approximately 8.7 percent, and the rate on 30-year bonds was 9.2 percent. While the long-term rate did exceed the short-term rate, the small difference produced a gently rising, almost flat, yield curve.

Financial Markets and the Transfer of Savings

After working and earning income, my Auntie Bea's advice was to "spend a little, give a little, and save a little." Each year I take that advice. After I decide not to spend and to save, I have to make an additional decision: what to do with my savings. Should I put the funds in a bank or buy stock or shares in a mutual fund? I'm not going to let the funds sit idle. I want to put them to productive use to earn a return.

This process is not limited to individuals. Firms also have savings. Earnings that are not distributed and retained are saved, and management will have to decide what to do with the savings. Perhaps the funds will be used for investments in plant and equipment and other productive assets. Management could also invest the funds in financial assets for short periods of time prior to the acquisition of assets such as plant and equipment. The financial managers of governments go through the same thought process. The government collects tax revenues but does not necessarily spend the funds immediately. The funds may be placed in short-term investments to earn a return. The same principles apply to nonprofit organizations such as charitable foundations. In each case, the current savings are invested to earn a return.

When I spend my income, the funds are returned to the economy, and presumably they are returned when I give to charities. Savings are not spent; they represent a command over resources that I am not using. How are these funds returned to the economy? The answer revolves around the role of financial markets. Financial markets are the mechanism to transfer these savings to productive uses. The process of transferring savings into investments is a primary, perhaps the most important, function of the financial system. The process of transferring savings into investments leads to the creation of financial claims such as stock and debt instruments such as bonds. These securities are issued to tap the various sources of savings.

Two basic methods exist for transferring funds from savers to users. First is the direct investment. This transfer occurs when you start your own business and invest your savings in the operation. A direct transfer also occurs when securities are initially sold to investors in the "primary" market. Firms and governments issue securities, which may be sold directly to the general public through investment bankers. (The process of issuing and selling securities through investment bankers is covered in the next chapter.)

Once the securities are created, they may be subsequently bought and sold ("traded"). A second important purpose of financial markets is the creation of markets in *existing* securities. These "secondary" markets, however, do not transfer funds to the users of funds; they transfer ownership of securities among various investors. Sellers trade their securities for cash, and buyers trade cash for the securities. (Secondary markets are not limited to financial assets. The markets for land or antiques are secondary markets. No new assets are created; there is only the transfer of ownership of an existing asset.) Trading in existing securities through secondary markets such as the New York Stock Exchange receives substantial coverage in the financial press and is covered in Chapter 4.

The Indirect Transfer Through Financial Intermediaries

When new securities are issued, funds are directly transferred from savers to firms. While the ultimate effect is the same, the transfer through financial intermediaries is less direct. The funds are initially lent to the intermediary, and the intermediary subsequently lends the funds to the ultimate users. To obtain the funds, the financial intermediaries create *claims on themselves*. This creation of claims is an important distinction. An investment banker facilitates an initial sale; securities brokers and secondary markets facilitate subsequent sales. Investment bankers, brokers, and securities exchanges do not create claims on themselves. They are not financial intermediaries but rather function as middlemen who facilitate the buying and selling of new and existing securities.

When a saver deposits funds in a financial intermediary such as a bank, that individual receives a claim on the bank (the account) and not on the firm (or individual or government) to whom the bank lends the funds. If the saver had lent the funds directly to the ultimate users and they failed, the saver would sustain a loss. This loss may not occur if the saver lends the money to a financial intermediary. If a financial intermediary makes a bad loan, the saver does not sustain the loss unless the financial intermediary fails. Even then the saver may not sustain a loss if the deposits are insured. The combination of the intermediary's diversified portfolio of loans and the insurance of deposits has made financial intermediaries a primary haven for the savings of many risk-averse investors. (Diversification is an important topic in finance and is covered at length in Chapter 8 on the analysis of risk.)

To tap these savings, a variety of intermediaries has evolved. These include commercial banks, thrift institutions (savings and loan associations, mutual savings banks, and credit unions), and life insurance companies. Many savers are probably not aware of the differences among these financial intermediaries. They offer similar services and pay virtually the same rate of interest on deposits.

This blurring of the distinctions among the various financial intermediaries is the result of changes in the regulatory environment. Under the Depository Institutions Deregulation and Monetary Control Act of 1980 (more commonly referred to as the Monetary Control Act of 1980), all depository institutions (commercial banks, savings and loan associations, mutual savings banks, and credit unions) became subject to the regulation of the Federal Reserve. The Federal Reserve's powers extend to the types of accounts these institutions may offer and the amount that the various depository institutions must hold in reserve against their deposits.

Although the Federal Reserve has supervisory power over depository institutions' portfolios, the Monetary Control Act of 1980 gave the managements of various financial institutions more flexibility to vary their loan portfolios. In addition, each depository institution was granted the right to borrow funds from the Federal Reserve. The net effect of these reforms has been to reduce the differentiation among the various types of financial intermediaries. Thus, for most individuals the difference between the local commercial bank and the local savings and loan association is slight.

Commercial Banks

In terms of size, commercial banks are the most important depository institution. The total amount of deposits and loans made by commercial banks is given in Exhibit 2.1. Commercial banks' importance to business is evident, as loans to firms exceeded $1,279 billion and accounted for 10.9 percent of commercial banks' total assets. Commercial banks are also a prime source of funds to consumers, with consumer loans accounting for 6.9 percent of banks' total assets. Most of the loans to firms and households are for a relatively short term (for instance, less than one to five years to maturity). Commercial banks tend to stress loans that must be paid off ("mature") quickly. This emphasis on short maturities is the result of the rapid turnover of bank deposits (especially demand deposits) and the need for banks to coordinate their portfolios with changes in the economic environment and the level of interest rates.

The primary liabilities of commercial banks are their deposits: checking accounts (demand deposits) and various types of savings and time deposits. These deposits constitute 49.3 percent of the banks' sources of finance. Demand deposits are payable on demand. The owner of a checking account may demand immediate cash, and funds in the account may be readily transferred by check.

EXHIBIT 2.1
Assets and Liabilities of Commercial Banks as of January 2010 (in billions)

Assets		
Cash (currency and coins), cash items in process, and deposits with the Federal Reserve	$ 1,314.1	11.2%
U.S. government securities	1,447.4	12.3
Other securities	891.4	7.6
Loans		
Commercial and industrial	$ 1,279.6	10.9
Real estate	3,757.0	32.0
Loans to individuals	813.4	6.9
Interbank and other loans	219.4	1.9
Other assets	2,051.2	17.4
	$11,753.5	100.0%

Liabilities		
Demand deposits, savings accounts and CDs	$ 5,799.5	49.3
Large time deposits	1,888.9	16.1
Other borrowings and liabilities	2,794.8	23.8
Equity (net worth)	1,270.3	10.8
	$11,735.5	100.0%

Source: Data available at the Federal Reserve Web site **http://www.federalreserve.gov**.

Savings accounts, money market accounts, and certificates of deposit are interest-bearing accounts. Funds deposited in a regular savings account may be withdrawn at will. Time deposits, which are referred to as certificates of deposit (or CDs, as they are commonly called), are issued for a fixed term, such as six months or two years. The saver may redeem the CD prior to maturity but must pay a penalty, such as the loss of interest for one quarter. For CDs issued in denominations of $100,000 or larger, the rate of interest and the length of time to maturity are mutually agreed upon by the bank and the saver with the funds. These "jumbo CDs" may be subsequently sold, as there is a secondary market in CDs with denominations exceeding $100,000. Since large-denomination CDs may be bought and sold, they are often referred to as negotiable CDs to differentiate them from smaller-denomination CDs, which cannot be sold but may be redeemed prior to maturity (usually with a penalty).

For denominations of less than $100,000, the bank establishes the terms and offers the CD to the general public. If the public finds the terms unattractive (perhaps the rate of interest is less than that offered by competing banks), the bank does not receive deposits. Thus, it is not surprising that the terms offered by one bank are similar to the terms offered by competing banks; differences tend to be small or very subtle, such as the frequency with which interest is added to the principal. (The more frequently the interest is added, or compounded, the more interest the depositor earns, as interest earns additional interest.)

The remaining liabilities of the commercial bank include other borrowings from a variety of sources. For example, commercial banks borrow from each other and borrow from the Federal Reserve. The last entry on the commercial bank's balance sheet in Exhibit 2.1 is stockholders' equity, which represents the stockholders' investment in the firm.

While Exhibit 2.1 shows the various sources of funds available to commercial banks, it also illustrates that the various types of deposits are the most important. Checking and savings accounts and time deposits constitute almost 50 percent of the banks' sources of finance. The exhibit also indicates that total deposits greatly exceed stockholders' equity. Commercial banks have a large amount of debt outstanding when it is realized that the deposits are loans to the banks by households, firms, and governments.

Certificate of deposit (CD)

Time deposit issued by a bank with a specified interest rate and maturity

Negotiable CD

Certificate of deposit issued in amounts of $100,000 or more whose terms are individually negotiated between the bank and the saver and for which there exists a secondary market

Thrift Institutions

As the name implies, thrift institutions are a place for savers, especially individuals with modest sums, to deposit funds. The money is then loaned by the thrift to borrowers in need of the funds. There are essentially two types of thrifts: mutual savings banks and savings and loan associations (S&Ls). Mutual savings banks developed in the early 1800s to encourage savings. Many had colorful names (for example, Merchant Seaman's Bank) that indicated their origins. A mutual savings bank is owned by its depositors, but the bank itself is managed by a board of trustees. While a mutual savings bank may view its depositors as owners and not creditors, the owners may readily withdraw their funds. Thus, mutual savings banks must have sufficient liquidity to meet withdrawals.

Savings and loan associations developed later, primarily as a source of mortgage loans. Initially, S&L members (depositors) pooled their money to build housing. (The members were, in effect, the owners of the S&L.) Members borrowed the funds and when all the borrowed funds were repaid, the association was dissolved. Since these S&Ls were self-liquidating, they could not grow. They simply served a specific need of their members.

Today the S&L has evolved into a thrift institution that accepts deposits from anyone and makes a variety of loans. S&Ls, however, continue to place more emphasis on mortgage loans than do commercial banks. To attract deposits, S&Ls (and other thrifts) tend to pay a rate of interest that is slightly higher than the rates paid by commercial banks.

Regulation of Commercial Banks and Thrift Institutions

Commercial banks and other savings banks are subject to government regulation, whose purpose is to protect the banks' creditors, especially their depositors. The very nature of banking implies that when a commercial bank fails, substantial losses could be sustained by the bank's depositors. This is exactly what occurred during the Great Depression of the 1930s, when the failure of many commercial banks imposed substantial losses on depositors. These losses led to increased regulation of commercial banks and the establishment of federal deposit insurance, both of which are designed to protect depositors. Such protection promotes a viable banking system and eases the flow of savings into investment.

The regulation of banks comes from both state and federal banking authorities and the Federal Deposit Insurance Corporation. Banks that have national charters must join the Federal Reserve and are subjected to its regulation as well as to examination by the Comptroller of the Currency, which is the federal agency that grants national bank charters. Banks with state charters are regulated by the individual state banking commissions and are subject to regulation by the Federal Reserve. These various authorities regulate and supervise such facets of a bank's operations as its geographic location, the number of banks and branches in an area, and the types of loans and investments the bank may make.

Reserves

Required reserves

Funds that banks must hold against deposit liabilities

Commercial banks and all other depository institutions (savings and loan associations, mutual savings banks, and credit unions) must keep funds in reserve against their deposit liabilities (that is, required reserves). The minimum amount that all banks must maintain as a reserve is determined by the Federal Reserve. While holding reserves against deposit liabilities may increase the safety of the deposits, such safety is not the prime reason for having reserve requirements. As will be explained in Chapter 5, the reserve requirement is one of the tools of monetary control. This element of control, not safety, is the reason for having a reserve requirement against the deposit liabilities of banks.

The amount of the reserve requirement varies with the type of account. For example, as of January 2010, checking accounts had a reserve requirement of 10 percent. (The first $55.2 million in checking accounts have a reserve requirement of 3 percent.) Time deposits have no reserve requirements.

Commercial banks may hold their reserves in two forms: (1) cash in the vault or (2) deposits with another bank, especially the Federal Reserve. If the bank's reserve requirement is 10 percent for demand deposits and the bank receives $100 cash in a checking account, it must hold $10 in reserve against the new demand deposit. The entire $100 in cash is considered part of the bank's total reserves, but the bank must hold only $10 against the deposit liability. The bank may choose to hold $1 of the required reserves in cash in the vault (to meet cash withdrawals) and $9 in the Federal Reserve. The remaining $90 are funds that the bank does not have to hold in reserve. In this example, these **excess reserves** (the difference between the bank's total reserves and its required reserves) total $100 − $10 = $90. A commercial bank's excess reserves may be lent to borrowers or used for some other purpose, such as purchasing government securities. If a commercial bank does not have any excess reserves, it is said to be "fully loaned up." To acquire additional income-earning assets, such as a government security or a business loan, the bank would have to acquire additional excess reserves.

Commercial banks (and other depository institutions) may deposit their reserves in a Federal Reserve bank, or they may deposit their reserves in other banks called **correspondent banks**. Correspondent banks in many cases are large, metropolitan commercial banks. These large correspondent banks frequently provide additional services. For example, they have efficient mechanisms for clearing checks that facilitate check clearing for smaller banks. The correspondent banks also have research staffs and give management advice and investment counsel. Thus, they are important to the well-being of the small, local banks. Of course, the correspondent banks are willing to provide these services because a small bank's deposits are like any other deposits: they are a source of funds that the larger banks may use. The large commercial banks use the funds deposited in them by small banks to purchase income-earning assets.

In addition to the required reserves, commercial banks also hold **secondary reserves**. These are high-quality, short-term marketable securities such as U.S. government securities (Treasury bills) that may be readily sold. Thus, short-term marketable securities offer a bank both a source of interest income and a means to obtain funds quickly to cover a shortage in its reserves.

The importance of reserves and reserve requirements cannot be exaggerated. The commercial banking system, through the process of loan creation, can expand or contract the nation's supply of money. The ability of commercial banks and other depository institutions to lend depends on their excess

Excess reserves

Reserves held by a bank in excess of those it must hold to meet its reserve requirement

Correspondent bank

Major bank with which a smaller bank has a relationship to facilitate check clearing and to serve as a depository for reserves

Secondary reserves

Short-term securities, especially Treasury bills, held by banks to increase their liquidity reserves. Thus anything that affects their reserves alters their ability to lend and create money and credit. Many financial transactions affect commercial banks' reserves, including the federal government's methods of financing a deficit or the open market operations of the Federal Reserve.

Deposit Insurance

Federal government deposit insurance is one of the positive results of the Great Depression of the 1930s. The large losses sustained by commercial banks' depositors led to the establishment of the Federal Deposit Insurance Corporation (FDIC). The establishment of FDIC has significantly increased the general public's confidence in the banking system. As of this writing, FDIC insures deposits to $250,000. Thus, if a commercial bank should fail, FDIC will reimburse depositors up to the $250,000 limit. Since most individuals do not have that much on deposit, these individuals know that their funds are safe. (If you have more than $250,000, you may obtain the same degree of safety by placing amounts up to $250,000 in different banks.) The $250,000 limit does mean that large depositors, including many corporations, are not fully insured and do stand to take losses should a bank fail.

All commercial banks that are members of the Federal Reserve System must purchase insurance from FDIC, and many state banking authorities also require that FDIC insurance be carried by their state nonmember banks. However, some state banking authorities do not require federal deposit insurance. Also foreign banks that are licensed to operate in the United States do not have to carry FDIC insurance.

Besides offering deposit insurance, FDIC has further increased public confidence in the banking system through its powers of bank examination. By exercising this power to examine banks, FDIC, along with other regulatory agencies, has improved bank practices. The improved bank practices plus the deposit insurance have improved the quality of banking. However; the establishment of FDIC and other regulatory agencies has not eliminated bank failures, for banks do fail.

Such failures became common occurrences as a result of the financial crisis that started in 2008. During 2007, only three banks failed. However, the number of bank failures increased to 25 during 2008 and rose dramatically to 140 during 2009. An additional 90 failures occurred during the first six months of 2010. While most of these failures were small banks, losses were not sustained by the many individuals who deposited modest sums with the failed commercial banks. If necessary, such depositors received full reimbursement by FDIC. Thus, for most individuals, depositing funds in a commercial bank does not subject the funds to risk of loss.

If a bank does fail, FDIC generally seeks to merge that bank into a stronger bank. The transfer of deposits saves FDIC from having to reimburse depositors. For example, when Washington Mutual failed during 2008, its assets were acquired by JPMorgan Chase. Its depositors and customers became depositors and customers of the acquiring bank. There was no interruption of banking services, and depositors did not sustain losses. If, however, such a merger cannot be arranged, the failed bank may be liquidated, in which case the depositors receive reimbursement up to the legal limit.

Life Insurance Companies

Life insurance companies also perform the role of a financial intermediary because they receive the funds of savers, create a claim on themselves, and lend the funds to borrowers. Since other types of insurance companies do not perform this financial intermediary role, a distinction has to be made between them and life insurance companies. Other types of insurance, such as property and liability insurance, are exclusively services that the individual buys. The price of the insurance is related to the cost of the product, just as the cost of any service, such as a movie or an electrician, is related to the cost of producing the service. Of course, the property and liability insurance companies invest the funds they receive from policyholders. However, suppliers of other services will also use the funds they receive. In neither case is there a transfer of savings to borrowers.

The feature that differentiates life insurance from other forms of insurance and makes life insurance companies financial intermediaries is that life insurance may provide more than insurance against premature death. Ordinary and universal life insurance policies and endowments contain two elements, the insurance and a savings plan. The policy's premiums cover both the cost of the insurance and the savings program. As long as the policy is in force, the policy accumulates cash value, which is the savings component of the policy. Many savers find such policies attractive because the periodic payments assure them of insurance plus a savings program. Others find them unattractive because the interest rate paid on the savings may be less than can be earned on alternative investments.

Life insurance companies use the proceeds from the policies to acquire income-earning assets. While life insurance companies compete with commercial banks for granting loans, they serve different financial markets. Commercial banks stress short-term, liquid loans and are a primary source of short-term finance. Life insurance companies, however, do not need to stress short-term liquidity. Mortality tables are scientifically constructed. A life insurance company can predict with accuracy the volume of death benefits that the company will have to pay and can construct a portfolio of long-term assets that meets the forecast benefits. Since long-term investments tend to earn higher interest rates than short-term debt, a life insurance company will seek to have a substantial amount of its funds in these more profitable investments. This strategy is illustrated in Exhibit 2.2, which presents selected assets for MetLife. The value of MetLife's long-term bond portfolio is almost 27 times the size of its holdings of cash and other short-term securities. (The features of these various debt instruments are covered in Chapter 22.)

Long-term bonds		
Treasury bonds	$ 25.4	11.1%
State and local government bonds	7.2	3.2
Corporate bonds	104.9	46.1
Foreign government bonds	11.9	5.2
Mortgage-backed securities	72.8	32.0
Other bonds	5.4	2.4
Total bonds	$227.6	100.0%

Other investments	
Mortgages	$ 50.9
Stock	3.1
Cash and cash equivalents	8.3

Source: 2009 MetLife 10-K Report.

Pension Plans

The role of a pension plan is to accumulate assets for workers so that they will have funds for retirement. Funds are periodically put in the pension plan by the saver, the employer, or both. The money deposited with the fund then is used to purchase income-earning assets. The saver's funds grow over time as additional contributions are paid into the pension plan, and the funds already in the plan earn income and appreciate in value.

Many pension plans exist, but not all of them really perform the function of financial intermediaries. Many pension plans do not invest or lend the money directly to borrowers. Instead they may purchase *existing* securities, such as the stock of IBM; that is, the pension plan participates in the secondary, not the primary, market for securities. For a pension plan to serve as a financial intermediary, it must pass the funds directly to a borrower or invest them directly in a firm.

This distinction between pension plans may be illustrated by the pension plans used by many colleges and universities for their employees. Funds may be contributed by both the employer and the employee to the Teachers Insurance and Annuity Association (TIAA) or to the College Retirement Equity Fund (CREF). The actual dollar amount of the contribution varies with the school and the employee's salary. The funds may be contributed to either plan or may be split between the two plans.

CREF primarily purchases existing corporate stock. Money that flows into CREF does not go to the companies that issued the stock. Instead, the money goes to the seller of the stock, who may have purchased the shares many years ago. TIAA purchases an entirely different type of portfolio that stresses debt, especially mortgages. In this case funds are transferred from savers to borrowers, and the pension plan is acting as a financial intermediary. It creates a claim on itself when it receives the savers' funds, and it receives a claim from borrowers when the funds are lent to finance purchases. The transfer of purchasing power from saver to borrower by an intermediary that creates claims on itself is the role of a financial intermediary. Hence, TIAA is an example of a pension plan that does serve as a financial intermediary.

Money Market Mutual Funds and Money Market Instruments

One of the most important financial institutions is the mutual fund that invests on behalf of individuals. However, most of these funds are not financial intermediaries in the sense that they borrow from savers and lend the funds to the ultimate users. It is true that they do create claims on themselves, since investors own shares in the funds (in other words, the investors own equity claims). Whether the fund is a financial intermediary depends on what it does with the money raised by selling the shares: Does it acquire newly issued securities or buy previously issued securities?

If the fund buys securities in the secondary markets, it is not serving as a financial intermediary. No money is transferred to a firm, government, or individual seeking to borrow funds. Instead, the money is transferred to another investor who is seeking to liquidate a position in the particular security.

Of course, a mutual fund could buy newly issued securities. Some funds specialize in purchasing shares of emerging and new firms, and to the extent that these funds participate in the primary market, they are operating as financial intermediaries. Other mutual funds specialize in government securities, which may be purchased when the bonds are issued. Such funds also serve as financial intermediaries, transferring the money of savers to the ultimate users of the money. Most mutual funds, however, do not serve as financial intermediaries, as they primarily buy and sell existing securities.

Money market mutual fund

Investment company that invests solely in short-term money market instruments

Even though most mutual funds are not financial intermediaries, there is one major exception—the money market mutual fund that acquires short-term securities. While these are secondary markets in some money market instruments, money market mutual funds tend to acquire newly issued short-term debt instruments. These securities are then held until they are redeemed at maturity, at which time the process is repeated.

The development of these funds and their explosive growth was one of the most important developments in the financial markets. The initial growth was nothing short of phenomenal, as total assets rose from less than $10 billion in 1975 to over $1.6 trillion in 30 years. This immediate popularity may be explained by three factors: safety of principal, liquidity, and interest rates that exceed the rates paid by banks. The shares are safe since the money funds acquire short-term debt obligations whose values are subject to minimal price fluctuations. In addition, these debt obligations tend to have high credit ratings, so there is minimal risk of default. Individuals may withdraw money invested in the money funds (that is, redeem shares) at will. This ease of converting to cash with minimal chance of loss means these shares are among the most liquid assets available to savers.

The money funds invest in a variety of short-term securities that include the negotiable CDs discussed earlier. Other money market instruments include the short-term debt of the federal government (Treasury bills), commercial paper issued by corporations, repurchase agreements (commonly referred to as repos), banker's acceptances, and tax anticipation notes. Of course, the individual investor may also directly acquire these securities, but the large denomination of some short-term securities (for example, the minimum denomination of negotiable CDs is $100,000) excludes most investors.

The safest short-term security is the U.S. Treasury bill (commonly referred to as a T-bill), which is issued by the federal government. Before the political confrontation over the federal budget in 1995, there was no question that the federal government would retire the principal and pay the interest on its obligations. (The pricing of T-bills and the calculation of yields earned on the bills and other discounted short-term securities are covered in Chapter 17.) The short term of the bills also implies that if interest rates were to rise, the increase would have minimum impact on the bills, and the quick maturity means that investors could reinvest the proceeds in the higher-yielding securities.

Commercial paper is an unsecured short-term note issued by a corporation as an alternative to borrowing funds from commercial banks. Since the paper is usually unsecured, only firms with excellent credit ratings are able to sell it; hence, the risk of default is small, and the repayment of principal is virtually assured.

A repurchase agreement (repo) is a sale of a security in which the seller agrees to buy back (repurchase) the security at a specified price at a specified date. Repos are usually executed using federal government securities, and the repurchase price is higher than the initial sale price. The difference between the initial sale price and the repurchase price is the source of the return to the holder of the security. By entering into the repurchase agreement, the investor (the buyer) knows exactly how much will be made on the investment and when the funds will be returned.

Banker's acceptances are short-term promissory notes guaranteed by a bank. These acceptances arise through international trade. Suppose a firm ships goods abroad and receives a draft that promises payment after two months. If the firm does not want to wait for payment, it can take the draft to a commercial bank for acceptance. Once the bank accepts the draft (and stamps it "accepted"), the draft may be sold. The buyer purchases the draft for a discount, which becomes the source of the return to the holder. Bankers' acceptances are considered to be good short-term investments because they are supported by two parties: the firm on which the draft is drawn and the bank that accepts the draft.

Tax anticipation notes are issued by states or municipalities to finance current operations before tax revenues are received. As the taxes are collected, the proceeds are used to retire the debt. Similar notes are issued in anticipation of

U.S. Treasury bill (T-bill)

Short-term debt instrument issued by the federal government

Commercial paper

Unsecured short-term promissory notes issued by the most creditworthy corporations

Repurchase agreement (repo)

Sale of a short-term security in which the seller agrees to buy back the security at a specified price

Banker's acceptances

Short-term promissory note guaranteed by a bank

Tax anticipation note

Short-term government security secured by expected tax revenues

EXHIBIT 2.3
Distribution of Money
Market Mutual Funds'
Assets as of January 2010
(in billions)

Commercial paper	$ 511.8	27.6%
U.S. government and agency securities	257.7	13.9
Repurchase agreements	159.5	8.6
Eurodollar certificates of deposit	98.3	5.3
Negotiable certificates of deposit	571.1	30.8
Corporate notes	115.0	6.2
Other	139.1	7.5
	$ 1,852.5	100.0%

Source: Derived from *Investment Institute 2010 Mutual Fund Fact Book,* available at the Investment Company Institute Web site **http://www.ici.org**.

revenues from future bond issues and other sources, such as revenue sharing from the federal government. While these anticipation notes do not offer the safety of Treasury bills, the interest is exempt from federal income taxation. (The interest paid on debt issued by state and local governments is exempt from federal income taxation. These securities are discussed in Chapter 22 on bonds.) Commercial banks and securities maintain secondary markets in them, so the notes may be sold if the firm needs cash.

In addition to domestic short-term securities, money market mutual funds invest in Eurodollar certificates of deposit (Eurodollar CDs). These are similar to domestic negotiable CDs except they are issued either by branches of domestic banks located abroad or by foreign banks. Like domestic negotiable CDs, Eurodollar CDs are *denominated in U.S. dollars,* and they may be bought and sold because a secondary market exists. Eurodollar CDs offer a small yield advantage because they are not quite as liquid as domestic negotiable CDs and because they carry the additional risk of being issued in a foreign country.

Money market mutual funds can invest in any of the preceding money market instruments (negotiable certificates of deposit, Treasury bills, commercial paper, repurchase agreements, banker's acceptances, and tax anticipation notes). Exhibit 2.3 shows aggregate distribution of money market fund assets. As may be seen in the exhibit, commercial paper and negotiable CDs constitute about half of these funds' assets, so the money funds are a major source of finance to the government and corporations.

Although the money funds as a whole own a wide spectrum of money market instruments, some of the funds do specialize. Schwab U.S. Treasury Money Fund, for example, invests solely in U.S. government securities or securities that are collateralized by obligations of the federal government. Other Schwab money funds invest in a wider spectrum of short-term debt obligations. For example, as of December 31, 2009, Schwab Money Fund had 14.0 percent of its assets in federal government agency obligations, 39.8 percent in negotiable CDs, 29.6 percent in commercial paper, and the remaining percentage in various other short-term assets, such as repurchase agreements.

Competition for Funds

A commercial bank or any financial intermediary can lend only what has been lent to it. Unless the bank is able to induce individuals, firms, and governments to make deposits, that bank will be unable to grant loans and make investments. This general statement holds for all financial intermediaries. None can make investments without a source of funds. Whether these claims on the intermediaries are called life insurance policies or savings accounts or shares in money market mutual funds, the essential point remains the same. No financial intermediary can exist without its sources of funds.

Conversely, if funds flow out of financial intermediaries, all intermediaries will be able to hold fewer assets (that is, make fewer loans). Unless the outflow is reversed, it will tend to increase the cost of credit as the intermediaries raise the rates of interest they charge in order to ration their remaining lending capacity.

In addition to the aggregate flows into and out of all financial intermediaries, credit markets may feel the impact of flows among financial intermediaries. Funds deposited in one particular bank are not deposited in another competitive bank. If an individual saver has funds to invest and chooses a money market mutual fund instead of the local savings and loan association, it is the mutual fund that can lend the funds and not the savings and loan association. From the standpoint of the borrowers, it would not matter which intermediary makes the loans if all financial intermediaries had similar portfolios. But the portfolios of various financial intermediaries do vary.

These differences can have an important implication. A transfer of funds from one intermediary (for example, a savings and loan association) to another (such as a money market mutual fund) can have an important impact on the supply of credit available to a particular sector of the economy. Although the total supply of credit is unaffected (because the money market fund can lend only what the savings and loan association loses), there will be a redistribution of credit from those who borrow from savings and loan associations to those who borrow from the money funds. The money market mutual fund now has more funds to acquire short-term securities. Simultaneously, the flow of funds out of the savings and loan association reduces its capacity to grant mortgage loans. Such a redistribution of funds from savings and loan associations to money market mutual funds will be felt by the construction industry and home buyers as the supply of mortgage money declines.

As this discussion implies, financial intermediaries compete with each other for funds. This competition occurs through yields and services offered. If a particular intermediary did not offer competitive rates, funds would flow from it to those intermediaries offering higher yields. Thus, differentiation among the intermediaries on the basis of yields tends to be small.

Historically, financial intermediaries have been categorized on the basis of services or products offered. Today, however, this is only partially true. In the past, savers bought life insurance through insurance agents, bought stocks through securities brokers, and invested funds in a savings account in a bank. Those days of specialization are disappearing. Insurance agents, stockbrokers, and bankers today offer a wide spectrum of services and financial products. For example, many commercial banks offer savers not only the traditional services of savings and checking accounts but other products as well, such as brokerage services (to compete with stockbrokers), money market accounts (to compete with money market mutual funds), and pension plans (to compete with insurance companies and mutual funds). Such product competition also applies to savings banks. Savings and loan associations offer a variety of savings accounts as well as checking accounts, life insurance, and brokerage services.

Summary

Financial markets transfer savings by individuals, firms, and governments into productive investments. This transfer occurs directly when new securities are issued or indirectly through financial intermediaries. Financial markets also transfer existing securities among investors.

Money is anything that is generally acceptable to pay for goods and services and to retire debt. Liquidity refers to the ease of converting nonmonetary assets into money. The narrow definition of the money supply (M-1) is the sum of coins, currency, and demand deposits. A broader definition (M-2) adds saving accounts and small certificates of deposit to M-1.

Interest rates help allocate scarce credit among competing uses for the funds. The structure of yields relates the interest rate to the length of time that the debt will be outstanding. The structure of yields is often summarized by a yield curve. Generally the yield curve is positively sloped, which indicates that the longer the borrower has the use of the funds, the greater is the cost of funds. However, there have been periods when the yield curve was negative and short-term rates exceeded long-term rates. There have also been periods when the yield curve was flat; short-term and long-term rates were equal and there was no differentiation between the cost of short-term and long-term funds.

Funds are transferred from savers to borrowers through a system of financial intermediaries. The intermediaries borrow from savers and then lend the funds to their ultimate users. Financial intermediaries include commercial banks, thrift institutions, life insurance companies, pension plans, and money market mutual funds. All financial intermediaries compete for funds, since an individual intermediary can acquire a portfolio of assets only if it can obtain funds. The deregulation of the banking system has increased competition among the various intermediaries and blurred the distinctions among them, allowing them to offer products and services that previously were the exclusive domain of a particular intermediary.

In terms of size, commercial banks are the most important financial intermediary. These banks make a variety of loans but tend to stress loans that are quickly repaid. Other financial intermediaries, such as savings and loan associations and life insurance companies, make longer-term loans.

Recent developments in financial intermediaries include the large growth in money market mutual funds. Money market mutual funds compete directly with banks; they offer the advantages of somewhat higher yields and almost comparable safety. While the shares are not federally insured as are the deposits in banks, the short-term nature of their portfolios affords the saver safety of principal.

Money marker mutual funds own a variety of short-term debt securities issued by corporations (commercial paper), commercial banks (negotiable CDs), and governments. Government short-term debt obligations include U.S. Treasury bills and tax anticipation notes. Other short-term money market instruments include repurchase agreements, banker's acceptances, and Eurodollar CDs. Each of these securities is a means for the issuer to raise short-term funds, and each is a place for investors, especially money market mutual funds, to commit funds for a short period of time.

Review Objectives

Now that you have completed this chapter, you should be able to

1. Define money and determine how the money supply is measured (pp. 15–17).
2. Develop a yield curve and contrast positive and negative yield curves (pp. 18–19).
3. Differentiate the direct and indirect transfer of savings to users of funds (pp. 19–21).
4. Enumerate the primary assets and liabilities of a commercial bank (pp. 21–23).
5. Describe several regulations that apply to the banking system (pp. 24–27).
6. Differentiate required and excess banks reserves (pp. 24–26).
7. Explain the role of FDIC (pp. 26–27).
8. Compare the assets of life insurance companies and commercial banks (p. 22 and p. 27).
9. Contrast the various money market instruments (pp. 29–31).

Relationships

1. An increase in currency _____ the supply of money (M-1).
2. Transferring funds in a demand deposit to a savings account _____ M-1 and _____ M-2.
3. During most periods of history, increasing the term of a loan (time to maturity) _____ the rate of interest.
4. Depositing cash in a checking account _____ required reserves.
5. Transferring funds in a savings account to a checking account _____ commercial banks' excess reserves.

6. If the Federal Reserve increases banks' reserve requirement, it _____ the banks' ability to lend.

7. If the Federal Reserve decreases banks' reserve requirement, existing bank deposits _____.

Answers

1. increases

2. decreases; does not affect (no change)

3. increases

4. increases

5. decreases

6. decreases

7. are not affected (no change)

Investment Banking

Two basic methods exist for transferring funds from savers to users. The indirect transfer occurs through a financial intermediary such as a bank. You lend funds to the bank, which in turn lends the funds to the ultimate borrower. (The role of commercial banks and the various types of financial intermediaries was covered in Chapter 2.) The alternative is the direct sale of securities to investors in the primary market.

While most purchases of stocks (and bonds) occur in the secondary markets such as the New York Stock Exchange, the initial sales occur in the primary markets. The primary and secondary markets perform different functions, but both are important financial institutions. Secondary markets increase your willingness to buy securities and primary markets are the means by which your savings are transferred to firms and governments.

The initial sale of a security in the primary market is often executed with the assistance of investment bankers. While this initial sale occurs only once, it is exceedingly important, because it is the process by which securities come into existence. If firms and governments did not issue securities, you would have to find alternative uses for your savings. Firms and governments, however, do need funds, and they tap your savings through issuing and selling new securities in the primary markets. The secondary markets provide you with a means to sell these securities (or buy more) once they have been issued.

This chapter also briefly describes the major federal laws that govern the issuing and subsequent trading in securities. The purpose of this legislation is not to ensure that you will earn a positive return. Instead its purpose is to ensure that you and all investors receive timely and accurate information. You continue to bear the risk associated with buying stocks and bonds.

The Transfer of Funds to Business

One purpose of financial markets is to facilitate the transfer of funds from individuals (and firms and governments) with funds to invest to those individuals (and firms and governments) that need funds. One method is an indirect transfer through a financial intermediary such as a commercial bank. The other method is the direct investment in the firm by the general public. This transfer occurs when you start your own business and invest your savings in the operation. But the direct transfer is not limited to investing in your own business. Firms (and governments) also raise funds by selling securities directly to the general public.

The Role of Investment Bankers

Investment banker

Middleman who brings together investors and firms (and governments) issuing new securities

Initial public offering (IPO)

First sale of common stock to the general public

While companies could sell securities directly to you (and some do sell modest amounts of securities through programs such as the dividend reinvestment plans described in Chapter 20), the majority of these sales are executed through investment bankers. In effect, an investment banker serves as a middleman to channel money from investors to firms and governments that need the funds. If this sale is the *first* sale of common stock, it is referred to as an initial public offering (IPO). Exhibit 3.1 is the title page for the initial public offering of Yahoo! common stock and is used to illustrate the process of an initial public offering.

Firms sell securities when internally generated funds are insufficient to finance the desired level of spending and when the management believes it is advantageous to obtain outside funding from the general public. Such public funding may increase interest in the firm and avoid some of the restrictive covenants required by financial institutions.

Most sales of new securities are made with the assistance of investment bankers. Unfortunately, the term *investment banker* may be confusing, since investment bankers are often not bankers and generally do not invest. Instead they are usually a division of a brokerage firm such as Goldman, Sachs & Co., Donaldson, Lufkin & Jenerette Securities Corporation, or Montgomery Securities. (See Exhibit 3.1.) Although these firms may own securities, they do not necessarily buy and hold newly issued securities in their own accounts for investment purposes. Instead they are the middlemen that bring together individuals with funds to invest and the firms that need financing.

Underwriting

Purchase of an issue of new securities for subsequent sale by investment bankers; the guaranteeing of the sale of a new issue of securities

The firm in need of funds approaches the investment bankers to discuss an underwriting. If the investment bankers guarantee the sale, they make a "firm commitment" to raise a specified amount of money. In effect, the underwriters buy the securities with the intention to sell them to the general public. By

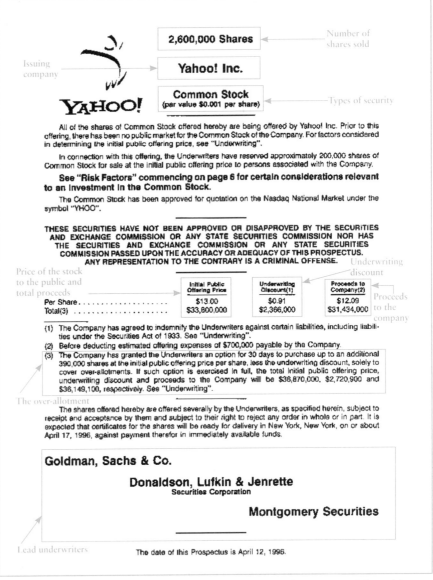

2,600,000 Shares — Number of shares sold

Issuing company — Yahoo! Inc.

Common Stock
(par value $0.001 per share) — Types of security

All of the shares of Common Stock offered hereby are being offered by Yahoo! Inc. Prior to this offering, there has been no public market for the Common Stock of the Company. For factors considered in determining the initial public offering price, see "Underwriting".

In connection with this offering, the Underwriters have reserved approximately 200,000 shares of Common Stock for sale at the initial public offering price to persons associated with the Company.

See "Risk Factors" commencing on page 6 for certain considerations relevant to an Investment in the Common Stock.

The Common Stock has been approved for quotation on the Nasdaq National Market under the symbol "YHOO".

THESE SECURITIES HAVE NOT BEEN APPROVED OR DISAPPROVED BY THE SECURITIES AND EXCHANGE COMMISSION OR ANY STATE SECURITIES COMMISSION NOR HAS THE SECURITIES AND EXCHANGE COMMISSION OR ANY STATE SECURITIES COMMISSION PASSED UPON THE ACCURACY OR ADEQUACY OF THIS PROSPECTUS. ANY REPRESENTATION TO THE CONTRARY IS A CRIMINAL OFFENSE.

Price of the stock to the public and total proceeds / Underwriting discount / Proceeds to the company

	Initial Public Offering Price	Underwriting Discount(1)	Proceeds to Company(2)
Per Share	$13.00	$0.91	$12.09
Total(3)	$33,800,000	$2,366,000	$31,434,000

(1) The Company has agreed to indemnify the Underwriters against certain liabilities, including liabilities under the Securities Act of 1933. See "Underwriting".
(2) Before deducting estimated offering expenses of $700,000 payable by the Company.
(3) The Company has granted the Underwriters an option for 30 days to purchase up to an additional 390,000 shares at the initial public offering price per share, less the underwriting discount, solely to cover over-allotments. If such option is exercised in full, the total initial public offering price, underwriting discount and proceeds to the Company will be $38,870,000, $2,720,900 and $36,149,100, respectively. See "Underwriting".

The over-allotment

The shares offered hereby are offered severally by the Underwriters, as specified herein, subject to receipt and acceptance by them and subject to their right to reject any order in whole or in part. It is expected that certificates for the shares will be ready for delivery in New York, New York, on or about April 17, 1996, against payment therefor in immediately available funds.

Goldman, Sachs & Co.

Donaldson, Lufkin & Jenrette
Securities Corporation

Montgomery Securities

Lead underwriters

The date of this Prospectus is April 12, 1996.

Source: Reproduced with permission of Yahoo! Inc. © 2000 by Yahoo! Inc. YAHOO! and the YAHOO! logo are trademarks of Yahoo! Inc.

agreeing to buy the securities, the underwriters guarantee the sale and bear the risk associated with the sale. If the investment bankers are unable to sell the securities to the general public, they must still pay the agreed-on sum to the issuing firm. Failure to sell the securities imposes losses on the underwriters, who must remit funds for securities that have not been sold to the general public.

Because an underwriting starts with a particular brokerage firm, which manages the underwriting, that firm is called the originating house. The originating

Syndicate

Selling group formed to market a new issue of securities

house may not be a single firm if the negotiation involves several investment bankers. In that case, several firms join together to manage the underwriting. The originating house usually does not sell all the securities but forms a syndicate. The syndicate is a group of brokerage houses that joins together to underwrite and market a specific sale of securities. The firms that manage the sale are often referred to as the *lead underwriters*. In the Yahoo! illustration, 17 additional firms joined the three lead underwriters to sell the securities.

The use of a syndicate has several advantages. The syndicate has access to more potential buyers, and using a syndicate reduces the number of securities that each firm must sell, which also increases the probability that the entire issue will be sold. Thus, syndication makes possible both the sale of a large offering and a reduction in the risk borne by each member of the selling group.

Best efforts agreement

Contract with an investment banker for the sale of securities in which the investment banker does not guarantee the sale but does agree to make the best effort to sell the securities

If the investment bankers do not want to bear the risk of the sale, they can agree to sell the securities through a best efforts agreement. The investment bankers do not underwrite the sale and do not guarantee that a specified amount of money will be raised. Instead, the investment bankers agree to make their best efforts to sell the securities, but the risk of the sale is borne by the issuing firm. If the securities do not sell, the firm does not receive the funds. While most sales of new securities are by underwriting, small issues of risky securities are often best efforts sales.

Pricing a New Issue

Because most sales of new securities are underwritings, the pricing of securities is crucial. If the initial offer price is too high, the syndicate will be unable to sell the securities. When this occurs, the investment bankers have two choices: (1) to maintain the offer price and to hold the securities in inventory until they are sold, or (2) to let the market find a lower price level that will induce investors to purchase the securities. Neither choice benefits the investment bankers.

If the underwriters purchase the securities and hold them in inventory, they either must tie up their own funds, which could be earning a return elsewhere, or must borrow funds to pay for the securities. The investment bankers must pay interest on these borrowed funds. Thus, the decision to support the offer price of the securities prevents the investment bankers from investing their own capital elsewhere or (more likely) requires that they borrow the funds. In either case, the profit margin on the underwriting is decreased, and the investment bankers may even experience a loss on the underwriting.

Instead of supporting the price, the underwriters may choose to let the price of the securities fall. The inventory of unsold securities can then be sold at the lower price. The underwriters will not tie up capital or have to borrow money from their sources of credit. If the underwriters make this choice, they force losses on themselves when they sell the securities at less than cost. But they also cause the customers who bought the securities at the initial offer price to lose. The underwriters certainly do not want to inflict losses on these customers, because the underwriters' market for future new security issues will vanish. Therefore, the investment bankers try not to overprice a new issue of securities, for overpricing will ultimately result in their suffering losses.

There is also an incentive to avoid underpricing new securities. If the issue is underpriced, all the securities will readily be sold, and their price will rise because demand will have exceeded supply. The buyers of the securities will be satisfied, for the price of the securities will have increased as a result of the underpricing. The initial purchasers of the securities reap windfall profits, but these profits are really at the expense of the company whose securities were underpriced. If the underwriters had assigned a higher price to the securities, the company would have raised more capital.

Although there are reasons for the underwriters to avoid either underpricing or overpricing, there appears to be a greater incentive to underprice the securities. Studies have found that initial purchases earned higher returns as the buyers were given a price incentive to buy the new offering.[1] Subsequent buyers, however, did not fare as well, and any initial underpricing appears to disappear soon after the original offering. In addition, many initial public offerings subsequently underperform the market during the first years after the original sale.

Marketing New Securities

Preliminary prospectus (red herring)

Initial document detailing the financial condition of a firm that must be filed with the SEC to register a new issue of securities

Securities and Exchange Commission (SEC)

Government agency that enforces the federal securities laws

Registration

Process of filing information with the SEC concerning a proposed sale of securities to the general public

Once the terms of the sale have been agreed upon, the managing house may issue a preliminary prospectus. The preliminary prospectus is often referred to as a *red herring*, a term that connotes the document should be read with caution as it is not final and complete. (The phrase "red herring" is derived from British fugitives' rubbing herring across their trails to confuse pursuing bloodhounds.) The preliminary prospectus informs potential buyers that the securities are being registered with the Securities and Exchange Commission (SEC) and may subsequently be offered for sale. Registration refers to the disclosure of information concerning the firm, the securities being offered for sale, and the use of the proceeds from the sale.[2]

The preliminary prospectus describes the company and the securities to be issued; it includes the firm's income statement and balance sheets, its current activities (such as a pending merger or labor negotiation), the regulatory bodies to which it is subject, and the nature of its competition. The preliminary prospectus is thus a detailed document concerning the company and is, unfortunately, usually tedious reading.

The preliminary prospectus does not include the price of the securities. That will be determined on the day that the securities are issued. If security prices decline or rise, the price of the new securities may be adjusted for the change in market conditions. In fact, if prices decline sufficiently, the firm has the option of postponing or even canceling the underwriting.

---

[1]See Seth Anderson, *Initial Public Offerings* (Boston: Kluwer Academic Publishers, 1995).

[2]While there are exceptions, generally unregistered corporate securities may not be sold to the general public. The debt of governments (e.g., state municipal bonds), however, is not registered with the SEC and may be sold to the general public. Information concerning the SEC may be obtained from **http://www.sec.gov**, the Securities and Exchange Commission's home page.

After the SEC accepts the registration statement, a final prospectus is published. The SEC does not approve the issue as to its investment worth but does affirm that all required information has been provided and that the prospectus is complete in format and content. Except for changes that are required by the SEC, the final prospectus is virtually identical to the preliminary prospectus. Information regarding the price of the security, the proceeds to the company, the underwriting discount, and any more recent financial data is added. As may be seen in Exhibit 3.1, Yahoo! Inc. issued 2,600,000 shares of common stock at a price of $13.00 to raise a total of $33,800,000. The cost of the underwriting (also called *flotation costs* or *underwriting discount*) is the difference between the price of securities to the public and the proceeds received by the firm. In this example, the cost is $0.91 a share for a total cost of $2,366,000, which is 7.5 percent of the proceeds received by Yahoo!

The issuing company frequently grants the underwriter an over-allotment to cover the sale of additional shares if there is sufficient demand. In this illustration, Yahoo! granted the underwriters the option to purchase an additional 390,000 shares, which would raise the total proceeds received by Yahoo! to $36,149,100.

Volatility of the Market for Initial Public Offerings

The new issue market (especially for initial public offerings of common stock, or IPOs) can be extremely volatile. Periods have occurred when the investing public seemed willing to purchase virtually any security that was being sold (e.g., the dot-com period during the late 1990s). There have also been periods during which new companies were simply unable to raise money, and large companies did so only under onerous terms.

The new issue market is volatile not only regarding the number of securities that are offered but also regarding the price changes of the new issues. When the new issue market is "hot," it is not unusual for the prices to rise dramatically. Yahoo!'s stock was initially offered at $13 and closed at $33 after reaching a high of $43 during the first day of trading.

Few new issues perform as well as Yahoo!, and many that initially do well subsequently fall on hard times. Boston Chicken (parent of Boston Market) went public at $20 a share and rose to $48½ by the end of the first day of trading. The company's rapid expansion overextended the firm's ability to sustain profitable operations. Boston Chicken filed for bankruptcy, and the stock traded for a few pennies a share. (One of the questions facing the holders of any IPO whose stock price rises dramatically is whether the initial performance can be continued, or at least sufficiently maintained so that the price does not fall.)

All firms, of course, were small at one time, and each one had to go public to have a market for its shares. Someone bought the shares of IBM, Microsoft, and Johnson & Johnson when these firms initially sold shares to the general public. The new issue market offers the opportunity to invest in emerging firms, some of which may achieve substantial returns for those investors or speculators who are willing to accept the risk. It is the possibility of large rewards that makes the new issue market so exciting. However, if the past is an indicator of the future, many firms that go public will fail and will inflict losses on those investors who have accepted this risk by purchasing securities issued by the small, emerging firms.

Shelf Registrations

The previous discussion was cast in terms of firms initially selling their stock to the general public (that is, the "initial public offering" or "going public"). Firms that have previously issued securities and are currently public also raise funds by selling new securities. If the sales are to the general public, the same basic procedure applies. The new securities must be registered with and approved by the SEC before they may be sold to the public, and the firm often uses the services of an investment banker to facilitate the sale.

There are, however, differences between an initial public offering and the sale of additional securities by a publicly held firm. The first major difference concerns the price of the securities. Because a market already exists for the firm's stock, the problem of an appropriate price for the additional shares is virtually eliminated. This price will approximate the going market price on the date of issue. Second, because the firm must periodically publish information (for instance, the annual report) and file documents with the SEC, there is less need for a detailed prospectus. Many publicly held firms construct a prospectus describing a proposed issue of new securities and file it with the SEC. This document is called a "shelf registration." After the shelf registration has been accepted, the firm may sell the securities whenever the need for funds arises. For example, Dominion Resources filed a shelf registration that covered debt securities, preferred stock, common stock, and rights to purchase stock. Such a shelf registration gives Dominion Resources considerable flexibility. Not all the various types of securities have to be issued, and specific securities can be sold quickly if the firm deems that conditions are optimal for the sale.

Private placement

Nonpublic sale of securities to a financial institution

In addition to public sales of securities, firms may raise funds through private placements, which are nonpublic sales of securities. Such sales are made to venture capital firms or mutual funds that specialize in emerging firms. Small firms are often unable to raise capital through traditional sources. The size of the issue may be too small or the firm perceived as too risky for an underwriting through an investment banker. Venture capitalists thus fill a void by acquiring securities issued by small firms with exceptional growth potential.

Of course, not all small firms with exceptional growth potential realize that potential. Venture capitalists often sustain large losses on these investments, but their successes can generate large returns. If a venture capitalist invests $1,000,000 in five firms and four fail but one grows into a successful business, the one large gain can more than offset the investments in the four losers.

The venture capitalist's success depends on the ability to identify quality management and new products with market potential. While venture capitalists must negotiate terms that will reward their risk taking, they must not stifle the entrepreneurial spirit necessary to successfully manage an emerging business.

Once the firm does grow and achieve success, the securities purchased by the venture capitalist may be sold to the general public as part of the initial public offering. Many public offerings of securities combine a sale of new securities to raise funds for the firm and a sale of securities by existing stockholders. These holdings are often composed of shares originally purchased by the venture capitalists who are using the initial public sale as a means to realize their profits on their investments in the successful firm.

The Regulation of New Public Issues of Corporate Securities

The securities industry is subject to a large amount of regulation. Since the majority of securities cross state borders, the primary regulation is at the federal level. The purpose of this regulation is to protect the investing public by providing investors with information to help prevent fraud and the manipulation of securities prices. The regulation in no way assures you that you will make profits on your investments. It is not the purpose of the regulation to protect you from your own mistakes.

Federal regulation developed as a direct result of the debacle in the securities markets during the early 1930s. The first major pieces of legislation were the Securities Act of 1933 and the Securities Exchange Act of 1934. These are concerned with issuing and trading securities. The 1933 act covers new issues of securities, and the 1934 act is devoted to trading in existing securities. To administer these acts, the Securities and Exchange Commission (commonly called the SEC) was established.[3]

Full-disclosure laws

Federal securities laws requiring the timely disclosure of information that may affect the value of a firm's securities

These acts are also referred to as the full-disclosure laws, for their intent is to require companies with publicly held securities to inform the public of facts relating to the companies. A firm can issue new securities only after filing a registration statement with the SEC. The SEC will not clear the securities for sale until it appears that all material facts that may affect the value of the securities have been disclosed. The SEC does not comment on the worthiness of the securities as an investment. It is assumed that once you have received the required information you can make your own determination of the quality of the securities as an investment.

---

[3]The SEC home page (**http://www.sec.gov**) includes investor assistance and complaints, basic information concerning the SEC and its rule-making and enforcement powers, and specialized information for small business. The home page also provides entry to the EDGAR database. EDGAR is an acronym for Electronic Data Gathering Analysis and Retrieval, which is the government's database of SEC filings by public companies and mutual funds. All publicly held companies are required to file financial information electronically. From this site, an investor may obtain (download) a firm's 10-K and other required documents.

10-K report

Required annual report filed with the SEC by publicly held firms

Once the securities are sold to the general public, companies are required to keep current the information on file with the SEC. This is achieved by having the firm file an annual report (called the 10-K report) with the SEC. The 10-K report has a substantial amount of factual information concerning the firm, and this information may be sent to stockholders as the company's annual report. (Companies will, on request, send stockholders a copy of the 10-K report without charge.)

Firms are also required to release during the year any information that may materially affect the value of their securities. Information concerning new discoveries or major lawsuits or strikes is disseminated to the general public. The SEC has the power to suspend trading in a firm's securities if the firm does not release this information. This is a drastic act and is seldom used, for most firms continually have news releases that inform the investing public of significant changes affecting the firm. Sometimes the firm itself will ask to have trading in its securities stopped until a news release can be prepared and disseminated.

The disclosure requirements do not insist that the firm tell everything about its operations. Every firm has trade secrets that it does not want known by its competitors. The purpose of full disclosure is not to stifle the corporation but (1) to notify the investors so they can make informed decisions and (2) to prevent the firm's employees from using privileged information for personal gain. It should be obvious that employees may have access to information before it reaches the general public. Such inside information can enhance their ability to profit by buying or selling the company's securities before the announcement is made. Such profiteering from inside information is illegal. Officers and directors of the company must report their holdings and any changes in their holdings of the firm's securities with the SEC. Thus, it is possible for the SEC to determine if transactions are made prior to public announcements.

Inside information, however, is not limited to individuals who work for a firm. The concept applies to people who work for another firm that has access to privileged information. For example, accountants, lawyers, advertising agency employees, and creditors have access to inside information. Certainly a firm's investment bankers will know if a firm is anticipating a merger, seeking to take over another company, or intending to issue new securities. These investment bankers are, in effect, insiders. Neither they, nor anyone to whom they give this information, may legally use the information for personal gain.

Securities Investor Protection Corporation (SIPC)

Federal agency that insures investors against failure by brokerage firms

Another source of regulation of securities markets is the Securities Investor Protection Corporation (SIPC). This agency is similar in purpose to FDIC, for SIPC is designed to protect investors from failure by brokerage firms. SIPC insurance applies to those investors who leave securities and cash with brokerage firms. If the firm were to fail, these investors might lose part of their funds and investments. SIPC insurance is designed to protect investors from this type of loss. The insurance, however, is limited to $500,000 per customer, of which only $100,000 applies to cash balances. Hence, if you leave a substantial amount of securities and cash with a brokerage firm that fails, you are not fully protected by the insurance. To increase coverage, some brokerage firms carry additional insurance with private companies to protect their customers.

Sarbanes-Oxley Act of 2002

The large increase in stock prices experienced during 1998 and into 2000, and the subsequent decline in prices, may partially be attributed to fraudulent (or at least questionable) accounting practices and securities analysts' touting of stocks. These scandals led to the creation of the Sarbanes-Oxley Act, which was intended to restore public confidence in the securities markets. While it is too early to determine the ramifications of Sarbanes-Oxley, its range and coverage are extensive. The main provisions encompass:

- The independence of auditors and the creation of the Public Company Accounting Oversight Board
- Corporate responsibility and financial disclosure
- Conflicts of interest and corporate fraud and accountability

Sarbanes-Oxley created the Public Company Accounting Oversight Board, whose purpose is to oversee the auditing of the financial statements of publicly held companies. The board has the power to establish audit reporting rules and standards and to enforce compliance by public accounting firms. Firms and individuals who conduct audits are prohibited from performing nonaudit services for clients that they audit.

Corporate responsibility and financial disclosure require a publicly held firm's chief executive officer (CEO) and chief financial officer (CFO) to certify that the financial statements do not contain untrue statements or material omissions. These officers are also responsible for internal controls to ensure that they receive accurate information upon which to base their certifications of the financial statements. Corporate personnel cannot exert improper influence on auditors to accept misleading financial statements. Directors and executive officers are also banned from trading in the firm's securities during blackout periods when the firm's pensions are not permitted to trade the securities. Personal loans to executives and directors are prohibited, and senior management must disclose purchases and sales of the firm's securities within two business days.

Conflicts of interest revolve around the roles played by securities analysts and by investment bankers. Investment bankers facilitate a firm's raising of funds. Analysts determine if securities are under- or overvalued. Both are employed by financial firms such as Merrill Lynch. If a securities analyst determines that a stock is overvalued, this will damage the relationship between the investment bankers and the firm wishing to sell the securities. Hence, there is an obvious conflict of interest between the securities analysts and the investment bankers working for the same financial firm.

These two divisions need to be independent of each other. While the financial firms asserted that a "firewall" did exist between the investment bankers and the securities analysts, the actions of the securities analysts often implied the opposite. Sarbanes-Oxley strengthens the firewall. Investment bankers' ability to preapprove a securities analyst's research reports is restricted. Individuals concerned with investment banking activities cannot supervise securities analysts. Retaliation against securities analysts for negative reports is prohibited. An analyst must disclose whether he or she owns securities or received compensation from the companies covered by the analyst. Penalties for violating Sarbanes-Oxley and existing corporate fraud laws that prohibit the destruction of documents and impeding or obstructing investigations were increased, with penalties including fines and imprisonment of up to 20 years.

Summary

All firms must have a source of funds to acquire assets and retire outstanding debt. One possible source for these funds includes savers who are not currently using all of their income to buy goods and services. The transfer of these funds may occur indirectly through a financial intermediary or directly through the purchase of securities issued by firms.

When a firm (or government) issues new securities, it usually employs the services of investment bankers to facilitate the sale. The investment bankers act as a middleman between the firm and investors. In many cases, the investment bankers underwrite the securities and guarantee the issuing firm a specified amount of money. The investment bankers buy the securities with the intention of reselling them to the investing public.

New issues of corporate stocks and bonds that are sold to the general public must be registered with the Securities and Exchange Commission (SEC). The registration provides individuals with information so they may make informed investment decisions. The SEC also enforces the federal securities laws that govern the trading of corporate stocks and bonds in the secondary markets.

Investors' accounts with brokerage firms are insured by the Securities Investor Protection Corporation (SIPC). This insurance covers up to $500,000 an individual's securities held by a broker, but many brokerage firms carry more insurance. The intent of SIPC is to increase public confidence in the securities industry by reducing the risk of loss from a failure by a brokerage firm. The most recent securities legislation was the Sarbanes-Oxley Act of 2002. Fraudulent corporation activities, misleading accounting practices, and the resulting severe stock market price declines reduced investor confidence. By increasing corporate responsibility and financial disclosure requirements, creating stronger firewalls between investment bankers and securities analysts, and increasing the punishment for violations, Sarbanes-Oxley is designed to help restore investor confidence in the securities markets.

Review Objectives

Now that you have completed this chapter, you should be able to

1. Explain the role of investment bankers (pp. 37–43).
2. Describe the components of a public sale of securities (pp. 38–41).
3. Differentiate a best-effort agreement from a firm commitment (pp. 39–40).
4. Explain the purpose of a shelf registration and a private placement (pp. 42–43).
5. Identify the regulatory body that enforces the federal securities laws (p. 43).
6. State the primary purpose of the federal securities laws (pp. 43–46).

Internet Assignment

Initial public offerings occur frequently. Go to a calendar of new offerings, select a company that has just issued stock or is about to issue stock, and track the price for a week after the IPO. Did the price increase by more than 10 percent after the IPO? Possible sites include Hoover's IPO Central (**http://www.hoovers.com/global/ipoc**) or IPO Monitor (**http://ipomonitor.com**). You may also search for sites using Google by typing in "IPO."

Securities Markets

An anonymous sage once suggested, "A fool and his money are soon parted." The stock market is definitely one place where such separation may occur. On Monday, October 19, 1987, the Dow Jones Industrial Average plummeted 508 points, a 22.6 percent decline in one day. That decrease in aggregate stock prices exceeded the decline that occurred on October 28, 1929. On that fateful day, the value of the market declined only 12.8 percent!

Of course, you could point out that those are just two examples from one day of trading. Over time the stock market has risen. That is true; over time the stock market has risen, but there have been extended periods when the stock market declined. From 2000 through 2002, aggregate stock price fell for three consecutive years. If you bought stock in January 2000 and maintained your position, you probably had a loss three years later at the end of December 2002. Think about that statement—virtually everyone who purchased stocks near the end of 1999 and the beginning of 2000 had a loss on the purchases at the end of 2002!

The stock market did not exceed its 2000 highs until the fall of 2007. In October the Standard & Poor's 500 stock index reached 1576, but that was only marginally higher than the 1517 reached in September 2000. Stock prices then immediately started to decline, and in less than two years the S&P 500 fell to a low of 667 in March 2009. That is a decline of over 57 percent in less than two years! In mid-2010 the index stood around 1000, or 37 percent below the 2007 historic high.

There certainly is no question that investing in stocks involves the potential for loss. Without the possibility of loss, there would be no possibility of gain. Of all the financial institutions, the stock market may be the best known. While the stock market is certainly fascinating and well known, its purpose is often misunderstood. The primary function of a stock market is not to raise funds for firms but to transfer securities from sellers like you and me to buyers like you and me. There is no net change in the number of securities in existence; no funds are transferred to firms. All that occurs is a transfer of ownership from the seller to the buyer.

Stock markets are *secondary markets* that facilitate the transfer of existing securities among investors. This transfer is extremely important, for owners know a secondary market exists in which they may sell their securities. The ease with which securities may be sold and converted into cash increases the willingness of investors to buy and hold stocks and bonds and thus increases the ability of firms to issue securities. Without secondary markets, investors would be reluctant to buy the shares when a firm initially issued them.

This chapter considers securities markets, especially the stock market. The mechanics of investing, the role of brokers and securities dealers, cash versus margin accounts, long and short positions, and foreign securities are covered. The chapter ends with a discussion of the efficient market hypothesis, which suggests that over a period of years few investors will outperform the market.

Market Makers

Millions of shares and billions of dollars change hands every day. The buyers and sellers never meet; instead the securities markets impersonally transfer the stocks (and bonds) from the sellers to the buyers. The transfers may occur on an organized exchange, such as the New York Stock Exchange (NYSE), or through a less formal market called the over-the-counter (OTC) market. While there are organizational differences between the exchanges and the OTC markets, from your perspective as a potential investor, they work essentially the same.

Suppose you want to buy a stock such as IBM or Google. IBM trades through the NYSE and Google trades through the OTC markets, but in either case you buy the stock through a broker. The broker does not actually sell you the stock but acts *as your agent*. The stock is purchased from a securities dealer. Even if you use a discount brokerage firm or buy and sell on-line through the Internet, the stock is sold to you by a securities dealer. The Securities and Exchange Act of 1934 defines a dealer as anyone who engages in the "business of buying and selling securities for his *own account*."

This buying and selling by dealers for their own accounts has the effect of making a market in the securities, and dealers in the over-the-counter securities are referred to as "market makers." Dealers for securities traded on the New York Stock Exchange and the American Stock Exchange are referred to as specialists.

In either case, the market makers and specialists offer to buy securities from any seller and to sell securities to any buyer. They make a market in the security, so you and other investors are able to buy and sell when you wish. Without market makers, you would not be able to readily buy and sell stocks and bonds. Market makers set specified prices at which they will buy and sell the security. For example, a market maker may be willing to purchase a stock at $20 and sell it at $21. The security is then quoted 20–21, which are the bid and ask prices. The market maker is willing to purchase (bid) the stock at $20 and to sell (ask) the stock for $21.

Transactions are either round or odd lots. A round lot is the basic unit of trading and for stock is usually 100 shares. Smaller transactions, such as 55 shares, are odd lots. For some stocks the round lot differs from 100 shares. For example, for inexpensive stocks a round lot may be 500 or 1,000 shares. The importance of the distinction between odd and round lots has diminished over time, especially in the stock market. You can easily buy or sell 55, or 555, or 5,555 shares of IBM. The same does not apply to the bond markets. You will not be able to buy or sell $55, $555, or $5,555 of an IBM bond. The unit of trading is $1,000 and even that may be too small to execute a trade; the minimum unit of trading may be $5,000 or $10,000 face value of the bond. In some cases the minimum unit may be $100,000.

The difference between the bid and the ask is the spread, and this spread, like brokerage commissions, is part of the cost of investing. When you buy a security, the value of the security is the bid price, but you pay the ask price. Thus, the difference between the bid and the ask is a cost to you. If there are several market makers in a particular security, this spread will be small. If, however, there are only one or two market makers, the spread may be large (at least as a percentage of the bid price). The spread is also affected by the volume of transactions in the security and the number of shares the firm has outstanding. If there is a large volume of transactions or the number of outstanding shares is large, then there is usually a larger number of market makers. This increased competition reduces the spread between the bid and the ask. If the number of outstanding shares is small, the spread is usually larger.

The spread is one source of market makers' profits as they turn over the securities in their portfolios. Market makers also profit when the prices of the securities rise, for the value of their inventory of securities rises. (They also bear the risk if the value of any securities they hold were to fall.) The profits are a necessary facet of securities markets, for the profits induce the market makers to serve the crucial function of buying and selling securities. These market makers guarantee to buy and sell at the prices they quote. Thus you know (1) what the securities are worth at a point in time and (2) that there is a place to sell current security holdings or to purchase additional securities. For this service the market makers must be compensated, and this compensation is generated primarily through the spread between the bid and the ask.

Specialist

Market maker on an organized exchange

Bid and ask prices

Prices quoted by market makers at which they are willing to buy and sell securities

Round lot

Normal unit of trading in a security

Odd lot

Unit of trading that is less than a round lot

Spread

Difference between the bid and ask prices

While the bid and ask prices are set by the market makers, the level of these securities prices is set by investors. The market maker only guarantees to make a transaction at the bid-ask prices. If the market maker sets too low a price for a stock, a large quantity of shares will be demanded by investors. If the market maker is unable or does not want to satisfy this demand for the stock, this dealer will sell one round lot and increase the bid-ask prices. The increase in the price of the stock will (1) induce some holders of the stock to sell their shares and thereby replenish the market maker's inventory and (2) induce some investors wanting to buy the stock to drop out of the market.

If the market maker sets too high a price for the stock, there will be a large quantity of shares offered for sale. If the market maker is unable or does not want to absorb all these shares, the dealer may purchase a round lot and lower the bid-ask prices. The decline in the price of the stock will (1) induce some potential sellers to hold their stock and (2) induce some investors to enter the market and purchase the shares, thereby reducing any excess buildup of inventory by the market maker. Thus, while market makers may set the bid and ask prices for a security, they cannot set the general level of securities prices.

To set the general price level, market makers must be able to absorb excess securities into their inventory when excess supply exists and to sell securities from their inventory when excess demand exists. Buying these excess securities will require that the market makers pay for them, and selling securities will require that the market makers deliver the securities sold. No market maker has an infinite source of funds or securities. Although market makers may build up or decrease their inventory, they cannot indefinitely support the price by buying, nor can they stop a price increase by selling. The market maker's function is not to set the level of securities prices; all investors do that through buying and selling. The market maker's function is to facilitate the orderly process by which buyers and sellers of securities are brought together.

Composite Transactions

With the development of the Nasdaq stock market and mergers among stock exchanges (the American Stock Exchange merged with Nasdaq in 1998), the distinction among the various securities market has virtually disappeared. Since New York Stock Exchange securities trade on other exchanges (e.g., European exchanges), reporting in the financial press on listed securities includes all trades and is reported as the NYSE-Composite transactions.

Securities listed on an exchange also trade in the over-the-counter markets. The bulk of these trades are large transactions (e.g., 10,000 or more shares) and are often referred to as *block* trades. The participants in these markets are large institutional investors such as mutual funds, pension plans, and insurance companies who need to buy and sell large amounts of listed securities such as IBM, which trades on the NYSE. These institutional investors work through brokerage firms or market makers that complete the transactions.

Institutional investors can also avoid brokerage firms and securities dealers by using computerized trading systems such as *Instinet* (**http://www.instinet.com**), which provides bid and ask quotations and executes orders. Participation in *Instinet* is limited to financial institutions that subscribe to the service. These transactions are also reported in the composite transactions just like trades on the various exchanges.

The Mechanics of Investing in Securities

Market order

Order to buy or sell a security at the best current price

Day order

Order to buy or sell at a specified price that is canceled at the end of the day if it is not executed

Good-till-canceled order

Order to buy or sell at a specified price that remains in effect until it is executed by the broker or canceled by the investor

Commission

Payment to broker for executing an investor's buy and sell orders

Settlement date

Date by which payment for the purchase of securities must be made; date by which delivery of securities sold must be made

After deciding to purchase a security, you place a purchase order with a broker whose role is to buy and sell securities for customers. The broker and the market maker (the securities dealer) should not be confused, since they perform different, but crucial, roles in the mechanics of purchasing and selling securities. Brokers execute orders for customers. Securities dealers make a market; they buy and sell securities for their own accounts. Dealers bear the risk associated with their purchases and sales. Because brokers buy and sell for their customers' accounts, they do not bear the risk associated with fluctuations in securities prices. These risks are borne by the investors.

You may ask the broker to buy the security at the best price currently available, which is the asking price set by the market maker. Such a request is a market order. You are not assured of receiving the security at the currently quoted price, since that price may change by the time the order is executed. However, the order is generally executed at or very near the asking price.

You may enter a limit order and specify a price below the current asking price and wait until the price declines to the specified level. Such an order may be placed for one day (a day order), or the order may remain in effect indefinitely (a good-till-canceled order). Such an order remains in effect until it is either executed or canceled. If the price of the security does not decline to the specified level, the purchase is never made.

Once the purchase has been made, the broker sends you a confirmation statement (Exhibit 4.1). This confirmation statement gives the number of shares and type of security purchased (100 shares of Clevepak Corporation), the per unit price (12.13 or $12.13), and the total amount due ($1,264.00). The amount due includes the price of the security and the transaction fees. The major transaction fee is the brokerage firm's commission, but there may also be state transfer taxes and other miscellaneous fees. You have three business days after the date of purchase (8/16/XX) to pay the amount due and must make payment by the settlement date (8/19/XX). (The difference in the two dates is referred to as $t + 3$.)

Brokerage firms establish their own commission schedules, and it may pay to shop around for the best rates. Large investors are able to negotiate commissions, so that the brokerage costs are less than 1 percent of the value of the securities. Some brokerage firms offer investors discount rates that may reduce brokerage fees. You may further reduce commission costs by using on-line brokerage firms. If you feel comfortable using online trading and do not need

E X H I B I T 4.1
Confirmation Statement of
a Security Purchase

Confirmation Statement of a Security Purchase

Loch Lomond Securities
100 South Main Street
Richmond, Virginia 23219
(804) 555-1811

OFFICE ACCOUNT NO.	AE	TRADE DATE	SETTLEMENT DATE	TRANS. NO.	CUSIP NO.	EXCH	ORIG
45078	1	8/16/XX	8/19/XX	112	1667661		

YOU BOUGHT	YOU SOLD	SECURITY DESCRIPTION		
100		**CLEVEPAK CORP**	GROSS AMOUNT	1213 00

PRICE	INTEREST	
12.13	COMMISSION	51 00

STATE TAX
SERVICE CHG.
SEC/POST

AMOUNT DUE 1264 00

SYMBOL
CLV

PLEASE RETURN THIS COPY

WITH SECURITIES SOLD OR
PAYMENT IN THE AMOUNT DUE

BY SETTLEMENT DATE

IN THE ENCLOSED ENVELOPE

IN ACCORDANCE WITH YOUR INSTRUCTIONS WE ARE PLEASED TO CONFIRM THE ABOVE TRANSACTION FOR YOUR ACCOUNT AND RISK SUBJECT TO TERMS LISTED ON REVERSE SIDE

BRANCH COPY

regular brokerage services, you can obtain substantial reductions in commission costs by buying and selling securities over the Internet.

Margin

Investor's equity in a security position

You may purchase the security on margin, which is buying the stock with a combination of your cash and credit supplied by the broker. The phrase "on margin" can be confusing, since it is similar to buying "on credit." Margin is not the amount borrowed but is your equity in the security. This amount is often expressed as a percentage:

$$\text{Margin} = \text{Equity/Total value of the portfolio,}$$

so if you own stock worth $10,000 but owe $2,000, your margin is 80 percent ($8,000/$10,000).

Margin requirement

Minimum percentage, set by the Federal Reserve, of the total price that must be put up to buy securities

The margin requirement is the minimum percentage of the total price that you must pay and is set by the Federal Reserve Board. Individual brokers, however, may require more margin. The minimum payment required of the investor is the value of the securities times the margin requirement. Thus, if the margin requirement is 60 percent and the price plus the commission on 100 shares of Clevepak Corporation is $1,264.00, the investor must supply $758.40 in cash and borrow $505.60 from the broker, who in turn borrows the funds from a commercial bank. The investor pays interest to the broker on $505.60. The interest rate will depend on the rate that the broker must pay to the lending institution. The investor, of course, may avoid the interest charges by paying the entire $1,264.00 and not using borrowed funds.

Investors use margin to increase the potential return on the investment. Suppose you buy 50 shares at $20 a share for a total cost (excluding commissions) of $1,000. If the margin requirement is 60 percent, you put up $600 in cash and borrow $400 from your broker. If the price of the stock rises to $30, your position in the stock is worth $1,500. Your profit is $500, and you make 83.3 percent ($500/$600) on your funds invested in the stock. If you had not used margin and covered the entire cost ($1,000), your percentage return would have been 50 percent. The use of margin magnified your return. The use of borrowed funds to magnify your return is referred to as financial leverage.

Using margin works both ways. If the price of the stock falls to $15, the value of the 50 shares is now $750. You have lost $250 on the investment. Your percentage loss is 25 percent if you buy the stock with cash, but your percentage loss is 41.7 percent ($250/$600) if you buy the stock on margin. If you borrow money and commit less of your own funds, the percentage loss is magnified. Leverage is a two-edged sword! (These illustrations do not include [1] commissions on the stock purchases and sales and [2] interest on the borrowed funds. Both commissions and interest reduce the return you earn. Problems 3 and 4 at the end of this chapter add the interest expense, which reduces the profits on the stocks purchased through the use of margin.)

The use of margin could increase the broker's risk exposure. If the price of the stock declined sufficiently, it would wipe out your margin, but you would still owe the broker the funds borrowed to purchase the securities. If you then defaulted (did not pay off the loan), the broker would lose. Obviously brokers do not want to be at risk, so as the security's price and your margin decline, the broker will request additional collateral. This request, referred to as a "margin call," may be met by having you deposit cash or additional securities in the account. Once the cash and/or securities are placed in the account, your margin is increased. The restoration of the margin means that you, and not the broker, are at risk.

Delivery of Securities

Once the shares have been purchased and paid for, you must decide whether to leave the securities with the broker or to take delivery. (In the case of a margin account, you *must* leave the securities with the broker.) If the shares are left with the broker, they will be registered in the broker's name (that is, in the street name). The broker then becomes custodian of the securities and sends a monthly statement of the securities that are being held in the street name. The monthly statement also includes any transactions that have taken place during the month and any dividends and interest that have been received. You may leave the dividends and interest payments to accumulate with the broker or receive payment from the broker.

The primary reason for leaving securities with the broker is convenience, and the vast majority of investors (probably more than 95 percent) have their securities registered in the street name. You do not have to store the securities and can readily sell them, because they are in the broker's possession. Interest and dividend payments are received by the broker. You may have the money transferred to a bank account or held for subsequent investment. (The brokerage firm may also permit checks to be drawn against the account.)

Whether the investor ultimately decides to leave the securities with the broker or take delivery depends on the individual investor. If the securities are purchased on margin, you must leave the securities with the broker. If you frequently buy and sell securities (in other words, you are a "trader"), then the securities have to be left with the broker in order to facilitate the transactions.

The Short Sale

Long position

Purchase of securities in anticipation of a price increase

Short position

Sale of borrowed securities in anticipation of a price decrease

The previous discussion was limited to what is called a long position in which you purchase a stock and profit when its price rises. Of course, you will sustain a loss if the price of the stock declines. Can you earn a profit from a decline in the price of a stock? The answer is yes if you establish a short position. In a short sale, you *borrow* stock and sell it. If the price declines, you buy back the stock and pay off the loan (that is, return the borrowed stock). You earn a profit because the stock is bought for less than it was sold.

Perhaps this process is best understood through a simple illustration. A stock is selling for $39. You believe that the stock is overvalued and that the price will decline. You then borrow the stock through a broker and sell it for $39. Several weeks later the stock is selling for $25. You buy the stock for $25 and repay the loan (that is, return the stock to the broker). You made $14 a share because you purchased the stock for $25 and sold it for $39. Of course, if the price rises to $46, you would lose because you have to buy the stock at the higher price. In that case, the stock would be sold for $39 but would be bought at $46.

Short sales are common in business because a short sale is simply a *contract for future delivery*. When a school takes a student's tuition money before the semester begins, it enters into a contract for the future delivery of services (courses). This is a short position because if the price of providing the services falls, the school profits. If, however, the price of providing the services rises, the school loses. Entering into contracts for the future delivery of goods and services is common practice in business. In each case, the firm has made a short sale.

Measures of Securities Prices

Securities prices fluctuate daily, and many indexes have been developed to measure the price performance of securities. The best known and most widely quoted is the Dow Jones Industrial Average (DJIA) of 30 stocks. Dow Jones and Company also computes averages for 15 utility stocks and 20 transportation stocks as well as a composite index of all 65 stocks. The companies that compose the Dow Jones averages are among the largest, most well-established firms in the nation. Small firms and many firms that have grown into prominence during the last decade are excluded from the average. You should, however, not conclude that the Dow Jones Industrial Average is static. For example, Chevron, Goodyear, Sears, and Union Carbide were dropped and replaced with Home Depot, Intel, Microsoft, and AT&T. The rationale for the change was to make the DJIA more representative of the current stock market.

If you believe that the DJIA is too narrow, many other indexes are available for you to follow. The Standard & Poor's 500, NYSE Composite Index, and the Nasdaq index are among the most important and most frequently quoted. Other indexes and their composition are as follows:

Russell 1000: The largest 1,000 firms

Russell 2000: The next-largest 2,000 firms

Russell 3000: Combines the firms in the Russell 1000 and Russell 2000

Standard & Poor's 400 MidCap: Index of moderate-sized firms

Standard & Poor's 600 Small Cap: Index of relatively small firms

Standard & Poor's 1500 Index: Combines all the stocks in the S&P 500, S&P 400 MidCap, and the S&P 600 Small Cap

Value Line Stock Index: Index of all stocks covered by the Value Line Investment Survey

Wilshire 5000: Index of the market value of all NYSE, AMEX, and actively traded Nasdaq stocks (Although the name implies that the index covers 5,000 stocks, the actual composition exceeds 7,000 issues and covers virtually all publicly traded companies.)

In addition to the preceding aggregate measures of the market, there are indexes of subsets of the securities market. For example, Dow Jones daily publishes in the *Wall Street Journal* its specialty indexes that include Internet services, real estate investment trusts, and foreign countries such as the United Kingdom and Japan. There is even a Dow Jones Islamic Market index. This variety of indexes is important because, as is discussed in Chapter 27 on investment companies, there are mutual funds and exchange-traded funds that track an index instead of investing in individual stocks and bonds. Such funds permit you to take a position in the market or a subset of the market without the need to select specific securities.

While the composition of the various indexes obviously differs, that is not the only important distinction. How the indexes are calculated also differs. Averages of securities prices may be simple averages or weighted averages. As the name implies, a simple average adds the prices and divides by the number of entries. A value-weighted average multiplies the price of each stock by the number of shares outstanding. Firms such as AT&T and IBM have more than 1,700,000,000 shares outstanding. They have perceptibly more impact on a value-weighted index such as the S&P 500 than a firm like Shaw Group, a building engineering firm with only 69,100,000 outstanding shares.

How have stocks performed? The answer in part depends on the time period you select. For example, stock prices rose during the 1990s and then fell dramatically during 2000–2002. If you sold near the end of 1999, you probably did very well. But if you bought near the end of 1999, you probably sustained losses during the next three years. As of 2010, many stocks continued to sell perceptibly lower than the highs reached during the late 1990s. For example, Textron closed on December 31, 2009, at $18.81, which is 26 percent lower than its December 31, 1999, closing price of $25.50. (For the calculation of returns and how various investments have performed, please read Chapter 26.)

Foreign Securities

In addition to domestic securities, you may purchase foreign stocks and bonds. Foreign companies, like American companies, issue a variety of securities as a means to acquire funds. These securities subsequently trade on foreign OTC markets and foreign exchanges such as the stock exchanges in London, Paris, Tokyo, and other financial centers. Unless Americans and other foreigners are forbidden to acquire these securities, you can buy and sell stocks through these exchanges in much the same way that you purchase domestic American stocks and bonds. Thus, foreign securities may be purchased through the use of American brokers who have access to trading on these exchanges. In many cases this access is obtained through a correspondent relationship with foreign brokers.

American Depositary Receipts (ADRs)

Receipts issued for foreign securities held by a trustee

American securities markets do not actually trade foreign shares but trade receipts for the stock called American Depositary Receipts or ADRs. (ADRs are also referred to as American Depositary Shares.) Such receipts are created by large financial institutions, such as commercial banks, and are denominated in dollars. The ADRs are then sold to the American public and continue to trade in the United States.

The creation of ADRs greatly facilitates trading in foreign securities. Prices are quoted in dollars, and dividend payments are received in dollars. The ADR can represent any number of foreign shares. For example, each share of Telefonos de Mexico traded on the New York Stock Exchange represents 20 ordinary Mexican shares. The regular shares would be considered low-priced stocks in the United States. To make the prices comparable to U.S. securities prices, an ADR may represent 10, 15, or 20 Mexican shares.

In addition to stocks, Americans may also acquire bonds sold in foreign countries. There are basically three general types: (1) bonds issued by foreign firms; (2) bonds issued by foreign governments; and (3) bonds issued in foreign countries by American firms.

Bonds issued abroad by American firms are basically of two types, depending on the currency in which they are denominated. The American firms can sell bonds denominated in the local currency (for example, British pounds), or the firms can sell abroad bonds denominated in American dollars, called

Eurobonds

Bonds sold in a foreign country but denominated in the currency of the issuing firm

Eurobonds. This term applies even though the bonds may be issued in Asia instead of Europe. When an American firm issues a Eurobond, it promises to make payments in dollars. In this case the American investor will not have to convert the payments from the local currency (such as British pounds) back into dollars.

Competition in the Securities Markets

Competition in the Securities Markets

Efficient market hypothesis (EMH)

Theory that securities prices correctly measure the current value of a firm's future earnings and dividends

Economics teaches that markets will be competitive if there are many informed participants who may readily enter and exit. Both the stock and bond markets meet these conditions. Individuals may readily buy and sell securities, information is rapidly disseminated, and prices quickly change in reaction to changes in the economic and financial environment. The securities markets are among the most competitive markets in existence.

This competition among investors has led to the efficient market hypothesis (EMH), which asserts that securities markets are so competitive that the current price of a stock properly values the firm's future prospects—that is, the firm's future earnings and its dividends. If a firm's stock were perceived as undervalued, investors would rush to buy it, thus driving up its price. The converse would occur if the stock were perceived as overvalued, and the price would be driven down. Hence the current price is a true measure of the security's worth. For the individual investor, therefore, security analysis designed to determine if a stock is overpriced or underpriced is futile, because the stock is neither.

An important implication of this theory of efficient markets is that you cannot *consistently beat the market*; rather, you will earn a return consistent with the market return and the amount of risk you bear. The efficient market hypothesis suggests that the probability of your outperforming the market over any extended period is very small. That does not mean you cannot outperform (or underperform) the market during a short period of time. During a brief period, such as a year, some investors will earn a return that is higher than the return earned by the market. However, there is little chance that those individuals will be able to achieve superior results for an extended period of time (in other words, to outperform the market consistently).

One primary reason for the efficient market hypothesis is the speed with which securities prices adjust to new information. The hypothesis requires that prices adjust extremely rapidly as new information is disseminated. In the modern world of advanced communication, information is rapidly dispersed in the investment community. The market then adjusts securities prices in accordance with the impact of the news on the firm's future earnings and dividends. By the time that the individual investor has learned the information, securities prices probably will have already changed. Thus, the investor will not be able to profit from acting on the information.

This adjustment process is illustrated in Figure 4.1, which plots the daily closing price of Merck when the company pulled its drug Vioxx. The price of the stock fell over $12 from $45.07 to $33.00 in one day. Such price behavior is exactly what the efficient market hypothesis suggests: the market adjusts very rapidly to new information. By the time the announcement was reported in the financial press, it was too late for the individual investor to react, as the price change had already occurred.

If the market were not so efficient and prices did not adjust rapidly, some investors would be able to adjust their holdings and take advantage of differences in investors' knowledge. Consider the broken line in Figure 4.1. If some investors knew that the drug had been recalled but others did not, the former could sell

F I G U R E 4.1
Daily Closing Price of
Merck Stock (September 27,
2004–October 4, 2004)

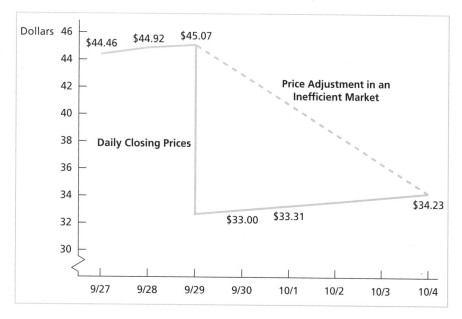

their holdings to those who were not informed. The price then could fall over a period of time as the knowledgeable sellers accepted progressively lower prices in order to unload their stock. Of course, if a sufficient number of investors had learned quickly of the recall, the price decline would be rapid as these investors adjusted their valuations of the stock in accordance with the new information. That is exactly what happened, because a sufficient number of investors were rapidly informed and the efficient market quickly adjusted the stock's price.

If an investor were able to anticipate the recall before it was announced, that individual could avoid the price decline. Obviously some investors did sell their shares just before the announcement, but it is also evident that some individuals bought those shares. Certainly one of the reasons for learning the material and performing the various types of analysis throughout this text is to increase your ability to anticipate events before they occur. However, you should realize that considerable evidence supports the efficient market hypothesis and strongly suggests that few investors will over a period of time outperform the market consistently.

While financial markets appear to be exceedingly efficient, some empirical evidence suggests that inefficiencies do exist. These inefficiencies are often referred to as "anomalies." As applied to financial markets, an anomaly is an investment strategy whose return exceeds the return that should be earned if the market were completely efficient.[1] Such inefficiencies tend to revolve

[1]For an excellent lay discussion of efficient markets, possible anomalies, and the implications of efficient markets for investing, see Burton Malkiel, *A Random Walk Down Wall Street*, 10th ed. (New York: W.W. Norton & Company, 2010). One implication of efficient markets is the use of a passive investment strategy. One possible passive strategy is explained in Richard Evans, *The Index Fund Solution* (New York: Simon & Schuster, 1999).

around particular investment strategies such as buying stocks in which insiders (e.g., management) are investing or buying stocks after an unusual event occurs, since the market may overreact. For example, an unexpected decline in earnings may lead to a large price decline in the price of the stock. After the market has digested the new earnings information, the price of the stock may subsequently rise.

Whether the inefficiencies are sufficiently large that you can take advantage of the anomaly and generate an excess return is open to debate. Essentially the argument becomes, if an investment strategy increases my return from 8.3 percent to 8.6 percent but I have more expenses (such as more commissions or higher taxes from securities trading), the increased return may not cover the additional costs. Thus, an anomaly could exist but its magnitude is insufficient to justify using it as an investment strategy. Or the anomaly may apply to large institutional investors but individuals may be unable to take advantage of the inefficiency.

Summary

Securities are traded on organized exchanges, such as the NYSE, or in the informal over-the-counter markets (Nasdaq). Securities are bought through brokers, who buy and sell for their customers' accounts. The brokers obtain the securities from dealers, who make markets in them. These dealers offer to buy and sell at specified prices (quotes), which are called the bid and the ask. Brokers and investors obtain these prices through an electronic system that transmits the quotes from the various dealers.

After securities are purchased, you must pay for them with either cash or a combination of cash and borrowed funds. When you use borrowed funds, you are buying on margin. Buying on margin increases both your potential return and potential risk of loss.

You may take delivery of securities or leave them with the broker. Leaving securities registered in the street name offers the advantage of convenience because the broker becomes the custodian of the certificates. Since the advent of the SIPC and its insurance protection, there is little risk of loss to the investor from leaving securities with the broker.

You may establish long or short positions. With a long position, you purchase stock in anticipation of its price rising. If the price of the stock rises, you may sell it for a profit. With a short position, you sell borrowed stock in anticipation of its price declining. If the price of the stock falls, you may repurchase it at the lower price and return it to the lender. The position generates a profit because the selling price exceeds the purchase price.

Both the long and short positions are the logical outcomes of securities analysis. If you think a stock is underpriced, a long position (purchase of the stock) should be established. If you believe a stock is overvalued, a short position (the sale of borrowed securities) is established. In either case, if you are correct, the position will generate a profit. Either position may, however, generate a loss if prices move against your expected price change.

American investors may purchase securities issued by foreign firms. This is usually accomplished through the purchase of American Depositary Receipts, or ADRs, which are issued by financial institutions and represent the foreign securities. You may also acquire securities such as Eurobonds—debt instruments issued abroad by American firms that are denominated in dollars instead of the foreign currency.

Securities markets are very competitive and efficient. New information is disseminated rapidly, and prices adjust quickly in response to the new information. The efficient market hypothesis suggests that few investors will be able to outperform the market over an extended period of time. Although you may outperform (or underperform) the market for a given period, consistently superior returns may be impossible to achieve.

Review Objectives

Now that you have completed this chapter, you should be able to

1. Distinguish between (a) organized exchanges and OTC markets, (b) brokers and securities dealers, (c) market orders and limit orders (pp. 49–52).

2. Trace the mechanics of a stock purchase or sale (pp. 52–55).

3. Explain the advantages and risk associated with buying stock on margin (pp. 53–54).

4. Contrast long and short positions in stocks (p. 55).

5. Illustrate the mechanics of a short sale (p. 55).

6. List several aggregate measures of the stock market (pp. 55–56).

7. Determine how American Depositary Receipts (ADRs) facilitate trading in foreign securities (p. 57).

8. Explain why an investor should not expect to outperform the market on a consistent basis (pp. 58–60).

Internet Assignment

Select ten stocks and set up a watch account. Be certain the companies are in different industries; you want a diversified portfolio to help manage your risk exposure! Invest $1,000 in each company starting with the closing price as of the day you set up the account. If the price of a share is $34.21, buy $1,000/$34.21 = 29 shares. A watch account at Yahoo! (**http://finance.yahoo. com**) will maintain the value of the account and your profit or loss on each stock if you enter the number of shares and the price paid per share. (If you prefer to use a watch account at another site, that is also acceptable.) For comparisons add an index such as the Standard & Poor's 500 stock index (ticker symbol: ^GSPC) or the Nasdaq index (^IXIC).

Problems

1. After an analysis of Lion/Bear, Inc., Karl O'Grady has concluded that the firm will face financial difficulty within a year. The stock is currently selling for $5 and O'Grady wants to sell it short. His broker is willing

to execute the transaction but only if O'Grady puts up cash as collateral equal to the amount of the short sale. If O'Grady does sell the stock short, what is the percentage return he loses if the price of the stock rises to $7? What would be the percentage return if the firm went bankrupt and folded?

2. Lisa Lasher buys 400 shares of stock on margin at $18 per share. If the margin requirement is 50 percent, how much must the stock rise for her to realize a 25 percent return on her invested funds? (Ignore dividends, commissions, and interest on borrowed funds.)

3. A year ago, Kim Altman purchased 200 shares of BLK, Inc. for $25.50 on margin. At that time the margin requirement was 40 percent. If the interest rate on borrowed funds was 9 percent and she sold the stock for $34, what is the percentage return on the funds she invested in the stock?

4. Barbara buys 100 shares of DEM at $35 a share and 200 shares of GOP at $40 a share. She buys on margin and the broker charges interest of 10 percent on the loan.

   a. If the margin requirement is 55 percent, what is the maximum amount she can borrow?

   b. If she buys the stocks using the borrowed money and holds the securities for a year, how much interest must she pay?

   c. If after a year she sells DEM for $29 a share and GOP for $32 a share, how much did she lose on her investment?

   d. What is the percentage loss on the funds she invested if the interest payment is included in the calculation?

5. A stock is currently selling for $45 a share. What is the gain or loss on the following transactions?

   a. You take a long position and the stock's price declines to $41.50.

   b. You sell the stock short and the price declines to $41.50.

   c. You take a long position and the price rises to $54.

   d. You sell the stock short and the price rises to $54.

6. A sophisticated investor, B. Graham, sold 500 shares short of Amwell, Inc. at $42 a share. The price of the stock subsequently fell to $38 before rising to $49 at which time Graham covered the position (that is, closed the short position). What was the percentage gain or loss on this investment?

7. You purchase 100 shares for $50 a share ($5,000), and after a year the price rises to $60. What will be the percentage return on your investment if you bought the stock on margin and the margin requirement was (a) 25 percent, (b) 50 percent, and (c) 75 percent? (Ignore commissions, dividends, and interest expense.)

8. Repeat Problem 7. to determine the percentage return on your investment but in this case suppose the price of the stock falls to $40 per share. What generalization can be inferred from your answers to Problems 7 and 8?

All the problems in this chapter compute what is called the "holding period return," which does not consider how long you held the stock. The difference between holding period returns and annualized returns is developed in Chapter 26 on investment returns.

In each problem, (1) determine the profit or loss, (2) determine the amount invested (i.e., did you buy the stock on margin or did you put up the full price), and (3) if you bought the stock on margin, calculate how much interest you paid.

Here are several examples.

1. You buy a stock for $100 and sell it for $140; what is the percentage return if the margin requirement is 40 percent and the interest rate of borrowed funds is 10 percent?

2. You sell a stock short for $100 and repurchase it for $140; what is the percentage return?

3. You buy a stock for $100 and sell it for $140; what is the percentage return?

4. You buy a stock for $100 and sell it for $60; what is the percentage return?

5. You sell a stock short for $100 and repurchase it for $60; what is the percentage return?

6. You buy a stock for $100 and sell it for $60; what is the percentage return if the margin requirement is 40 percent?

7. You buy a stock for $100 and sell it for $140; what is the percentage return if the margin requirement is 40 percent?

In each problem the starting price is $100 and the ending price is either $140 or $60, a change of $40.

1. In this illustration you borrow $60 and have to pay $6 in interest on the borrowed funds. This reduces your net gain to $34 ($40 − $6), so the percentage return is $34/$40 = 85%. While buying the stock on margin magnified the percentage return, the interest expense reduced the return.

2. In examples 1 through 5, you have a long position, which is premised on the price of the stock rising. In examples 6 and 7, you have a short position, which is premised on the price of the stock declining. In this example, since the price of the stock rises, you have to buy it back for a $40 loss, so the percentage loss is ($40)/$100 = −40%.

3. You make $40 on your long position, so the percentage return is $40/$100 = 40%.

4. You lose $40, so the percentage return is ($40)/$100 = −40%.

5. In this example, you repurchase the stock for a $40 gain, so the percentage return is $40/$100 = 40%.

6. The margin requirement is $40; you borrow $60 and put up $40 of your own funds. You lose $40, so the percentage loss is ($40)/$40 = −100%. Once again, buying the stock on margin magnified the return, except in this example it magnified the percentage loss.

7. The margin requirement is $40; you borrow $60 and put up $40 of your own funds. You make $40, so the percentage return is $40/$40 = 100%. Notice how buying the stock on margin magnified the percentage return on your funds.

Relationships

1. If stock prices decline, the S&P 500 _____.

2. An increase in the Russell 1000 suggests that stocks prices _____.

3. If an investor sells stock short and its price subsequently rises, the investor's loss _____.

4. An increase in the margin requirement _____ the amount an investor may borrow to buy stock.

5. An increase in the spread _____ the cost of investing.

6. Buying stock on margin instead of cash _____ risk.

7. If an investor uses borrowed funds to buy stock, the potential percentage loss is _____.

8. If you buy a stock (take a long position) and the price of the stock rises, your gain _____.

Answers

1. declines

2. increased

3. increases

4. decreases

5. increases

6. increases

7. increased

8. increases

The Federal Reserve

According to Will Rogers, "There have been three great inventions since the beginning of time: fire, the wheel, and central banking." Perhaps greatness should be disputed, but there is no denying the potential impact that the nation's central bank, the Federal Reserve (the "Fed"), can have on the economy through its impact on the supply of money and credit. This chapter covers the purpose and composition of the Fed, the importance that bank reserves play in the multiple expansion of money, and how the Fed's tools of monetary policy affect the lending capacity of the banking system. Through this impact the Fed alters the supply of money and interest rates.

The Federal Reserve, however, does not work in a vacuum. Other factors may also affect the supply and cost of credit. These include the fiscal policy of the federal government, the political environment, the saving habits of individuals, and expectations of inflation or deflation. For example, the federal government's deficit must be financed; someone has to lend the funds to cover the deficit. Will the Fed supply the credit required to finance the deficit or will this credit come at the expense of loans to corporations? The expectation of inflation may alter the cost of credit as lenders seek higher rates to compensate them for the loss of purchasing power. Will the Fed take steps to reduce the expectation of inflation? The Fed cannot act without considering the environment in which an action is taken or how it may produce a reaction that defeats the purpose of the Fed's policy.

The Role of the Federal Reserve

Monetary policy

Management of the money supply for the purpose of maintaining stable prices, full employment, and economic growth

The purpose of the Federal Reserve is to help achieve stable prices, full employment, and economic growth through the regulation of the supply of credit and money in the economy. Changing the supply of money and credit to achieve these three goals is called monetary policy.

The Federal Reserve (the "Fed") has several tools of monetary policy. The primary tool is open market operations, while secondary tools are the discount rate and reserve requirements. The Federal Reserve uses these monetary tools to expand or contract the supply of money to pursue the economic goals of prosperity with full employment and stable prices. When the Federal Reserve seeks to increase the supply of money and credit to help expand the level of income and employment, that is called an "easy" monetary policy. The process of executing such a policy is often referred to as "quantitative easing." When the Federal Reserve seeks to contract the supply of money and credit to help fight inflation, that is referred to as a "tight" monetary policy.

While controlling the supply of money and credit is the primary role of the Federal Reserve, it also serves other functions. These include supervisory power over depository institutions and the clearing of checks. The purpose of the supervisory power is to protect depositors from poor financial management by individual banks and includes enforcement of bank regulations and periodic examinations of banks. Periodic reports concerning a bank's loans, expenses, and earnings are also required. If the examinations and reports indicate that a bank is following unsound financial policies, the Federal Reserve can require the bank's management to correct the bank's actions. This ability to force a bank's management to change policy gives the Federal Reserve's supervisory powers real force. The mere existence of this force is generally sufficient to keep the vast majority of banks pursuing sound financial policies.

Clearing checks is a service provided banks by the Federal Reserve. The process of check clearing is illustrated by the flow chart in Exhibit 5.1. When a check is drawn on bank A and deposited in bank B, the clearing mechanism goes through the Federal Reserve. Although changes in technology such as electronic funds transfer have increased the speed with which checks clear and accounts are transferred, the process still goes through the Federal Reserve.

The Federal Reserve also serves as a depository institution for member banks, the U.S. Treasury, and foreign central banks. Banks deposit their reserves with the Federal Reserve, and the Treasury may deposit funds such as

E X H I B I T   5.1
The Process of Clearing Checks

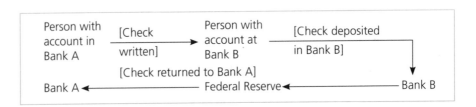

tax receipts in Federal Reserve banks. Foreign deposits arise as the result of international monetary transactions. Of all the different deposits, the most important are the reserves of banks. By altering their reserves, the Federal Reserve is able to alter the supply of money and the ability of banks to create loans. It is through the power of the Federal Reserve to create and destroy banks' excess reserves that credit is eased or tightened.

Structure of the Federal Reserve

Board of Governors

Controlling body of the Federal Reserve, whose members are appointed by the president of the United States

The power in the Federal Reserve is concentrated in a Board of Governors, consisting of seven people appointed by the president of the United States with the confirmation of the Senate. The appointments are for 14 years, and the terms are staggered so that one new appointment is made every two years. The chair of the Board of Governors is usually the major spokesperson for monetary policy and may act as an advisor to the president on economic policy. The power of the Board of Governors manifests itself in several ways through its power of appointment and control of open market operations.

District bank

One of twelve banks that compose the Federal Reserve

The country is divided into 12 districts, with a Federal Reserve bank in each district. Each district bank is managed by nine directors, three of whom are appointed by the Board of Governors. The remaining six directors are elected by member banks and represent the member banks, industry, commerce, and agriculture. By dividing the nation into districts, it is possible to have an individual reserve bank perform specialized financial services pertaining to its region. For example, the financial problems of rural regions may differ from those of urban areas. Decentralizing the central bank into districts permits a more flexible approach to regional financial problems. Since the city of New York is the financial center of the nation, the district bank in New York is the largest and most important individual reserve bank.

Member banks constitute the next component of the Federal Reserve. Commercial banks have either state or national charters. All banks with national charters must join the Federal Reserve. State banks have the option to join, but many do not choose to join. Since the Federal Reserve permits nonmember banks to use its check-clearing facilities and to borrow reserves, these services are available to all banks without their joining the system.

The member banks are required to invest capital in their district's Federal Reserve bank. The members are the owners of the Federal Reserve banks, and for this investment they receive a modest return on their capital from the earnings of the Federal Reserve. The source of these earnings is the interest earned on the U.S. government debt owned by the Federal Reserve. If the Federal Reserve earns profits that exceed its required payments to member banks, the excess profits are returned to the Treasury.

F I G U R E　5.1
Structure of the Federal
Reserve

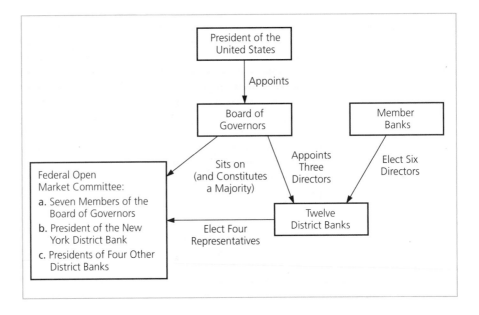

Federal Open Market
Committee

Part of the Federal Re-
serve that establishes
and executes monetary
policy

　　The last component of the Federal Reserve is the Federal Open Market
Committee, which has control over open market operations. Because open
market operations are the most important tool of monetary policy, this committee is a powerful component of the system. The committee consists of the
seven members of the Board of Governors and five presidents of the district
banks. The president of the New York district bank is a permanent member
of the committee, while the four remaining positions rotate among the district
bank presidents. By voting as a bloc, the Board of Governors has a majority
on the committee and has control of open market operations.
　　In summary, the important components of the Federal Reserve are
(1) the Board of Governors, (2) the district reserve banks, (3) the member
banks, and (4) the Federal Open Market Committee. This structure is summarized by Figure 5.1. Although the president of the United States appoints
the Board of Governors, and the member banks own the Federal Reserve, the
real power rests with the Board of Governors. It has this power because it
(1) appoints three of the nine directors of the district reserve banks, (2) composes
a majority of the Federal Open Market Committee, and (3) has regulatory authority over the commercial banks. Thus, the Board of Governors is individually the most important part of the Federal Reserve System.

The Expansion of Money and Credit

　　One way that the Federal Reserve affects the supply of money and credit is
through its impact on the reserves of banks, which alters their lending capacity. A small change in banks' reserves can produce a much larger change in

the money supply because of the fractional reserve system. Understanding the potential impact of monetary policy requires understanding how the banking system expands and contracts the supply of money and credit—that is, understanding how a fractional reserve banking system alters the supply of money.

Banks' ability to lend comes from investors: the depositors, general creditors, and owners who invest in various types of instruments (such as certificates of deposit or the bank's stock) issued by each bank. An individual bank can lend only what it obtains from its sources of finance, but, as is subsequently explained, the aggregate banking system can expand the supply of money. As this money flows among banks, the aggregate supply is increased. This increase is the result of the fractional reserve requirements established by the Federal Reserve.

This section is concerned with the banking system's ability to expand and contract the supply of money and credit. The next section will consider how the Federal Reserve affects the capacity of banks to lend and thus affects the supply of money and credit. Although the following discussion could become involved as different scenarios are considered, only one simple case is given, since the purpose of the discussion is to illustrate the expansion of money and credit and not to illustrate how differing assumptions may alter the amount of change in the money supply.[1]

The process of loan creation will be illustrated under the following assumptions: (1) Cash is always deposited in a demand deposit. (2) Banks hold no excess reserves; all excess reserves are loaned. (3) There are sufficient borrowers to consume the excess reserves of the banks. If these assumptions are violated, there are leakages within the system that decrease the potential expansion. For example, if individuals hold cash, that money is not deposited in a bank and hence cannot be lent by a bank. Such a holding of cash reduces the assets of banks and reduces their capacity to expand the supply of money and credit.

What is the potential effect of cash deposited in a checking account? The money supply (also referred to as M-1) is the sum of demand deposits plus coins and currency in circulation. Cash deposited into checking accounts does not change the money supply. All that is changed is the form of the money, from cash to demand deposits. Such transactions, however, are extremely important, for they increase the banks' ability to lend. When the banks use this ability and make loans, they expand the supply of money.

Consider what happens when $100 is deposited in a checking account. The $100 has been removed from circulation and replaced by the demand deposit. After the bank receives the $100 cash deposit, the $100 becomes part of the reserves of the bank. This $100 reserve is divided into two categories; (1) those reserves that must be held against the demand deposit, the required reserves, and (2) those reserves in excess of the reserve requirement, which are

---

[1]For a discussion of different scenarios under different assumptions, consult a money and banking text such as Lloyd Thomas, *Money, Banking, and Financial Markets* (Mason, Ohio: Thomson South-Western, 2006) or Frederic S. Mishkin, *The Economics of Money, Banking, and Financial Markets*, 9th ed. (Reading, Mass.: Addison-Wesley, 2009).

called excess reserves. If the reserve requirement is 10 percent, then $10 of the $100 cash reserve is required and $90 is excess reserves. These excess reserves are important because commercial banks use their excess reserves to acquire income-earning assets such as loans and securities. Depositing cash in a commercial bank thus gives it the ability to create loans, because the bank obtains a resource that it may lend—excess reserves. Banks do not lend and cannot lend their deposit liabilities.

If the bank grants a borrower a loan of $90, what effect will this transaction have on (1) the depositor, (2) the bank, and (3) the borrower? Since this transaction does not concern the depositor, it has no effect on the depositor. As far as the depositor is concerned, the bank still owes on demand $100. The borrower receives an asset—a demand deposit at the bank—and also incurs a liability, to the bank. The bank acquires an asset, the $90 loan, and the bank incurs a new liability, the $90 demand deposit. This deposit is the money that the borrower receives for the loan.

Why does the commercial bank create a new demand deposit instead of just lending the person the cash? The answer is that the bank does not want the borrower to remove the cash from the bank. The bank wants to keep that cash as long as possible, for it is part of the bank's reserves. The bank does realize that the borrower will spend the money and the reserves will probably be transferred to another bank, but the bank still wants the use of the reserves as long as possible.

Why does the borrower take out the loan? Obviously, the borrower does not want to leave the money in the bank and pay interest on the loan but intends to spend it. When the borrower does spend the money, the recipient of the check will either cash it or deposit it in a commercial bank. When the check is deposited, the probability of this bank and the borrower's bank being the same is quite small, since there are thousands of commercial banks in the country. When the check is deposited in the second bank, that bank sends the check to the first bank for payment. The first bank transfers $90 worth of reserves (the cash) to the second bank. This flow of deposits and reserves may be summarized by the following figure:

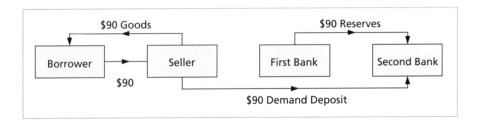

In summary, the loan made possible a purchase by the borrower, and thus a seller has made a sale that may not have occurred without the creation of the loan. Goods have flowed from the seller to the buyer. When the seller deposited the payment in a commercial bank, this caused reserves to flow between the seller's bank and the borrower's bank.

What is the net effect of this transaction on the money supply and amount of credit? Both have increased. There are $190 in demand deposits—the initial deposit of $100 in the first bank and the new deposit of $90 in the second bank. There has been a net increase in the money supply of $90. This $90 increase came through the process of loan creation, for there is now $90 in new credit. The act of depositing cash in a checking account led to a net increase in the supply of money through the process of loan creation.

The process of loan creation is not limited to the initial expansion of $90, for the second bank now has a new deposit. It must hold reserves against the new checking account. Since the reserve requirement is 10 percent, the bank must hold in reserve $9 ($90 × 0.1). It received $90 in reserves from the first bank when the check cleared. Thus, $81 of these reserves are excess reserves that the second bank may use to purchase an income-earning asset or grant a new loan. If the second bank grants a loan for $81, it creates a new demand deposit of $81. The borrower then purchases goods and services and pays for them with a check drawn on the new demand deposit. The $81 check then is deposited in a third bank and is cleared. This creates for the third bank a new deposit and transfers to it $81 in reserves from the second bank. The third bank divides these reserves into required reserves ($81 × 0.1 = $8.10) and excess reserves of $72.90. The third bank now has the capacity to acquire income-earning assets and create new loans.

This process of lending and passing reserves among commercial banks may continue until there are no more excess reserves. With each new loan there is expansion in the money supply. The net increase in new credit and in demand deposits is many times the initial deposit. This expansion is illustrated in Exhibit 5.2, which continues the multiple expansion for the first eight rounds. As may be seen in the table, each additional loan and new demand deposit

EXHIBIT 5.2
Multiple Expansion of the Supply of Money

	Initial Deposit = $100		Reserve Requirement = 10%	
	New Demand Deposits	Cumulative New Credit Created	Cumulative Required Reserves	Excess Reserves
1st bank	$100.00	$ 0.00	$ 10.00	$90.00
2st bank	90.00	90.00	19.00	81.00
3rd bank	81.00	171.00	27.10	72.90
4th bank	72.90	243.90	34.39	65.61
5th bank	65.61	309.51	40.95	59.05
6th bank	59.05	368.56	46.86	53.14
7th bank	53.14	421.70	52.17	47.83
8th bank	47.83	469.53	56.95	43.05
Final round	0	$900.00	100.00	0

(column 1) is smaller, but the sum of the new loans increases (column 2). As the total of demand deposits rises, required reserves also rise (column 3), so excess reserves must decline (column 4). Of course, it is this decline in excess reserves that causes each new loan to be smaller. Eventually, if the expansion continues indefinitely, the excess reserves will become zero and the total $100 in reserves will be required reserves.

If the expansion continues until there are no excess reserves, how much will the money supply increase? What is the increase in new loans? These questions may be answered by the following simple equation:

$$\frac{\text{Change in excess reserves}}{\text{Reserve requirement}} = \text{Change in the money supply} \qquad (5.1)$$

Equation 5.1 gives the increase in *both* new credit and the money supply. In the previous example, the cash deposit of $100 increased excess reserves by $90. Since the reserve requirement was 10 percent, the maximum possible expansion in the money supply and new credit is

$$\$90/0.1 = \$900.$$

Depositing $100 in a demand deposit permits an expansion of $900 of new money. Since the new money came through the creation of new credit, $900 is also the maximum possible increase in new credit. The change in the money supply and the change in credit thus is ten times the initial change in the excess reserves.

Cash Withdrawals and the Reduction in Reserves

In the previous example, cash was deposited in an account, which created new excess reserves and led to the expansion in the supply of money and credit. A cash withdrawal from a bank reverses the process and reduces the bank's reserves. If the bank has excess reserves, the withdrawal creates no problems for the bank, because it takes the funds out of its excess reserves. After the withdrawal, the bank's lending capacity is reduced because the bank has lost excess reserves.

The situation is different if the bank has no excess reserves. While the bank may be able to meet the withdrawal from its existing (and required) reserves, it now has a major problem: Its reserves are insufficient to meet its reserve requirements against its deposit liabilities. Thus, the bank must take some action to restore its reserves.

One possibility is to borrow the reserves from another bank. If bank A borrows reserves from bank B, bank A will now meet its reserve requirement. Will bank B meet its reserve requirement? The answer should be obvious. Bank B can make this loan only if it has excess reserves! The borrowing of reserves transfers reserves from one bank to another; it does not alter the total supply of reserves in the banking system. All that changes is the location of the reserves from bank B to bank A.

Federal funds market

Market in which banks borrow and lend excess reserves

The market for these reserves is called the federal funds market. Federal funds is one of the most well developed of all short-term credit markets. If a commercial bank lacks sufficient reserves against its deposit liabilities, it can borrow reserves from a commercial bank that has excess reserves. If a bank has excess reserves, it can put these funds to work by lending them in the federal funds market because the lending bank charges the borrowing bank interest for the use of the reserves.

Since the reserves may be needed for only a very short time, the loans made in the federal funds market are usually for extremely short periods (for example, a day). Thus, any commercial bank that has a temporary surplus of loanable funds may briefly lend them in the federal funds market and earn interest on the funds. The rate of interest is referred to as the federal funds rate. (This is something of a misnomer because the loans involve neither the federal government nor the Federal Reserve.) Any commercial bank that has a deficit in its reserves is able to borrow them for as short a period as necessary.

Federal funds rate

Interest rate charged by banks on overnight loans of reserves

If the banking system lacks excess reserves, the bank that experienced the cash withdrawal could borrow the reserves from the Federal Reserve. Unlike the banking system, the Federal Reserve has the power to create reserves. If bank A is short and all other banks lack excess reserves, then borrowing from the Federal Reserve creates the reserves needed by bank A. Of course, the Federal Reserve charges interest on this loan, just as bank B would charge bank A interest for the use of its reserves. This interest rate, called the discount rate, is a tool of monetary policy and is discussed in the next section on the tools of monetary policy.

Discount rate

Interest rate charged banks for borrowing reserves from the Federal Reserve

Suppose, however, that the banking system has no excess reserves and bank A does not want to borrow reserves from the Federal Reserve. What will happen? The bank will have to liquidate some of its assets, and because there are no excess reserves in the banking system, the multiple expansion illustrated previously works in reverse. The reduction in reserves will cause the supply of money and credit to contract. Just as the cash deposit leads to a multiple expansion, the withdrawal of cash when the banking system is fully loaned up will cause a multiple contraction in the money supply and in the supply of credit.

This process of a multiple contraction is illustrated in Exhibit 5.3, which essentially reverses the procedure illustrated in Exhibit 5.2. The initial cash withdrawal of $100 reduces demand deposits by $100 (column 1). Total reserves also decline by $100, but since required reserves decline by only $10 (column 3), the decline in total reserves of $100 means the bank is now short reserves by $90. The bank liquidates an asset worth $90 to replace its lost reserves and the shortage is transferred to the second bank. The second bank now loses $90 in deposits and reserves and the process is repeated. Unless the cash is returned to the banking system, the system must contract. The cumulative decline in demand deposits is given in the second column, and the fourth column presents the cumulative change in required reserves with each subsequent contraction. As in the case of the expansion in demand deposits, the maximum decrease in the money supply is $-\$900$ ($-\$90/0.1$) and the cumulative change in required reserves is $-\$100$, which is the amount of the initial cash withdrawal.

EXHIBIT 5.3
Multiple Contraction in the
Supply of Money

Final Round	Initial Withdrawal = $100		Reserve Requirement = 10%	
	Change in Demand Deposits	Cumulative Change in Demand Deposits	Reduction in Required Reserves	Cumulative Change in Required Reserves
1st bank	−$100.00	−$100.00	−$10.00	−$ 10.00
2st bank	−90.00	−190.00	−9.00	−19.00
3rd bank	−81.00	−271.00	−8.10	−27.10
4th bank	−72.40	−343.90	−7.29	−34.39
.	.	.	.	.
.	.	.	.	.
.	.	.	.	.
Final round	0	−$900.00	0	−$100.00

This contraction is precisely what happened during the Great Depression. (Remember the run on the bank George Bailey experienced in *It's a Wonderful Life?*) Banks had insufficient liquidity to meet withdrawals. Because the Federal Reserve did not put reserves into the system, many commercial banks were unable to meet the withdrawals and had to close their doors. Thus, a major role of the central bank should be to act as a source of reserves and liquidity to commercial banks when all other sources have been drained. The Federal Reserve, by its ability to create bank reserves, is able to create liquidity for banks when such liquidity is needed to meet withdrawals.

The previous discussion suggests that a flow of funds out of a bank can create a significant liquidity problem. An outflow of deposits reduces the individual bank's reserves. (Such cash withdrawals need not affect the reserves of the banking system if the funds are deposited in another bank.) The management of a bank is conscious of the impact of a flow of funds from the bank and takes steps to reduce the impact by seeking to match its loan portfolio and anticipated cash drains. Such matching would be simple if all deposits were 30-day certificates of deposit. The bank could assure having the funds to meet the CDs by making only 30-day loans. The maturing loans would cover the maturing CDs. If the CDs were renewed, then the banks could make new loans for an additional 30 days.

Of course, portfolio management of banks is not that simple because banks issue a variety of instruments to induce deposits. These range from very short-term deposits (such as demand deposits) to instruments that may not mature for many years (for example, a five-year CD). In addition, as is explained in Chapter 18, commercial banks grant lines of credit that permit the creditor to borrow varying amounts over a period of time. (Individuals also have access to lines of credit through credit cards such as VISA that offer cash advances.) Such loans mean that bankers do not know from day to day exactly how much will be loaned, nor do they know exactly when the loans will be repaid.

Management will have had experience with the rate at which deposits flow into and out of the bank, how many loans will be granted, and when they will be repaid. This knowledge permits the bank to construct a portfolio consistent with management's anticipated need for funds to meet withdrawals. However, there have been periods when a bank's managers have found themselves in precarious situations. This is especially true during periods when interest rates rise rapidly. Depositors may withdraw more funds than had been anticipated by the bank's management. Presumably these withdrawals are being made by savers seeking to earn a higher return in an alternative institution that competes with the accounts offered by the bank. Meeting these withdrawals can hurt the individual bank, especially if it must pay higher interest rates to raise the funds to meet the withdrawals. Unless the bank is also able to raise the rates it charges on its loans, the profitability of the bank is hurt, since its cost of funds is increased.

The Tools of Monetary Policy

As the previous discussion indicates, the reserves of commercial banks are an important component of the financial system. Anything that affects these reserves affects the ability of commercial banks to create money and credit. Ultimately, the control of the supply of money rests with the Federal Reserve. It is through the impact on banks' reserves that the Fed is able to affect interest rates and the economy.

The Federal Reserve has three primary tools for affecting the reserves of depository institutions: the reserve requirement, the discount rate, and open market operations. Each is important through its ability to change excess reserves and hence affect banks' lending capacity. In addition to these primary tools of monetary policy, the Federal Reserve has selective credit controls concerning real estate and consumer loans and the purchase of securities with borrowed funds (the margin requirement discussed in Chapter 4).

Reserve Requirement

Because all depository institutions must maintain reserves against their deposit liabilities, any change in these required reserves alters all banks' ability to lend. For example, if the current 10 percent reserve requirement for demand deposits is raised to 15 percent, every depository institution will need to increase its required reserves. While they previously had to hold $10 in reserves against every $100 in demand deposits, these banks will now have to hold $15 in reserves. Therefore, by simply increasing the reserve requirement, the Federal Reserve immediately decreases banks' capacity to grant loans. A decrease in the reserve requirement has the opposite effect, for it immediately increases banks' ability to lend.

Obviously this tool of monetary policy cannot be used to fine-tune the money supply to changing liquidity needs. Changing the reserve requirement is unable to produce subtle changes in the money supply, so it is rarely used as a tool of monetary policy. The major advantage of changing the reserve requirement is to release or absorb a large amount of excess reserves in one act. In addition, a change in the reserve requirement has an "announcement effect" that serves to indicate the seriousness of a particular Federal Reserve policy.

Discount Rate and the Target Federal Funds Rate

As was previously explained, the discount rate is the interest rate that the Federal Reserve charges banks when they borrow reserves to meet temporary shortages in their required reserves. A change in the cost of borrowing reserves alters banks' willingness to borrow from the Federal Reserve. A decrease in the discount rate may stimulate increased borrowing. An increase in the discount rate should discourage further borrowing and may cause banks to retire debt owed the Federal Reserve.

Although the discount rate may induce banks' behavior, it is a passive tool of monetary policy. The initiative for changes in the level of borrowing rests with the banks. The Federal Reserve may alter the discount rate, but it cannot force banks to borrow or to cease borrowing. An increase in the discount rate does not mean that the banks will cease borrowing and retire existing debt owed the Federal Reserve. If the banks are able to pass on to their customers the higher cost of borrowing, there may be little contraction in the level of credit. Furthermore, not all banks borrow from the Federal Reserve. Some banks prefer to remain free of this obligation. Thus, an increase in the discount rate will not affect the lending behavior of these banks.

During the 1960s, the Federal Reserve changed the discount rate infrequently. From 1960 to 1968 the rate was changed only seven times. In the 1970s the Federal Reserve altered the discount rate more frequently in response to changing economic conditions. For example, there was a rapid increase in the rate from 6½ percent in 1978 to a high of 13 percent in 1980. This doubling of the discount rate occurred during a period of inflation and high interest rates, when the Federal Reserve sought to restore more stable prices. As inflation and interest rates subsided, the Federal Reserve lowered the discount rate to encourage economic activity.

Changes in the reserve requirement occur infrequently and changes in the discount rate are intermittent, because there is a more effective means to alter the supply of money and credit. Currently, the Fed uses the federal funds rate and open market operations. The federal funds rate should not be confused with the discount rate. Recall that the federal funds rate is the interest rate charged by banks when they lend reserves to each other. Banks with excess reserves lend to banks needing reserves. Unlike the discount rate, the federal funds rate is not set by the Federal Reserve. Instead it is established by the demand and supply of funds available in the federal funds market. The Federal Reserve, however, can affect the supply of funds and thereby affect the federal funds rate. During

F I G U R E   5.2
Target Federal Funds Rate,
1995–2010

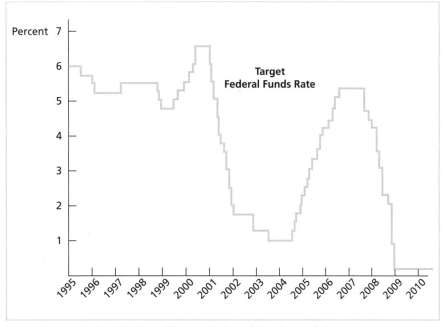

Source: Data available at the Federal Reserve Web site **http://www.federalreserve.gov**.

the 2000s, the Federal Reserve preferred to set a *target federal funds rate* and achieved that target through the use of open market operations.

Fluctuations in the target federal funds rate are illustrated in Figure 5.2, which presents the rate from 1995 into 2010. While the rate reached 6.5 percent during 2000, the Fed responded to subsequent sluggish economic growth by lowering the target federal funds rate. The rate declined virtually every month during 2001, and by mid-2003, the target rate stood at 1 percent.

A similar pattern occurred between 2007 and 2010. From 2004 through 2006, the Fed consistently raised the target federal funds rate to a high of 5.25 percent. During 2007, the Fed started to reduce the target rate. A pattern of consistent declines continued, and in some cases the decreases were not 0.25 percent but 0.5 and 0.75 percent. The financial crises and the subsequent recession resulted in the Fed lowering the target to virtually zero (0.0 – 0.25 percent) in 2008. Two years later the target remained at that historically low rate.

Open Market Operations

Open market
operations

Buying and selling of
U.S. Treasury securities
by the Federal Reserve

The target federal funds rate is achieved through the most important tool of monetary policy, open market operations, which is the purchase and sale of securities by the Federal Reserve. By buying and selling these securities, the Federal Reserve alters the supply of money in circulation and the reserves of the banking system. The Federal Reserve may buy and sell securities at any time and in any volume. Open market operations, then, are not only a means of changing the money supply and the availability of credit but also of fine-tuning the supply of money on a day-by-day basis.

If the Federal Reserve seeks to expand the supply of money, it purchases securities. After the transactions are negotiated, payments must be made, and the act of paying for the securities alters the money supply and the reserves of banks. Ownership of the securities is transferred to the Federal Reserve, and the Federal Reserve pays for the securities by writing a check drawn on itself, which the sellers deposit in banks. The banks clear the checks and receive payment in the form of reserves from the Federal Reserve. The total effect of these transactions is (1) to increase the supply of money because demand deposits are increased, and (2) to increase the reserves of the banking system. The required reserves of the banks rise, for the bank's deposit liabilities have risen. However, only a fraction of the increase in reserves will be required reserves. Thus, the excess reserves of the banks also rise.

When the Federal Reserve seeks to contract the money supply, it sells government securities. Once again, it is the payment for the purchased securities that alters the money supply and the capacity of banks to lend. If the public buys the securities, it draws down demand deposits, and the money supply and reserves of banks are decreased. The total effect of these transactions is (1) to decrease the money supply, because demand deposits are decreased, and (2) to decrease the total reserves of the banking system, because banks have fewer reserves on deposit in the Federal Reserve. Since only a percentage of these reserves was required against the deposit liabilities, the excess reserves of the bank were also decreased. Thus, by selling securities, the Federal Reserve decreases the supply of money and decreases the excess reserves of the banks, which reduces their ability to lend and create credit.

The Impact of Fiscal Policy on Credit Markets

Even though the Federal Reserve can affect the supply of money and credit in the economy, it does not have complete control over them. There are forces beyond its control that can affect the supply of money and credit. One of these forces is the fiscal policy of the federal government.

Fiscal policy

Taxation, expenditures, and debt management by the federal government

Fiscal policy is taxation, expenditures, and debt management by the federal government. Like monetary policy, fiscal policy may be used to pursue the economic goals of full employment, price stability, and economic growth. Like monetary policy, fiscal policy can affect the supply of money and the capacity of the banking system to lend.

Deficit

Disbursements exceeding receipts

Taxation or government expenditures by themselves do not alter the money supply. However, when government expenditures exceed revenues, this deficit must be financed. When government revenues exceed expenditures, the government must do something with this surplus. It is the financing of the deficit or disposing of the surplus that may affect the supply of money and the capacity of banks to lend.

Surplus

Receipts exceeding disbursements

If the federal government runs a deficit, it may obtain funds to finance the deficit by borrowing from (1) the general public, (2) banks, (3) the Federal

Reserve, and (4) foreign investors. If the federal government runs a surplus, it may retire debt held by (1) the general public, (2) banks, (3) the Federal Reserve, and (4) foreign investors. Securities issued to finance the deficit compete with other securities. A surplus has the opposite effect. In either case, a deficit or a surplus, the security markets and the banking system are not immune to the fiscal policy of the federal government. Financing a government deficit or investing any government surplus can have an impact on the money supply and commercial banks' reserves and, thus, have an impact on the supply and cost of credit.

Borrowing from the General Public

When the federal government operates at a deficit, it issues securities to finance the deficit. If the general public purchases the securities, funds are transferred from the general public to the Treasury. The Treasury, however, then spends the money to buy goods and services. (If the government did not spend the money, there would be no deficit!) When the Treasury pays for these goods and services, the public's bank deposits are restored as the money is transferred from the Treasury's account to the general public's accounts.

What is the change in the money supply and the reserves of the banks as a result of these transactions? The answer is none. There is no change in the money supply because there is no change in total demand deposits or cash. There is also no change in banks' ability to lend. All that occurs is that the government obtains goods and services from the public by borrowing from the public. In doing so, the Treasury's deficit does not affect the supply of money or the ability of banks to lend.

If the federal government were to run a surplus and use the funds to retire debt held by the general public, the preceding analysis still applies except in reverse. More money is received than spent (the surplus), but when the money is used to retire debt held by the general public, the funds are returned to the private sector. Money that initially flowed out of the private sector is returned. The money supply and the reserves of the banking system are not affected.

Borrowing from Banks

Suppose the federal government's deficit is financed by the banks—that is, the banks buy the government securities. For these purchases to occur, the banks must have excess reserves. From the banks' perspective, lending to the Treasury is essentially no different than lending to businesses or individuals. The money supply is expanded, but the capacity of the banks to lend is decreased because excess reserves are reduced. (The process of lending to the government at the expense of the private sector is sometimes referred to as "crowding out.")

The retiring of debt held by the banks has the opposite effect. The funds are returned to the bank system, which increases the bank's capacity to lend. It makes no difference if IBM retires a debt owed a commercial bank or if the Treasury pays off a Treasury security owned by the bank. In either case, the excess reserves of the banks are increased, and their capacity to lend is restored.

Borrowing from the Federal Reserve

Borrowing from the Fed to finance a deficit, however, is different from borrowing from the banking system. When the Federal Reserve buys the securities, the Treasury account at the Fed is increased. The Treasury spends these funds to buy goods and services, and the public deposits the payments in commercial banks. The Federal Reserve transfers funds from the Treasury's account to the banks' accounts.

The crucial question then becomes: What is the impact on the money supply and the ability of banks to lend when funds are transferred from the Treasury's account to the banks' account? The answer is twofold: (1) Total demand deposits rise when the public makes the deposits, and (2) total reserves of the banks are increased. (Remember that the banks' accounts at the Federal Reserve are reserves.) While required reserves increase to cover the new demand deposits, excess reserves are also increased. The ability of banks to create additional loans and further expand the money supply is enhanced. Thus, the net effect of the Federal Reserve's financing a federal government deficit is to increase both the money supply and the ability of banks to lend.

Once again the impact of a surplus is the exact opposite. If the Treasury were to run a surplus and use the funds to retire debt owed the Federal Reserve, both the money supply and the lending capacity of the banks are reduced. The tax collections that generate the surplus reduce the private sector's accounts at the banks. When the funds are transferred to the Treasury account, they reduce the deposit liabilities of the banks. This causes the money supply to decline and reduces the total reserves of the banking system. The reduction in the reserves decreases banks' excess reserves and, hence, decreases their ability to lend.

Borrowing from Foreign Sources

The federal government may also borrow abroad, in which case the securities are sold in foreign countries. When the funds from the sale are deposited in domestic banks, the banks' reserves are increased. From a domestic perspective, borrowing from abroad has the same impact as borrowing from the Federal Reserve. The money supply and the reserves of domestic banks are increased. The money supply and reserves of foreign banks, however, are *decreased*. (This conclusion assumes that the funds borrowed abroad by the Treasury are spent domestically. If the funds are spent abroad, the money flows back out of the country, so there is no net impact on the domestic monetary system.)

Retiring debt owed abroad reverses the flow of deposits. If a surplus is used to retire Treasury securities held by foreigners, the money flows out of the country. The outflow reduces the domestic money supply and the reserves of domestic banks. (If the foreigners were to deposit the proceeds in domestic banks, the net effect would be nil.) Just as selling securities abroad causes a domestic expansion in the money supply and the reserves of banks, retiring debt held abroad contracts the domestic money supply and reserves of banks.

The impact on the money supply and banks' reserves of these cases is summarized in Exhibit 5.4. Of these possibilities to finance a deficit or to repay existing debt, the greatest impact occurs when the transfers involve the Federal Reserve or foreign investors, because both the domestic money supply and the reserves of the banking system are affected. Financing a deficit by selling securities to the Federal Reserve or abroad has expansionary implications. Retiring debt held by the Federal Reserve or foreign investors will have the opposite effect. The domestic money supply and the reserves of domestic banks are decreased.

As this discussion indicates, a federal government deficit or surplus may have an impact on the supply of money and credit. If the Federal Reserve deems this impact to be undesirable, it may take actions to offset the impact. For example, if the deficit is financed by banks and this results in fewer loans to businesses and households, the Federal Reserve could create more reserves. The increase in reserves would be accomplished through open market operations. The Federal Reserve would buy securities, which restores reserves to the banking system. Thus, while the Federal Reserve cannot control the federal government's deficit or surplus, it can take action to reduce the impact on the supply of credit and on financial markets.

EXHIBIT 5.4
Summary of the Impact of Fiscal Policy on the Money Supply and the Reserves of Commercial Banks

	Change in Money Supply	Change in Total Reserves of Banks*	Change in Excess Reserves of Banks
Case I			
Borrowing from General Public	None	None	None
Retiring Debt Owed General Public	None	None	None
Case II			
Borrowing from Banks	Increase	None	Decrease
Retiring Debt Owed Banks	Decrease	None	Increase
Case III			
Borrowing from the Federal Reserve	Increase	Increase	Increase
Retiring Debt Owed the Federal Reserve	Decrease	Decrease	Decrease
Case IV			
Borrowing from Abroad	Increase	Increase	Increase
Retiring Debt Held Abroad	Decrease	Decrease	Decrease

*Excess reserves plus required reserves.

Impact of an Inflationary Economic Environment on Credit Markets

Inflation

General increase in prices with special emphasis on increases in consumer prices

Inflation is a general increase in prices. That is a very simple definition with two crucial words: *prices* and *general*. The first important word is *prices*, indicating what consumers pay to obtain goods and services. (*Prices* could also mean what producers must pay for plant and equipment, but when the word *inflation* is used, the implication is that the prices of consumer goods and services are rising.) The second important word is *general*. Inflation does not mean that all prices are rising but that the prices of most goods and services are increasing. The prices of some specific goods could be falling while most prices were rising.

Inflation is frequently expressed as a rate of increase in an index. The index that is most often used is the Consumer Price Index or CPI. The CPI is compiled monthly by the Bureau of Labor Statistics and is an aggregate of the prices of goods and services paid by consumers. Changes in the CPI are usually expressed in percentages such as 3 percent, meaning that prices as measured by the CPI are rising annually at a rate of 3 percent.

As consumers know, inflation has occurred virtually every year for decades. In 1984, the CPI approximated 100 but had risen to 216 by 2010. That is an annualized rate of approximately 3 percent, but the rate during individual years has varied perceptibly. During 1980, the rate of inflation reached 12 percent, but during the recent financial crisis (2008–2010), the CPI was virtually unchanged.

The most frequent explanation for inflation is excessive spending by consumers, firms, or governments. Generally this excess spending is financed by (or the result of) excessive creation of money and credit by governments and central banks. This cause is often summarized by the expression "too much money chasing too few goods."

The traditional tools for fighting inflation created by excessive demand are fiscal policy and monetary policy. With fiscal policy, government spending is reduced or taxes are increased. The reduction in government spending should decrease the demand for goods and services and help reduce the inflationary pressure. An increase in corporate income taxes reduces corporate profits, which cuts into the capacity of corporations to pay dividends and reinvest earnings. An increase in personal taxes reduces individuals' disposable income. All these tax increases reduce aggregate demand for goods and services and, therefore, should reduce the tendency for prices to rise.

If monetary policy is used to fight inflation, the Federal Reserve sells securities, raises the reserve requirement, and raises the discount rate. These actions reduce the supply of money, reduce banks' excess reserves, and increase the cost of credit (that is, interest rates). The reduction in the supply of money and the higher interest rates should reduce aggregate demand, which is causing prices to rise.

Even if the Federal Reserve does not raise interest rates, inflation will cause interest rates to rise. Inflation can redistribute resources from creditors to debtors (from lenders to borrowers), since the debtors will repay the creditors in the future with funds that purchase less. However, for such a redistribution to occur, the lenders would have to lack an awareness of inflation. If the lenders do anticipate the inflation, they certainly will take steps to protect the purchasing power of their funds. Such protection is achieved by charging more interest so their return equals or exceeds the rate of inflation.

If lenders do not fully anticipate inflation and do not earn a sufficient rate of interest, there will be a transfer of resources to borrowers from the lenders. The belief that savers will not correctly anticipate the severity of inflation has encouraged some individuals and firms to finance purchases through issuing debt. Thus, inflation (or at least the expectation of it) alters economic decision making and affects credit markets. Inflation encourages the use of debt financing to make current purchases.

Lenders, however, may certainly anticipate inflation just as borrowers may anticipate it. Expectations of inflation, then, should tend to drive up interest rates as (1) borrowers seek to obtain funds to purchase goods before their prices rise, (2) lenders seek to protect the purchasing power of their funds by requiring higher rates to compensate them for lending, and (3) the Federal Reserve tightens credit in an effort to retard the inflationary pressure.

Deflation

General decline in prices

The opposite of inflation is deflation, which is a general decline in prices. (Deflation should not be confused with "disinflation," a term that is sometimes used to indicate a decline in the rate of inflation.) Just as inflation benefits various investors and firms, falling prices may benefit some individuals and companies. Lower prices imply lower costs of goods sold and increased profits for some individual firms. Lower prices, however, also imply decreased revenues and profits for other firms. Lower oil prices contributed to the bankruptcy of Global Marine, which operated drilling rigs, but lower fuel prices benefited companies such as utilities that generate electricity. Consumers who heat their homes with oil furnaces also benefited from lower energy costs.

Recession

Period of at least six months during which the economy experiences increased unemployment and negative growth

Deflation is rare. Instead of falling prices, declining economic activity produces higher levels of unemployment and results in a recession, which is an increase in unemployment and a reduction in the nations' output for a period of at least six months. Until 2007, the economy experienced few recessions and they were relatively short and mild. However, the recession experienced from December 2007 through June 2009 was the severest economic downturn since the Great Depression of the 1930s. While prices remained stable and did not fall, the rate of unemployment rose from 5 percent in 2007 to over 10 percent. Even after the recession was officially declared over, the economy experienced sluggish growth at best, and the rate of unemployment consistently remained above 9 percent. To combat this economic environment, the Federal Reserve bought securities and lowered interest rates to historic lows. (See the discussion of the target federal funds rate and Figure 5.2 presented earlier in this chapter.) Simultaneously, the federal government pursued an expansionary fiscal policy and ran deficits that were primarily financed by the Federal Reserve buying the government securities. The immediate effectiveness of these actions was certainly a major source of political debate during the 2010 elections, and the long-term impact of the Federal Reserve's quantitative easing and the federal government's stimulus programs will not be known for years.

Summary

The Federal Reserve is the nation's central bank. Its purpose is to control the supply of money and credit in the nation. Through this control the Federal Reserve pursues the goals of monetary policy: higher levels of employment, stable prices, and economic growth.

Monetary policy works through its impact on banks' reserves. Since banking is organized under a system of fractional reserves, any transaction that puts reserves into the system will lead to expansion in the supply of money and credit. Transactions that take reserves out of the system will cause the supply of money and credit to contract unless there are excess reserves in the system to meet the reduction in the reserves.

The tools of monetary policy include open market operations, the reserve requirement, and the discount rate. Open market operations—the buying and selling of government securities by the Federal Reserve—are the most important tool of monetary policy and are used to establish a target federal funds rate. When the Federal Reserve seeks to expand the money supply, it buys securities. When it seeks to contract the money supply, it sells securities. Such purchases and sales affect the reserves of banks and thus alter their ability to lend. By altering banks' reserves, the Federal Reserve pursues its economic goals.

The fiscal policy of the federal government, like monetary policy, may have an impact on the money supply and the reserves of banks. When the federal government spends more than it receives in tax revenues, the resulting deficit must be financed. When the Federal Reserve supplies the funds to cover the deficit, the effect is the same as the Federal Reserve's purchasing securities. In both cases the money supply and the reserves of banks are increased.

The reverse occurs when the federal government runs a surplus in which receipts exceed expenses (the federal government's cash inflows exceed cash outflows). Unless the funds are returned to the economy, the money supply and bank reserves are diminished. By increasing expenditures or retiring debt held by the public, the funds are returned, and the impact on the banking system is reduced.

Inflation is a general increase in prices while deflation is a general decrease in prices. Recession is a period of rising unemployment. The anticipation of inflation affects financial decision making as individuals, financial managers, and creditors take actions designed to protect their purchasing power. Inflation encourages spending to acquire goods before prices rise farther and to finance the purchases with borrowed funds. Lenders, however, seek to protect themselves from inflation by charging a higher rate of interest to compensate for the inflation. During a period of inflation, the Federal Reserve will pursue a tight monetary policy and sell securities to reduce inflationary pressures. During a period of recession, the Federal Reserve does the opposite by purchasing securities and lowering interest rates to stimulate the economy.

Review Objectives

Now that you have completed this chapter, you should be able to

1. List the economic goals of monetary policy (p. 66).
2. Describe the structure of the Federal Reserve (pp. 67–68).
3. Explain how deposits in commercial banks lead to a multiple expansion in the money supply (pp. 68–72).
4. Define the federal funds rate (p. 73).
5. Illustrate how the tools of monetary policy are used to affect the supply of money and credit (pp. 75–78).
6. Determine which of the tools of monetary policy is the most important (pp. 77–78).
7. Explain how the Federal Reserve uses open market operations to affect the federal funds rate (pp. 77–78).
8. Identify the potential impact that a federal government deficit has on the monetary system (pp. 78–81).
9. Define inflation, deflation, and recession; explain how each is measured (pp. 82–84) and why inflation is associated with higher interest rates (pp. 82–83).

Internet Assignments

1. The Bureau of Labor Statistics, an agency within the U.S. Department of Labor, reports data concerning the aggregate economy. One possible measure of the direction of change is the rate of unemployment, which increases as the economy weakens. Go the bureau's Web page at http://stats.bls.gov and locate the unemployment rate. (It may be found under a section titled "Latest Numbers.") Based on recent changes in the unemployment rate, would you expect the Federal Reserve to tighten or ease credit in the immediate future?

2. The Federal Reserve publishes financial data concerning the money supply and interest rates. Go to its Web site address, http://www.federalreserve.gov, and locate the summary of economic conditions in the Beige Book. Does this summary support your answer to the previous question?

Relationships

1. Decreasing the reserve requirement should lead to _____ in the money supply.
2. A decrease in excess reserves implies _____ in the ability of banks to lend.
3. Cash withdrawals from banks _____ the reserves of banks.
4. Sales of securities by the Federal Reserve _____ the capacity of banks to lend.
5. An increase in the target federal funds rate suggests that short-term interest rates will _____.

6. An increase in the federal government's deficit financed by the Federal Reserve _____ the money supply.

7. Inflation is a general increase in prices; deflation is a general _____ in prices.

8. To fight inflation, the Federal Reserve _____ the money supply.

9. Changes in stock prices _____ the supply of money.

Answers

1. an increase
2. a decrease
3. decrease
4. decrease
5. increase
6. increases
7. decrease
8. decreases
9. do not affect (no change)

Nations do not live in a vacuum; they are not economically or politically independent of each other. Goods, services, and capital (investments) flow among nations, and these flows often have an impact on local employment, prices, and the banking system. This chapter is concerned with these currency flows.

The first section considers the price of one currency in terms of another, that is, the exchange rate. Changes in the prices of currencies alter the demand for a country's goods and services, which affects the level of economic activity. The flow of currencies also affects bank deposits and banks' capacity to lend. The next section describes the system of accounting for currency flows, the balance of payments. Emphasis is placed on the merchandise trade balance, which measures the importing and exporting of goods and services. Under the current monetary system, a deficit or surplus in the merchandise trade balance should produce changes in a currency's exchange rate. While temporary deficits may be met by a country's borrowing from the International Monetary Fund, the fundamental imbalance between the supply and demand for the currency has to be corrected for the currency to maintain a stable value.

Foreign Currencies and the Rate of Exchange

Domestic economies do not operate in a vacuum. Many consumers, firms, and governments buy and sell goods from and to foreign producers. Cars, electronic products and components, clothing, and some foods are illustrations of products that are imported. It is virtually impossible to buy goods in the United States that were produced solely in the United States. Even if the final goods were made here, these products often have parts that were made abroad.

Demand for foreign goods is also a demand for foreign money. Foreign merchants want payment in their nation's currency, and the buyers must acquire that currency. To acquire this money, the buyers use their nation's currency, which they offer in exchange for the foreign currency. If Americans want British goods, they must convert U.S. dollars into pounds. They offer (that is, supply) American dollars in exchange for British pounds. The opposite is true when British citizens buy American goods. To acquire the goods, they must have American dollars, and to obtain these dollars they supply British pounds in exchange for American dollars. Thus, demand for foreign goods (and demand for foreign currency) implies supplying the domestic currency.

Foreign exchange market

Market for the purchase and sale of currencies

The market for foreign currencies is called the foreign exchange market. Billions of dollars' worth of currencies are traded daily in the financial centers: New York, London, Tokyo, and Zurich. The price of one currency in terms of another is referred to as the exchange rate, and the prices of major currencies are reported in the financial press. A typical entry may be

Exchange rate

Price of a foreign currency; the value of one currency in terms of another

Country	U.S. $ Equivalent	Currency per U.S. Dollar
Britain (UK)	1.4345	$0.6971

These entries indicate that the dollar cost of the British (UK) pound is $1.4345 or that $1.00 buys 0.6971 pounds. The 0.6971 is derived by dividing $1 by the price of the pound: $1/$1.4345 = 0.6971 units of the British currency.

Currencies are also reported as "currency cross rates" in a table expressing currencies in term of each other. Typical entries for pesos, pounds, and dollars would be as follows:

	Dollar	Pound	Peso
Mexico	9.2215	13.228	. . .
UK	0.6971	. . .	0.07560
U.S.	. . .	1.4345	0.10844

The dollar column indicates that $1 buys 9.2215 Mexican pesos and 0.6971 British pounds. Reading across the U.S. row indicates that the pound costs $1.4345 and the Mexican peso costs $0.10844. Reading down the pound column indicates that 1 pound buys 13.228 pesos and $1.4345 U.S. dollars. Reading across the UK row indicates that $1.00 costs 0.6971 pounds and a peso costs 0.0756 pounds.

American demand for a foreign currency arises from importing goods and services; travel abroad; foreign investments in securities, plant, and equipment; and government spending. If you think about all the transactions that individuals and American firms have with foreign firms, individuals, and governments, you realize that a substantial demand exists for foreign currencies. Of course, this demand for foreign currencies implies a supply of American dollars.

Demand also exists for American dollars with which foreign individuals, firms, and governments purchase goods and securities. Ultimately the price of a currency depends on the supply of and the demand for that currency. An imbalance in the demand for or the supply of a currency causes its price to change. Excess demand generates a higher price, while excess supply depresses the price. Such price changes are often referred to as devaluations and revaluations. A devaluation (or depreciation) implies that one currency's value declines relative to all other currencies. A revaluation (or appreciation) implies that one currency's value rises relative to all other currencies.

How devaluation changes the price of one currency relative to all other currencies may be explained by a simple example. Assume that the British pound costs $1.50 in American dollars. If a good is priced at 2.5 pounds, it costs $3.75 in American money (2.5 times $1.50). If the British pound depreciates, it takes fewer dollars to buy a pound. Thus, if the pound is devalued by 10 percent, it takes 10 percent fewer dollars to buy a pound. The pound's price in terms of dollars falls from $1.50 to $1.35. The good now costs $3.375, because Americans can buy pounds at a lower price. The price of the good in terms of pounds is not reduced. It still costs 2.5 pounds, and hence its price to anyone holding pounds is unaltered. However, anyone holding a different currency can purchase pounds at the lower, devalued price. Thus depreciation does not lower prices to the domestic population but lowers the price of domestic goods to foreigners.

Conversely, devaluation also raises all foreign prices to the domestic population. The British now have to pay more pounds for foreign goods. Previously, a British pound purchased $1.50 worth of American goods. If a good cost $2.25, it cost 1.5 pounds ($2.25/$1.50). After the devaluation, the number of pounds necessary to purchase the good increases to 1.67 ($2.25/$1.35) because the value of the pound in terms of dollars declined. All foreign goods are more expensive to holders of British pounds because the pound buys smaller amounts of foreign currencies.

Since prices of goods and services are altered by the decline in the pound, the quantity demanded will also be altered. Holders of British pounds will demand fewer foreign goods because their prices are higher. Simultaneously, since other currencies can purchase more pounds, the quantity of British goods demanded will increase. British citizens will import fewer foreign goods, and the rest of the world will buy more British goods.

The opposite is true for a revaluation, which increases the value of one currency relative to another and raises the price of domestic goods to foreigners and lowers the price of all foreign goods to the domestic population. For example, if the British pound appreciates by 10 percent, the price of a pound in terms of dollars rises from $1.50 to $1.65. To foreigners, the prices of all British goods increase. Simultaneously, the British pound now buys more foreign money, for a pound purchases $1.65 worth of American goods. The increased prices of British goods should reduce the quantity demanded, while the reduced price of imports increases the quantity demanded.

Devaluation

Decrease (depreciation) in the price of one currency relative to other currencies

Revaluation

Increase (appreciation) in the price of one currency relative to other currencies

Thus, the appreciation reduces the demand for domestically produced goods and increases the demand for imports.

Under the current international monetary system, currency price changes occur daily. If the demand for a particular currency rises so that demand exceeds supply, the price of that currency rises relative to other currencies. If the supply of the currency exceeds the demand, the price falls. Because prices fluctuate every day, continual devaluations and revaluations occur as the prices of currencies vary in accordance with supply and demand. You might anticipate that the value of a major currency such as the European euro or the British pound would be stable in terms of dollars, but that expectation is not necessarily correct. For example, from 1982 to 1985, the British pound declined from over $2.40 to less than $1.20. That price decline is a devaluation of over 50 percent, which implies that the prices of dollar-denominated goods and services doubled for individuals using British pounds.

Effect on Banks' Reserves and the Domestic Money Supply

As was previously explained, foreign purchases cause international currency flows. The effect of these flows may be to alter the ability of domestic and foreign banks to create credit. This effect on banks' ability to create credit may be illustrated by the following example in which U.S. citizens buy goods in England. When the purchases are made, the Americans acquire goods and pay for them with a check drawn on an American bank. The British merchant deposits the check in a bank and obtains a new demand deposit.

The British bank has a new demand deposit and a check drawn on an American bank. The check is sent to the British central bank, the Bank of England. The Bank of England sends the check to the Federal Reserve, through which foreign banking transactions are cleared for payment.

Payment from the Federal Reserve can take a variety of forms. For example, the British central bank can request payment in British pounds or American dollars; that is, the Bank of England accepts an account at the Federal Reserve. Foreign central banks maintain accounts at the Federal Reserve just as the U.S. federal government keeps an account with the Federal Reserve. Such accounts can supply funds to British citizens when they make purchases in the United States. The British bank could request payment in another currency, such as European euros. Thus if the Bank of England needs a currency other than American dollars, payment could be made in a third currency.

If the Bank of England accepts an account at the Federal Reserve, the following transactions occur. The check is sent to the Federal Reserve for payment. The Bank of England receives the account, and the Federal Reserve issues a new claim on itself in payment for the check. This process is illustrated by the flowchart presented below. The check goes from the American citizen to the British citizen, passes through a British bank to the Bank of England to the Federal Reserve to the bank on which it was drawn.

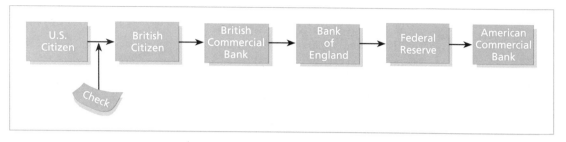

Funds are now lodged in the British banking system and have increased demand deposits and the reserves of the British banks. Since the funds are abroad, they are no longer part of the U.S. money supply. Demand deposits and reserves of banks in the United States are reduced. In effect, Americans now have British goods and services, and the British have a claim (represented by the account of the Bank of England at the Federal Reserve) on American goods and services.

If the British purchase American goods, the money is returned to the United States. Hence, if British people are purchasing American goods and services at the same time and at the same value at which Americans are buying British goods and services, the currency flows cancel each other. The dollars that go abroad are returned when the British purchase American goods, and there will be no net effect on the banking system. The same conclusion holds if the British use the American dollars to buy goods in another country, such as Germany, and if the Germans use the dollars to buy American goods. The dollars that flowed out to purchase English goods are returned to America. There is a balance in the flow of currencies, and the foreign transactions of all three nations are in balance.

If, however, the British do not exercise the claim on American goods or do not pass the claim to a third party that exercises the claim, the value of purchases of goods and services among nations is not equal, and one nation's currency is lodging itself in another nation. As is explained in the next section, the country doing the purchasing has a deficit in its balance of trade, while the other country has a surplus. The deficit nation is losing currency and receiving goods while the surplus nation is losing goods and receiving money. The importance of these transactions to the banking system in each nation is the effect the currency flows have on reserves of banks and on each nation's money supply. The reserves of banks and the money supply of the deficit nation are reduced, while the reserves of banks and the money supply of the surplus nation are increased. The potential for banks to expand and create credit is reduced in the deficit nation. But the converse is true in the surplus nation, for the ability of its banks to expand the money supply is increased.

Balance of Payments

The balance of payments is a record of all monetary transactions between a country and the rest of the world during a period of time. The balance of payments records transactions by double entry bookkeeping. Each transaction is recorded as both a debit and a credit, so the total of all debits must equal credits. However, individual parts or subsets of the balance of payments statement may have a surplus or deficit.

The essential parts of the balance of payments are (1) the current account, (2) the capital account, and (3) the official reserve account. The current account enumerates the value of goods and services imported and exported, government spending abroad, and foreign investment income for the time period. It is the broadest measure of a country's international trade in goods and services.

The difference between the value of imports and exports is often referred to as a country's "balance of trade." *If a country imports more goods than it exports, it is running a deficit in its "merchandise trade" account. If a country is exporting more goods than it imports, it is running a surplus.* A country can run a surplus or a deficit in its balance of trade but not in its balance of payments. For every credit in the balance of payments, there is a corresponding and offsetting debit, so the balance of payments must balance even though the current account may have a surplus or deficit.

The capital account consists of investment flows and measures capital investments made between the domestic country and all other countries. Capital investments include direct investments in plant and equipment in a foreign country and the purchases of foreign securities. Security transactions may be long or short term. Long-term transactions are purchases and sales of foreign bonds and stocks. Short-term capital transactions primarily take the form of changes in bank balances held abroad and in foreign money market securities.

The third account, the official reserve account, is a balancing account and reflects the change in a country's international reserves. If a country imports more than it exports or makes more foreign investments, its foreign reserves will decline. If a country exports more than it imports and experiences foreign investments, its holding of foreign reserves will rise. These changes in its reserves may also affect its drawing rights on its account with the International Monetary Fund. (The role of the IMF is discussed in the next section.)

An illustration of a balance of payments is presented in Exhibit 6.1. The exhibit is divided into the current account, the capital account, and the official reserve account. The vertical columns give the debits (−) and the credits (+). Credits represent currency inflows while debits are currency outflows, and the sum of the debits and credits must be equal.

The current account starts with merchandise exports, a credit of $224.40, and merchandise imports, a debit of $368.70. The difference ($224.40 − $368.70 = −$144.30) is the merchandise balance of trade, and since the amount is a negative number, that indicates a net currency outflow. The next entry is government spending abroad, a debit of $15.30. If a government spends abroad, that has the same impact on currency flows as individuals' spending abroad. It does not matter whether the government buys goods and services abroad or the nation's citizens buy foreign goods and services. Both are currency outflows (that is, both are debits).

Net income from investments abroad, a credit of $20.80, is a currency inflow. This currency inflow is the result of previous currency outflows. Current foreign investments in plant and equipment or in foreign securities require currency outflows that are reported in the capital account. These investments

Current account

Part of the balance of payments that enumerates the importing and exporting of goods and services by a nation over a period of time

Capital account

Part of the balance of payments that enumerates the importing and exporting of investments and long-term securities

Official reserve account

Part of the balance of payments that enumerates changes in a country's international reserves

E X H I B I T 6.1
Simplified Balance of
Payments for the Time
Period 12/31/X0 through
12/31/X1

	Debit (−)	Credit (+)	Balance
Current Account			
Exports		$224.40	
Imports	$368.70		
Balance of trade			$(144.30)
Government spending abroad	15.30		
Net income from investment abroad		20.80	
Balance on current account			$(138.80)
Capital Account			
Long-term			
Direct investment abroad	130.10		
Foreign investments in the country		117.60	
Purchases of foreign securities	27.40		
Foreign purchase of domestic securities		41.00	
Short-term			
Purchases of short-term foreign investments	9.30		
Foreign purchases of short-term investments		95.70	
Balance on capital account			87.50
Official Reserves			
Statistical adjustment		3.90	
Net change in foreign reserves		47.40	
	$550.80	$550.80	

may generate future income that will produce a currency inflow in the current account. Of course, foreign investors will also be earning income on their investments in the domestic country. For the country to experience a net currency inflow, the income received from the foreign investments must exceed the income paid foreign investors. In this illustration, the net investment income is a currency inflow of $20.80, which is reported in the credit column. A currency outflow would have been reported in the debit column.

The sum of all these transactions (−$138.80) is the balance on the current account. In this illustration, the net income from previous investments helped offset some of the currency outflow from the merchandise trade balance, but the total on the current account indicates a currency outflow.

The capital account represents currency flows resulting from investments in physical assets, such as plant and equipment, and financial assets, such as stocks and bonds. It also includes investments in short-term financial assets.

If a country has a net currency outflow in the current account, that outflow may be offset by an inflow in the capital account. If foreigners use the currency to make investments in that country, the money is returned. Correspondingly, if a country is running a surplus in its current account, it is receiving money it may use to invest in the foreign country. Such investments, of course, may be in actual physical assets or in financial assets. If the receiving country just holds the other country's cash, it is investing in a financial asset. However, the currency is usually invested in an income-earning asset, since holding the money itself earns nothing.

In this illustration, direct investments generate an outflow (a debit of $130.10), while direct foreign investments in the country generate an inflow (a credit of $117.60). Purchases of long-term foreign securities were $27.40, and foreign purchases were $41.00. Purchases of short-term foreign securities were $9.30, while foreign purchases were $95.70. The total credits on the capital account exceeded the debits by $87.50, indicating a cash inflow. If there had been a currency outflow (in other words, debits exceeded credits), the balance would be negative.

The sum of the currency inflows and outflows on the current and capital accounts still may not balance. The official reserve account is the final balancing item that equates the currency inflows and outflows. If there is a net credit balance on the current and capital accounts, there has to be a debit on the official reserve account. A net credit balance on the official reserve account indicates the opposite, a net debit on the current and capital accounts.

Transactions involving the reserve account can result when the country borrows or repays credit granted by the International Monetary Fund and when it uses or adds to its international reserves created by the IMF. Also, there is a statistical discrepancy account for errors and omissions. These errors can occur when transactions, such as illegal transactions, are not recorded. For example, if individuals in a politically unstable country smuggle out money to invest in a safe haven, the transaction may not be recorded on the country's current or capital accounts.

Of the three accounts in the balance of payments, the merchandise trade balance receives the most publicity. A debit on the merchandise trade account indicates that the country is importing more goods than it is exporting. The merchandise trade balance for the United States for 1980 through 2008 is presented in Figure 6.1. During the entire time period, a deficit existed in the merchandise trade balance, so dollars were flowing out of the country.

Those dollars did not disappear, and many were deposited in foreign banks. Such dollar-denominated deposits in banks in Europe are referred to as Eurodollars. A Eurodollar, then, is a deposit in a foreign bank denominated in dollars. (The bank need not be located in Europe; a dollar-denominated deposit in Hong Kong is also called a Eurodollar.) The creation of Eurodollar deposits has resulted in large banks accepting deposits in other currencies. A bank in London can have deposits denominated in euros, dollars, and yen as well as British pounds. Such deposits, like any deposits, are a source of funds that the bank can lend. Thus banks may create loans that are denominated in many currencies as well as loans denominated in their local currency.

Eurodollars

Deposit in a foreign bank denominated in dollars

FIGURE 6.1
U.S. Merchandise Trade
Balance, 1980–2008
(in billions)

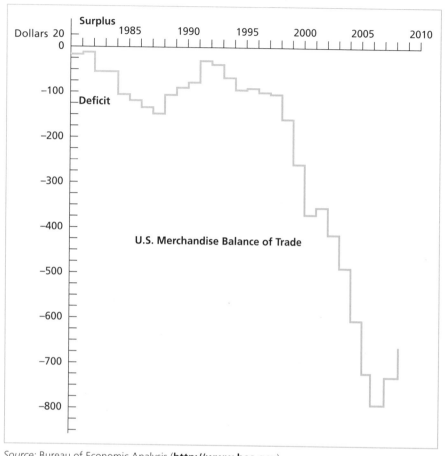

Source: Bureau of Economic Analysis (**http://www.bea.gov**).

The outflow of U.S. dollars that has resulted from the continuing deficit in the balance of trade has raised an important question: What happens if the foreign individuals, firms, banks, and governments no longer want to hold the dollars? For example, the United States has imported a significant amount of goods from China and has a large deficit in its balance of trade. Conversely, China now has large holdings of dollars. What would happen if the Chinese government were no longer willing to hold dollars? The answer is that they would seek to sell the dollars. The Chinese, however, could sell the dollars only if someone were willing to buy them. The increased supply drives down the dollar's price relative to other currencies.

Notice that the price falls to induce someone to buy (i.e., hold) the currency. The big question is, of course, what would happen if many holders of dollars were to seek to sell at the same time. The dollar's price would dramatically fall, and the U.S. prices of foreign goods and services would dramatically rise. Domestic interest rates in the United States would also increase as the sellers would demand higher rates to hold dollar-denominated debt. And higher interest rates would not bode well for the domestic levels of employment. While the ultimate impact of a run on the dollar is at best speculative, the effect on the domestic economy and on the country's global political stature would certainly be felt.

The Role of the International Monetary Fund

The U.S. dollar is the currency for many international transactions. Participants in international markets are willing to hold dollars and dollar-denominated securities even though the country has been experiencing a deficit in the balance of trade. Such willingness need not apply to other currencies. If a country consistently has a deficit on the current account, the potential for a disequilibrium exists. If foreigners become unwilling to accept the additional currency and to hold additional financial assets, a disequilibrium will occur. Such a situation cannot exist indefinitely. One country cannot continually experience a currency outflow. Eventually the other countries will cease to hold the currency or financial assets denominated in that currency.

One temporary solution to a currency outflow is for a country to draw on its reserves at the International Monetary Fund. The IMF, which was created by the Bretton Woods agreements of 1944, oversees the international monetary order. The initial agreement created a pool of currencies contributed by the countries that joined the IMF. These funds are made available to countries with temporary balance of payments difficulties. The primary contributors to this fund are the major economic powers: the United States, the United Kingdom, Germany, France, and Japan.

If a country experiences a currency outflow, it may draw from the pool of currencies. The drawings are, in effect, a purchase of foreign currencies that is paid for by the country's currency. Each drawing increases the amount of the deficit country's currency held by the IMF. The drawings are to be reversed in three to five years by the country's repurchasing of its currency with foreign exchange. Of course, to acquire the foreign exchange, the country must cease experiencing currency outflows and start experiencing currency inflows.

As the country draws currencies from the IMF, it is required to take corrective action to stop the currency outflow. Responsibility for this action generally falls on the country experiencing the currency outflow and not on the countries receiving the currency inflow. Under a system of flexible exchange rates, the adjustment comes through changes in the value of currencies. An excess supply of one currency relative to other currencies causes its price to decline, which increases the quantity demanded of its products and hence of its currency. An excessive currency inflow would have the opposite effect. The increased demand for its currency (the currency inflow) causes the value of the currency to rise, making goods more expensive to foreigners and reducing the quantity demanded.

The importance of the IMF primarily revolves around the less-developed world economies. The more advanced economies (developed countries, or DCs) are often differentiated from the emerging economies (or "less-developed countries," or LDCs) such as Chile, Korea, or Thailand. Freely fluctuating exchange rates act as a constraint on the advanced economies by allocating their currencies. Such countries may not need to borrow funds from the IMF, as changes in exchange rates alter the demand for and supply of their currencies. For less-developed nations, however, the ability to borrow funds may be crucial for continued economic growth. When the IMF grants these countries loans, it also lends credibility to their debt. A country that complies with the IMF's demand for corrective action is able to borrow from other sources.

While the major free-world economic powers operate under a system of fluctuating rates, some countries do not permit the value of their currency to freely fluctuate. Instead they "peg" the value of their currency to a particular currency (for example, the U.S. dollar) or to an index or "basket" of currencies. Since the value of a basket of currencies may be more stable than the value of an individual currency, the value of the currency pegged to the basket may be more stable than if the currency were tied to the U.S. dollar or the euro. If a country that pegs its currency to another currency or basket of currencies experiences a consistent outflow, it has to adjust the value of its currency relative to the pegged currency or basket of currencies. A large devaluation (say, 10 percent) may occur overnight as the deficit nation's government lowers the value of its currency to discourage imports and encourage exports in an effort to stop the currency outflow. For example, Finland devaluated the markka (Fmk) in an effort to encourage exports and tourism. The devaluation made Finland one of the cheapest European countries to visit. If foreign travel in Finland did increase, the influx of tourists would, of course, generate a currency inflow.

In reality, some countries do manipulate their currencies for political and economic purposes. While a deficit in the merchandise trade balance indicates a currency outflow, a surplus indicates the opposite. The country is exporting more goods and services and receiving funds. During the 2000s, China consistently exported more goods to the United States and other countries than it imported. This surplus in the merchandise trade balance contributed to the rapid growth of the Chinese economy, which the Chinese government wanted to maintain. Since a higher currency price would discourage exports, it would also dampen economic growth. The Chinese yuan was pegged to the dollar, but the Chinese government would not increase the dollar cost of the yuan. This refusal to revalue the currency was a major source of friction between the U.S. and Chinese governments.

Summary

International currency flows occur when individuals, firms, and governments buy goods and services and make investments in foreign countries. To make these purchases and investments, they must purchase the foreign currency. The value of one currency in terms of another is the exchange rate, and for many currencies that rate varies daily in response to the supply and demand for the currency. If a country imports more than it exports, it experiences a deficit in its merchandise trade balance. Currency flows out of the country, which reduces bank deposits and the reserves of the banking system. The opposite occurs when the country experiences a currency inflow. Funds are deposited in domestic banks, which increases their ability to lend.

Imbalances in international currency flows result in changes in the value of one currency relative to other currencies. An outflow should cause the value of the currency to decline and the value of other currencies to rise. While currency outflows lead to devaluations, inflows lead to revaluation and the exchange rate increases.

Currency flows arising from foreign trade and foreign investments are recorded on a nation's balance of payments, which is a system of double entry bookkeeping for recording international monetary transactions. While a nation may have a deficit or surplus in its current or capital accounts, the balance of payments must balance. If a country has a short-term problem such as a deficit in its current account, it may purchase foreign exchange from the International Monetary Fund. The nation is then required to take corrective action to stop the outflow of its currency and to repurchase its currency with foreign exchange within three to five years.

Review Objectives

Now that you have completed this chapter, you should be able to

1. Express the value of a currency in terms of another currency (pp. 87–88).

2. Explain why the demand for one currency implies the supplying of another currency (pp. 88–89).

3. Differentiate devaluations and revaluations and their impact on the demand for foreign goods and services (pp. 88–89).

4. Illustrate how international currency flows may affect a nation's supply of money and credit (pp. 90–91).

5. Describe the components of a nation's balance of payments (pp. 91–96).

6. Differentiate deficits and surpluses in the merchandise trade balance (pp. 96–97).

Problems

1. Given the following information, determine the balance on the United States' current account and capital accounts:

imports	$211.5
net income from foreign investments	32.3
foreign investments in U.S.	7.7
government spending abroad	4.6
exports	182.1
U.S. investments abroad	24.7
foreign securities bought by U.S.	4.9
U.S. securities bought by foreigners	2.8
purchase of short-term foreign securities	6.5
foreign purchases of U.S. short-term securities	9.1

2. If the price of a British pound is $1.82, how many pounds are necessary to purchase $1.00?

3. Last year Leather Boot, Inc. had investments in Paris worth 500,000 euros. At that time, the euro was worth $1.20. Today the euro is trading for $1.30. What is the gain or loss in value of the inventory expressed in dollars and in euros?

Additional Problems with Answers

1. The dollar cost of the European euro is $1.30.

   a. You are planning a trip to Europe and read that a hotel charges 120 euros per night. What is the cost to you in dollars?

   b. Your dollar will buy how many euros?

   c. After completing your trip, you have 100 euros that you want to convert back to dollars. How many dollars will you receive?

2. What is the nation's trade balance on its current account and capital account given the following information? Is the nation experiencing a cash inflow (outflow) on its current account and its capital account? Was there a net currency inflow or outflow?

imports	$206
exports	250
direct investments abroad	34
foreign investments in the country	16
foreign purchases of domestic securities	33
purchases of foreign securities	87
net income from foreign investments	71
government spending abroad	33

Answers

1. a. The hotel room will cost you $156 ($1.30 × 120).

   b. The dollar will buy 0.769231 euros ($1/$1.30).

   c. You will receive $130 for the 100 euros.

2.

Current account	Debit	credit
Exports		$250
Imports	$206	
Government spending abroad	33	
Net income from investment abroad		71
Balance on current account		$ 82

Capital account		
Direct investment abroad	34	
Foreign investment in U.S.		16
Purchases of foreign securities	87	
Foreign purchases of U.S. securities		33
Balance on capital account	$72	

In this problem there is a net credit balance on current account but a net debit on the capital accounts. The net of the two accounts is a credit of $10, which means there is a currency inflow.

Relationships

1. If a currency appreciates, the prices of domestic goods are _____.

2. If the dollar cost of the British pound rises, prices denominated in pounds _____ for individuals holding pounds.

3. In the foreign exchange market, an increase the U.S dollar implies _____ in the cost of British pounds or Japanese yen.

4. An increase in foreign purchases _____ a surplus in the balance of trade.

5. If the dollar cost of the British pound rises, prices denominated in dollars _____ for individuals holding dollars.

6. If exports are increased, the mechandise trade balance is _____.

7. Under flexible exchange rates, an increase in currency outflows (e.g., an increase in foreign purchases) should lead to a _____ in the value of currency.

8. If a currency is devalued, the cost of foreign currencies _____.

Answers

1. not changed (no impact)
2. are not affected (no change)
3. decrease
4. decreases
5. are not affected (no change)
6. decreased
7. decrease
8. increases

Financial Tools

S everal techniques are common to financial management from both a personal and a business perspective. All investments are made in the present and their returns occur in the future. All investments involve risk, and financial statements are used to analyze a company's performance.

Before proceeding to personal investing, security valuation, and business finance, Part 2 covers tools that will be used in almost every chapter of the remainder of this text. The first is the time value of money (Chapter 7), which is crucial to financial decision making. It helps answer such questions as

If I invest $3,000 a year for 30 years and earn 9 percent annually, how much will I have in my account?

If I buy a home and take out a $200,000 mortgage at 6 percent for 25 years, what will be my periodic payments?

If my company buys equipment for $100,000 and it generates cash flow of $31,500 for five years, what will be the return on the investment?

These are but a few of the numerous questions that involve the time value of money, and being able to answer them is crucial to your business and investment decisions.

Since all investments involve risk, there has to be a means to measure and manage it. Chapter 8 presents the sources of risk, two methods to measure risk, and the first technique for risk management (the construction of a diversified portfolio). Other techniques for risk management will appear through the remainder of this text as they are appropriate.

The measurement of risk uses statistics. The theory of portfolio diversification uses concepts developed from the economic theory of consumer behavior. Financial analysis also uses accounting data. Chapter 9 reviews the basic components of three accounting statements: the balance sheet, the income statement, and the statement of changes in financial position. The accounting data are then used to illustrate various ratios that are employed to analyze a firm's financial position and its performance.

The concepts and methods covered in Part 2 are crucial to the study of finance. You may already know some of this material, in which case you must determine the extent to which you need to review. Take the material in Part 2 seriously. A strong background and understanding of time value, risk measurement, and analysis of financial statements will make comprehending Parts 3 through 5 easier.

The Time Value of Money

A s Benjamin Franklin so aptly put it, "Money makes money. And the money that money makes makes more money." That is the essence of the time value of money: A dollar received in the future is not equivalent to a dollar received in the present, and time value brings them together.

Perhaps no topic in this text is more important than the time value of money. It permeates finance and facilitates your answering many financial questions. For example, if you place $1,000 in your retirement account each year for 30 years, how much will you accumulate? Of course, you have to know how much you expect to earn each year. If that rate is 8 percent, you will have $122.345.90 if you start contributing to the account today. Even if you procrastinate until the end of the year to make the first contribution, you still have $113,283.20. For a total investment of only $30,000, you will have over $110,000. If you increase the amount to $3,000 annually, the final amount exceeds $330,000.

You are considering purchasing a town house that will require that you borrow $250,000. You are curious what the annual payments will be for the mortgage. In order to answer that question you will need to know the length of the mortgage and the interest rate. If the term is 25 years and the rate is 6.7 percent, your annual payment will be $20,876.10. That's a lot of money and over the 25 years you will have paid out $521,902.20 to purchase the $250,000 town house.

Within five years, you want $100,000 to start a business restoring cars. How much must you save annually to achieve your dream? If you can earn 7 percent on your funds, you need to save $17,389 each year to accumulate the $100,000. If you can wait for ten years, the required amount drops to $7,238, but the cost will likely increase. If inflation is 2.7 percent annually, you will need $130,528 to buy what cost $100,000 10 years earlier. You will need to invest $9,447 annually to have $130,528 after ten years if you earn 7 percent each year.

All of these examples illustrate the time value of money and how the concept may be applied to your everyday life. Financial managers have to make similar calculations. For example, if an investment in plant and equipment costs $12,000,000 and will generate cash flow of $3,210,000 for seven years, what is the investment's return? The cash outflow is in the present but the cash inflows are in the future. Time value equates these cash inflows and outflows and determines the return. Once the expected return is determined, the financial manager can decide whether or not to proceed and make the investment.

This chapter covers four basic time value cases: (1) the future value of a dollar, (2) the present value of a dollar, (3) the future value of an annuity, and (4) the present value of an annuity. Each is explained and illustrated using interest tables and a financial calculator. (How you may use Excel to solve these problems is explained in Appendix E to this text.) Several additional examples are provided to illustrate how time value concepts are applied to solve many financial problems. Since these calculations appear throughout this text, the time to learn them is now, or a substantial proportion of this text (and any financial textbook) will be incomprehensible. Consider yourself forewarned.

The Future Value of a Dollar

If you deposit $100 in a savings account that pays 5 percent annually, how much money will be in the account at the end of the year? The answer is easy to determine: $100 plus $5 interest, for a total of $105. The answer is derived by multiplying $100 by 5 percent, which gives the interest earned during the year, plus the initial principal. That is,

$$\text{Initial principal} + (\text{Interest rate} \times \text{Initial principal}) = \text{Principal after one year}$$
$$\$100 + 0.05(\$100) = \$105.$$

How much will be in the account after two years? This answer is obtained in the same manner by adding the interest earned during the second year to the principal at the beginning of the second year; that is, $105 plus 0.05 times $105 equals $110.25. After two years the initial deposit of $100 will have grown to $110.25; your savings account will have earned $10.25 in interest. This total interest is composed of $10 (interest on the initial principal) and

$0.25 (interest that has accrued during the second year on the $5 in interest earned during the first year). This earning of interest on interest is called compounding. Money that is deposited in savings accounts is frequently referred to as being compounded, for interest is earned on both the principal and the previously earned interest.

Compounding

Process by which interest is paid on interest that was previously earned

The words *interest* and *compounded* are frequently used together. For example, banks may advertise that interest is compounded daily for savings accounts. In the previous example, interest was earned only once during the year—that is, compounded annually. In many cases interest is compounded quarterly, semiannually, or even daily. The more frequently it is compounded (the more frequently the interest is added to the principal), the more rapidly the interest is put to work to earn even more interest.

Future value of a dollar

Amount to which a single payment will grow at some rate of interest

How much will be in your account at the end of 20 years or 25 years? You could determine the answers by the same process, but that would be a lot of tedious work. Fortunately, there are easier ways to determine the future value of a dollar (that is, how much will be in your account after any given number of years at any given interest rates). The process may be done by using (1) an interest table, (2) an electronic calculator, or (3) a computer program such as Excel. This discussion employs interest tables and financial calculators. Excel is illustrated in the Excel review in Appendix E at the end of the text.

The equation for the future value of a dollar is as follows:

$$P_0(1 + i)^n = P_n. \tag{7.1}$$

P represents the present value (amount or principal), i is the rate of interest, and n is the number of time periods. The subscript 0 represents the present and subscripts $1, 2 \ldots n$ represent periods 1, 2, and on through the nth period. In this form, the equation for the future value of a dollar is a simple equation in the following general form:

$$A \times B = C.$$

A is the present value, B is the interest factor, and C is the future value. Thus, the future value equation states:

$$\text{Present value} \times \text{Interest factor} = \text{Future value};$$

that is,

$$P_0 \times (1 + i)^n = P_n.$$

Notice that the interest factor for the future value of a dollar (*FVIF*) is

$$FVIF = (1 + i)^n. \tag{7.2}$$

The interest factor for the future value of one dollar (and all subsequent interest factors in this chapter) has two components: a percentage or interest rate

(i), and the number of time periods (n). Throughout this text, these components will be symbolized in the following general form: $IF(I, N)$. For example, the future value of $100 at 5 percent at the end of 20 years will be written as

$$P_0 \times FVIF\ (5I, 20N) = P_{20}.$$

$FVIF$ indicates the interest factor for the future value of a dollar; $5I$ represents the 5 percent, and $20N$ represents the 20 time periods. When the values are entered into the equation, the future value is

$$\$100(2.653) = \$265.30.$$

The interest factor, 2.653, is found in the first table of Appendix A. The interest rates are read horizontally at the top. The number of periods (such as years or months) is read vertically along the left-hand margin. To determine the future value of $100 at 5 percent for 20 years, locate the interest factor 2.653 and multiply by $100. For 25 years, the interest factor is 3.386, so your account will grow to $338.60 ($100 × 3.386) if the interest rate is 5 percent.

The future value of a dollar grows with increases in the length of time and in the rate of interest. These relationships are illustrated in Figure 7.1. If $1 is compounded at 5 percent interest (AB on the graph), it will grow to $1.28 after five years and to $1.63 after 10 years. However, if $1 is compounded at 10 percent interest (AC on the graph), it will grow to $2.59 in 10 years. These cases illustrate the basic nature of compounding: The longer the funds continue to grow and the higher the interest rate, the higher will be the final value.

Notice that doubling the interest rate more than doubles the amount of interest. When the interest rate is doubled from 5 percent to 10 percent, interest accumulated in 10 years rises from $0.63 at 5 percent to $1.59 at 10 percent.

FIGURE 7.1
Future Value of One Dollar

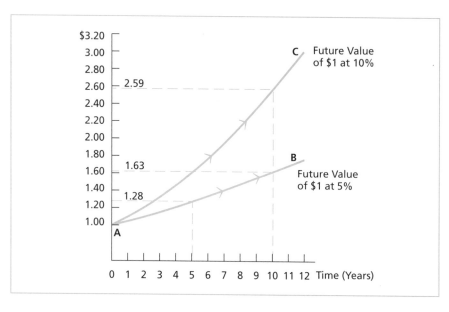

The same conclusion applies to doubling the number of years. When the dollar is compounded annually for five years at 5 percent, the interest earned is $0.28 but rises to $0.63 after 10 years. These conclusions are the result of the fact that compounding involves a geometric progression. The $(1 + i)$ is raised to some power (n).

Time value problems may be illustrated with time lines, which place time periods and payments on a horizontal line. For the previous example, the time line would be

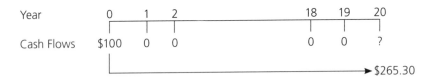

The initial cash outflow of $100 invested at 5 percent grows to $265.30 at the end of 20 years. Notice that the arrow represents the direction of time. When the process is reversed and the future is being brought back to the present (as is illustrated in the next section), the arrow will point to the left.

It is important not to confuse "simple interest" and "compounding." Simple interest is the result of multiplying an amount, the interest rate, and time. In the previous illustration, if simple interest applied, the amount earned would be

$$\$100 \times 20 \times 0.05 = \$100,$$

and the total in the account would be

$$\$100 + 100 = \$200.$$

This amount is perceptibly less than the $265.30 determined using compound interest. When the interest is compounded, the earned interest is $165.30 and not $100.

Simple interest is appropriate only if you withdraw the interest each period so there is no compounding or if there is only one period. Obviously, there can be situations when the interest is withdrawn each period and when payments are made only once. However, in most of the examples used in this text, funds are not withdrawn and payments are made over a number of periods. Thus, compounding is appropriate and generally used throughout this text.

Solving Time Value Problems Using Financial Calculators

Before proceeding to the next case involving time value, the present value of a dollar, it is useful to illustrate how problems may be solved using a financial calculator. Although differences exist among models, financial calculators generally have five special keys:

N I or % PV PMT FV

These keys represent the time period (N), the interest rate (I or % for each time period), the amount in the present (PV for *present value*), the periodic payment (PMT for *annuity payment*, which will be discussed later in this chapter), and the amount in the future (FV for *future value*).

To illustrate how easy financial calculators are to use, consider the previous example of the future value of a dollar in which $100 grew to $265.30 after 20 years when the annual interest rate was 5 percent. Using a financial calculator, enter the present amount (PV = −100), the interest rate (I = 5), and time (N = 20). Since there are no annual payments, be certain that PMT is set equal to zero (PMT = 0). Then instruct the calculator to determine the future value (FV = ?). The calculator should arrive at a future value of $265.33. (The small difference in the answers is the result of the interest tables being rounded off to three places.)

You may wonder why the present value was entered as a *negative* number. Financial calculators consider payments as either cash *inflows* or cash *outflows*. Cash inflows are entered as positive numbers, and cash outflows are entered as negative numbers. One of the cash flows must be an inflow (a positive number), and one must be an outflow (a negative number). In the above example, the initial amount is an outflow because the individual invests the $100. The resulting future amount is a cash inflow because the investor receives the terminal amount. That is, the investor gives up the $100 (the outflow) and after 20 years receives the $265.33 (the inflow).

The cash flows could be reversed. Suppose a firm borrows $100 at 5 percent for 20 years. How much will it have to repay? In this form, the initial $100 is a cash inflow (funds received) and the future amount will be a cash outflow when the loan is repaid. To determine that amount, enter the present amount (PV = 100), the interest rate (I = 5), and number of years (N = 20), the payment (PMT = 0), and instruct the calculator to determine the future value (FV = ?). The calculator determines the future value to be −265.33. The firm will have to repay $265.33, and since that is a cash outflow, the calculator gives a negative number.

Problems involving time value permeate this text and are illustrated with the use of both interest tables and financial calculators. Illustrations using interest tables employ the following general form: *FVIF(I,N)* to represent the interest factor, with the *FV* indicating the future value of a dollar and the *i* indicating the interest rate for *n* time periods. Financial calculator illustrations use the following general form:

PV = ?
I = ?
N = ?
PMT = ?
FV = ?

followed by the answer. When applied to the preceding illustration, the form is

$$PV = \$-100$$
$$I = 5$$
$$N = 20$$
$$PMT = 0$$
$$FV = ?$$
$$FV = \$265.33$$

The illustration is placed in the margin, so that it does not break the flow of the written text.

The Present Value of a Dollar

Present value

Current value of a dollar to be received in the future

In the preceding section, we examined the way in which a dollar is compounded over time. In this section, we will consider the reverse situation. How much is a dollar that will be received in the future worth today? For example, how much will a payment of $1,000 after 20 years be worth today if the funds earn 5 percent annually? Instead of asking how much a dollar will be worth at some future date, the question asks how much that future dollar is worth today. This is a question of present value. The process by which this question is answered is called discounting. Discounting determines the present value of funds that are to be received in the future.

In the earlier section, the future value of a dollar was calculated by Equation 7.1:

Discounting

Process of determining present value

$$P_0(1 + i)^n = P_n.$$

Discounting reverses this equation. The present value (P_0) is determined by dividing the future value (P_n) by the interest factor $(1 + i)^n$. This is expressed in Equation 7.3:

$$P_0 = \frac{P_n}{(1 + i)^n}. \tag{7.3}$$

The future amount is discounted by the appropriate interest factor to determine the present value. For example, if the interest rate is 6 percent, the present value of $100 to be received five years from today is

Time Line

0 1 2 3 4 5

Year

Cash 0 0 0 0 $100
flow $74.73 ←

$$P_0 = \frac{\$100}{(1 + 0.06)^5},$$

$$P_0 = \frac{\$100}{(1.338)},$$

$$P_0 = \$74.73.$$

Equation 7.3, like the equation for the future value of a dollar, breaks down into three simple components: the amount in the future, the amount in the present, and the interest factor that links the present and future values. Thus, the future amount times the interest factor for the present value of a dollar is

$$A \times B = C$$

$$P_n \times PVIF\,(I, N) = P_0.$$

$PVIF(I, N)$ represents the interest factor for the present value of a dollar and is equal to:

$$PVIF = \frac{1}{(1 + i)^n}. \tag{7.4}$$

For example, if the interest rate is 6 percent, the present value of $100 to be received five years from today is

$$P_0 = \$100 \times PVIF(6I, 5N).$$

Function Key	Data Input
FV =	100
I =	6
N =	5
PMT =	0
PV =	?
Function Key	Answer
PV =	−74.73

You may determine the present value by using the interest table for the present value of a dollar (Appendix B). This table presents the interest factors for selected interest rates and periods. The interest rates are read horizontally at the top, and the number of periods is read vertically along the left-hand side. To determine the present value of $100 that you will receive in five years if the current interest rate is 6 percent, multiply $100 by the interest factor, which is found in the table under the vertical column for 6 percent and in the horizontal row for five years. The present value of $100 is

$$\$100 \times 0.747 = \$74.70.$$

The $100 you will receive after five years is currently worth only $74.70.

Notice that the present value interest table is constructed so you multiply even though according to Equation 7.4, you are dividing. Since $\$1/(1 + 0.06)^5 = 0.747$, you multiply $100 by 0.747. Also notice that the answer in the margin derived using a financial calculator is essentially the same. The small difference is the result of rounding off.

The present value of a dollar depends on the length of time before it will be received and the interest rate. The farther into the future the dollar will be received and the higher the interest rate, the lower is the present value of the dollar. This is illustrated by Figure 7.2, which gives the relationship between the present value of a dollar and the length of time at various interest rates. Lines AB and AC give the present value of a dollar at 4 percent and 7 percent, respectively. As may be seen in this graph, a dollar to be received after 20 years is worth considerably less than a dollar to be received after five years when both are discounted at the same percentage. At 4 percent (line AB) the current value of $1 to be received after 20 years is only $0.456, whereas $1 to be received after five years is worth $0.822. Also, the higher the interest rate

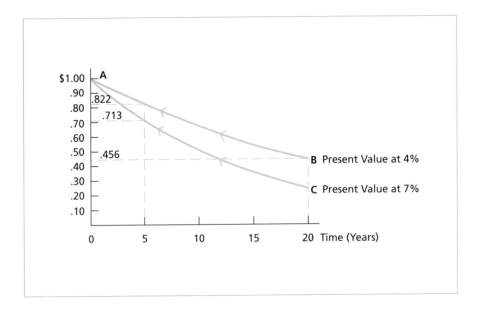

(or discount factor), the lower is the present value of a dollar. For example, the present value of $1 to be received after five years is $0.822 at 4 percent, but it is only $0.713 at 7 percent.

The Future Value of an Annuity of a Dollar

Annuity

Series of equal, annual payments

Future value of an annuity

Amount to which a series of equal payments will grow at some rate of interest

Annuity due

Annuity in which the payments are made at the beginning of the time period

Ordinary annuity

Annuity in which the payments are made at the end of the time period

How much will be in your savings account after three years if $100 is deposited annually and the account pays 5 percent interest? This is similar to the future value of a dollar except that the payment is not a single deposit but a series of annual deposits. If the payments are equal (for example, rent or a loan repayment schedule), the series is called an annuity. The above question illustrates the future value of an annuity.

To determine how much will be in the account you must consider not only the interest rate earned but also whether deposits are made at the beginning of the year or the end of the year. If each deposit is made at the beginning of the year, the series is called an annuity due. If the deposits are made at the end of the year, the series is an ordinary annuity. A car loan with an initial down payment and payments made at the end of each month is an illustration of an ordinary annuity. An apartment lease with payments at the beginning of each month is an illustration of an annuity due.

These differences in payments are illustrated in the following time lines for a $100 annuity paid over three years. The time line for an annuity due is

The time line for an ordinary annuity payments is

Notice that in both cases the time period is three years and that three $100 payments are made. The only difference is the timing of the payments: at the end of each year for the ordinary annuity and at the beginning of each year for the annuity due.

This difference in the timing of payments affects the future value of an annuity, because the difference in timing affects the interest earned. The difference in earned interest is illustrated in Exhibit 7.1 for deposits in an account that pays 5 percent annually. The exhibit gives the payments, their timing, the interest earned, and the amount in the account at the end of each year for an ordinary annuity (the top half of the exhibit) and an annuity due (bottom half). Even though the total deposits in each case were $300, the difference in the timings results in a difference in interest earned. For example, the initial $100 deposit for the annuity due earns three interest payments while the initial deposit for the ordinary annuity earns only two interest payments. Since the annuity due payments are made at the beginning of each year, the annuity due earns more interest ($31.01 versus $15.25) and thus has the higher terminal value. As will be illustrated later in the chapter, the greater the interest rate and the longer the time period, the greater will be this difference in the terminal values.

The procedures for determining the future value of an annuity due (*FVAD*) and the future value of an ordinary annuity (*FVOA*) are stated formally in Equations 7.5 and 7.6, respectively. In each equation, *PMT* represents the equal, periodic payment, *i* represents the rate of interest, and *n* represents the number of years that elapse from the present until the end of the period. For the annuity due, the equation is

$$FVAD = PMT(1 + i)^1 + PMT(1 + i)^2 + \cdots + PMT(1 + i)^n. \quad (7.5)$$

When this equation is applied to the previous example in which $i = 0.05, n = 3$, and the annual payment $PMT = \$100$, the accumulated sum is

$$FVAD = \$100(1 + 0.05)^1 + \$100(1 + 0.05)^2 + \$100(1 + 0.05)^3$$
$$= \$105 + \$110.25 + \$115.76$$
$$= \$331.01.$$

For the ordinary annuity, the equation is

$$FVOA = PMT(1 + i)^0 + PMT(1 + i)^1 + \cdots + PMT(1 + i)^{n-1}. \quad (7.6)$$

E X H I B I T   7.1   Flow of Deposits and Interest Payments for the Future Value of an Ordinary Annuity and the Future Value of an Annuity Due

		Ordinary Annuity						
Date	**1/1/×1**	**12/31/×1**	**1/1/×2**	**12/31/×2**	**1/1/×3**	**12/31/×3**	**Total**
Deposit		$100.00		$100.00		$100.00	$300.00
Interest received				5.00		10.25	15.25
Amount in the account at end of period	$0	$100.00	$100.00	$205.00	$205.00	$315.25	$315.25

		Annuity Due						
Date	**1/1/×1**	**12/31/×1**	**1/1/×2**	**12/31/×2**	**1/1/×3**	**12/31/×3**	**Total**
Deposit	$100.00		$100.00		$100.00		$300.00
Interest received		5.00		10.25		15.76	33.01
Amount in the account at end of period	$100.00	$105.00	$205.00	$215.25		$331.01	$331.01

When this equation is applied to the previous example, the accumulated sum is

$$FVOA = \$100(1 + 0.05)^0 + \$100(1 + 0.05)^1 + \$100(1 + 0.05)^{3-1}$$
$$= \$100 + \$105 + \$110.25$$
$$= \$315.25.$$

As with the future value of a dollar and the present value of a dollar, the future value of an annuity of a dollar is determined by the simple equation:

$$A \times B = C.$$

In this case, that is

$$PMT \times FVAIF(I,N) = FVA,$$

in which PMT represents the periodic payment, the annuity, and $FVAIF(I,N)$ is the interest factor for the future value of an annuity at I percent and N time periods.

The value of the interest factor for the future value of an annuity may be found in the appropriate interest table. Appendix C presents the interest factors for the future value of an ordinary annuity. The number of periods is read vertically at the left, and the interest rates are read horizontally at the top. To ascertain the future value of the ordinary annuity in the previous example, find the interest factor for the future value of an annuity at 5 percent for three years (3.152). So the future value of the ordinary annuity is

$$\$100 \times 3.152 = \$315.20.$$

This is the same answer that was derived by determining the future values of each $100 deposit and totaling them. The slight difference in the two answers is the result of rounding off.

The future value of an annuity of a dollar compounded annually depends on the number of payments (that is, the number of years over which deposits are made) and the interest rate. The longer the time and the higher the interest rate, the greater will be the sum that will have accumulated in the future. This is illustrated by Figure 7.3. Lines AB and AC show the value of the annuity at 4 percent and 8 percent, respectively. After five years the value of the $1 annuity will grow to $5.87 at 8 percent but to only $5.42 at 4 percent. If these annuities are continued for another five years for a total duration of 10 years, they will be worth $14.49 and $12.01, respectively. Thus, both the rate at which the annuity compounds and the length of time affect the annuity's value.

Future Value of an Annuity Due

The previous paragraphs illustrated the use of an interest table to determine the future value of an ordinary annuity. Annuity interest tables are usually provided only for ordinary annuities, but these interest factors may be easily converted into interest factors for annuities due. That conversion is achieved by multiplying the factor by $1 + i$. For example, the interest factor for the future value of an ordinary annuity at 5 percent for three years is 3.152, so the interest factor for an annuity due for three years at 5 percent is

$$3.152(1 + .05) = 3.3096.$$

F I G U R E   7.3
Future Sum (or Value) of an
Annuity of One Dollar

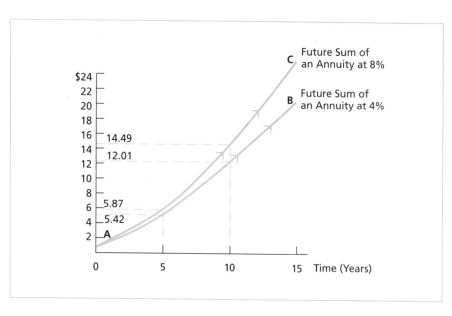

If this interest is applied to the example of $100 deposited in a bank at 5 percent for three years with the deposits starting immediately, the terminal value is

$$\$100(3.3096) = \$330.96.$$

The difference between the terminal value of the two kinds of annuity payments can be substantial as the number of years increases or the interest rate rises. Consider an individual retirement account (IRA) in which you invest $2,000 annually for 20 years. If the deposits are made at the end of the year (an ordinary annuity) and the rate of return is 7 percent, the terminal amount will be

$$\$2,000(40.995) = \$81,990.$$

However, if the investments had been made at the beginning of each year (an annuity due), the terminal amount would be

$$\$2,000(40.995)(1 + 0.07) = \$87,729.30.$$

The difference is $5,739.30! Almost $6,000 in additional interest is earned if the investments are made at the beginning, not at the end, of each year.

The difference between the ordinary annuity and the annuity due becomes even more dramatic if the interest rate rises. Suppose the above IRA offered 12 percent instead of 7 percent. If the deposits are made at the end of each year, the terminal value is

$$\$2,000(72.052) = \$144,104.$$

If the deposits are made at the beginning of the year, the terminal value will be

$$\$2,000(72.052)(1 + 0.12) = \$161,396.48.$$

The difference is now $17,292.48.

The Present Value of an Annuity of a Dollar

Present value of an annuity

Current value of a series of equal payments to be received in the future

In financial analysis you are often concerned with the present value of an annuity. For example, you may expect to receive $100 at the end of each year for three years and want to know how much this series of annual payments is currently worth if 6 percent can be earned on invested funds. Notice the payments are made at the end of the year, so this is an illustration of an ordinary annuity. If the payments had been made at the beginning of the year, the series of payments would be an annuity due.

One method for determining the current worth of this ordinary annuity is to calculate the present value of each $100 payment (find the appropriate interest

Time Line

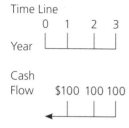

factors in Appendix B and multiply them by $100) and to add these individual present values. That is obviously a tedious job; there has to be an easier way.

The easier way is, of course, to use an interest table for the present value of an annuity or a financial calculator. This process may be seen by considering the equation for the present value of an annuity (Equation 7.7):

$$PV = \frac{PMT}{(1 + i)^1} + \cdots + \frac{PMT}{(1 + i)^n}$$

$$PV = \sum_{t=1}^{n} \frac{PMT}{(1 + i)^t}. \tag{7.7}$$

The present value (*PV*) of equal, annual payments (*PMT*) is found by discounting each payment at the appropriate interest rate (*I*) and summing them from the first payment though the last (*n*) payment. Equation 7.7 may be written as:

$$PV = (PMT)\left(\sum_{t=1}^{n} \frac{1}{(1 + i)^t} \right).$$

Once again this is a simple equation in the general form of

$$A \times B = C.$$

The annual annuity payment is multiplied by an interest factor to determine the present value of an ordinary annuity:

$$PMT \times PVAIF(I,N) = PV.$$

PMT is the annuity payment, *PVAIF(I,N)* is the interest factor for the present value of an ordinary annuity of $1.00 at *I* percent for *N* time periods, and *PV* is the present value of the annuity. The interest factors for the present value of an ordinary annuity of $1.00 are given in Appendix D. The interest rates are read horizontally along the top, and the number of periods is read vertically at the left. To determine the present value of an annuity of $100 that is to be received for three years when interest rates are 6 percent, find the interest factor for three years at 6 percent (2.673) and then multiply $100 by this interest factor. The present value of this annuity is $267.30, which is the price you would be willing to pay now in exchange for three future annual payments of $100, when the return on alternative investments is 6 percent.

As with the present value of a dollar, the present value of an annuity is related to the interest rate and the length of time over which the annuity payments are made. The lower the interest rate and the longer the duration of the annuity, the greater is the current value of the annuity. Figure 7.4 illustrates the relationship between the duration of the annuity and the present value of the annuity at various interest rates. As may be seen by comparing lines AB and AC, the lower the interest rate, the higher is the present dollar value.

CALCULATOR SOLUTION	
Function Key	Data Input
FV =	0
PMT =	100
I =	6
N =	3
PV =	?
Function Key	Answer
PV =	− 267.30

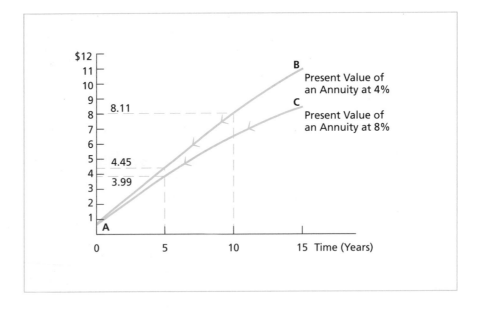

For example, if payments are to be made over five years, the present value of an annuity of $1 is $4.45 at 4 percent but only $3.99 at 8 percent. The longer the duration of the annuity, the higher is the present value; hence, the present value of an annuity of $1 at 4 percent is $4.45 for five years, whereas the present value is $8.11 for 10 years.

Present Value of an Annuity Due

Interest tables for the present value of an annuity are usually provided for ordinary annuities, but there are situations when a financial manager or investor needs the present value of an annuity due. For example, a lease in which the payments start now is an example of an annuity due.

Just as the interest factors for the future value of an ordinary annuity may be adjusted for an annuity due, so can the interest factors for the present value of an ordinary annuity be converted into interest factors for the present value of an ordinary annuity be converted into interest factors for the present value of an annuity due. The conversion is simple: multiply the interest factor by $1 + i$. In the previous example, the interest factor for the present value of an ordinary annuity of $1 at 6 percent for three years is 2.673. That interest factor may be converted into the interest factor for the present value of an annuity due of $1 at 6 percent for three years as follows:

$$2.673(1 + .06) = 2.833.$$

Thus the present value of an annuity due of $100 for three years at 6 percent is worth $283.30 ($100 × 2.833).

Notice that the present value of an annuity due is greater than the present value of an ordinary annuity ($283.30 versus $267.30 in these illustrations).

The reason is that an annuity due's first payment is made immediately while the ordinary annuity makes the first payment at the end of the year. You can put the funds to work earning interest for you sooner. This difference in the timing of the payments increases the value of the annuity due.

Illustrations of Compounding and Discounting

The previous sections have explained the various computations involving time value. This section illustrates them in a series of problems that an investor or financial manager may encounter. These illustrations are similar to examples that are used throughout the text. If you understand these examples, comprehending the rest of the text material should be much easier, because the emphasis can then be placed on the analysis instead of on the mechanics of the calculations.

1. An employer offers to start a pension plan like a 401(k) for a 45-year-old employee. The plan is to place $1,000 at the end of each year in an account that earns 6 percent annually. The employee wants to know how much will be in the account by retirement at age 65.

   This is an example of the future value of an ordinary annuity. The payment is $1,000 annually, and it will grow at 6 percent for 20 years. The fund will thus grow to

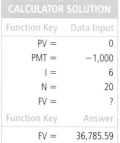

CALCULATOR SOLUTION

Function Key	Data Input
PV =	0
PMT =	−1,000
I =	6
N =	20
FV =	?
Function Key	Answer
FV =	36,785.59

$$FVA = PMT(1 + i)^0 + \cdots + PMT(1 - i)^{n-1}$$

$$= \$1{,}000(1 + 0.06)^0 + \cdots + \$1{,}000(1 + 0.06)^{19}$$

$$= \$1{,}000[FVAIF(6I, 20N)]$$

$$= \$1{,}000(36.786) = \$36{,}786.$$

2. The same employer decides to place a lump sum in an account that earns 6 percent and to draw on the account to make the annual payments of $1,000. After 20 years all the funds in the account will be depleted. How much must be deposited initially in the account?

   This is an example of the present value of an ordinary annuity. The annuity of $1,000 per year at 6 percent for 20 years is worth how much today? The present value (the amount of the initial deposit necessary to fund the annuity) is

$$PVA = \sum_{1}^{n} \frac{PMT}{(1 + i)} + \cdots + \frac{PMT}{(1 + i)^n}$$

$$= \frac{\$1{,}000}{1 + 0.06} + \cdots + \frac{\$1{,}000}{(1 + 0.06)^{20}}$$

PART 2 Financial Tools

$$= \$1,000[PVAIF(6I,20N)]$$

$$= \$1,000(11.470) = \$11,470.$$

Thus, the employer need deposit only $11,470 in an account that earns 6 percent to meet the $1,000 pension payment for 20 years.

You should notice the difference between the answers in the last two examples. In the first, a set of payments earns interest, and thus the future value is larger than just the sum of the 20 payments of $1,000. In the second, a future set of payments is valued in present terms. Since future payments are worth less today, the current value is less than the sum of the 20 payments of $1,000.

Examples 1 and 2 are two means for the employer to obtain the same objective (i.e., to fund the pension plan). In the first example, the employer contributes the $1,000 each year. In the second example, the employer makes one payment and then draws on the amount to make the annual $1,000 payments. The net result is the same: $1,000 is paid into the employee's pension plan each year. The results are the same because $11,470 today is mathematically equivalent to $1,000 a year for 20 years at 6 percent.

3. You buy a stock for $10 and expect its price to increase 9 percent annually. After 10 years, you plan to sell the stock. What is your anticipated sale price? This question illustrates the future value of a dollar, and that future value is

$$P_n = P_0(1 + i)^n$$

$$P_{10} = \$10(1 + 0.09)^{10}$$

$$P_{10} = \$10(FVIF\ 9I,\ 10N)$$

$$P_{10} = \$10(2.367) = \$23.67.$$

You anticipate selling the stock for $23.67.

4. You sell a stock for $23.67 that was held for 10 years. You earned a return of 9 percent. What was the original cost of the stock? This is an example of the present value of a dollar discounted back at 9 percent for 10 years. The purchase price was

$$P_0 = \frac{P_n}{(1 + i)^n}$$

$$P_0 = \frac{\$23.67}{(1 + 0.09)^{10}}$$

$$P_0 = \$23.67(PVIF\ 9I,\ 10N)$$

$$P_0 = \$23.67(0.422) = \$9.98 \approx \$10.$$

The stock cost $10 when you purchased it.

5. Examples 3 and 4 are two views of the same investment. In (3), your investment grew to $23.67, while in (4) you determined the cost of the stock knowing the sale price and the return. Another version of this problem is as follows. You bought a stock for $10, held it for 10 years, and then sold it for $23.67. What was the return on the investment? This is a common question because you often know the purchase and sale prices and want to know the return. (This question reappears in Chapters 14, 23, and 26 on yields and returns.)

If you are using interest tables, either the future value or the present value of a dollar may be used. If the future value table (Appendix A) is used, the question is: $10 grows to $23.67 in 10 years at what rate? The answer is

$$P_0(1 + x)^n = P_n$$

$$\$10(1 + x)^n = \$23.67.$$

$$\$10[FVIF(?I, 10N)] = \$23.67$$

$$FVIF(?I, 10N) = 2.367.$$

CALCULATOR SOLUTION	
Function Key	Data Input
PV =	−10
N =	10
PMT =	0
FV =	23.67
I =	?
Function Key	Answer
I =	9

The interest factor, 2.367, is found in the future value table on the row for 10 years. That makes the rate 9 percent.

If the present value table (Appendix B) is used, the question asks what discount rate (x) at 10 years will bring $23.67 back to $10. The answer is

$$P_0 = \frac{P_n}{(1 + x)^n}$$

$$\$10 = \frac{\$23.67}{(1 + x)^{10}}$$

$$\$10 = \$23.67[(PVIF\ ?I, 10N)]$$

$$PVIF\ (?I, 10N) = \frac{\$10}{\$23.67} = 0.422.$$

The interest factor is 0.422, which may be found in the present value of a dollar table for 10 years in the 9 percent column. Thus, this problem may be solved by the proper application of either the compound value or present value tables.

Examples 1 through 4 illustrate the future and present values of a dollar and of an annuity. Example 5 is different because you know the beginning and ending values and must determine the interest rate or rate of return. The text discussion shows how the answer may be derived using either future value or present value of a dollar interest tables. The margin note illustrates the calculator solution.

6. An investment pays $50 per year for 10 years, after which $1,000 is returned to the investor. If you can earn 6 percent, how much is this investment worth? This question really contains two questions: What is the present value of an annuity of $50 at 6 percent for 10 years, plus what is the present value of $1,000 after 10 years at 6 percent? The answer is

$$PV = \sum_{1}^{n} \frac{PMT}{(1+i)^1} + \cdots + \frac{PMT}{(1+i)^n} + \frac{P_n}{(1+i)^n}$$

$$= \frac{\$50}{(1+0.06)^1} + \cdots + \frac{\$50}{(1+0.06)^{10}} + \frac{\$1,000}{(1+0.06)^{10}}$$

$$= \$50[PVAIF(6I, 10N)] + \cdots + \$1,000[PVIF(6I, 10N)]$$

$$= \$50(7.360) + \$1,000(0.558) = \$926,$$

in which 7.360 and 0.558 are the interest factors for the present value of an annuity of a dollar and the present value of a dollar, respectively, both at 6 percent for 10 years (Appendixes D and B, respectively). This example illustrates that many investments may involve both a series of payments (the annuity component) and a lump-sum payment. This particular investment illustrates a bond, the valuation of which is discussed in Chapter 23.

Throughout the remainder of this text there will be numerous applications of the concept of the time value of money. Time value plays an exceedingly important role in finance because decisions must be made today while the returns occur in the future. Before completing this section, let's do two more illustrations that may directly apply to you at some point in your life.

7. You purchase a home for $100,000, make a down payment of $20,000, and borrow the balance ($80,000). The mortgage loan is for 25 years and the rate of interest is 8 percent. What is the annual payment required by this loan? (Mortgage payments are usually made monthly, but to keep this illustration simple, assume the payment is made annually.) This problem is a common application of the time value of money, and even if the lender makes the calculation, you can answer the question to determine what the mortgage payment will be before asking for the loan.

This problem differs from the previous annuity illustrations, which asked you to determine the future value or present value. In this problem, you know the present value of the annuity (the amount borrowed or $80,000), the number of years (25), and the interest rate (8 percent). The unknown is the annuity payment that is required to pay the interest and retire the loan. Since the payments will be made at the end of each year, the mortgage is an illustration of an ordinary annuity. Since the loan is being made in the present, the problem requires the use of the present value interest table. That is

$$\$80,000 = PMT[PVAIF(8I,25N)]$$

$$\$80,000 = PMT(10.675)$$

$$PMT = \frac{\$80,000}{10.675} = \$7,494,15.$$

Thus, the annual mortgage payment is $7,494.15.

Now that we know your annual payment required to make the loan is $7,494.15, you can split the payment into the interest payment and the principal repayment. (This division may be important, since you may be able to deduct the interest payment on the mortgage for federal income taxation.) Since the interest rate is 8 percent and the initial amount of the loan is $80,000, the interest during the first year is $6,400. The balance of the payment ($1,094.15) reduces the amount owed to $78,905.85.

Since the amount owed is reduced, the interest paid during the second year declines to $6,312.47 (0.08 × $78,905.85). The annual payment remains $7,494.15, so the balance owed is reduced by $1,181.68 ($7,494.15 − $6,312.47). The balance owed after the second year is $77,724.17. This type of calculation is used to generate a repayment schedule, which is referred to as a *loan amortization schedule.*

Such a schedule is illustrated in Exhibit 7.2. The first column gives the number of the payment, and the second and third columns break the payment into the payments for interest and principal repayment. The last column gives the balance due on the loan. As payments are made (1) the amount of the outstanding principal declines, (2) the amount of interest paid each period declines, and (3) the rate at which the principal is repaid increases. In the early years of a mortgage, most of the payment covers the interest charges, but during the later life of the mortgage, most of the payment retires the principal.

8. Your 85-year-old Auntie Bea has to enter a nursing home that charges $8,000 a month ($96,000 a year). You have power of attorney and sell her home for $470,000. Excluding any other sources of income (such as social security payments) and any other expenses (for example, doctors), how long will her money last if you are able to earn 8 percent annually? This may strike you as a morbid situation, but it is a real problem facing many elderly individuals and their families. Actually your Auntie Bea is better off than many elderly. She had a house and was able to live in it until age 85.

Once again this problem is an illustration of an annuity. The known variables are (1) the amount of money Auntie Bea has in the present ($470,000), (2) the rate she will earn on the funds (8 percent), and (3) the amount of the annuity payment ($96,000). The unknown is the number

EXHIBIT 7.2
Selections from a Loan
Amortization Schedule
for an $80,000 Mortgage
at 8 Percent for 25 Years
(Annual Payment =
$7,494.15)

Number of Payment	Interest Payment	Principal Repayment	Balance of Loan
1	$6,400.00	$1,094.15	$78,905.85
2	6,312.47	1,181.68	77,724.17
—			
—			
12	4,942.78	2,551.52	59,233.29
13	4,738.66	2,755.64	56,477.65
—			
—			
24	1,069.15	6,425.16	6,939.17
25	555.13	6,939.17	.00

of years that the funds will last. Since she has the money now, this is another illustration of the present value of an annuity. Auntie Bea's problem is set up as follows:

$$\$470,000 = \$96,000[PVAIF(8I,?N)]$$

$$PVAIF(8I,?N) = \frac{\$470,000}{\$96,000} = 4.896.$$

CALCULATOR SOLUTION

Function Key	Data Input
PV =	470,000
I =	8
FV =	0
PMT =	−96,000
N =	?
Function Key	Answer
N =	6.46

Looking up this factor in the table for the present value of an annuity at 8 percent derives an answer of six to seven years. Auntie Bea's assets will cover the nursing home until after she reaches the age of 91. Since life expectancy for a female age 85 is about 6.5 to 7.0 years, Auntie Bea is in relatively good shape financially. Of course, if she lives longer than her life expectancy, there may be a financial problem unless a greater rate of return can be earned on her funds or if she has other sources of income. There may also be a problem if she earns a return of less than 8 percent. For example, at 4 percent, her funds will be exhausted in slightly more than five years, which is less than her life expectancy.

Before proceeding to nonannual compounding, let's recap the eight illustrations. Examples 1 and 2 illustrate the future value and the present value of an ordinary annuity. Examples 3 and 4 illustrate the future value and present value of a dollar. Example 5 solves for the rate of interest or rate of return when the present and the future amounts are given. Example 6 combines the present value of a dollar and the present value of an annuity, while example 7 illustrates the amortization of a mortgage loan. Example 8 requires that you determine how long a current amount will last as you draw down the funds through a series of equal, annual payments. Each example is typical of a financial problem you may encounter during your career or your life. Being able to answer them can only increase your ability to solve financial problems that you will subsequently experience.

Nonannual Compounding

Nonannual
compounding

Payment of interest more
frequently than once a
year

You should have noticed that in all the previous examples, compounding occurred only once a year. Compounding can and often does occur more frequently, such as twice a year (or semiannually). Nonannual compounding
requires that the equations presented earlier be adjusted. This section extends
the discussion of the compound value of a dollar to include compounding for
periods other than a year.

This explanation, however, is limited to the future value of a dollar. Similar adjustments must be made in the future value of an annuity, the present
value of a dollar, or the present value of an annuity when the funds are compounded more frequently than annually.

Converting annual compounding to other time periods necessitates two
adjustments in Equation 7.1. First, a year is divided into the same number of
time periods as the funds that are being compounded. For semiannual compounding, a year consists of two time periods, whereas for quarterly compounding the year comprises four time periods.

After adjusting for the number of time periods, you adjust the interest
rate to find the rate per time period. This is done by dividing the stated interest rate by the number of time periods per year. If the interest rate is 8 percent
compounded semiannually, 8 percent is divided by 2, giving an interest rate of
4 percent earned in each time period. If the annual rate of interest is 8 percent
compounded quarterly, the interest rate is 2 percent ($0.08 \div 4$) in each of the
four time periods.

These adjustments may be expressed in more formal terms by modifying
Equation 7.1 as follows:

$$P_0\left(1 + \frac{i}{c}\right)^{n \times c} = P_n. \tag{7.8}$$

The only new symbol is c, which represents the frequency of compounding.
The interest rate (i) is divided by the frequency of compounding (c) to determine the interest rate in each period. The number of years (n) is multiplied by
the frequency of compounding to determine the number of time periods.

The application of this equation may be illustrated by a simple example.
You invest $100 in an asset that pays 8 percent compounded quarterly. What
will the future value of this asset be after five years? In other words, $100 will
grow to what amount after five years if it is compounded quarterly at 8 percent? Algebraically, that is

$$P_5 = P_0\left(1 + \frac{i}{c}\right)^{n \times c}$$

$$= \$100\left(1 + \frac{0.08}{4}\right)^{5 \times 4}$$

$$= \$100(1 + 0.02)^{20}.$$

In this formulation you are earning 2 percent for 20 time periods. To solve this equation, the interest factor for the compound value of a dollar at 2 percent for 20 periods (1.486) is multiplied by $100. Thus, the future value is

$$P_5 = \$100(1.486) = \$148.60.$$

The difference between compounding annually and compounding more frequently can be seen by comparing this problem with a problem in which the values are identical except that the interest is compounded annually. The question then is: $100 will grow to what amount after five years at 8 percent compounded annually? The answer is

$$P_5 = \$100(1 + 0.08)^5$$
$$= \$100(1.469)$$
$$= \$146.90.$$

This sum, $146.90, is less than the amount that was earned when the funds were compounded quarterly. We may conclude that the more frequently interest is compounded, the greater will be the future amount.

Periods of Less Than One Year

All the previous illustrations and problems had time periods of a year or more. There are, however, many situations in finance that occur in time periods of less than a year. For example, a wholesaler may lend to a retailer for a period of 30 days, or a cash manager may acquire a three-month short-term security. The retailer may need to know the annual cost of the credit and the cash manager may want to determine the annual rate of return being earned on the security. These are but two illustrations that involve the time value of money for less than a year.

As with nonannual compounding, the basic time value of money equations may be applied to solve these problems. Suppose the cash manager invests $98,543 that will return $100,000 at the end of 45 days. What is the annual rate of return? The future value of a dollar Equation 7.1 may be used to solve the problem as follows:

$$P_0(1 + i)^n = P_n.$$

P_0 is the initial amount ($98,543) and P_n is the terminal amount ($100,000) received after the 45-day time period (n = 45 days or 45/365 = 0.1233 of a year). Thus the equation is

$$\$98,543(1 + i)^{0.1233} = \$100,000.$$

To isolate the unknown, divide $100,000 by $98,543 and raise both sides of the equation by reciprocal of 0.1233 (1/0.1233 = 8.1103):

$$[(1 + i)^{0.1233}]^{8.1103} = [\$100,000/\$98,543]^{8.1103}$$

$$(1 + i) = 1.014785^{8.1103} = 1.12641,$$

and subtract 1:

$$i = 1.12641 - 1 = 12.641\%.$$

The annualized rate of interest to the borrower (the rate of return to the lender) is 12.641 percent. This is a compound rate of interest that assumes that the lender is able to invest $98,543 and have it grow to $100,000 every 45 days and that the borrower uses $98,543 every 45 days and retires the loan by paying $100,000.

Many situations in short-term financial decision making involve this type of calculation. A financial manager or corporate treasurer may borrow short-term funds, receiving an amount such as $98,543 and agreeing to repay $100,000 after a specified period of time. Such discounted loans are common, especially for short periods of time less than a year. (See, for instance, the section on calculating yields on money market securities in Chapter 17 and the cost of bank loans, commercial paper, and trade credit in Chapter 18.) The determination of the annualized percentage cost of the loans to the borrowers (or the yields to the lenders) is essentially the same as any time value problem, only the period is less than a year instead of greater than a year.

Summary

Money has time value. A dollar to be received in the future is worth less than a dollar received today. You will forgo current consumption only if future growth in your funds is possible. Such appreciation is called compounding. The longer the funds compound and the higher the rate at which they compound, the greater will be the amount of funds in the future.

The opposite of compounding is discounting, which determines the present value of funds that are to be received in the future. The present value of a future sum depends both on how far in the future the funds are to be received and on the discount rate.

Compounding and discounting are applied both to single payments and to series of payments. If the payments in a series are equal and made annually, the series is called an annuity.

The ability to compare future dollars with present dollars is crucial to financial decision making. Many financial decisions involve the current outlay of funds, for investments are made in the present. The returns on these investments occur in the future. The concepts presented in this chapter are basic to an understanding of the valuation of securities, the cost of a loan, and capital budgeting.

Summary of the Equations for the Interest Factors

Each of the four cases involving time value has interest factors. Each interest factor has a percentage (interest rate) and time (number of time periods). The equations for the interest factors are as follows:

Future value of a dollar (*FVIF*):

$$(1 + i)^n.$$

Present value of a dollar (*PVIF*):

$$\frac{1}{(1 + i)^n}.$$

Future value of an ordinary annuity (*FVAIF*):

$$\frac{(1 + i)^n - 1}{i}.$$

Present value of an ordinary annuity (*PVAIF*):

$$\frac{1 - \dfrac{1}{(1 + i)^n}}{i} = \frac{1 - (1 + i)^{-n}}{i}.$$

Review Objectives

Now that you have completed this chapter, you should be able to

1. Solve time value of money problems.
2. Interpret the results of your solutions.
3. Contrast compounding (p. 106) and discounting (pp. 110–112).
4. Use an interest table or a financial calculator (pp. 108–110).
5. Differentiate an ordinary annuity from an annuity due (p. 112).
6. Explain why the present value of an annuity of $100 for 10 years is less than the future value of the same annuity (pp. 119–120).
7. Construct a loan amortization schedule (pp. 122–123).

Problems

1. An investment generates $10,000 per year for 25 years. If you can earn 10 percent on other investments, what is the current value of this investment? If its current price is $120,000, should you buy it?

2. A company has two investment possibilities, with the following cash inflows:

Investment	Year 1	Year 2	Year 3
A	$1,400	1,700	1,800
B	$1,500	1,500	1,500

If the firm can earn 7 percent in other investments, what is the present value of investments A and B? If each investment costs $4,000, is the present value of each investment greater than the cost of the investment? (This question is a very simple example of one method of capital budgeting [Chapter 14]. This technique permits the firm to rank alternative investments and help select the potentially most profitable investment.)

3. If you currently earn $50,000 and inflation continues at 4 percent for 10 years, how much must you make to maintain your purchasing power?

4. If you bought a $50,000 home in 1980 and sold it in 2010 for $250,000, what would be the annual rate of price appreciation during the 30 years?

5. You purchase a stock for $20 and expect its price to grow annually at a rate of 8 percent.

   a. What price are you expecting after five years?

   b. If the rate of increase in the price doubled from 8 percent to 16 percent, would that double the *increase* in the price? Why?

6. You are 25 years old and inherit $65,000 from your grandmother. If you wish to purchase a $100,000 boat to celebrate your 30th birthday, what compound annual rate of return must you earn?

7. You invest $1,000 in a certificate of deposit that matures after 10 years and pays 5 percent interest, which is compounded annually until the certificate matures.

   a. How much interest will you earn if the interest is left to accumulate?

   b. How much interest will you earn if the interest is withdrawn each year?

   c. Why are the answers to *a* and *b* different?

8. A self-employed person deposits $3,000 annually in a retirement account (called a Keogh account) that earns 8 percent.

   a. How much will be in the account when the individual retires at the age of 65 if the savings program starts when the person is age 40?

   b. How much additional money will be in the account if the saver defers retirement until age 70 and continues the contributions?

   c. How much additional money will be in the account if the saver discontinues the contributions at age 65 but does not retire until age 70?

9. A 45-year-old woman decides to put funds into a retirement plan. She can save $2,000 a year and earn 9 percent on this savings. How much will she have accumulated if she retires at age 65? At retirement how much can she withdraw each year for 20 years from the accumulated savings if the savings continue to earn 9 percent?

10. You annually invest $1,500 in an individual retirement account (IRA) starting at the age of 20 and make the contributions for 10 years. Your twin sister does the same starting at age 30 and makes the contributions for 30 years. Both of you earn 7 percent annually on your investment. Who has the larger amount at age 60?

(Problems 8 through 10 illustrate the basic elements of pension plans. A sum of money is systematically set aside. It earns interest so that by retirement a considerable amount has been accumulated. Then the retired person draws on the fund until it is exhausted, or until death occurs, in which case the remainder of the fund becomes part of the estate. Of course, while the retired person draws on the fund, the remaining principal continues to earn interest.)

11. If a parent wants to have $100,000 to send a newborn child to college, how much must be invested annually for 18 years if the funds earn 9 percent? (Any current student who subsequently becomes a parent and wants to send a child to college should make this calculation early in the child's life.)

12. A widow currently has a $93,000 investment yielding 9 percent annually. Can she withdraw $16,000 a year for the next 10 years?

13. Each year you invest $2,000 in an account that earns 5 percent annually. How long will it take for you to accumulate $50,000?

14. You want your salary to double in six years. At what annual rate of growth must your salary increase to achieve your goal?

15. An investment offers to pay you $10,000 a year for five years. If it costs $33,520, what will be your rate of return on the investment?

16. Auntie Kitty sells her house for $200,000, which is then invested to earn 6 percent annually. If her life expectancy is 10 years, what is the maximum amount she can annually spend on a nursing home, doctors, and taxes?

17. You are offered $900 after five years or $150 a year for five years. If you can earn 6 percent on your funds, which offer will you accept? If you can earn 14 percent on your funds, which offer will you accept? Why are your answers different?

18. An investment costs $61,446 and offers a return of 10 percent annually for 10 years. What are the annual cash inflows anticipated from this investment?

19. You are offered an annuity that will pay $10,000 a year for 10 years (that is, 10 payments) *starting after five years have elapsed*. If you seek an annual return of 8 percent, what is the maximum amount you should pay for this annuity?

20. You purchase a town house for $140,000. After a down payment of $30,000, you obtain a mortgage loan at 9 percent that requires annual payments for 15 years.

    a. What are the annual payments?

    b. How much of the first payment goes to pay the interest?

    c. What is the remaining mortgage balance after the first payment is made?

21. You contribute $1,000 annually to a retirement account for 8 years and stop making payments at the age of 25. Your twin brother (or sister . . . whichever applies) opens an account at age 25 and contributes $1,000 a year until retirement at age 65 (40 years). You both earn 10 percent on your investments. How much can each of you withdraw for 20 years (that is, ages 66 through 85) from the retirement accounts?

    (Each of the previous problems may be readily solved using interest tables and financial calculators. There are, however, problems that are not easily solved using interest tables. For example, solving for the return on an investment that involves both an annuity and a single payment is a tedious process if you use interest tables. The same applies if the cash flows vary each year. However, a financial calculator may readily solve these problems.

    Problems 28–30 illustrate this reality. All three are easily solved using a financial calculator but require that you employ a reiterative process when you are using interest tables. That is, you set up the equation and select a rate. If the results equate the two sides of the equation, you have solved the problem and determined the return. If not, you have to repeat the process until you have selected the rate that equates the two sides. After doing a couple of these problems, you may decide that learning how to use a financial calculator or a program such as Excel is worth the effort.)

22. Uncle Fred recently died and left $325,000 to his 50-year-old favorite niece. She immediately spent $100,000 on a town home but decided to invest the balance for her retirement at age 65. What rate of return must she earn on her investment over the next 15 years to permit her to withdraw $75,000 at the end of each year through age 80 if her funds earn 10 percent annually during retirement?

23. You win a judgment in an auto accident for $100,000. You immediately receive $25,000 but must pay your lawyer's fee of $15,000. In addition, you will receive $2,500 a year for 20 years for a total of $50,000, after which the balance owed ($25,000) will be paid. If the interest rate is 7 percent, what is the current value of your settlement?

24. A $1,000,000 state lottery prize is spread evenly over 10 years ($100,000 a year), or you may take a lump distribution of $654,000. If you can earn 7 percent, which alternative is better?

25. You wish to retire in 12 years and currently have $50,000 in a savings account yielding 5 percent annually and $100,000 in quality "blue chip" stocks yielding 10 percent. If you expect to add $30,000 at the end of each year to your stock portfolios, how much will you have in your retirement fund when you retire? What rate of return must you earn on your retirement funds if you want to withdraw $102,000 per year for the next 15 years after retiring?

26. A firm must choose between two investment alternatives, each costing $100,000. The first alternative generates $35,000 a year for four years. The second pays one large lump sum of $157,400 at the end of the fourth year. If the firm can raise the required funds to make the investment at an annual cost of 10 percent, which alternative should be preferred?

27. A savings and loan association finances your 25-year, $100,000, 9-percent mortgage. How much interest does the S&L collect on the loan in the second year?

28. You purchase a building for $900,000, collect annual rent (after expenses) of $120,000 and sell the building for $1,000,000 after three years. What is the annual return on this investment?

29. You buy a stock for $1,000 and expect to sell it for $900 after four years but also expect to collect dividends of $120 a year. Prove that the return on this investment is less than 10 percent.

30. You purchase a stock for $10,000 and collect $400 at the end of each year in dividends. You sell the stock for $11,300 after four years. What was the annual return on your $10,000 investment?

**Additional
Problems
with Answers**

Now that you have done numerous time value problems, here are a few more for additional practice. Answers are provided after the problems to facilitate correcting your work.

1. A firm has only $10,000 to invest and must choose between two projects. Project A returns $12,400 after a year while project B pays $15,609 after three years. If management wants to earn 10 percent on an investment, which alternative should be selected based on the present value of the cash inflows?

2. A firm can annually earn $1,000 in investment A for three years and $1,080 in investment B for three years. Both investments cost $2,500. Management uses 10 percent to discount cash flows; however, B is the riskier alternative, so management decides to use 16 percent. Based on this information, which investment is the better alternative?

3. A firm borrows $9,600 for five years at 9 percent. The loan requires the firm to repay the interest and principal in equal, annual payments that cover the interest and principal. The interest is determined on the declining balance that is owed. What are the annual payments and the amount by which the loan is reduced during the first year?

4. A corporation promises to pay you $4 a year for 20 years and $100 after 20 years. What is the maximum amount you would pay for the security if you wanted to earn 8 percent?

5. A firm buys a short-term money market instrument for $9,791 and receives $10,000 after 180 days. What is the rate earned on this short-term investment?

6. A company leases equipment for five years. The equipment costs $5,000, and the owner (called the "lessor") wants to earn 10 percent on the lease. What should be the lease payments?

7. If a firm has $12,400 to invest and can earn 14 percent, how much will the firm have after two years?

8. A firm has only $10,000 to invest and must choose between two projects. Project A returns $12,400 after a year while project B pays $15,609 after three years. If management wants to select the investment with the higher return, which alternative should be chosen?

9. If a corporation promises to pay you $60 a year for three years and $1,000 after three years, what is the maximum amount you would lend if you wanted to earn 8 percent?

10. A firm borrows $9,791 and agrees to pay $10,000 after 180 days. What is the interest rate on this short-term loan?

Answers

1. A: $12,400/(1 + 0.1) = $12,400 \times 0.909 = $11,272

   or

   A: $FV = 12,400$; $PMT = 0$; $N = 1$; $I = 10$, and $PV = ?$

   $PV = -11,276$

   B: $15,609/(1 + 0.1)^3$ = $15,609 \times 0.751 = $11,727

   or

   B: $FV = 15,609$; $PMT = 0$; $N = 3$; $I = 10$, and $PV = ?$

   $PV = -11,727$

   The present value of investment B is higher and, therefore, B is preferred.

2. A: $1,000 \times 2.487 = $2,487

   or

   A: $FV = 0$; $PMT = 1,000$; $N = 3$; $I = 10$, and $PV = ?$

   $PV = -2,487$

   B: $1,080 = $1,080 \times 2.248 = $2,428

   or

   B: $FV = 0$; $PMT = 1,080$; $N = 3$; $I = 16$, and $PV = ?$

   $PV = -2,426$

   Even though investment B pays more, the higher discount rate more than offsets the higher income. (Risk adjustments are discussed in Chapter 14.)

3. The amount of each payment:

   $PMT = \$9,600/3.890 = \$2,467.87$

   or

   $FV = 0; PV = 9,600; N = 5; I = 9;$ and $PMT = ?$

   $PMT = 2,468.09$

   The payment is split into interest ($864 for the first year) and princi-pal. The principal reduction is the total payment minus the interest, which is $2,467.87 − \$864 = \$1,603.87$ using the interest table and $2,468.09 − \$864 = \$2,404.09$ using a financial calculator. (This problem illustrates the term loan discussed in Chapter 19 and is es-sentially the same as the mortgage loan illustrated in Exhibit 7.2 in the body of this chapter.)

4. $\$4(9.818) + \$100(0.215) = \$60.77$

   or

   $FV = 100; PMT = 4; N = 20; I = 8,$ and $PV = ?$

   $PV = -60.73$

   This problem illustrates the valuation of a preferred stock (see Chap-ter 24) in which the company pays you a $4 dividend every year and redeems the security for $100 at the end of 20 years. Notice that prob-lems 4 and 9 are essentially the same. Both ask you to determine the maximum amount that you would be willing to pay for the asset. Val-uation is an essential concept in finance, and in each case the process is essentially the same: What are future cash flows worth today?

5. $\$9,791 = \$10,000/(1 + r)^{0.4932}$

   $r = 4.38\%$

   or

   $FV = 10,000; PMT = 0; N = 180/365 = 0.4932; PV = 9,791,$ and $I = ?$

   $I = 4.38$

6. $PMT = \$5,000/3.791 = \$1,319$

   or

   $PV = -5,000; FV = 0; N = 5; I = 10;$ and $PMT = ?$

   $PMT = 1,319$

   If the owner receives payments of $1,319 for five years, the return from the lease is 10 percent. (Leases are covered in Chapter 19.)

7. $\$12,400(1 + 0.14)^2 = \$12,400(1.300) = \$16,120$

   or

   $PV = -12,400; PMT = 0; N = 2; I = 14;$ and $FV = ?$

   $FV = 16,115$

Problem 7 helps resolve the conflict illustrated in problems 1 and 8. If you invest the $12,400 received in year one at 14 percent for two years, the terminal value is $16,120, which exceeds the amount ($15,609) received at the end of the third year from investment B. So investment A is preferred.

8. $A: \$10,000 = \$12,400/(1 + r)$

   $IF = \$10,000/\$12,400 = 0.8065$

   $r = 24\%$

   or

   $A: FV = 12,400; PMT = 0; N = 1; PV = -10,000,$ and $I = ?$

   $I = 24$

   $B: \$10,000 = \$15,609/(1 + r)^3$

   $IF = \$10,000/\$15,609 = 0.06407$

   $r = 16\%$

   or

   $B: FV = 15,609; PMT = 0; N = 3; PV = -10,000,$ and $I = ?$

   $I = 16\%$

   The percentage return on investment A is higher and, therefore, A is preferred. You should note that problems 1 and 8 illustrate two methods for selecting investments and the answers are contradictory. The process of choosing between alternative investments is discussed in Chapter 14.

9. $\$60(2.577) + \$1,000(0.794) = \$948.62$

   or

   $FV = 1,000; PMT = 60; N = 3; I = 8,$ and $PV = ?$

   $PV = -948.46$

   This problem illustrates the valuation of a $1,000 bond (see Chapter 23) in which the company pays you $60 in interest every year and repays the $1,000 at the end of three years.

10. $\$9,791 = \$10,000/(1 + r)^{0.4932}$

    $r = 4.38\%$

    or

    $FV = 10,000; PMT = 0; N = 180/365 = 0.4932; PV = 9,791,$ and $I = ?$

    $I = 4.38$

    Problems 5 and 10 illustrate short-term investments and short-term loans, which are covered in Chapters 17 and 18. The rate of interest paid by the borrower is the same as the return earned by the lender. (Answers will be marginally different if you interpret 180 days as half a year, in which case $N = 0.5$.)

Relationships

1. The future value of an annuity _____ if payments are made at the beginning of the year instead of at the end of the year.

2. If the number of years is increased, the future value of an annuity of a dollar _____.

3. The present value of an annuity _____ as the interest rate increases.

4. More frequent compounding _____ the future value of a dollar.

5. If interest rates decline, the future value of an annuity of a dollar _____.

6. The use of margin to buy a stock _____ the present value of the investment.

7. An increase in the rate of interest _____ the present value of an annuity due and _____ the future value of an annuity due.

8. If the number of years is increased, the future value of a dollar _____.

9. If interest rates increase, the future value of a dollar _____.

Answers

1. increases
2. increases
3. decreases
4. increases
5. decreases
6. has no impact on (no change)
7. decreases; increases
8. increases
9. increases

CHAPTER 8

Risk and Its Measurement

I n *War As I Knew It*, George Patton wrote, "Take calculated risks; that is quite different from being rash." I once bought a bond that offered an annual return of 15 percent. Unfortunately, the company failed, and I lost virtually every dollar I invested in the bond. I knew the bond was a high-risk security and took what I considered to be an acceptable calculated risk, but I lost.

Since the future is uncertain, you too must take calculated risks. The reward for taking those risks is the anticipated return. Some investors deal with risk on an intuitive basis, but measures of risk are available. Even if you never compute these statistical measures, you need to know them, since you will encounter them when analyzing financial assets.

This chapter provides an elementary introduction to the measurement of risk. While the chapter starts with different uses for the word *return*, the bulk of the chapter is devoted to risk measurement. The first is the dispersion around the return or central tendency and is called a "standard deviation." The second measure is an index of the volatility of an asset's return relative to a base, such as the return on the market. This measure is referred to as a "beta" coefficient.

Standard deviations and beta coefficients are hard to avoid if you do financial management or investment analysis. For example, beta coefficients may be used to help determine the required return that is necessary to justify the purchase of a stock. Both measures are used to evaluate the performance of portfolio managers. While the chapter does illustrate how standard deviations and beta coefficients are calculated, you may never have to calculate them. (If you do, a spreadsheet program such as Excel does the mechanics virtually instantaneously.) What you need to know is how to use and interpret these measures of risk. Hence the emphasis in this text is on their usage and not the mechanics of their calculation.

The Return on an Investment

Return

What is earned on an investment: the sum of income and capital gains generated by an investment

All investments are made in anticipation of a return. This applies to individuals and also to the financial managers of firms. An investment may offer a return from either of two sources. The first is the flow of income. A savings account yields a flow of interest income. The second source of return is capital appreciation. If you buy stock and its price increases, you earn a capital gain. All investments offer potential income and/or capital appreciation. Some investments, like the savings account, offer only income. Other investments, such as an investment in land, may offer only capital appreciation. In fact, some investments may require expenditures (for example, property tax) on the part of the investor.

Investors and financial managers make investments because they anticipate a return. It is important to differentiate between *the expected return* and *the realized return*. The expected return is the incentive for accepting risk, and it must be compared with the required return, which is the return necessary to induce you to bear the risk. The required return includes (1) what you may earn on alternative investments, such as the risk-free return available on Treasury bills, and (2) a premium for bearing risk that includes compensation for the expected inflation rate and for fluctuations in securities prices. Specification of this required return, however, requires a measurement of risk. Thus, discussion of the required return will be deferred until after the discussion of the measures of risk.

Required return

Return necessary to induce an individual to make an investment

Expected return depends on individual expected outcomes and the probability of their occurrence. For example, an investor may say, "Under normal economic conditions, which occur 60 percent of the time, I expect to earn a return of 10 percent on an investment in this stock. However, there is a 20 percent chance the economy will grow more rapidly and the company will do well, in which case I will earn 15 percent. Conversely, there is a 20 percent chance the economy will enter a recession and the company will do poorly, in which case I will earn only 5 percent." Given the possible outcomes and their probabilities, what is the return this investor can anticipate?

The answer to this question depends on the outcomes and the probability of their occurring (in other words, the probability of the economy growing more rapidly, growing at a normal rate, or entering into a recession). Since the investor believes these probabilities are 20 percent, 60 percent, and 20 percent, respectively, the expected return on the investment is

$$0.2 \times 15\% + 0.6 \times 10\% + 0.2 \times 5\% = 10\%.$$

Notice that the expected return is a weighted average of the individual expected outcomes and the probability of occurrence. If the individual expected outcomes had been different, the expected return would differ. For example, if the investor had expected the returns to be 19 percent, 9 percent, and 2 percent, the expected return on the investment would be

$$0.2 \times 19\% + 0.6 \times 9\% + 0.2 \times 2\% = 9.6\%.$$

If the probabilities had been different, the expected return would also differ. If, in the first illustration, the probabilities had been 15 percent, 50 percent, and 35 percent, the expected return would be

$$0.15 \times 15\% + 0.5 \times 10\% + 0.35 \times 5\% = 9\%.$$

Thus, a change in either the expected returns of the individual outcomes or their probability of occurrence causes the expected return on the investment to change.

The Sources of Risk

Risk

Possibility of loss; the uncertainty that the anticipated return will not be achieved

Risk is the uncertainty that the realized return will not equal the expected return (that is, the expected return may not be achieved). If there were no uncertainty, there would be no risk. In the real world, there is uncertainty, which requires the financial manager or investor to analyze possible outcomes and assess the investment's risk. Of course, the realized outcome may be better than expected, but the emphasis in the analysis of risk is on the negative: the outcome will be worse than expected.

Since financial decisions are made in the present but the results occur in the future, risk permeates all financial decision making. The future is not certain; it is only expected. However, sources of risk can be identified. These are frequently classified into "diversifiable" risk and "nondiversifiable" risk or "unsystematic risk" and "systematic risk." (Both sets of terms are used to differentiate the sources of risk.) A diversifiable risk (or unsystematic risk) refers to the risk associated with the individual asset. Since the investor buys specific assets, such as the stock of IBM or the bonds of Verizon, that individual must bear the risk associated with each specific investment.

Diversifiable risk (Unsystematic risk)

Risk associated with individual events that affect a particular asset; firm-specific risk that is reduced through the construction of diversified portfolios

Business risk

Risk associated with the nature of a business

The sources of diversifiable risk are the business and financial risks associated with the individual firm. Business risk refers to the nature of the firm's operations, and financial risk refers to how the firm finances its assets (that is, whether the firm uses a substantial or modest amount of debt financing). For example, the business risk of United Airlines depends on such factors as the cost of fuel, the capacity of planes, and changes in demand. The financial risk associated with United Airlines depends on how it finances its planes. Were the assets acquired by leasing, by retaining earnings, or by issuing bonds, preferred stock, or common stock? The use of debt obligations and lease obligations increases financial risk while the use of equity financing reduces financial risk.

Financial risk

Risk associated with the types of financing used to acquire assets

Although business and financial risk differ (one is concerned with the nature of the firm's operations and the other with how management chooses to finance its operations), management uses financial leverage to affect the firm's total risk exposure. As is explained in Chapter 13 on the cost of capital, management may reduce the firm's cost of funds by using financial leverage. However, increased use of financial leverage increases risk and raises the cost of funds. The problem facing management is to determine what combination of debt and equity financing minimizes the cost of funds. That combination is the firm's optimal capital structure and uses debt financing without excessively increasing the firm's financial risk.

Business and financial risk are *firm specific* and are the source of unsystematic, diversifiable risk. As is illustrated later in this chapter, the construction of a diversified portfolio reduces diversifiable risk. This reduction occurs because the events that decrease the return on one asset may increase the return on another. Notice there is little relationship between the returns on the individual assets; hence the name "unsystematic risk."

The possible beneficial effect of combining different assets in a portfolio may be intuitively grasped by considering the purchase of the stocks of an airline and an oil driller (for example, United Airlines and Schlumberger). Higher oil prices may reduce the earnings of the airline but increase the profits of the drilling operation. Lower oil prices may have the opposite impact; thus, combining the stocks of these two firms will reduce the risk associated with the portfolio. Of course, the risk associated with each individual asset remains the same, but from your perspective, the risk associated with the portfolio is what matters and not the risk associated with the individual asset.

Although the previous illustration applies to an individual's portfolio, the same concept applies to a firm. The financial managers of firms also bear the risk associated with specific assets. A firm invests in particular pieces of inventory, acquires specialized plant and equipment, and extends credit to specific buyers (that is, accounts receivable). Inventory may not sell, equipment may become obsolete, and debtors may default. The financial manager thus bears the unsystematic risk associated with each individual asset acquired by the firm in much the same way that the individual bears the unsystematic risk associated with individual stocks and bonds.

Because firms face unsystematic risk, the advantages associated with diversification may also apply. For example, General Electric (GE) has operations in energy, health care, aviation and transportation, water, consumer products, and finance. Such a strategy reduces the unsystematic risk associated with individual industries and products. Many mergers have been justified (perhaps rationalized) on the grounds that combining two firms with similar, but different, product lines will create a stronger firm with a better and more diversified assortment of goods and services for sale.

Even though a firm may seek a broader mix of products, diversification primarily remains the responsibility of investors. Firms cannot achieve as diversified a mix of assets as is possible in an individual's portfolio, which can include real estate, savings accounts, collectibles, and shares in mutual funds as well as the stocks and bonds issued by a variety of firms and governments.

Nondiversifiable risk (Systematic risk)

Risk associated with fluctuations in securities prices and other nonfirm-specific factors: market risk that is not reduced through the construction of diversified portfolios

Market risk

Risk associated with fluctuations in securities prices

Interest rate risk

Risk associated with changes in interest rates

Reinvestment rate risk

The risk associated with reinvesting earnings on principal at a lower rate than was initially earned

Purchasing power risk

Uncertainty that future inflation will erode the purchasing power of assets and income

Nondiversifiable (or systematic risk) refers to those sources that are not reduced through the construction of a diversified portfolio. These include fluctuations in securities prices, changes in interest rates, reinvestment rates, inflation, and fluctuations in exchange rates. Even though diversification does not affect these sources of risk, they may be managed through the use of derivatives such as options and futures contracts. See the discussion in Chapter 28 and 29.

Market risk is the risk associated with movements in securities prices, especially stock prices. If you buy a stock and the market as a whole declines, the price of the specific stock will probably fall. Conversely, if the market increases, the price of the stock will probably also tend to increase.

Interest rate risk is the risk associated with fluctuations in interest rates. Suppose that a financial manager borrows funds under one set of terms only to have interest rates subsequently fall. If the financial manager had waited, the cost of these borrowed funds would have been lower. Movements in interest rates also affect securities prices, especially the prices of fixed income securities, such as bonds and preferred stock. As explained in Chapter 23, there is an inverse relationship between changes in interest rates and securities prices. Thus, a rise in interest rates will drive down securities prices and inflict a loss on investors in fixed income securities.

Reinvestment rate risk refers to the risk associated with reinvesting funds generated by an investment. If you receive interest or dividends, these funds could be spent on goods and services. For example, individuals who live on a pension consume a substantial portion, and perhaps all, of the income generated by their assets. Other investors, however, reinvest their investment earnings in order to accumulate wealth.

Suppose you want to accumulate a sum of money and purchase a $1,000 bond that pays $100 a year and matures after 10 years. The anticipated annual return based on the annual interest and the amount invested is 10 percent ($100/$1,000). You want to reinvest the annual interest, and the question then becomes what rate will be earned on these reinvested funds: Will the return be more or less than the 10 percent initially earned? The essence of reinvestment rate risk is this: Will you earn more or less on the reinvested funds?

Purchasing power risk is the risk associated with inflation. A conservative investor may deposit funds in a savings account that pays a modest rate of interest. If the rate of inflation exceeds the rate of interest, the investor sustains a loss.

The rate of inflation has varied perceptibly. During the early 1980s, the annual rate of inflation rose to over 10 percent, and purchasing power risk became a major concern of financial managers and investors. These individuals were forced to take actions designed to reduce the impact of inflation. Variable interest rate bonds and variable rate mortgages are examples of two debt instruments that were developed in response to the risk associated with the loss of purchasing power. Subsequently, the rate of inflation declined and the impact of purchasing power risk diminished. During 2008–2010, inflation was virtually nonexistent. However, the risk associated with inflation has not disappeared. Inflation may certainly reappear, so its impact should still be considered when making financial decisions.

While the impact of inflation has diminished, another source of risk has become more prominent: the risk associated with the fluctuations of the dollar relative to other currencies. This exchange rate risk is the risk associated with fluctuations in the prices of foreign moneys. Many firms make and receive payments in foreign countries, and Americans travel abroad, making payments in foreign currencies. In addition, many individuals and financial managers make foreign investments. Any foreign investment subjects the investor to risk from changes in the value of the foreign currency. The dollar value of a foreign currency can rise, thus increasing the return when the funds are converted back to dollars. The value of the foreign currency can also fall, however, reducing the return on the investment when converted back to dollars.

In addition to exchange rate risk, there is also the risk associated with the governments of specific countries. This "country risk" or sovereign risk applies to investing in the debt obligations of a specific country and the possibility that the government will default. Such default has been considered slight if not nonexistent, but during 2010, the possibility of default by Portugal, Ireland, Italy, Greece, or Spain (sometimes referred to as PIIGS) was a major source of uncertainty in world financial markets.

The various sources of risk appear repeatedly throughout this text, since risk and its management are an integral part of financial decision making. Neither the financial manager nor the investor can stop fluctuations in stock prices or interest rates. Nor can they stop inflation, fluctuations in exchange rates, or government default. However, these individuals can seek to earn a return that compensates them for bearing nondiversifiable risk or can use strategies designed to reduce the impact of these sources of risk.

Exchange rate risk

Risk of loss from changes in the value of foreign currencies

Sovereign risk

The risk associated with a government defaulting on its debt obligations

The Standard Deviation as a Measure of Risk

As was stated earlier, risk is concerned with the uncertainty that the realized return will not equal the expected return. One measure of risk, the standard deviation, emphasizes the extent to which the return differs from the average or expected return. An alternative measure of risk, a beta coefficient, is an index of the return on an asset relative to the return on a portfolio of assets (for example, the return on a stock relative to the return on the Standard & Poor's 500 stock index). This section considers the standard deviation as it is used to measure risk, while beta coefficients are explained later in the chapter.

The standard deviation measures the dispersion around an average value. As applied to investments, it considers an average return and the extent to which individual returns deviate from the average. If there is very little difference between the average return and the individual returns, the dispersion will be small. If there is a large difference between the average return and the individual returns, the dispersion will be large. The larger this dispersion, the greater the risk associated with the investment.

Standard deviation

Measure of dispersion around an average value; a measure of risk

Beta coefficient

Index of systematic risk; measure of the volatility of a stock's return relative to the market return

This measurement is perhaps best illustrated by a simple example. Consider the returns on two stocks over a period of nine years:

Return Year	Return Stock A	Return Stock B
1	13.5%	11.0%
2	14.0	11.5
3	14.25	12.0
4	14.5	12.5
5	15.0	15.0
6	15.5	17.5
7	15.75	18.0
8	16.0	18.5
9	16.5	19.0
average return	15.0%	15.0%

The average return over the nine years is the same for both stocks, 15 percent, but annual returns differ. Stock A's individual returns were close to the average return. The worst year generated a 13.5 percent return while the best year generated a 16.5 percent return. None of the individual returns deviated from the average by more than 1.5 percent. Stock B's individual returns differ from the average return, ranging from a low of 11 percent to a high of 19 percent. With the exception of year 5, all the returns deviate from the average by more than 1.5 percent.

Even though both stocks achieved the same average return, common sense suggests that B was riskier than A. The individual returns are more dispersed around the average return and this implies greater risk. The larger dispersion means there were periods with smaller returns (or larger losses, if applicable) from the investment. Of course, there were periods when the returns were greater, which would be expected if the risk were greater, but even so, the average return from B only matched the average return from A.

How may this dispersion be measured? One possible answer is the standard deviation. Since the standard deviation measures the tendency of the individual returns to cluster around the average return, it may be used as a measure of risk. The larger the dispersion, the greater the standard deviation and the larger the risk associated with the particular investment.

The standard deviation is easily calculated using a computer program. (For the use of Excel to compute the standard deviation, see Appendix E.) The manual process may be illustrated using the above example for stock A. The standard deviation for stock A's returns is calculated as follows:

1. Subtract the average return from the individual observations.
2. Square this difference.
3. Add these squared differences.
4. Divide this sum by the number of observations less 1.
5. Take the square root.

For stock A the standard deviation is determined as follows:

Individual Return	Average Return	Difference	Difference Squared
13.50%	15%	−1.5	2.2500
14	15	−1	1.0000
14.25	15	−0.75	0.5625
14.50	15	−0.5	0.25
15	15	0	0
15.50	15	0.5	0.25
15.75	15	0.75	0.5625
16	15	1	1.000
16.50	15	1.5	2.2500
		The sum of the squared differences:	8.1250

The sum of the squared differences divided by the number of observations less 1:

$$\frac{8.1250}{9-1} = 1.0156$$

The square root: $\sqrt{1.0156} = 1.01$.

Thus, the standard deviation is 1.01.

The investor must then interpret this result. Plus and minus one standard deviation has been shown for normal distributions to encompass approximately 68 percent of all observations (in this case, that is 68 percent of the returns). The standard deviation for stock A is 1.01, which means that approximately two-thirds of the returns fall between 13.99 percent and 16.01 percent.[1] These returns are simply the average return (15 percent) plus 1.01 and minus 1.01 percent (that is, plus and minus the standard deviation).

For stock B the standard deviation is 3.30, which means that approximately 68 percent of the returns fall between 11.7 percent and 18.3 percent. B's returns have a wider dispersion from the average return, and this fact is indicated by a greater standard deviation.

These differences in the standard deviations are illustrated in Figure 8.1, which plots the various returns on the horizontal axis and the frequency of their occurrence on the vertical axis. While the example used only nine years, Figure 8.1 is drawn as if there were a large number of observations. Most of A's returns are close to the average return, so the frequency distribution is narrower and taller. The frequency distribution for B's returns is lower and wider, which indicates the greater dispersion in that stock's returns (that is, the standard deviation for stock B is 3.30 versus 1.01 for A).

---

[1] A square root is a positive (+) or negative (−) number. The square root of 9 is +3 and −3 because (3) (3) = 9 and (−3) (−3) = 9. However, in the calculation of the standard deviation, only positive numbers are used (that is, the sum of the squared differences), so the square root must be a positive number.

FIGURE 8.1
Distribution of the Returns
of Two Stocks

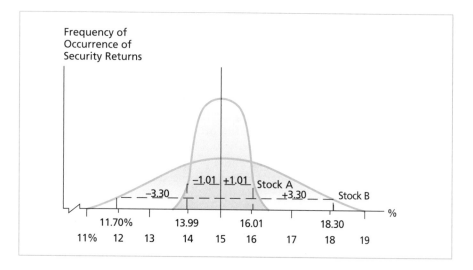

FIGURE 8.1
Distribution of the Returns
of Two Stocks

In the previous example, historical returns were used to illustrate the standard deviation as a measure of risk. The same concept may be used to measure the risk associated with expected returns. Consider stock A: An investor believes there is a 20 percent chance of a 15 percent return, a 60 percent chance of a 10 percent return, and a 20 percent chance of a 5 percent return. The expected average return is 10 percent. However, there is dispersion around that expected return, and once again this dispersion may be measured by the standard deviation. In this case, the standard deviation is 3.162, which is calculated as follows:

(1) Expected Individual Return	(2) Expected Average Return	(3) Difference (1) − (2)	(4) Difference Squared	(5) Probability of Occurrence	(6) Difference Squared Times the Probability (4) × (5)
15	10	5	25	0.2	5.0
10	10	0	0	0.6	0.0
5	10	−5	25	0.2	5.0

Sum of the weighted squared differences: 10.0
Square root of 10 (the standard deviation): 3.162

If the expected returns or the probabilities of occurrence were different, the standard deviation would be different. For example, if the expected returns for stock B were 20 percent, 10 percent, and 0 percent and the probabilities were the same, the expected return would be 10 percent $(0.2(20\%) + 0.1(60\%) + 0.0(20\%) = 10\%)$. The standard deviation around stock B's expected return is 6.325. Since 6.325 is larger than 3.162, this indicates a larger dispersion in the expected return for stock B.

The larger dispersion around the expected return implies that the investment is riskier, because you are less certain of the return. The larger the dispersion, the greater is the chance of a smaller gain (or larger loss). Correspondingly, there is a greater chance of a larger return. However, this potential for increased gain means you will be bearing additional risk. Stock A involves less risk; it has the smaller dispersion. Because the expected returns on both investments are the same, obviously stock A is to be preferred since it has less risk.

Although the preceding discussion was limited to the return on an individual security and the dispersion around that return, the concepts can be applied to an entire portfolio, such as a mutual fund's portfolio. (For instance, Morningstar provides the standard deviation of mutual fund returns in its database.) A portfolio also has an average return and dispersion around that return. While you are concerned with the return and the risk associated with each investment, the return and risk associated with the portfolio as a whole is more important. This aggregate is, of course, the result of the individual investments and of each one's weight in the portfolio (that is, the value of each asset, in proportion to the total value of the portfolio).

Consider a portfolio consisting of the following three stocks:

Stock	Return
1	8.3%
2	10.6
3	12.3

If 25 percent of the total value of the portfolio is invested in stocks 1 and 2 and 50 percent is invested in stock 3, the return is more heavily weighted in favor of stock 3. The return is a weighted average of each return times its proportion in the portfolio.

Return	×	Weight (percentage value of stock in proportion to total value of portfolio)	=	Weighted average
8.3%	×	0.25	=	2.075%
10.6	×	0.25	=	2.650
12.3	×	0.50	=	6.150

The return is the sum of these weighted averages.

$$
\begin{array}{r}
2.075\% \\
2.650 \\
\underline{6.150} \\
10.875\%
\end{array}
$$

The previous example is generalized in Equation 8.1, which states that the return on a portfolio r_p is a weighted average of the returns of the individual assets $[(r_1) \cdots (r_n)]$, each weighted by its proportion in the portfolio $(w_1 \cdots w_n)$:

$$r_p = w_1(r_1) + w_2(r_2) + \cdots + w_n(r_n). \tag{8.1}$$

Thus, if a portfolio has 20 securities, each plays a role in the determination of the portfolio's return. The extent of that role depends on the weight that each asset has in the portfolio. Obviously those securities that compose the largest part of the individual's portfolio have the largest impact on the portfolio's return.[2]

Unfortunately, an aggregate measure of the portfolio's risk (or the portfolio's standard deviation) is more difficult to construct than the weighted average of the returns. This happens because securities prices are not independent of each other. However, although securities prices do move together, there can be a difference in these price movements. For example, prices of stocks of firms in homebuilding may be more sensitive to recession than stock prices of utilities, whose prices may decline only moderately. These relationships among the assets in the portfolio must be considered in the construction of a measure of risk associated with the entire portfolio. In more advanced texts, these inner relationships among stocks are called *covariation*.

Risk Reduction Through Diversification—An Illustration

The development of a measure of covariation and the calculation of a portfolio's standard deviation go beyond the scope of this text. The concept, however, may be illustrated by considering the returns earned on two specific stocks, Public Service Enterprise Group and Mobil Corporation. Public Service Enterprise Group is an electric and gas utility whose stock price fell with higher interest rates and inflation. Prior to its merger with Exxon, Mobil was a resource company whose stock price rose during inflation in response to higher oil prices but fell during the 1980s as oil prices weakened and inflation receded. Thus, what was positive for one company was negative for the other.

The annual returns (dividends plus price change) on investments in these two stocks are given in Figure 8.2. As may be seen in the graph, there were periods when the returns on the two stocks moved in opposite directions. For example, during 1978, an investment in Public Service Enterprise Group generated a loss while an investment in Mobil produced profits. The converse occurred during 1981 as Public Service Enterprise Group's stock price rose. From 1980 to 1985, the stock price of Public Service Enterprise Group doubled, but the price of Mobil's stock declined.

---

[2]The same general equation may be applied to expected returns, in which case the expected return on a portfolio, $E(r_p)$, is a weighted average of the expected returns of the individual assets $[E(r_1) \cdots E(r_n)]$ each weighted by its proportion in the portfolio $(w_1 \cdots w_n)$:

$$E(r_p) = w_1 E(r_1) + w_2 E(r_2) + \cdots + w_n E(r_n).$$

FIGURE 8.2 Annual Returns

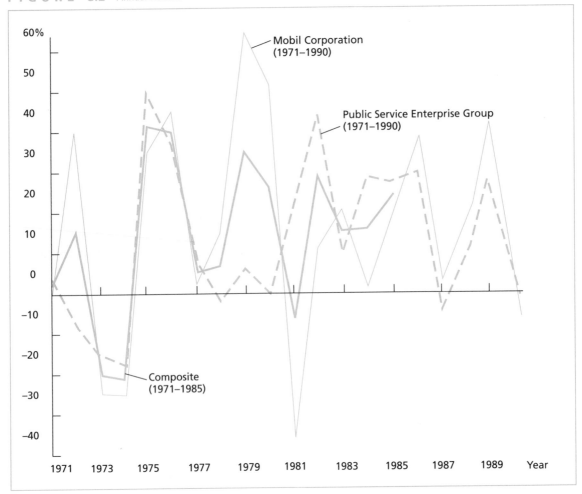

Figure 8.3 presents a scatter diagram of the returns on these two stocks. The horizontal axis presents the annual return on Public Service Enterprise Group, while the vertical axis presents the annual return on Mobil Corporation. As may be seen in the graph, the individual points lie throughout the plane representing the returns. For example, point A represents a positive return on Mobil but a negative return on Public Service Enterprise Group, and point B represents a positive return on Public Service Enterprise Group but a negative return on Mobil.

Combining these securities in a portfolio reduced the individual's risk exposure. The line representing the composite return runs between the lines representing the returns on the individual securities. Over the entire period, the average annual returns on Mobil and Public Service Enterprise Group were

FIGURE 8.3
Scatter Diagrams of
Returns

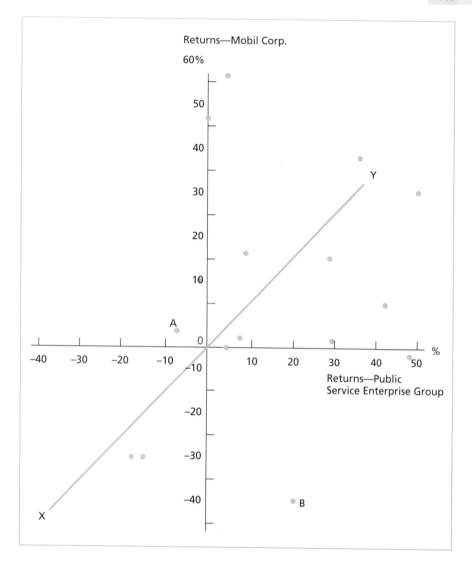

15.7 percent and 14.7 percent, respectively. The average annual return on the composite was 15.2 percent. The risk reduction (the reduction in the dispersion of the returns) can be seen by comparing the standard deviations of the returns. For the individual stocks, the standard deviations were 27.8 percent and 21.5 percent, respectively, for Mobil and Public Service Enterprise Group. However, the standard deviation for the composite return was 19.4 percent, so the dispersion of the returns associated with the portfolio is less than the dispersion of the returns on either stock by itself.

Why is there less dispersion for the portfolio than for the individual stocks? The answer is that the returns are not highly correlated. Correlation may be measured by a statistical concept: the "correlation coefficient." The numerical value of the correlation coefficient ranges from $+1.0$ to -1.0.[3] If the two variables move exactly together (that is, if there is a perfect positive correlation between the two variables), the numerical value of the correlation coefficient is 1.0. If the two variables move exactly opposite of each other, the correlation coefficient equals -1.0. All other possible values lie between these two extremes. Low numerical values, such as -0.12 or $+0.19$, indicate little relationship between the two variables.

The correlation coefficient relating the returns on Mobil and Public Service Enterprise Group stocks is 0.148, so there was little relationship between the returns on the two stocks. This lack of correlation is visible in Figure 8.3. If there were a high positive correlation between the two returns, the points would lie close to the line XY. Instead, the points are scattered throughout the figure. Thus, there is little correlation between the two returns, which is why combining the two securities reduces the individual's risk exposure.

Combining Mobil and Public Service Enterprise Group reduced risk because it decreased the dispersion of the portfolio, and this lower dispersion was the result of the low correlation between the returns. However, two additional points should be made. First, just because diversification was achieved in the past does not imply it will be achieved in the future. If the returns become positively correlated, combining the two stocks will not achieve diversification. This positive correlation appears to have occurred since 1985 because the returns appear to have moved together during that period. (The composite return has been omitted from 1985 through 1990 to better illustrate the close movement between the returns on the two stocks.) This suggests that investing in Mobil and Public Service Enterprise Group during 1985 to 1990 had little impact on diversification. Second, to the extent that diversification reduces risk, it affects only the risk associated with specific assets. Other sources of risk remain. Diversification does not reduce the risk associated with fluctuations in securities prices, inflation, changes in interest rates, the reinvestment rate, or fluctuations in exchange rates.

In effect, *a diversified portfolio reduces unsystematic risk*. The risk associated with each individual investment is reduced by accumulating a diversified portfolio of assets. Even if one company fails (or does extremely well), the impact on the portfolio as a whole is reduced through diversification. Distributing investments among different industries, however, *does not eliminate the other sources of risk*. For example, the value of a group of securities will tend to follow the market values in general. The price movements of securities will be mirrored by the diversified portfolio; hence the investor cannot eliminate this source of systematic risk.

This reduction in unsystematic risk is illustrated in Figure 8.4. The vertical axis measures units of risk, and the horizontal axis gives the number of securities. Since market risk is independent of the number of securities in the

---

[3]The computation of the correlation coefficient is explained in statistics textbooks. See, for instance, David R. Anderson, Dennis J. Sweeney, and Thomas A., Williams, *Statistics for Business and Economics*, 10th ed. (Mason, Ohio: South-Western, 2008). For the purpose of this discussion, all that is necessary is that low values (i.e., 0.2 to –0.2) indicate, at best, a weak relationship between the two variables.

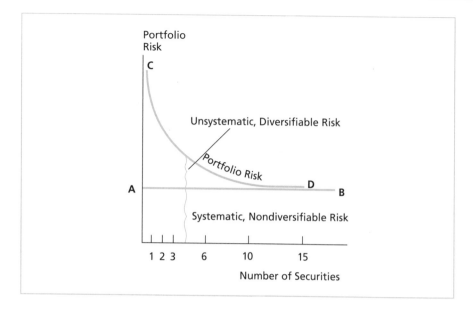

portfolio, this element of risk is illustrated by a line, AB, that runs parallel to
the horizontal axis. Regardless of the number of securities that an individual
owns, the amount of market risk remains the same.

Portfolio risk

Total risk associated
with owning a portfolio;
sum of systematic and
unsystematic risk

Portfolio risk (or the sum of systematic and unsystematic risk) is indicated
by line CD. The difference between line AB and line CD is the unsystematic
risk associated with the specific securities in the portfolio. The amount of unsystematic risk depends on the number of securities held. As this number increases, unsystematic risk diminishes; this reduction in risk is illustrated in
Figure 8.4, in which line CD approaches line AB. For portfolios consisting of
10 or more securities, the risk involved is primarily systematic.

Such diversified portfolios, of course, do not consist of 10 public utilities
but of a cross section of American and foreign securities. Investing $20,000 in
10 stocks ($2,000 for each) may achieve a reasonably well diversified portfolio.
Although such a portfolio may cost more in commissions than two $10,000
purchases, the small investor achieves a diversified mixture of securities, which
should reduce the risk of loss associated with investment in a specific security.
Unfortunately, the investor must still bear the systematic risk associated with
investing.

Beta Coefficients

The computation of a standard deviation for a portfolio of any size is impractical for the individual investor, because it requires the correlation among the
individual stock returns. For a portfolio of three stocks (A, B, and C), you
need to know the correlation among stocks A and B, A and C, and B and C.

If the portfolio has four stocks (A, B, C, and D), then you need the correlation between A and B, A and C, A and D, B and C, B and D, and C and D. Consider the number of correlations that would be necessary for a portfolio of 20 stocks!

Fortunately there is an alternative. The previous discussion of diversification suggested that if a portfolio is sufficiently diversified, unsystematic risk is virtually erased. The remaining risk is the result of nondiversifiable, systematic risk. Is there a measure of systematic risk and may it be used instead of a standard deviation to indicate the risk associated with an asset or with a well-diversified portfolio?

The answer is yes. This measure of the systematic risk associated with an asset is called a *beta coefficient*. While the concept may be applied to any asset, the usual explanation employs common stock. A beta coefficient is an index of risk that quantifies the responsiveness of a stock's return to changes in the return on the market. Since a beta coefficient measures a stock's return relative to the return on the market, it measures the systematic risk associated with the stock.

Beta coefficients have become widely used by financial analysts to measure the risk associated with individual stocks. The concept is also applied to portfolios, as betas are computed for mutual funds, in which case they compare the return on the fund with the return on the market. (Portfolio betas are weighted averages of the individual betas in the portfolio.) While the use of betas permeates finance, it is important to realize that these coefficients are only a *relative measure of risk*. They tell you nothing about how the market itself will fluctuate!

A beta coefficient of 1 means that the stock's return moves exactly with an index of the market as a whole. A 10 percent increase in the market produces a 10 percent increase in the return on the specific stock. Correspondingly, a 10 percent decline in the market results in a 10 percent decline in the return on the stock. A beta coefficient of less than 1 implies that the return on the stock tends to fluctuate less than the market as a whole. A coefficient of 0.7 indicates that the stock's return will rise only 7 percent as a result of a 10 percent increase in the market but will fall by only 7 percent when the market declines by 10 percent. A coefficient of 1.2 means that the return on the stock will rise by 12 percent if the market increases by 10 percent, but the return on the stock will decline by 12 percent when the market declines by 10 percent.

The greater the beta coefficient, the more market (systematic) risk is associated with the individual stock. High beta coefficients may indicate higher returns during rising markets, but they also indicate greater losses during declining markets. Stocks with high beta coefficients are referred to as "aggressive." The converse is true for stocks with low beta coefficients, which should underperform the market during periods of rising stock prices but outperform the market as a whole during periods of declining prices. Such stocks are referred to as "defensive."

This relationship between the return on a specific security and the market index as a whole is illustrated in parts (a) and (b) of Figure 8.5. In each graph,

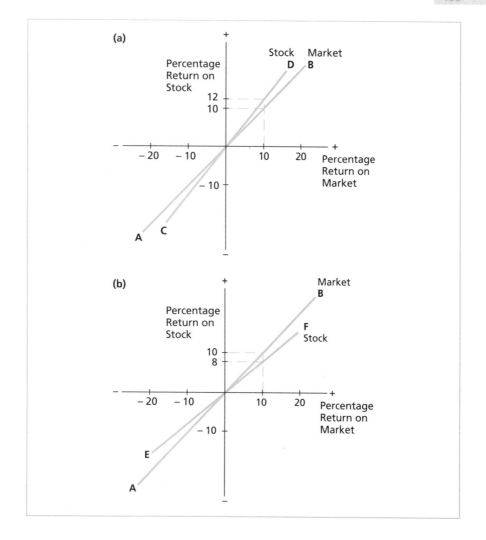

the horizontal axis represents the percentage return on the market index, and the vertical axis represents the percentage return on the individual stock. The line AB, which represents the market, is the same in both graphs. It is a positively sloped line that runs through the point of origin and is equidistant from both axes (it makes a 45-degree angle with each axis).

Part (a) of Figure 8.5 illustrates a stock with a beta coefficient greater than 1. Line CD represents a stock whose return rises and declines more than the market's return. In this case, the beta coefficient is 1.2, so when the market index is 10 percent, this stock's return is 12 percent.

Part (b) of Figure 8.5 illustrates a stock with a beta coefficient of less than 1. Line EF represents a stock whose return rises (and declines) more slowly than that of the market. In this case, the beta coefficient is 0.8, so when the market's return is 10 percent, this stock's return is 8 percent.

EXHIBIT 8.1
Selected Beta Coefficients

Company	Beta Coefficient
ExxonMobil	0.37
Verizon Communications	0.57
Heinz	0.63
IBM	0.68
GE	1.68
Alcoa	2.11
Harley Davidson	2.37
Bank of America	2.58

Source: Data obtained from **http://finance.yahoo.com**.

Beta coefficients do vary among firms. This is illustrated in Exhibit 8.1, which presents the beta coefficients for selected firms found through the Internet at Yahoo! Some firms (such as Verizon Communications) have relatively low beta coefficients, while the coefficients for other firms (such as Alcoa) are much higher. If you are willing to bear more risk, you may be attracted to those stocks with the higher beta coefficients, because when stock market prices rise, these stocks tend to outperform the market. If you are less inclined to bear risk, you may prefer the stocks with low beta coefficients. You may forgo some potential return during rising market prices but should suffer smaller losses during declining markets.

To be useful, beta coefficients must be reliable predictors of future stock price behavior. For example, if you desire stocks that will be stable, you will probably purchase stocks with low beta coefficients. An investor selecting a stock with a beta coefficient of 0.6 will certainly be upset if the market prices decline by 10 percent and this stock's price falls by 15 percent, since a beta coefficient of 0.6 indicates that the stock price should decline by only 6 percent when market prices decline by 10 percent.

Unfortunately, beta coefficients can and do change over time. (The beta for Bank of America was less than 1.0 in 2005 but rose to over 2.5 in 2010.) Therefore, you should not rely solely on these coefficients in selecting a particular security. However, beta coefficients do give you some indication of the systematic risk associated with specific stocks and thus can play an important role in the selection of a security.

Unlike the beta coefficients for individual securities, the beta coefficient for a portfolio composed of several securities is fairly stable over time. Changes in the different beta coefficients tend to average out; while one stock's beta coefficient is increasing, the beta coefficient of another stock is declining. A portfolio's historical beta coefficients, then, can be used as a tool to forecast its future beta coefficient, and this projection should be more accurate than forecasts of an individual security's beta coefficient.

Since a portfolio's beta coefficient is stable, the investor can construct a portfolio that responds in a desired way to market changes. For example, the average beta coefficient of the portfolio illustrated in Exhibit 8.1 is approximately 1.37. If an equal dollar amount were invested in each security, the value of the portfolio should be more volatile than the market, even though individual beta coefficients are less than 1. Hence, the beta coefficient for the portfolio may be a more useful tool than the beta coefficients for individual securities.

Regression Analysis and the Estimation of Beta Coefficients

A statistical technique, regression analysis, is used to estimate a stock's beta coefficient. (This section may be omitted without loss of continuity.) As was previously explained, a beta coefficient is a measure of the responsiveness of a stock's return to movements in securities prices in general. While it is not known exactly how a stock's return will react to future changes in the market, it is possible to measure historical responsiveness. For example, observations of the past relationship between the return on the market (r_m) and the return on stock A (r_s) are as follows:

Return on the Market (r_m)	Return on Stock A (r_s)
14%	13%
12	13
10	12
10	9
5	4
2	−1
−1	2
−5	−7
−7	−8
−12	−10

Each observation represents the return on the stock and the return on the market for a period of time (for instance, a week). These data are plotted in Figure 8.6 with each point representing one set of observations. For example, point A represents a 4 percent increase in the return on the stock in response to a 5 percent increase in the market. Point B represents a 7 percent decrease in the return on the stock in response to a 5 percent decline in the return on the market.

FIGURE 8.6
Observations Relating the
Return on a Stock to the
Return on the Market

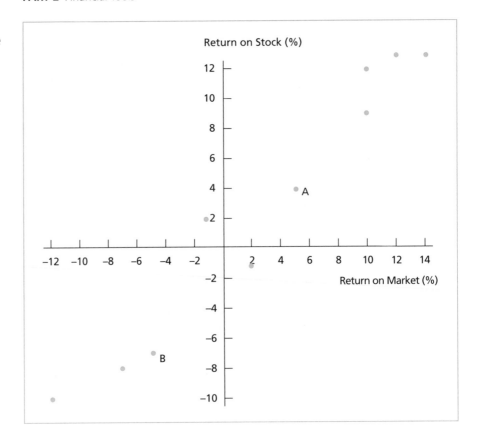

Individual observations, like points A and B, tell very little about the systematic risk of the stock, but all the observations, taken as a whole, may. The individual observations are summarized by linear regression analysis, which is used to compute an equation relating the return on the stock (r_s, the dependent variable) to the return on the market (r_m, the independent variable). The regression analysis computes the y-intercept (a) and the slope (b) for the following equation:

$$r_s = a + br_m.$$

This slope is the beta coefficient.

Like the correlation coefficient presented earlier in this chapter, regression analysis is a statistical concept. The actual computations of the intercept and the slope are generally performed by a computer program. A manual demonstration of the process is presented in Exhibit 8.2, in which the following equation is derived:

$$r_s = -0.000597 + 0.9856r_m.$$

EXHIBIT 8.2
The Computation of a Beta Coefficient

X (r_m)	Y (r_s)	X^2	Y^2	XY
0.14	0.13	0.0196	0.0169	0.0182
0.12	0.13	0.0144	0.0169	0.0156
0.10	0.12	0.0100	0.0144	0.0120
0.10	0.09	0.0100	0.0081	0.0090
0.05	0.04	0.0025	0.0016	0.0020
0.02	−0.01	0.0004	0.0001	−0.0002
−0.01	0.02	0.0001	0.0004	−0.0002
−0.05	−0.07	0.0025	0.0049	0.0035
−0.07	−0.08	0.0049	0.0064	0.0056
−0.12	−0.10	0.0144	0.0100	0.0120
$\Sigma X = 0.28$	$\Sigma Y = 0.27$	$\Sigma X^2 = 0.0788$	$\Sigma Y^2 = 0.0797$	$\Sigma XY = 0.0775$

n = the number of observations (10).

$$b = \frac{n\Sigma XY - (\Sigma X)(\Sigma Y)}{n\Sigma X^2 - (\Sigma X)^2}$$

$$= \frac{(10)(0.0775) - (0.28)(0.27)}{(10)(0.0788) - (0.28)(0.28)}$$

$$= \frac{0.07750 - 0.756}{0.7880 - 0.0784} = 0.9856.$$

The a is computed as follows:

$$a = \frac{\Sigma Y}{n} - b\frac{\Sigma X}{n}$$

$$= \frac{0.27}{10} - (0.9856)\frac{0.28}{10} = -0.000597.$$

The estimated equation is $r_s = -0.000597 + 0.9856\, r_m$.

This equation is given as line XY in Figure 8.7, which reproduces Figure 8.6 and adds the regression line. As may be seen from the graph, line XY runs through the individual points. Some of the observations are above the line while others are below it. However, all the points are close to the line.

This regression equation can be used to forecast the expected return on the stock. If the individual anticipates that the market return will be 20 percent, the stock should yield a return of

$$r_s = -0.000597 + 0.9856(20\%) = 19.7\%.$$

As with any forecast, this result may not be realized, because factors other than the increase in the market may affect the stock's return. (These factors are

FIGURE 8.7

Regression Equation Relating the Return on a Stock to the Return on the Market

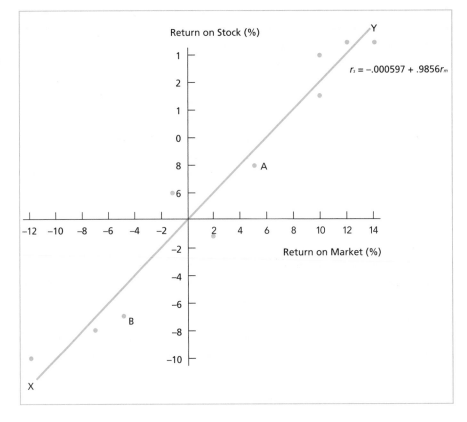

the unsystematic risk associated with the stock.) The predictive power of this particular beta may be excellent, because the individual observations lie close to the estimated regression line. That indicates a high correlation between the two variables. The actual correlation coefficient is 0.976, which indicates a strong, positive relationship between the return on the stock and the return on the market. A correlation coefficient of 1.0 indicates a perfect, positive relationship. Most of the fluctuations in the individual returns on the stock were caused by fluctuations in the return on the market. Of course, this high correlation may not continue in the future, but unless some fundamental change in the firm were to occur, the beta coefficient may be an excellent forecaster of the future responsiveness of the stock to changes in the market.

The Capital Asset Pricing Model and an Investment's Required Return

The development of beta coefficients and a theory of risk reduction through diversification were exceedingly important to the process of asset valuation. As is explained in several places in this text, an asset's value is the present value of future cash flows. These cash flows are discounted back to the present at the asset's required return. The capital asset pricing model or CAPM is one method used to determine that required return. The CAPM specifies the relationship between risk and return that is used either to value or to judge an asset's expected return. (Valuation expresses an asset's present worth in monetary units such as dollars. An asset's return is expressed in percentages.) If an asset's value exceeds its cost or if an asset's expected return exceeds the required return, the asset is purchased. Either method produces the same decision, since the only difference is the units of measure.

Capital asset pricing model (CAPM)

Model used in the valuation of an asset that specifies the required return for different levels of risk

The CAPM builds on the proposition that additional risk requires a higher return. This return has two components: (1) what may be earned on a risk-free asset, such as a federally insured savings account or a U.S. Treasury bill, plus (2) a premium for bearing risk. Since unsystematic risk is reduced through diversification, a stock's risk premium is the additional return required to bear the nondiversifiable, systematic risk associated with the stock.

This risk-adjusted required return (k) is expressed in Equation 8.2:

$$k = \text{risk-free rate} + \text{risk premium}. \tag{8.2}$$

The risk premium is composed of two components: (1) the additional return that investing in securities in general offers above the risk-free rate and (2) the volatility of the particular security relative to the market as a whole. The volatility of the individual stock is measured by the beta coefficient (β), and the additional return is measured by the difference between the expected return on the market (r_m) and the risk-free rate (r_f). This differential ($r_m - r_f$) is the risk premium that is required to induce the individual to purchase risky assets.

To induce the investor to purchase a particular stock, the risk premium associated with the market must be adjusted by the market risk associated with the individual security. This risk adjustment uses the stock's beta coefficient, which indicates the stock's volatility relative to the market. The risk adjustment is achieved by multiplying the security's beta coefficient by the difference between the expected return on the market and the risk-free rate. Thus the risk premium for the individual stock is

$$\text{risk premium} = (r_m - r_f) \beta. \tag{8.3}$$

The return required for investing in a particular stock is found by substituting this risk premium into Equation 8.3. Thus the required return is

$$\text{required return} = r_f + (r_m - r_f) \beta. \tag{8.4}$$

The relationship between various levels of risk and the required return indicated by Equation 8.4 is illustrated in Figure 8.8. Risk, as measured by the beta coefficient, is given on the horizontal axis while the required return, measured as a percentage, is on the vertical axis. If the risk-free rate is 7 percent

FIGURE   8.8
Relationship between Risk
and the Required Return

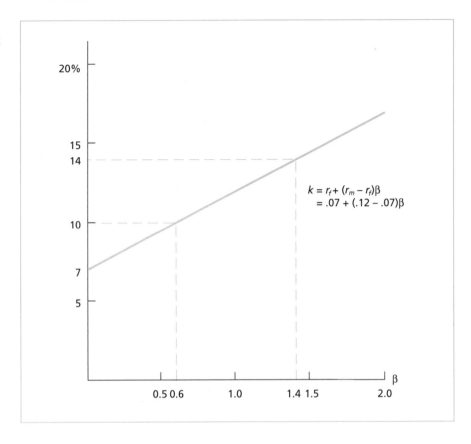

and the expected return on the market is 12 percent, then the required rate of return on a stock with a beta coefficient of 0.6 is

$$k_A = 0.07 + (0.12 - 0.07)0.6 = 0.10 = 10\%.$$

If a stock has a beta coefficient equal to 1.4, the required return is

$$k_B = 0.07 + (0.12 - 0.07)1.4 = 0.14 = 14\%.$$

The stock with the higher beta coefficient has the higher required return because it is riskier.

The preceding specification of the required rate of return reappears several times in this text. It is part of the firm's cost of capital in Chapter 13 and is used to value common stock in Chapter 21. Since the cost of capital is part of the capital budgeting models covered in Chapter 14, the required return has an impact on the financial manager's decision to invest in plant and equipment.

Summary

Investments are made in anticipation of a return, which is a flow of income and/or price appreciation. Individuals and financial managers make investments in anticipation of a return, but the realized return may differ from the expected return. That is the element of risk. The future is uncertain.

There are several sources of risk. These include the risk associated with the specific asset (diversifiable, unsystematic risk) and the nondiversifiable, systematic risk from fluctuations in securities prices, changes in interest rates, reinvestment rates, inflation, and fluctuations in exchange rates.

The construction of a diversified portfolio reduces the risk associated with the particular asset. By owning a variety of assets whose returns are not highly positively correlated, the investor reduces unsystematic risk without necessarily reducing the potential return on the portfolio as a whole. Unfortunately, the construction of a diversified portfolio does not reduce the other sources of risk.

Risk may be measured by an asset's (or portfolio's) standard deviation, which measures the dispersion around the realized return (in the case of historical returns) or the expected return (in the case of anticipated returns). The larger the dispersion of the returns, the greater the risk.

An alternative measure of risk determines the responsiveness of an asset's return relative to the market as a whole. This measure, called a beta coefficient, is an index of the systematic risk associated with the asset. The larger the beta coefficient, the greater the systematic risk associated with the security, since its return has risen or fallen more rapidly than the return on the market as a whole.

Beta coefficients are used to determine an investor's required rate of return. This capital asset pricing model specifies the required return and includes (1) the risk-free rate that may be earned on very safe investments plus (2) a risk premium. The risk premium includes a premium for purchasing risky assets instead of the risk-free asset, plus an adjustment for the systematic risk associated with the particular investment.

Review Objectives

Now that you have completed this chapter, you should be able to

1. Describe the expected, required, and realized returns (pp. 138–139).

2. List and contrast the sources of risk (pp. 139–142).

3. Differentiate the standard deviation and the beta coefficient as measures of risk (p. 142 and p. 151).

4. Explain why larger standard deviations and higher beta coefficients indicate increased risk (pp. 142, 143, 153).

5. Explain what condition must be met for diversification to occur (pp. 149–150).

6. Compute the required return specified in the capital asset pricing model (pp. 158–160).

7. Illustrate the relationship between beta and the required return (pp. 159–160).

**Internet
Assignments**

1. Beta coefficients change over time. Exhibit 8.1 illustrates beta coefficients obtained through Yahoo! Update these beta coefficients. Have they changed, and what are the implications of any changes (i.e., has the company become more or less risky)?

2. Beta coefficients may differ if you obtain them from different sources. These discrepancies occur because various sources use different time periods or a different measure of the market when calculating beta coefficients. Using different sources, obtain the betas for the same companies in Exhibit 8.1 and compare with the betas you obtained in the previous assignment. Are the numerical values of the betas different? Possible sites include

> Google finance (**www.google.com/finance**)
> Reuters (**http://reuters.com**)
> MSN Money (**http://moneycentral.msn.com**).

Your school may subscribe to services such as Mergent Online (**http://www.mergent.com**), in which case you may also use those sources.

Problems

1. You are considering two stocks and have determined the following information:

Stock A	Return	Probability of the Return
	18%	25%
	14	50
	10	25

Stock B	Return	Probability of the Return
	22%	10%
	12	60
	11	30

a. Which of the two stocks has the higher expected return?

b. Which stock is riskier?

c. Given your answers to the two previous questions, what stock is preferred?

2. What is the required return on an investment with a beta of 1.3 if the risk-free rate is 4 percent and the return on the market is 11 percent? If the expected return on the investment is 14 percent, what should you do?

3. You are considering buying stock A. If the economy grows rapidly, you may earn 30 percent on the investment, while a declining economy could result in a 20 percent loss. Slow economic growth may generate a return of 6 percent. If the probability is 15 percent for rapid growth, 20 percent for a declining economy, and 65 percent for slow growth, what is the expected return on this investment?

4. You expect to invest your funds equally in four stocks with the following expected returns:

Stock	Expected Return
A	16%
B	14
C	10
D	8

At the end of the year, each stock had the following realized returns:

Stock	Realized Return
A	–6%
B	18
C	3
D	–22

Compare the portfolio's expected and realized returns.

5. Stock A has a risk premium of 6.5 percent. If Treasury bills yield 6.2 percent and the expected return on the market is 10.5 percent, what is the stock's beta coefficient?

6. Two stocks, A and B, have beta coefficients of 0.8 and 1.4, respectively. If the expected return on the market is 10 percent and the risk-free rate is 5 percent, what is the risk premium associated with each stock?

7. You are considering investing in three stocks with the following expected returns:

Stock A	7%
Stock B	12
Stock C	20

What is the expected return on the portfolio if an equal amount is invested in each stock? What would be the expected return if 50 percent of your funds is invested in stock A and the remaining funds are split evenly between stocks B and C?

8. Two investments generated the following annual returns:

	Investment X	Investment Y
19X0	10%	16%
19X1	20	18
19X2	30	15
19X3	20	20
19X4	10	21

a. What is the average annual return on each investment?

b. What is the standard deviation of the return on investments X and Y?

c. Based on the standard deviation, which investment was riskier?

9. A portfolio consists of assets with the following expected returns:

Technology stocks	20%
Pharmaceutical stocks	15
Utility stocks	10
Savings account	5

a. What is the expected return on the portfolio if the investor spends an equal amount on each asset?

b. What is the expected return on the portfolio if the investor puts 50 percent of available funds in technology stocks, 10 percent in pharmaceutical stocks, 24 percent in utility stocks, and 16 percent in the savings account?

10. Consider a $30,000 portfolio consisting of three stocks. Their values and expected returns are as follows:

Stock	Investment	Expected Return
A	$ 5,000	12%
B	10,000	10
C	15,000	14

What is the weighted-average expected return on the portfolio?

Additional Problems with Answers

The following problems are primarily concerned with illustrating the computation of weighted averages. While the chapter illustrates how to compute the standard deviation and simple linear regression, these computations may be readily done through a statistics package such as is available in Excel.

1. You purchase a stock but realize that the return will be affected by economic conditions. If the economy is growing at or above 4 percent, you anticipate a return of 12 percent. If the economy is growing at between 0 and 4 percent, you anticipate a return of 5 percent. If the economy is contracting, the anticipated return is −3 percent. You believe that the probabilities of each case occurring is 30 percent, 55 percent,

and 15 percent, respectively. What is your anticipated return on the investment?

2. Four possible investments and their anticipated returns are

Savings accounts	2%
Corporate debt	5%
Corporate equities	9%
Derivatives	15%

A financial planner suggests that your great-aunt Agnes invest 30 percent in savings accounts, 45 percent in corporate debt, and 25 percent in corporate equities. The same financial planner suggests that you invest 5 percent in the savings accounts, 25 percent in corporate debt, 60 percent in corporate equities, and 10 percent in derivatives. What are the anticipated returns on both portfolios? Why are they different?

3. Stock A has a beta of 1.3, but stock B has a beta of only 0.45. You expect the market to increase by 7.3 percent and you could earn 1.9 percent in a risk-free asset. What is the required return for each stock? If you invest $3,500 in stock A and $6,500 in stock B, what is the portfolio beta?

Answers

1. Both Problems 1 and 2 illustrate weighted averages. The difference is that Problem 1 applies to one asset while Problem 2 applies to a portfolio.

The return on the security is a weighted average:

$$(0.30)(0.12) + (0.55)(0.05) + (0.15)(-0.03) = 0.059 = 5.9\%.$$

2. The anticipated returns on the portfolios are weighted averages:

Agnes's portfolio:

$$(0.30)(0.02) + (0.45)(0.05) + (0.25)(0.09) + (0)(0.15)$$

$$= 0.051 = 5.1\%$$

Your portfolio:

$$(0.05)(0.02) + (0.25)(0.05) + (0.60)(0.09) + (0.10)(0.15)$$

$$= 0.0825 = 8.25\%$$

The returns differ because you have the riskier portfolio. Notice, however, that your recommended portfolio includes safe assets (the savings account) and income-producing assets (the corporate debt), while Agnes's portfolio does not contain any risky derivatives.

3. The required return is

$$k = r_f + (r_m + r_f)\,\beta$$

For stock A the required return is

$$k = 0.019 + (0.073 - 0.019)\,1.3 = 0.0892 = 8.92\%.$$

For stock B the required return is

$$k = 0.019 + (0.073 - 0.019)\,0.45 = 0.0433 = 4.33\%.$$

Stock A's beta exceeds 1.0, so the required return exceeds the market return. (The beta for the market is 1.0.) Stock B's beta is less than 1.0, so the required return is less than the market return.

If you invest 35 percent of your portfolio in A and 65 percent in B, the beta of the portfolio is

$$(0.35)\,(1.3) + (0.65)\,(0.45) = 0.75.$$

The beta for the portfolio is a weighted average of the betas. One stock is more volatile than the market and the other is less volatile, but the weighted average indicates that the portfolio as a whole should be less volatile than the market (i.e., the beta is less than 1.0).

Relationships

1. Diversification _____ portfolio risk.

2. An increase in the risk-free rate _____ the required return.

3. A decrease in the expected return on the market _____ the required return.

4. A decrease in the beta coefficient _____ systematic risk.

5. Increased return _____ a firm's beta coefficient.

6. Diversification _____ expected return.

7. An increase in the numerical value of a standard deviation implies _____ variability.

8. Diversification _____ systematic risk.

9. An increase in the standard deviation suggests that risk has _____.

Answers

1. decreases
2. increases
3. decreases
4. decreases
5. does not change (no impact)
6. does not change (Diversification reduces risk.)
7. increased
8. does not change (Diversification reduces the impact of asset-specific risk.)
9. increased

Analysis of Financial Statements

" A nnual income twenty pounds, annual expenditure nineteen nineteen six, result happiness. Annual income twenty pounds, annual expenditure twenty pounds ought and six, result misery." As Charles Dickens so aptly expressed it in *David Copperfield*, the difference between operating at a profit or at a loss may be just a few pennies. This bottom line, however, plays an important role both in the financial decisions made by management and in how management's performance is perceived by the public. Management wants to make those decisions that increase the value of the firm, which include decisions affecting the firm's profitability.

By enumerating revenues and expenses in a firm's income statement (or statement of profit or loss, as it is sometimes called), accountants determine if a firm's operations are profitable. Earnings are not, however, synonymous with cash. Revenues and expenses are not the same as cash receipts and cash disbursements. Not all sales are for cash; some are for credit. Not all expenses require the disbursement of cash; depreciation is a noncash expense.

This chapter is initially concerned with financial statements and depreciation. If you know this material, the first half of the chapter may be omitted, and you can progress to the second half: the study of a firm's financial statements through ratio analysis, (page 189). Ratio analysis is a popular tool with creditors, investors, and management because the ratios may be easily computed and readily interpreted. Creditors and investors employ ratio analysis to establish the ability of the firm to service its debt and earn profits for the owners. Management may use the analysis as (1) a planning device, (2) a tool for control, or (3) a means to identify weaknesses in the firm.

Ratios can be classified into five groups. Liquidity ratios seek to determine if a firm can meet its current obligations as they come due. Activity ratios tell how rapidly assets flow through the firm. Profitability ratios measure performance, while leverage ratios measure the extent to which the firm uses debt financing. Coverage ratios measure the ability to make (or cover) specific payments.

General Accounting Principles

Accounting statements provide financial information concerning an enterprise. Although the emphasis in this text is their application to firms, financial statements may be constructed for governments (for example, the local municipality), nonprofit organizations (such as the Metropolitan Opera), or individuals. In all cases these statements show the financial condition of the entity and its assets and how they were financed. This information can then be used to aid financial decision making.

To be useful in decision making, financial statements must be *reliable, understandable, and comparable.* Reliability requires the statements to be objective and unbiased. The data included on the statements should be verifiable by independent experts. This does not mean that two accountants working with the same information will construct identical financial statements. Individual opinions and judgments may lead to different financial statements. An example that involves the accountant's judgment is the allowance for doubtful accounts receivable. Two accountants may establish differing amounts that will affect the firm's financial statements. A larger allowance reduces accounts receivable (and total assets) and decreases earnings. However, it should not be concluded that two accountants will construct widely different statements. While the financial statements may differ, the amount of differentiation should be modest.

Accountants' second goal is that financial statements be understandable. The statement should be presented in an orderly manner and be readable by informed laypersons as well as professionals. Investors and other individuals who use financial statements need not know all the principles used to construct a financial statement. However, an intelligent individual should be able to read a firm's financial statements and have some idea of the firm's profitability, its assets and liabilities, and its cash flow.

Comparability requires that one set of financial statements can be compared to the same financial statements constructed over different accounting periods. The principles used to construct one year's statements should be used for subsequent years. If the principles being applied are changed, the previous years' statements should be restated. If the firm's operations change, the financial statements should also reflect these changes. If, for example, the firm discontinues part of its operations, its sales, expenses, and profits for previous years should be restated. If this adjustment is not made, the users of the

PART 2 Financial Tools

financial statements will be unable to compare the firm's financial condition and performance over a period of time for its continuing operations.

To increase the objectivity of financial statements, a general framework for accounting and financial reports has been established by the Financial Accounting Standards Board (FASB). Accounting principles that are "generally accepted" also receive the support of the American Institute of Certified Public Accountants and the Securities and Exchange Commission (SEC). These bodies establish the principles under which financial statements are constructed. The principles, however, are not static. Their conceptual framework changes over time with changes in the business environment and the needs of the statements' users. For example, increases in foreign investments and fluctuations in the value of foreign currencies have generated a need for better methods of accounting for these foreign investments. This problem, plus others such as inflation, pension liabilities, and stock options, have resulted in changes in accounting principles as the profession seeks to improve the informational content of financial statements.

The Balance Sheet

Stockholders' equity

Firm's net worth; stockholders' investment in the firm; the sum of stock, paid-in capital, and retained earnings

Consolidated balance sheet

Parent company's balance sheet, which summarizes and combines the balance sheets of the firm's various subsidiaries

Current assets

Short-term assets that are expected to be converted into cash during the fiscal year

Long-term assets

Assets that are expected to be held for more than a year, such as plant and equipment

What have the owners invested in a firm? One method of answering this question is to construct a balance sheet that enumerates what a business owns (that is, its assets) and what it owes (that is, its liabilities) and to calculate the difference. This difference is called the net worth or the stockholders' equity in the firm.

Exhibit 9.1 presents a simplified balance sheet for H. J. Heinz Company. This balance sheet (and the other financial statements presented later in this chapter) are published in the firm's annual report. This balance sheet combines the financial information for all the firm's subsidiaries and hence is called a consolidated balance sheet. The assets are divided into three groups: (1) current assets, which are expected to be used and converted into cash within a relatively short period of time; (2) long-term assets, which are those assets with a life span exceeding a year; and (3) other assets, such as investments in other firms' stocks. The liabilities and stockholders' equity are presented next, frequently on the right-hand side of the balance sheet across from the assets. Although it is not necessary for a balance sheet to be arranged in this manner, many firms use this general form which clearly enumerates the assets, liabilities, and equity of the firm.

While current assets are listed in order of liquidity (cash, accounts receivable, and inventory), the following discussion considers each asset in reverse order. Raw materials are first acquired and converted into finished goods. This inventory is then sold, at which time the firm receives either an account receivable or cash.

Firms must have goods or services (or both) to sell. These goods are the firm's inventory. Not all inventory is ready for sale. Some of the goods may be unfinished ("work-in-process"), and there also may be inventories of raw materials. The financial analyst should remember that only finished goods are available for sale. Considerable time and additional cost may be involved to process the raw materials into finished goods. Therefore, much of a firm's inventory may not be salable and cannot be converted into cash. According to the H. J. Heinz balance sheet, total inventory was $1,237,613 in 2009. (Actual figures are 1,000 times the numbers used in the text.)

EXHIBIT 9.1
H. J. Heinz Company
Consolidated Balance
Sheet (in thousands)

As of the end of the fiscal year	2009	2008
Current assets		
Cash and cash equivalents	$ 373,145	$ 617,687
Receivables (net of allowances)	1,171,797	1,161,481
Inventories		
Finished goods and work-in-process	973,983	1,100,735
Raw materials and packaging	263,630	277,481
Total inventories	1,237,613	1,378,216
Prepaid expenses	125,765	139,492
Other current assets	36,701	28,690
Total current assets	2,945,021	3,325,566
Property, plant, and equipment		
Land	76,193	56,007
Buildings	775,217	842,198
Equipment	3,258,152	3,502,071
Less accumulated depreciation	2,131,260	2,295,563
Total property, plant, and equipment	1,978,302	2,104,713
Other noncurrent assets (goodwill, trademarks, and intangibles)	4,740,861	5,134,764
Total assets	$9,664,184	$10,565,043
Liabilities and Shareholders' Equity		
Current liabilities		
Short-term debt	$61,297	124,290
Long-term debt due within a year	4,341	328,418
Accounts payable	1,113,307	1,247,479
Accrued salaries and wages	324,599	390,895
Other accrued liabilities	485,406	487,656
Income taxes	73,896	91,322
Total current liabilities	2,052,746	2,670,060

(Continued)

EXHIBIT   9.1
(Continued)

Long-term liabilities		
Long-term debt	5,076,186	4,730,946
Deferred taxes	345,749	409,186
Other long-term liabilities	685,512	867,031
Total long-term liabilities	6,381,400	6,007,163

Shareholders' equity		
Preferred stock	70	70
Common stock	107,774	107,774
(431,096 shares issued, $0.25 par value)		
Additional capital	737,917	617,811
Retained earnings	6,525,719	6,129,008

Less:		
Treasury shares at cost	4,881,842	4,905,755
Other adjustments	1,269,700	61,090
Total shareholders' equity	1,219,938	1,887,820
Total liabilities and shareholders' equity	$9,664,184	$10,565,043

Source: Adapted from H. J. Heinz Company, *Annual Report,* 2009.

While the balance does present both finished goods and raw materials, they are aggregated. (Balance sheets sent to stockholders often aggregate categories. Presumably management would have access to disaggregated data and thus would know the amount of inventory that is finished goods and the amount that is raw materials.)

When goods or services are sold, the firm receives either cash or a promise of payment in the future. A credit sale generates an account receivable, which represents money that is due to the firm. Heinz has $1,171,797 in receivables; this is a net figure obtained by subtracting the doubtful accounts from the total amount of receivables. Since a firm does not always obtain payment from all its accounts receivable, it is necessary to make an allowance for these "doubtful accounts." Only the net realizable figure is included in the tabulation of the firm's assets.

A cash sale generates the asset "cash" for the firm. Since holding cash will earn nothing, some of it may be invested in short-term money instruments (often referred to as "cash equivalents"). Cash and short-term money instruments may be combined under a classification called cash and cash equivalents. For Heinz, cash and short-term marketable securities total $373,145. This money is available to meet the firm's immediate financial obligations.

Account receivable

Account arising from a credit sale that has not been collected

Cash and cash equivalents, accounts receivable, and inventory are the major short-term assets. Other current assets include the "prepaid expense," which arises when an expense is paid before it occurs. For example, an insurance premium is paid at the beginning of the policy. The premium payment generates the asset, prepaid expenses. This asset is consumed (reduced) while the policy is in force, so at the end of the term of the policy, the prepaid expense account is reduced to zero. In 2009, total current assets amounted to $2,945,021. These short-term assets will flow through the firm during its fiscal year and will be used to meet its financial obligations that must be paid during the year. The total value and the nature of these assets are important in determining the firm's ability to meet its current obligations.

Long-term assets include the firm's property, plant, and equipment, which are used for many years. The firm's employees utilize these long-term assets in conjunction with the current assets to create the products or services that the company offers for sale. The type and quantity of long-term assets that a company uses vary with the industry. Some industries, such as utilities and transportation, require numerous plants and extensive equipment. Firms in these industries must have substantial investments in long-term assets in order to operate. Not all companies choose to own these assets; instead, they may rent them, which is called leasing. Regardless of whether the firm leases or owns these assets, it must have the use of the long-term assets to produce the company's output.

As of the end of fiscal 2009, Heinz had $1,978,302 invested in buildings and equipment. This is a net number and includes the original investment in fixed assets minus depreciation. Depreciation is important because it is the process of allocating the cost of the fixed assets over a period of time. The value of long-term assets on a firm's balance sheet is reduced over time as the assets are used.

Land is also a long-term asset and may be included in fixed assets. Unlike investments in plant and equipment, land is not depreciated but is carried on the books at its cost or purchase price. Land values, however, may increase, in which case the accountants could increase the land's value on the books. Such revaluations rarely occur, so many firms have hidden assets whose book values understate their market values. (Revaluations rarely occur because the revaluation creates taxable income.)

Hidden assets

Assets that have appreciated in value but are carried on the balance sheet at a lower value, such as their original cost

The remaining entry on the asset side of the balance sheet is "other non-current assets," which may include stock in other companies, goodwill, intangibles, and trademarks. Even though stock in other companies may be sold and converted into cash, it is often considered separate from the firm's current assets and classified as a long-term asset. Goodwill occurs when one company buys another but pays more than the book value (the accounting value) of the acquired firm. For example, if company A buys company B for $100 but the book value is only $60, then the acquiring firm accounts for the $40 difference as goodwill. Intangibles may include patents and trademarks. For a firm such as Heinz, trademarks, patents, and copyrights are often significant assets that contribute to the value of the firm.

The total assets are the sum of the current assets ($2,945,021), the property, plant, and equipment ($1,978,302), and the other assets ($4,740,861) for a total of $9,664,184 in 2009. These assets are financed by the claims of creditors and stockholders—the firm's liabilities and equity.

The firm's liabilities are divided into two groups: current liabilities, which must be paid during the fiscal year, and long-term liabilities, which are due after the fiscal year. Current liabilities are primarily accounts payable and short-term loans. Just as the firm sells on credit, it may also purchase goods and raw material on credit. This trade credit is short-term and is retired as goods are produced and sold, and receivables collected. Heinz had $1,113,307 in accounts payable. Its short-term debt amounted to $61,297.

Additional current liabilities include long-term debt that is due to be paid in the current fiscal year ($4,341) and accruals, which cover items such as wages and salaries that have been earned but not paid ($324,599). Other accrued liabilities may include interest on the firm's outstanding debt and payments for the use of patents, as well as income taxes. For Heinz these current liabilities were $485,406 and $73,896. The sum of all the current liabilities was $2,052,746.

Long-term debt obligations must be retired at some time after the current fiscal year. Such obligations may include bonds that are outstanding and mortgages on real estate. These long-term debts represent part of the permanent financing of the firm because these funds are committed to financing the business for a long time. Short-term liabilities are usually not considered part of the firm's permanent financing because these liabilities must be paid within a relatively short period. For Heinz, the long-term liabilities consist primarily of long-term debt ($5,076,186 in 2009). On other financial statements, a breakdown of the various debt issues (if the debt consists of more than one issue) may be given in a footnote that appears after the body of the financial statement.

Other noncurrent liabilities may include deferred taxes, which arise from the differences in the timing of when the taxes are incurred and when they are paid. For example, a firm may make a profitable installment sale and report the earnings in its current fiscal year. Even though the tax liability is incurred during the present year, the firm does not make the tax payment until it receives the installments. Thus, the tax payments are deferred. These deferred taxes appear on the balance sheet in a separate account from the current taxes due, which must be paid within the fiscal year and hence are a current liability.

Stockholders' (or shareholders') equity completes the balance sheet. The initial entry is preferred stock (if the firm has preferred stock outstanding, and many do not). Heinz has a trivial amount of preferred stock ($70). The next entry is for common stock ($107,774), which is the product of the number of shares outstanding (431,096) and their par value ($0.25). Next is additional capital ($737,917). By far the largest entry is the retained earnings ($6,525,719), which represents the firm's earnings over time that were not distributed. The last two entries include "other adjustments," which could have arisen from losses on foreign exchange transactions, and share repurchases.

Current liability

Debt that must be paid during the fiscal year

Long-term liability

Debt that becomes due after one year

Many firms have repurchased their stock and hold these shares "in the treasury." The shares could be retired, but if the firm wanted to resell them to the general public, the shares would have to be reregistered with the SEC. Because the treasury stock is held for future purposes, it is not retired, which avoids the cost associated with reregistering the shares. Over time, Heinz has repurchased stock for which it paid $4,881,842, which is subtracted from its total equity. (Notice that the reduction in equity is the cost to repurchase the stock and not what the shares were initially sold for.)

Such repurchases have been common after periods of falling stock prices. Repurchases also occur when management believes the shares to be under-valued and uses the firm's cash to reduce the number of shares outstanding instead of using the cash for other purposes. The purchases may be made on the open market or through privately negotiated sales. The latter may occur when a single stockholder wants to sell a large block, in which case the seller may approach management concerning the possible sale of the shares back to the firm.

Firms may also repurchase their stock as a defensive tactic against an attempted takeover. The repurchase of shares owned by public stockholders increases management's proportionate ownership in the firm. The repurchased shares may be resold to "friendly hands," an investor who will support current management. For example, the shares may be repurchased by the employee pension plan. If the trustees of the pension plan support current management, the sale strengthens management's position against a hostile takeover.

Book value

Firm's total assets minus total liabilities; equity; net worth

Book value per share

Book value divided by number of shares outstanding

The book value of a firm is the equity that the investors have in the firm—the sum of common stock, additional paid-in capital, and retained earnings minus the repurchases and the adjustments ($1,219,938). This sum represents the common stockholders' investment in the firm. Individual investors are pri-marily concerned with the value of a share of stock and not with the value of all the shares. To obtain the book value per share, the total equity available to common stock is divided by the number of shares outstanding. For Heinz, the per share book value in 2009 was $2.83. This amount is the accounting value of each of the shares held by the firm's stockholders.

If Heinz were to cease operations, sell its assets, and pay off its liabilities, the owners would receive the remainder. If the assets and liabilities are accurately measured by their dollar values on the balance sheet, the book value equals the amount that stockholders would receive in the liquidation. However, as we will discuss later, the book value may not be an accurate measure of the market value of the firm or its assets.

Since a balance sheet presents a firm's assets, liabilities, and equity, it is a summary of the firm's financial condition at a particular point in time. It shows how funds were raised and how they were allocated. The balance sheet for Heinz indicates that in 2009, Heinz owned total assets valued at $9,664,184. These are the resources that the firm has to use, and (excluding the investment in the common stock of other firms) are allocated between short-term and long-term assets.

Heinz had liabilities of $8,444,246 and equity of $1,219,938 in 2009. The sum of the liabilities and equity must equal the sum of the assets, for it is the liabilities and equity that finance the acquisition of the assets. The assets could not have been acquired if creditors and owners had not provided the funds. For Heinz, the balance sheet indicates that liabilities finance 87.4 percent and that equity finances 12.6 percent ($1,219,938/$9,664,184) of the total assets. Thus, the balance sheet indicates the proportion of the assets financed with debt and the proportion financed with equity.

Two additional points need to be made about balance sheets. First, a balance sheet is constructed at the end of a fiscal period (for example, a year). It indicates the value of the assets and liabilities and the net worth at that particular time. Since financial transactions occur continuously, the information contained in a balance sheet may become outdated rapidly. Second, the values assigned to the assets need not mirror their market value. Instead, the values of the assets may be overstated or understated. For example, the firm owns accounts receivable, not all of which will be paid. Although the firm does allow for these potential losses in an effort to make the balance sheet entries more accurate, the allowances may be insufficient, and the value of the assets may be overstated. Conversely, the value of other assets may be understated. The land on which the plant is built may have increased in value but may continue to be carried on the company's books at its cost.

For the book value of the firm to be a true indication of its worth, all the assets on the balance sheet should be valued at their market prices; however, this practice is not necessarily followed. Accountants suggest that assets be valued conservatively: (1) at the cost of the asset, or (2) at its market value, depending on which is less. Such conservatism is prudent but may result in assets having hidden or understated value if their appreciation is not recognized. Because of these accounting methods, the book value of the equity or net worth of a firm may not be a good measure of its liquidation or market value.

The Income Statement

Income statement

Financial statement that summarizes revenues and expenses for a period of time to determine profit or loss

The income statement tells investors how much accounting income or profits the company has earned during a period of time (for example, its fiscal year). It is a summary of revenues and expenses and indicates the firm's accounting profits or losses. It is not, however, a summary of cash receipts and disbursements. (Receipts and disbursements are considered in the cash budget, which is discussed in Chapter 16.)

Exhibit 9.2 provides the 2009 and 2008 income statements for H. J. Heinz Company. The statements start with a summary of the firm's sources of revenues: net sales (total sales minus returns) of $10,148,082 in 2009. Next follows a summary of the cost of goods sold ($6,564,447). The difference between the net sales and the cost of goods sold is the gross profit ($3,583,635). Then the selling, administrative expenses, and depreciation are subtracted to determine the operating earnings or earnings before interest and taxes ($1,571,685). (If the firm has other sources of income—for instance, dividends received—they are added to the operating earnings to determine the company's total

EXHIBIT 9.2
H. J. Heinz Company
Statement of Income
(in thousands, except per
share data)

For the fiscal year ending April	2009	2008
Sales	$10,148,082	$10,070,778
Cost of products sold	6,564,447	6,390,086
Gross profit	3,583,635	3,680,692
Selling and administrative expense	2,089,983	2,111,725
Operating income	1,493,652	1,568,967
Other income	78,033	(27,836)
Earnings before interest and taxes	1,571,685	1,541,131
Interest income	64,150	41,519
Interest expense	339,635	364,856
Taxes	373,128	372,896
Net income	923, 072	844,925
Earnings per common share	$ 2.90	2.63
Cash dividends per share	$ 1.66	1.52

Source: Adapted from H. J. Heinz Company, *Annual Report,* 2009.

earnings before interest and taxes.) To determine net earnings, net interest expense ($339,635 − 64,150) and taxes ($373,128) must be subtracted from the 1,571,685, which yields net earnings of $923,072.

Stockholders are generally not concerned with total earnings but with earnings per share. The bottom line of the income statement shows the earnings per share (EPS = $2.90), which is net earnings divided by the number of shares outstanding. This $2.90 is the amount of earnings available to each share of common stock.

Notice that earnings per share ($2.90) may not be simply earnings divided by the number of shares outstanding at the end of the year. Since the firm may issue or repurchase stock throughout the year, it does not have the use of the funds for the entire year. The funds raised by issuing shares (or the funds used to repurchase shares) could not generate current income. Thus, shares outstanding are averaged over the year, and this average is used to determine earnings per share.

H. J. Heinz could report two earnings per share figures. One alternative uses outstanding shares (or an average of outstanding shares). Fully diluted earnings per share includes shares that will be issued if or when stock options are exercised. Although these shares are not currently outstanding, it is reasonable to assume they will become outstanding as employees exercise their options to buy the stock. Providing fully diluted earnings per share acknowledges that the earnings will be spread over more shares when (and if) the options are exercised and more shares become outstanding.

When the firm earns profits, management must decide what to do with these earnings. There are two choices: (1) to pay out the earnings to stockholders in the form of cash dividends, or (2) to retain the earnings. The retained earnings on the balance sheet are the sum of all the firm's undistributed earnings that have accumulated but that have not been paid out in dividends during the company's life. These retained earnings are used to finance the purchase of assets or to retire debt. How this year's earnings were used does not appear on the income statement. The income statement merely summarizes revenues and expenses during the fiscal year and indicates whether the firm produced a net profit or loss.

Statement of Cash Flows

Accountants, financial managers, and investors have increased their emphasis on analyzing a firm's ability to generate cash. This emphasis has led to the creation of the "statement of cash flows," which determines the changes in the firm's holdings of cash and cash equivalents and serves as a linkage between the income statement (which determines if the firm operated at a loss or at a profit) and the balance sheet (which enumerates the firm's assets, liabilities, and equity).

Statement of cash flows

Financial statement summarizing cash inflows and cash outflows

The statement of cash flows is divided into three sections: (1) operating activities, (2) investment activities, and (3) financing activities. In each section it enumerates the inflow and outflow of cash. The cash inflows are

1. a decrease in an asset,
2. an increase in a liability, and
3. an increase in equity.

The cash outflows are

1. an increase in an asset,
2. a decrease in a liability, and
3. a decrease in equity.

The statement of cash flows starts with a firm's earnings and works through various entries to determine the change in the firm's cash and cash equivalents. This process is illustrated in Exhibit 9.3. H. J. Heinz starts with earnings of $923,072. Since earnings are not synonymous with cash, adjustments must be made to put earnings on a cash basis. The first adjustment is to add back all noncash expenses and deduct noncash revenues. The most important of these adjustments is usually depreciation, the noncash expense that allocates the cost of plant and equipment over a period of time. (The various methods used to depreciate plant and equipment are covered later in this chapter.) Other noncash expenses may include depletion of raw materials and the amortization of intangible assets, such as goodwill. In this illustration, H. J. Heinz has depreciation and amortization expense of $281,375 in 2009, so that amount is added to the firm's earnings.

An increase in deferred taxes is added to earnings plus noncash expenses. Earnings are determined after subtracting taxes owed for the time period but not necessarily paid. The firm may be able to defer paying some taxes to the future, so these deferred taxes do not result in a current outflow of cash. Although taxes actually paid are a cash outflow, deferred taxes recognized during the time period are not a cash outflow and are added back to earnings to determine the cash generated by operations.

In 2009, Heinz experienced an increase in deferred taxes of $108,081, which is added back to determine cash from operation. A decrease in deferred taxes would indicate that previously deferred taxes were paid and were a cash outflow. In that case, the change in deferred taxes would be subtracted.

The next set of entries refers to changes in the firm's current assets and liabilities resulting from operations. Some of these changes will generate cash while others will consume it. If accounts receivable increase, that means during the accounting period the firm has experienced a net increase in credit sales. These credit sales do not generate cash until the receivables are collected, so an increase in accounts receivable is a cash outflow. In 2009, Heinz's receivables increased, so there was a cash outflow of $10,866. The outflow is represented by the minus sign before the amount. Conversely, if accounts receivable had declined, it would mean the firm collected more receivables than it granted. Such a positive collection would result in a cash inflow. Since a decline in accounts receivable produces a positive inflow, the dollar amount of the decline would be presented as a positive number on the statement.

An increase in inventory, like an increase in accounts receivable, is a cash outflow. More inventory is purchased than is sold, so there is a cash outflow. If the firm's inventory declines, it experiences a cash inflow. A reduction in inventory indicates that less inventory was purchased than was sold. This cash inflow would be added to determine cash generated by operations. During 2009, inventory decreased, and this $50,731 cash inflow is added to determine cash generated by operations.

These effects on cash by changes in accounts receivable and inventory also apply to other current assets. An increase in any current asset, other than cash or cash equivalents, is a cash outflow, while a decrease is a cash inflow. For example, if the firm prepays an insurance policy or makes a lease or rent payment at the beginning of the month, these payments are cash outflows. However, they are also increases in the asset prepaid expense; thus, the increase in the asset represents a cash outflow.

In additional changes in current assets, normal day-to-day operations will alter the firm's current liabilities. Wages will accrue and other trade accounts may change. During 2009, Heinz's accrued wages and taxes increased, which were cash inflows. Accounts payable, however, were reduced. This $62,934 is an outflow. (If payables increase, that is a cash inflow because the cash has not been paid out.)

The sum of the adjustments and changes in current assets and liabilities gives the net cash generated (or consumed) by operations. In 2009, Heinz's operations generated cash of $1,166,882.

The next part of the statement of cash flows analyzes the firm's investments in long-term assets. The acquisition of plant and equipment requires a cash outflow while the sale of plant and equipment generates cash (an inflow). Expanding firms will need additional investment in plant and equipment, which

EXHIBIT 9.3
H. J. Heinz Company
Statement of Cash Flows
for 2009 (in thousands)

Operating activities	
Net income	923,072
Depreciation and amortization	281,375
Deferred taxes	108,081
Other	−197,409

Change in current asset and liabilities	
Receivables	−10,866
Inventory	50,731
Accounts payable	−62,934
Accruals	24,641
Income taxes	61,216
Other	−11,025
Cash provided by operating activities	1,166,882

Investing activities	
Purchases of plant and equipment	−292,121
Proceeds from sale of plant and equipment	5,407
Acquisitions	−293,898
Other	−180,582
Cash used for investing activities	−761,194

Financing activities	
Payment of long-term debt	−427,417
Proceeds from sale of long-term debt	853,051
Payment for short-term debt	−483,666
Dividends	−525,293
Purchases of stock	−181,431
Other	248,420
Cash used for financing activities	−516,336
Effect of exchange rate changes	−133,894
Net (decrease)/increase in cash	−244,542
Cash at the beginning of the year	617,687
Cash at the beginning of the year	373,145

Source: H. J. Heinz Company, *Annual Report*, 2009.

consumes cash. A firm with excess capacity may sell plant and equipment, which generates cash. During 2009, Heinz acquired $292,121 in new plant. This acquisition is a cash outflow, so the amount is negative. The firm also sold plant for $5,407, which is an inflow. After additional entries, the net amount of these investment activities is a negative $761,194. The negative number indicates that net investments in plant and equipment required a cash outlay.

The third part of the statement of changes in cash flows covers the financing decisions of the firm. Issuing new debt or new stock produces a cash inflow. Retiring debt, redeeming stock, or paying cash dividends are cash outflows. Financing decisions can be either long- or short-term. An increase in a short-term liability, such as a bank loan, or a long-term liability, such as a bond outstanding, is a source of cash. A reduction in these accounts, however, requires a cash outflow. An increase in equity is also an inflow of cash while a reduction in equity is a cash outflow.

Besides paying cash dividends ($525,293), Heinz financing activities included repayment of debt ($427,417) and issuing new long-term debt ($853,051). Heinz also repurchased stock ($181,431) and participated in other financing activities such as borrowing from commercial banks. The net of the financing activities was a cash outflow of $516,336.

The final part of the statement presents the firm's cash position at the end of the time period. Cash at the end of the accounting period is determined by the amount of initial cash and by the change in cash. Heinz's cash inflow from operations was $1,166,882 but its investment activities resulted in a cash outflow of $761,194. Financing activities resulted in a cash outflow of $516,336, so after combining the cash flows from operations, investments, and financing, cash outflows exceeded inflows by $244,542. Since the firm began the year with $617,687, it ends the year with $373,145 in cash.

The bottom line of the statement of cash flows is the firm's cash position at the end of the accounting period. If the firm uses more cash than it generated, its cash holdings (or cash equivalents) will decline. Conversely, if the firm's cash inflows exceed the outflows, its cash and cash equivalents will rise.

What does the statement add to the financial analyst's knowledge? By placing the emphasis on cash, the statement permits the analyst to see where the firm generated cash and how this money was used. In the example in Exhibit 9.3, Heinz generated cash from earnings and the noncash depreciation expense. Since these are part of operating activities, they are "internally" generated funds. How was this cash used? The answer is primarily to purchase plant and inventory, pay dividends, and retire long-term debt. Since the internally generated cash was insufficient to cover the cash outflows, Heinz needed "external" sources of funds.

Limitations of Accounting Data

Accounting statements have inherent weaknesses, but that does not excuse you from employing accounting data. You need to be aware of the limitation and interpret the financial statements in light of these weaknesses.

First, accounting data do not take into account nonmeasurable items, such as the quality of the research department or the marketing performance of the firm. Performance is measured solely in terms of money, and the implication of accounting data is that if the firm consistently leads its industry (or is at least above average), its management and divisions are qualitatively superior to its competitors. A relationship probably does exist between performance and superior financial statements. The strong financial statements of Coca-Cola or Johnson & Johnson mirror the quality of their management and of their research and marketing staffs. However, many firms may be able to improve their financial position temporarily and achieve short-term superior performance that cannot be maintained.

Second, accounting statements that are available to the public give aggregate data. Although the company's management has access to itemized data, individual investors or security analysts may not receive sufficiently detailed information to guide investment decisions. For example, a company may not give its sales figures according to product lines. Aggregate sales data do not inform the public as to which of the company's products are its primary sources of revenue. The use of aggregate numbers in the firm's income statements and balance sheets may hide important information that the investor or securities analyst could use in studying the company.

Third, accounting data may be biased. For example, the valuation of assets by the lower of either cost or market value may result in biased information if the dollar value of the assets has significantly risen (as may occur during periods of inflation). Such increases in value are hidden by the use of the historical cost, and thus the accounting statements do not give a true indication of the current value of the firm's assets. If the value of the assets has risen and this is not recognized by the accounting data, the return earned by the company on its assets is overstated. If the true value of the assets were used to determine the return that the firm earns on its assets, the rate would be lower.

Fourth, accounting data provided by management may not be accurate or sufficiently challenged by auditors. The accounting statements of publicly held firms must be audited by an independent certified public accountant (CPA). These audits, which are an official examination of accounts, must be performed annually. After conducting an audit, the CPA issues an "auditor's opinion" that attests to the *fairness* of the financial statements and their *conformity* with generally accepted accounting principles. By fairness, accountants mean that the statements are not misleading. This auditor's opinion must be included in the firm's annual report. On occasion, the opinion may include a discussion of specific factors that affect specific details in the financial statements. In this case the opinion is said to be "qualified."

Since audits are done by independent accountants, investors are supposed to have confidence in the financial statements. The auditors, however, may lack knowledge in specific areas and accept management's data. For example, the auditors may accept the estimates of the firm's engineers because the auditors lack the specialized knowledge to challenge the estimates. In addition, the auditors may not challenge management presentations of gray areas, which are open to interpretation. (The acceptance of Enron's off–balance sheet operations were justified on that basis.) Thus, auditing financial statements does not guarantee the accuracy of the statements. The financial analyst or investor should realize that audited financial statements are not absolute truths but include judgments that may affect the accuracy of the financial statements.

Responsibility for accuracy rests with management. One of the purposes of the Sarbanes-Oxley Act of 2002 was to improve accuracy by requiring the chief executive officer (the CEO) and the chief financial officer (the CFO) of publicly held corporations to certify that the financial statements do not contain untrue statements or material omissions. Penalties for violating these provisions include fines and possible imprisonment. While Sarbanes-Oxley legal requirements should increase the accuracy of financial statements, their construction still requires judgments that can affect the final numbers.

Depreciation

Straight-line depreciation

Allocation of the cost of plant and equipment by equal amounts over a period of time

Accelerated depreciation

Allocating the cost of plant and equipment in such a way that a larger proportion of an asset's cost is recovered during the earlier years of the asset's life

Depreciation was previously defined as the allocation of the cost of a fixed asset such as plant or equipment over a period of time. It is important because the annual noncash depreciation expense reduces the firm's taxable income, which reduces its taxes. Since depreciation is a noncash expense, it is added back to earnings to determine the firm's cash flow from operations.

While a fixed asset may be depreciated, that does not tell you the rate or amount by which the asset may be depreciated each year. If the allocation of the cost is the same dollar amount each year, the firm is using straight-line depreciation. The allocation, however, may be in larger dollar amounts during the initial years and smaller amounts during the later years of the investment's life. This allocation system is called accelerated depreciation. As will be illustrated below, the advantage of accelerated depreciation is that it allocates the cost of the asset faster and, therefore, recoups most of the cost of the investment quicker *and* initially reduces the firm's income taxes.

Depreciation expense arises in the following way. A firm has the following balance sheet:

Firm X Balance Sheet as of 12/31/XX			
Assets		**Liabilities and Equity**	
Cash	$1,000	Debt	$500
		Equity	$500

The only asset is cash provided by investors (the equity) and creditors (the debt). In order to produce some product, the firm uses $400 of the cash to acquire equipment. After the purchase, the balance sheet is

Assets		**Liabilities and Equity**	
Cash	$600	Debt	$500
Equipment	$400	Equity	$500

The $400 cash was spent when the equipment was acquired; thus the firm no longer has these funds.

The firm anticipates that the equipment will operate for several years. For example, the firm may anticipate that the equipment may last four years, after which time it will have to be junked and replaced. If the firm anticipates that the $400 machine will have a useful life of four years, the firm depreciates the machine on a straight-line basis for $100 a year. This is determined by using the following formula:

$$\text{Annual depreciation} = \frac{\text{Cost}}{\text{Anticipated useful life in years}}. \tag{9.1}$$

Annual depreciation is

$$\frac{\$400}{4} = \$100.$$

In effect the firm is saying that $100 worth of the machine is depreciated or consumed each year and that at the end of four years the machine is totally consumed and valueless.

The importance of depreciation expense on profit and corporate income tax is illustrated as follows. If the output produced by the firm's machine is sold for $800, and if, after operating and administrative expenses of $500, the firm has earnings of $300, is the $300 a true statement of the earnings? The answer is no, because no allowance has been made for the $100 of the machine's value that has been consumed to produce the output. The true profit is not $300 but $200, which is $300 gross earnings minus the $100 depreciation expense. The firm now pays corporate income tax on its earnings of $200 and not on the earnings before the depreciation expense. If the corporate income tax rate is 25 percent, the firm pays $50 (0.25 × $200) in taxes instead of the $75 (0.25 × $300) it would have to pay if the depreciation expense were omitted. Since the depreciation expense reduces the firm's earnings, it also reduces its income taxes.

Since the firm bought the equipment in the first year, it might seem reasonable to add the entire cost of the equipment to the firm's expenses for that year. In that case would the firm have a true statement of its earnings? The answer is "no" because the firm's costs are incorrectly stated. The firm's expenses would be $900, which includes the $500 operating expense and the $400 cost of the equipment. The firm would be operating at a loss of $100 ($800 revenues minus $900 expenses). This understates the earnings because the equipment's entire value was not consumed during the year. Only one-fourth of its value was consumed during the first year. Hence, only one-fourth of the equipment's value should be charged (or "expensed") against the firm's annual revenues. Overstating depreciation, like understating depreciation, alters the firm's earnings.

That depreciation affects cash flow may be seen by continuing the example. The $100 depreciation expense did not involve an outlay of cash. The operating and administrative expenses do require an outlay of cash. (The outlay of cash occurred when the machine was initially purchased and not while it was being used. Depreciation is a noncash expense item that allocates the initial cash outlay over a period of time.) Because no cash is expended by the firm as a result of the depreciation expense, depreciation is said to be a source of cash flow because it is recouping the original outlay for the machine. Therefore, depreciation increases the flow of cash in the firm.

This seemingly contradictory statement (that an expense will increase the firm's cash flow) may be illustrated by constructing the following simple income statement for the firm:

Sales	$800
Operating expenses	500
Income before depreciation	300
Depreciation	100
Taxable income	200
Taxes	50
Net income	$150

Only the operating expenses ($500) and the tax ($50) required a disbursement of cash. The firm has $250 ($800 – $550) left. This is the $150 profit and the $100 depreciation expense that is added back to the profits to obtain the cash flow generated by operations. Thus, cash flow is the earnings (after taxes) plus depreciation expense. The firm has $250 that it may use and $100 of the cash is the result of the depreciation expense. The firm must now decide what to do with the $100 generated by the depreciated asset. For example, management may use the cash to restore the depreciated asset, purchase a different asset, retire outstanding debt, or make payments to stockholders.

Accelerated Depreciation

Conceptually, accelerated depreciation is no different from straight-line depreciation except that a greater proportion of the asset's purchase price is depreciated in the early years of the asset's life. Depreciation charges are larger when the plant and equipment are new and smaller when the plant and equipment are old. This variation in the expense, of course, alters the firm's earnings. When the depreciation charge is larger, the firm's profits and corporate income taxes are smaller. By using accelerated depreciation the firm initially is able to decrease earnings and taxes but increase its cash flow (that is, accelerated depreciation initially increases the sum of earnings plus depreciation expense).

Plant and equipment are generally depreciated under the modified accelerated cost recovery system (MACRS), which uses the schedules given in Exhibit 9.4. The first column presents the year, and the other columns present (for the given classes of depreciable assets) the proportion of the asset's cost that may be depreciated in that year. For example, if an asset is to be depreciated over five years, 32 percent of the cost of that asset is written off in the second year.

Modified accelerated cost recovery system (MACRS)

Type of accelerated depreciation that became law under the tax revision of 1981 and hat was revised under the 1986 Tax Reform Act

PART 2 Financial Tools

Recovery Year	Percentage of Cost Depreciated Over:					
	3 Years	5 Years	7 Years	10 Years	15 Years	20 Years
1	33.00%	20.00%	14.28%	10.00%	5.00%	3.79%
2	45.00	32.00	24.49	18.00	9.50	7.22
3	15.00	19.20	17.49	14.40	8.55	6.68
4	7.00	11.52	12.49	11.52	7.69	6.18
5		11.52	8.93	9.22	6.93	5.71
6		5.76	8.93	7.37	6.23	5.28
7			8.93	6.55	5.90	4.89
8			4.46	6.55	5.90	4.52
9				6.55	5.90	4.46
10				6.55	5.90	4.46
11				3.29	5.90	4.46
12					5.90	4.46
13					5.90	4.46
14					5.90	4.46
15					5.90	4.46
16					3.00	4.46
17						4.46
18						4.46
19						4.46
20						4.46
21						2.25

The number of years that may be used for depreciating a particular asset is similar to the asset's economic life. For example, cars and light trucks are depreciated over five years, and office equipment is depreciated over seven years. An asset, however, may be used for longer than the period allowed to write off its cost. Prior to the establishment of the accelerated cost recovery system (ACRS) and its subsequent modification (MACRS), depreciation was determined by the asset's useful life. Thus, a piece of equipment that had an expected useful life of 10 years would be depreciated over 10 years. Under current law, that equipment would be classified as a seven-year asset, and the seven-year schedule would be applied.

Two additional observations should be made. First, a close look at the schedules presented in Exhibit 9.4 reveals that the depreciation schedules are one year longer than the stated number of years. For example, the depreciation of a five-year asset occurs over six years. This is because depreciation is based on the assumption that assets are purchased evenly throughout the year. On the average, assets are only owned for half of the year in which they are acquired. Second, the depreciation schedules do not consider any residual value that the asset may have. Thus, an asset classified as depreciable under the seven-year schedule will have no value at the end of the eighth year according to the depreciation schedule, even though in reality it may have some residual value.

Methods of Depreciation Compared

All methods of depreciation allocate the cost of plant and equipment over a period of time. The differences relate to their effects on the firm's earnings and thus to their effects on the firm's taxes and the cash flow from the investments. Straight-line depreciation and the accelerated cost recovery system are compared in Exhibit 9.5 for an asset that costs $1,000 and is depreciated over 10 years. (The exhibit employs a $1,000 asset to facilitate the comparison of straight-line and accelerated depreciation. As of 2003, under section 179, the firm may immediately deduct ["write off"] up to $25,000 of the cost of equipment.) The first section of this table illustrates straight-line depreciation over the asset's economic life. Notice the half-year convention also applies to straight-line depreciation. Since the average asset is owned for six months, only half of the annual depreciation expense is deducted the first year. To fully depreciate the asset, the final deduction occurs in the 11th year in the exhibit.

The second section illustrates the accelerated cost recovery system, which classifies the asset as a seven-year asset. The first column gives the year and the second column gives the firm's operating revenues after all expenses except depreciation. The third column gives the depreciation expense for each of the years. The remaining four columns illustrate the effects of depreciation expense. The fourth column presents the firm's taxable income; the fifth column gives the income taxes (assuming a tax rate of 25 percent), and the sixth column gives the net income or profit after the taxes. The seventh column gives the firm's cash flow, which is the sum of its earnings after taxes and its depreciation expenses. As may be seen in the table, the accelerated method of depreciation initially (1) reduces the firm's taxable income, which reduces its taxes, and (2) increases the firm's cash flow.

The table, however, also illustrates that the accelerated method of depreciation increases the firm's income and taxes and reduces its cash flow in the later years of the asset's life. Actually, the total depreciation expense, net income after taxes, taxes, and cash flow over the asset's life are the same for both methods of depreciation. This can be seen by adding the depreciation expense, taxes, net income, and cash flow columns. The sums are equal for both methods.

If accelerated depreciation does not reduce the firm's taxes and increase its cash flow over the life of the asset, what is its advantage? The answer to this question is the timing of the taxes and the cash flows. Accelerated depreciation increases the firm's cash flow during the early years of the asset's life and delays the payment of taxes to the later years of the asset's life. Accelerated depreciation increases the cash flow now, so the firm has the cash to invest and increase earnings. By deferring taxes, the firm is receiving a current loan in the form of deferred taxes from the federal government. And equally important, this loan has no interest cost.

Year	Income before Depreciation	Depreci- ation Expense	Income before Taxes	Income Taxes	Net Income after Taxes	Cash Flow
Straight-Line Depreciation						
1	$300	$ 50	$250	$ 62.50	$ 187.50	$ 237.50
2	300	100	200	50.00	150.00	250.00
3	300	100	200	50.00	150.00	250.00
4	300	100	200	50.00	150.00	250.00
5	300	100	200	50.00	150.00	250.00
6	300	100	200	50.00	150.00	250.00
7	300	100	200	50.00	150.00	250.00
8	300	100	200	50.00	150.00	250.00
9	300	100	200	50.00	150.00	250.00
10	300	100	200	50.00	150.00	250.00
11	300	50	250	62.50	187.50	237.50
Totals		$1,000		$575.00	$1,725.00	$2,725.00
Accelerated Cost Recovery						
1	$300	$ 142.80	$157.20	$ 39.30	$ 117.90	$ 260.70
2	300	244.90	55.10	13.78	41.32	286.22
3	300	174.90	125.10	31.28	93.82	268.72
4	300	124.90	175.10	43.78	131.32	256.22
5	300	89.30	210.70	52.67	158.03	247.33
6	300	89.30	210.70	52.67	158.03	247.33
7	300	89.30	210.70	52.67	158.03	247.33
8	300	44.60	255.40	63.85	191.55	236.15
9	300	—	300.00	75.00	225.00	225.00
10	300	—	300.00	75.00	225.00	225.00
11	300	—	300.00	75.00	225.00	225.00
Totals		$1,000.00		$575.00	$1,725.00	$2,725.00

In effect, the federal government, by permitting accelerated depreciation, is granting firms interest-free loans that may be used to earn more profits. Accelerated depreciation is another of those devices that the federal government uses to influence behavior. By granting accelerated depreciation, the federal government encourages firms to invest in plant and equipment. Encouraging such investments should increase both the productive capacity of the nation and the level of employment, for workers must build the plant and equipment and operate it after it has been installed.

Ratio Analysis of Financial Statements

Accounting data are often used to analyze a firm's financial condition. Such analysis may be conducted by creditors to measure the safety of their loans. Investors also analyze financial statements to learn how well management is performing. The profitability of the firm may be perceived in the financial statements. In addition, management analyzes the data in financial statements to identify weaknesses in the firm, which, if corrected, may increase the firm's profitability and value.

The ratios used in financial analysis can be classified into the following groups: (1) liquidity, (2) activity or asset utilization, (3) profitability, (4) leverage, and (5) coverage. Liquidity ratios indicate the ability of the firm to meet its short-term obligations as they come due. Activity ratios are concerned with the amount of assets a firm uses to support its sales. The more rapidly assets turn over, the fewer assets the firm needs to generate sales. High turnover of inventory and accounts receivable also indicates how quickly the firm is able to convert these current assets into cash. Profitability ratios are a measure of performance; they indicate what the firm earns on its sales, assets, and equity. Leverage ratios are concerned with the firm's capital structure, or the extent to which debt is used to finance the firm's assets. Coverage ratios indicate the extent to which the firm generates operating income to cover an expense.

Time series analysis

Analysis of a firm over a period of time

Cross-sectional analysis

Analysis of several firms in the same industry at a point in time

These ratios may be computed and interpreted from two viewpoints. They may be compiled for a period of years to perceive trends; this is time series or trend analysis. The ratios may be computed at the same time for several firms within an industry; this is cross-sectional analysis. Time series and cross-sectional analysis may be used together. Rarely will all the ratios indicate the same general tendency. When they are taken as a group, the ratios should give you an indication of the direction in which the firm is moving and how it compares with other firms in its industry.

The analysis of financial statements through ratios can be a very useful tool for financial managers, investors, and creditors, who may use this type of analysis to ascertain how the firm is performing over time and relative to its competition. The ratios will tend to indicate trends, such as a deterioration in the firm's profitability. Such time series analysis of financial statements may indicate future difficulties while there is still time to take remedial action.

Even if the firm is not experiencing a deteriorating financial position, its performance may be inferior to other firms within its industry. A cross-sectional analysis of firms will indicate if the particular firm is performing up to the norms of the industry. To make such comparisons, you must have access to industry averages. The most widely known industry averages are the ratios compiled by Dun & Bradstreet and published annually in *Dun's Review*. Firms are classified by their SIC (Standard Industrial Classification) numbers, and the ratios are subdivided by the size of the firm.

Robert Morris Associates, a national association of bank loan officers, also publishes industry averages in its annual publication *Statement Studies*.

The sources of its data are financial statements acquired by commercial banks from firms receiving loans. The firms are classified by their SIC numbers.

Individual investors and creditors may find calculating their own ratios to be useful, since they may stress the ratios most applicable to the intended use of the analysis. For example, commercial banks and other lending institutions are concerned with the capacity of the borrower to service the loan (to pay the interest and repay the principal). Thus, ratios concerning the borrower's use of debt or the coverage of interest payments are important. Loan officers will use such ratios in credit reviews and in decisions to grant new loans.

If you do an analysis of a firm's financial statements and compare the results to published sources, you may have problems. First, published industry averages are based on last year's financial statements, reducing the comparability of the data with current-year financial ratios. Second, the individual firm may not fit neatly into one of the industry categories. Large firms, such as Pepsi, have operations in a variety of related fields (for example, soft drinks *and* snack foods), which reduces the comparability of ratios computed for similar, but not identical, firms (for example, Coca-Cola). Third, even if industry averages are presented for firms in comparable industries, the problem of comparing firms of different sizes remains. This problem is obvious for large size differentials (such as the local "ma and pa" grocery store compared with a large supermarket chain). But the problem may also apply when comparing larger firms in an industry. For example, are the ratios for a small grocery store comparable to the ratios for a large operation, such as Safeway or Food Lion?

Although there are problems with the application of ratio analysis, it remains a convenient means to analyze a firm's financial condition. You certainly should not discard the analysis because there may be difficulties with its application or interpretation. Used with other tools of financial analysis, ratio analysis of financial statements can give a clear indication of the firm's performance and its direction. The analysis can be a harbinger of things to come and as such may indicate that action should be taken now to correct a small problem before it grows into a major source of financial embarrassment.

In the sections that follow, several ratios are discussed and illustrated. These ratios do not exhaust all the possible ratios, and certainly you may find that in a specific occupation additional ratios or more sophisticated versions of some of the ratios presented here are needed. The purpose of this chapter is only to illustrate how ratios are compiled, interpreted, and used, employing the balance sheet as of the end of the 2009 fiscal year (Exhibit 9.1), and income statement for the 2009 fiscal year (Exhibit 9.2), of H. J. Heinz Company.

Before proceeding, you also need to be forewarned that several ratios have more than one definition. The definition used by one analyst may differ from that used by another. These differences can arise from averaging the data in two financial statements. (See, for instance, the two approaches to inventory turnover discussed below.) Another source of differences can be what is included or excluded. (See, for instance, the various definitions of the debt ratios.) You cannot assume that the analysis obtained from one source is comparable to that provided by an alternative source. This problem may be particularly acute now that analysis of financial statements can be found on the Internet. Of course, you can avoid this problem by performing the analysis yourself!

Liquidity Ratios

Liquidity is the ease with which assets may be converted into cash without loss. If a firm is liquid, it will be able to meet its bills as they come due. Thus, liquidity ratios are useful not only to short-term creditors of the firm, who are concerned with being paid, but also to the firm's management, who must make the payments.

The Current Ratio

Current ratio

Ratio of current assets to current liabilities: measure of liquidity

The current ratio is the ratio of current assets to current liabilities:

$$\text{Current ratio} = \text{Current assets/Current liabilities.}$$

It indicates how well the current liabilities, which must be paid within a year, are "covered." For Heinz, the current assets are $2,945,021 and the current liabilities are $2,052,746; thus, the current ratio is

$$\frac{\$2,945,021}{\$2,052,746} = 1.43,$$

which indicates that for every dollar that the firm must pay within the year, there is $1.43 in an asset that is either cash or should become cash during the year.

For most industries it is desirable to have more current assets than current liabilities. It is sometimes asserted that it is desirable to have at least $2 in current assets for every dollar in current liabilities (a current ratio of at least 2:1). If the current ratio is 2:1, then the firm's current assets could deteriorate in value by 50 percent and the firm still would be able to meet its short-term liabilities. While such rules of thumb are convenient, they need not apply to all industries. For example, electric utilities usually have current liabilities that exceed their current assets. Does this worry short-term creditors? No, because the short-term assets are of high quality (accounts receivable from electricity users). Should a person fail to pay an electric bill, the company will cut off service, and this threat is usually sufficient to induce payment. The higher the quality of the current assets (in other words, the higher the probability that these assets can be converted to cash at their stated value), the smaller the need for the current ratio to exceed 1:1. The reason for selecting a current ratio such as 2:1 as a rule of thumb is that creditors frequently believe that not all current assets will be converted into cash, and to protect themselves the creditors want a current ratio of at least 2:1.

Although management also wants to know if the firm has sufficient liquid assets to meet its bills, the current ratio may have an additional use to management. A low current ratio is undesirable because it indicates financial weakness. A high current ratio may also be undesirable, for it may imply that the firm is not using funds economically. For example, the firm may have issued long-term debt and used it to finance too much inventory or accounts receivable. The high current ratio may also indicate that the firm is not taking advantage of available short-term financing. Since short-term debt tends to be cheaper than long-term debt, failure to use short-term debt may reduce profitability. Thus, a high or low numerical value for the current ratio could signal that the management of short-term assets and liabilities needs changing.

The Quick Ratio

Although the current ratio gives an indication of the ability of the firm to meet its current liabilities as they come due, the ratio does have limitations. It is an aggregation of all current assets and does not differentiate among current assets with regard to their degrees of liquidity. The ratio considers inventory that may be sold after three months on credit (payment for which in turn may not be collected for several additional months) as no different from cash or a short-term government security.

Since it may take months before inventory is sold and turned into cash, a variation on the current ratio is the ratio of all current assets except inventory divided by current liabilities. This ratio is called the quick ratio or *acid test* (both terms are used for this ratio) and is expressed as follows:

Quick ratio (acid test)
Current assets excluding inventory divided by current liabilities; measure of liquidity

$$\text{Quick ratio} = \frac{\text{Current assets} - \text{Inventory}}{\text{Current liabilities}}$$

For Heinz the quick ratio is

$$\frac{\$2,945,021 - \$1,237,613}{\$2,052,746} = 0.83,$$

which is lower than the current ratio of 1.43 determined previously. The difference is, of course, the result of inventory that the company is carrying. A low quick ratio indicates that the firm may have difficulty meeting its obligations as they come due. The quick ratio, however, does not indicate that the firm will fail to pay. The ability to meet the obligations will be influenced by such factors as (1) how quickly cash flows into the firm, (2) the firm's ability to raise additional capital, (3) how rapidly obligations come due, and (4) the relationship the company has with its suppliers and their willingness to extend credit. The quick ratio simply indicates how well the current liabilities are covered by cash and assets that may be converted into cash relatively quickly. In effect, the quick ratio considers that not all current assets are equally liquid and is a more stringent measure of liquidity than the current ratio.

The quick ratio is sometimes defined as

$$\text{Quick ratio} = \frac{\text{Cash} + \text{Cash equivalents} + \text{Accounts receivable}}{\text{Current liabilities}}$$

The two definitions will give the same answer if the firm's current assets are limited to cash, marketable securities, accounts receivable, and inventory. Some firms, however, do have other current assets, such as prepaid expenses, in which case the choice of definition will affect the numerical value of the quick ratio. For Heinz, the quick ratio using the alternative definition is

$$\frac{\$373,145 + \$1,171,797}{\$2,052,746} = 0.75.$$

This value is lower and may be preferred, since you do not want to overstate the firm's capacity to pay its current liabilities as they come due.

The Components of the Current Assets

Another approach to liquidity is to rank the current assets with regard to their degree of liquidity and determine each one's proportion of total current assets. The most liquid current asset is cash. Next are cash equivalents, such as Treasury bills or negotiable certificates of deposit. Then comes accounts receivable, and, finally, inventory. For Heinz the proportion of each asset to total current assets is as follows:

Current Asset	Proportion of Total Current Assets
Cash and cash equivalents	12.7%
Accounts receivable	39.8
Inventory	42.0
Other	5.5

The table indicates that 12.7 percent of the firm's assets are cash and short-term securities, and inventory accounts for 42.0 percent of current assets.

Since this technique determines each asset's proportion of current assets, it gives an indication of the degree of liquidity of the firm's current assets. If a large proportion of the current assets is inventory, the firm is not very liquid. The decomposition of the current assets according to their degree of liquidity, along with the quick ratio, gives management, creditors, and investors a better measure of the ability of the firm to meet its current liabilities as they come due than the current ratio provides. These ratios, then, are a basic supplement to the current ratio and should be used to analyze the liquidity of any firm, such as Heinz, that carries a significant amount of inventory in its operations.

Activity Ratios

Activity ratios indicate how rapidly the firm is turning its assets (for example, inventory and accounts receivable) into cash. Two activity ratios that are frequently encountered are inventory turnover and receivables turnover (the average collection period or days sales outstanding). The more rapidly the firm turns over its inventory and receivables, the more rapidly it acquires cash. Hence, high turnover indicates that the firm is rapidly receiving cash and is more able to pay its liabilities as they come due. High turnover, however, need not imply that the firm is maximizing profits. For example, high inventory turnover may indicate that the firm is selling items for a lower price in order to induce quicker sales. The rapid collection of accounts receivable may indicate that the firm is offering too large a cash discount to buyers to increase collections of receivables. High turnover of inventory or receivables is not desirable by itself and may be indicative of management decisions that reduce earnings. Comparison must be made with industry averages in order to have some basis for making assertions that the turnover is too slow or too rapid.

Inventory Turnover

Inventory turnover

Speed with which inventory is sold

Inventory turnover may be defined as annual sales divided by average inventory. That is,

$$\text{Inventory turnover} = \frac{\text{Sales}}{\text{Average inventory}}.$$

Since all assets must be financed, the more rapidly the inventory turns over, the less are the financing needs of the firm. Since Heinz's 2008 year-end inventory was $1,378,216, the inventory turnover for 2009 is

$$\frac{\text{Sales}}{\text{Average inventory}} = \frac{\$10,148,082}{(\$1,237,613 + \$1,378,216)/2} = 7.8.$$

This indicates that annual sales are 7.8 times the level of inventory. Inventory turns over 7.8 times a year or about every 1.5 months ($12/7.8 = 1.5$). The turnover may be expressed in days by dividing the number of days in a year by the inventory turnover. Thus, in this illustration Heinz holds an average item of inventory for 47 days ($365/7.8 = 47$). Since management can anticipate that on the average, inventory will be held for 47 days, management will need to find financing for that period of time to carry the inventory.

Inventory turnover may also be defined as cost of goods sold divided by average inventory. Accountants in particular may prefer to use cost of goods sold, because accounting places much emphasis on the determination of cost. Financial analysts and creditors may prefer to use sales in order to stress how rapidly the inventory flows into sales. In addition, Dun & Bradstreet uses sales instead of costs in its "Key Business Ratios." Hence, analysts must use sales to inventory if they are comparing a specific firm with the Dun & Bradstreet industry averages.

Either definition, however, is acceptable provided that the user is consistent. If the cost of goods sold is used instead of annual sales, all inventory turnover ratios used as a basis of comparison must also use cost of goods sold instead of annual sales. This points out the need for the person using ratio analysis to be aware of the definitions and to apply the definitions consistently. Otherwise, the analysis may be biased.

Receivables Turnover

Receivables turnover

Speed with which accounts receivable are collected

Receivables turnover is defined as annual credit sales divided by receivables. Thus, the receivables turnover ratio is expressed as follows:

$$\text{Receivables turnover} = \frac{\text{Annual credit sales}}{\text{Accounts receivable}}.$$

An alternative definition substitutes annual sales for annual credit sales. That is,

$$\text{Receivables turnover} = \frac{\text{Annual sales}}{\text{Accounts receivable}}.$$

Either definition is acceptable as long as it is applied consistently. (The analyst may also use average accounts receivable instead of year-end accounts receivable.) While management can use either definition, investors may be limited to the data provided by the firm. If annual credit sales are not reported by the firm, the investor will have no choice but to use annual sales instead of annual credit sales.

The Heinz income statement does not give annual credit sales, so the first definition cannot be used. When the second definition is used, receivables turnover is

$$\text{Receivables turnover} = \frac{\$10,148,082}{\$1,171,797} = 8.7.$$

Average collection period (days sales outstanding)

Number of days required on the average to collect an account receivable

Note that 8.7 times a year is about every 42 days (365/8.7).

An alternative means to measure receivables is the average collection period or "days sales outstanding." The average collection period is

$$\text{Average collection period} = \frac{\text{Receivables}}{\text{Sales per day}}.$$

For Heinz, sales per day are $10,148,082/365, or $27,803. (A 360-day year is often used as a convenience. As stated previously, any definition may be acceptable, as long as it is applied consistently.) The average collection period is

$$\$1,171,797/\$27,803 = 42 \text{ days}.$$

This implies that when the firm makes a credit sale instead of a cash sale, it can expect payment in 42 days. (The average collection period may also be calculated by dividing 365 by the receivables turnover.) This is essentially the same information derived by the receivables turnover rate. If it takes the firm 42 days to collect its receivables, they are turning over about 8.7 times a year. By stressing the number of days necessary to collect the receivables, the average collection period (days sales outstanding) may be easier to interpret.

Turnover ratios employing current assets need to be interpreted cautiously. These ratios are dealing with dynamic measurements, since they are concerned with how long it takes for an event to occur. Turnover ratios may be biased if the firm has (1) seasonal sales; (2) sales that do not occur evenly during the fiscal year; or (3) growth in inventory, accounts receivable, or sales during the fiscal year. Under these circumstances, the use of year-end figures may produce ratios that are biased.

The potential bias may be seen in the following example, which presents the monthly inventory of a firm that has a seasonal type of business. During the year, inventory is accumulated in anticipation of large sales during the Christmas season.

Month	Inventory at End of Month	Sales during the Month
January	$ 100	$ 50
February	100	50
March	200	50
April	200	50
May	300	50
June	400	50
July	500	50
August	700	50
September	1,000	400
October	1,000	1,300
November	1,200	2,000
December	300	1,200
Total sales		$5,300

If year-end inventory and yearly sales figures are employed, the inventory turnover is 17.67 ($5,300/$300), which indicates that inventory is turning over almost every 21 days (365/17.67). This, however, is misleading because it fails to consider the large buildup of inventory that occurred during the middle of the year. In this case the use of year-end inventory figures increases the inventory turnover. The inventory turnover appears to be more rapid than it actually was.

Several means exist to help alleviate this problem. For example, the average of the monthly inventories may be used instead of the year-end inventory. The monthly average inventory is $500 (total inventory acquired during the year divided by 12). When this figure is used with the annual sales, the turnover is 10.6, or about 34 days. This is slower than the turnover indicated when the year-end inventory figures were used. Other methods for removing the potential bias may be to construct monthly turnover ages or moving averages. The point is that turnover ratios may be subject to bias and, hence, may be misleading. In order for ratios to be helpful, you need to recognize the potential bias and take steps to remove it.

Fixed Asset and Total Asset Turnover

Fixed asset turnover

Ratio of sales to fixed assets; measure of fixed assets necessary to generate sales

In addition to the turnover ratios that analyze the speed with which the firm turns over its current assets, there are also turnover ratios that employ the firm's long-term (fixed) assets and total assets. The fixed asset turnover ratio is defined as

$$\text{Fixed asset turnover} = \frac{\text{Sales}}{\text{Fixed assets}}$$

For Heinz, the fixed asset turnover is

$$\frac{\$10,148,082}{\$1,978,302} = 5.1.$$

This indicates that sales are 5.1 times fixed assets (land, plant, and equipment). The more rapidly fixed assets turn over (the higher the ratio), the smaller the amount of plant and equipment the firm is employing. Many firms, such as utilities, must have substantial investment in plant and equipment to produce the output they sell. (A utility such as Southern Company has a fixed asset turnover of 0.4, which indicates the company has $2.50 invested in plant and equipment for every $1 of revenues.) Other firms, especially retailers, or those providing services, may need only modest amounts of fixed assets.

Total asset turnover

Ratio of sales to total assets: measure of total assets required to generate sales

Total asset turnover measures how many assets are used to generate sales. The definition of total asset turnover is

$$\frac{\text{Sales}}{\text{Total asset turnover}} = \text{Total assets}$$

For Heinz the total asset turnover is

$$\frac{\$10,148,082}{\$9,664,184} = 1.05.$$

This indicates the firm needs $1.00 in assets for every $1.05 generated in revenues.

By computing all the turnover ratios (in other words, the average collection period, inventory turnover, fixed asset turnover, and total asset turnover), the financial manager may be able to identify weak areas. For example, if the firm's accounts receivable and inventory turnover ratios are comparable to those for the industry but its total asset or fixed asset turnover is low, then the problem has to be the management of the firm's fixed assets. Once problems are identified, further analysis and remedial action can be directed toward the source of the problem.

Profitability Ratios

Operating profit margin

Ratio of operating income to sales; percentage earned on sales before deducting interest expense and taxes

Profitability ratios are measures of performance that indicate what the firm is earning on its sales or assets or equity. (The words profit, income, and earnings are often synonymous. Operating income is defined as earnings before interest and taxes, and, in most cases, that is sufficient unless the firm has extraordinary or nonrecurring items included in earnings before interest and taxes. Although management will report these items as a separate entry, they may be reported as part of income before interest and taxes, in which case the earnings are not indicative of operating income.) The operating profit margin is earnings before interest and taxes (EBIT) divided by sales, and the net profit margin is the ratio of earnings after interest and taxes to sales.

$$\text{Operating profit margin} = \frac{\text{Earnings before interest and taxes}}{\text{Sales}}$$

Net profit margin

Ratio of earnings after interest and taxes to sales; percentage earned on sales

$$\text{Net profit margin} = \frac{\text{Earnings after interest and taxes}}{\text{Sales}}$$

Computing both of these ratios may appear unnecessary, but it is best to compute both. Management then can see the effect of changes in interest expense and taxes on profitability. If management computed only the net profit margin, an increase in tax rates or interest rates would decrease the profit margin even though there had been no internal deterioration in the profitability of the firm's operations.

For Heinz, the operating profit margin is

$$\text{Operating profit margin} = \frac{\$1,571,685}{\$10,148,082} = 15.5\%,$$

and the net profit margin is

$$\text{Net profit margin} = \frac{\$923,072}{\$10,148,082} = 9.1\%.$$

These indicate that the company earns $0.155 before interest and taxes for every dollar of sales and $0.091 after interest and taxes for every dollar of sales.

In addition to the operating profit margin and the net profit margin, some financial analysts compute the gross profit margin, which is

Gross profit margin

Ratio of revenues minus cost of goods sold to sales; percentage earnings on sales before considering operating expenses, interest, and taxes

$$\text{Gross profit margin} = \frac{\text{Revenues} - \text{Cost of goods sold}}{\text{Sales}}$$

For Heinz, the gross profit margin is

$$\text{Gross profit margin} = \frac{\$3,583,635}{\$10,148,082} = 35.317\%.$$

This ratio indicates that the firm earns $0.35 on every dollar of sales before considering administrative, advertising, depreciation, and financing expenses. The gross profit margin is sensitive only to changes in the cost of goods sold; it is not affected by other operating expenses. The operating profit margin, however, is affected by all operating expenses. By analyzing both the gross profit margin and the operating profit margin, the analyst can determine whether changes in the cost of goods sold or changes in other operating expenses are affecting the firm's earnings before interest and taxes (that is, its operating income).

Return on total assets

Ratio of earnings to total assets; percentage earned on assets

Other profitability ratios measure the return on total assets and the return on equity. The return on total assets is earnings divided by assets and measures what a firm earns on its resources.

$$\text{Return on total assets} = \frac{\text{Earnings after interest and taxes}}{\text{Total assets}}$$

Return on equity

Ratio of earnings to owners' equity; percentage earned on equity

The return on equity is earnings divided by the equity or the net worth of the firm.

$$\text{Return on equity} = \frac{\text{Earnings after interest and taxes}}{\text{Equity}}$$

Equity is defined as the sum of the common stock, the additional paid-in capital, and the retained earnings. Return on equity measures the return the firm is earning on its stockholders' investment. (If the company has any preferred stock, the ratio must be adjusted by subtracting the dividends paid the preferred stockholders from the earnings and subtracting the par value of the preferred stock from the equity. Since the common stockholders are interested in the return on their investment, the preferred stock should not be included in determining the return on the common stock equity.) For Heinz, the return on total assets is

$$\text{Return on total assets} = \frac{\$923,072}{\$9,664,184} = 9.6\%.$$

The return on the equity is

$$\text{Return on equity} = \frac{\$923,072}{\$1,219,938} = 75.7\%.$$

This indicates that the firm returns $0.096 for every dollar invested in assets and $0.757 for every dollar invested by the common stockholders.

In addition to the return on total assets and return on equity, some financial analysts compute the return generated by operating income (earnings before interest and taxes, or EBIT). This ratio, which may be referred to as the basic earning power, is

Basic earning power

Ratio of operating income to total assets; measure of the firm's ability to generate income before considering interest and taxes

$$\text{Basic earning power} = \frac{\text{EBIT}}{\text{Total assets}}$$

and it measures what the firm earns on its assets independently of (1) how the assets were financed and (2) the taxes the firm has to pay. For Heinz, its basic earning power is

$$\text{Basic earning power} = \frac{\$1,571,685}{\$9,664,184} = 16.3\%,$$

which indicates that $1 of the firm's assets generates $0.163 in operating income (that is, income before paying interest and taxes).

This ratio may be particularly important to long-term creditors who are concerned with the capacity of management to generate earnings after meeting operating expenses. Since operating expenses are paid prior to debt service, the greater the basic earning power, the safer should be the creditors' interest payments.

Leverage Ratios

Debt/net worth ratio

Ratio of debt to equity; debt divided by equity

Among the more frequently computed ratios are leverage ratios, which measure the firm's use of debt financing. The two most commonly used ratios to measure financial leverage are (1) debt to equity, which is often referred to as the debt/net worth ratio, and (2) debt to total assets, which is commonly referred to as the debt ratio. These ratios are as follows:

Debt ratio

Total debt divided by total assets; proportion of assets financed by debt; a measure of financial leverage

$$\text{Debt/net worth ratio} = \frac{\text{Debt}}{\text{Equity}}$$

$$\text{Debt ratio} = \frac{\text{Debt}}{\text{Total assets}}$$

Because Heinz's total debt is $8,434,146 (that is, the sum of current liabilities and long-term debt), the values of these ratios are

$$\frac{\text{Debt}}{\text{Equity}} = \frac{\$8,434,146}{\$1,219,938} = 6.91.$$

$$\frac{\text{Debt}}{\text{Total assets}} = \frac{\$8,434,146}{\$9,664,184} = 87.3\%.$$

The debt-to-equity ratio indicates that there is $6.91 debt for every dollar of equity. The debt-to-assets ratio indicates that debt is financing 87.3 percent of the firm's assets.

Leverage ratios are aggregate ratios. They use total debt and do not differentiate between short-term and long-term debt. The debt-to-equity ratio uses total equity and does not differentiate between preferred and common stock financing. (If the firm has both preferred and common stock outstanding, you may define the debt-to-net-worth ratio as debt/common equity.) The debt-to-total-assets ratio uses total assets and does not differentiate between current and long-term assets.

You may disaggregate the data. For example, if the emphasis is on long-term debt financing, current liabilities may be removed so that the debt ratio becomes

$$\frac{\text{Long-term debt}}{\text{Total assets}}$$

This ratio indicates the extent to which long-term debt is financing the firm's assets.

For many purposes the use of aggregate numbers does not pose a problem, for the debt ratio is measuring the proportion of the total assets that creditors (both short- and long-term) are financing. The smaller the proportion of total assets that creditors are financing, the larger the decline in value of the assets that may occur without threatening the creditors' position. Leverage ratios thus give an indication of financial risk. Firms that have high leverage ratios are considered riskier, because there is less cushion to protect creditors if the value of the assets deteriorates. For example, the debt ratio for Heinz is 87.3 percent. This indicates that the value of the assets may decline by 12.7 percent (100% − 87.3%) before the equity is destroyed, leaving only enough assets to pay off the debt. If the debt ratio had been 30 percent, then a 70 percent decline in the value of the assets would endanger the creditors' position.

Leverage ratios are not only an indication of risk to creditors but also of risk to stockholders, for firms that are highly financially leveraged are riskier equity investments. If the value of the assets declines or if the firm should experience declining sales and losses, the equity is wiped out more quickly for financially leveraged firms than for unleveraged firms. Hence, leverage ratios are important indicators of risk for stockholders as well as for creditors.

EXHIBIT 9.6
Ratio of Total Debt to Total
Assets for Selected Firms

Industrial/Manufacturing	Debt Ratio
Textron	85.1%
Alcoa	67.6
Tupperware	64.4
Coca-Cola	48.0
Merck	47.3
Illinois Tool Works (ITW)	45.1

Source: 2009 annual reports and 10-K reports.

Leverage ratios differ significantly among firms. The debt ratios (debt to total assets) for several large companies are presented in Exhibit 9.6. The table has been arranged in descending order from the highest debt ratio to the lowest. The debt ratios calculated for Exhibit 9.6 use total debt. The ranking of the ratios may differ if only noncurrent debt is used. For example, the Coca-Cola Company debt ratio declines from 48.0 percent to only 19.7 percent if current liabilities are excluded from the calculation.

The ratios may also differ from debt ratios reported by the firms in their annual reports. For example, the management of the Coca-Cola Company uses a different definition of the leverage ratios: total debt to total capital. Total capital is defined as equity plus interest-bearing debt. Since interest-bearing debt excludes accruals and payables, that definition differs from either total assets used in the debt ratio or total equity used in the debt-to-equity ratio.

For the individual firm, there may exist an optimal proportion of debt to total assets. Finding this optimal capital structure of debt and equity financing is important to maximizing the value of a firm, and Chapter 13 discusses the optimal capital structure of a firm. It is sufficient for now to suggest that finding the optimal use of financial leverage may benefit the common stockholder by increasing the per share earnings of the company and permitting faster growth and larger dividends. If, however, the firm is too financially leveraged or *undercapitalized*, potential investors may be less willing to invest, and creditors will require a higher interest rate to compensate them for the increased risk. Thus, leverage ratios, which measure the use of financial leverage by the firm, are among the most important ratios that managers, creditors, and investors may calculate.

Several ratios may be combined to analyze a firm. One such technique is the DuPont system, which was designed by that firm's management to measure a firm's earning power. The system combines net profit margin, total asset turnover, and leverage to determine the return on the firm's equity. Essentially, the DuPont system determines the return on equity by multiplying three things: (1) the net profit margin, (2) total asset turnover, and (3) an equity multiplier (used to indicate the amount of leverage).

DuPont system

Measure of earning capacity that combines asset turnover, profitability, and financial leverage

The product of the net profit margin and total asset turnover determines the return on assets. That is,

$$\text{Return on assets} = \frac{\text{Net profits}}{\text{Sales}} \times \frac{\text{Sales}}{\text{Assets}} = \frac{\text{Net profit}}{\text{Assets}}$$

The product of the return on assets and the ratio of assets to equity (the equity multiplier) determines the return on equity. That is,

$$\text{Return on equity} = \frac{\text{Net profits}}{\text{Assets}} \times \frac{\text{Assets}}{\text{Equity}}$$

Thus, the DuPont system is

$$\text{Return on equity} = \frac{\text{Net profits}}{\text{Sales}} \times \frac{\text{Sales}}{\text{Assets}} \times \frac{\text{Assets}}{\text{Equity}} = \frac{\text{Net profits}}{\text{Equity}}$$

In the DuPont system, financial leverage is measured by the ratio of assets to equity (the equity multiplier mentioned earlier). This ratio is the reciprocal of the ratio of equity to total assets. Since the ratio of equity to total assets indicates the proportion of assets financed by equity, it is a measure of financial leverage. The smaller the proportion of assets financed by equity (or the larger the proportion of the assets financed by debt), the larger will be the ratio of assets to equity, and, for a given return on assets, the greater will be the return on equity.

The DuPont system is illustrated in Exhibit 9.7, which presents the general layout of the system and applies it to the financial statements of Heinz. While the end product of the system (the return on equity) is no different than the simple ratio of earnings to equity, the layout of the analysis facilitates locating internal sources of a firm's problems.

In addition to combining profitability, turnover, and leverage in one analysis, the system facilitates comparisons of firms in one industry with firms in different industries. Some firms, such as grocery stores, have rapid inventory turnover but small profit margins. These low profit margins may appear to indicate that the firms are not very profitable. Other firms, such as furniture stores, may have large profit margins but slow inventory turnover. If profit margins are considered in a vacuum, such firms appear to be very profitable. If these conclusions were true, owners of grocery stores would convert them to furniture stores. This does not occur, however, because the return on equity may be similar for both firms when profitability, turnover, and leverage are considered together. A furniture store may turn over its inventory only twice a year; thus, it has to have large profit margins to compensate for its low turnover. Both firms may earn the same return for their stockholders when profitability, turnover, and leverage are taken together, and the DuPont system does just that by integrating them in one analysis.

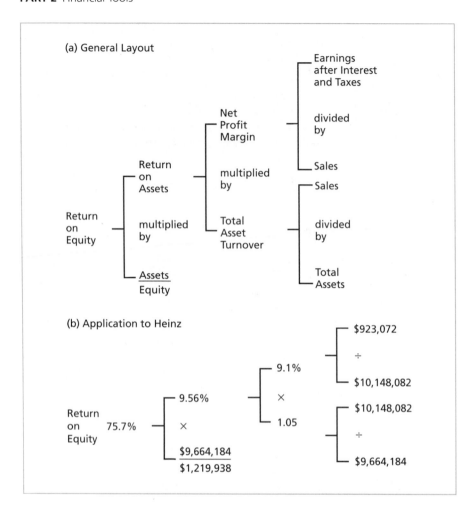

Coverage Ratios

In addition to the ratios previously covered in this chapter, the financial analyst may compute coverage ratios, which indicate the ability of the firm to service (to "cover") some payment, such as interest. All coverage ratios consider the funds available to meet a particular expense relative to that expense. The most common coverage ratio is times-interest-earned, which measures the ability of the firm to meet its interest obligations. That ratio is

**Times-interest-
earned**

Ratio of operating
income (EBIT) to inter-
est expense; measure
of the safety of a debt
instrument

$$\text{Times-interest-earned} = \frac{\text{Earnings before interest and taxes}}{\text{Annual interest charges}}$$

A ratio of 2 indicates that the firm has $2 in operating income for every $1 in interest expense. The numerator uses operating income (EBIT), since interest is paid after other expenses but before taxes. The higher the numerical value of the ratio, the safer should be the interest payment. For Heinz, the times-interest-earned ratio is

$$\text{Times-interest-earned} = \frac{\$1,571,685}{\$339,635} = 4.63.$$

This indicates that Heinz had operating income of $4.63 for every $1 in interest expense, which suggests that the firm should easily meet its interest obligations.

Ability to cover interest expense is important, for failure to meet interest payments as they come due may throw the firm into bankruptcy. Deterioration in the times-interest-earned ratio gives an early warning to creditors and investors, as well as to management, of a deteriorating financial position and an increased probability of default on interest payments.

Analysis of Financial Statements and the Internet

Several ratios have been defined and illustrated using H. J. Heinz Company's financial statements. An obvious question arises: How is this information used? A set of ratios by themselves has little meaning; there has to be some comparison. One possible comparison is to compute the ratios over time to determine changes in the firm's financial position (that is, to use time series analysis). You would compute the various ratios for a period such as five years to determine if the firm's performance or financial condition has changed.

An alternative approach employs competing or comparable firms (a cross-sectional analysis). An immediate problem arises. H. J. Heinz manufactures food products. Should it be compared to Campbell Soup or Tyson Foods, which manufacture *different* food products?

No matter which approach you select, you may have to compute many ratios. An alternative approach is to use the Internet. Several of the basic ratios covered in this chapter may be found via the Internet. See, for example, Yahoo! **http://finance.yahoo.com**, MSN Money **http://moneycentral.com,** and Motley Fool **http://www.fool.com**. You have only to enter the company's ticker symbol (HNZ for Heinz) to start the search.

You should, however, be forewarned that various sources do not necessarily provide the same ratios and that the numerical values for the same ratio may differ. The differences could be the result of the time periods used. One source may use the firm's last fiscal year (or last quarter) while an alternative source computes the ratios using the last 12 months (trailing 12 months or TTM). Different definitions of a particular ratio could also explain the numerical differences. For example, the return on equity could be earnings divided by total equity or earnings divided by common equity. Even if the definitions and time periods are the same, different data may be used in the calculations. For example, the net profit margin is earnings divided by sales. One source may use earnings that have not been adjusted for nonrecurring items while another source may use adjusted earnings.

These differences pose a problem for anyone using ratios from different sources to make comparisons. One obvious solution is for the individual to compute the ratios, in which case the definitions and time periods can be applied consistently. A more pragmatic method may be to select one source and use it exclusively. The choice could depend on which source provides the desired ratios. Some sources also provide comparisons of firms in the same industry or let the individual compare firms in different industries.

Summary   This chapter covered three essential financial statements. A balance sheet enumerates at a point in time what a firm owns (its assets), what it owes (its liabilities), and what owners have invested in a firm (its equity). An income statement enumerates a firm's revenues and expenses over a period of time and determines if a firm operated at a profit or for a loss. The statement of cash flows enumerates the flow of cash into and out of a firm over a period of time.

After a firm acquires fixed assets, they are depreciated, which is the allocation of the cost of plant and equipment over a period of time. Under straight-line depreciation, the same dollar amount is subtracted from revenues each year. Under accelerated depreciation, the initial cost of the investment is reduced more rapidly, for larger dollar amounts are subtracted during the early years of an investment's life. Thus, accelerated depreciation permits the cost of the investment to be written off faster, which initially reduces the firm's earnings and taxes. Since depreciation is a noncash expense, accelerated depreciation initially increases the cash flow from the investment. This increased cash flow may be reinvested to increase the profitability of the firm.

Rules for depreciation are established by Congress and the Internal Revenue Service. Since accelerated depreciation writes off an investment more rapidly and increases the cash flow generated by the investment, it encourages capital spending. By altering depreciation schedules, the federal government induces behavior consistent with the economic goals of full employment, stable prices, and economic growth.

Ratio analysis provides a convenient method to analyze a firm's financial statements, for the ratios are easily computed and readily permit comparisons. Since publicly held corporations must give financial information to stockholders, ratio analysis may be employed not only by management and creditors but also by stockholders.

Liquidity ratios measure the capacity of the firm to meet its current obligations as they come due. Activity ratios indicate how rapidly assets flow through the firm and how many assets are used to generate sales. Profitability ratios measure performance; leverage ratios indicate the use of debt financing; coverage ratios measure the capacity of the firm to make certain payments, such as interest. Once the ratios have been computed, the results may be compared over a series of years or compared with other firms within the industry. Such comparisons should help the analyst perceive the firm's position within the industry, as well as trends that are developing.

Review Objectives	Now that you have completed this chapter, you should be able to	

1. Define the basic components of a firm's balance sheet, income statement, and statement of cash flows (pp. 170–181).
2. Differentiate among assets, liabilities, revenues, expenses, income, cash, and retained earnings (pp. 170–176).
3. Enumerate the sources of several limitations to accounting data (pp. 181–183).
4. Compute and interpret the financial ratios covered in the chapter (pp. 189–205).
5. Illustrate the difference between cross-sectional and time series analysis (pp. 189–191 and 205–206).

Internet Assignments

1. Obtain the most recent financial statements of H. J. Heinz Company (HNZ) and update the ratios illustrated in the text. Have there been any changes in the firm's financial position as indicated by the ratios?
2. Use an Internet source and compare the profitability and leverage ratios for the following retail firms:
   1. Gap, Inc. (GPS)
   2. Limited Brands, Inc. (LTD)
   3. Pier 1 Imports (PIR)
   4. Target Corp. (TGT)
   5. Wal-Mart Stores (WMT)

   Rank the firms on the basis of (a) use of debt financing and (b) profitability.

Problems

1. Two firms have sales of $1 million each. Other financial information is as follows:

Firm	A	B
EBIT	$150,000	$150,000
Interest expense	20,000	75,000
Income tax	50,000	30,000
Debt	400,000	700,000
Equity	600,000	300,000

   What are the operating profit margins and the net profit margins for these two firms? What are their returns on assets and on equity? Why are they different?

2. Joseph Berio is a loan officer with the First Bank of Tennessee. Red Brick, Incorporated, a major producer of masonry products, has applied for a short-term loan. Red Brick supplies building material throughout the

southern states, with brick plants located in Tennessee, Alabama, Georgia, and Indiana.

Mr. Berio knows that brick production is affected by two factors: the cost of energy and the state of the building industry. First, manufacturing bricks uses a significant amount of energy. Red Brick, Inc. has recently converted many oil-fired kilns to coal kilns, which are cheaper to operate. To finance these conversions, the company has recently issued a substantial amount of long-term debt that must be retired over the next 25 years.

Second, brick sales are very sensitive to activity in the building industry, especially new housing starts. The industry frequently follows a pattern of boom and bust, with sales and earnings responding to changes in the demand for building products.

Currently the economy is experiencing a severe recession, and housing starts have fallen more than 40 percent from the previous year. While the south and southwest have not experienced such a severe decline, housing starts there have declined 25 percent.

Red Brick, Inc. has not been immune to the economic environment. Sales have declined, and although the firm has reduced production, inventory has increased. The firm needs the short-term loan to finance its inventory. Mr. Berio must decide whether to grant or deny the loan. Such loans have been made to Red Brick in the past and have always been repaid when the economic picture improved.

The firm's income statement and balance sheet are given in Exhibit 1. Exhibit 2 presents both a ratio analysis of Red Brick's previous year's financial statements and the industry averages of the ratios.

To help decide whether to grant the loan, Mr. Berio computes several ratios and compares the results with the ratios given in Exhibit 2.

a. What strengths and weaknesses are indicated by this analysis?

b. What may explain why the debt ratio exceeds the industry average? Is that necessarily a weakness in this case?

c. As a banker, is Mr. Berio more concerned with the firm's liquidity or its return on equity?

d. Based on the above analysis, should Mr. Berio grant the loan? Justify your position.

EXHIBIT 1
Income Statement
and Balance Sheet
for Red Brick

Red Brick Income Statement (for the period ending December 12/31/20X1)	
Sales	$210,000,000
Cost of goods sold	170,000,000
Administrative expenses	26,000,000
Operating income	$ 14,000,000
Interest expense	13,000,000
Taxes	400,000
Net income	$ 600,000

Red Brick Balance Sheet as of 12/31/20X2			
Assets		**Liabilities and Stockholders' Equity**	
Cash	$ 600,000	Accounts payable	$ 39,000,000
Accounts receivable	33,000,000*	Notes payable	11,000,000
Inventory	75,400,000†	Long-term debt	45,000,000
Plant and equipment	132,000,000	Stockholders' equity	146,000,000
	$241,000,000		$241,000,000

*90% of sales are on credit.
†Previous year's inventory was $52,000,000.

EXHIBIT 2
Selected Ratios for
Red Brick and Industry
Averages

	Company's Ratios (Previous Year)	Industry Average
Current ratio	4:1	2.2:1
Quick ratio	2:1	0.8:1
Inventory turnover	4.7×	4.6×
Average collection period	39 days	49 days
Debt ratio (debt/total assets)	39%	30%
Times-interest-earned	4.1	3.7
Return on equity	13.8%	14.1%
Return on assets	8.2%	10.2%
Operating profit margin	14.1%	15.2%
Net profit margin	8.8%	8.8%

3. You prefer to extend credit on the assumption that you will be paid in full within 30 days of the sales. Firm X has average inventory of $600,000 with all cash sales (no credit sales) of $6,000,000. If you extend credit to this firm, can you expect to be paid on time?

4. Assume Lasher's Kitchen has pretax earnings of $75,000 after depreciation expense of $15,000. If the firm's tax rate is 35 percent, what is its cash flow from operations?

5. Fill in the blanks (_____) with the correct entries.

Assets		**Liabilities and Stockholders' Equity**	
Current assets		Current liabilities	
Cash	$ 250,000	Accounts payable	$ 620,000

Accounts receivable (_____ less) allowance for doubtful accounts of $20,000)	1,320,000	Notes payable to banks	130,000
		Accrued wages	
		Taxes owed	100,000
Inventory	1,410,000	Total current liabilities	$1,250,000
Total current assets	_____		
Land	_____	Long-term debt	_____
Plant and equipment ($2,800,000 less accumulated depreciation _____)	2,110,000	Stockholders' equity Preferred stock Common stock ($1 par, 750,000 shares authorized, 700,000 outstanding)	1,000,000 _____
Total assets	$5,390,000	Retained earnings	_____
		Total stockholders' equity	$3,140,000
		Total liabilities and equity	_____

6. ABCD Corporation has credit sales of $10,640,000 and receivables of $1,520,000.

   a. What is the receivables turnover?

   b. What is the average collection period (days sales outstanding)?

   c. If the company offers credit terms of 30 days, are its receivables past due?

7. An asset costs $200,000 and is classified as a 10-year asset. What is the annual depreciation expense for the first three years under the straight-line and the modified accelerated cost recovery systems of depreciation?

8. Given the following information, construct the firm's balance sheet:

Cash and cash equivalents	$ 300,000
Accumulated depreciation on plant and equipment	800,000
Plant and equipment	5,800,000
Accrued wages	400,000
Long-term debt	4,200,000
Inventory	6,400,000

Accounts receivable	4,100,000
Preferred stock	500,000
Retained earnings	7,700,000
Land	1,000,000
Accounts payable	2,100,000
Taxes due	100,000
Common stock	$ 10 par
Common shares outstanding	150,000
Current portion of long-term debt	$ 300,000

9. From the following information, construct a simple income statement and a balance sheet:

Sales	$1,000,000
Finished goods	200,000
Long-term debt	300,000
Raw materials	100,000
Cash	50,000
Cost of goods sold	600,000
Accounts receivable	250,000
Plant and equipment	400,000
Interest expense	80,000
Number of shares outstanding	100,000
Earnings before taxes	220,000
Taxes	100,000
Accounts payable	200,000
Other current liabilities	50,000
Other expenses	100,000
Equity	450,000

10. If a corporation earns $270,000 and the payout ratio (proportion distributed) is 30 percent, what is the change in retained earnings?

11. A firm has earnings of $12,000 before interest, depreciation, and taxes. A new piece of equipment is installed at a cost of $10,000. The equipment will be depreciated over five years, and the firm pays 25 percent of its earnings in taxes. What are the earnings and cash flows for the firm

in years 2 and 5, using the two methods of depreciation discussed in the chapter? What is the source of the difference in earnings and cash flow?

12. If a firm has the following sources of finance,

Current liabilities	$100,000
Long-term debt	350,000
Preferred stock	75,000
Common stock	225,000

earns a profit of $35,000 after taxes, and pays $7,500 in preferred stock dividends, what is the return on assets, the return on total equity, and the return on common equity?

13. If a firm has sales of $25,689,000 a year, and the average collection period for the industry is 45 days, what should this firm's accounts receivable be if the firm is comparable to the industry?

14. Given the following information, compute the current and quick ratios:

Cash	$100,000
Accounts receivable	357,000
Inventory	458,000
Current liabilities	498,000
Long-term debt	610,000
Equity	598,000

15. A firm with sales of $500,000 has average inventory of $200,000. The industry average for inventory turnover is four times a year. What would be the reduction in inventory if this firm were to achieve a turnover comparable to the industry average?

16. A firm with annual sales of $8,700,000 increases its inventory turnover from 4.5 to 6.0. How much would the company save annually in interest expense if the cost of carrying the inventory is 10 percent?

Additional Problem with Answers

This chapter illustrated the computation of financial ratios that appear throughout this text using H. J. Heinz Company financial statements for 2009. Simplified Heinz balance sheet and income statement for 2010 are provided below. Compute the ratios in this chapter and compare the results to those in the chapter. Does it appear that the firm's financial condition has improved or deteriorated?

H. J. Heinz Company Consolidated Balance Sheet (in millions)	
As of the end of the fiscal year	2010
Assets	
Current assets	
Cash and cash equivalents	$ 483.3
Receivables (net of allowances)	1,045.3
Inventories	1,249.1
Other current assets	273.4
Total current assets	3,051.1
Property, plant, and equipment	
Land	77.2
Buildings	842.3
Equipment	3,546.0
Less accumulated depreciation	2,373.8
Total property, plant, and equipment	2,091.7
Other noncurrent assets (goodwill, trademarks, and intangibles)	4,932.8
Total assets	$ 10,075.6
Liabilities and Shareholders' Equity	
Current liabilities	
Short-term debt	$43.6
Long-term debt due within a year	151.7
Accounts payable	1,007.5
Other accrued liabilities	972.6
Total current liabilities	2,175.4
Long-term liabilities	
Long-term debt	4,559.2
Deferred taxes	665.1
Other long-term liabilities	727.6
Total long-term liabilities	5,951.9
Shareholders' equity	1,891.3
Total liabilities and shareholders' equity	$10,075.6

H. J. Heinz Company Statement of Income	
For the fiscal year ending April	2010
Sales	$10,495.0
Cost of products sold	6,700.7
Gross profit	3,794.3
Selling and administrative expense	2,350.8
Operating income	1,443.5
Other income	(18.2)
Earnings before interest and taxes	1,425.3
Interest expense	295.2
Taxes	358.5
Net income	$ 882.3
Earnings per common share	$ 2.73
Cash dividends per share	$ 1.68

Source: Adapted from H. J. Heinz Company, *Annual Report*, 2010.

Answers

	2010	2009
1. Liquidity ratios:		
Current ratio:		
$\dfrac{\text{Current assets}}{\text{Current liabilities}}$	$\dfrac{\$3,051.1}{\$2,175.4} = 1.40$	1.43
Quick ratio:		
$\dfrac{\text{Current assets} - \text{inventory}}{\text{Current liabilities}}$	$\dfrac{\$3,051.1 - 1,249.1}{\$2,175.4} = 0.83$	0.83
2. Activity ratios		
Inventory turnover:		
$\dfrac{\text{Annual sales}}{\text{Average inventory}}$	$\dfrac{\$10,495}{(\$1,249.1 + 1,237.6)/2} = 8.4$	7.8
Receivables turnover:		
$\dfrac{\text{Annual sales}}{\text{Accounts receivable}}$	$\dfrac{\$10,495}{\$1,045.3} = 10.0$	8.7
Days sales outstanding:		
$\dfrac{\text{Receivables}}{\text{Sales per day}}$	$\dfrac{\$1,045.3}{\$10,495/365} = 36.4$	42.0
Fixed asset turnover:		
$\dfrac{\text{Annual sales}}{\text{Fixed assets}}$	$\dfrac{\$10,495}{\$2,091.7} = 5.0$	5.1

Total asset turnover:

$$\frac{\text{Annual sales}}{\text{Total assets}} \qquad \frac{\$10,495}{\$10,076} = 1.04 \qquad 1.05$$

3. Profitability ratios

Gross profit margin:

$$\frac{\text{Sales} - \text{Cost of goods sold}}{\text{Sales}} \qquad \frac{\$10,495 - 6,701}{\$10,495} = 56.67 \qquad 35.3\%$$

Operating profit margin:

$$\frac{\text{Operating earnings}}{\text{Sales}} \qquad \frac{\$1,425.3}{\$10,495} = 13.87 \qquad 15.5\%$$

Net profit margin:

$$\frac{\text{Earnings after taxes}}{\text{Sales}} \qquad \frac{\$882.3}{\$10,495} = 8.4\% \qquad 9.1\%$$

Return on assets:

$$\frac{\text{Earnings after taxes}}{\text{Total assets}} \qquad \frac{\$882.3}{\$10,076} = 8.8\% \qquad 9.6\%$$

Return on equity:

$$\frac{\text{Earnings after taxes}}{\text{Equity}} \qquad \frac{\$882.3}{\$1,891.3} = 46.7\% \qquad 75.7\%$$

4. Leverage ratios

Debt/net worth:

$$\frac{\text{Debt}}{\text{Equity}} \qquad \frac{\$2,175,4 + 5,951.9}{\$1,891.3} = 4.3 \qquad 6.9\%$$

Debt ratio:

$$\frac{\text{Debt}}{\text{Total assets}} \qquad \frac{\$8.127.3}{\$10,075} = 0.81\% \qquad 0.87\%$$

5. Coverage ratios

Times-interest-earned:

$$\frac{\text{Earnings before interest and taxes}}{\text{Annual interest expense}} \qquad \frac{\$1,425.3}{\$295.3} = 4.8 \qquad 4.6$$

Heinz's ratios indicate little change between 2009 and 2010. Receivables and inventory turned over somewhat faster in 2010, but profitability based on the net profit margin, return on assets, and return on equity was lower. Generally a firm's ratios are stable from one year to the next as they are in this illustration. If, however, the ratios consistently move in one direction, a fundamental change may have occurred. This suggests that financial managers and financial analysts should seek to determine the cause and significance of any change.

Relationships

1. The sale of a fixed asset for more than its book value _____ taxes owed.

2. Increased depreciation expense _____ return on equity.

3. Collecting an account receivable _____ the debt ratio.

4. An increase in depreciation expense _____ earnings and _____ cash flow.

5. Operating at a loss _____ the debt ratio.

6. If a firm's current ratio increases, the firm's liquidity position _____.

7. An increase in taxes _____ the coverage ratio times-interest-earned.

8. A decrease in debt _____ on days sales outstanding.

9. Increased use of trade credit (accounts payable) to acquire inventory _____ days sales outstanding.

10. If a firm sells plant for less than its book value, total asset turnover _____ and return on equity _____.

11. Earnings that are not distributed as dividends (i.e., are retained) _____ equity.

12. Collecting an account receivable _____ return on assets.

13. The use of the modified accelerated cost recovery system of depreciation (MACRS) instead of straight-line depreciation initially _____ the return on equity.

14. Increasing the firm's cash _____ fixed asset turnover.

15. Selling inventory for a loss _____ the quick ratio.

16. An increase in interest expense _____ the firm's operating profit margin.

17. If a firm repurchases shares, total asset turnover _____.

18. The return on equity _____ if inventory is sold for a loss.

19. An increase in long-term debt such as selling bonds _____ the quick ratio.

20. Buying inventory with credit (accounts payable) _____ total asset turnover.

Answers

1. increases
2. decreases
3. does not affect (no change)
4. decreases; increases
5. increases
6. increases
7. does not affect (no change)
8. has no impact (no change)
9. has no impact on (no change)
10. increases; decreases
11. increase
12. does not affect (no change)
13. decreases
14. does not affect (no change)
15. increases
16. does not affect (no change)
17. increases
18. decreases
19. increases
20. decreases

Corporate Finance

I n 2010, ExxonMobil (XOM) had assets of $233,323,000,000. Imagine managing that many assets! PetMed Express (PETS) had assets of $104,200,000 (.045 percent of ExxonMobil's assets). Someone also had to be responsible for the management of PetMed Express's assets, and the financial managers of both ExxonMobil and PetMed Express must find financing to carry their respective firms' assets.

Although managing these firms' assets is important, it may have little impact on you or me (unless we work for either firm). Financing these assets, however, may have an impact on us. It is the savings of individuals, other firms, and governments that form the source of finance that permits ExxonMobil and PetMed Express to acquire their assets. The well-being of our investments may very much be affected by the management of these firms' assets. Even if we don't directly invest in either firm, we may own shares in mutual funds or pension plans that do invest in ExxonMobil or PetMed Express.

Parts 1 and 2, (and Part 4, to come) of this text cover areas in finance that touch the lives of everyone: financial institutions and the individual's investments. This section is devoted to financial management from the business perspective. While few individuals may become financial managers, many may have contact with specific components of corporate finance (for example, how ExxonMobil finances its assets). And, of course, an individual who becomes an entrepreneur and operates his or her own business will be facing many of the same decisions required of the corporate financial manager but without the specialists available in any large corporation!

The chapters in Part 3 cover a variety of corporate financial decisions: the management of short- and long-term assets, how these assets should be financed, which combination of debt and equity funds is optimal, how to plan when the firm will need finance, how to analyze the firm's performance, and whether the firm should grow through investments in plant and equipment. Financial decisions permeate virtually all business decisions, since most business decisions have financial implications. Thus, it is desirable for nonfinance students to be aware of the components of financial decision making. Such knowledge should facilitate individuals' communicating and advancing within the business community.

CHAPTER 10

Forms of Business and Corporate Taxation

The remainder of this text covers basic financial management from a business perspective. While the topics apply to all firms, they are most applicable to corporations with sufficient resources to do the analysis. If, however, you are contemplating starting your own business, much of this material will apply to your operation. Knowledge of the material in the next 10 chapters should increase your ability to manage the business profitably.

This chapter is a brief review of the forms of business and corporate taxation. If you have previously learned this material, please move on to the next chapter, which covers the first tools used to help make business financial decisions.

Sole Proprietorships, Partnerships, and Corporations

Most businesses can be classified as either sole proprietorship, partnership, or corporation. (Other forms of business include syndications, trusts, and joint stock companies.) By far the largest is the sole proprietorship. According to the U.S. Economic Census, there were 17,176,000 sole proprietorships but only 1,759,000 partnerships and 4,710,000 corporations. (Census data are available at the U.S. Census Bureau's Web site, **http://www.census.gov.**) Corporations, however, generated the most revenues ($15,890 billion) and profits ($915 billion) while sole proprietorships had revenues of $870 billion and profits of $187 billion. Obviously, corporations own the majority of the nation's productive capacity, generate most of the sales, and earn most of the profits. Sole proprietorships are primarily "ma and pa" operations that are limited to small businesses like the corner store. However, many large corporations had modest beginnings, and American business is filled with stories of a talented person building a small business into an industrial leader.

Sole proprietorship

Firm with one owner

A sole proprietorship, as the name implies, has one owner. The firm may employ other people and may borrow money, but the sole proprietor bears the risk of ownership and reaps the profits if they are earned. These are important elements of a sole proprietorship, for the firm has no existence without its proprietor. The firm is not a legal entity that can be held responsible for its actions. The sole proprietor is responsible for the firm's actions and is legally liable for the firm's debts. Sole proprietors bear the risk of ownership, and this risk is not limited to their personal investments. They can lose more than the money invested in their businesses, because the sole proprietor can be held liable for the debts incurred to operate the business. However, since the sole proprietorship is not a legal entity, the firm pays no income taxes. Any profits are considered to be income for the sole proprietor and are subject only to personal income taxation.

Partnership

Firm formed by two or more individuals, each of whom is liable for the firm's debts

A partnership is similar to a proprietorship except that there are at least two owners (or partners) of the business. While a partnership may have as few as two owners, there is no limit to the number of partners. A partnership has no life without its partners. The partners are the owners, and they reap the rewards and bear the risks of ownership. Each of the partners contributes something to the firm, and this contribution need not be money. For example, several partners may contribute funds while others contribute expertise.

The rights and obligations of the partners are established when the partnership is formed. The most important of these are the partners' shares of profits and the extent of their liability. In the simplest case, each partner contributes some percentage of the funds necessary to run the business and receives this percentage of the profits. However, not all partnership agreements are this simple. For example, if one partner contributes cash and the other contributes expertise, the division of profits may not be 50–50. Instead, the distribution will be mutually established by the partners.

When forming a partnership, it is important to have a written agreement that spells out the rights and duties of each partner. In general, all the partners bear the risk of enterprise. Each partner is liable for the total debt of the firm, so the individual partner's liability is not limited to his or her contribution to the business. While creditors initially seek settlement of claims from the firm, they can sue the partners for payment if the firm fails to meet the claims. If one partner is unable to pay the prorated share of these obligations, the other partners are liable for these debts. In addition, a partner's share in the firm may be seized to settle personal debts. While the creditors must initially sue the individual for personal obligations, if these cannot be met the creditors then have a claim on the partnership. These claims and counterclaims may be complex, but the general order is that personal creditors have an initial claim on the partners' personal assets, and the firm's creditors have the initial claim on the partnership's assets. If personal assets are insufficient to meet the individual's obligations, creditors may make a claim against that partner's share of the partnership. If the firm's assets are insufficient, the partnership's creditors may make claims against the individual partners.

Limited partnership

Partnership in which some of the partners have limited liability and are not liable for the partnership's debts

There is a type of partnership that grants limited liability to certain partners. These partnerships are called limited partnerships; in these, the limited

Limited liability

Individual's personal liability extending only to his or her investment in the firm

Corporation

Economic unit created by a state, having the power to own assets, incur liabilities, and engage in specific activities

Charter

Document specifying the relationship between a firm and the state in which the firm is incorporated

Bylaws

Document specifying the relationship between a corporation and its stockholders

partners are liable only for their contributions. While these partners have limited liability, they have no control over the operation of the firm. Such control rests with the remaining (or general) partners, who have unlimited liability. This form of partnership is popular for risky types of enterprises, such as oil and gas drilling operations, prospecting and mining, and real estate. Shares in several limited partnerships (for example, Kinder Morgan Energy Partners LP [KMP]) trade on the New York Stock Exchange. These partnerships are analogous to mutual funds, since neither pays income tax. The partnerships distribute earnings to the partners, who are responsible for the appropriate tax.

A corporation is an artificial, legal economic unit established by a state. Every corporation must be incorporated in a state. Variations in the individual state laws have caused some states to become more popular than others for forming a corporation. Under the state laws, the firm is issued a certificate of incorporation that gives the name, the location of the principal office, the purpose, and the number of shares of stock (shares of ownership) that are authorized (that is, the number of shares that the firm may issue). In addition to the certificate of incorporation, the firm receives a charter that specifies the relationship between the corporation and the state. At the initial meeting of stockholders, bylaws are established that set the rules by which the firm is governed (for example, the voting rights of the stockholders).

In the eyes of the law, a corporation is a legal entity that is separate from its owners. It may enter contracts and is legally responsible for its obligations. This significantly differentiates corporations from sole proprietorships and partnerships. Once a firm incorporates, the owners of the corporation are liable only for the amount of their investment in the company. Owners of corporations have "limited liability," and this limited liability is a major advantage of incorporating. Creditors may sue the corporation for payment if the corporation defaults on its obligations, but the creditors cannot sue the stockholders.

For many small corporations, however, limited liability does not exist. Creditors often ask that the stockholders pledge their personal assets to secure a small corporation's loans. Thus, if the corporation defaults, the creditors may seize assets that the shareholders have pledged. If this occurs, the liability of the shareholders is not limited to their initial investment. Limited liability does apply in substance to large corporations that have assets to pledge or sufficient credit ratings to receive unsecured loans. Thus, an investor knows that on purchasing the stock in a corporation such as IBM or Merck, the maximum amount that can be lost is the amount of the investment. If the firm goes bankrupt, the creditors cannot seize the assets of the stockholders. Such limited liability is a major advantage of incorporating a firm, for large corporations (for example, United Airlines and Enron) do go bankrupt.

A second advantage of incorporating is permanence. Since the corporation is established by the laws of the state, it is permanent until dissolved by the state. Proprietorships and partnerships cease when one of the owners dies or goes bankrupt. The partnership must be re-formed in order to continue to operate. Corporations, however, continue to exist when one of the owners dies. The stock becomes part of the deceased owner's estate and is transferred to the heirs. The company continues to operate, and a new corporation is not formed. Permanence offers a major advantage for incorporating if the owners envision the firm growing in size and operating for many years, since the expense of re-forming the relationship among the owners is avoided.

A third potential advantage of incorporation is the ease with which title of ownership may be transferred from one investor to another. All that is necessary for such transfer is for the investor to sell the shares of stock (which are evidence of ownership) and have the name of the new owner recorded on the corporation's record of stockholders. Such transfers occur daily through organized securities exchanges like the New York Stock Exchange.

Incorporating may also offer the company the advantage of being able to raise large sums of money by issuing bonds and stock. Limited liability for stockholders, the potential for capital gains, and the existence of secondary markets in which the securities can be bought or sold are advantages associated with incorporating that do not exist for the unincorporated firm. Corporations like IBM can issue new bonds or stock to raise capital. Even companies with lower credit ratings may be able to raise funds by issuing new securities even though they will have to pay a higher rate of interest to induce investors to buy the securities.

S Corporations and Limited Liability Companies (LLC)

One option that stockholders of small corporations may elect permits them to have the advantages associated with corporations (such as permanence, limited liability, and ease of transfer) without the disadvantage of double taxation (the taxation of corporate income and the subsequent taxation of dividends received by the stockholders). If a corporation has 35 or fewer stockholders, the firm may elect to be taxed as an S corporation. If the firm does elect to be taxed as an S corporation, its income is not subject to federal corporate income taxation. Instead, the firm's earnings are taxed as income to its stockholders. Thus, the tax treatment is the same as for partnership or sole proprietorship income.

S corporation

Corporation that is taxed as if it were a partnership

While electing S corporate status circumvents the problem of double taxation, it also means that the individual stockholders are responsible for the appropriate income taxes. This taxation applies even if the corporation does not distribute its earnings as dividends. If the firm retains earnings for reinvestment, the stockholders have to pay taxes on the undistributed earnings. If management desires to retain earnings to finance future growth, the election to be taxed as an S corporation would be the incorrect decision. The firm would be better off having its earnings taxed at the corporate level and retaining (not distributing) its earnings.

An alternative to the S corporation is the limited liability company (LLC), which is a new form of business that has grown in popularity since it received favorable tax treatment from the IRS. Such companies may qualify for tax purposes to be treated as partnerships; that is, there is no income tax at the firm level. Income (or loss) flows through to the owners, who pay the appropriate federal income tax. Although both LLCs and S corporations are not taxed at the firm level, they are different. An S corporation can have no more than 35 stockholders, who must be U.S. citizens or resident aliens. LLCs are not subject to this limitation. Foreign investors, corporations, or partnerships may own stock in an LLC.

LLCs also offer the advantage of limited liability. The owners of the LLC are not liable for the debts of the company. While such limited liability applies to limited partnerships, there are important differences between LLCs and limited partnerships. The latter must have at least one general partner who manages the firm and is responsible for its debts. LLCs do not have this constraint. Owners of the firm may actively participate in its management and not be personally liable.

Corporate Taxation

Sole proprietorships and partnerships are not subject to income taxes. Earnings generated by these firms flow through to the owners, who pay the appropriate income taxes. Many corporations, however, are subject to taxation by various levels of government. Income, capital gains, and even property may be subject to taxation. This discussion is limited to the federal corporate income tax.

As of January 2010, the federal corporate tax structure was as follows:

Taxable Corporate Income	Marginal Tax Rate
$0–50,000	15%
$50,001–75,000	25
$75,001–100,000	34
$100,001–335,000	39
$335,001–10,000,000	34
$10,000,001–15,000,000	35
$15,000,001–18,333,333	38
over $18,333,333	35

If a corporation earns $40,000, the tax is

$$\$40,000 \times 0.15 = \$6,000.$$

If the earnings are $70,000, the income tax is

$$(\$50,000 \times 0.15) + (\$20,000 \times 0.25) = \$12,500.$$

The tax is computed on the income in both tax brackets and the two amounts are summed. That is, $50,000 is taxed at 15 percent and the remaining $20,000 is taxed at 25 percent, so the total tax owed is $12,500.

If the firm earns $200,000, the tax is

$$(\$50,000 \times 0.15) + (\$25,000 \times 0.25) + (\$25,000 \times 0.34)$$
$$+ (\$100,000 \times 0.39) = \$61,250.$$

Notice that as corporate income rises, the tax rate rises to 35 percent, but there are income levels taxed at 39 and 38 percent. The 39 percent tax bracket recaptures the benefits of the lower 15 and 25 percent brackets. The 38 percent tax bracket recaptures the benefit of the 34 percent bracket. Once corporate income exceeds $18,333,333, *all* corporate income is taxed at 35 percent.

Under this tax structure, the maximum rate applies to virtually all corporations of significant size. Certainly for publicly held firms, an investor should view corporate income taxes as approximately one-third of earnings before taxes. If the corporation's tax rate is lower, the investor may ask why. A current lower tax rate can suggest a temporary tax aberration such as tax loss carried forward (covered in the next section). Such temporary benefits may not continue in the future, so that lower current taxes could imply higher taxes and lower after-tax earnings in the future.

Taxation of Corporate Losses

Not all corporations are profitable. Some operate at a loss, and this loss, like earnings, has tax consequences. All firms must report earnings and pay appropriate income taxes each fiscal year. But a firm operates for many years, during which it may operate at a loss for some years and generate earnings during other years. The federal corporate tax laws permit losses from one year to offset earnings from profitable years, so that over a number of years, it is the firm's net earnings after losses that are taxed and not just the earnings in profitable years.

If a corporation operates at a loss during the current fiscal year, the loss is carried back to offset income earned in the previous years. (The corporation may elect to carry the loss forward, which may be desirable if management expects to be in a higher tax bracket in the future.) If the loss is carried back, the corporation receives a refund for previously paid taxes. If any loss remains because the total loss exceeded the earnings of the previous years, the remaining loss is carried forward for up to 15 years to offset future earnings. In this case, the carry forward of the loss erases future taxes.

The impact of the carry-back and carry-forward of losses may be seen by considering the following illustrations. In each case the corporation has a loss in the current year (that is, year 4). The corporate income tax rate is assumed to be 30 percent. The carry-back is assumed to be three years. (The laws concerning carry-back and carry-forward are often changed by Congress and the IRS. For current regulations, consult the IRS Web site: **www.irs.gov**.) The loss in year 4 of $1,000 is used to offset the total earnings in years 1 and 2, and $200 of the earnings in year 3. Thus, the $120 in taxes paid in each of years 1 and 2 and $60 of the taxes paid for year 3 are refunded in year 4. The $1,000 loss in year 4 recaptures the taxes paid in years 1 and 2 and part of year 3's taxes.

	Year					
Case A	**1**	**2**	**3**	**4**	**5**	**6**
Earnings	$400	400	400	(1,000)	400	400
Taxes	$ 120	120	120	0	120	120
(Tax refund)				($300)		
Net taxes paid (after refund)	0	0	$ 60	0	120	120

Two important points need to be made. First, notice that the loss is initially used against year 1's income. If that income does not exhaust the loss, the residual is carried to year 2 to offset that year's income. Once again if the earnings do not exhaust the loss, the residual is carried to year 3. The loss is carried forward to years 5, 6, and so on only if it exceeds the sum of the earnings in years 1, 2, and 3. Second, notice that the loss is used first against year 1's and not against year 3's income. The loss is carried back three years and then any remaining loss is moved forward.

	Year						
Case B	**1**	**2**	**3**	**4**	**5**	**6**	**7**	**8**
Earnings	$400	400	400	(1,500)	—	—	—	—
Taxes	$ 120	120	120	0	—	—	—	—
(Tax refund)				($360)				
Net taxes paid (after refund)	0	0	0	0				

In case B, the loss in year 4 exceeds the combined earnings of years 1 through 3 (the $1,500 loss versus the $1,200 combined earnings), so the remaining $300 loss will be carried forward to offset income earnings in subsequent years. The entire $360 previously paid in taxes will be refunded, and the corporation will not have to pay corporate federal income tax on the next $300 of earnings. Of course, this future tax savings depends on the firm's generating future earnings, and in this illustration there are, as of now, no future earnings, so this potential tax saving may be lost.

	Year						
Case C	**1**	**2**	**3**	**4**	**5**	**6**	**7**	**8**
Earnings	—	—	—	($1,500)	400	600	800	1,000
Taxes	—	—	—	0	$120	180	240	300
(Tax refund)	—	—	—	—	($120)	(180)	(200)	—
Net taxes paid (after refund)	—	—	—	0	0	0	$40	300

In case C, the firm had no earnings or losses in the first three years, so the entire $1,500 loss is carried forward. The order of carry-forward is chronological, so the entire $400 profit in year 5 is offset as are the earnings of $600 in year 6. The earnings in years 5 and 6 are offset by only $1,000 of year 4's $1,500 loss. The remaining $500 is used to partially offset the $800 earned in year 7. After year 7, however, the entire loss has been used to offset income, so any income earned in year 8 ($1,000) will be subject to federal corporate income tax.

Summary
Most firms are sole proprietorships, partnerships, or corporations. The differences among them are related to the number of owners, permanence of the business, ease of transferring ownership, owners' liability, and taxation. The development of S corporations and limited liability companies (LLCs) has blurred the distinctions between corporations and other forms of business.

In terms of revenues and earnings, corporations are the most important form of business. Corporations are established in a state and receive a charter from the state that specifies the relationship between the state and the corporation. The relationship between the company and its owners (stockholders) is specified in the bylaws. The advantages associated with large publicly held corporations includes permanence, ease of transfer of ownership, and limited liability.

Businesses are subject to taxation by federal and state governments. Federal corporate income tax rates rise to 35 percent as the firm's taxable income increases. If the corporation operates at a loss, the loss may be carried back three years to offset earnings that were previously taxed. This carry-back results in the corporation receiving a tax refund. If the previous three years' income are more than offset by the loss, any remaining loss is carried forward to offset future earnings. This carry-forward may be extended up to 15 years; however, for the loss carry-forward to produce tax savings, the corporation must generate earnings in the future.

Review Objectives
Now that you have completed this chapter, you should be able to

1. Enumerate the differences and similarities among the forms of business (pp. 220–224).

2. Calculate the amount of taxes owed given an amount of taxable income (p. 224).

3. Calculate the tax refund for a given loss (pp. 225–227).

Problems
1. Given the following information, what is the corporation's federal tax obligation?

Taxable income:	$2,000
Taxable income:	$65,000
Taxable income:	$1,000,000
Taxable income:	$50,000,000

2. Over the last five years, corporation A has been consistently profitable. Its earnings before taxes were as follows:

Year	1	2	3	4	5
Earnings	$1,000	3,000	4,300	5,200	4,400

a. If the corporate tax rate was 25 percent, what were the firm's income taxes for each year?

b. Unfortunately, in year 6 the firm experienced a major decline in sales, which resulted in a loss of $10,800. What impact will the loss have on the firm's taxes for each year if the permitted carryback is two years?

Additional Problems with Answers

1. What are the 2010 corporate income tax obligations of the following companies, given their earnings?

Corporation A	$ 75,000
Corporation B	500,000
Corporation C	(2,000)

2. Over a period of years the earnings of Linvale's Fruit, Inc. have fluctuated, as may be seen in the following table. If the firm's tax rate is 20 percent, what are the taxes paid, taxes refunded, and loss carryforward for each year?

Year	1	2	3	4	5
Earnings	$1,000	(2,000)	1,500	3,000	(2,000)

Answers 1. Corporation A owes $50,000(0.15) + $25,000(0.25) = $13,750.

Corporation B owes $50,000(0.15) + $25,000(0.25) + $25,000 (0.34) + 235,000(0.39) + 165,000(0.34) = $170,000.

Corporation C operated at a loss and has no corporate income tax obligation.

2.

Year	1	2	3	4	5
Earnings	$1,000	(2,000)	1,500	3,000	(2,000)
Taxes paid	$ 200	0	100	600	0
Taxes refunded	0	200	0	0	400
Tax loss carried forward	0	1,000	0	0	0

Notice that the $2,000 losses in years 2 and 5 produced different results. In year 2, the loss offset earnings of $1,000 in the previous year, and the $1,000 balance was carried forward, so only $500 in earnings was taxed. In year 5, the $2,000 loss offsets $500 in income from year 3 and $1,500 from year 4. Year 3 income had been previously reduced by the $1,000 carry-forward from year 2, so the year 5 loss only had to offset $500. Since the year 5 loss offsets income from years 3 and 4, there is no carry-forward to year 6.

CHAPTER 11

Break-Even Analysis and the Payback Period

Management needs methods for selecting long-term investments in plant and equipment. These techniques can range from the simple to the complex. This chapter covers two variations on a simple method for making investment decisions. In both cases the emphasis is on avoiding losses. The first, referred to as break-even analysis, asks how much output must be produced in order to cover all costs, that is, to break even. The second, referred to as the payback period, asks how quickly will the firm recoup the cost of an investment.

Notice that neither technique considers earnings, and neither considers the time necessary to achieve breaking even and recovering the costs. Since the emphasis is solely on covering all costs, it would be possible to select an investment that is never profitable.

For large firms, these techniques are not acceptable. For the management of a small company, this analysis is better than no analysis and may be acceptable on pragmatic grounds. At least determining the level of output necessary to avoid losses and how long it will take to recover the costs of an investment tells management some basic, useful information. While the analysis cannot determine whether a decision will generate earnings, it does help management decide which new products should be developed and what markets should be entered. If a new product's forecasted level of sales cannot break even, production should not proceed! If an investment requires many years to recoup its costs, management may not proceed but will devote the firm's scarce resources elsewhere.

Break-Even Analysis

Break-even analysis

Technique used to determine that level of output at which total expenses equal total revenues (resulting in neither profits nor losses)

Break-even analysis determines the level of sales that generates neither profits nor losses and hence causes the firm to "break even." Break-even analysis also permits management to see the effects on the level of profits of (1) fluctuations in sales, (2) fluctuations in costs, and (3) changes in fixed costs relative to variable costs. Break-even analysis is based on the following three mathematical relationships: the relationship between (1) output and total revenues (sales), (2) output and variable costs of production, and (3) output and fixed costs of production.

The relationship between output and total revenues (TR) is the number of units sold (Q) times the price (P) for each unit. This may be expressed as a simple equation: Total revenue equals price times quantity sold. In symbolic form this equation is expressed as follows:

$$TR = P \times Q. \tag{11.1}$$

The larger the number of units that are sold at a given price, the larger the firm's total revenue. This relationship is illustrated in the first three columns of Exhibit 11.1, which presents the costs and revenues of a firm used in break-even analysis. The first column gives the price of the product and the second column the quantity sold. Multiplying these two gives the total revenue in the third column. For example, since the per-unit price is $2.00, the total revenue for a level of sales of 1,000 units is $2,000.

In Figure 11.1, total revenue is illustrated as a straight line that runs through the origin, for at zero units of output there can be no revenues. As

EXHIBIT 11.1
Relationships between Output and Revenues, Output and Costs, and Output and Profits

1 P	2 Q	3 TR	4 FC	5 V	6 VC	7 TC	8 Profits (losses)
$2	$ 0	$ 0	$1,000	$1	$ 0	$1,000	($1,000)
2	200	400	1,000	1	200	1,200	(800)
2	400	800	1,000	1	400	1,400	(600)
2	600	1,200	1,000	1	600	1,600	(400)
2	800	1,600	1,000	1	800	1,800	(200)
2	1,000	2,000	1,000	1	1,000	2,000	0
2	1,200	2,400	1,000	1	1,200	2,200	200
2	1,400	2,800	1,000	1	1,400	2,400	400
2	1,600	3,200	1,000	1	1,600	2,600	600
2	1,800	3,600	1,000	1	1,800	2,800	800
2	2,000	4,000	1,000	1	2,000	3,000	1,000

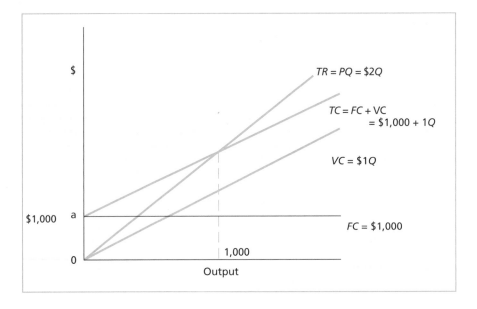

output is increased, total revenue increases. The rate at which total revenue increases (the slope of the line) is the price of the output. This rate is constant, for each additional unit of output is assumed to be sold at the given price.

Costs of production are divided into two classes: (1) costs that vary with production, such as labor expense; and (2) costs that do not vary with output, such as administrative expense or interest charges. This classification of costs is arbitrary, for fixed costs may become variable, and variable costs may become fixed. For example, a company may change its management personnel and change its fixed administrative expense. Union contracts may convert some variable costs into fixed costs. For example, a union contract may require severance pay. The firm may then be reluctant to lay off workers, and thus the labor cost becomes fixed and independent of the level of output. These qualifications make the actual classification of costs into fixed and variable more difficult, but they do not invalidate the concept that some costs are fixed and independent of the level of output, while other costs vary with the level of output.

Fixed costs (FC) do not vary with the level of output, which may be expressed by the following simple equation:

Fixed costs

Those costs that do not vary with the level of output

$$\text{Fixed costs} = \text{Constant.} \tag{11.2}$$

In Exhibit 11.1, the fourth column gives the fixed costs of operation. These fixed costs are $1,000 whether the firm produces 10 or 100 units of output. The relationship between output and fixed costs is shown in Figure 11.1 as a horizontal line (FC) that crosses the y-axis at a, the fixed dollar amount ($1,000). The line FC has no slope, because fixed costs neither rise nor fall with the level of output. They are independent of the level of output.

Variable costs

Those costs that vary
with the level of output

Variable costs (*VC*) change with the level of output: The more output the firm produces, the larger the total variable costs of production. This relationship may also be expressed by a simple equation:

$$VC = \text{Per-unit variable cost} \times \text{Quantity} = VQ. \qquad (11.3)$$

The equation states that variable costs are per-unit variable costs times quantity of output, in which *V* is the per-unit variable cost of production. As the level of output rises, variable costs rise in proportion to the increase in output. This relationship is shown in the fifth and sixth columns in Exhibit 11.1, which give the per-unit variable cost ($1) and total variable costs of production. At zero level of output there are no variable costs. Each additional unit of output then adds $1 to the firm's variable costs. Thus, at 200 units of output these costs are $200, and at 1,000 units of output these costs have risen to $1,000.

The total variable costs are represented in Figure 11.1 by the line *VC*. The variable costs line passes through the origin, which indicates that if operations were to cease, the firm would have no variable costs of operation. This is different from fixed costs, which still exist even if the firm ceases production. For example, during a strike variable labor costs cease, but certain costs (such as interest or depreciation) do not disappear just because the firm stops production. A plant that is not operating because of a strike will not be generating output and sales, which puts pressure on management to settle the strike before the fixed costs become an intolerable burden.

Total costs

Sum of fixed and variable
costs

Total costs (*TC*) of production are the sum of fixed costs and variable costs (*TC* = *FC* + *VC*). In Exhibit 11.1, total costs of operation are shown in the seventh column, which is the sum of columns 4 and 6. In Figure 11.1, the total costs are illustrated by *TC*, which is the vertical summation of *FC* and *VC*.

Total revenues

Price times quantity sold

When a firm breaks even, its total costs of production are equal to its total revenues, and the firm is neither making profits nor experiencing losses. If the firm were to produce less, it would experience losses. Management knows that it must maintain at least that level of output in order to cover all its costs. If management does not believe that the break-even level of output can be produced and sold, it must make changes. For example, it may decide to produce the output but also find a means to reduce the per-unit costs of production.

At the break-even point, total costs must equal total revenue, that is

$$TR = TC. \qquad (11.4)$$

Next, substitute Equations 11.1, 11.2, and 11.3 into Equation 11.4 and solve for the break-even level of output (Q_B):

$$PQ_B = FC + VQ_B$$

$$PQ_B - VQ_B = FC$$

$$Q_B(P - V) = FC$$

$$Q_B = \frac{FC}{P - V}. \qquad (11.5)$$

Since *FC* is the fixed cost of production and *V* is the per-unit variable cost of output, the equation for the break-even level of output is

$$\text{Break-even level of output} = \frac{\text{Fixed costs}}{\text{Price of product} - \text{Per-unit variable cost}}$$

Notice that Equation 11.5 employs a subscript. While *Q* represents any level of output, the subscript *B* indicates a particular level of output. In this case, it represents that level of output that equates revenues and costs, so the firm "breaks even."

If this equation is applied to the example in Exhibit 11.1, the break-even level of output is:

$$Q_B = \frac{\$1,000}{\$2 - \$1}$$

$$Q_B = 1,000.$$

This answer is the same as that obtained in the eighth column of Exhibit 11.1, which gives the profits of the firm. These profits are determined by subtracting column 7 (total costs) from column 3 (total revenues). The break-even point is also illustrated in Figure 11.1. As may be seen in Figure 11.1 and Exhibit 11.1, the firm's total cost exceeds its total revenue for all levels of output below 1,000, and the firm makes a profit at all levels of output greater than 1,000. It breaks even when it produces and sells 1,000 units of output.

Uses for Break-Even Analysis

Management may express breakeven in terms of the firm's entire operations. In the 2005 Agere Systems letter to stockholders, management discussed steps being taken to improve operations and reduce losses. These changes included selling operations, closing facilities to reduce fixed costs, and reducing the number of employees. Management expressed these actions as "necessary to lower our breakeven point and improve our financial performance."

Besides indicating the level of output that must be achieved to avoid losses, break-even analysis is a means for management to analyze the effects of changes in prices and costs. For example, what would be the effect of a decline in the price of the product in Exhibit 11.1? If, as the result of increased competition, the price of the product were to fall from $2.00 (column 1 of the exhibit) to $1.50, break-even analysis indicates that the firm would now have to sell at least 2,000 units of output [$1,000/($1.50 − $1.00) = 2,000] to meet its total costs. While the decrease in price may produce an increase in sales, can management anticipate increased sales sufficient to absorb 2,000 units of output? An example of a change in costs may be the suggestion of the advertising department for a stepped-up campaign to increase sales. Management may use break-even analysis to ascertain by how much the level of output must be expanded to cover the increased advertising expense. If the advertising campaign adds $0.25 per unit to the cost of the item, the break-even point becomes

$$\frac{\$1,000}{\$2 - \$1.25} = 1,333.$$

The advertising campaign will result in losses to the firm unless a level of sales of 1,333 units can be anticipated.

Break-even analysis may also be used to analyze the substitution of fixed for variable costs (for example, the substitution of equipment for labor). Though the equipment may be cost-effective, it may require a higher level of sales in order for the firm to break even. If the higher level of sales cannot be achieved, the substitution may convert a profitable firm into one that operates at a loss. (The implications of substituting fixed costs for variable costs are discussed and illustrated in the next chapter in the section on operating leverage.)

The Payback Period

Payback period

Period of time necessary to recoup the cost of an investment

The payback period determines how long is required for an investment's cash inflows to recover an investment's cost (the initial cash outflow). If an investment costs $1,000 and the annual cash inflows are $250, the payback period is four years ($1,000/$250). If four years are an acceptable period of time to recover the initial cost, the investment is made. Notice that management must determinate what is an acceptable time period, and that determination may be subjective.

The payback period may also be used to rank alternative investments. The more rapidly the initial cash outflow is recovered, the more preferred the investment. If four $1,000 investments have the following cash inflows:

Year	A	B	C	D
1	$250	$334	$400	$100
2	250	333	300	200
3	250	333	200	300
4	250	—	100	400
5	250	—	—	—

investment B would be preferred since it recoups the $1,000 in three years while the other investments take four years.

Obviously, the payback method is a simple means to rank alternatives and select investment projects. There are many flaws in the technique, but it is better to use the payback method than to make long-term investment decisions without using any capital budgeting techniques. The inability to accurately predict the future suggests that emphasizing the near future may be a desirable, or at least pragmatic, means to select among investment alternatives.

The criticisms of the payback method illustrate why other capital budgeting techniques are superior. The weaknesses include the following: (1) the cost of funds (the cost of capital discussed in Chapter 13) is omitted, (2) the timing of the cash flow is ignored, and (3) cash inflows after the payback period are disregarded. Each of these weaknesses will be discussed briefly. How these limitations may be overcome will be subsequently examined in the sections on the net present value and internal rate of return methods of capital budgeting in Chapter 14.

Neglecting to consider the cost of capital means that alternative uses of the money are ignored. The firm must raise funds to acquire an investment, and these funds have a cost, the cost of capital. An investment should be able to earn a return sufficient to compensate investors for the use of their capital. Since the payback period is concerned only with recouping the investment's cost, it says nothing about the investment's return.

This weakness is compounded when the other weaknesses are considered. Consider investments C and D in the table. The payback method's inability to differentiate the timing of the cash flows means that, if strictly applied, the method cannot distinguish between investment C's and investment D's cash flows. Both have payback periods of four years. Of course, C is superior, since the cash inflow in the early years is greater, which provides funds that can be reinvested elsewhere.

The third limitation is that payback does not consider cash inflows received after the payback period. The failure to consider cash flows after the payback period results in selecting investments B, C, and D before A. Common sense indicates that A is superior. B, C, and D recoup only the $1,000 cost. They offer no return. An investment must generate cash flow after the payback period to be profitable, and even then the investment might not be selected when the cost of capital is used in the analysis.

Although the payback method is consistently criticized, it is nevertheless used, because (1) it is readily understood, (2) it is easy to apply, and (3) it avoids making projections into the more distant future. The more uncertain the future, the stronger may be the case for use of the payback method. Thus, while the payback method has little support on theoretical grounds, it has support on pragmatic grounds. It is easy to perform and places the emphasis on the immediate return of the cost of the investment. The management of a small business may simply lack the time, knowledge, or capacity to do more sophisticated types of capital budgeting.

Summary   The break-even level of output occurs when revenues exactly cover expenses. Revenues depend on the number of units sold and their price. Total expenses depend on fixed costs, which are independent of the level of production, and variable costs, which rise and fall with changes in the level of output. Although break-even analysis does not determine the most profitable level of output, it is a useful tool when management anticipates introducing a new product or substituting fixed costs for variable costs.

The payback period determines the time necessary for an investment's cash inflows to recapture the investment's cost or initial cash outflow. Investments with the fastest payback are preferred. Like break-even analysis, the payback period does not determine an investment's profitability or its contribution to the value of the firm. The technique also has major weaknesses such as its failure to consider the timing of cash inflows.

Both the break-even analysis and the payback period calculation are relatively easy to perform and easily interpreted. For these reasons, a firm's calculation management may justify the use of either technique on pragmatic grounds. This justification may be particularly true for a small firm whose management lacks the time and resources to perform a more detailed and theoretically correct analysis.

Review Objectives

Now that you have completed this chapter, you should be able to

1. Differentiate fixed from variable costs (pp. 231–233).
2. Calculate the break-even level of output (pp. 233–234).
3. Identify a potential use for break-even analysis (pp. 234–235).
4. Determine an investment's payback period (pp. 235–236).
5. Enumerate several weaknesses associated with the payback period as a method for selecting long-term investments (pp. 235–236).

Problems

1. Three investments cost $5,000 each and have the following cash flows. Rank them on the basis of their payback periods. Does the ranking make intuitive sense?

Year	A	B	C
1	$2,000	$3,000	$ 500
2	2,000	2,000	1,000
3	2,000	1,000	3,000
4	2,000	500	7,000
5	2,000	0	9,000

2. The manufacturer of a product that has a variable cost of $2.50 per unit and total fixed cost of $125,000 wants to determine the level of output necessary to avoid losses.

   a. What level of sales is necessary to break even if the product is sold for $4.25? What will be the manufacturer's profit or loss on the sales of 100,000 units?

   b. If fixed costs rise to $175,000, what is the new level of sales necessary to break even?

   c. If variable costs decline to $2.25 per unit, what is the new level of sales necessary to break even?

PART 3 Corporate Finance

d. If fixed costs were to increase to $175,000, while variable costs declined to $2.25 per unit, what is the new break-even level of sales?

e. If a major proportion of fixed costs were noncash (depreciation), would failure to achieve the break-even level of sales imply that the firm cannot pay its current obligations as they come due? Suppose $100,000 of the above fixed costs of $125,000 were depreciation expense. What level of sales would be the *cash* break-even level of sales?

3. Management believes it can sell a new product for $8.50. The fixed costs of production are estimated to be $6,000, and the variable costs are $3.20 a unit.

a. Complete the following table at the given levels of output and the relationships between quantity and fixed costs, quantity and variable costs, and quantity and total costs.

Quantity	Total Revenue	Variable Costs	Fixed Costs	Total Costs	Profits (Loss)
0					
500					
1,000					
1,500					
2,000					
2,500					
3,000					

b. Determine the break-even level using the above table and use Equation 11.5 to confirm the break-even level of output.

c. What would happen to the total revenue schedule, the total cost schedule, and the break-even level of output if management determined that fixed costs would be $10,000 instead of $6,000?

4. The management of a firm wants to introduce a new product. The product will sell for $4 a unit and can be produced by either of two scales of operation. In the first, total costs are

$$TC = \$3,000 + \$2.8Q.$$

In the second scale of operation, total costs are

$$TC = \$5,000 + \$2.4Q.$$

a. What is the break-even level of output for each scale of operation?

b. What will be the firm's profits for each scale of operation if sales reach 5,000 units?

c. One-half of the fixed costs are noncash (depreciation). All other expenses are for cash. If sales are 2,000 units, will *cash receipts cover cash expenses* for each scale of operation?

d. The anticipated levels of sales are the following:

Year	Unit Sales
1	4,000
2	5,000
3	6,000
4	7,000

If management selects the scale of production with higher fixed cost, what can it expect in years 1 and 2? On what grounds can management justify selecting this scale of operation? If sales reach only 5,000 a year, was the correct scale of operation chosen?

5. A firm has the following total revenue and total cost schedules:

$$TR = \$2Q.$$

$$TC = \$4,000 + \$1.5Q.$$

a. What is the break-even level of output? What is the level of profits at sales of 9,000 units?

b. As the result of a major technological breakthrough, the total cost schedule is changed to:

$$TC = \$6,000 + \$0.5Q.$$

What is the break-even level of output? What is the level of profits at sales of 9,000 units?

Additional Problems with Answers

1. The price of a product is $32 per unit. A firm can produce this good with variable costs of $20 per unit and total fixed costs of $10,000.

a. What is the break-even level of output?

b. What is the break-even level of output if fixed costs increase to $18,000 but variable costs decline to $14 per unit?

2. An item sells for $5. Variable costs of production are $3, and the fixed costs are $3,000.

a. What are the equations relating costs to output, revenues and output, and profits or losses?

b. Reconstruct a table similar to the illustration in Exhibit 11.1.

c. What is the break-even level of output?

d. What are the profits or losses at sales of 800, 1,200, and 2,000 units?

Answers   1. a. Break-even level of output: $10,000/$32 − $20) = 833 units

b. Break-even level of output: $18,000/($32 − $14) = 1,000 units

2. a. $VC = \$3Q$
   $FC = \$3,000$
   $TC = \$3,000 + 3Q$
   $TR = \$5Q$
   Profit/loss $= TR - TC = \$5Q - (\$3,000 + 3Q)$

b.

P	Q	TR	FC	V	VC	TC	Profit/loss
$5	400	2,000	3,000	3	1,200	4,200	(2,200)
5	800	4,000	3,000	3	2,400	5,400	(1,400)
5	1,000	5,000	3,000	3	3,000	6,000	(1,000)
5	1,200	6,000	3,000	3	3,600	6,600	(600)
5	1,600	8,000	3,000	3	4,800	7,800	200
5	2,000	10,000	3,000	3	6,000	9,000	1,000
5	2,500	12,500	3,000	3	7,500	10,500	2,000

c. Break-even level of output:

$$Q = FC/(P - V)$$
$$= 3,000/(5 - 3) = 1,500 \text{ units}$$

Confirmation:

P	Q	TR	FC	V	VC	TC	Profit/loss
5	1,500	7,500	3,000	3	4,500	7,500	0

d. Profit/loss at 800 units: ($1,400)
   1,200 units: ($600)
   2,000 units: $1,000

Relationships

1. An increase in price without a decrease in units sold _____ total revenue.

2. An increase in fixed costs _____ variable costs.

3. A decrease in per unit variable costs _____ fixed costs.

4. An increase in per unit variable costs _____ the break-even level of output.

5. An increase in the cost of a investment _____ the payback period.

6. If an investment's cash flow is $100 a year, an increase in the number of years _____ the payback period.

7. An increase in inflows _____ the payback period.

Answers

1. increases

2. does not affect (no change)

3. does not affect (no change)

4. increases

5. increases

6. does not affect (no change)

7. decreases

D israeli suggested that "what we anticipate seldom occurs; what we least expected generally happens." Few individuals anticipated the housing bubble and the subsequent decline in real estate values. The unanticipated happened. The excessive use of debt financing and the default on those mortgages magnified the losses that investors and individual homeowners experienced. (For a narrative of a few individuals who did anticipate the mortgage defaults and who made fortunes betting against by "shorting" those mortgages, read Michael Lewis, *The Big Short* [New York: W. W. Norton, 2010].)

Leverage is among the most important topics in finance. For firms, there are two sources of leverage. Operating leverage refers to the use of fixed factors of production such as plant and equipment relative to variable factors of production. A substitution of machinery for labor may produce the same level of output and alter the firm's operating income, but the substitution may also increase the volatility of operating income and risk. Financial leverage refers to the use of debt financing instead of equity financing. Substituting debt for equity may alter net income and the return on equity but may also increase the volatility of net income and risk.

This chapter considers only two topics: operating and financial leverage and their impact on the firm's net earnings and risk. In the minds of some managers, leverage is the "name of the game." By successfully using leverage, management is able to increase the return on equity and increase the value of the firm. But the use of leverage also increases risk. Excessive risk is counterproductive and may decrease the value of the firm. Certainly there has to be a best or optimal use of leverage that increases returns without unduly increasing risk.

This chapter, however, considers only leverage's impact on operating and net income and risk. The optimal combination of debt and equity financing is covered in the next chapter on the cost of capital and the optimal capital structure.

Operating Leverage

A given level of output may be produced with different combinations of factors of production. One farmer and one tractor may plow a field, but the same result could be achieved with more workers using hoes. While this example is exaggerated, it does illustrate that if the objective is a plowed field, there is more than one method to achieve the same results.

Operating leverage

Use of fixed factors of production (fixed costs) instead of variable factors of production (variable costs) to produce a level of output

If a firm uses more fixed factors of production (fixed costs) instead of variable factors (variable costs), it is employing operating leverage. Plowing the field with one farmer plus a tractor instead of several farmers with hoes illustrates using more fixed costs (the cost of the tractor) instead of variable costs (the cost of each farmer). Using several farmers instead of buying the tractor gives you flexibility. You can reduce your costs by reducing your workforce. Or you can increase output by adding another worker, in which case your costs increase. If, however, you have purchased the tractor, your costs are the same whether the tractor is extensively used or spends most of the day sitting idle in the shed.

Operating leverage is the use of fixed factors (fixed costs) instead of variable costs. Operating leverage is also a major source of risk. Consider Exhibit 12.1. In part (a) fixed costs are $1,000 and variable costs per unit are $1.00. In part (b) fixed costs and variable costs differ. For all levels of output, the fixed costs of production are $1,500, and the variable costs decline to $0.70 per unit. Since management has substituted fixed for variable costs, per unit variable costs are lower. You can immediately see that losses are greater ($1,500 versus $1,000) if the firm produces no output and the break-even level of output is increased from 1,000 to 1,154 units. The important consideration, however, it that once break-even level of output is passed, earnings rise more rapidly. Previously, an increase of 250 units increased profits by $250. After the substitution, an increase of 250 units increases profits by $325. Expanding sales will produce larger earnings, but the converse is also true. Declining sales will generate larger losses. This is, of course, the risk associated with using more operating leverage. Management may magnify earnings but also increases the risk of larger losses.

Fixed Asset Turnover: A Measure of Operating Leverage

If a firm has substantial fixed costs, it has a large amount of operating leverage. One means to measure operating leverage is the ratio of sales to fixed assets, which in Chapter 9 was referred to as fixed asset turnover. Low fixed asset turnover indicates that the firm uses a substantial investment in plant and equipment and that such investments are necessary to generate sales. Fixed assets have costs (such as depreciation) that occur regardless of the amount of

EXHIBIT 12.1
Relationship among
Output, Revenues, Costs,
and Profits/Losses

(a) Fixed costs = $1,000; variable costs = $1.00

Price (per unit)	Quantity	Total Revenue	Fixed Costs	Variable Costs	Total Variable Costs	Total Costs (per unit)	Profits/ Losses
$2	0	$ —	$1,000	$1.00	$ 0.00	$1,000.00	($1,000.00)
2	250	500	1,000	1.00	250.00	1,250.00	(750.00)
2	500	1,000	1,000	1.00	500.00	1,500.00	(500.00)
2	750	1,500	1,000	1.00	750.00	1,750.00	(250.00)
2	1,000	2,000	1,000	1.00	1,000.00	2,000.00	0.00
2	1,250	2,500	1,000	1.00	1,250.00	2,250.00	250.00
2	1,500	3,000	1,000	1.00	1,500.00	2,500.00	500.00
2	1,750	3,500	1,000	1.00	1,750.00	2,750.00	750.00
2	2,000	4,000	1,000	1.00	2,000.00	3,000.00	1,000.00
2	2,250	4,500	1,000	1.00	2,250.00	3,250.00	1,250.00
2	2,500	5,000	1,000	1.00	2,500.00	3,500.00	1,500.00

(b) Fixed costs = $1,500; variable costs = $0.70

Price (per unit)	Quantity	Total Revenue	Fixed Costs	Variable Costs	Total Variable Costs	Total Costs (per unit)	Profits/ Losses
$2	0	$ —	$1,500	$0.70	$ 0.00	$1,500.00	($1,500.00)
2	250	500	$1,500	0.70	175.00	1,675.00	(1,175.00)
2	500	1,000	$1,500	0.70	350.00	1,850.00	(850.00)
2	750	1,500	$1,500	0.70	525.00	2,025.00	(525.00)
2	1,000	2,000	$1,500	0.70	700.00	2,200.00	(200.00)
2	1,154	2,308	$1,500	0.70	807.80	2,307.80	0.20
2	1,250	2,500	$1,500	0.70	875.00	2,375.00	125.00
2	1,500	3,000	$1,500	0.70	1,050.00	2,550.00	450.00
2	1,750	3,500	$1,500	0.70	1,225.00	2,725.00	775.00
2	2,000	4,000	$1,500	0.70	1,400.00	2,900.00	1,100.00
2	2,250	4,500	$1,500	0.70	1,575.00	3,075.00	1,425.00
2	2,500	5,000	$1,500	0.70	1,750.00	3,250.00	1,750.00

sales. Once these fixed costs are covered, earnings tend to rise more rapidly than the earnings of a firm whose costs vary with the amount of sales.

Exhibit 12.2 presents the ratio of revenues to fixed assets (fixed asset turnover) for three firms with revenues and fixed assets in excess of $10 billion. The table ranks the firms from the lowest to highest sales (revenues) to fixed assets and provides each firm's industry. As may be expected, Southern Company must have substantial investment in plant and equipment to generate revenues. For every $1 in revenues, the firm had over $2.56 in fixed assets. The need for substantial investments also applies to an oil refiner (ConocoPhillips). Other firms may not need large investments in plant and equipment to generate sales. Microsoft generates $7.79 for every $1 invested in fixed assets.

EXHIBIT 12.2
Ratio of Revenues to Fixed
Assets of Selected Firms
(Revenues and Assets in
Billions)

Firm	Industry	Revenues	Fixed Assets	Sales to Fixed Assets
Southern Company	Gas and electric utility	$ 15.7	$40.1	0.39
ConocoPhillips	Oil refining	152.8	87.7	1.74
Microsoft	Computer hardware and software	58.4	7.5	7.79

Source: 2009 annual reports.

Operating Leverage and Risk

The previous discussion suggests that operating income will rise and fall more rapidly for a firm with operating leverage. This section compares the operating leverage for two industries, airlines and retailing, and shows how operating leverage affects the level of risk associated with each industry.

The airline industry is an excellent example of an industry that has a large amount of operating leverage. A large proportion of airlines' costs is fixed (such as depreciation on the planes and equipment). Other costs are also fixed. Once the plane is in the air, the cost of the flight is virtually the same whether the plane carries one person or a full load. The difference between breakeven and a profitable flight is often a matter of a few passengers. Once this break-even number of passengers is reached, the profitability of the flight rises rapidly, because the fixed costs are being spread over an increasing number of passengers. Thus, once a profitable level of operation is reached, the level of profits rises rapidly with further increases in passengers carried.

Retailing is an entirely different type of operation. A firm may have few fixed costs (such as rent for the building) and many variable costs. As the firm expands output, these variable costs (for instance, wages and cost of goods sold) also expand. Such operations do not have a large amount of operating leverage, for as sales expand there is not a large increase in earnings.

Figure 12.1 compares an airline with a retailer to illustrate how changes in sales have a larger impact on the earnings of the firm with the higher degree of operating leverage. The top half of the figure is a break-even chart for an airline; the bottom half is a break-even chart for a retailer. For ease of comparison, both the break-even level of output (Q_B) and the total revenue curve (TR) are identical for both firms. The difference between the two firms rests entirely upon their cost curves. The retailer has lower fixed costs (0R versus 0S), but the total cost curve for the retailer rises more rapidly.

The effect of these differences in costs (that is, the difference in operating leverage) can be seen by moving along the horizontal axis. If output increases from Q_B to Q_1, the earnings are greater for the airline than for the retailer (AB versus CD). If output decreases from Q_B to Q_2, the losses are greater for the airline than for the retailer (EF versus GH). The airline experiences greater fluctuations in earnings and losses for the same change in revenues because it has the higher degree of operating leverage.

F I G U R E   12.1
Break-Even Analysis and
Fluctuations in Earnings for
an Airline and a Retailer

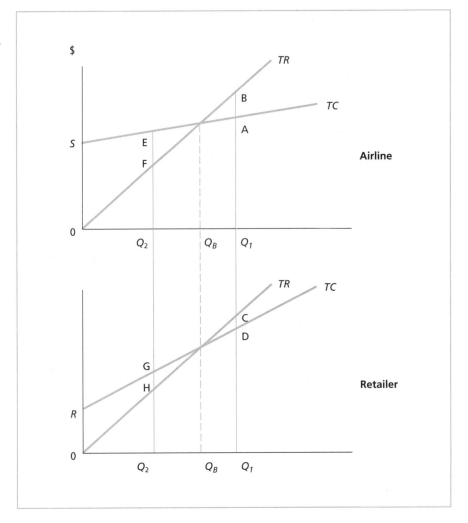

These fluctuations in earnings imply that the airline is the riskier firm. In periods of declining sales, it will experience greater losses than the retailer. Firms with more operating leverage are riskier because their earnings are more variable. While firms with less operating leverage may not achieve a rapid increase in earnings as sales expand, they will not experience rapid declines in earnings when sales decline. Most of their costs are variable costs that also decrease with the decline in output and sales.

These differences in operating leverage indicate that some businesses are inherently more risky than others. For the individual firm, risk emanates from two sources: the nature of the business and how the business is financed (*business risk* and *financial risk*). Airlines, then, have a high degree of business risk, while retailers, especially those selling staples such as food and clothing, may not have this high degree of business risk.

Financial Leverage

Financial leverage

Use of another person's or firm's funds in return for agreeing to pay a fixed return for the funds; the use of debt or preferred stock financing

The previous section demonstrated how the use of operating leverage may increase the firm's operating income, but increased operating leverage is associated with more volatility. Small changes in sales and revenues are magnified and the firm becomes riskier. The use of debt financing instead of equity has the same impact on net income. Small changes in revenues are magnified; increased use of financial leverage may increase the firm's return on equity, but the firm becomes riskier.

Financial leverage occurs when the firm enters into fixed contracts to obtain funds. When a firm issues debt such as bonds (and preferred stock, which pays a fixed dividend) or borrows from a bank, the firm enters into a contract. This contract requires the firm to meet certain fixed obligations, such as interest payments and principal repayment. The firm, however, may earn more with the funds than it has agreed to pay. In the simplest terms, a firm may borrow funds at 10 percent and earn 12 percent. The additional 2 percent accrues to the owners (that is, the equity) and increases the return earned by the stockholders.

How financial leverage works may be shown by a simple example. Firm A needs $100 capital to operate and may acquire the money from the owners of the firm. Alternatively, it may acquire part of the money from stockholders and part from creditors. If the management acquires the $100 from stockholders, the firm uses no debt financing and is not financially leveraged. The firm would have the following simple balance sheet:

Assets		Liabilities and Equity	
Cash	$100		
		Equity	$100

Once in business the firm generates the following simplified income statement:

Sales	$100
Expenses	80
Earnings before interest and taxes	$ 20
Taxes (40%)	8
Net earnings	$ 12

What return has the firm earned on the owner's investment (that is, the return on equity)? The answer is 12 percent, for the investors contributed $100 and the firm earned $12 after taxes. The firm may pay the $12 to the investors in cash dividends or may retain the $12 to help finance future growth. Either way, however, the owners' return on their equity is 12 percent.

By using financial leverage, management may be able to increase the owners' return on their investment. What happens to their return if management is able to borrow part of the capital needed to operate the firm? The answer depends on (1) what proportion of the total capital is borrowed, and (2) the interest rate that must be paid to the creditors. If management borrows 40 percent ($40) of the firm's capital at an interest cost of 5 percent, the balance sheet becomes:

Assets		Liabilities and Equity	
Cash	$100	Debt	$40
		Equity	$60

Because the firm borrowed $40, it is now obligated to pay interest. Thus, the firm has a new expense that must be paid before it has any earnings for the common stockholder. The simple income statement becomes:

Sales	$100.00
Expenses	80.00
Earnings before interest and taxes	$ 20.00
Interest expense	2.00
Taxable income	$ 18.00
Taxes	7.20
Net earnings	$ 10.80

The use of debt causes the net profit to decline from $12 to $10.80. What effect does this method of financing have on the owners' return? It increases from 12 percent to 18 percent! How does this reduction in the net profit produce an increase in the owners' return? The answer is that the owners invested only $60, and that $60 earned them $10.80. They made 18 percent on their money, whereas previously they had earned only 12 percent.

There are two sources of the additional return. First, the firm borrowed money and agreed to pay a fixed return of 5 percent. The firm, however, was able to earn more than 5 percent with the money, and this additional earning accrued to the owners of the firm. Second, the entire burden of the interest cost was not borne by the firm. The federal tax laws permit the deduction of interest as an expense before determining taxable income. The greater the corporate income tax rate, the greater the portion of this interest expense borne by the government. In this case 40 percent, or $0.80, of the interest expense was borne by the government in lost tax revenues. If the corporate income tax rate were 50 percent, the government would lose $1.00 in taxes by permitting the deduction of the interest expense.

As illustrated in the previous example, a firm's management may increase the owners' return by the use of debt (financial leverage). By increasing the proportion of the firm's assets that are financed by debt, management is able to increase the return on the equity. Exhibit 12.3 shows the effect of various levels of debt financing (as measured by the debt ratio) on (1) the net earnings for the firm, and (2) the return on the investors' equity. The table was constructed using a 40 percent tax rate. The rate of interest is assumed to be

E X H I B I T   12.3
Relationship between the
Debt Ratio and the Return
on Equity

Debt Ratio (Debt/Total assets)	0%	20	50	70	90
Amount of debt outstanding	$ 0	20	50	70	90
Equity	$100	80	50	30	10
Sales	$100	100	100	100	100
Expenses	$ 80	80	80	80	80
Earnings before interest and taxes	$ 20	20	20	20	20
Interest expense (5% interest rate)	$ 0	1	2.50	3.50	4.50
Taxable income	$ 20	19	17.50	16.50	15.50
Income taxes (40% tax rate)	$ 8	7.60	7.00	6.60	6.20
Net earnings	$ 12	11.40	10.50	9.90	9.30
Return on equity	12%	14.25	21.0	33.0	93.0

5 percent no matter what proportion of the firm's assets are financed by debt. This unrealistic assumption will be dropped later in the chapter. Figure 12.2 plots the return on equity presented in Exhibit 12.3. From both the table and the figure you may see that as the debt ratio rises, the return on the owners' equity not only rises but rises at an increasing rate. This dramatically indicates how the use of financial leverage may increase the return on a firm's equity.

F I G U R E   12.2
Use of Financial Leverage
and the Return on Equity

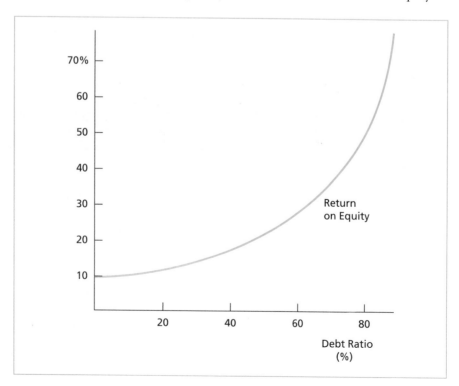

Financial Leverage and Risk

Because the use of financial leverage increases the owners' return on equity, the question becomes: Why not use ever-increasing amounts of debt financing? The answer is that as the firm becomes more financially leveraged, it becomes riskier. This increase in risk raises (1) the potential for fluctuations in the owners' returns, and (2) the interest rate that the creditors charge for the use of their money.

That the use of financial leverage increases the potential risk to the owners may be seen by employing the simple example presented in the previous section. What happens to the return on equity if sales decline by 10 percent (from $100 to $90) and expenses remain the same? The income statements for the financially unleveraged and leveraged firms become:

	Unleveraged Firm (0% Debt Ratio)	Leveraged Firm (40% Debt Ratio)
Sales	$90.00	$90.00
Expenses	80.00	80.00
Earnings before interest and taxes	$10.00	$10.00
Interest	—	2.00
Taxable income	$10.00	$ 8.00
Taxes (40% tax rate)	4.00	3.20
Net profit	$ 6.00	$ 4.80

The 10 percent decline in sales produces declines in the earnings and the return on the owners' investment in both cases. For the unleveraged firm the return is now 6 percent ($6/$100); for the financially leveraged firm the return plummets from 18 percent to 8 percent ($4.80/$60).

Why does the return decline more for the leveraged firm than for the unleveraged firm? The answer rests with the fixed interest payment. When the firm borrowed the funds, it agreed to make a fixed interest payment. This agreement is a legal obligation stipulating that the firm must pay or default on the loan. The fixed interest payment, which was a source of the increase in the owners' return when sales were $100, causes the larger decline in the owner's return when the firm's sales decline. If the firm had been even more leveraged (if the debt ratio had been greater), the decline in the return on equity would have been even larger. This suggests a general conclusion: The greater the proportion of a firm's assets that are financed by fixed obligations, the greater the potential variability in the owners' return. Small changes in revenues or costs will produce larger fluctuations in the firm's net earnings.

Firms that use large amounts of financial leverage are viewed by creditors as being risky. Creditors may refuse to lend to a highly leveraged firm or do so only at higher rates of interest or more stringent loan conditions. As the interest rate

EXHIBIT 12.4
Relationship between
Increased Interest Rates
and the Return on Equity
(Tax Rate = 40 Percent)

Debt Ratio	0%	20	50	70
A				
Earnings before interest and taxes	$20.00	20.00	20.00	20.00
Interest at 5 percent	NA	$ 1.00	2.50	3.50
Taxable income	$20.00	19.00	17.50	16.50
Taxes (40% rate)	$ 8.00	7.60	7.00	6.60
Net earnings	$12.00	11.40	10.50	9.90
Return on equity	12.00%	14.25	21.00	33.00
B				
Earnings before interest and taxes	$20.00	20.00	20.00	20.00
Interest rate	NA	6.00%	10.00	12.00
Interest	NA	$ 1.20	5.00	8.40
Taxable income	$20.00	18.80	15.00	11.60
Taxes (40% rate)	$ 8.00	7.52	6.00	4.64
Net earnings	$12.00	11.28	9.00	6.96
Return on equity	12.00%	14.10	18.00	23.20

increases, the owners' return on their equity in the firm diminishes. This may be seen in the example presented in Exhibit 12.4, which illustrates what happens to the investors' return as the interest rate rises. The first case (A) illustrates the return if the interest rate is held constant as more debt is employed. The second case (B) assumes that interest rates rise as the debt ratio increases to compensate creditors for the increased risk. The bottom row in each case gives the return on the owners' equity, and, as would be expected, the increased interest expense causes the owners' return to diminish. This may be seen by comparing the bottom lines of both cases. However, even though the return may diminish when the interest rate rises, it might still exceed the return obtained when no debt was used, in which case financial leverage would still be favorable.

As long as the return on the assets financed by debt exceeds the after-tax cost of debt (that is, the interest rate adjusted for the tax savings), financial leverage is favorable and will increase the return on the owners' investment. This after-tax cost of debt is

$$k_d = i(1 - t). \qquad (12.1)$$

The after-tax cost of debt (k_d) depends on the interest rate (i) and the firm's marginal tax rate (t). The larger the tax rate, the smaller the effective cost of debt, because the tax savings that result from deducting the interest expense from taxable income are larger. This after-tax cost of debt is the true cost of using debt financing. While the interest rate paid for the use of borrowed funds obviously affects the cost of borrowing, it is the after-tax cost of borrowing that determines if financial leverage is favorable.

The use of the effective cost of debt to determine if financial leverage is favorable may be illustrated with the first example presented in this chapter. When the firm did not use debt financing, it earned 12 percent on its assets after taxes. However, the effective cost of debt was only

$$0.05(1 - 0.4) = 0.03 = 3\%,$$

so financial leverage was favorable. As long as the firm could borrow at an effective cost of 3.0 percent and put those funds to work at 12 percent, financial leverage would be favorable.

Actually, in this illustration financial leverage would have been favorable if the interest rate had been 12, 15, or even 18 percent, because the effective cost of debt after adjusting for taxes would have been 7.2, 9, and 10.8 percent, respectively. It is only at 20 percent that financial leverage would have become unfavorable, for then the interest charges would have risen sufficiently to absorb every dollar earned on the borrowed money. If the firm had financed operations with $60 equity and $40 debt at 20 percent, it would have had the following income statement:

Sales	$100.00
Expenses	80.00
Earnings before interest and taxes	$ 20.00
Interest expense	8.00
Taxable income	$ 12.00
Taxes	4.80
Net earnings	$ 7.20

The return on equity is 12 percent ($7.20/$60), which is exactly the return earned on the equity by the unleveraged firm.

Why can the interest rates be so high and financial leverage still be favorable? A major reason is the ability of the firm to deduct the interest expense before determining taxable income. Only when the after-tax cost of debt exceeds the return earned on the firm's assets acquired by debt financing is financial leverage unfavorable. In the above example, the after-tax cost of debt must rise to 12 percent (20 percent before-tax cost of debt) before financial leverage becomes unfavorable.

The ability to deduct the interest expense encourages the use of debt financing. Corporations whose federal income tax rate is 35 percent share almost a third of their interest expense with the federal government. From the firm's viewpoint, $1.00 paid in interest to creditors reduces the firm's taxes by $0.35. The true interest cost of $1.00 interest expense is only $0.65, and thus the tax laws become a major incentive to use financial leverage.

Financial Leverage Through Preferred Stock Financing

In the preceding sections financial leverage was achieved through the use of debt. Financial leverage may also be acquired through the use of preferred stock, because preferred stock has a fixed dividend. (The fixed dividend is analogous to the fixed interest payments.) The differences between debt and preferred stock financing are that the dividend on the preferred stock is neither a contractual obligation nor a tax-deductible expense. The fact that the dividend is not a contractual obligation is the primary advantage of preferred stock financing. Preferred stock is less risky for the firm than debt financing. If the firm is unable to meet the dividend payment, the owners of the preferred stock cannot force the firm to make the payment. In the case of debt, if the firm fails to pay the interest, the creditors can take the firm to court to force payment or force bankruptcy.

Although preferred stock financing is a less risky means to acquire financial leverage, the other difference between it and debt financing argues strongly against the use of preferred stock. Since interest is a tax-deductible expense and the preferred dividends are not, the effective cost of debt financing is cheaper. If a firm borrows at 8 percent, the true cost is reduced as a result of the tax laws. If a firm issues preferred stock and pays an 8 percent dividend, the true cost to the firm is 8 percent. Because the cost of debt financing is shared with the government, firms tend to use debt instead of preferred stock as a means to obtain financial leverage.

The inability to deduct preferred dividends reduces the impact of financial leverage. The difference in the return to the common stockholder that results from the use of debt and preferred stock financing is illustrated in the following example. The firm issues $50 worth of common stock and needs an additional $50. It may issue either $50 of debt with a 5 percent interest rate or $50 of preferred stock with a 5 percent dividend. In both cases the firm acquires $50 and pays out $2.50 in either interest or dividends. However, the earnings available to the common stockholder are larger when debt is used instead of preferred stock. This is shown in the following income statements:

	Debt Financing	Preferred Stock Financing
Sales	$100.00	$100.00
Expenses	80.00	80.00
Earnings before interest and taxes	$ 20.00	$ 20.00
Interest	2.50	—
Taxable income	$ 17.50	$ 20.00
Taxes (50 percent)	8.75	10.00
Net earnings	$ 8.75	$ 10.00
Preferred dividends	—	2.50
Earnings available to common stock	$ 8.75	$ 7.50

When debt financing is used, the earnings available to the common stockholders are $8.75, while they are only $7.50 when the preferred stock is used. Thus, the return on the common stockholders' investment is larger (17.5 percent versus 15 percent) when debt financing is used. The ability of the firm to share the interest expense with the federal government encourages the use of debt financing instead of preferred stock financing. The use of preferred stock financing has declined over time, and this decline is partially explained by the unfavorable tax treatment afforded preferred stock.

Summary

Operating leverage brings to the foreground the importance of fixed costs relative to variable costs. Firms that have large fixed costs have operating leverage. These firms must achieve a higher level of sales to break even. Firms with costs that fluctuate with the level of output do not have operating leverage; they may achieve profits at a lower level of production. However, once profitable levels of output are achieved, the firm with more operating leverage will experience more rapid increases in operating income for given changes in production. This increased variability of operating income increases the business risk associated with the firm.

All assets must be financed. There are two basic sources of finance: debt and equity. If a firm uses debt financing, it is financially leveraged. If the firm is able to earn more with the funds acquired by issuing debt than it must pay in interest, the residual accrues to equity. By successfully using debt financing, the firm increases the owners' return on their investment.

Although the successful use of debt financing increases the return on equity, it also increases financial risk. If the firm experiences a decline in sales or profit margins, it must still pay the interest and retire the principal. Failure to do so may result in bankruptcy. Thus, while the use of debt financing may increase the return on equity during periods of success and growth, the opposite may be true during periods of difficulty. Then the use of debt financing reduces the return on equity, as the firm must meet the fixed obligations of its debt financing.

Review Objectives

Now that you have completed this chapter, you should be able to

1. Determine the sources of operating and financial leverage (pp. 243 and 247).
2. Explain the impact of leverage on operating income and net income (pp. 243–245).
3. Illustrate the impact of substituting fixed for variable cost on the volatility of earnings (pp. 245–246).
4. Explain how the use of financial leverage affects the return on equity (pp. 248–249).
5. Determine the cost of debt (pp. 250–252).
6. Contrast debt and preferred stock as a source of financial leverage (pp. 253–254).

Problems

1. Fill in the table using the following information.
   Assets required for operation: $10,000
   Firm A uses only equity financing
   Firm B uses 30% debt with a 6% interest rate and 70% equity
   Firm C uses 50% debt with a 10% interest rate and 50% equity
   Firm D uses 50% preferred stock financing with a dividend rate of 10%
   and 50% equity financing
   Earnings before interest and taxes: $1,000

	A	B	C	D
Debt	$	$	$	$
Preferred stock				
Common stock				
Earnings before interest and taxes				
Interest expense				
Earnings before taxes				
Taxes (40% of earnings)				
Preferred stock dividends				
Net earnings				
Return on common stock				

What happens to the return on the stockholders' investment as the amount of debt increases? Why is the rate of interest greater in case C? Why is the return lower when the firm uses preferred stock instead of debt? Why does the use of preferred stock involve less risk for the firm than a comparable use of debt financing?

2. Firm A has $10,000 in assets entirely financed with equity. Firm B also has $10,000 in assets, but these assets are financed by $5,000 in debt (with a 10 percent rate of interest) and $5,000 in equity. Both firms sell 10,000 units of output at $2.50 per unit. The variable costs of production are $1, and fixed production costs are $12,000. (To ease the calculation, assume no income tax.)

   a. What is the operating income (*EBIT*) for both firms?

   b. What are the earnings after interest?

   c. If sales increase by 10 percent to 11,000 units, by what percentage will each firm's earnings after interest increase? To answer the question, determine the earnings after taxes and compute the percentage increase in these earnings from the answers you derived in part *b*.

   d. Why are the percentage changes different?

3. Fill in the table using the following information.
   Assets required for operation: $2,000
   Case A—firm uses only equity financing
   Case B—firm uses 30% debt with a 10% interest rate and 70% equity
   Case C—firm uses 50% debt with a 12% interest rate and 50% equity

	A	B	C
Debt outstanding	$	$	$
Stockholders' equity			
Earnings before interest and taxes	300	300	300
Interest expense			
Earnings before taxes			
Taxes (40% of earnings)			
Net earnings			
Return on stockholders' equity	%	%	%

What happens to the rate of return on the stockholders' investment as the amount of debt increases? Why did the rate of interest increase in case C?

Additional Problems with Answers

No concept is more important in finance than the use of leverage. While there are two types of leverage, operating leverage and financial leverage, emphasis is usually placed on financial leverage. Operating leverage, the use of fixed costs instead of variable costs, varies among industries. In many cases firms in a particular industry such as electric utilities have no choice. Most of their assets have to be fixed plant and equipment, so these firms have substantial operating leverage.

Financial leverage involves choice. Management decides to finance the operations with debt instead of equity. While using debt financing may increase the return on equity, it also increases the firm's risk. The terms of the debt contracts must be met or the firm will be in default. The risk associated with debt financing certainly came to the foreground during 2008 when the excessive use of financial leverage was one of the primary causes of the 2008 financial crisis.

1. Given the various debt ratios, fill in the table and determine the firm's earnings and return on equity. The firm's earnings before interest and taxes (*EBIT*) are $10,000 and total assets are $100,000. The tax rate is 35 percent, and the rate of interest on debt is 6 percent. What impact did the use of additional debt financing have on the return on equity?

Debt ratio	0%	20	40	60
Debt outstanding				
Stockholders' equity				
Earnings before interest and taxes				
Interest expense				
Earnings before taxes				
Taxes				
Net earnings				
Return on stockholders' equity				

2. Complete the table using the following information.
   Assets required for operation: $10,000
   Firm A—the firm uses only equity financing
   Firm B—the firm uses 30% debt with a 10% interest rate and 70% equity
   Firm C—the firm uses 50% debt with a 12% interest rate and 50% equity

	A	B	C
Debt outstanding			
Stockholders' equity			
Earnings before interest and taxes	$1,000	$1,000	$1,000
Interest expense			
Earnings before taxes			
Taxes (40% of earnings before taxes)			
Net earnings			
Return on stockholders' equity			

What happens to the return on the stockholders' investment as the usage of debt increases? Why did the rate of interest increase in case C?

Answers   1. As the firm uses more debt financing, the return on equity increases because the firm earns more on the funds than it agrees to pay interest.

Debt ratio	0%	20	40	60
Debt outstanding	$0	20,000	40,000	60,000
Stockholders' equity	$100,000	80,000	60,000	40,000
Earnings before interest and taxes	$10,000	10,000	10,000	10,000
Interest expense	$0	1,200	2,400	3,600
Earnings before taxes	$10,000	8,800	7,600	6,400
Taxes	$3,500	3,080	2,660	2,240
Net earnings	$6,500	5,720	4,940	4,160
Return on stockholders' equity	6.50%	7.15	8.23	10.40

2.

	A	B	C
Debt outstanding	$0	3,000	5,000
Stockholders' equity	$10,000	7,000	5,000
Earnings before interest and taxes	$1,000	1,000	1,000
Interest expense	$0	300	600
Earnings before taxes	$1,000	700	400
Taxes (40% of earnings before taxes)	$400	280	160
Net earnings	$600	420	240
Return on stockholders' equity	6.0%	6.0%	4.8%

In this illustration, the return on the stockholders' investment does
not increase as the amount of debt increases. In C, the return actually
decreases. The use of financial leverage causes the return on equity to
decrease, since the after-tax cost of debt $[0.12(1 - 0.4) = 0.72 = 7.2\%]$
exceeds the 6 percent the firm earns on its assets ($600/$10,000) before
using debt financing. The additional risk to the lenders from firm C's
use of financial leverage explains why the interest rate increases.

Relationships

1. An increase in operating leverage _____ risk.
2. An increase in operating leverage _____ fixed asset turnover.
3. A decrease in financial leverage _____ risk.
4. An increase in financial leverage _____ fixed asset turnover.
5. If a firm issues bonds, financial leverage _____.
6. An increase in the successful use of financial leverage _____ the return on equity.
7. An increase in the tax rate _____ the cost of debt.
8. An increase in the use of preferred stock _____ financial leverage.
9. A decrease in the tax rate _____ the cost of preferred stock.
10. A decrease in sales _____ interest expense.

Answers

1. increases
2. decreases
3. decreases
4. does not affect (no change)
5. increases
6. increases
7. decreases
8. increases
9. does not affect (no change)
10. does not affect (no change)

What process is used to select a stock (see discussion of stocks in Chapter 21)? One answer to this question is that you determine the value of the stock and compare that value to the price of the stock. That is, you discount future cash flows to determine their present value. If the present value exceeds the stock's price, you buy the stock. If the present value is less than the price, you sell it if you own it. If you do not own the stock and are willing to bear the risk, you sell the stock short.

Alternatively, you can estimate the stock's return, compare it with your required return, and act accordingly. If the expected return exceeds your required return, you purchase the stock. If the expected return is less than the required return, you sell it. Either technique leads you to the same conclusion; the only substantive difference between the two is the units. Valuation is expressed in dollars while returns are in percentages.

The process for making investment decisions is the same for a firm's managers. They either compare the present value of future cash inflows with the current cost of the investment or they compare the investment's expected return with the required return. The terminology used may differ from the terms used in stock selection, but the process is the same.

The process for investing in plant and equipment requires an estimate of the cost of funds used to finance the purchase of the asset. That cost is referred to as the *cost of capital* and depends on the cost of the various sources of funds. A firm may borrow from a variety of sources and may issue preferred and common stock to raise funds. Lenders and stockholders are not altruistic. Creditors demand interest payments, and stockholders want a return from dividends and price appreciation. All sources of funds have a cost, so the question becomes: What is the best combination of debt and equity financing that *minimizes* the firm's cost of capital? That combination is referred to as the firm's *optimal capital structure*.

This chapter is concerned with the determination of the cost of capital and the firm's optimal capital structure; the following chapter uses this cost of capital to select among various competing uses for the firm's capital. This chapter begins with the costs of the various components in the firm's capital structure. This is followed by a discussion of the weighted cost of capital and the determination of the optimal capital structure. Once this capital structure has been determined, it should be maintained, as it generates the lowest cost of funds.

Maintaining the optimal capital structure does not mean the cost of capital is fixed. The cost of additional finance may rise even though the optimal capital structure is maintained, so it is necessary to differentiate between the average cost of capital and the cost of additional funds, which is the marginal cost of capital. The chapter ends by tying the cost of capital to the value of the firm's stock and showing how the excess use of financial leverage will lead to a higher cost of capital and lower valuation of the stock.

Components of the Cost of Capital

Optimal capital structure

Combination of debt and equity financing that minimizes the average cost of capital

Although the use of financial leverage may increase the return on stockholders' equity, it may also increase the risk associated with the firm. This suggests a question: What is the best combination of debt and equity financing? This best combination of the firm's sources of finance is its optimal capital structure. The optimal capital structure takes advantage of financial leverage without unduly increasing financial risks. In effect, it minimizes the overall cost of finance to the firm.

To determine the optimal capital structure, the financial manager must first establish the cost of each source of finance and then determine which combination of these sources minimizes the overall cost. This minimum cost of capital is important, because the financial manager must be able to judge investment opportunities. The selection of investments requires knowledge of the firm's cost of capital because an investment must earn a return sufficient to cover the cost of the funds used to acquire the asset. Thus, the determination of the firm's cost of capital is necessary for the correct application of the capital budgeting techniques that are explained in the next chapter.

This section is devoted to the determination of the costs of the components of the firm's capital structure. After these costs have been determined, the financial manager constructs a weighted average of the various costs. By varying the mix of sources of capital and recomputing the weighted averages, the optimal capital structure is determined.

Cost of Debt

As is explained in the previous chapter, the effective, after-tax cost of debt (k_d) depends on the interest rate (i), the corporate income tax rate (t), and risk. For a given risk class, the after-tax cost is

$$k_d = i(1 - t). \tag{13.1}$$

For example, if the interest rate is 7.6 percent and the tax rate is 35 percent, the after-tax cost of debt is

$$.076(1 - 0.35) = 0.0494 = 4.94\%.$$

Notice that the cost of debt is not the interest rate, but the interest rate adjusted for the tax write-off of the interest expense. Also notice that the cost of debt depends on the current rate of interest. It is not the interest rate at which the firm issued debt in the past. If a firm has debt outstanding that was issued 10 years ago with a fixed interest rate above or below the current interest rate, it is the *current interest rate that is used to determine the firm's current cost of capital.* When the older debt was issued, the previous rate was used to determine the firm's cost of capital at that time. Current cost is the interest rate that the firm must presently pay to borrow the money, adjusted for the current tax deduction.

The cost of debt is affected by any flotation costs associated with issuing new securities and by the term of the debt. Flotation costs paid to investment bankers reduce the proceeds of the sale and increase the interest cost per dollar borrowed. The larger the flotation costs, the greater the effective interest rate will be.

The cost of debt also depends on its term. Short-term debt generally carries a lower yield (lower interest cost) than long-term debt. If the firm issues long-term debt, the interest expense will probably be higher than if the firm had used short-term financing. However, by using long-term debt, the firm avoids the problems of retiring or rolling over (refunding) short-term debt, thus avoiding the risk associated with refinancing short-term debt.

The cost of debt also depends on the riskiness of the firm. The risk is related to the nature of the business (business risk) and to the use of financial leverage (financial risk). The more the firm uses debt financing, the greater will be the potential for it to fail to meet its debt obligations. This increase in the risk of default means that as the firm's use of financial leverage increases, the interest rate on borrowed money will increase. This is illustrated by the line k_d in Figure 13.1. Initially, the cost of debt may be stable, as the firm uses

F I G U R E 13.1
Cost of Debt

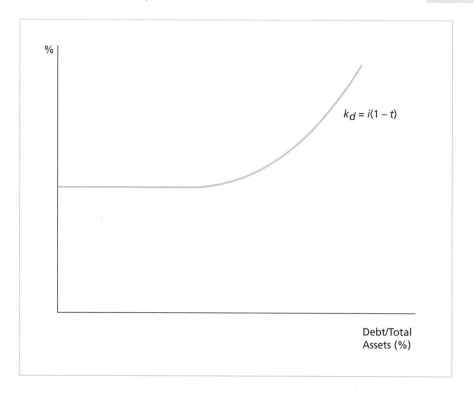

more financial leverage without increasing risk for the creditors. As the use of debt increases, the cost of debt starts to rise, because creditors demand more interest to compensate them for the increased risk of loss.

Cost of Preferred Stock

The price or value of preferred stock depends on the dividend and the yield required to induce investors to buy the shares. The equation for the valuation of a perpetual preferred stock is

$$P_p = \frac{D_p}{k_p}.$$

P_p is the price of the preferred stock, D_p is the dividend paid by the preferred stock, and k_p is the return required by investors to induce them to buy the stock. This equation may be rearranged to isolate the yield or the firm's cost of preferred stock.

$$P_p \times k_p = D_p$$

$$k_p = \frac{D_p}{P_p}. \tag{13.2}$$

As may be seen from this equation, the cost to the firm of the preferred stock depends on its dividend and the price that investors are willing to pay for the stock. If the prefherred stock pays a $1.00 dividend and sells for $12.00, the cost of the preferred stock to the firm is

$$k_p = \frac{\$1.00}{\$12.00} = 0.0833 = 8.33\%.$$

The 8.33 percent is the cost of the funds if the firm currently uses preferred stock financing.

For a new issue of preferred stock, the company should use the net price after selling the stock, which deducts the expense of selling the shares. For example, if this firm issued new preferred shares and had to pay an underwriting fee of 7 percent, it would net only $11.16 [$12.00(1 − 0.07)] per share. Thus, the cost of preferred stock financing would be

$$k_p = \frac{\$1.00}{\$11.16} = 8.96\%.$$

The cost of selling new shares to the public raises the cost of preferred stock. In this case, the cost increased by over half a percentage point.

From the viewpoint of the firm, the cost of preferred stock is higher than the cost of debt. This cost differential results from federal income tax laws; the *interest is tax deductible while the preferred dividend payments are not.* The increased cost of preferred stock argues for the use of debt. In recent years, there has been relatively little preferred stock financing compared to debt financing. While the preferred stock does not legally bind the firm to pay dividends and meet other indenture agreements, its additional cost overshadows these advantages.

Cost of Common Stock

The cost of common stock is the return required by investors to buy the firm's common stock. This cost of common equity is an opportunity cost: it is the return that investors could earn on comparable, alternative uses for their money. This cost applies both to existing shares and to new shares being issued by the firm.

Since the cost of common stock is an opportunity cost, there is no identifiable expense such as interest that the financial manager may use to determine the cost of these funds. However, the financial manager knows that the *cost of common stock exceeds the cost of debt.* No tax advantage is associated with equity, because dividends are paid in after-tax dollars (that is, dividends are not tax deductible), while interest is paid in before-tax dollars (that is, interest is a tax-deductible expense). In addition, common stock represents ownership and, therefore, is a riskier security than the firm's debt obligations. Although the firm is legally obligated to pay interest and meet the terms of indentures of its debt agreements, there is no legal obligation for the firm to pay dividends.

Since equity is riskier than debt to the investor, one means to estimate the cost of equity is to start with the interest rate paid to the holder of debt and add a risk premium. In this specification the cost of equity is

$$k_e = i + \text{Risk premium.} \tag{13.3}$$

Here k_e is the cost of equity and i is the interest rate being paid on new issues of debt (the current rate of interest unadjusted for the tax advantage). The risk premium associated with the common stock is then added to the interest rate. Although the financial manager knows the interest rate, the amount of the risk premium is not known. Quantifying the amount of this premium could be considered making an educated guess or, if you are a cynic, a matter of conjecture.

An alternative approach to the determination of the cost of equity is the capital asset pricing model (CAPM) presented in Chapter 8 and used in Chapter 21 to value common stock. In the CAPM, the required return on equity was

$$k_e = r_f + (r_m - r_f)\text{beta.}$$

In this specification, the cost of equity depends on the risk-free rate of interest (r_f) plus a risk premium. The risk premium depends on (1) the difference between the return on the market as a whole (r_m) and the risk-free rate and (2) the firm's beta coefficient, which measures the systematic risk associated with the firm.

Since this required return is the return necessary to induce investors to buy the stock, it may be viewed as the firm's cost of equity. Notice that to make the CAPM operational, the financial manager needs estimates of the risk-free rate, the return on the market, and the beta coefficient. Thus, the financial manager encounters the same problems making the CAPM operational as you face using the model as a tool for the valuation of common stock. However, the approach is theoretically superior to using the interest rate on the firm's bonds and adding on a risk premium, as it more precisely specifies the risk premium associated with investing in the stock.

A third approach defines the cost of equity in terms of investors' expected return on the stock; that is, the expected dividend yield plus expected growth (that is, capital gains). In Chapter 21, the return on common stock (r) was

$$r = \text{Dividend yield} + \text{Growth rate}$$

$$r = \frac{D_0(1 + g)}{P} + g. \tag{13.4}$$

As with the CAPM approach, the financial manager has to make this model operational. Although the current dividend and the price of the stock are known, estimates must be made of the future capital gains. This is, of course, the same problem you would face trying to use the common stock valuation model (the dividend-growth model) in Chapter 21.

While the three approaches appear to be different, they are essentially the same. The interest rate plus risk premium method and the CAPM method are similar. However, the CAPM specifies more clearly the risk premium in terms of the return on a risk-free security, the return on the market, and the systematic risk associated with the individual firm.

The CAPM method and the expected return method are identical if it is assumed that financial markets are in equilibrium. If that assumption holds, the required return found using the CAPM would also be the investors' expected return determined by using the expected dividend yield plus the expected capital gain. For example, if the expected return exceeded the required return, investors would drive up the price of the stock, causing the expected return to fall. If the expected return were less than the required return, the opposite would occur. Investors would seek to sell the shares, which would drive down their price and increase the yield. These changes will cease when the market is in equilibrium and the required return is equal to the expected return.

The same argument may be expressed in terms of a stock's valuation and its price. If the price of the stock is less than the valuation, investors bid up the price. If the price exceeds the valuation, investors seek to sell, which drives down the price. The incentive for stock prices to cease changing occurs when the price and the valuation are equal. Thus, if the equity markets are in equilibrium, a stock's price must equal its valuation, and the required return equals the expected return.

If the equity markets are in equilibrium, the stock's price may be substituted for its value in the dividend-growth model ($V = P$):

$$P = \frac{D_0(1 + g)}{k_e - g}.$$

By rearranging terms, the required return is

$$k_e - g = \frac{D_0(1 + g)}{P}$$

$$k_e = \frac{D_0(1 + g)}{P} + g. \tag{13.5}$$

In this form, the required return is the sum of the dividend yield plus the capital gain. This is identical to the investor's return and may be used as the cost of common equity.

Equation 13.5 expresses the cost of equity under the assumption that the firm does not have to issue new shares. The cost of equity is the cost of retained earnings. If the firm were to issue additional shares, it would not receive the market price of the stock because it would have to pay the flotation costs associated with selling new stock. To adjust for this expense, the flotation costs (F) must be subtracted from the price of the stock to obtain the net proceeds to the firm. This cost of new shares (k_{ne}) is expressed as

$$k_{ne} = \frac{D_0(1 + g)}{P - F} + g. \tag{13.6}$$

Obviously, the greater the flotation costs, the smaller will be the amount obtained from the sale of each new share, and the greater will be the cost of the equity.

The following example illustrates how the above model of the cost of common stock is used. A firm's earnings are growing annually at the rate of 7 percent. The common stock is currently paying $0.935 a share, and this dividend will grow annually at 7 percent so that the year's dividends will be $1 [or $D_0(1 + g) = 1]. If the common stock is selling for $25, the firm's cost of common stock is

$$k_e = \frac{\$0.935(1 + 0.07)}{\$25} + 0.07$$

$$= 0.04 + 0.07 = 0.11 = 11\%.$$

This tells management that investors currently require an 11 percent return on their investment in the stock. That return consists of a 4 percent dividend yield and the 7 percent growth. Failure on the part of management to achieve this return for the common stockholders will result in a decline in the price of the common stock.

If the firm has exhausted its retained earnings and must issue new stock, the cost of common stock must rise to cover the flotation costs. If these costs are $1 a share (4 percent of the price of the stock), the firm nets $24 per share, and the cost of equity is

$$k_{ne} = \frac{\$0.935(1 + 0.07)}{\$25 - \$1} + 0.07$$

$$= 0.0417 + 0.07 = 11.17\%.$$

The cost of equity is now higher. The firm must earn 11.17 percent in order to cover the flotation costs and investors' required return.[1]

As this discussion indicates, the cost of common equity may be viewed from the standpoint of the investor or of the firm. The investors' required return is the cost of equity to the firm, because this return must be met for investors to commit their funds to the firm. Failure to meet this cost will result in a lower value of the stock as investors move their funds to alternative investments. The lower stock price increases the cost of raising funds through a new issue of stock. The lower stock price will also hurt the firm's employees, if their compensation is tied to the value of the stock.

In addition to the dividend and the potential for growth, the value of the firm also depends on risk. Increased risk increases the required return; equity

---

[1]Flotation costs are a cash outflow that occurs when the securities are issued. This expense is capitalized on the balance sheet as an asset that is depreciated or "amortized" over the lifetime of the security (for example, the flotation costs associated with a 10-year bond issue are written off over 10 years). The depreciation generates a cash inflow that recaptures the flotation costs. Although writing off the capitalized asset restores the initial cash outflow, the timings of the outflows and of the inflows differ. The outflow occurs first, which raises the cost of a new issue of securities.

F I G U R E   13.2
Cost of Equity

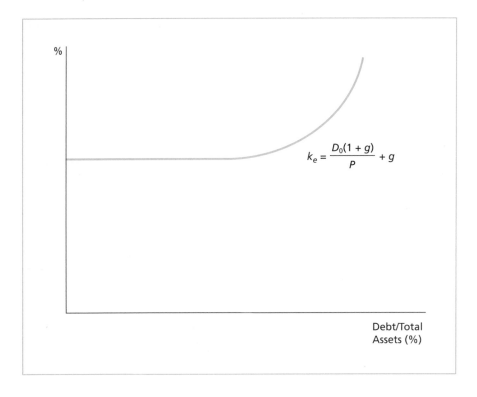

F I G U R E   13.2
Cost of Equity

funds become more expensive. The firm will have to earn a higher return on its investments to compensate equity investors for the additional risk.

Risk partially depends on the nature of the business (business risk) and partially on how management finances the firm's operations (financial risk). The relationship between financial risk and the cost of equity is illustrated in Figure 13.2, which relates the cost of equity (k_e) to the firm's use of financial leverage. The same relationship between the cost of debt and the firm's use of financial leverage was previously illustrated in Figure 13.1. In both cases, the cost of equity and the cost of debt may be initially stable, but ultimately both of these costs start to rise as the firm becomes more financially leveraged and hence more risky.

Cost of Capital: A Weighted Average

Cost of capital

Weighted average of the costs of a firm's sources of finance

The cost of capital to the firm is a weighted average of the costs of debt, preferred stock, and common stock. The weights depend on the proportion of the firm's assets financed by each source. Management should determine the optimal combination of the various sources that minimizes the weighted-average cost of funds and maximizes the value of the owners' investment in the firm.

Determining the firm's optimal capital structure requires understanding how the weighted-average cost of funds is derived. This section develops the weighted average cost of funds. The next section illustrates determination of the optimal capital structure.

Management has calculated that the current cost of each type of financing is as follows:

Cost of debt	5.20%
Cost of preferred stock	8.96
Cost of common stock (retained earnings)	11.00

The proportion (the weights) of the firm's assets financed by each type of financing is

Debt	40%
Preferred stock	10
Common stock (retained earnings)	50

To find the cost of capital, multiply the proportion of each component of the optimal capital structure by its respective costs and add the results. For this firm that yields:

	Cost × Weight = Weighted Cost
Debt	5.20% × 0.40 = 2.080%
Preferred stock	8.96 × 0.10 = 0.896
Common stock	11.00 × 0.50 = 5.500
	Cost of capital = 8.476%

The process of determining the cost of funds is generalized in Equation 13.7,

$$k = w_1 k_d + w_2 k_p + w_3 k_e. \qquad (13.7)$$

The equation states that the cost of capital (k) is a weighted average in which the costs of debt (k_d), preferred stock (k_p), and equity (k_e) are weighted by the extent to which they are used (that is, w_1, w_2, and w_3, respectively). These weights, along with the cost of each source, then determine the overall cost of funds. In the above illustration, the cost of capital is

$$k = (0.4)5.20 + (0.1)8.96 + (0.5)11.00 = 0.08476 = 8.476\%.$$

For this firm the weighted-average cost of capital is 8.476 percent. The firm must earn at least 8.476 percent on its investments to justify using its sources of finance. It is this cost of capital that will be used in the next chapter to determine whether a firm should make a particular investment in plant and equipment (that is, the cost of capital will be the discount factor used in capital budgeting).

If a firm does earn 8.476 cents after taxes on the investment of a dollar, then the firm has 2.080 cents to pay the interest, 0.896 cent to pay the dividends on the preferred stock, and 5.5 cents to pay dividends on the common stock or to reinvest in the company so that it may grow. The 8.476 cents covers the cost of each individual component of the firm's cost of capital.

If the company earns more than 8.476 percent, it can pay its debt expense and the preferred stock dividends, and it will have more than is necessary to meet the expected return of the common stockholders. For example, if the firm earns 10 percent (10 cents), 2.080 cents is paid to creditors and 0.896 cents goes to the preferred stockholders. That leaves 7.024 cents for the common stockholders, which exceeds the 5.5 cents required as a return on common stock. The firm may increase its dividends or increase its growth rate by reinvesting the earnings. Either way, investors will bid up the price of the stock. Since the return on an investment in the stock exceeded investors' required return, the value of this firm is increased.

The Optimal Capital Structure

The previous section illustrated the determination of the firm's weighted cost of capital. In that illustration, the cost of debt was less than the cost of equity because debt is less risky to the investor and the borrower may deduct interest payments before determining taxable income. If debt costs less than equity, couldn't management reduce the firm's cost of capital by substituting cheaper debt for more expensive equity? The answer is both "yes" and "no." As management *initially* substitutes cheaper debt, the cost of capital declines. However, as debt finances a larger proportion of the firm's assets and the firm becomes more financially leveraged, the costs of both debt and equity rise. What management needs to determine is the optimal combination of debt and equity financing that minimizes the firm's cost of capital. This trade-off between debt and equity is well understood by many corporate executives and is illustrated by the following statement taken from a Coca-Cola annual report. "Our company maintains debt levels we consider prudent based on our cash flow, interest coverage, and percentage of debt to capital. We use debt financing to lower our overall cost of capital, which increases our return on shareowners' equity."

The process of determining the optimal capital structure is illustrated in Exhibit 13.1. The first column in the table presents the proportion of debt financing. The second and third columns give the after-tax cost of debt and the cost of equity, respectively. (To ease the calculation, it is assumed that this firm has no preferred stock.) The cost of debt is less than the cost of equity, and both are initially constant over a range of debt ratios. The costs of both debt and equity start to rise as the firm becomes more financially leveraged. The fourth column presents the weighted-average cost of capital, which incorporates the cost of debt and the cost of equity, weighted by the proportion of assets financed by each.

Proportion of Debt Financing	Cost of Debt	Cost of Equity	Weighted Cost
0%	4%	10.0%	10.00%
10	4	10.0	09.40
20	4	10.0	08.80
30	4	10.0	08.20
40	4	10.5	07.90
50	5	11.5	08.25
60	6	13.0	08.80
70	8	15.0	10.10
80	10	18.0	11.60
90	15	22.0	15.70

If the firm is entirely financed by equity, the weighted-average cost of capital is the cost of equity. When the firm begins to substitute the cheaper debt financing for equity financing, the weighted-average cost of capital is reduced. As the use of debt increases, the weighted-average cost of capital initially declines.

However, this decline does not continue indefinitely as the firm substitutes additional cheaper debt. Eventually, both the cost of debt and the cost of equity begin to increase, because creditors and investors believe that more financial leverage increases the riskiness of the firm. At first, the increases in the cost of debt and the cost of equity may be insufficient to stop the decline in the weighted cost of capital. But as the costs of debt and equity continue to increase, the average cost of capital reaches a minimum and then starts to increase. In the table, this optimal capital structure occurs at 40 percent debt (40 percent debt financing to 60 percent equity financing). As additional debt is used, the costs of both debt and equity rise sufficiently that the cost of capital increases.

This determination of the optimal capital structure is also illustrated by Figure 13.3, which plots the cost of debt (k_d), the cost of equity (k_e), and the weighted-average cost of capital (k) given in Exhibit 13.1. As is readily seen in the graph, when the use of debt increases, the weighted-average cost of capital initially declines, reaches a minimum at debt of 40 percent $(D_1 = 40\%$ and $k_1 = 7.9\%)$, and then starts to increase.

The optimal capital structure is reached at the minimum point on the weighted-average cost of capital structure. The financial manager should acquire this combination of financing because it involves the lowest cost of funds.

This minimum cost of capital should be used to judge potential investments; it will be employed in the capital budgeting techniques discussed in the next chapter. As the firm expands and makes additional investments in plant and equipment, it must also expand its sources of financing. These additional sources should maintain the firm's optimal capital structure. Additional (or marginal) investments are financed by additional (or marginal) funds. As long as the optimal capital structure is maintained, additional funds should cost the

FIGURE 13.3
Cost of Capital

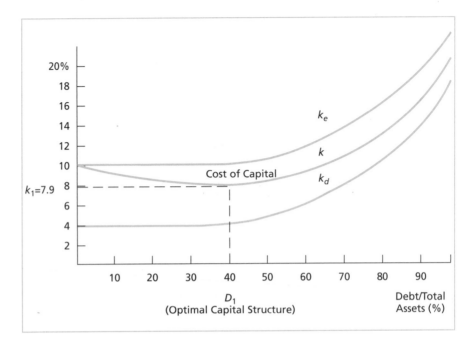

same as the weighted average (that is, the weighted marginal cost of funds is equal to the firm's average cost of capital). Of course, if the additional investments increase the riskiness of the firm or the flotation costs associated with issuing new securities rise, then the cost of the additional funds will increase. In that case, which is discussed in the next section, the cost of the marginal funds will exceed the firm's weighted-average cost of capital.

For many firms, the optimal capital structure is a range of debt financing. In the example presented in Exhibit 13.1 and Figure 13.3, the weighted-average cost of capital evidences little variation for debt financing ranging from 30 percent to 50 percent. This indicates that the positive impact of debt financing in lowering the firm's cost of capital is achieved when 30 percent of the firm's assets are debt financed. Additional use of debt has little impact on the cost of capital until more than 50 percent of the assets are debt financed. Thus, the optimal capital structure may be viewed as a range of debt-to-equity financing and not just a specific combination of debt to equity.

That the optimal capital structure is a range and not a specific combination is important from a practical viewpoint. New issues of debt or common stock may be made infrequently, and when debt or stock is issued, the dollar amount of the issue may be substantial. Because of the cost of issuing them, a firm will not sell new securities for a trivial amount of money. Thus, when new securities are issued, the proportions of debt and equity financing are altered. If the optimal capital structure were not a range, every new issue of securities would alter the firm's cost of capital. Since the optimal debt structure is a range, a firm has flexibility in issuing new securities and may tailor the security issues to market conditions. For example, if management anticipates that interest rates will increase in the future, it may choose to issue debt now and use equity financing at some future date. This flexibility in the type of securities issued is in part the result of the fact that the optimal capital structure is a range of debt-to-equity financing. But even the existence of a range does not mean that (1) a firm can always use the same type of financing, or (2) it is not important for a firm to seek the optimal capital structure. Finding the optimal capital structure is required if management wants to maximize the value of the firm.

The Marginal Cost of Capital

Marginal cost of capital

Cost of additional sources of finance

Once the optimal capital structure has been determined, the financial manager should maintain it. Preserving the optimal capital structure, however, does not necessarily mean that the cost of capital is constant. The cost of additional funds (the marginal cost of capital) can rise. If the cost of debt or the cost of equity increases as the firm uses more debt and equity financing, the marginal cost of capital will rise, even though the optimal capital structure is preserved. For example, the cost of common stock depends on whether the firm is using retained earnings or issuing new shares. New shares cost more than retained earnings because of flotation costs. The marginal cost of capital will increase when new shares are issued even though the optimal combination of debt and equity financing is preserved.

Consider the illustration in Exhibit 13.1, in which the optimal cost of capital was 7.9 percent with 40 percent debt and 60 percent equity. That cost consisted of the 4 percent after-tax cost of debt and the 10.5 percent cost of equity. This cost of equity is the cost of retained earnings because these equity funds are used before the firm would issue new (and more expensive) common stock.

Suppose, however, the firm has additional investment opportunities that would require more than its retained earnings. It could borrow all the necessary funds, which would increase the firm's use of financial leverage. Such a course of action would be undesirable because the firm would no longer be maintaining its optimal capital structure. To maintain the optimal capital structure, the firm will have to issue additional shares (and pay the associated flotation costs) and simultaneously borrow some additional funds if it wants to make these investments. The firm must borrow 40 percent of the additional funds and issue new shares to cover the remaining 60 percent of the additional financing. The impact of the increase in the cost of equity due to the flotation costs is to increase the cost of capital, even though the proportion of debt to equity is maintained.

To illustrate this increase in the cost of capital, suppose the 10.5 percent cost of equity consisted of the following dividend yield and growth rate:

$$k_e = \frac{\$0.95(1 + 0.055)}{\$20} + 0.055$$

$$k_e = \frac{\$1.00}{\$20} + 0.055 = 0.05 + 0.055 = 10.5\%.$$

Once retained earnings are exhausted, the firm will have to issue new shares with a flotation cost of $1.00 per share, so the firm nets $19 per share. The cost of these new shares (k_{ne}) is

$$k_{ne} = \frac{\$0.95(1 + 0.055)}{\$20 - \$1} + 0.055$$

$$k_{ne} = \frac{\$1.00}{\$19} + 0.055 = 0.0526 + 0.055 = 10.76\%.$$

The cost of the common stock rises from 10.5 percent to 10.76 percent and the firm's cost of capital rises to

$$k = (0.4)(4\%) + (0.6)(10.76\%) = 8.056\%.$$

The cost of capital has risen from 7.9 percent to 8.056 percent even though management is maintaining the optimal capital structure of 40 percent debt and 60 percent equity.

Which of these two costs (7.9 percent and 8.056 percent) does the firm use when making investment decisions? The answer depends on how many investment opportunities the firm has. If the firm has insufficient opportunities to consume its retained earnings, the cost of capital is 7.9 percent. However, after the retained earnings are exhausted and new shares must be sold, the firm's cost of capital rises to 8.056 percent. Then, 8.056 percent should be used to judge additional investment opportunities because that is the firm's cost of capital.

The following example will illustrate this process of making additional investments and maintaining the optimal capital structure as the cost of finance changes. Currently, the firm desires to make six $1,000,000 investments for a total cost of $6,000,000. (Remember, the techniques for selecting investments will be discussed in the subsequent chapter. In reality, the determination of the cost of capital and the decision to make long-term investments are tied together, but only one piece of the puzzle can be discussed at a time!) The firm has $10,000,000 in assets financed 40 percent with debt and 60 percent with equity. This optimal capital structure was determined earlier and has a cost of capital of 10.5 percent. The information used to determine that cost of capital was

1. an after-tax cost of debt of 4 percent,
2. a current dividend of $0.95, which will rise to $1.00 during the year,
3. a stock price of $20,
4. a growth rate of 5.5 percent.

During the period when the desired investments are to be made, the firm will generate retained earnings of $1,200,000. In addition, the firm's creditors have informed management that if the firm borrows more than $2,000,000, the rate of interest will have to be increased, even if the firm maintains its capital structure. The impact of this increase will raise the after-tax cost of debt to 5 percent. What will be the marginal cost of each additional dollar to the firm?

This is the most complicated question posed in this chapter. Management knows the optimal capital structure is 40 percent debt and that this structure should be retained. For every additional $400,000 of borrowed funds, the firm must have $600,000 in new equity. Thus, the $1,200,000 in new retained earnings will support $800,000 in additional borrowed capital for a total of $2,000,000 in new finance. The cost of these funds is

$$k = (0.4)(4\%) + (0.6)(10.5\%) = 7.9\%.$$

That is, the cost of the first $2,000,000 in additional funds (that is, the marginal cost) is 7.9 percent. However, $2,000,000 will not cover all the investment opportunities.

Since an additional $4,000,000 is needed to make all the desired investments, the financial manager decides to issue $2,400,000 in additional stock $(0.6 \times \$4,000,000)$; $2,400,000 in additional stock will support $1,600,000 in additional debt and still maintain the 40 percent debt financing. What will be the cost of the additional funds? If the after-tax cost of debt remains 4 percent and the cost of new shares is 10.76 percent, the firm's cost of capital is

$$k = (0.4)(4\%) + (0.6)(10.76\%) = 8.056\%.$$

However, does the after-tax cost of debt remain at 4 percent? The answer is yes only for the first $2,000,000; above that, additional debt has an after-tax cost of 5 percent. The financial manager anticipated borrowing $800,000 to be used in conjunction with the $1,200,000 in retained earnings and $1,600,000 to be used with the $2,400,000 raised through the issuing of new shares. That is a total of $2,400,000. Only the first $2,000,000 will have an after-tax cost of 4 percent. The last $400,000 will cost 5 percent. Once again, the cost of capital changes even though the optimal combination of debt and equity financing is maintained. The cost of capital now rises to

$$k = (0.4)(5\%) + (0.6)(10.76\%) = 8.456\%.$$

These different costs of capital are illustrated in Figure 13.4, which presents the firm's marginal cost of capital. As additional funds are needed, the marginal cost of capital rises. The first increase occurs at $2,000,000, when the firm runs out of retained earnings. The second increment occurs at $5,000,000, when the firm runs out of borrowing capacity with the lower after-tax cost of debt.

How are these amounts ($2,000,000 and $5,000,000) determined? These breaks in the marginal cost of capital schedule may be determined by the following equation:

$$\text{Break point} = \frac{\text{Amount of funds available at given cost}}{\text{Proportion of that component in the capital structure}}. \quad (13.8)$$

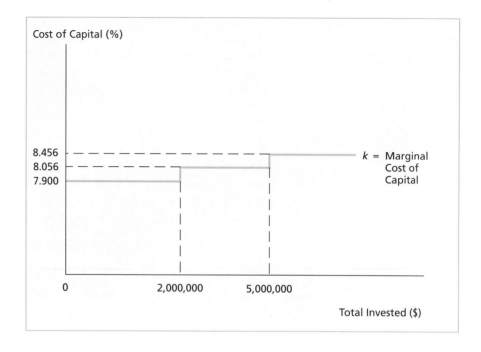

For example, there were $1,200,000 of available retained earnings, and equity constituted 60 percent of the capital structure. Thus, the break point for the retained earnings is

$$\text{Break point (retained earnings)} = \frac{\$1,200,000}{0.6} = \$2,000,000.$$

The cost of capital of the first $2,000,000 uses the lower cost of retained earnings (10.5 percent) in the calculation. Once $2,000,000 is exceeded, the higher cost of new stock (10.76 percent) must be used.

The same logic applies to the cost of debt. The break point for debt is

$$\text{Break point (chapter debt)} = \frac{\$2,000,000}{0.4} = \$5,000,000.$$

As long as the total funds raised are less than $5,000,000, the lower after-tax cost of debt applies (4 percent), but if the total capital exceeds $5,000,000, the higher after-tax cost of debt must be used (5 percent).

When these individual pieces are put together, the cost of capital for different amounts of funds is

$$\$0 - \$2,000,000: (0.4)(4\%) + (0.6)(10.5\%) = 7.9\%$$

$$\$2,000,001 - \$5,000,000: (0.4)(4\%) + (0.6)(10.76\%) = 8.056\%$$

$$\text{above } \$5,000,000: (0.4)(5\%) + (0.6)(10.76\%) = 8.456\%.$$

This is, of course, the schedule of the marginal costs of funds presented in Figure 13.4, which illustrates the increments in the marginal cost of capital and at what level of total funds these increments occur.

The Optimal Capital Structure and the Value of the Firm's Stock

The successful use of financial leverage increases the return on the firm's equity and increases earnings per share. Earnings per share increase because as the firm uses more debt financing and becomes more financially leveraged, it issues fewer shares. Since earnings are spread over fewer shares, per share earnings increase. Does this increased use of debt and higher per share earnings lead to a higher stock price? What is the relationship between the optimal capital structure and the price of the stock?

These are important and difficult questions that are developed more fully in advanced texts on finance. The following discussion can, at best, only indicate the relationship among the components of the cost of capital, the optimal capital structure, and stock valuation.

Since the goal of management is to maximize the value of the firm's stock, the optimal capital structure is that combination of debt and equity financing that maximizes the value of the stock. The financial manager substitutes debt for equity as long as this substitution increases per share earnings without unduly increasing the risk associated with debt financing. The increase in per share earnings, when coupled with only a moderate addition to risk, should increase the value of the stock. However, if the firm continues to substitute debt for equity and use more financial leverage, the element of risk will increase sufficiently to offset the advantage of higher per share earnings. The net effect is to cause the value of the shares to fall.

This trade-off is illustrated in Exhibit 13.2. The firm needs $1,000, so the financial manager considers the impact of borrowing the funds. In part I, the first row presents the amount of debt to be issued in increments of $100. The second line presents the before-tax cost of the debt (the interest rate), and the third line gives the cost of equity. As the firm becomes more financially leveraged, the before-tax cost of debt and the cost of equity rise. The fourth line indicates that as the firm uses more debt financing, the number of shares outstanding is reduced (fewer shares will have to be issued to raise the necessary capital).

Part II presents a simple income statement for the firm as it uses more debt. Operating income ($250) is the same regardless of the choice of financing. As more debt is used (and as the rate of interest charged rises), interest expense rises, reducing taxable earnings and, correspondingly, reducing taxes. The lower taxes do not completely offset the higher interest payments, so net income declines. Earnings per share, however, rise because the smaller earnings are spread over a fewer number of shares.

Parts III and IV present the value of the stock and the cost of capital at the various combinations of debt and equity financing. Initially, the use of

EXHIBIT 13.2 Determination of the Optimal Capital Structure Using Market Value of Stock

I.

Amount of debt	$ 0	$100	$200	$300	$400	$500	$600
Interest rate	10%	10%	10%	11%	12%	14%	16%
Cost of equity	15%	15%	15.5%	16.6%	17.8%	19.4%	21.5%
Number of shares outstanding	10	9	8	7	6	5	4

II.

Earnings before interest & taxes	$250	$250	$250	$250	$250	$250	$250
Interest	$ —	$ 10	$ 20	$ 33.0	$ 48.0	$ 70	$ 96.0
Earnings before taxes	$250	$240	$230	$217.0	$202.0	$180	$154.0
Tax (at 40%)	$100	$ 96	$ 92	$ 86.8	$ 80.8	$ 72	$ 61.6
Net income	$150	$144	$138.00	$130.20	$121.20	$108.00	$ 92.40
Earnings per share	$ 15	$ 16	$ 17.25	$ 18.60	$ 20.20	$ 21.60	$ 23.10

III.

Value of a share	$100	$106.67	$ 111.29	$112.05	$ 113.48	$ 111.34	$ 107.44

IV.

Cost of capital	15%	14.1%	13.6%	13.6%	13.56%	13.9%	14.36%

financial leverage increases the value of the stock. These values are derived using the dividend-growth model:

$$V = \frac{D_0(1 + g)}{k_e - g}.$$

To simplify the illustration, assume that all earnings are distributed. Therefore, the value of the stock is

$$V = \frac{D_0(1 + g)}{k_e - g} = \frac{\text{Earnings per share}}{k_e},$$

when $g = 0$. Thus, when per share earnings are $17.25 (at $200 debt), the value of the stock is $17.25/0.155 = $111.29.

As may be seen in part III, the value of the stock initially rises because the firm is successfully employing financial leverage. However, as the firm becomes more financially leveraged, the increased risk starts to offset the advantage of financial leverage. The value of the stock reaches a maximum and then starts to decline.

The combination of debt and equity financing that maximizes the value of the stock also is the firm's optimal capital structure. This is illustrated in part IV, which presents the cost of capital. In this illustration, the minimum cost of capital occurs when the firm seeks to use $400 in debt so that 40 percent of its assets are financed with debt and 60 percent with equity. At that capital structure, the minimum cost of capital is

$$k = w_d(k_d)(1 - t) + w_e(k_e)$$
$$= (0.4)(0.12)(1 - 0.4) + (0.6)(0.178) = 13.56\%.$$

Exhibit 13.2 presents the same concept that was illustrated in Exhibit 13.1 but ties together the maximization of the value of the stock with the minimization of the firm's cost of funds. The combination of debt and equity financing that minimizes the cost of capital will also maximize the value of the stock. This statement has intuitive appeal. If the financial manager is able to minimize the firm's cost of funds, that should benefit the firm's owners. If the financial manager is not minimizing the cost of capital, the firm will not be as attractive to investors, and the value of the equity will be reduced. Thus, maximizing the value of the firm requires minimizing the cost of capital.

Cost of Capital: Review and Problem Areas

No topic in this text is more important than the determination of a firm's cost of funds and its optimal capital structure. As the previous discussion indicated, this determination is a complex procedure that in reality is difficult to apply. The following discussion reiterates some of the problem areas and reveals others that until now have been swept under the carpet.

First, to determine the cost of capital, the financial manager must know all the component costs. As was previously mentioned, the estimation of the cost of equity requires information (the future growth rate in dividends, the firm's beta coefficient, the appropriate risk-free rate, the expected return on the market, and so on) that is not readily observable. Inaccurate estimates will produce an inaccurate measure of the cost of equity and an inaccurate estimate of the cost of capital.

Second, the financial manager needs to know how the market will value the shares after the financing decision is made. This is, of course, impossible to know. Obviously, the financial manager makes the financing decision in anticipation of the market treating the shares in a particular way, but conditions change, and the anticipated correct financial structure in one environment may not be correct in a different environment. The large use of debt financing leverage generated lower stock prices for many firms during the 2007–2008 financial crisis.

Third, the discussion examined the optimal capital structure in terms of maximizing the value of a firm's stock. That may be acceptable for publicly held firms, but the vast majority of businesses are not publicly held. Even though most privately held firms are small, the determination of their cost of capital remains important. (As is explained in the next chapter, this determination is a critical part of the decision to invest in plant and equipment.) The financial managers of small, private firms cannot know the current value of their firm's equity or the impact their decisions will have on that value.

Fourth, a notable theory in finance contends that a firm's capital structure may be irrelevant. This conclusion is derived from several important assumptions, one of which is that if a firm uses too little financial leverage, investors can substitute their own leverage for the firm's. Consider a firm with no debt financing. Investors can borrow money to buy the stock (that is, buy the stock on margin). In such a case, the stockholders are substituting their own leverage for the firm's use of financial leverage. If the firm uses a large amount of financial leverage, the stockholders can then hold portfolios of cash and the stock, which reduces the impact of the firm's large use of financial leverage. By having stockholders alter their portfolios to offset a firm's use of financial leverage, one can reason that an optimal capital structure is irrelevant. What is important is the operating income the firm generates, and not how that income is divided between creditors in the form of interest payments and owners in the form of dividends and capital gains.[2]

---

[2]For a discussion of this proposition and the theory that dividend policy is irrelevant, see the latest edition of an advanced text on corporate finance, such as Eugene Brigham and Michael Ehrhardt, *Financial Management: Theory and Practice*, 13th ed. (Mason, Ohio: South-Western College Publishing, 2010).

Summary

All assets must be financed. While there may be a variety of securities, there are ultimately only two sources: debt and equity. If the firm uses debt financing or preferred stock financing, it is financially leveraged. If the firm uses financial leverage, it increases risk, which may increase the cost of the components of the firm's capital structure.

One component of the capital structure, the cost of debt, depends on the interest rate that must be paid and the tax saving associated with the deductibility of interest payments. Another component, the cost of preferred stock, depends on the dividend that is paid and the net proceeds from the sale of the preferred stock. The third component, the cost of common equity, depends on whether the firm uses retained earnings or issues new shares of stock. New equity is more expensive because of the flotation costs associated with the sale of the new shares.

The cost of common stock is an opportunity cost concept: It is the return necessary to induce investors to own the stock. This cost may be determined by adding an equity premium to the interest rate paid creditors such as bondholders. An alternative approach to determine the cost of common stock is to use the capital asset pricing model, which incorporates the return on a risk-free security, the return on the market as a whole, and the systematic (market) risk associated with the stock. A third approach uses the expected dividend yield and expected growth to determine the cost of common stock.

Management's task is to determine the best combination of debt and equity financing, that is, to determine the firm's optimal capital structure. That structure takes advantage of financial leverage without unduly increasing risk. That combination of debt and equity financing minimizes the overall cost of capital and minimizes the value of the common stock.

Once the optimal capital structure has been determined, that combination of debt and equity should be maintained. However, even if the proportions are maintained, the marginal cost of capital may increase as the firm has to pay flotation costs and issue riskier debt with a higher interest rate to raise additional funds.

Review Objectives

Now that you have completed this chapter, you should be able to

1. Identify the components of a firm's capital structure (p. 261).
2. Differentiate among the factors that affect the cost of debt, the cost of preferred stock, and the cost of common stock (pp. 262–268).
3. Compute the cost of capital (pp. 268–270).
4. Explain why a firm's cost of capital changes with changes in its capital structure (pp. 270–273).
5. Determine the firm's optimal capital structure (pp. 270–273).
6. Distinguish between the average and marginal cost of funds (pp. 273–277).
7. Explain the relationship between the optimal capital structure and the value of a firm's stock (pp. 277–279).

Problems

1. A firm's current balance sheet is as follows:

Assets	$100	Debt	$10
		Equity	$90

a. What is the firm's weighted-average cost of capital at various combinations of debt and equity, given the following information?

Debt/Assets	After-Tax Cost of Debt	Cost of Equity	Cost of Capital
0%	8%	12%	?
10	8	12	?
20	8	12	?
30	8	13	?
40	9	14	?
50	10	15	?
60	12	16	?

b. Construct a pro forma balance sheet that indicates the firm's optimal capital structure. Compare this balance sheet with the firm's current balance sheet. What course of action should the firm take?

Assets	$100	Debt	$?
		Equity	$?

c. As a firm initially substitutes debt for equity financing, what happens to the cost of capital, and why?

d. If a firm uses too much debt financing, why does the cost of capital rise?

2. The management of a conservative firm has adopted a policy of never letting debt exceed 30 percent of total financing. The firm will earn $10,000,000 but distribute 40 percent in dividends, so the firm will have $6,000,000 to add to retained earnings. Currently the price of the stock is $50; the company pays a $2 per share dividend, which is expected to grow annually at 10 percent. If the company sells new shares, the net to the company will be $48. Given this information, what is the

a. cost of retained earnings;

b. cost of new common stock?

The rate of interest on the firm's long-term debt is 10 percent and the firm is in the 32 percent income tax bracket. If the firm issues more than $2,400,000, the interest rate will rise to 11 percent. Given this information, what is the

c. cost of debt;

d. cost of debt in excess of $2,400,000?

The firm raises funds in increments of $3,000,000 consisting of $900,000 in debt and $2,100,000 in equity. This strategy maintains the capital structure of 30 percent debt and 70 percent equity. Develop the marginal cost of capital schedule through $12,000,000. What impact would each of the following have on the marginal cost of capital schedule?

e. the firm's income tax rate increases

f. the firm retains all of its earnings and the price of the stock is unaffected

g. $12,000,000 is insufficient to meet attractive investment opportunities

3. a. Given the following, determine the firm's optimal capital structure:

Debt/Assets	After-Tax Cost of Debt	Cost of Equity
0%	8%	12%
10	8	12
20	8	12
30	9	12
40	9	13

50	10	15
60	12	17

b. If the firm were using 60 percent debt and 40 percent equity, what would that tell you about the firm's use of financial leverage?

c. What two reasons explain why debt is cheaper than equity?

d. If the firm were using 30 percent debt and 70 percent equity and earned a return of 11.7 percent on an investment, would this mean that stockholders would receive less than their required return of 12 percent? What return would stockholders receive?

4. Sun Instruments expects to issue new stock at $34 a share with estimated flotation costs of 7 percent of the market price. The company currently pays a $2.10 cash dividend and has a 6 percent growth rate. What are the costs of retained earnings and new common stock?

5. HBM, Inc. has the following capital structure:

Assets	$400,000	Debt	$140,000
		Preferred stock	20,000
		Common stock	240,000

The common stock is currently selling for $15 a share, pays a cash dividend of $0.75 per share, and is growing annually at 6 percent. The preferred stock pays a $9 cash dividend and currently sells for $91 a share. The debt pays interest of 8.5 percent annually, and the firm is in the 30 percent marginal tax bracket.

a. What is the after-tax cost of debt?

b. What is the cost of preferred stock?

c. What is the cost of common stock?

d. What is the firm's weighted-average cost of capital?

6. The financial manager of a firm determines the following schedules of cost of debt and cost of equity for various combinations of debt financing:

Debt/Assets	After-Tax Cost of Debt	Cost of Equity
0%	4%	8%
10	4	8
20	4	8
30	5	8
40	6	10
50	8	12
60	10	14
70	12	16

   a. Find the optimal capital structure (that is, optimal combination of debt and equity financing).

   b. Why does the cost of capital initially decline as the firm substitutes debt for equity financing?

   c. Why will the cost of funds eventually rise as the firm becomes more financially leveraged?

   d. Why is debt financing more common than financing with preferred stock?

   e. If interest were not a tax-deductible expense, what effect would that have on the firm's cost of capital? Why?

Additional Problems with Answers

1. a. What is the cost of debt and retained earnings if the interest rate is 10 percent, the federal corporate income tax rate is 30 percent, the firm's anticipated growth rate is 12 percent, the current dividend is $0.50, and price of the stock is $12?

   b. What is the weighted-average cost of capital if the firm uses 24 percent debt and 76 percent equity?

   c. If the firm has limited funds available, such as limited earnings and retained earning, then additional funds will cost more. The firm has $2,300,000 in retained earnings, after which it will have to issue new shares. How much total funding can it obtain before it must issue additional shares if equity constitutes 76 percent in the firm's capital structure?

   d. If the firm exhausts its retained earnings and must issue additional shares, the cost of equity includes flotation costs. If these costs are $1 per share, what is the cost of new equity?

   e. What is the firm's cost of capital if it must issue additional shares?

2. a. Given the following schedules,

Debt/Assets	Cost of Debt	Cost of Equity
0%	4%	12%
10	4	12
20	5	12
30	5	12
40	6	13
50	6.5	14
60	7	15.5
70	8	17
80	9.5	18

what is the firm's cost of capital at the various combinations of debt and equity?

b. What is the firm's optimal capital structure? Complete the balance sheet showing that combination of debt and equity financing.

Balance Sheet for Firm X as of XX/XX/20XX			
Assets	$2,000	Debt Equity	$2,000

c. If the firm earns $10 on every $100 of assets, will the stockholders receive more or less than their required rate of return if the firm uses its optimal combination of debt and equity financing?

Answers   1. a. Cost of debt $= \$10(1 - .3) = .07 = 7\%$

Cost of equity (retained earnings) $= \$0.50(1 + .12)/\$12 + .12 = 16.7\%$

b. Weighted cost of capital (k): $k = w_1 k_d + w_2 k_p + w_3 k_e$. The new symbol (w) represents the weight of each source of funds in the firm's capital structure. If the firm uses 24 percent debt, and 76 percent equity, the cost of capital is

$$k = (0.24)(.07) + (0.76)(.167) = 14.372\%.$$

c. Once the firm has exhausted its retained earnings and must issue additional shares, the cost of equity increases. Where this break point occurs is determined by the following equation:

$$\text{Break point} = \frac{\text{Amount of funds available at a given cost}}{\text{Proportion of that component in the capital structure}}$$

If the firm has $2,300,000 in retained earnings, the break point occurs at $2,300,000/.76 = \$3,026,315$. After the firm raises $3,026,315 (that is., $726,315 in debt and $2,300,000 in retained earnings), it will have to issue new shares as it will have exhausted the retained earnings.

d. Cost of new equity is

$$\$0.50(1 + .12)/(\$12 - \$1) + .12 = 17.1\%.$$

e. The cost of capital now uses the cost of new equity (17.1%) instead of 16.7%, so the cost of capital becomes

$$k = (0.24)(.07) + (0.76)(.171) = 14.676\%.$$

2. a. The cost of capital is a weighted average at each combination of debt to equity financing. For example, if the firm uses 10 percent financing and 90 percent equity financing, the weighted average is

$$(0.1)(4\%) + (0.90)(12\%) = 11.2\%.$$

The cost of capital at the various combinations of debt and equity are as follows:

Debt/Assets	Cost of Debt	Cost of Equity	Cost of Capital
0%	4%	12%	12%
10	4	12	11.2
20	5	12	10.6
30	5	12	9.9
40	6	13	10.2
50	6.5	14	10.25
60	7	15.5	10.4
70	8	17	10.7
80	9.5	18	11.2

Notice how the cost of capital initially declines as the firm substitutes cheaper debt for equity, but starts to rise as the firm becomes financially leveraged. The optimal combination that minimizes the weighted average occurs with 30 percent debt financing and 70 percent equity financing. At the combination, the balance is as follows:

Balance Sheet for Firm X as of XX/XX/20XX			
Assets	$2,000	Debt	600
		Equity	1,400
			$2,000

c. If the firm earns 10 percent on assets, it is earning $200. Since the cost of debt is 5 percent, the firm pays $30 in interest expense ($600 × 0.05). Because $170 is left for stockholders, the return on equity, is 12.14 percent ($170/1,400). Notice that by successfully using financial leverage, the return on the equity is increased.

Relationships

1. An increase in the tax rate _____ the cost of debt.
2. Increased use of debt financing initially _____ the cost of capital.
3. A decrease in the price of stock _____ the cost of capital.
4. A decrease in a stock's beta coefficient _____ the required return, which _____ the cost of capital.
5. An increase in interest rates _____ the cost of capital.
6. A decrease in the cost of an investment in plant or equipment _____ the cost of capital.
7. If a firm increases its use of equity financing, the debt ratio _____.
8. Flotation costs _____ the cost of capital.
9. A decrease in the tax rate _____ the cost of preferred stock.
10. Moving toward the firm's optimal capital structure should _____ the value of the firm.
11. The cost of selling new securities _____ the cost of capital even if the optimal capital structure is maintained.
12. Increasing the amount of debt in excess of the optimal capital structure _____ the firm's financial risk.

Answers

1. decreases
2. decreases
3. increases
4. decreases; decreases
5. increases
6. does not affect (no change)
7. decreases
8. increase
9. does not affect (no change)
10. increase
11. increases
12. increases

According to Henry David Thoreau, "Goodness is the only investment that never fails." Many financial managers and investors are certainly aware from experience that some investments do fail! But according to Gilbert and Sullivan, "Nothing venture, nothing win." While Gilbert and Sullivan were referring to love, the concept obviously applies to investing. You can't win if you are not in the game, and that is the dilemma facing financial managers and all investors. You have to make investments in order to earn a return, but you also bear the risk that you will achieve the expected return.

This chapter covers long-term investments in plant and equipment. According to its annual report, ConocoPhillips committed over $10 billion to additional plant, equipment, and exploration during 2009. That is a substantial investment in long-term assets for just one year. A much smaller firm, Travel Centers of America, whose total assets are less than 1 percent of ConocoPhillips' total assets, acquired $11 million in plant and equipment.

The managements of both firms had to decide which long-term investments to make. This selection process is capital budgeting. Capital budgeting answers such questions as: (1) Should an old machine be replaced with a new machine? (2) Should the level of operation of the firm be expanded by purchasing new plant and equipment? or (3) Which of two competing new machines should the firm purchase? These decisions are crucial to the life and profitability of the firm. Since capital budgeting techniques aid in this decision-making process, they are crucial to increasing the wealth of the firm and its stockholders.

This chapter is concerned with the methods of capital budgeting. Initially the discussion is directed to the determination of the appropriate cash inflows

and outflows from an investment. The bulk of Chapter 14 describes and illustrates the net present value and internal rate of return methods of capital budgeting. All the illustrations use simple numbers. Although few investments cost
$1,000 or generate cash inflows of $400 a year for four years, such examples
facilitate the explanation.

The chapter then explores using net present value and internal rate of
return to choose between mutually exclusive investments. Although net present value and internal rate of return often result in the same ranking of competing investments, the possibility of different rankings does exist. This section
includes a discussion of what may cause conflicting rankings and how they
may be resolved.

The last section of Chapter 14 introduces risk analysis into capital budgeting. Virtually all investments involve risk, and the techniques used to integrate
risk into the analysis of securities also apply to the analysis of plant and equipment. This integration may be achieved by altering an investment's cash flow or
the cost of capital used to discount an investment's cash flow. Risk adjustments
are an involved topic, so this coverage can only introduce you to techniques
that are developed in advanced courses covering capital budgeting.

Valuation and Long-Term Investment Decisions

The process for investing in plant and equipment is essentially the same as that
for investing in securities. In Chapter 23, the current value of a bond is determined by discounting the future interest payments and principal repayment
by the yield on comparable debt instruments. In Chapter 21, future dividend
payments and the growth in the firm's dividend are discounted back to the
present by the required return to determine the value of a stock. Both models
are illustrations of discounted cash flows: Future cash inflows are discounted
back to the present and compared with the cost (cash outflows) necessary to
make the investment.

An investment in plant and equipment is conceptually no different than
an investment in a stock or bond. Investments in plant and equipment require
management to estimate future cash inflows, discount them back to the present at the firm's cost of capital, and compare this present value with the cost
of making the investment. This process of determining the value of investment

Capital budgeting

The process of selecting long-term investments, primarily plant and equipment

in plant and equipment and selecting among various long-term investments is referred to as capital budgeting.

Although an investment in plant and equipment may conceptually be the same as an investment in a long-term financial asset, there are important differences. Valuing and buying or selling existing securities transfer existing wealth. The buyer gives cash for the security and the seller receives cash for the security. There is a transfer of assets between the two participants. Many investments in plant and equipment, however, *create new wealth*. The new plant and equipment will be used to create new products and services. If these new products are profitable, they should increase the value of the firm. That is, the creation of new wealth by the firm translates into a higher price for its stock.

Some of these investments are obvious, such as supporting research to develop new products or acquiring new plant and equipment to expand output and enter new markets for existing products. Capital budgeting techniques, however, are also applied to such decisions as whether to replace existing plant and equipment before the end of their useful life or whether to refund a bond issue prior to maturity. In some cases, such as the acquisition of corporate headquarters, long-term investment decisions must be made even though no specific cash inflow may be generated by or identified with the investments.

Occasionally, long-term investment decisions are beyond the control of the financial manager. Installing pollution control equipment required by environmental legislation and meeting new safety standards require mandatory investments by the firm. The choice is not whether to make the investment but which of the competing means to employ. Of course, the firm could cease the operation and thereby avoid making the required investment, but in many cases that is not a realistic option. Car manufacturers are not going to cease building cars to avoid making an investment in equipment that installs a newly required safety improvement.

Some long-term investments rapidly generate returns; others require years to develop and then may never generate a profit. For example, a pharmaceutical company may spend a large amount on research that never successfully generates a new drug. Merck stated in its annual report that long-term growth would come through its commitment to research. Such commitment requires current cash outflows. Presumably, Merck's management must determine which of the drugs being developed are potentially the most profitable and will contribute to the growth of the firm and increase the value of Merck's stock.

Importance of Cash Flow

All investments involve costs. In some cases, these cash outflows may be readily identifiable. When Hertz acquires new cars, their cost is known. Other cash outflows associated with the investment may not be so readily identifiable.

Will Hertz have to invest in additional storage and maintenance facilities? Will it have to open additional rental outlets? Will it have to hire more employees and invest in their training? These cash outflows associated with the new cars could be substantial and convert what on the surface appears to be a profitable investment into a money-losing proposition.

In addition to identifying and quantifying cash outflows, the financial manager must estimate the investment's cash inflows. For investments that produce existing products, such estimates may be relatively easy. New products, however, or proposals to enter new markets require estimates of sales and expenses that are not readily available. These estimates are susceptible to built-in biases. If management desires to enter a new field, it may make overly optimistic estimates of future cash flows. The history of business is replete with illustrations of firms entering new markets, taking a beating, and retreating. RCA started to manufacture computers in direct competition with IBM, and Midway Airlines entered the Philadelphia market in direct competition with USAir. Both decisions were probably made after much discussion and analysis of anticipated cash flows. Both failed.

The statement of cash flows was discussed in Chapter 9, and noncash depreciation expense was added back to earnings to determine cash flow from operations. (Depletion, which occurs as natural resources are used, and amortization, which is the process of allocating the cost of an intangible or nonphysical asset, are also noncash expenses that contribute to the firm's cash flow.) Notice that the emphasis is not on accounting earnings. Depreciation (and depletion and amortization expenses), the deferral of income taxes from the current accounting period to another, or a change in current assets, such as an increase in accounts receivable or inventory, affect cash flows. It is the investment's impact on these cash flows that is important for the decision to invest in a long-term asset.

Consider the following situation, in which the financial manager must decide whether to acquire new equipment that costs $50,000 and requires an outlay of $5,000 to install. To make the decision, the financial manager must determine the cash flow generated by the investment. The $5,000 installation charge is a current cash outflow that is recaptured over the same five years that the equipment is depreciated. Estimated annual operating earnings generated by the equipment are $17,200 before the annual depreciation expense. In addition, the firm's investment in inventory rises by $2,000 and its accounts receivable increase by $3,000. These increases in inventory and accounts receivable are cash outflows that require additional funds. In the fifth year the inventory and accounts receivable are restored to their current levels (in other words, before the investment in the equipment). At that time the equipment is removed at a cost of $4,500. If the income tax rate is 20 percent, what are (1) the accounting earnings and (2) the cash flow generated by the investment?

PART 3 Corporate Finance

The answers to these two questions for years 1, 2 through 4, and 5 are as follows:

	Year 1	Years 2–4	Year 5
Determination of earnings:			
Earnings before depreciation and taxes	$17,200	$17,200	$17,200
Depreciation	10,000	10,000	10,000
Depreciation of installation expense	1,000	1,000	1,000
Removal expense	0	0	4,500
Taxable income	6,200	6,200	1,700
Taxes (20%)	1,240	1,240	340
Net income	$ 4,960	$ 4,960	$ 1,360
Determination of cash flows:			
Net income	$ 4,960	$ 4,960	$ 1,360
Depreciation	10,000	10,000	10,000
Depreciation of installation expense	1,000	1,000	1,000
Change in inventory and accounts receivable	(5,000)	0	5,000
Cash flow	$10,960	$15,960	$17,360

The forecasted earnings are $4,960 per year in years 1 through 4 and $1,360 in year 5, but the cash flows are $10,960 in year 1, $15,960 per year in years 2 through 4, and $17,360 in year 5. How can the earnings and cash flows be so different?

In each year, operating income is reduced by the depreciation of both the equipment and installation expense, which has been capitalized. (To simplify the illustration, the requirement that depreciation not start until after six months have passed [the "half-year" convention] is ignored. In reality, the installation expense would be added to the cost of the equipment to determine the depreciable base and that amount would be spread over the time period. This presentation, however, illustrates that depreciation includes other costs associated with putting the equipment into use, such as commissions and installation expenses.) These expenses are noncash expenses that reduce income for tax purposes. Notice also that there is a removal expense in year 5. Since that occurs at the end of the investment's life, it is not depreciated; it is expensed, which reduces taxable income in the fifth year. It is possible for the opposite to occur if the equipment is sold and cash is received. (If the sale is for more than the asset's book value, the sale also increases taxable income and taxes.)

The net income in years 1 through 5 does not represent cash. Cash flow is determined by adding back the noncash expenses and making any other adjustments that generate or consume cash. In each year, the $11,000 in noncash expenses are added back to net income. (Remember that the cash outflow occurred when the equipment was purchased and the installation costs were paid.) Adding back noncash expenses increases the cash flow generated by the investment. Conversely, in year 1, the investment requires an increase in inventory and accounts receivable. These increases are cash outflows that reduce the investment's cash flow in year 1. However, when inventory and accounts receivable are reduced in year 5 to their former levels, cash is released. The reductions in inventory and accounts receivable are sources of funds that contribute to the investment's cash flow in year 5.

The difference between net income and the cash flow is immediately obvious from a comparison of the two bottom lines. An investment of $55,000 ($50,000 to buy the equipment plus $5,000 in installation expense) generates $4,960 in profits in years 1 through 4 and only $1,360 in year 5. That does not appear to be an attractive investment—$55,000 to generate less than $5,000 in profits for each of the five years. However, the same investment generates $10,960 in cash in year 1, $15,960 in years 2 through 4, and $17,360 in year 5. The firm more than earns back the initial $55,000 cash outlay. From this perspective, the investment looks more attractive.

Just because the investment now looks more attractive is not justification to make it. Instead, the financial manager should apply one or more of the following methods of capital budgeting to determine if the investment constitutes a wise use of the firm's scarce resource, its capital.

Introduction to Discounted Cash Flow Methods of Capital Budgeting

Two methods for capital budgeting are net present value (NPV) and internal rate of return (IRR). Both are discounted cash flows techniques. Future cash flows are brought back to the present; that is, both techniques explicitly use the time value of money. Both techniques recognize that (1) investment decisions are made in the present, (2) the cash inflows are generated in the future, and (3) the cash inflows must be compared to the investment's cash outflows required to make the investment.

Net present value (NPV)

Present value of an investment's cash flows minus the cost of the investment

Net present value and internal rate of return use the same essential information but process it in different ways. Net present value (NPV) discounts future cash inflows at the firm's cost of capital to determine the present value of the investment. This present value is then compared to the present cost (cash outflows) of making the investment. Internal rate of return (IRR) determines the return that equates the present value of the cash inflows and the cash outflows of the investment. This return is then compared to the cost of capital necessary to make the investment.

Internal rate of return (IRR)

Rate of return that equates the present value of an investment's cash flows with the cost of making the investment

Although the two techniques are similar, there is one essential difference: the treatment of the discount factor that each employs. This difference may be important when the two techniques give conflicting signals as to which investments should be selected. Although this conflict may not occur, the possibility does exist and will be illustrated in the section devoted to selecting between mutually exclusive investments.

The initial discussion will be devoted to explaining and illustrating net present value and internal rate of return. Several symbols will be used:

- C: the investment's cost (the initial cash outflow)
- $CF_1, CF_2, \ldots CF_n$: the cash inflows generated by the investment in years 1, 2, and on through the last year (n)
- n: the number of years in which the investment generates cash inflows
- PV: the present value of the investment's cash inflows
- NPV: the net present value (PV minus C)
- k: the firm's cost of capital
- r: the investment's internal rate of return

The cash inflows and number of years are estimated, so these payments cannot be known with certainty. Initially, the discussion will avoid the question of risk; no adjustment is made for riskier investments. The inclusion of risk is discussed later in this chapter.

Net Present Value

The net present value technique of capital budgeting determines the present value of the cash inflows and subtracts from this present value the cost of the investment. The difference is the net present value. This process is illustrated by the following example. A firm is considering an investment that costs $1,000 and has the following estimated cash inflows:

Year	Investment A Cash Inflow
1	$400
2	400
3	400
4	400

Should management make this investment? To answer this question, management needs to know the net present value of the cash flows. To determine the net present value, the firm must know the cost of funds used to acquire the asset (the cost of capital, discussed in the previous chapter). If the cost of capital is 8 percent, the present value of the investment is the sum of the present value of each cash flow discounted at 8 percent. The following illustrates the process of determining the present value of this investment:

Year	Cash Inflow	× Interest Factor	= Present Value
1	$400	0.926	$370.40
2	400	0.857	342.80
3	400	0.794	317.60
4	400	0.735	294.00
			$\Sigma = 1{,}324.80$

The individual present values are summed to obtain the present value of the investment. In this case, the present value is $1,324.80. Since the cost of making the investment is $1,000, the net present value (*NPV*) is

$$NPV = \$1,324.80 - \$1,000 = \$324.80.$$

Since the net present value is *positive*, the investment more than covers all the cost of the funds. *The additional* NPV *increases the value of the firm* so the investment should be made.

This process is applied to all of the firm's investment opportunities to determine their net present values. Suppose the firm is considering the following investments in addition to the one previously discussed:

| Year | Cash Inflows Investment | | |
	B	C	D
1	$295	$250	$357
2	295	150	357
3	295	330	357
4	295	450	357

Management determines the net present value of each investment. The general procedure used for investment A is repeated for each investment.

For investment B the net present value is

$$NPV = \$295(3.312) - \$1,000 = \$977 - \$1,000 = (\$23).$$

(3.312 is the interest factor for the present value of an annuity of $1 at 8 percent for four years.) Since the net present value of investment B is *negative*, the firm should *not* make the investment.

The net present values of investments C and D are ($47) and $182, respectively. (You should verify these results to test your ability to compute an investment's net present value.) These results give the following ranking of all four investments:

Investment	Net Present Value
A	$325
D	182
B	(23)
C	(47)

The firm should make investments A and D (for a total outlay of $2,000) because their net present values are positive. The firm should reject investments B and C because their net present values are negative. Notice that the firm accepts *all investments whose net present values are positive.*

The net present value technique of capital budgeting may be stated in more formal terms. First, determine the present value (*PV*) by discounting the cash inflow (*CF*) generated each year by the firm's cost of capital (*k*). Thus, the present value of an investment is

$$PV = \frac{CF_1}{(1 + k)^1} + \frac{CF_2}{(1 + k)^2} + \cdots + \frac{CF_n}{(1 + k)^n}. \tag{14.1}$$

Second, determine the net present value (*NPV*) of the investment by subtracting the cash outflow (*C*) of the investment from the present value. That is,

$$NPV = PV - C. \tag{14.2}$$

If the net present value is positive, the investment should be made. If the net present value is negative, the firm should not make the investment. The acceptance and rejection criteria for the net present value method of capital budgeting are summarized as follows:

Accept the investment if
$PV - C = NPV \geq 0.$

Reject the investment if
$PV - C = NPV < 0.$

If the *NPV* = 0, the firm is at the margin. The investment neither contributes to nor detracts from the value of the firm. It does, however, cover the cost of funds. Investors earn their required return, so the investment should be made.

Internal Rate of Return

The internal rate of return method of capital budgeting determines the rate of return that equates the present value of the cash inflows and the present value of the cash outflows of the investment. This particular rate of return is called the internal rate of return because it is a rate that is unique (internal) to that investment. In effect, the internal rate of return method sets up the following equation:

$$\text{Present cost} = \text{Present value of the cash inflows.} \tag{14.3}$$

The method may be illustrated by the same examples used to illustrate the net present value approach. The information for investment A is substituted into the equation for determining present value. That is,

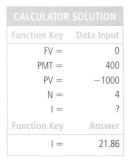

CALCULATOR SOLUTION

Function Key	Data Input
FV =	0
PMT =	400
PV =	−1000
N =	4
I =	?
Function Key	Answer
I =	21.86

$$\$1,000 = \frac{\$400}{(1 + r)^1} + \frac{\$400}{(1 + r)^2} + \frac{\$400}{(1 + r)^3} + \frac{\$400}{(1 + r)^4}.$$

Then the equation is solved for the unknown r, the internal rate of return. Since the investment is an annuity, the calculation is easy:

$1,000 = $400 × interest factor for the present value of an annuity of $1 for four years.

Solving for the interest factor ($PVAIF$, $?I$, $4N$) gives

$$\$400 \ (PVAIF, \ ?I, \ 4N) = \$1,000$$

$$PVAIF, \ ?I, \ 4N = \$1,000/\$400 = 2.50.$$

Then, 2.50 must be found in the interest table for the present value of an annuity for four years ($n = 4$). This yields an internal rate of return of approximately 20 percent (21.86 percent using a financial calculator).

Should the firm make this investment? The answer is "yes" because the internal rate of return exceeds the firm's cost of capital. This investment's internal rate of return exceeds 20 percent, which is greater than the firm's 8 percent cost of capital. Thus, the investment should be made.

As with the net present value, the financial manager computes the internal rate of return for each investment. For investment B, that is

$$\$1,000 = \frac{\$295}{(1+r)^1} + \frac{\$295}{(1+r)^2} + \frac{\$295}{(1+r)^3} + \frac{\$295}{(1+r)^4}$$

$$\$1,000 = \$295/PVAIF, \ ?I, \ 4N$$

$$PVAIF, \ ?I, \ 4N = \$1,000/\$295 = 3.389.$$

Locating 3.389 in the interest table for the present value of an annuity for four years, we find the internal rate of return is 7 percent. Since 7 percent is less than the cost of capital, the investment should not be made.

The internal rates of return for investments C and D are computed in the same manner. Since investment D is an annuity, its internal rate of return may be computed in the same manner as those of investments A and B, and its internal rate of return is 16 percent. Investment C, however, is not an annuity. Unless you are using a financial calculator that accepts uneven cash inflows or a computer program that computes internal rates of return, you will have to solve the problem through the use of trial and error. Select a rate such as 10 percent and determine the present value of the cash inflows. If this present value equals $1,000, you have solved for the internal rate of return. That is,

$$\$1,000 = \frac{\$250}{(1+0.1)^1} + \frac{\$150}{(1+0.1)^2} + \frac{\$330}{(1+0.1)^3} + \frac{\$450}{(1+0.1)^4}$$

$$= \$250(0.909) + \$150(0.826) + \$330(0.751) + \$450(0.683)$$

$$= \$227.25 + \$123.90 + \$247.83 + \$307.35 = \$906.33.$$

Since the present value of the cash inflows is less than $1,000, 10 percent is too large. A lower rate is selected and the process is repeated until the present values of the cash inflows and outflows are equal. That occurs at approximately 6 percent:

$$\$1,000 \approx \$250(0.943) + \$150(0.890) + \$330(0.840) + \$450(0.792)$$

$$\approx \$235.75 + \$133.50 + \$277.20 + \$356.40 = \$1,002.85.$$

Given these internal rates of return, the ranking of the four investments is

Investment	Internal Rate of Return
A	20%
D	16
B	7
C	6

The firm should make investments A and D because their internal rates of return exceed the firm's cost of capital but should reject investments B and C because their internal rates of return are less than the firm's cost of capital (less than 8 percent). The total cost of these investments is $2,000, and once again notice that the firm makes *all investments whose internal rates of return exceed the firm's cost of capital.* Like the net present value method of capital budgeting, the internal rate of return assumes that the firm has the funds or can obtain the funds necessary to make all the acceptable investments.

The process for the calculation of the internal rate of return should seem familiar, since you have made this calculation before. It appears in Chapter 7 on the time value of money. See in particular Example 5 on page 121 and Problems 28–30 on page 132. The calculation was also used to determine a bond's yield to maturity. See the section "Yield to Maturity" in Chapter 23. Actually the yield to maturity is a bond's internal rate of return if all the interest payments are made and the bond is retired for its face value at maturity. This process is used in Chapter 26 on historical returns earned by various investments such as stock. The return on an investment in stock equates the initial cost of an investment (a cash outflow) and the cash inflows generated by dividend payments and subsequent sale of the stock. The annualized return on any investment is its internal rate of return.

The internal rate of return method of capital budgeting may be summarized in symbolic terms. The internal rate of return is that value, r, that equates

$$C = \frac{CF_1}{(1 + r)^1} + \cdots + \frac{CF_n}{(1 + r)^n} = \sum_{t=1}^{n} \frac{CF_t}{(1 + r)^t} \qquad (14.4)$$

and the criteria for accepting an investment are

if $r \geq k$, accept the investment,

if $r < k$, reject the investment.

If $r = k$, once again the firm is at the margin. The investment neither contributes to nor detracts from the value of the firm but does cover the cost of funds, including the owners' required return.

While the preceding are the acceptance criteria, management may not accept all investments with an internal rate of return greater than the cost of capital. Instead, management may establish a higher rate of return (or hurdle rate) that is used as the acceptance criterion for selecting investments. For example, if the cost of capital is 10 percent, the firm may make all investments with an internal rate of return in excess of 15 percent. Such a hurdle rate helps the firm adjust for risk because it excludes the investments with the lowest anticipated internal rates of return.

Hurdle rate

Return necessary to justify making an investment; often set higher than the firm's cost of capital

Net Present Value and Internal Rate of Return Compared

The internal rate of return and net present value methods of capital budgeting are very similar. Both methods use all the cash flows generated by an investment, and both consider the timing of those cash flows. Both methods explicitly incorporate the time value of money into the analysis. When the two methods are compared,

Net present value:

$$NPV = \frac{CF_1}{(1 + k)^1} + \cdots + \frac{CF_n}{(1 + k)^n} - C$$

Internal rate of return:

$$C = \frac{CF_1}{(1 + r)^1} + \cdots + \frac{CF_n}{(1 + r)^n}$$

the difference is the discount factor. The net present value approach uses the firm's cost of capital to discount the cash inflows. The internal rate of return method determines the rate of return that equates the present value of the cash inflows and the present cost or outflows. The use of different discount factors results in different statements of the acceptance criteria. For the net present value approach, an investment must yield a net present value equal to or greater than zero to be accepted. For the internal rate of return method, the investment's internal rate of return must be equal to or exceed the firm's cost of capital to be accepted.

While the obvious difference between the two techniques is the discount factor and the resulting difference in the statement of the acceptance criteria, the different discount factors have an important and subtle assumption. That assumption involves the reinvestment rate. The net present value technique assumes that funds earned in years 1, 2, and so on are *reinvested at the firm's cost of capital*. The internal rate of return assumes that the funds earned in years 1, 2, and so on are *reinvested at the investment's internal rate of return*.

Consider the investment used earlier in the chapter to illustrate both techniques. It had the following cash flows:

Year	Cash Inflow
1	$400
2	400
3	400
4	400

When the cost of capital was 8 percent, the net present value of the investment was determined to be $324.80. The reinvestment assumption requires that the $400 received in year 1 be invested for the next three years at 8 percent. The $400 received in year 2 will be reinvested for the next two years at 8 percent, and the $400 received in year 3 will be reinvested for one year at 8 percent. If these funds are not reinvested at 8 percent, the net present value will not be $324.80. If the reinvestment rate is higher, the net present value will exceed $324.80; if the reinvestment rate is lower, the net present value will be lower than $324.80.

When the internal rate of return technique was applied to the above cash inflows, the return was calculated to be approximately 22 percent. The reinvestment assumption requires that all the cash inflows be reinvested at that rate. Thus, the $400 received in the first year must be reinvested at 22 percent for the next three years, and the same reinvestment rate is required for each of the subsequent cash inflows. If these reinvested funds earn less than 22 percent, the true internal rate of return is less than 22 percent. If these reinvested funds earn more than 22 percent, the internal rate of return is greater than 22 percent.

In many investment decisions, the actual reinvestment rate may not be important. It would not be important in the above illustration if that were the only investment considered by the financial manager. However, when the financial manager must rank investments and select among competing investments (as will be required in the next section), the realized reinvestment rate may be crucial to the decision-making process.

If the financial manager cannot determine the rate at which the funds will be reinvested, then there is a strong argument for preferring the net present value technique over the internal rate of return. The assumption that the cash inflows will be reinvested at the firm's cost of capital is a more conservative assumption. Consider the above illustration. The net present value technique assumed the $400 received in the first year would be reinvested at 8 percent, while the internal rate of return required a reinvestment rate of 22 percent. Certainly, it should be easier to reinvest the funds at the lower rate. Furthermore, if no such investment can be found, the cash may always be used to reduce the firm's capital. The $400 cash generated during the first year, for example, could be used to retire some of the debt and equity issued to make the investment. Since these funds cost 8 percent, their retirement means the financial manager is able to save this cost even if he or she is unable to earn more elsewhere.

Ranking Investment Alternatives

In the preceding section, the firm made all investments in which the net present value was positive or those in which the internal rate of return exceeded the firm's cost of capital. Since the firm made all investments that met these criteria, there was no need to rank investments. However, there are circumstances in which the management will need to rank investments and choose among the alternatives.

Mutually exclusive investments

Two investments for which the acceptance of one automatically excludes the acceptance of the other

The need to rank investments occurs when the investments are mutually exclusive. Mutually exclusive investments occur when selecting one alternative automatically excludes another investment. For example, when land is used for one type of building, it cannot be used for a different type of structure. Mutually exclusive investments also occur if a number of investments achieve similar results. Once one of the alternative investments is selected, the others are excluded. Students are well aware of this type of problem. If you select one class at period A, all other classes at that period are excluded. Or, if you select one section of a finance course, all other sections are excluded. These choices are mutually exclusive.

Once mutually exclusive investments exist, it is necessary to rank investment proposals in order to make the most profitable investments first. In some cases such ranking may pose no problem. Consider the following hypothetical investment proposals. Each costs $1,000 and has a net present value and internal rate of return as listed:

New Investment	Net Present Value	Internal Rate of Return
A	$22	19%
B	43	37
C	5	9
D	6	10

A and B are mutually exclusive, and C and D are mutually exclusive. Therefore, B is selected and A is excluded, and D is selected over C. Both the net present value and internal rate of return techniques select B over A and D over C. Notice also that investment D is made but that A is not, even though A has a higher net present value than D. This occurs because the acceptance of B automatically excludes A. The acceptance of D is immaterial to the acceptance of A, because A's acceptance depends on its net present value relative to B and not to any other investment.

In the preceding example, both the net present value and internal rate of return techniques selected B over A and D over C. The question becomes: Do the two techniques always produce the same rankings? The answer is "no." There are two situations in which the rankings may diverge: The timings of the cash flows differ or the costs of the investments differ. These disparities are, of course, immaterial if the investments are independent. The firm may select (or reject) any of the investments. But these differences may be crucial if the firm must select between investments A and B when net present value favors A while internal rate of return favors B. The financial manager, in effect, must favor one of the two methods of capital budgeting for determining which of the two long-term investments to make.

Differences in the Timing of Cash Flows

Consider the following two mutually exclusive investments. Each investment costs $10,000, but the cash inflows occur in different time periods.

	Cash Inflows	
Year	**A**	**B**
1	$12,400	—
2	—	—
3	—	$15,609

The cash inflow of investment A is earned in year 1, while investment B has a higher dollar cash inflow but takes longer to earn those funds. Since the two investments are mutually exclusive, the firm must choose between the two alternatives. This requires that the financial manager rank the two investments.

The determination of the net present value and internal rate of return for each investment is easy. If the firm's cost of capital is 10 percent, the net present value of each investment is

$$NPV_A = \frac{\$12,400}{(1 + 0.1)} - \$10,000 = \$12,400(0.909) - \$10,000$$

$$= \$11,272 - \$10,000 = \$1,272.$$

$$NPV_B = \frac{\$15,609}{(1 + 0.1)^3} - \$10,000 = \$15,609(0.751) - \$10,000$$

$$= \$11,722 - \$10,000 = \$1,722.$$

The internal rate of return for each investment is

$$\$10,000 = \frac{\$12,400}{(1 + r_A)} \text{ and } \$10,000 = \frac{\$15,609}{(1 + r_B)^3}.$$

Solving for r_A for investment A yields:

$$\$12,400 \ IF = \$10,000$$

$$IF = \frac{10,000}{12,400} = 0.8065 \text{ and } r_A = 24\%.$$

Solving for r_B for investment B yields:

$$\$15,609 \ IF = \$10,000$$

$$IF = \frac{10,000}{15,609} = 0.6407 \text{ and } r_B = 16\%.$$

A summary of these results is

	Investment A	Investment B
Net present value	$1,272	$1,722
Internal rate of return	24%	16%

Immediately, the financial manager faces a quandary. Investment A has the higher internal rate of return, while investment B has the higher net present value. Which investment is preferable? If the investments were not mutually exclusive, the firm would make both. However, in this case the investments are mutually exclusive, and management must choose between the two alternatives. The question then becomes how to resolve the conflicting signals.

The reconciliation is built around the answer to a second question: What will the firm do with the cash inflow generated by investment A in year 1 (that is, what is the reinvestment rate)? Certainly the firm will not let these funds sit but will invest them in year 2. If the firm selects investment B, it receives the funds in year 3 and thus cannot reinvest them in years 1 and 2. The choice between investment A and investment B depends on what the firm can do with the cash generated in year 1 by investment A. In effect, the firm must consider a third investment that starts in year 2 and is purchased with the funds generated by investment A.

Suppose the firm could reinvest the $12,400 at 14 percent for the next two years. What is the terminal value of the investment? That is, what is the future value of investment A if the reinvested funds grow annually at 14 percent for two years? The answer is

$$\$12,400(1 + 0.14)^2 = \$12,400(1.300) = \$16,120.$$

If the $12,400 is reinvested at 14 percent for two years, the terminal value of investment A is $16,120, which is greater than the final value of investment B ($15,609). Thus, the conflicting signals from the net present value and internal rate of return methods are resolved. The firm should make investment A because its terminal value ($16,120) exceeds the terminal value ($15,609) of investment B.

In the illustration, the conflict was resolved in favor of investment A. This, however, need not have been the case. Suppose the firm could have invested the

$12,400 received in year 1 at only 12 percent instead of 14 percent. Would the firm still have selected investment A? The answer is "no," because at 12 percent the $12,400 would grow to only

$$\$12,400(1 + 0.12)^2 = \$12,400(1.254) = \$15,549.60.$$

If the cash inflow is reinvested at 12 percent, the terminal value of investment A is $15,549.60, which is smaller than investment B's terminal value ($15,609). Thus, investment B would be selected.

As these illustrations demonstrate, reconciling the conflict between the net present value and the internal rate of return depends on what the firm can do with the cash inflows that it earns in the early years of an investment's life. If the firm has alternatives that offer high returns, the choice will be the investment with the higher initial cash inflows even though it may have the lower net present value. The lower net present value is offset by the returns earned when the cash is reinvested at profitable rates. The converse is true when the initial cash inflows are reinvested at less profitable rates. Then, the funds earned through reinvesting are not sufficient to justify making the investment with the lower net present value, and thus the conflict is resolved in favor of the investment with the higher net present value but longer time horizon.

This general conclusion is illustrated in Figure 14.1, which presents a profile of the net present value of both investments at various costs of capital.

F I G U R E   14.1
Net Present Value Profiles for Investments A and B

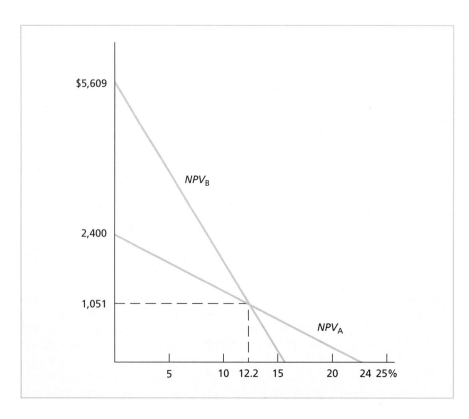

If the discount factor is 0 percent, then the net present values of investments A and B are $2,400 and $5,609, respectively. As the discount factors rise, the net present values fall. If the discount factors are sufficiently high, the net present values fall to zero. This occurs at 24 percent for investment A and 16 percent for investment B, which are each investment's internal rate of return. Since the internal rate of return equates the cost of an investment with the present value of its cash inflows, the net present value must equal zero.

The net present value of investment B exceeds the net present value of investment A as long as the discount factor is less than 12.2 percent.[1] When the discount factor is less than 12.2 percent, the net present value method selects investment B. However, if the discount factor exceeds 12.2 percent, investment A's net present value is higher; therefore, investment A would be preferred. Thus, as long as the discount factor (the firm's cost of capital) exceeds 12.2 percent, the net present value and the internal rate of return give the same ranking: A is preferred to B. However, if the cost of capital is less than 12.2 percent, the two techniques produce a contradictory ranking that raises the reinvestment question. If the reinvestment rate is less than 12.2 percent, investment B is to be preferred; the funds earned through the reinvestment of investment A's earlier cash inflows do not offset investment B's higher net present value.

Differences in Cost

The previous section showed that differences in the timing of cash flows may lead to conflicting rankings of investments by net present value and internal rate of return. The same problem may arise if there is a difference in the cost of two mutually exclusive investments. Consider the following mutually exclusive investments:

	Investment	
	A	B
Cost	$1,000	$600
Cash flow year 1	$1,150	$700
Cost of capital: 10 percent		

----

[1] The two discount factors are equal when

$$\frac{\$12,400}{(1 + r)} = \frac{\$15,609}{(1 + r)^3}$$

$$\frac{(1 + r)^3}{(1 + r)} = \frac{\$15,609}{\$12,400}$$

$$(1 + r)^2 = 1.2588$$

$$1 + r = \sqrt{1.2588}$$

$$r = 1.122 - 1$$

$$r = 12.2\%.$$

All the cash inflow occurs in year 1 but the costs of the investments differ. (In the previous illustration the cash inflows occurred in different years and the costs of the investments were equal.) The net present values of the two investments are

$$NPV_A = \$1,150(0.909) - \$1,000 = \$45.35$$

$$NPV_B = \$700(0.909) - \$600 = \$36.30.$$

The internal rate of return for A is

$$\$1,000 = \$1,150/(1 + r_A)$$

$$1 + r_A = \$1,150/\$1,000 = 1.15$$

$$r_A = 1.15 - 1 = 0.15 = 15\%.$$

The internal rate of return for B is

$$\$600 = \$700/(1 + r_B)$$

$$1 + r_B = \$700/\$600 = 1.167$$

$$r_B = 1.167 - 1 + 0.167 = 16.7\%.$$

A summary of these results is

	Investment A	Investment B
Net present value	$45.35	$36.30
Internal rate of return	15%	16.7%

Once again there is a conflict. The net present value of A exceeds the net present value of B, but their internal rates of return are reversed. B's internal rate of return exceeds A's internal rate of return.

The cause of the conflict is the difference in the amount invested. Investment A costs more, and those additional funds earn 15 percent. These earnings contribute to the investment's net present value, so the *NPV* of A exceeds the net present value of B, even though B earns a higher rate of return on the small amount invested.

The conflict may be resolved by asking what the firm can do with the money it saves by selecting B instead of A. If there were no alternative investment for the $400, the conflict is resolved in favor of A. Even though A's internal rate of return is lower, it is better to invest $1,000 and increase the value of the firm by $45.35 than to invest $600 and increase the value of the firm by $36.30. (Fifteen percent on $1,000 is better than 16.5 percent on $600 and 0 percent on $400.)

Assuming a return of 0 percent is unreasonable, since the firm can always save its cost of capital. (Management can save 10 percent by repurchasing stock and retiring debt.) Therefore, the worst alternative return is not 0 percent but the cost of capital.

If the firm earns 10 percent on $400 and 16.7 percent on $600, the return on $1,000 is a weighted average:

$$(0.4)(10) + (0.6)(16.7) = 14.02\%.$$

Obviously, 14.02 percent is inferior to the 15 percent internal rate of return on investment A, which uses the entire $1,000. If the firm earns 13 percent on $400 and 16.7 percent on $600, the return on $1,000 is

$$(0.4)(13) + (0.6)(16.7) = 15.22\%,$$

in which case combining investment B with the additional investment is superior to investing the entire amount in investment A.

The same conclusion may be seen by using net present value. The net present value of investment B is added to the net present value of the additional investment. For example, if the $400 is invested at 10 percent, the cash inflow at the end of the first year is $440 (the return of the $400 invested plus 10 percent). The net present value of investment B plus the additional $400 investment is

$$NPV = \$700(0.909) + \$440(0.909) - (\$600 + \$400)$$
$$= \$1,036 - \$1,000 = \$36,$$

which is inferior to the $45 offered by investment A. Earning only 10 percent does not increase the total NPV and does not increase the value of the firm. The total is obviously inferior to the $45 offered by investment A.

If, however, the $400 were invested at 13 percent so the cash flow at the end of the year is $452, the net present value of investment B plus the additional $400 is

$$NPV = \$700(0.909) + \$452(0.909) - (\$600 + \$400)$$
$$= \$1,047 - \$1,000 = \$47.$$

Investment B is now the preferred choice, because its net present value when combined with the net present value of the additional investment is higher than the net present value of all the funds invested in A.

As the previous examples illustrate, the net present value and internal rate of return approaches to capital budgeting are not free from problems. Although in many cases these problems will not arise, they may if the financial manager must select among alternative investments, all of which may be acceptable by themselves. Is there any reason to prefer one technique over the other? The answer is "yes." Many individuals prefer the internal rate of return because it may be easier to interpret. Rates of return are frequently used in finance (for example, the yield to maturity on a bond that is discussed in Chapter 23 is an illustration of a rate of return) and many comparisons use percentages (the return on assets or return on equity are expressed as a percentage). This has led many financial managers to be more comfortable with the internal rate of return than with the absolute numbers generated by net present value. However, net present value is the more conservative technique and may be preferred.

This conservatism is the result of the reinvestment assumption. If an investment generates cash flow, the worst case for reinvesting the cash is to return the funds to the firm's sources of finance. The cost of these funds is the firm's cost of capital, so if the financial manager retires some of these sources, he or she is at least meeting the firm's alternative use for the cash. Since net present value assumes that all cash inflows are reinvested at the firm's cost of capital, there is no reason to believe that this assumption will not be met. If the financial manager is able to find even better alternative uses for the cash flow, then such reinvestment should increase the value of the firm.

Such may not be the case when the internal rate of return is used, since that technique assumes that the cash inflows are reinvested at the internal rate of return. Of course, it may be possible to reinvest the cash inflows at a higher rate and realize a higher return, which would, of course, increase the value of the firm. But if the cash flow is invested at a lower rate, the realized return will not be the internal rate of return. If failure to consider the reinvestment rate were to lead to incorrect investment decisions (as was previously illustrated when choosing between mutually exclusive investments), the technique could result in a reduction in the value of the firm.

The Introduction of Risk into Capital Budgeting

In the previous sections, net present value (NPV) and internal rate of return (IRR) were used to analyze and select long-term investments. In the case of net present value, the future cash flows were discounted back to the present at the firm's cost of capital. The resulting present value was subtracted from the cost of the investment (the initial cash outflow) to determine the NPV. If the NPV was positive, the investment was made because the investment contributed to the value of the firm. In the case of the internal rate of return, the rate that equated future cash inflows to the current cost was compared to the cost of capital. If the IRR exceeded the cost of capital, the investment was made because, once again, the investment increased the value of the firm.

All future cash flows must be projections; they have to be expected values. Although these cash flows are uncertain, the degree of uncertainty differs among alternative investments. Previously, the applications of net present value and the internal rate of return implicitly assumed that the risk associated with each investment was the same. That is, all cash flows were treated as if they were known; no attempt was made to adjust the estimated cash inflows for uncertainty. In addition, the cost of capital was not adjusted for the risk associated with an individual investment.

Some investments, however, are riskier than others, and some investments may be risky by themselves but are not risky when taken in a portfolio context. These investments may actually reduce the firm's risk exposure. Thus the first step for the inclusion of risk into the capital budgeting process is to decide whether a project should be analyzed solely by itself as if it were a stand-alone project that has no impact on the risk associated with the firm or its owners. If an investment is not to be analyzed as a stand-alone project, the financial manager must consider the impact of the investment on the risk exposure of the firm or of the owners. Does the investment reduce the risk associated with the firm? This is, of course, the same consideration you make when adding another security to your portfolio: Does the investment diversify the portfolio?

It is easier by far to analyze a project's risk from the stand-alone perspective and avoid asking the question: How does the investment affect the firm's or stockholders' risk? Conceptually, this is incorrect, since investments are not made in a vacuum, but in many cases, analysis of the stand-alone risk is sufficient. Many investment projects are small, relative to the firm's total assets, and will have little or no impact on the risk exposure of the firm. For example, if Limited Brands acquires a centralized warehouse to hold clothing prior to distribution to its stores, this investment may have little, if any, impact on the firm's risk. In addition, new projects are often similar to current operations. These investments offer little potential for diversification and cannot change the firm's or stockholders' risk exposure.

If the investment is analyzed in portfolio context, the question essentially is this: Does the investment reduce the owners' risk? If investors have constructed well-diversified portfolios, the answer has to be "no." The stockholders in many publicly held companies do hold well-diversified portfolios, so the firm's investment in additional plant or equipment in all probability offers little potential for diversification.

If the owners do not hold well-diversified portfolios, the answer could be "yes." If the investment reduces the correlation between the return on the company's stock and the return on the other securities held in the individual's portfolio, then the potential for diversification exists. This potential may be especially important for small, closely held (or nonpublic) firms in which the business is the owner's primary asset. A risky investment that reduces the overall risk of the firm could be advantageous because the owner's risk exposure is reduced.

For many firms, the potential for portfolio effects may be ignored simply on pragmatic grounds. Because the financial manager does not know the stockholders' willingness to bear risk or whether they have constructed well-diversified portfolios, it may be impossible to incorporate potential portfolio effects in the analysis of a particular investment. In addition, stockholders may alter their portfolios for changes in risk. If a long-term investment in plant or equipment makes the firm riskier, stockholders may substitute less-risky securities in their portfolios to reduce their risk exposure. Conversely, if the financial manager makes investments that reduce risk and stockholders prefer a riskier strategy, the investors may buy the stock on margin (that is, buy the stock with borrowed funds). Thus, the impact of a firm's particular investment on stockholders may not concern the financial manager, since the stockholders can adjust their own portfolios to the level of risk they are willing to accept.

Risk Adjustments in Capital Budgeting

After deciding to include risk in capital budgeting analysis, the next step is to determine how it may be incorporated into the techniques. Consider the equation for the determination of the net present value:

$$NPV = \frac{CF}{(1 + k)^1} + \cdots + \frac{CF_n}{(1 + k)^n} - \text{Cost.}$$

The investment's cost (cash outflows) are known, so the incorporation of risk must either affect the project's estimated cash inflows (the numerator) or affect the cost of capital used to discount the inflows (the denominator). The problem facing the financial manager is how to make the adjustment operational.

If the financial manager is concerned with an investment's stand-alone risk, the emphasis is placed on the variability of the estimated cash inflows. One possible technique, "sensitivity analysis," determines the impact on the cash inflow by altering one variable at a time. The analysis starts with the expected cash inflows and then changes one of the inputs used to determine the cash flows. "What if" the price of the product were increased and all other variables, such as the cost of production, were held constant? What impact would the change have on the investment's estimated cash inflows? The more sensitive the change in the cash inflows to the change in the variable, the greater is the risk associated with the investment. If sales respond to the change in price, then the cash inflows will also respond. Conversely, if revenues are insensitive to changes in price, the estimated cash inflows are more certain and less risky. Similar reasoning is applied to several variables to determine the sensitivity of the net present value to each variable. Sensitivity analysis requires a large number of calculations, but by using a spreadsheet model, the financial manager determines the sensitivity of the net present value to the relevant variables and better understands the risk associated with the investment.

An alternative approach, "scenario analysis," adds the probability of outcomes. It asks not only what will be the impact on the cash inflows and the net present value if variables are changed, but also what is the likelihood of the change. Consider the following investment whose anticipated net present value responds to changes in the economy. The states of the economy, the investment's estimated net present value associated with each state of the economy, and the probability of occurrence are as follows:

State of the Economy	Probability of Occurrence	Net Present Value
Recession	.20	$ 0
No growth	.30	100
Mild growth	.50	300

The expected net present value is an average of each scenario weighted by the probability of occurrence. That is,

Net Present Value = $(.20)(\$0) + (.30)(\$100) + (.50)(\$300) = \$180$.

The variability of the cash inflows is measured by the standard deviation of the cash flows, which is calculated as follows:

(1) Individual NPV	(2) Expected NPV	(3) Difference (1) − (2)	(4) Difference Squared	(5) Probability of Occurrence	(6) Difference Squared Times the Probability (4) × (5)
$ 0	$180	$ 180	$32,400	.2	$ 6,480
100	180	−80	6,400	.3	1,920
300	180	−120	14,400	.5	7,200
			Sum of the weighted squared differences:		15,600

The standard deviation is the square root of the sum of the weighted squared differences:

$$\sqrt{15,600} = 125.$$

The larger the standard deviation, the larger is the variability of the outcome and hence the greater the risk associated with the investment. (The same calculation was illustrated in Chapter 8 on risk measurement.)

The standard deviation is an absolute number and should not be compared to the standard deviations of other investments. Comparisons are made by calculating the coefficient of variation, which is the standard deviation divided by the expected value. In this illustration, the standard deviation is 125 and the expected net present value is $180, so the coefficient of variation is $125/\$180 = 0.69$.

Since the numerical value of the coefficient of variation is a relative number, it may be compared to the same statistic for all investments in order to rank them. Suppose two investments have different net present values ($100 and $1,000), and their standard deviations are $10 and $20, respectively. The standard deviation of the second investment is larger, but when the standard deviation is expressed relative to the NPV, the resulting coefficient is smaller: $10/\$100 = 0.1$ versus $20/\$1,000 = 0.02$. The variability of the second investment is smaller, which indicates more certainty and less risk. An investment's coefficient of variation may also be compared to the coefficient of variation of the firm's typical investment to determine if the specific project is more or less risky than the firm's average investment.

Sensitivity analysis and scenario analysis are means to bring risk into capital budgeting by adjusting an investment's cash inflows. An alternative approach that also adjusts the cash inflow employs "certainty equivalents."

Certainty equivalents attempt to express expected cash inflows as certain cash inflows. For example, suppose a risky $1,000 investment is expected to generate the following cash inflows:

Year	1	2	3
	$300	$445	$568

All the cash inflows are expected and none is certain. An alternative use for the $1,000 is a three-year $1,000 U.S. Treasury bond that pays $100 annually and repays the $1,000 at maturity. These expected cash inflows are as follows:

Year	1	2	3
	$100	$100	$1,100

Because the expected cash inflows are to be paid by the federal government, they are virtually assured and hence are certain.

If the firm's cost of capital is 12 percent and that rate is used to discount the Treasury bond's cash flows, the net present value is

$$NPV = \$100(0.893) + \$100(0.797) + \$1,100(0.712) - \$1,000$$

$$= \$952.20 - \$1,000 = (\$47.80).$$

The net present value is negative and an investment in the bond will not be made. However, the risky alternative's net present value is

$$NPV = \$300(0.893) + \$445(0.797) + \$568(0.712) - \$1,000$$

$$= \$1,026.98 - \$1,000 = \$26.98.$$

Because the net present value is positive, the investment would be made.

The decision to make the risky investment and not make the certain investment may not be correct once risk is integrated into the analysis. Because risk has not been considered, the NPVs are not comparable. The question becomes: Can the two sets of cash flows be expressed on a common basis? Certainty equivalents attempt to answer that question.

Suppose the financial manager believes that cash flows from the risky investment are only equivalent to 95 percent of the certain investment and this percentage declines by 5 percent with each subsequent year. From this individual's perspective, the certainty equivalents of the cash flows are

Year	1	2	3
	(0.95)$300	(0.90)$445	(0.85)$568
	$285.00	$400.50	$482.80

After this adjustment to express the cash flows as if they were certain, should the investment be made? Once again the cash flows must be brought back to the present. To determine the present value, a new question arises: What is the appropriate rate to discount the cash flows? The answer cannot be the firm's cost of capital, for that cost encompasses the risk associated with the firm's sources of finance. Instead the appropriate discount rate is the risk-free return, because the cash flows are now considered to be the equivalent of certain cash inflows.

In this illustration, the risk-free, three-year Treasury bond offered 10 percent, so that rate may be applied to the investment's cash inflows that have been expressed in risk-free terms. When 10 percent is applied to the certainty equivalent cash flows, the net present value becomes:

$$NPV = 285.00(0.909) + \$400.50(0.826) + \$482.80(0.751) - \$1,000$$
$$= \$952.46 - \$1,000 = (\$47.54).$$

Because the NPV is negative, the investment should not be made.

Although certainty equivalents may be used to adjust the cash flows for risk, it should be obvious that the method has a major problem. How are the certainty equivalents determined? Essentially, the analyst assigns the values. Two financial managers could, and probably would, assign different certainty equivalents and, hence, come to opposite conclusions about the desirability of making the investment. This lack of objectivity is a major weakness in the technique and explains why financial managers may be reluctant to use it.

Adjusting the Discount Rate

Previously, risk was introduced into capital budgeting by adjusting the cash inflows. Alternative techniques adjust the cost of capital by adding a risk premium to the discount factor for riskier projects and reducing the discount factor for less-risky projects. The problem facing the financial manager is the determination of the risk premium.

One possible method requires a qualitative judgment by the financial manager. The cost of capital is the required return to be used for investments of average risk. If the firm is expanding known products into new markets that are comparable to existing markets, then the use of the cost of capital may be justified. However, if the financial manager is considering new products, then a risk premium is added to the cost of capital. Conversely, if the new products are less risky than the typical investment made by the firm, the cost of capital may be reduced.

Consider the following example. The financial manager has the following risk-adjusted cost of capital schedule:

Project Risk	Risk-adjusted Cost of Capital
Low risk	6.5%
Average risk	8.5
High risk	10.5
Exceedingly high risk	12.5

These risk-adjusted costs of capital act as hurdle rates that are applied to different projects. If the net present value approach is used, the adjusted cost of capital is used to discount the estimated cash inflows. If, after using the adjusted cost of capital, the net present value is positive, the investment is made. If the internal rate of return approach is used, the adjusted cost of capital is used as the criterion for decision making. If an investment's internal rate of return exceeds the appropriate cost of capital, the investment is made.

This approach, like the certainty equivalent approach, presents a problem: How is risk to be measured, and how much of a risk premium should be added? One possibility is to measure risk using the variability of the cash flows. As the variability of the cash inflows increases, the risk premium is increased. This approach, however, still does not tell the financial manager how large a risk premium should be added to the firm's cost of capital. The amount of a risk premium remains a judgment call by the financial manager.

An alternative means to measure risk is to use the beta coefficients discussed in Chapter 8. In that chapter, beta coefficients were used to indicate the volatility of a stock's return relative to the volatility of the market. Beta coefficients are applied in Chapter 21 as part of the capital asset pricing model's specification of the required return for the valuation of common stock. The same concept may be applied to adjust for risk in capital budgeting. The risk-adjusted required return (the risk-adjusted cost of capital) for an investment (k_a) is

$$k_a = r_f + (k - r_f)\beta.$$

Here k is the firm's cost of capital used for the typical or average investment made by the firm, r_f is the risk-free rate, and β is the beta coefficient associated with the investment being considered. If the risk-free rate is 3 percent and the firm's cost of capital is 9 percent, the general equation for the risk-adjusted required return is

$$k_a = 0.03 + (0.09 - 0.03)\beta.$$

This equation is illustrated by line xy in Figure 14.2, which indicates that as risk increases (the beta increases), the required return increases. If an investment has an estimated beta of 1.2, it is riskier than the typical investment made by the firm. The adjusted required return is

$$k_a = 0.03 + (0.09 - 0.03)1.2 = 0.102 = 10.2\%,$$

which exceeds the firm's cost of capital. If an investment has a beta of 0.7, it is less risky than the firm's typical investment. Its adjusted required return is

$$k_a = 0.03 + (0.09 - 0.03)0.7 = 0.072 = 7.2\%.$$

This return is less than the firm's cost of capital, because this particular investment is less risky than the average investment made by the firm.

F I G U R E   14.2

Relationship between
Project Risk and Required
Return

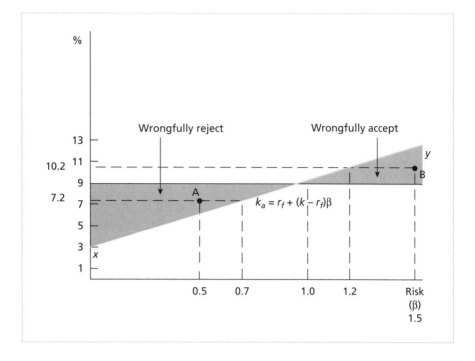

Failure to make this risk adjustment can lead to wrongfully rejecting an acceptable investment or to wrongfully accepting an inferior investment. Consider investment A in Figure 14.2. It offers a return of 7.2 percent, which is less than the 9 percent required return for the typical investment made by the firm. Since a 7.2 percent return is less than 9 percent, the investment would be rejected.

This rejection, however, is made prior to considering the risk associated with the investment. If the beta is 0.5, the required return for this investment is

$$0.03 + (0.09 - 0.03)0.5 = 6.0\%.$$

Since the investment offers 7.2 percent, on a risk-adjusted basis, it should be accepted.

The opposite situation, the acceptance of an inferior investment, is also possible. Consider investment B in Figure 14.2. It offers a return of 10.2 percent, which exceeds the 9 percent required return for the typical investment made by the firm. Since a 10.2 percent return is greater than 9 percent, the investment would be accepted.

This acceptance is made prior to considering the risk associated with the investment. If the beta is 1.5, the required return for this investment is

$$0.03 + (0.09 - 0.03)1.5 = 12.0\%.$$

Since the investment offers 10.2 percent, on a risk-adjusted basis, it should be rejected.

As the above illustrations suggest, investments with a beta coefficient of less than 1.0 and a return of less than 9 percent may be incorrectly rejected, and investments with a beta greater than 1.0 and a return exceeding 9 percent may be incorrectly accepted. These wrongful rejection and acceptance decisions are indicated by the shaded areas in Figure 14.2. All investments that offer an internal rate of return that lies above line *xy* are acceptable because the return exceeds the risk-adjusted required return. All investments that offer an internal return that lies below line *xy* are not acceptable because that return is less than the risk-adjusted cost of capital. There the internal rates of return are less than the risk-adjusted required return.

Although this discussion suggests means to incorporate risk in the capital budgeting process, making these risk adjustments operational is difficult. The inclusion of risk increases the accuracy of capital budgeting only if the estimates of risk are accurate. Consider a pharmaceutical firm whose investment in research may take years to develop and to receive government approval to market a new product. How can the firm estimate the beta for such an investment? In Chapter 21, betas are used to value a stock. The estimation of the stock's beta was relatively easy. The historical returns on the stock and the market are known. The biggest problems to estimate the beta and subsequently employ it were (1) determining which measure of the market to use and (2) after estimating the beta, assuming that the historical beta was an accurate measure of the current beta. Although these are important problems, they pale when compared to the problem of estimating a beta for a nonexistent product that may result from a firm's investment in research and development.

Thus, for the financial manager, the problem is not whether to include risk in capital budgeting, but how to accurately measure it. In some cases this measurement is highly subjective, so the selection of investments is also subjective. Accurate data are obviously crucial to capital budgeting decisions. Estimating an investment's future cash flows is no easy task, so it should hardly be any surprise that the measurement of the investment's risk is an exceedingly difficult task.

Summary

Capital budgeting is the process for making long-term investment decisions, such as whether to expand plant and equipment. This chapter covered two methods for selecting long-term investments: the net present value and the internal rate of return.

The net present value (NPV) technique determines the present value of an investment's cash inflows and subtracts the current cash outflows to determine the net present value. If the net present value is positive, the investment is selected. If the financial manager must rank competing investments, those investments with the highest net present value are selected first.

The internal rate of return (IRR) determines the discount factor that equates the present value of an investment's cash inflows and outflows. If this internal rate of return exceeds the firm's cost of capital, the investment should be made. If the financial manager must rank competing investments, those investments with the highest internal rates of return are selected first.

The rankings determined by the net present value and the internal rate of return may conflict. Such conflicts can occur when there are differences in the costs of the investments or differences in the timing of their cash flows. Reconciliation of the conflicts may be achieved by analyzing the reinvestment rates. If the financial manager must choose between the net present value and the internal rate of return techniques, the net present value is to be preferred since it makes the more conservative assumption concerning the reinvestment of cash flow (that is, the cash inflows are reinvested at the firm's cost of capital).

Both the net present value and the internal rate of return capital budgeting techniques use forecasted cash inflows. These forecasts are expected values and cannot be known with certainty. An investment's risk may be analyzed on a stand-alone basis in which the financial manager considers only the risk associated with the investment. An investment's risk, however, may also be analyzed in a portfolio context in which the impact on the firm and its owners is considered. If a portfolio approach is used, risky investments whose returns are poorly or even negatively correlated with the returns from other investments may reduce the firm's risk exposure. The lack of correlation has a diversification effect that reduces the firm's risk.

There is also the possibility for a long-term investment in plant or equipment to reduce the owners' risk. If stockholders do not have well-diversified portfolios, investments by the firm that are not positively correlated with the owners' portfolios reduce their risk. This may be especially important for the owners of a small, privately held firm whose portfolios may not be independent of the firm. For large, publicly held companies, however, it is reasonable to assume that the stockholders have well-diversified portfolios and that any portfolio effects on these investors will be minimal or nonexistent.

The analysis of risk may be incorporated into capital budgeting either by adjusting an investment's expected cash inflows or by adjusting the firm's cost of capital. Estimated cash inflows may be restated based on the probability of their occurring or on an estimate of their certainty equivalents. The firm's cost of capital may be adjusted using a risk premium or by applying the capital asset pricing model, which employs beta coefficients. These betas measure the volatility of an investment's return relative to the volatility of the return on the firm's typical or average investment. Although adjusting either the cash inflows or the cost of capital may be used, the problem facing the financial manager is the measurement of risk and not the application of the risk adjustment.

Review Objectives

Now that you have completed this chapter, you should be able to

1. Distinguish between an investment's earnings and its cash flows (pp. 291–293).

2. Calculate an investment's net present value and internal rate of return (pp. 294–299).

3. Determine if an investment should be made, using NPV and IRR (pp. 294–299).

4. Describe the reinvestment assumption employed by NPV and IRR methods of capital budgeting (pp. 299–301).

5. Define mutually exclusive investments and be able to select among them (pp. 301–308).

6. Differentiate stand-alone and portfolio risk (p. 309).

7. Explain how cash inflows may be adjusted for the probability of their occurrence (pp. 310–313).

8. Adjust the firm's cost of capital for difference in risk associated with long-term investments (pp. 313–315).

9. Illustrate how certainty equivalents and beta coefficients may be used to adjust for risk when applying NPV and IRR (pp. 313–316).

Problems

1. You purchase machinery for $23,958 that generates cash flow of $6,000 for five years. What is the internal rate of return on the investment?

2. The cost of capital for a firm is 10 percent. The firm has two possible investments with the following cash inflows:

	A	B
Year 1	$300	$200
2	200	200
3	100	200

a. Each investment costs $480. What investment(s) should the firm make according to net present value?

b. What is the internal rate of return for the two investments? Which investment(s) should the firm make? Is this the same answer you obtained in part *a*?

c. If the cost of capital rises to 14 percent, which investment(s) should the firm make?

3. A firm has the following investment alternatives:

	Cash Inflows		
	A	B	C
Year 1	$1,100	$3,600	—
2	1,100	—	—
3	1,100	—	$4,562

Each investment costs $3,000; investments B and C are mutually exclusive, and the firm's cost of capital is 8 percent.

a. What is the net present value of each investment?

b. According to the net present values, which investment(s) should the firm make? Why?

   c. What is the internal rate of return on each investment?

   d. According to the internal rates of return, which investment(s) should the firm make? Why?

   e. According to both the net present values and internal rates of return, which investments should the firm make?

   f. If the firm could reinvest the $3,600 earned in year 1 from investment B at 10 percent, what effect would that information have on your answer to part *e*? Would the answer be different if the rate were 14 percent?

   g. If the firm's cost of capital had been 10 percent, what would be investment A's internal rate of return?

   h. The payback method of capital budgeting selects which investment? Why? (Review Chapter 11, if necessary.)

4. The chief financial officer has asked you to calculate the net present values and internal rates of return of two $50,000 mutually exclusive investments with the following cash flows:

	Project A Cash Flow	Project B Cash Flow
Year 1	$10,000	$ 0
2	25,000	22,000
3	30,000	48,000

If the firm's cost of capital is 9 percent, which investment(s) would you recommend? Would your answer be different if the cost of capital were 14 percent?

5. A firm's cost of capital is 12 percent. The firm has three investments to choose among; the cash flows of each are as follows:

	Cash Inflows		
	A	B	C
Year 1	$395	—	$1,241
2	395	—	—
3	395	—	—
4	—	$1,749	—

Each investment requires a $1,000 cash outlay, and investments B and C are mutually exclusive.

   a. Which investment(s) should the firm make according to the net present values? Why?

   b. Which investment(s) should the firm make according to the internal rates of return? Why?

c. If all funds are reinvested at 15 percent, which investment(s) should the firm make? Would your answer be different if the reinvestment rate were 12 percent?

6. Management of TSC, Inc. is evaluating a new $90,000 investment with the following estimated cash flows:

Year	Cash Flow
1	$10,000
2	25,000
3	40,000
4	50,000

If the firm's cost of capital is 10 percent and the project will require that the firm spend $15,000 to terminate the project, should the firm make the investment?

7. An investment with total costs of $10,000 will generate total revenues of $11,000 for one year. Management thinks that since the investment is profitable, it should be made. Do you agree? What additional information would you want? If funds cost 12 percent, what would be your advice to management? Would your answer be different if the cost of capital is 8 percent?

8. An investor purchases a bond for $949. The bond pays $60 a year for three years and then matures (it is redeemed for $1,000). What is the internal rate of return on that investment?

9. Management of a firm with a cost of capital of 12 percent is considering a $100,000 investment with annual cash flow of $44,524 for three years.

   a. What are the investment's net present value and internal rate of return?

   b. The internal rate of return assumes that each cash flow is reinvested at the internal rate of return. If that reinvestment rate is achieved, what is the total value of the cash flows at the end of the third year?

   c. The net present value technique assumes that each cash flow is reinvested at the firm's cost of capital. What would be the total value of the cash flows at the end of the third year, if the funds are reinvested at the firm's cost of capital?

   d. Why does management know that the reinvestment assumption for the net present value method can be achieved but that achieving the reinvestment assumption for the internal rate of return is uncertain?

10. (This problem combines material from Chapters 13 and 14.) The financial manager has determined the following schedules for the cost of funds:

Cost of Debt Ratio	Cost of Debt	Equity
0%	5%	13%
10	5	13
20	5	13
30	5	13
40	5	14
50	6	15
60	8	16

a. Determine the firm's optimal capital structure.

b. Construct a simple pro forma balance sheet that shows the firm's optimal combination of debt and equity for its current level of assets.

Assets	$500	Debt	—
		Equity	—
			$500

c. An investment costs $400 and offers annual cash inflows of $133 for five years. Should the firm make the investment?

d. If the firm makes this additional investment, how should its balance sheet appear?

Assets	—	Debt	—
		Equity	—

e. If the firm is operating with its optimal capital structure and a $400 asset yields 20.0 percent, what return will the stockholders earn on their investment in the asset?

11. Investments Quick and Slow cost $1,000 each, are mutually exclusive, and have the following cash flows. The firm's cost of capital is 10 percent.

	Cash Inflows	
	Q	S
Year 1	$1,300	$386
2	—	386
3	—	386
4	—	386

a. According to the net present value method of capital budgeting, which investment(s) should the firm make?

b. According to the internal rate of return method of capital budgeting, which investment(s) should the firm make?

c. If Q is chosen, the $1,300 can be reinvested and earn 12 percent. Does this information alter your conclusions concerning investing in Q and S? To answer, assume that S's cash flows can be reinvested at its internal rate of return. Would your answer be different if S's cash flows were reinvested at the cost of capital (10 percent)?

12. A firm has the following investment alternatives. Each one lasts a year.

Investment	A	B	C
Cash inflow	$1,150	560	600
Cash outflow	$1,000	500	500

The firm's cost of capital is 7 percent. A and B are mutually exclusive, and B and C are mutually exclusive.

a. What is the net present value of investment A? Investment B? Investment C?

b. What is the internal rate on investment A? Investment B? Investment C?

c. Which investment(s) should the firm make? Why?

d. If the firm had unlimited sources of funds, which investment(s) should it make? Why?

e. If there were another alternative, investment D, with an internal rate of return of 6 percent, would that alter your answer to part *d*? Why?

f. If the firm's cost of capital rose to 10 percent, what effect would that have on investment A's internal rate of return?

13. A firm, whose cost of capital is 10 percent, may acquire equipment for $113,479 and rent it to someone for a period of five years.

a. If the firm charges $36,290 annually to rent the equipment, what are the net present value and the internal rate of return on the investment? Should the firm acquire the equipment?

b. If the equipment has no estimated residual value, what must be the minimum annual rental charge for the firm to earn the required 10 percent on the investment?

c. If the firm can sell the equipment at the end of the fifth year for $10,000 and receive annual rent payments of $36,290, what are the net present value and the internal rate of return on the investment? What is the impact of the residual?

d. If the $10,000 residual resulted in the firm charging only $34,290 for the rental payments, what is the impact on the investment's net present value?

14. If the cost of capital is 9 percent and an investment costs $56,000, should you make this investment if the estimated cash flows are $5,000 for years 1 through 3, $10,000 for years 4 through 6, and $15,000 for years 7 through 10?

15. Management of Braden Boats, Inc., is considering an expansion in the firm's product line that requires the purchase of an additional $175,000 in equipment with installation costs of $15,000 and removal expenses of $2,500. The equipment and installation costs will be depreciated over five years using straight-line depreciation. The expansion is expected to increase earnings before depreciation and taxes as follows:

Years 1 and 2	Years 3 and 4	Year 5
$70,000	$80,000	$60,000

The firm's income tax rate is 30 percent and the weighted-average cost of capital is 10 percent. Based on the net present value method of capital budgeting, should management undertake this project?

16. A risky $30,000 investment is expected to generate the following cash flows:

Year	1	2	3
	$14,000	$15,750	$18,000

The probability of receiving each cash inflow is 90, 80, and 70 percent, respectively. If the firm's cost of capital is 12 percent, should the investment be made?

17. A firm has the following investment alternatives. Each costs $13,000 and has the following cash inflows.

	Year			
Cash Flow	1	2	3	4
A	$4,300	$4,300	$4,300	$4,300
B	3,500	5,000	4,500	4,000
C	4,800	6,000	3,000	2,000

Investment A is considered to be typical of the firm's investments. Investment B's cash flows vary over time but are considered to be less certain. Investment C's cash flows diminish over time but because most of the cash flows occur early in the investment's life, they are considered to be more certain. The firm's cost of capital is 10 percent, but the financial manager uses a hurdle rate of 8 percent for less-risky projects and 12 percent for riskier projects.

a. Based on the cost of capital, should any of the investments be made?

        b. If the financial manager uses a risk-adjusted cost of capital, should any of the investments be made?

        c. Would the answers to *a* and *b* be different if the three investments were mutually exclusive?

18. A risky $400,000 investment is expected to generate the following cash flows:

Year	1	2	3	4
	$145,300	$175,445	$156,788	$145,000

        a. If the firm's cost of capital is 10 percent, should the investment be made?

        b. An alternative use for the $400,000 is a four-year U.S. Treasury bond that pays $28,000 annually and repays the $400,000 at maturity. Management believes that the cash inflows from the risky investment are equivalent to only 75 percent of the certain investment, which pays 7 percent. Does this information alter the decision in *a*?

Additional Problems with Answers

1. What is the net present value and internal rate of return for an investment that costs (cash outflow) $1,000 and will generate annual cash inflows of $400 for five years if the firm's cost of capital is 10 percent?

2. An investment costs $10,000 and will generate annual cash inflows of $1,550 for 10 years. According to the net present value and internal rate of return methods of capital budgeting, should the firm make this investment if its cost of capital is 10 percent?

3. You are considering two investments that cost $10,000 each but can mak only one of them (that is, the two investments are mutually exclusive). The firm's cost of capital is 12 percent.

	Cash Inflows	
Year	A	B
1	$12,400	—
2	—	—
3	—	—
4	—	$19,400

        a. Based on net present value, which investment should you make?

        b. Based on internal rate of return, which investment should you make?

        c. If the cash inflow received in year 1 by investment A is reinvested at 16 percent, would that affect your investment decision?

4. A firm has two $1,000, mutually exclusive investment alternatives with the following cash inflows. The cost of capital is 6 percent.

	Cash Inflows	
Year	A	B
1	$175	$1,100
2	175	—
3	175	—
4	175	—
5	175	—
6	175	—
7	175	—
8	175	—

a. What is the internal rate of return on each investment? Which investment should the firm make?

b. What is the net present value of each investment? Which investment should the firm make?

c. If the cash inflows can be reinvested at 8 percent, which investment should be made?

5. What is the net present value for an investment that costs (cash outflow) $1,000 but has a probability of 80 percent that it will generate annual cash inflows of $500 for five years? The firm's cost of capital is 10 percent.

Answers The equations for the net present value and the internal rate of return are as follows.

Present value of an investment (PV):

$$PV = \frac{CF_1}{(1 + k)} + \cdots + \frac{CF_n}{(1 + k)^n}$$

Net present value (NPV):

$$NPV = PV - C$$

Internal rate of return (IRR):

$$C = \frac{CF_1}{(1 + r)} + \cdots + \frac{CF_n}{(1 + r)^n}$$

Definitions of the symbols:

C cost of the investment (cash outflow)

r internal rate of return

k cost of capital

$CF_1 \ldots CF_n$ cash flow in years 1 through n

These equations apply in general to all investments. The net present value tells you if the present value of the cash inflows exceeds the current cash outflows (the cost of the investment). If the net present value is equal to or greater than 0, the investment should be made. The internal rate of return determines the rate that equates the present value of the cash inflows with the current cash outflow. If the internal rate of return from the investment exceeds the cost of funds necessary to make the investment, the investment should be made.

1. If an investment costs (cash outflow) $1,000, will generate annual cash inflows of $400 for five years, and the firm's cost of capital is 10 percent, the NPV and IRR are

Present value (PV):

$$PV = \frac{\$400}{(1 + .1)} + \cdots + \frac{400}{(1 + .1)^5}.$$

Net present value (NPV):

$$NPV = PV - C = \$400(3.791) - \$1,000 = \$516.40.$$

The interest factor for the present value of an annuity at 10 percent for five years is 3.791. If a financial calculator is used,

$$PMT = 400; FV = 0; N = 5; I = 10; PV = ?$$

After determining the PV ($1,516.31), subtract the cost ($1,000) to determine the net present value. In this illustration the net present value is positive, so the firm should make the investment.

Internal rate of return (IRR):

$$C = \frac{\$400}{(1 + r)} + \cdots + \frac{400}{(1 + r)^5}.$$

The use of tables is easy if the future payment is (1) a single amount or (2) an annuity. In this example, the five payments are equal, so the present value of an annuity table may be used. The equation collapses as follows:

$1,000 = \$400 \, (PVAIF \, ?I, \, 5N)$ and $PVAIF = \$1,000/400 = 2.5$.

Using the interest tables, r is approximately 28 percent. To use a calculator, enter:

$PV = -1000; FV = 0; PMT = 400;$ and $N = 5$. I is the unknown. After entering the data in the calculator, $I = 28.65$.

The internal rate of return (28 percent) exceeds the firm's cost of capital (10 percent); hence the firm should make the investment. Notice that both the net present value and internal rate of return methods of capital budgeting conclude that the firm should make the investment.

2. Present value (PV):

$$PV = \frac{\$1,550}{(1 + .1)} + \cdots + \frac{1,550}{(1 + .1)^5}.$$

Net present value (NPV):

$$NPV = PV - C = \$1,550(6.145) - \$10,000 = (\$476).$$

The interest factor for the present value of an annuity at 10 percent for 10 years is 6.145.

$$PMT = 1550; FV = 0; N = 10; I = 10; PV = ? = 9524$$

$$NPV = \$9,524 - \$10,000 = (\$476).$$

Internal rate of return (IRR):

$$C = \frac{\$1,550}{(1 + r)} + \cdots + \frac{\$1,550}{(1 + r)^{10}}.$$

$$PV = 10,000; FV = 0; PMT = 1500; N = 10; I = ? = 8.88$$

$$\$1,000 = \frac{\$1,550}{(1 + r)} + \cdots + \frac{\$1,550}{(1 + r)^{10}}.$$

At 9 percent: $1,000 exceeds $1,550 × 6.418 = $995; the internal rate of return is less than 9 percent.

$$PMT = 1500; PV = 1000; FV = 0; N = 10; I = ? = 8.8$$

The net present value is negative and the internal rate of return (8.88 percent) is less than the firm's cost of capital (10 percent). The firm should not make the investment. In Problem 1, the investment should be made. In Problem 2, the investment should not be made. Notice once again that both the net present value and internal rate of return methods of capital budgeting conclude that the firm should not make investment B.

3. In this problem, the cash inflows occur at different times and the investments are mutually exclusive.

a. Net present value investment A:

$$NPV = \$12,400/(1 + 0.12) - \$10,000 = \$1,071.$$

$$FV = 12400; PMT = 0; I = 12; N = 1; PV = ? = 11071$$

Net present value investment B:

$$NPV = \$19,390/(1 + 0.12)^4 - \$10,000$$

$$= \$19,390(0.636) - \$10,000 = \$2,332.$$

$$FV = 19390; PMT = 0; I = 12; N = 4; PV = ? = 12322$$

The NPV indicates that both investments are acceptable, but since they are mutually exclusive, you accept B because its NPV is larger.

b. Internal rate of return investment A:

$$\$10,000 = \$12,400/(1 + r).$$

$$PVIF = \$10,000/\$12,400 = 0.806 \text{ so IRR} = 24\%.$$

$$FV = 12400; PMT = 0; N = 1; PV = 10000; I = ? = 24$$

Internal rate of return investment B:

$$\$10,000 = \$19,400/(1 + r)^4.$$

$$PVIF = \$10,000/\$19,400 = 0.515 \text{ so IRR} = 18\%.$$

$$FV = 19400; PMT = 0; N = 4; PV = 10000; I = ? = 18$$

Both the NPV and IRR indicate that investment A is acceptable, but since they are mutually exclusive, you accept A because its IRR is larger.

c. There is an obvious conflict since the NPV and IRR select different alternatives. One means to reconcile the conflict is to determine the reinvestment of the cash flow from investment A. If that cash flow can be reinvested at 16 percent for three years, the terminal value is

$$\$12,400(1 + 0.16)^3 = \$12,400(1.561) = \$19,356.$$

$$PV = 12400; N = 3; I = 16; PMT = 0; FV = ? = 19355$$

Since $19,355 is less than $19,400, investment B is preferred.

4. This problem is another version of Problem 3 except that investment A is an annuity while B is a single payment.

a. Internal rate of return investment A:

$$\$1,000 = \$175(IFAPV).$$

$$IFAPV = \$1,000/\$175 = 5.714.$$

The IRR is between 7 and 8 percent.

$$FV = 0; PMT = 175; N = 8; PV = 1000; I = ? = 8.14$$

Internal rate of return investment B:

$$\$1,000 = \$1,100/(1 + r)^1.$$

PVIF = 0.909, so the IRR is = 10%.

FV = 1100; PMT = 0; N = 1; PV = 1000; I = ? = 10

Both the NPV and IRR indicate that investment A is acceptable, but since they are mutually exclusive, you accept B because its IRR is larger.

b. Net present value investment A:

$$NPV = \$175(6.210) - \$1,000 = \$87.$$

FV = 0; PMT = 175; I = 6; N = 8; PV = ? = 1087

Net present value investment B:

$$NPV = \$1,100(0.943) - \$1,000 = \$37.$$

FV = 1100; PMT = 0; I = 6; N = 1; PV = ? = 38

The NPV indicates that both investments are acceptable, but since they are mutually exclusive, you accept A because its NPV is larger.

Once again there is a conflict since you cannot make both investments. If the cash inflows are reinvested at 8 percent, the terminal values are

Investment A: $175(FVAIF for 8 years at 8 percent)

= $175(10.637) = $1,861.

PV = 0; N = 8; I = 8; PMT = 175; FV = ? = 1,861

Investment B: $1,100(FVIF for 7 years at 8 percent)

= $1,100(1.714) = $1,885.

Since $1,885 exceeds $1,861, investment B is preferred. (Notice that the reinvestment of the $1,100 occurs for seven years and not eight years.)

5. This problem essentially repeats Problem 1 but adds a risk adjustment. The investment costs (cash outflow) $1,000 and will generate annual cash inflows of $500 for five years. However, the cash inflow's probability of occurrence is 80 percent; the firm's cost of capital is 10 percent.

Present value (PV):

$$PV = \frac{(0.8)(\$500)}{(1 + .1)} + \cdots + \frac{(0.8)(\$500)}{(1 + .1)^5}$$

Net present value (NPV):

$$NPV = PV - C = \$400(3.791) - \$1,000 = \$516.40$$

Notice that the cash inflows are adjusted for the probability of occurrence. Lower probabilities would reduce the investment's cash inflows and their net present value. In this illustration the net present value is positive, so the firm should make the investment. If a financial calculator is used,

$$PMT = 400; FV = 0; N = 5; I = 10; PV = ?.$$

After determining the PV ($1,516.31), subtract the cost ($1,000) to determine the net present value.

Relationships

1. Increased depreciation expense _____ cash flow.

2. Increased taxes may result from a _____ in depreciation.

3. An increase in the cost of capital _____ an investment's net present value (NPV).

4. A decrease in the cost of capital _____ an investment's internal rate of return (IRR).

5. An increase in interest rates _____ net present values.

6. A decrease in the cost of an investment _____ an investment's IRR.

7. Decreased depreciation expense _____ an investment's NPV.

8. If the reinvestment rate increases, an investment's terminal value _____.

9. If the risk associated with an investment increases, the investment's IRR _____.

10. An increase in risk should _____ an investment's NPV.

Answers

1. increases
2. decrease
3. decreases
4. does not affect (no change)
5. decreases
6. increases
7. decreases
8. increases
9. does not change (no impact)
10. decrease

n *Don Quixote*, Cervantes suggested that to be "forewarned" is to be "fore-armed." To be forearmed is the purpose of planning. Forecasting financial needs and constructing financial plans should forewarn management of possible future problems. Even if no major problems are identified, these financial plans will help determine if, and when, external financing will be needed.

This process of identifying problems and developing plans for adjusting to change is illustrated by two firms concerned with different facets of health care. Owens & Minor is one of the nation's two largest wholesale distributors of medical and surgical supplies. Schering-Plough was one of the nation's premier pharmaceutical firms prior to its acquisition by Merck in 2009. The 1995 year was a difficult one for Owens & Minor, as regulators, customers, and health care providers became increasingly cost conscious. Even though sales rose over 20 percent, Owens & Minor operated at a loss and the value of its stock declined. In its 1995 annual report, management detailed several plans and initiatives to improve quality of service, raise performance of underperforming divisions, focus on inventory control, and increase cash flow.

During the same period, the management of Schering-Plough faced the same economic environment, but 1995 was another record year for Schering-Plough. In its 1995 annual report, management reported sales had grown to over $5 billion, new products had been developed, and plans were made for future spending of almost $700 million on research and development. Management realized that the downward pressure on health care costs required they plan for the continual development of new and superior products so that Schering-Plough would be able to continue to compete.

By the mid-2000s, the situations were reversed. Owens & Minor experienced consistent growth in revenues and earnings. The company periodically raised its cash dividend, and the price of the stock rose. Schering-Plough, however, reported lower revenues and lower per share earnings, which led to a dividend reduction. The patent on one of Schering-Plough's most important drugs, Claritin, expired, leading to increased competition from generic drug firms. The Food and Drug Administration (FDA) raised compliance issues with the company's manufacturing processes, and Merck's and Pfizer's problems with pain-relieving drugs for arthritis cast a pall over the entire industry. Obviously, anticipating change and developing plans for solving those challenges were just as important in the mid-2000s for the management of Schering-Plough as planning had been for the management of Owens & Minor in the mid-1990s.

Although planning applies to all facets of a firm's operations, it is particularly important for the financial health of a company. Management needs to forecast the anticipated asset levels to plan for their financing. Without funds, a firm cannot grow, and the time to plan for tomorrow's financing needs is today. This chapter illustrates two techniques, the percent of sales and regression analysis, which may be used to forecast future assets and liabilities. If these forecasted sources of funds do not cover the forecasted desired uses of funds, management is forewarned. It can now plan how to acquire the necessary financing to achieve the anticipated expansion in assets.

Planning

Planning is the process of establishing goals and identifying courses of action (strategies) to meet the goals. Planning is like a road map; it helps point out the roads (or the alternative methods) to reach the destination (or the goal). In finance, the goal of management is often stated as the maximization of the value of the firm. The facets of the financial manager's job, such as the decision to acquire plant and equipment or how to finance the firm's assets, are means to obtain the desired goal of increasing the value of the firm.

The financial manager, however, does not work in a vacuum but must work within the framework of the firm. The management of a firm encompasses marketing, production, and administration as well as finance. The senior executives in charge of a firm's functional areas and operations develop a strategic plan. This plan is a general guide for the management of a firm and encompasses the development of new products through research and development, the expansion of current markets and the identification of new markets for existing products, the control of costs and operations, the expansion (or contraction) of plant and equipment required by changes in anticipated sales, and the financing of additional plant and equipment.

Financial management is one part of the strategic plan, as is planning for marketing and production. Financial planning is a process of anticipating future needs and establishing courses of action today to meet financial objectives in the future. Thus, financial management and planning are concerned with when funds will be needed and how much will be available from internally generated sources. The need for external sources raises such questions as: Should the firm use long- or short-term credit? What is the best combination of debt-to-equity financing?

In a sense, virtually every chapter in this text is concerned with financial planning. For example, several chapters consider the variety of debt instruments and stock. Chapter 13 puts these pieces together by discussing the optimal combination of debt and equity financing. This information is required before investments in plant and equipment (capital budgeting, discussed in Chapter 14) can be undertaken.

Several specific techniques are used in the planning process. For example, break-even analysis, which determines the level of output and sales necessary to avoid sustaining losses, is covered in Chapter 11. This type of analysis helps establish long-term plans, as the management seeks to reduce costs or increase revenues if it appears that the firm will operate at a loss. Break-even analysis, along with the capital budgeting techniques considered in Chapter 14, is a crucial component of long-term financial planning.

This chapter adds two more tools (the percent of sales and regression analysis) to facilitate the planning process. By identifying the firm's expected cash inflows and outflows and forecasting the anticipated levels of assets, liabilities, and retained earnings, these methods determine if a firm will need additional financing. If the answer is "yes," then management can plan how to raise the funds. If the forecasts indicate that the firm will have excess funds, management can plan how to use these funds.

Fluctuations in Asset Requirements

Firms must have assets in order to operate. The amount and type of assets vary with each industry. Airlines and utilities have primarily plant and equipment. Retailers must carry current assets, such as inventory. Firms providing services may have few assets. Other than space (which may be rented), the local barbershop or travel agency may operate with few assets.

Just as the amount and type of assets required for operations vary with each industry, the level of a firm's assets within an industry also changes. For example, a firm that sells swimming pools will not want to stock pools during the winter. Sales are obviously seasonal. Firms whose sales are primarily seasonal (or cyclical, such as homes) will experience periodic increases and decreases in the level of assets needed for their operations.

These fluctuations are illustrated in Figure 15.1, which presents the levels of various assets over a period of time. Fixed assets (0A) are given and do not vary. Current assets have been divided into two groups: those that remain at a particular level (AB) and those that vary (BC). The firm may carry a minimum amount of inventory and may always have some accounts receivable. In addition, the firm has current assets that vary over time. The level of inventory will fluctuate with anticipated changes in demand, which in turn will generate differing amounts of accounts receivable and cash. These fluctuations in the levels of inventory, accounts receivable, and cash are illustrated by CD in Figure 15.1.

The firm may also require additional assets as it expands. As the firm grows, some assets automatically expand with the level of sales. For example, the level of inventory expands to meet the higher volume of sales. Other assets, especially long-term assets such as plant and equipment, will not spontaneously expand with the level of output. Initially, the existing plant and equipment will be used more intensively. The number of shifts will be increased, or employees may work overtime. However, if the expansion of sales continues, management will expand the firm's investment in plant and equipment.

This difference is illustrated in Figure 15.2. The left-hand side illustrates those assets that increase with expanding output. This relationship is shown by the steadily increasing line AA that represents the level of these assets at each level of sales. The right-hand side illustrates those assets that are increased only after a higher level of sales has been achieved. From zero sales to sales of S_1, the level of plant and equipment remains constant. After the level of S_1 has been obtained, further increases in the level of output require expansion in the plant and equipment. The level of fixed assets rises from A_1 to A_2. This higher level of assets is maintained until sales rise from S_1 to S_2, when plant and equipment must be further expanded. The level of fixed assets then is increased to A_3.

In the discussion that follows, it is initially assumed that the firm can expand the level of production without having to increase capacity. Thus, only those assets that spontaneously fluctuate with the level of sales will be affected by an increase (or decrease) in sales. After explaining how the percent of sales

F I G U R E 15.1
Fluctuations in Assets over Time

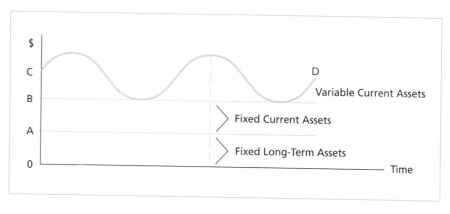

F I G U R E 15.2
Relationships between
Sales and Various Assets

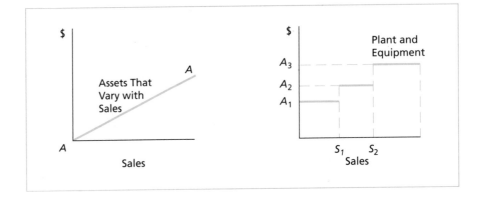

F I G U R E 15.2
Relationships between
Sales and Various Assets

may be used to forecast assets and liabilities, the assumption that the firm has excess capacity is relaxed, so that expanding the level of sales requires more investment in plant and equipment. Since all assets must be financed, the forecasted expansion in assets forewarns the financial manager of the firm's future need for funds.

Forecasting External Financial Requirements: Percent of Sales

Percent of sales

Forecasting technique that assumes specific assets and liabilities will vary directly with the level of sales

The percent of sales technique for forecasting financial requirements isolates the assets and liabilities that *spontaneously change with the level of sales* and expresses each as a percent of sales. These percentages are then used to forecast the level of each asset and liability. The forecasted increase in the level of assets must be financed and the increased level of liabilities will automatically finance some of the increase in assets. The difference between the increases in the assets and the liabilities must be financed by other means.

What assets vary with the level of sales? Consider a firm with the following balance sheet:

Assets		Liabilities	
Cash	$ 100	Accounts payable	$ 200
Accounts receivable	300	Bank note payable	200
Inventory	300	Other current liabilities	100
Plant and equipment	500	Long-term debt	300
	$1,200	Equity	400
			$1,200

Several of the assets will vary with the firm's level of sales. A higher level of sales will require that the firm carry more inventory and will also increase the accounts receivable, as credit sales should expand if all sales increase. The level of cash may also rise with increased cash sales, and management may want to increase its level of cash holdings to meet the expanded liquidity needs, such as the payroll associated with higher sales volume. (Notice the difference between the two sets of assumptions. Inventory and accounts receivable *will* increase. Cash *may* increase. The difference is important.)

While cash, inventory, and accounts receivable increase as sales rise, other assets do not automatically expand. For example, plant and equipment may not be increased but will be used at a higher level of capacity. If the level of sales rises sufficiently, more plant and equipment will need to be acquired, but no automatic increase in these fixed assets must occur as sales volume increases.

All the assets that increase with the higher level of sales must be financed. The funds to finance these assets must come from somewhere, and one source is any liability that also spontaneously expands with the level of sales. If liabilities increase sufficiently, they will cover the expansion in assets, but if they do not, the firm will have to find additional financing to operate at the higher level of sales.

Accounts payable are the primary liabilities that increase with expanded sales, because the firm's suppliers increase goods sold to the firm on credit. Other liabilities, such as accrued wages and salaries, also automatically expand. The other short-term liabilities, such as bank notes payable and the current portion of long-term debt due this fiscal year, do not spontaneously expand with the level of sales and thus are not automatic sources of financing.

The previous balance sheet may illustrate how the percent of sales technique of forecasting works. After those assets and liabilities that spontaneously vary with the level of sales are identified, they are expressed as a percent of sales. Thus, if the firm has inventory of $300 and sales of $2,000, inventory is 15 percent of sales ($300/$2,000). The following exhibit expresses as a percentage of sales all the assets and liabilities in the previous balance sheet that are assumed to vary with the level of sales:

Assets		Liabilities	
Cash	5%	Accounts payable	10%
Accounts receivable	15%		
Inventory	15%		

The percent of sales for the assets and liabilities that do not automatically increase with the level of sales is not calculated. Thus, as may be seen from the exhibit, the ratio of all assets that vary with sales is 35 percent, and the ratio of liabilities is 10 percent.

Once the percentages have been determined, the anticipated level of sales is multiplied by each percentage to determine the anticipated level of each asset and liability necessary to sustain that level of sales. For example, if management anticipates that the level of sales will rise to $2,400 (a 20 percent increase), the percent of sales technique will forecast the following level of assets and liabilities for each asset and liability that varies with sales:

Assets		Liabilities	
Cash	$120	Accounts payable	$240
Accounts receivable	360		
Inventory	360		

In this case the percent of sales forecasting method states that the level of inventory ($300) will rise to $360 ($2,400 × 0.15), the level of accounts receivable ($300) will be $360 ($2,400 × 0.15), and the level of cash ($100) will be $120 ($2,400 × 0.05). The automatic expansion in assets is $140, which may be found by multiplying the increase in sales ($400) by 35 percent, which is the sum of the ratios of all assets that vary with the level of sales.

Concurrently with the increase in assets, accounts payable will rise to $240 ($2,400 × 0.10). The total increase in assets is $140, while the increase in liabilities is $40. This $40 increase in liabilities will finance only part of the increase in assets. Thus, $100 ($140 − $40) of assets will require other sources of financing. Management may expect that the firm will operate at a profit, and these earnings could be retained to finance the additional assets. But earnings after taxes would have to be $100 to finance the expansion in assets. If management cannot anticipate after-tax profits of $100, an outside source of finance (such as a bank loan) will have to be found to finance the anticipated increase in assets necessitated by the increase in sales.

If management anticipates earning 5 percent on the total sales and retaining 60 percent of the earnings, the forecasted increase in equity is

$$(0.05)(\$2,400)(0.6) = \$72.$$

Given this increase in equity and the forecasted levels of the current assets and current liabilities, management may construct the following pro forma balance sheet:

Assets		Liabilities	
Cash	$ 120	Accounts payable	$ 240
Accounts receivable	360	Bank note payable	200
Inventory	360	Other current liabilities	100
Plant and equipment	500	Long-term debt	300
	$1,340	Equity	472
			$1,312

The balance sheet entries include the forecasted entries (the assets and liabilities that spontaneously changed with the level of sales); the entries that did not change, such as the long-term debt; and the new equity, which is the old equity plus the earnings that are to be retained.

Immediately it is obvious that the balance sheet *does not balance*. The forecasted increase in the assets *exceeds* the forecasted increase in the liabilities and equity. Total assets exceed total liabilities and equity by $28. To achieve the forecasted increase in assets, the firm will have to find $28 in *additional* funding. Without these additional sources, the expansion in assets cannot occur. However, this is a forecasted and not an actual balance sheet, so management now has the task (and presumably the time) to obtain the additional sources of finance.

Management has several options. Any increase in equity, any increases in liabilities, or any decrease in assets will help provide the needed financing. For example, the dividend policy may be changed to reduce dividends and increase the retention of earnings. Another possibility may be to seek an additional bank loan. If management decides not to reduce dividends, but instead to increase borrowing from the bank by $28, the pro forma balance sheet becomes

Assets		Liabilities	
Cash	$ 120	Accounts payable	$ 240
Accounts receivable	360	Bank note payable	228
Inventory	360	Other current liabilities	100
Plant and equipment	500	Long-term debt	300
	$1,340	Equity	472
			$1,340

The balance sheet now balances; the sum of the projected assets equals the sum of the projected liabilities plus equity.

This example illustrates the importance of the assumption regarding the increase in cash. The firm needed $28 because the expansion in the uses of funds (i.e., the forecasted cash outflows) exceeded the forecasted expansion in sources (i.e., the forecasted inflows). If the $20 increase in cash could be avoided, the need for additional funds would be reduced to $8. If the firm could reduce its cash from $100 to $92 (i.e., reduce the cash by $8), there would be no need for additional financing.

So far, three possible solutions to the need for additional finance have been considered: (1) borrowing more from the bank, (2) retaining more earnings (distributing less in dividends), and (3) drawing down existing cash. These are not the only possible solutions. Any decrease in an asset and any increase in a liability or equity is a cash inflow. Management's dilemma is to determine which of the numerous possibilities is the best solution to the forecasted problem.

You should note that in this example, the forecasted increase in assets exceeds the forecasted increase in liabilities plus equity. That result indicates the need for additional funds. If the forecasted increase in assets were less than the forecasted increase in liabilities plus equity, forecasted cash inflows exceed outflows. Management would then have to decide what to do with the funds. Once again, numerous possibilities exist, ranging from increased dividend payments to the repurchase of stock or retiring existing debt. One common practice is to park the funds in a short-term money market security such as a Treasury bill.

Many companies do invest any excess funds in money market securities. (The variety of these instruments is covered in Chapter 2 in the section "Money Market Mutual Funds and Money Market Instruments." Money market securities are often reported under the general heading of cash equivalents on the firm's balance sheet.) Even firms that have operated at a loss may have substantial investments in cash equivalents. For example, Ford Motor Company, which operated at a loss during 2008 and reported a modest profit in 2009, held cash and cash equivalents exceeding $22.0 billion at the end of its 2008 fiscal year. Substantial holdings of cash equivalents suggest the firm may be financially strong and able to pay its current obligations as they come due even though it is currently operating at an accounting loss.

The Percent of Sales Summarized as an Equation

The previous section illustrates the percent of sales technique of forecasting, which asserts that if an asset or liability is some percent of sales and sales expand by some percentage, then the assets and liabilities will also expand by the same percentage. This relationship is illustrated in Figure 15.3. The horizontal axis represents the level of sales, and the vertical axis shows the level of inventory. (A similar graph may be drawn for any asset or liability that varies with sales.)

The relationship between inventory and sales is summarized by the following equation:

$$I = bS. \tag{15.1}$$

I is inventory; S is the level of sales; and b is the percent of sales, which is also the slope of the line. Once this percentage is known, it is easy to predict the

FIGURE 15.3
Relationship between Inventory and Sales

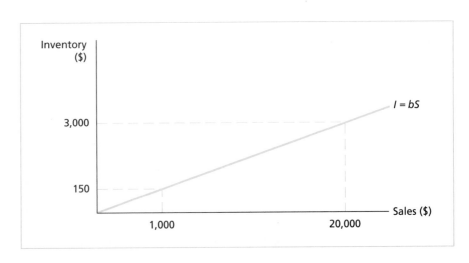

level of inventory associated with any level of sales. Thus, if sales are $1,000, inventory will be $150 ($1,000 × 0.15). If sales expand to $20,000, inventory must expand to $3,000 ($20,000 × 0.15). By this method, all that is necessary to forecast the level of the asset is (1) the ratio of the current level of that asset to current sales and (2) the anticipated level of sales.

The financial manager may use a simple equation that summarizes (1) all the assets and liabilities that vary with sales, (2) the profits the firm earns on its projected sales, and (3) the distribution of those earnings. The equation, summarizing the percent of sales forecasting method, is

External funding requirements =

$$\left[\left(\frac{\text{Assets that vary with sales}}{\text{Sales}} \right) \times \begin{array}{c} \text{Change} \\ \text{in} \\ \text{sales} \end{array} - \left(\frac{\text{Liabilities that vary with sales}}{\text{Sales}} \right) \times \begin{array}{c} \text{Change} \\ \text{in} \\ \text{sales} \end{array} \right] \begin{array}{c} \text{Increase in} \\ - \ \text{retained} \\ \text{earnings.} \end{array}$$

In symbolic form this equation for external funding requirements (EFR) is

$$EFR = \left[\frac{A}{S} (\Delta S) - \frac{L}{S} (\Delta S) \right] - (PS_1)R. \qquad (15.2)$$

Although this equation may look formidable, it is not. The equation states that the firm's requirements for outside financing equal the funds needed to finance those assets generated by the projected change (Δ) in sales (S) minus the funds generated by the change in sales and the increase in retained earnings. Both the assets and liabilities that vary with the level of sales are expressed as a percent of current sales (A/S and L/S, respectively). The *additional* retained earnings depend on the profit margin of the firm's *projected sales* (PS_1) and the proportion of the earnings that are retained (R).

Suppose that a firm with sales of $10,000 has the following balance sheet:

Assets		Liabilities	
Accounts receivable	$ 3,000	Accounts payable	$ 2,500
Inventory	2,000	Long-term debt	4,000
Plant and equipment	8,000	Equity	6,500
	$13,000		$13,000

Accounts receivable, inventory, and accounts payable vary with sales; the other entries do not. If the firm expands sales from $10,000 to $12,000, these assets and liabilities will spontaneously increase. Accounts receivable and inventory are 50 percent of sales, while accounts payable are 25 percent of sales. Thus, the first part of the equation is

$$EFR = (0.5)(\$2,000) - (0.25)(\$2,000) = \$1,000 - \$500.$$

The $1,000 is the projected cash outflow required by the expansion in the assets. The $500 is the projected cash inflow from the expansion in the forecasted liabilities.

If the firm earns 5 percent on its total sales and distributes 30 percent of its earnings as dividends, it retains the remaining 70 percent. The addition to retained earnings is

$$(0.05)(\$12,000)(0.7) = \$420.$$

This is also a cash inflow, so the total cash inflows are

$$\$500 + \$420 = \$920.$$

The projected inflows minus the projected outflows give the firm's external need for funds. In this example, the external funds needed are

$$
\begin{aligned}
EFR &= (0.5)(\$2,000) - (0.25)(\$2,000) - (0.05)(\$12,000)(0.70) \\
&= \$1,000 - \$500 - \$420 \\
&= \$80.
\end{aligned}
$$

The spontaneous increase in current assets requires $1,000. The spontaneous increase in liabilities generates only $500, and the firm retains only $420 of its earnings generated on its projected sales. Thus, the firm needs $80 of external financing to cover the anticipated increase in assets.

By this analysis the financial manager now knows that the firm will need more funds. One possible internal source is to distribute fewer dividends (retain more earnings). If the firm retained all its earnings, its need for outside funding would be

$$
\begin{aligned}
EFR &= (0.5)(\$2,000) - (0.25)(\$2,000) - (0.05)(\$12,000)(1) \\
&= \$1,000 - \$500 - \$600 \\
&= (\$100).
\end{aligned}
$$

The firm would have sufficient funds. It would have *excess* funds of $100 and would not need outside finance to cover the expansion in assets spontaneously generated by the increase in sales.

The percent of sales forecasting method is one technique for predicting the firm's need for outside finance. Unfortunately, the method may produce inaccurate estimates. If such estimates understate financial needs, finding additional credit rapidly may be difficult. If the technique overpredicts the financial needs, it may cause the firm to borrow more than is necessary and cause the firm to pay unnecessary interest expense.

The source of the problem is the assumption that the current percentage will hold for all levels of sales. This assumption need not be true; for example, the firm may be able to economize on inventory as it becomes larger, so that inventory as a percent of sales declines as the level of sales rises. The converse may also be true as sales decline. The firm may continue to carry items even though sales have diminished, or there may be a lag after the decline in sales before the firm recognizes which items are moving slowly and ceases to carry them. Thus, inventory as a percent of sales may rise when the level of sales declines.

Although the percent of sales technique of forecasting may produce biased estimates, it is still employed as a forecasting tool for two reasons. First, it is simple and pragmatic. Second, if the change in sales is relatively small, the estimate may not be significantly biased. The larger the increase in sales, the greater the bias will be; but if management is concerned with only a small change in the level of sales, the percent of sales method of forecasting financial needs may be sufficient.

Forecasting External Financial Requirements: Regression Analysis

An alternative to the percent of sales is regression analysis, which uses the relationship between the asset or liability and sales over several years. For example, Exhibit 15.1 depicts a firm's level of inventory and sales for the last five years. This information indicates a positive relationship between the level of inventory and sales, but inventory as a percent of sales has declined. If this decline continues, the use of a percentage determined from only one year's observations will overpredict the level of inventory.

This relationship between sales and inventory is plotted in Figure 15.4, which also indicates a positive trend, since the points are rising. Using the graph in this form, however, may be difficult. For example, it would be difficult to project the level of inventory if the level of sales were to rise to $2,500. This problem can be overcome if the points are expressed as an equation.

Figure 15.5 reproduces the points in Figure 15.4 but in addition passes a line through the points so that the relationship between inventory and sales is expressed by the following simple linear equation:

$$I = a + bS. \tag{15.3}$$

Year	Sales	Inventory	Inventory as a percent of sales
1	$1,000	$400	40%
2	1,200	470	39
3	1,400	500	36
4	1,700	530	31
5	2,000	600	30

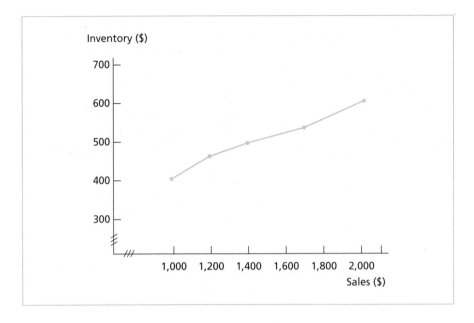

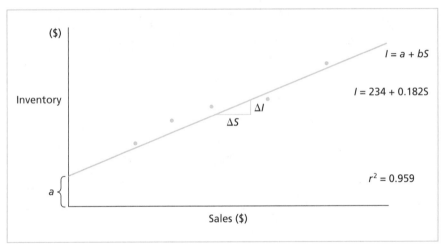

The vertical intercept, a, gives the level of inventory the firm carries even when it has only the minimal amount of sales. The rate at which the line rises is the slope, $\Delta I/\Delta S$, and this is represented by the symbol b. Regression analysis estimates numerical values for a and b, the intercept and the slope.

For this firm, regression analysis indicates that the equation for the relationship between inventory and sales is

$$I = \$234.28 + 0.182S.$$

The $234.28 is the y-intercept and indicates the level of inventory if there were no sales. The 0.182 is the slope of the line and indicates that for an increase in sales of $1,000, the level of inventory will increase by $182. (How the equation may be estimated manually and by using Excel are illustrated in Exhibits 15.2 and 15.3.)

Once the equation has been estimated, it can be used to forecast the level of inventory for any level of sales. For example, if sales are $3,000, the equation estimates that the level of inventory will be $780, which is obtained by substituting $3,000 for sales and solving for inventory:

$$\text{Inventory} = \$234.28 + 0.182(\$3,000)$$
$$= \$780.28.$$

Figure 15.5 indicates that the relationship between sales and inventory is close, since the individual observations (that is, the individual points) lie close to the regression line. Such closeness indicates a high correlation between the independent variable (sales) and the dependent variable (inventory).

This correlation may be measured by the "correlation coefficient" or the "coefficient of determination." In statistics these are often symbolized as r or r^2, respectively. As was explained in Chapter 8, in which regression analysis was used to estimate a stock's beta coefficient, the numerical value of the correlation coefficient ranges from $+1.0$ to -1.0. If the two variables move exactly together (if there is a perfect positive correlation between the independent and dependent variables), the numerical value of the correlation coefficient is 1.0. If the two variables move exactly opposite of each other, the

EXHIBIT 15.2
Manual Calculation of the Regression Equation

X	Y	X²	Y²	XY
1,000	400	1,000,000	160,000	400,000
1,200	470	1,440,000	220,900	564,000
1,400	500	1,960,000	250,000	700,000
1,700	530	2,890,000	280,900	901,000
2,000	600	4,000,000	360,000	1,200,000
$\Sigma X = 7,300$	$\Sigma Y = 2,500$	$\Sigma X^2 = 11,290,000$	$\Sigma Y^2 = 1,271,800$	$\Sigma XY^2 = 3,765,000$

n = number of observations (5).

$$\text{slope} = b = \frac{n\Sigma XY - (\Sigma X)(\Sigma Y)}{n\Sigma X^2 - (\Sigma X)^2}$$

$$= \frac{(5)(3,765,000) - (7,300)(2,500)}{(5)(11,290,000) - (7,300)(7,300)} = 0.182.$$

$$\text{intercept} = a = \frac{\Sigma Y}{n} - b\frac{\Sigma X}{n}$$

$$= \frac{2,500}{5} - (0.182)\frac{7,300}{5} = 234.28.$$

EXHIBIT 15.3
Excel Estimation of the
Regression Equation

Sales: the independent or X variable
Inventory: the dependent or Y variable
Locate the regression program in Excel under Tools. Enter the data.

	A	B	C
	Year	Inventory	Sales
1			
2	1	400	1,000
3	2	470	1,200
4	3	500	1,400
5	4	530	1,700
6	5	600	2,000

Column A gives the years and columns B and C are used for inventory and sales.
The data for inventory are in cells B2 through B6, and the data for sales are in cells
C2 through C6.
    Where the regression program asks for the Y variable, type in b2:b6. For the X
variable, type in c2:c6. Have the output placed somewhere other than over the data,
such as A8. Excel quickly determines the equation to be

$$\text{Inventory} = \$234.34 + 0.182\text{Sales.}$$

(How Excel is used to perform regression analysis is explained in more detail in
Appendix E devoted to using Excel.)

correlation coefficient equals -1.0. All other possible values lie between these
two extremes. Numerical values near 0, such as -0.12 or $+0.19$, indicate little
relationship between the two variables.
    The coefficient of determination is the square of the correlation coeffi-
cient and measures the proportion of the variation in the dependent variable
explained by movement in the independent variable. Thus, if the correlation
coefficient is 0.1, the coefficient of determination is 0.01 (0.1^2), which indicates that the movement in the independent variable explains very little of the
movement in the dependent variable.
    Computation of these two coefficients is part of statistics, and the com-
puter programs that estimate the regression equation routinely give the numerical values of the correlation coefficient and the coefficient of determination.
(The regression output from Excel includes these coefficients.) The interpretation of the coefficients is potentially useful to the financial manager who
is concerned with the accuracy of the estimated equation. The coefficient of
determination (the r^2) gives the proportion of the variability in inventory that
is explained by the variability in sales. In this illustration the r^2 is 0.959, which
indicates a very close relationship between sales and inventory. The high r^2
should increase the financial manager's confidence in using the regression
equation to forecast inventory as sales change.
    Such a close correspondence between the variables need not occur, but
regression analysis will still summarize the relationship. For example, consider

the relationships between sales and inventory presented in Exhibit 15.4 and Figure 15.6.

In case A, the individual observations relating sales and inventory are scattered throughout the graph, but the regression technique still estimates an equation summarizing the individual observations. The correlation is low, with an r^2 of only 0.216, so the quality of the equation as a forecasting tool is questionable.

The same conclusion concerning the forecasting ability of the estimated equation applies to case B. In this case, the individual observations for all levels of sales between $1,000 and $2,000 lie above the line. However, regression analysis still estimates an equation that summarizes the relationship between sales and inventory. While the quality of the equation is rather high ($r^2 = 0.813$), the forecasting ability of the estimated equation is suspect.

This example points out a possible problem with simple linear regression analysis. First, the actual relationship between the variables may not be a straight line. Case B in Figure 15.6 implies that the relationship between inventory and sales is curvilinear. The dots rise but appear to taper off as the level of sales increases. By visual inspection the true relationship between sales and inventory appears to be the curved line AB drawn through the points. An equation for this curved line should give more reliable forecasts than the simple straight line (linear) equation that was previously estimated.

Another potential source of difficulty with simple linear regression is the possibility of several variables affecting the dependent variable. For example, the level of inventory may be affected not only by sales but also by the availability of the goods, the season of the year, or the cost of credit. That appears to be the situation in case A in Figure 15.6 because the relationship between inventory and sales is weak. Something other than sales must explain the level of inventory.

These problems with simple linear regression may be solved by using nonlinear regression analysis or multiple regression, which includes more than one independent variable. Both of these statistical techniques are covered in more advanced texts.

Although nonlinear and multiple regression analysis will not be developed here, it is desirable to compare simple linear regression with the percent of sales technique for forecasting. The percent of sales is the simple case of regression analysis in which there is no intercept and the slope is determined by the origin and one observation. The percent of sales technique assumes that

EXHIBIT 15.4		
Relationships between Sales and Inventory		

Sales	Case A Inventory	Case B Inventory
$1,000	$400	$400
1,200	380	550
1,400	600	600
1,700	500	700
2,000	450	750

FIGURE   15.6   Relationships between Sales and Inventory

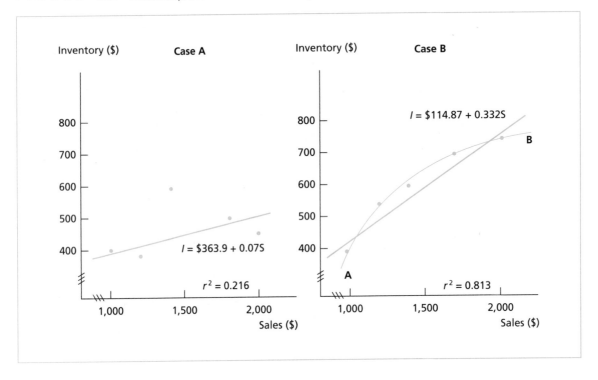

the present ratio of inventory to sales will remain constant, and it takes that ratio as the slope of the equation. On the basis of that assumption, the technique then projects the level of inventory. Regression analysis, however, does not make that assumption and formulates an equation using several observations that relate inventory and sales.

The differences in the predictive power of the two techniques are illustrated in Exhibit 15.5, which is based on the previous example. The first column gives the level of sales, and the second and third columns give the estimated levels of inventory. The second column uses the percent of sales method, which assumes that the ratio of inventory to sales is constant (30 percent). The third column uses the regression equation ($I = \$234.28 + 0.182S$), which was formulated on the basis of data for past levels of inventory and sales.

As may be seen in the exhibit, the higher the anticipated level of sales, the larger the estimated level of inventory. But the estimated level of inventory is larger for the percent of sales method than for the regression technique. The percent of sales technique may be overestimating the desired level of inventory. For example, if as the firm grows and there are economies in inventory management, the level of inventory need not continue to grow at the same rate. Thus, the ratio of inventory to sales will decline. Under these circumstances, regression analysis gives a better estimate of the desired level of inventory and is the more accurate predictor.

Sales	Percent of Sales Forecast (Inventory = 0.30 Sales)	Regression Analysis Forecast (Inventory = $234.28 + 0.182 Sales)
$1,500	$450	$507.28
2,000	600	598.28
2,500	750	689.28
3,000	900	780.28

Forecasting External Financial Requirements: Changes in Fixed Assets

In the previous sections it was assumed that as the firm expanded sales, only those assets that spontaneously changed with the level of sales varied. Such expansion of sales can occur only if the firm has excess capacity. In this section, the firm must expand its fixed assets, as well as those assets that spontaneously change with the level of sales.

To ease the explanation, the example used for the percent of sales is continued. The firm has the following balance sheet:

Assets		Liabilities	
Cash	$ 100	Accounts payable	$ 200
Accounts receivable	300	Bank note payable	200
Inventory	300	Other current liabilities	100
Plant and equipment	500	Long-term debt	300
	$1,200	Equity	400
			$1,200

Sales were $2,000 and they are expected to increase to $2,400. If the net profit margin on sales is 10 percent and the firm retains 40 percent of its earnings, the percent of sales method forecasts the following projected balance sheet entries:

Assets		Liabilities	
Cash	$ 120	Accounts payable	$ 240
Accounts receivable	360	Bank note payable	200
Inventory	360	Other current liabilities	100
Plant and equipment	500	Long-term debt	300
	$1,340	Equity	496
			$1,336

Cash, accounts receivable, inventory, and accounts payable all increase because it is assumed that they spontaneously change with the level of sales. Equity increases by $96, since the firm earns $240 on its sales ($2,400 × 0.1 = $240) and retains 40 percent of its earnings ($240 × 0.4). The other entries remain the same because they do not change with the level of sales.

In the example, assets increase by $140 while liabilities and equity increase by $136. The projected balance sheet, of course, does not balance; the difference of $4 equals the projected shortage of funds. The financial manager would have to plan for this $4 in additional finance to cover the projected expansion in assets. Because the required amount is so modest, it is safe to assume that finding the additional finance would not be a major problem.

Suppose, however, that the expansion in sales also requires an increase of $200 in fixed assets. The projected balance sheet would become:

Assets		Liabilities	
Cash	$ 120	Accounts payable	$ 240
Accounts receivable	360	Bank note payable	200
Inventory	360	Other current liabilities	100
Plant and equipment	700	Long-term debt	300
	$1,540	Equity	496
			$1,336

The firm's need for finance is larger (that is, $204), since the expansion in sales cannot be achieved in this example without an expansion in plant and equipment.

What choices are available to the financial manager to raise the required $204? Actually, the financial manager has several options. First, the holdings of cash could be reduced to acquire another asset. Second, a larger proportion of the earnings could be retained instead of being distributed. Earnings that are retained, of course, could help finance the projected expansion in assets. Third, the firm could issue additional debt, such as bonds, or issue additional stock to raise the cash to acquire other assets.

Obviously, the financial manager has several possible courses of action. As is discussed in Chapter 13, one of the questions is what combination of debt and equity financing is the most desirable to finance the expansion. The use of debt financing may increase the return earned by the owners, but the additional use of financial leverage also increases the risk associated with the firm. For the purposes of this discussion, assume that the financial manager decides to (1) reduce the holdings of cash to $80, which releases $40, (2) distribute only 40 percent of earnings and thus retain $144 instead of $96, and (3) float additional debt to cover the remaining deficiency. After these changes occur, the projected balance sheet becomes:

Assets		Liabilities	
Cash	$ 80	Accounts payable	$ 240
Accounts receivable	360	Bank note payable	200
Inventory	360	Other current liabilities	100
Plant and equipment	700	Long-term debt	416
	$1,500	Equity	544
			$1,500

Management has solved the financial problem by using a combination of reducing existing cash, issuing more long-term debt, and retaining earnings. That is, of course, not the only possible solution. Frequently many possible means are available to solve a problem. It is management's obligation to work through various solutions to determine which are feasible and which one best enhances the value of the firm.

Summary

Management constructs strategic plans that establish general goals for a firm. The strategies designed to meet the goals are executed by the various executives responsible for a firm's operations, marketing, and finance. Financial plans must fit within the general strategic plan of a firm. These plans require forecasts of when a firm will need outside sources of finance.

Some assets, such as accounts receivable and inventory, automatically expand with increases in a firm's sales. Other assets, such as plant and equipment, have to be increased after a firm reaches a certain level of sales. Once capacity is reached, further expansion will require additional investment in plant and equipment.

All assets have to be financed, so projecting a firm's level of assets is crucial to the financial health of a firm. One forecasting technique uses the percent of sales. It expresses all assets and liabilities that spontaneously change with the level of sales as a percent of sales. That percentage is then used to forecast the future level of these assets and liabilities as sales increase. A more sophisticated forecasting technique uses estimated equations (regression analysis) to estimate the level of assets and liabilities associated with various levels of sales.

Either technique may be used to construct a projected balance sheet that indicates a firm's estimated future assets, future liabilities, and future equity. If the estimated assets exceed the estimated liabilities plus equity, the financial manager must plan today to find the finance required by the forecast of the firm's future assets.

Review Objectives

Now that you have completed this chapter, you should be able to

1. Identify the assets and liabilities that spontaneously vary with the level of sales (pp. 334–335).

2. Illustrate the percent of sales method of forecasting (pp. 336–343).

3. Use regression analysis to forecast assets and liabilities that change with sales (pp. 343–349).

4. Explain how dividend policy affects the need for external financing (pp. 349–351).

5. Add the impact of changes in any assets that do not spontaneously change with sales (pp. 349–351).

Problems

1. SLM, Inc., with sales of $1,000, has the following balance sheet:

SLM, Incorporated Balance Sheet as of 12/31/X0			
Assets		Liabilities and Equity	
Accounts receivable	$ 200	Trade accounts payable	$ 200
Inventory	400	Long-term debt	600
Plant	800	Equity	600
	$1,400		$1,400

It earns 10 percent on sales (after taxes) and pays no dividends.

a. Determine the balance sheet entries for sales of $1,500 using the percent of sales method of forecasting.

b. Will the firm need external financing to grow to sales of $1,500?

c. Construct the new balance sheet and use newly issued long-term debt to cover any financial deficiency.

2. EMM, Inc. has the following balance sheet:

EMM, Incorporated Balance Sheet as of 12/31/X0			
Assets		Liabilities and Equity	
Cash	$ 1,000	Accounts payable	$ 5,300
Accounts receivable	7,200	Bank note payable	3,200
Inventory	6,100		
Long-term assets	4,200	Equity	10,000
	$18,500		$18,500

a. If the firm expects sales to rise from $20,000 to $25,000, what are the forecasted levels of accounts receivable, accounts payable, and inventory?

b. Will the expansion in accounts payable cover the expansion in inventory and accounts receivable?

c. If the firm earns 12 percent on sales after taxes and retains all of these earnings, will it cover its estimated needs for short-term financing?

d. Construct a new balance sheet that incorporates the issuing of additional short-term debt to cover any needs for additional finance. Assume cash remains $1,000. If cash also increases proportionately with sales, what impact will the increase in cash have on the firm's need for funds?

3. EEM, Inc. has the following balance sheet:

EEM, Incorporated Balance Sheet as of 12/31/X0			
Assets		**Liabilities and Equity**	
Cash	$ 1,000	Accounts payable	$ 5,300
Accounts receivable	7,200	Bank note payable	3,200
Inventory	6,100		
Long-term assets	4,200	Equity	10,000
	$18,500		$18,500

It has estimated the following relationships between sales and the various assets and liabilities that vary with the level of sales:

$$\text{Accounts receivable} = \$3,310 + 0.35 \text{ Sales,}$$

$$\text{Inventory} = \$2,264 + 0.28 \text{ Sales,}$$

$$\text{Accounts payable} = \$1,329 + 0.22 \text{ Sales.}$$

a. If the firm expects sales of $25,000, what are the forecasted levels of the balance sheet items above?

b. Will the expansion in accounts payable cover the expansion in inventory and accounts receivable?

c. If the firm earns 12 percent on sales after taxes and retains all of these earnings, will it cover its estimated needs for short-term financing?

d. Construct a new balance sheet that incorporates the issuing of additional short-term debt to cover any needs for additional finance. Assume cash remains $1,000.

e. Compare your answers in parts *a–d* with your answers to parts *a–d* in Problem 2.

4. BBP, Inc., with sales of $500,000, has the following balance sheet:

BBP, Incorporated Balance Sheet as of 12/31/X0			
Assets		**Liabilities and Equity**	
Cash	$ 25,000	Accounts payable	$ 15,000
Accounts receivable	50,000	Accruals	20,000
Inventory	75,000	Notes payable	50,000
Current assets	150,000	Current liabilities	85,000
Fixed assets	200,000	Common stock	100,000
		Retained earnings	165,000
Total assets	$350,000	Total liabilities and equity	$350,000

The firm earns 15 percent on sales and distributes 25 percent of its earnings. Using the percent of sales, forecast the new balance sheet for sales of $600,000 assuming that cash changes with sales and that the firm is not operating at capacity. Will the firm need external funds? Would your answer be different if the firm distributed all of its earnings?

5. With sales of $350,000, MJM, Inc. is operating at capacity but management anticipates that sales will grow 25 percent during the coming year. The company earns 10 percent on sales and distributes 50 percent of earnings to stockholders. Its current balance sheet is as follows:

MJM, Incorporated Balance Sheet as of 12/31/X0			
Assets		**Liabilities and Equity**	
Cash	$ 7,500	Accounts payable	$ 38,000
Accounts receivable	30,000	Accruals	45,000
Inventory	65,000	Notes payable	0
Current assets	102,500	Current liabilities	83,000
Plant and equipment	100,000	Common stock	70,000
		Retained earnings	49,500
Total assets	$202,500	Total liabilities and equity	$202,500

a. In addition to cash, which assets and liabilities will increase with the increase in sales and by how much if the percent of sales is used to forecast the increases?

b. How much external finance will the firm need?

c. If cash did not increase but could be maintained at $7,500, what impact would the lower cash have on the firm's need for external finance?

d. If the firm distributed 25 percent instead of 50 percent of its earnings, would it need external finance?

e. Construct a new balance sheet assuming that cash increases with the increase in sales and the firm distributes 50 percent of its earnings to stockholders. If the firm needs external finance, acquire the funds by issuing a short-term note to a commercial bank. Compare this financing strategy to the strategies implied by the answers to parts c and d.

6. HBM, Inc. had sales of $10 million and a net profit margin of 7 percent in 20X0. Management expects sales to grow to $12 million and $14 million in 20X1 and 20X2, respectively. Management wants to know if additional funds will be necessary to finance this anticipated growth. Currently, the firm is not operating at full capacity and should be able to sustain a 25 percent increase in sales. However, further increases in sales will require $2 million in plant and equipment for every $5 million increase in sales. The firm's balance sheet is as follows:

HBM, Incorporated Balance Sheet as of 12/31/X0			
Assets		Liabilities and Equity	
Cash	$1,500,000	Accruals	$1,500,000
Accounts receivable	2,000,000	Accounts payable	1,000,000
Inventory	1,500,000	Notes payable	500,000
Plant and equipment	3,000,000	Long-term debt	3,000,000
		Equity	2,000,000
	$8,000,000		$8,000,000

Management has followed a policy of distributing at least 70 percent of earnings as dividends. Management believes that the percent of sales method of forecasting is sufficient to answer the question, "Will outside funding be necessary?" In order to use this technique, management has assumed that accounts receivable, inventory, accruals, and accounts payable will vary with the level of sales. Cash will not change.

a. Prepare projected balance sheets for 20X1 and 20X2 that incorporate any necessary outside financing. Any short-term funds that are required should be obtained through a loan from the bank, and any excess short-term funds should be appropriately invested. Any long-term financing that is needed should be obtained through long-term debt and/or appropriate reductions in short-term assets.

b. If the firm did not distribute 70 percent of its earnings, could it sustain the expansion without issuing additional long-term debt?

c. If the firm's creditors in part a require a current ratio of 2:1, would that affect the firm's financing in 20X1 and 20X2? If so, what additional actions could the firm take?

d. If the percent of sales forecasts are replaced with the following regression equations:

$$\text{Accounts receivable} = \$100,000 + 0.12 \text{ Sales,}$$

$$\text{Inventory} = \$250,000 + 0.15 \text{ Sales,}$$

$$\text{Accruals} = \$100,000 + 0.07 \text{ Sales,}$$

$$\text{Accounts payable} = \$250,000 + 0.08 \text{ Sales,}$$

what is the firm's need for outside funding (if any) in 20X1 and 20X2?

e. If the firm's creditors in part *d* required a current ratio of 2:1, would that affect the firm's financing in 20X1 and 20X2? If so, what additional actions could the firm take?

7. RRM, Inc. has the following balance sheet:

RRM, Incorporated Balance Sheet as of 12/31/X0			
Assets		**Liabilities and Equity**	
Cash	$ 3,200	Accruals	$ 4,900
Marketable securities	2,000	Accounts payable	17,050
Accounts receivable	17,130	Notes payable	7,000
Inventory	19,180		
		Long-term debt	22,000
		Common stock	20,000
Plant and equipment	41,000	Retained earnings	11,560
	$82,510		$82,510

Sales are currently $160,000, but management expects sales to rise to $200,000. The net profit margin is expected to be 10 percent, and the firm distributes 60 percent of its earnings as dividends.

Management is concerned about the firm's need for external funding to cover the expansion in assets required by the expansion in sales. To achieve sales of $200,000, management will have to *expand plant by $10,000* and expects to *increase its holdings of cash by $1,000*. However, the holding of marketable securities may be reduced to zero.

a. According to the percent of sales and the additional information, will the firm need external financing, and, if so, how much?

b. Construct a pro forma balance sheet indicating the forecasted new entries for sales of $200,000. If the firm has excess funds, they should be invested in marketable securities. If the firm needs funds, these should be covered by issuing new long-term debt.

8. BHM, Inc. has the following balance sheet:

BHM, Incorporated Balance Sheet as of 12/31/X0			
Assets		**Liabilities and Equity**	
Cash	$ 1,000	Accounts payable	$16,000
Marketable securities	2,000	Accruals	4,100
Accounts receivable	14,130	Bank loan payable	5,000
Inventory	17,180	Long-term debt	12,000
Plant and equipment	31,000	Common stock	10,000
		Retained earnings	18,210
	$65,310		$65,310

Sales are currently $80,000 but are *expected to fall* to $60,000, which will require a contraction of assets. Since the firm is contracting, management would like to retire the long-term debt; however, the terms of the issue do not permit a partial repayment. Management would like to retain the short-term bank loan, but the bank will not renew the loan if the renewal results in the firm having a current ratio of less than 2:1. Since the firm is contracting, management would like to increase the marketable securities by $1,500 to meet emergencies. However, if the firm needs funds to retire debt, management is willing to liquidate all the marketable securities. The firm's historical profit margin on sales of 10 percent and the firm's policy of distributing 30 percent of earnings will be maintained.

To help forecast the firm's future financial position, fill in all the anticipated entries in the following balance sheet using the percentage of sales applied to accounts receivable, inventory, accounts payable, and accruals prior to any change in the firm's debt structure:

BHM, Incorporated Balance Sheet as of 12/31/X0			
Assets		**Liabilities and Equity**	
Cash	$1,000	Accounts payable	$1,000
Marketable securities		Accruals	
Accounts receivable		Bank loan payable	
Inventory		Long-term debt	
Plant and equipment		Common stock	
		Retained earnings	
	$		$

Then, construct a new pro forma balance sheet that incorporates all the anticipated changes in the assets, liabilities, and equity assuming that the firm pays the dividend, and answer the following questions. If the firm has excess cash, add it to the existing cash.

a. Can the firm retain the short-term bank loan?

b. Can the firm retire the long-term debt?

c. If the firm distributed no dividends and retained all of its earnings, could the firm retire the long-term debt?

Additional Problems with Answers

As Yogi Berra so aptly put it, "It's tough to make predictions, especially about the future." But firms must plan for their financial needs, and this planning requires predicting (forecasting) the anticipated level of assets and how they will be financed. The problems in this chapter consider various facets of that process, and these sample problems replicate several of the chapter's problems.

1. What is the level of inventory if inventory is 40 percent of sales and sales are $3,000?

2. What is the forecasted level of inventory for sales of $3,000 if the estimated equation relating inventory to sales is

$$I = \$250 + 0.34S?$$

3. A firm has the following balance sheet:

Assets		Liabilities and Equity	
Cash	$ 100,000	Accounts payable	$ 200,000
Marketable securities	100,000	Accruals	100,000
Accounts receivable	400,000	Short-term bank loan	100,000
Inventory	200,000	Long-term debt	200,000
Plant and equipment	400,000	Common stock	300,000
		Retained earnings	300,000
	$1,200,000		$1,200,000

Sales are currently $2,000,000. You expect sales to rise by 10 percent to $2,200,000, which will require an expansion of assets. You have an estimated regression equation relating inventory to sales but use percent of sales to forecast the other assets and liabilities that change with sales (e.g., accounts receivable, inventory, accounts payable, and accruals). The regression equation for inventory is

$$\text{Inventory} = \$15,000 + .1\text{Sales}$$

Since the firm is expanding, an additional $100,000 investment in plant and equipment is required. You want to retain the $100,000 in marketable securities and the $100,000 in cash. The net profit margin on sales is 5 percent and historically the firm has distributed 40 percent of earnings as cash dividends.

To forecast the firm's future financial position, fill in all the *anticipated* entries in the following projected balance sheet:

Assets		Liabilities and Equity	
Cash	$	Accounts payable	$
Marketable securities		Accruals	
Accounts receivable		Bank loan	100,000
Inventory		Long-term debt	200,000
Plant and equipment		Common stock	300,000
		Retained earnings	
	$_____		$_____

Based on the forecasts, answer the following questions:

a. What are the forecasted earnings and how much will be retained?

b. How much external financing will the firm need? How do you know?

c. Even if the firm can obtain additional bank loans, why may this be an undesirable strategy?

d. If the firm must maintain a debt ratio of less than 0.5 (50 percent), can the firm finance a shortage with debt?

e. If the firm sold its marketable securities, would that source of funds cover any shortage?

f. Would increasing the dividend cover any shortage?

4. A firm has the following balance sheet:

Assets		Liabilities and Equity	
Cash	$ 1,000	Accounts payable	$ 15,000
Marketable securities	15,000	Accruals	10,000
Accounts receivable	14,000	Short-term bank loan	15,000
Inventory	30,000	Long-term debt	22,000
Plant and equipment	40,000	Common stock	20,000
		Retained earnings	18,000
	$100,000		$100,000

Sales are currently $100,000, but you expect them to decrease by 20 percent to $80,000, which will require a contraction of assets. You have historically used the percent of sales technique to forecast selected assets and liabilities (i.e., accounts receivable, inventory, accounts payable, and accruals) that spontaneously change with sales.

Other factors that will affect the forecast include (1) the short-term bank loan *must be retired*, (2) the plant and equipment are aging and they must be expanded by $10,000 to reverse sales decline, (3) the net profit margin on sales is 10 percent, and (4) the firm does not distribute dividends. In addition, you want to maintain the holdings of marketable securities. However, if the firm needs funds, you could liquidate the marketable securities but prefer to issue long-term debt.

To help forecast the firm's future financial position, fill in the forecasted entries prior to any changes in the firm's use of long-term debt. Some of the numbers have been provided, and since the entries are anticipated, the sum of the two sides need not be balanced.

Assets		Liabilities and Equity	
Cash	$ 1,000	Accounts payable	$
Marketable securities	15,000	Accruals	
Accounts receivable		Bank loan	
Inventory		Long-term debt	22,000
Plant and equipment	50,000	Common stock	20,000
		Retained earnings	
	$____		$____

Based on your projections, answer the following questions:

a. Does the firm need additional finance? If the firm needs external finance, how much is necessary to cover its financial needs?

b. If the firm liquidates its marketable securities, will that cover its needs for finance?

c. The terms of the long-term debt's indenture will not permit additional long-term debt if the firm's current ratio is less than 2:1. Does the firm meet this condition?

d. If the firm liquidates the marketable securities, would the answer to *c* be different?

e. Will issuing additional debt violate this condition?

f. Construct a new balance sheet that incorporates the financing changes and meets the conditions. If the firm has excess funds, add them to cash.

Answers

1. The first problem illustrates the percent of sales. This technique uses the current percentage to forecast the level of any asset or liability that spontaneously changes with sales. In this illustration forecasted inventory is

$$I = bS$$

$$I = .4(\$3{,}000) = \$1{,}200$$

2. The second problem illustrates using an estimated regression equation. The relationship between any asset or liability that changes with sales may be expressed as an equation. If only one variable such as sales is used, the simple, linear equation is

$$I = a + bS.$$

In this application, inventory is

$$I = \$250 + 0.34(\$3{,}000) = \$1{,}270.$$

3. The forecasted balance sheet:

Assets		Liabilities and Equity	
Cash	$ 100,000	Accounts payable	$ 220,000
Marketable securities	100,000	Accruals	110,000
Accounts receivable	440,000	Bank loan	100,000
Inventory	235,000	Long-term debt	200,000
Plant and equipment	500,000	Common stock	300,000
		Retained earnings	366,000
	$1,375,000		$1,296,000

Accounts receivable, accounts payable, and accruals are forecasted using the percent of sales. If sales rise by 10 percent, each of these entries also increases by 10 percent. Inventory uses the regression equation. The forecasted level of inventory is $15,000 + .1($2,200,000) = $235,000. Cash, marketable securities, the bank loan, long-term debt, and common stock remain unchanged.

Based on the forecasts, the answers are as follows.

a. The forecasted earnings: $0.05 \times \$2{,}200{,}000 = \$110{,}000$.

The addition to retained earnings: $66,000.

40 percent of the earnings are distributed ($44,000) and 60 percent are retained ($66,000), so retained earnings increases to $300,000 + $66,000 = $366,000.

b. External financing needed: $79,000.

The sum of the forecasted assets is $1,375,000, and the forecasted liabilities plus equity is $1,296,000. Since forecasted assets exceed forecasted liabilities plus equity, there is a shortage. The firm will need $79,000 in financing to cover the increase in assets.

c. The firm should not use short-term loans to finance long-term expansion in plant and equipment.

d. If the firm were to cover the shortage by issuing debt, the debt ratio (total debt/total assets) will be

$$(\$220,000 + 110,000 + 100,000 + 200,000 + 79,000/\$1,375,000$$
$$= 709,000/1,375,000 = 51.5\%.$$

Since the firm must maintain a debt ratio of less than 50 percent, it cannot finance the shortage by issuing debt.

e. Since the firm has $100,000 in marketable securities, selling those securities and using the funds would cover the shortage.

f. Increasing the dividend would not cover the need for funds. It would do the opposite and increase the need for external finance.

4. The forecasted balance sheet:

Assets		Liabilities and Equity	
Cash	$ 1,000	Accounts payable	$ 12,000
Marketable securities	15,000	Accruals	8,000
Accounts receivable	11,200	Bank loan	0
Inventory	24,000	Long-term debt	22,000
Plant and equipment	50,000	Common stock	20,000
		Retained earnings	26,000
	$101,200		$88,000

a. The firm needs $13,200.

b. If the firm liquidates its marketable securities it will raise $15,000, which covers its need for funds.

c. The current ratio before liquidating the marketable securities:

$$(\$1,000 + 15,000 + 11,200 + 24,000)/(\$12,000 + 8,000)$$
$$= \$51,200/\$20,000 = 2.6$$

The firm meets the condition.

d. If the firm liquidates the marketable securities, it does not meet the condition:

$$($1,000 + 11,200 + 24,000)/($12,000 + 8,000)$$
$$= $36,200/$20,000 = 1.8.$$

Failing to meet the condition implies the firm cannot sell the marketable securities, use the funds to cover the shortage, and subsequently issue long-term debt for other purposes.

e. Issuing long-term debt does not change the current ratio because the debt is not a current liability. This implies the firm can use long-term debt to cover the shortage.

f. The new forecasted balance sheet that incorporates all the changes:

Assets		Liabilities and Equity	
Cash	$ 1,000	Accounts payable	$ 12,000
Marketable securities	15,000	Accruals	8,000
Accounts receivable	11,200	Bank loan	0
Inventory	24,000	Long-term debt	35,200
Plant and equipment	50,000	Common stock	20,000
		Retained earnings	26,000
	$101,200		$101,200

The firm issued $13,200 in long-term debt for a total of $35,200 ($22,000 + 13,200). The new debt covers the firm's needs for funds and the projected balance sheet balances.

Relationships

1. An increase in assets _____ the need for funding.

2. A decrease in the retained earnings _____ the need for external financing.

3. If a greater proportion of earnings are retained, the need for external financing _____.

4. The sale of plant _____ the need for external financing.

5. Acquiring inventory with the firm's cash _____ the need for external financing.

6. A reduction in a firm's net profit margin _____ the need for external financing.

7. If a firm is operating at less than full capacity and expands, its financing needs _____.

8. When a regression equation is used to forecast, an increase in sales _____ the equation's estimated slope.

9. When a regression equation is used to forecast, an increase in the coefficient of determination (r^2) _____ the confidence in the forecast.

Answers

1. increases

2. increases

3. decreases

4. decreases

5. does not affect (no change)

6. increases

7. are not affected (no change)

8. does not affect (no change)

9. increases

Other chapters cover a variety of tools that management may use to plan and make financial decisions. These include break-even analysis, net present value, internal rate of return, and methods for forecasting. This chapter describes the cash budget.

While budgets may be constructed for any time period, the cash budget is primarily a tool to analyze the day-to-day timing of cash flow. Cash receipts and disbursements are rarely synchronized. When disbursements precede receipts, cash must be obtained from somewhere, or the firm will be unable to pay its bills as they come due. The cash budget, which enumerates expected cash receipts and disbursements, forecasts when the firm will need funds and when it will generate the cash to retire any short-term loans that covered the cash deficiencies.

This is a short chapter that covers only one topic: the cash budget. Unfortunately, budgeting is not exciting but it is crucial to the financial health of the firm. The chapter lays out a simple form for constructing a cash budget. You may prefer a different form or different layout. The substance and bottom line, however, remains the same and answers the following questions: When does the cash come in and when does it go out? Will the firm need short-term funds, and when can it retire any short-term loans?

The Cash Budget

Cash budget

Projected financial statement that enumerates cash receipts and disbursements for a period of time

To help determine when the firm will need external funds (for example, a commercial bank loan) to cover cash disbursements, the financial manager may construct a cash budget. This is simply a table that enumerates all the firm's cash outlays and cash receipts. A cash budget is not synonymous with an income statement, which enumerates revenues and expenses. Some revenues may not be cash. For example, a credit sale generates revenues but the cash will not immediately be collected. The same applies to a purchase on credit. While such purchases may be expenses, the actual cash outlay occurs in the future. In addition, the firm may make some cash payments that are not expenses. For example, principal repayment requires an outlay of cash but is not an expense.

The term *budget* is often encountered in conjunction with financial planning and decision making. All budgets are estimates of anticipated receipts and disbursements for a period of time. Individual households as well as firms may construct such plans, and certainly the budget of the federal government is one of the most discussed documents that emanate from Washington, D.C. In each case these budgets are planning devices, as their construction requires that financial managers anticipate when outlays will be made and receipts collected.

In addition to being planning devices, budgets can be used as tools of control. Individual departments within the firm can have budgets that constrain their ability to spend or require that excess spending decisions be made by higher management. The budgets then act as a constraint on the firm's divisions and give management more internal control of the firm's operations. The budget may also be used as a tool to judge performance. Was the budget maintained? Which divisions within the firm overextended their budgets? By comparing the actual performance with the anticipated performance, management may be able to identify sources of financial problems.

The period of time for a budget is variable and depends on the purpose of the budget. Some budgets may be for short periods, such as six months. A firm with seasonal or fluctuating sales may develop a budget that covers the season. Other budgets may cover many years. A public utility may have a budget for capital spending on plant and equipment that covers planned receipts and disbursements for 5 to 10 years.

Budgets are particularly useful planning tools for short time periods. A cash budget may be constructed for three or six months and then used to predict the short-term needs of the firm for cash. The cash budget helps the financial manager to determine if cash is needed and *when* it is needed. This element of time is crucial, for the financial manager can contact sources of short-term credit before the funds are needed. Such early contact indicates that management is aware of its financial needs, and this should increase the confidence of lenders in the firm's management. Such confidence may result in more favorable terms, which reduce the cost of the funds.

The Differences between a Cash Budget and an Income Statement

The cash budget and income statement have similarities, but it is important for you to know their differences. Both are constructed over a period of time such as a month or quarter or year. (A balance sheet is constructed at *a point in time*; so the differences between it and a cash budget are easier to perceive.) Income statements enumerate revenues and expenses. Cash budgets enumerate receipts and disbursements. Income statements are on an accrual basis. A credit sale accrues revenues and is reported on the income statement. Since no cash is received until the receivable is collected, the credit sale would be excluded from the cash budget. The anticipated collection of the receivable would appear on the cash budget.

Other important differences include the treatment of depreciation and the repayment of debt. Depreciation is a noncash expense that allocates the cost of a long-term investment over a period of time. This allocation is an expense on the income statement, but since there is no cash disbursement, depreciation does not appear on the cash budget. The retirement of debt is not an expense and is excluded from the income statement. Retiring debt, however, requires a cash disbursement and would appear on a cash budget.

These illustrations help clarify the differences between the two financial statements. The purpose of the income statement is to determine earnings, and earnings are not synonymous with cash. The purpose of the cash budget is to determine when cash will be needed. While both use similar information, the two statements are perceptibly different and should not be confused.

The Cash Budget Illustrated

The cash budget is basically a table relating time, disbursements, and receipts. The units of time may be months, weeks, or even days. The cash items are grouped into inflows (receipts) and outflows (disbursements). The difference between the inflows and outflows is the summary or bottom line that indicates to the financial manager whether to expect excess cash that needs to be invested or cash deficiencies that must be financed.

The construction of a cash budget for the fall season is illustrated by the following example. The financial manager has determined the anticipated levels of sales for the next seven months:

May	$15,000	August	50,000	November	10,000
June	20,000	September	40,000		
July	30,000	October	20,000		

Thirty percent of the sales are for cash, and 70 percent are on credit. Of the credit sales, 90 percent are paid after one month, and 10 percent are paid after two months. Thus, the financial manager expects that of the anticipated sales of $15,000 in May, $4,500 will be for cash ($15,000 × 0.3) and $10,500 will be on credit ($15,000 × 0.7). Of these credit sales, $9,450 will be collected after one month ($10,500 × 0.9), and $1,050 will be collected after two months ($10,500 × 0.1).

If the firm has other assets that will become cash during the time period, those assets must also be included in the cash budget. For example, if the firm owns a $10,000 U.S. Treasury bill that will be paid on June 1, $10,000 must be included in the cash budget. Since the purpose of the cash budget is to determine the excess or shortage of cash that the firm will experience, all cash receipts must be included in the budget.

In this case, the firm's sales are seasonal, so it will increase inventory in anticipation of the seasonal business. As the inventory is produced, the firm must pay for labor and materials. The estimated disbursements for wages and materials for the season are as follows:

May	$ 3,000	August	30,000	November	3,000
June	25,000	September	10,000		
July	38,000	October	5,000		

EXHIBIT 16.1
Monthly Cash Budget (for a Firm's Fall Season)

	May	June	July
Part 1			
1 Anticipated sales	$15,000	$20,000	$30,000
2 Cash sales	4,500	6,000	9,000
3 Accounts collected (one-month lag)		9,450	12,600
4 Accounts collected (two-month lag)			1,050
5 Other cash receipts		10,000	
6 Total cash receipts	**4,500**	**25,450**	**22,650**
Part 2			
7 Variable cash disbursements	3,000	25,000	38,000
8 Fixed cash disbursements	3,000	3,000	3,000
9 Other cash disbursements			
10 Total cash disbursements	**6,000**	**28,000**	**41,000**
Part 3			
11 Cash gain (or loss) during the month (line 6 minus line 10)	(1,500)	(2,550)	(18,350)
12 Cash position at beginning of month	12,000	10,500	7,950
13 Cash position at end of month (line 12 plus line 11)	10,500	7,950	(10,400)
14 Less desired level of cash	(10,000)	(10,000)	(10,000)
15 Cumulative excess (or shortage) of cash (line 13 minus line 14)	**500**	**(2,050)**	**(20,400)**

These estimated disbursements indicate that the increase in inventory occurs in June, July, and August. The sales, however, occur primarily in July, August, and September. There is a lag in sales after the buildup of inventory; thus there will be a drain on the firm's cash.

Besides the cash outlays that vary with the level of output, the firm has fixed disbursements that do not vary with the level of operations. These include interest and rent of $1,000 a month and administrative expenses of $2,000 a month for a total of $3,000 a month. The firm also has to make an estimated quarterly income tax payment in September of $2,500 and a payment of $1,000 on August 1 to retire part of a debt issue. Management likes to maintain a minimum cash balance of $10,000 as a safety valve in case of emergency. The firm's cash position at the beginning of May is $12,000, which exceeds the desired minimum level for the cash balance.

The financial manager now uses this information to obtain estimates of the monthly net increase or decrease in the firm's cash position. The monthly cash budget is illustrated in Exhibit 16.1. The first part of the table presents the estimated cash that the firm receives monthly. The first line of the table gives the sales, and the next three lines give the cash generated by the sales: line 2 enumerates the cash sales; line 3 gives the collections that occur on

EXHIBIT 16.1
(*Continued*)

August	September	October	November	December	January
$50,000	$40,000	$20,000	$10,000		
15,000	12,000	6,000	3,000		
18,900	31,500	25,200	12,600	6,300	
1,400	2,100	3,500	2,800	1,400	700
35,300	**45,600**	**34,700**	**18,400**		
30,000	10,000	5,000	3,000		
3,000	3,000	3,000	3,000		
1,000	2,500				
34,000	**15,500**	**8,000**	**6,000**		
1,300	30,100	26,700	12,400		
(10,400)	(9,100)	21,000	47,700		
(9,100)	21,000	47,700	60,100		
(10,000)	(10,000)	(10,000)	(10,000)		
(19,100)	**11,000**	**37,700**	**50,100**		

the credit sales after one month; and line 4 gives the credit collections that occur two months after the sales. The arrows show when May's credit sales yield cash receipts. Line 5 gives other sources of cash receipts (for instance, the $10,000 Treasury bill). The sum of lines 2 through 5 is the monthly cash receipts and is given in line 6.

The second part of the table enumerates the firm's monthly cash disbursements. Line 7 gives the monthly disbursements that vary with the level of sales, while line 8 gives the disbursements that do not vary with the level of sales (the interest, rent, and administrative expenses). Line 9 gives other cash disbursements (the $2,500 tax payment and the $1,000 debt retirement payment). The sum of the monthly cash payments is given in line 10.

The third part of the table summarizes the first two parts and indicates whether the firm has a net inflow or outflow of cash during the month. Thus, the cash budget establishes whether the firm has excess cash that it can use to purchase short-term income-earning assets (such as a U.S. Treasury bill) or has insufficient cash, which requires that the firm find short-term financing. Line 11 is the difference between lines 6 and 10; it gives the net inflow or outflow of cash during the month. Line 12 gives the firm's cash position at the beginning of the month. The sum of lines 11 and 12 equals the firm's cash position at the end of the month, which is given in line 13. Notice that the cash position can be negative (see July, for example), which indicates the cash outflow exceeded the cash inflow plus the cash from the preceding time period. The minimum desired level of cash is given in line 14. The difference between cash position at the end of the month and the desired minimum level of cash is given in line 15 of the table. This is the bottom line! It indicates that the firm will have excess cash or that it will have a cash deficiency.

How is the information contained in the cash budget interpreted? Consider the month of May. The firm has a net cash outflow of $1,500 (line 11), but the firm began the month with $12,000 in cash. It has enough to cover the anticipated cash drain and maintain its desired level of cash holdings. This is indicated in line 15, which shows that there is excess cash of $500 over the desired cash balance level.

During June, cash disbursements once again exceed receipts (by $2,550). The extent to which the cash expenditures exceed the receipts, however, is reduced by the receipt of the $10,000 payment from the Treasury bill. It appears that the financial manager was previously aware of the firm's cash needs in June and July and purchased a short-term security that matured in June. Even with this extra inflow of cash, the cash position at the end of the month drops to $7,950 (line 13), which is less than the desired level of cash balances by $2,050 (line 15). The financial manager would then have to decide either to let the cash position fall below the desired minimum or to borrow the $2,050 to maintain the desired minimum level of cash. (Notice that the cash gain [or loss] for a given month is equal to the difference between the cumulative excess (or shortage) between that month and the preceding month. Thus in June, the cash loss of $2,550 is equal to the change in cumulative cash from May to June. During the month, cash fell from a positive $500 to a negative $2,050 for a total decline in cash of $2,550.)

In July the difference between the cash outflows and cash receipts grows even larger. Anticipated cash payments exceed cash receipts by $18,350, before allowance is made for the desired minimum level of cash. When the actual cash outflow and the desired level of cash are added, the cumulative shortage is $20,400 (line 15). Thus, the financial manager can anticipate that the firm will need $20,400 of short-term financing to cover the firm's cash needs for June and July. In August, cash receipts slightly exceed disbursements, so the cumulative shortage falls to $19,100. After August, the firm's cash position improves dramatically as the cash from collections flows into the firm. In September the firm will have generated a cash inflow of $30,100. After September the firm's cash position continues to improve, and the cumulative excess cash grows to $50,100 by the end of November. Thus, the financial manager can anticipate having excess cash that can be used to purchase a short-term income-earning asset that matures when the cycle begins again.

If the financial manager decides to maintain the $10,000 minimum cash balance and to borrow from the bank the funds necessary to cover the cash shortages, the firm will have a short-term bank loan outstanding in June, July, and August. The loan will be fully retired by the end of September, at which time the firm will start to accumulate excess cash, which may be invested in short-term securities. That is the bottom line.

In summary, this cash budget helps establish when the firm will need external short-term finance and when the short-term loan will be repaid. In this example, the financial manager can anticipate how much cash the firm will need in June, July, and August, and he or she also knows when the firm will generate sufficient cash to retire the short-term loan. Thus, the financial manager can approach the lender with estimates of (1) the firm's cash needs and (2) when the firm will be able to repay the loan. This information is important for the lender, who is concerned with earning interest and being repaid the principal. From the lender's viewpoint, a cash budget is more important than the firm's income statement, since it shows how the cash will be used and when repayments will be made.

Preparing the cash budget also permits the financial manager to shop around for terms. Since the financial manager is able to anticipate the firm's financial needs, he or she is able to arrange for the necessary financing in advance. Such planning should increase the bargaining position of the borrower and may result in more favorable credit terms.

Summary

The cash budget enumerates cash receipts and cash disbursements and enables management to plan for the firm's short-term cash needs. Cash receipts and cash disbursements are rarely synchronized. If disbursements precede receipts, the cash must be obtained from some source. Conversely, if receipts precede disbursements, the excess funds may be invested.

The cash budget forecasts both the timing and the amount of a firm's receipts and disbursements. If there is an anticipated shortage, management can plan for necessary short-term financing. Knowing when the funds will be needed and when short-term loans can be repaid should facilitate obtaining the funds at a lower interest cost to the firm.

Review Objectives

Now that you have completed this chapter, you should be able to

1. Differentiate receipts and disbursements (p. 366).
2. Contrast the cash budget with the income statement (p. 367).
3. Explain the purpose of the cash budget (pp. 366–367).
4. Construct a cash budget (pp. 367–371).
5. Interpret a cash budget's bottom line (pp. 370–371).

Problems

1. A firm has the following monthly pattern of sales:

January	$ 100
February	300
March	500
April	1,000
May	500
June	300

Sixty percent of the sales are on credit and are collected after a month. The company pays wages each month that are 60 percent of sales and has fixed disbursements (for example, rent) of $100 a month. In March it receives $200 from a bond that matures; in April and June it makes a tax payment of $200. Management maintains a cash balance of $150 at all times. Construct a cash budget that indicates the firm's monthly needs for short-term financing. Its beginning cash position is $150.

2. Management wants to know if there will be a need for short-term financing in February. Essential information is as follows:

a. Estimated sales for January and February are $1 million and $800,000, respectively.

b. Sixty percent of sales are for cash and 40 percent are credit sales that are collected the next month.

c. Cash disbursements that vary with sales are 40 percent of sales.

d. Fixed operating disbursements are $300,000 a month.

e. Depreciation expense is $50,000 a month.

f. A tax payment of $100,000 is due in January.

g. A bond payment of $300,000 is owed and will be due in February.

h. The cash balance at the beginning of January is $12,000.

i. Management seeks a minimum cash balance of $10,000.

j. December credit sales were $100,000.

3. Redo the cash budget in Exhibit 16.1.

a. Assume that the desired minimum level of cash is $4,000 instead of $10,000. What is the change in the firm's need for funds?

b. Assume that 60 percent of sales are for cash instead of 30 percent and the pattern of collections remains the same (90 percent after one month and 10 percent after two months). What is the change in the firm's need for funds?

c. Assume that both the desired minimum level of cash and sales change as in parts *a* and *b*. What is the revised cash budget's "bottom line"?

4. Given the following information, complete the cash budget:

a. Collections occur one month after the sale.

b. January's credit sales were $80,000.

c. The firm has a certificate of deposit for $40,000 that matures in April.

d. Salaries are $145,000 a month.

e. The monthly mortgage payment is $25,000.

f. Monthly depreciation is $20,000.

g. Property tax of $35,000 is due in February.

	February	March	April
Sales	$150,000	$200,000	$250,000
Cash sales	30,000	20,000	60,000
Collections	—	—	—
Other receipts	—	—	—
Total cash receipts	—	—	—
Salaries	—	—	—
Other disbursements	—	—	—
Total cash disbursements	—	—	—
Net change during the month	—	—	—
Beginning cash	30,000	—	—
Ending cash	—	—	—
Required level of cash	10,000	10,000	10,000
Excess cash or (shortage)	—	—	—

5. Given the following information, construct the firm's cash budget for the given months and answer the questions.
   - All sales are for credit and collections occur after 30 days.
   - A $100,000 Treasury bill matures in March.
   - Monthly fixed disbursements are $25,000.
   - Variable disbursements are 40 percent of sales and occur one month prior to sales. (Variable cash disbursements are given for April.)
   - A tax payment of $30,000 is due in April.
   - A payment of $50,000 is to be received in February.
   - The initial cash is $20,000.
   - The minimum required cash balance is $10,000.

	January	February	March	April
Sales	—	$200,000	$230,000	$200,000
Cash sales	—	—	—	—
Collections	—	—	—	—
Other receipts	—	—	—	—
Total cash receipts	—	—	—	—
Variable disbursements	—	—	—	$70,000
Fixed disbursements	—	—	—	—
Other disbursements	—	—	—	—
Total cash disbursements	—	—	—	—
Net change during the month	—	—	—	—
Beginning cash	$20,000	—	—	—
Ending cash	—	—	—	—
Required cash	$10,000	—	—	—
Excess cash to invest	—	—	—	—
Cash borrowed	—	—	—	—

a. At the end of March, what are the firm's (1) accounts receivable, (2) marketable securities, and (3) accounts payable?

b. What is the maximum amount that the firm may have to borrow? If your answer is "None," give a reason that verifies your answer.

c. If the firm used accelerated depreciation instead of straight-line depreciation, how would that affect the cash budget?

Continue the illustration in Exhibit 16.1 and construct the cash budget for December through May. Anticipated sales for December through May are as follows:

December	$5,000
January	15,000
February	25,000
March	40,000
April	35,000
May	15,000.

Thirty percent of the sales are for cash and 70 percent are on credit. Of the credit sales, 90 percent are collected one month after sale and 10 percent as collected two months after the original sale. Other anticipated receipts include a $1,000 tax refund in December.

Forecasted variable cash disbursements are as follows:

December	$12,000
January	14,000
February	31,000
March	29,000
April	14,000
May	7,000.

The firm must retire a $25,000 loan in January. Since the $25,000 loan is retired in January, the desired level of cash will be reduced to $6,000 starting in February.

After competing the cash budget, answer the following questions:

1. What are the firm's accounts receivable at the end of March?
2. What are the firm's cash, amount borrowed, and short-term marketable securities at the end of March?
3. What is the amount borrowed during February?
4. What is the maximum amount borrowed and when is the loan retired?
5. In May, can the firm acquire money market securities? What are several possible money market securities the firm may acquire?

Answer   The cash budget for the period December through May:

	December	January	February	March	April	May
Part 1						
Sales	$5,000	$15,000	$25,000	$40,000	$35,000	$15,000
Cash sales	1,500	4,500	7,500	12,000	10,500	4,500
Accounts collected (one-month lag)	6,300	3,150	9,450	15,750	25,200	22,050
Accounts collected (two-month lag)	1,400	700	350	1,050	1,750	2,800
Other cash receipts	1,000					
Total cash receipts	10,200	8,350	17,300	28,800	37,450	29,350
Part 2						
Variable cash disbursements	12,000	14,000	31,000	29,000	14,000	7,000
Fixed cash disbursements	3,000	3,000	3,000	3,000	3,000	3,000
Other cash disbursements		25,000				
Total cash disbursements	15,000	42,000	34,000	32,000	17,000	10,000
Part 3						
Cash gain (or loss)	(4,800)	(33,650)	(16,700)	(3,200)	20,450	19,350
Cash at beginning of month	60,100	55,300	21,650	4,950	1,750	22,200
Cash at end of month	55,300	21,650	4,950	1,750	22,200	41,550
Less desired level of cash	(10,000)	(10,000)	(6,000)	(6,000)	(6,000)	(6,000)
Cumulative excess (or shortage) of cash	45,300	11,650	(1,050)	(4,250)	16,200	35,550

1. At the end of March, the firm has not collected $28,000 of March sales ($40,000 − 12,000) and $1,750 of February sales ($25,000 − 7,500 − 15,750) for a total receivables of $29,750.

2. At the end of March, the firm is holding $6,000 in cash, has loans of $4,250, and no short-term marketable securities.

3. During February the firm borrows $1,050. The cash outflow of $16,700 more than wipes out the $11,650 that the firm had in excess cash and uses some of the desired cash. To maintain $6,000 in cash, the firm must borrow $1,050 ($11, 650 + 10,000 − 16,700 = $4,950, which is $1,050 less than $6,000.)

4. The maximum amount borrowed is $4,250 in April and the loan is retired in May.

5. The firm has a total of $41,550 at the end of May. After meeting the $6,000 desired level of cash, the firm has $35,500 that may be invested in short-term money market securities such as Treasury bills, negotiable certificates of deposit, and commercial paper. (Note that $35,500 may be too small to invest in most money market securities, since their unit of trading is larger. The firm could invest in shares in money market mutual funds that acquire the various short-term money market instruments.)

Relationships

1. An increase in the collection of accounts receivable _____ the firm's cash.

2. An increase in fixed disbursements _____ the firm's cash.

3. Paying accounts payable slower _____ the firm's need for cash.

4. An increase in depreciation _____ the firm's taxes.

5. If a loan requires the firm to increase its holding of cash, disbursements are _____.

6. Retiring a debt obligation such as a mortgage _____ earnings and _____ cash.

7. An increase in credit sales _____ the firm's cash.

Answers

1. increases
2. decreases
3. decreases
4. decreases
5. not affected (no change)
6. does not affect (no change); decreases
7. does not affect (no change)

Management
of Current Assets

"Yesterday is a canceled check; tomorrow is a promissory note; today is ready cash." This quote from Hubert Tinley catches the management of current assets. The essential objective is to increase the speed with which current assets flow up the balance sheet; that is, to increase the speed with which inventory is sold, receivables are collected, and cash is put to work. If the cash is not immediately needed to acquire more inventory, acquire plant and equipment, or retire debt, it may be invested in short-term securities such as corporate commercial paper or U.S. Treasury bills to earn interest income.

The amount of cash and cash equivalents that some firms carry is substantial. VF Corporation, maker of Lee and Wrangler jeans and other casual wear, held $382 million in cash and short-term investments at the beginning of 2010. The Coca-Cola Company, one of the country's leaders in soft drinks, had more than $9.1 billion in cash and marketable securities, which accounted for 52.1 percent of the company's total current assets.

Other firms may have little cash. In 2005, Chesapeake Corporation, a manufacturer of specialty paperboard packaging, reported cash of $54.3 million. This modest amount was 16.1 percent of the firm's total current assets and less than 4 percent of Chesapeake's total assets. Such lack of liquidity suggested that the firm may have had financial difficulty. And in less than three years, Chesapeake Corporation declared bankruptcy.

This chapter and the next one consider the management of working capital: current assets and current liabilities. This chapter is devoted to the management of the firm's cash and other current assets; the subsequent chapter covers the sources of short-term funds. Current assets flow through the firm.

Inventory is acquired and subsequently sold for cash or on credit. Accounts receivable are collected, and the cash is used to acquire other income-producing assets or to retire debt. The cycle is then repeated as the firm acquires new inventory for sale.

This chapter begins with a discussion of the firm's working capital policy, its operating cycle, and the choice between long-run and short-term financing. This is followed by a discussion of inventory management: the inventory cycle and the EOQ, or economic order quantity. The next section considers the management of accounts receivable: the establishment of credit policy and the analysis of accounts receivable. Once these accounts are collected, the firm receives cash, so the chapter concludes with a discussion of the various short-term securities that may be acquired by the financial manager as temporary parking places for the firm's cash.

Working Capital and Its Management

Working capital

Short-term assets; cash, cash equivalents, accounts receivable, and inventory

Net working capital

Difference between current assets and current liabilities

Working capital policy

Management of short-term assets and liabilities

A firm's day-to-day operations center around generating sales and managing current assets and current liabilities. Although the determination whether to invest in new plant and equipment or refund a bond issue is obviously important, such decisions may be made intermittently. Management, however, is continuously concerned with current assets and how they are financed. Managing inventory, selling the inventory, collecting accounts receivable, investing temporary excess cash, raising short-term funds, and meeting current obligations as they come due require decisions on a daily basis.

A firm's current assets are often referred to as its working capital. The difference between its current assets and current liabilities is its net working capital. How a firm manages its short-term assets and short-term liabilities is its working capital policy. Management of working capital is important to a firm's well-being because most business failures can be related to the mismanagement of current assets and their financing. Excess investment in inventory, inability to collect accounts receivable or retire its own accounts payable, or excessive use of short-term finance can rapidly destroy a firm that previously generated earnings and appeared to be profitable.

The two essential questions regarding working capital are: What should be the level of the various current assets? and, How should these assets be financed? The second question divides into two additional questions: Should management use sources of short-term or long-term finance? and, What specific sources should be used? The answers to these questions vary among industries and among firms within a given industry.

The Impact of the Operating Cycle on Working Capital Policy

Working capital policy is affected by the firm's operating cycle and by the fact that cash receipts and disbursements are rarely synchronized. The longer the operating cycle, the greater will be the firm's investment in current assets. Also, the less synchronization of receipts and disbursements, the greater will be the need for working capital.

In order to have product to sell, the firm needs inventory. Some firms (Macy's and Limited Brands) purchase finished goods (inventory) that may be immediately sold. Other companies, such as VF Corporation, manufacture the goods (Wrangler and Lee jeans, and Healthtex children's clothes) bought by Macy's and Limited Brands. These manufacturing companies acquire raw materials and employ labor to transform the raw materials into finished goods. The carrying of raw materials, work-in-process, and finished goods requires a source of funds. Paying the firm's suppliers and the labor that processes raw materials into finished goods also requires funds. However, the finished goods generate funds only after they are sold, and if the sales are on credit, funds are obtained only when the accounts receivable are collected.

This operating cycle is illustrated in Exhibit 17.1, which presents a time line in which a firm acquires raw materials, processes them, sells its inventory, collects its credit sales, and pays its creditors. The whole process is compressed into a month, and the firm's balance sheet is given as each step in the operating cycle occurs. On January 1, the firm buys $100 worth of raw materials on credit from its suppliers. At that point in time, the firm has $100 in assets financed by $100 in accounts payable. On January 10, the firm's workers convert the raw materials into finished goods. This adds $50 to the value of the raw materials, and the firm owes accrued wages of $50. The firm now has $150 in assets financed by the accounts payable ($100) and the accrued wages ($50).

On January 20, the goods are sold on credit for $190. The firm's assets become the $190 accounts receivable, which are financed by the $100 in accounts payable, $50 in accrued wages, and $40 in retained earnings. On January 30, the accounts receivable are collected, so the firm now has $190 in cash. On January 31, all the liabilities are paid off, so the firm's cash declines to $40. The accounts payable and accrued wages cease, and the firm retains the $40 in earnings, which finances the $40 in cash. The operating cycle is complete. The goods have been produced and sold, and the accounts receivable have been collected. The firm now has cash and is ready to repeat the cycle.

For some firms, this process may occur over an extended period of time. Consider a building contractor. A house takes several months to complete, during which time raw materials are converted into the finished product. The contractor needs short-term financing during the construction process. However, once the house is sold, the builder may rapidly collect payment, as a commercial bank or savings and loan association issues a mortgage loan to the buyer, who in turn immediately pays the builder. For homebuilders, the need for working capital and short-term funds is primarily a need to finance construction—not to carry accounts receivable generated by the sale. (A construction company may reduce its operating cycle by requiring payment as segments of the structure are completed. Such percentage of completion contracts are common in construction.)

EXHIBIT 17.1 The Operating Cycle

January 1	January 10	January 20	January 30	January 31
Firm buys raw materials ($100) from suppliers.	Workers convert raw materials into finished goods; workers are owed $50.	Goods are sold on credit for $190.	Accounts receivable are collected.	All liabilities are paid off.
Raw materials $100 — Accounts payable $100	Finished goods $150 — Accounts payable $100, Accrued wages 50	Accounts receivable $190 — Accounts payable $100, Accrued wages 50, Retained earnings 40	Cash $190 — Accounts payable $100, Accrued wages 50, Retained earnings 40	Cash $40 — Accounts payable $0, Accrued wages 0, Retained earnings 40

Firms in other industries may not have as great a need for working capital because their operating cycle differs or is shorter. Consider a public utility, such as Public Service Electric & Gas, that generates electric power. This firm's primary assets are plant and equipment. It has little inventory, and its primary short-term assets are accounts receivable, which are continually being collected as customers pay their utility bills. An electric utility does not experience the same buildup of short-term assets as the building contractor. Instead, the utility bills some of its customers each day and receives payment each day. It needs fewer short-term sources of funds than many other firms because there is a virtual synchronization of payments and receipts.

A firm's working capital policy is also affected by the nature of its sales (especially if the sales are cyclical or seasonal), the firm's credit policy (its willingness to sell on credit), and management's willingness to bear risk. Cyclical or seasonal sales are not evenly spread over a period of time. Management may increase the firm's investment in inventory in preparation for the period of increased sales (for example, the winter season at Macy's). The firm will need funds to carry the inventory. Once the inventory is sold, there may still be a need for financing if the sales are for credit. After these accounts receivable are collected, the firm uses the cash to retire the liabilities that financed the initial increase in inventory and the subsequent accounts receivable.

A firm's credit policy may also affect working capital. A lenient or easy credit policy is designed to increase sales, so the firm sells its inventory more rapidly. However, a lenient credit policy generates more accounts receivable that the firm must carry, and may retard its collection of cash. Such a policy requires the firm to have sufficient sources of funds to carry the additional receivables.

Management's willingness to bear risk also affects working capital policy. A conservative management may carry more inventory to be certain that sales are not lost from lack of goods in stock or to protect against work stoppages. The increased inventory requires financing. Willingness to bear risk also affects management's choice of funding for the firm's short-term assets. As is explained in the next section, the use of short-term instead of long-term funds to finance short-term assets increases the element of risk, because additional risks are associated with refunding the debt and changes in the short-term rate of interest.

Financing and Working Capital Policy

All assets must be financed. One of the most important tasks facing a financial manager is the choice of financing. Various sources of long-term financing were previously discussed (from the investor's perspective) in Chapters 20 through 25 on bonds and preferred and common stock. The next chapter considers specific sources of short-term finance, while this section covers the trade-off between sources of short-term and long-term finance and how that trade-off affects the risk associated with a firm's working capital policy.

Exhibit 17.1 illustrated that a firm's current assets vary through the operating cycle. As a firm's current assets rise, its sources of finance also must increase. In the illustration, the increase in assets was covered by increases in accounts payable and accrued wages. These are, of course, not the only possible sources, but a major principle of finance suggests that a financial manager should match the sources of finance with their use.

Short-term sources of finance, such as a loan from a commercial bank, require frequent refunding; long-term debt and equity do not require frequent refunding, which makes them appropriate for financing long-term assets. The firm should not use short-term sources to finance long-term assets. It may be years before the long-term assets generate funds; the short-term loans, however, must be repaid during the current fiscal year. Unless this credit can be refunded (for instance, the funds borrowed from one source can be used to retire the debt from another source) or renewed, management will face a substantial problem meeting its short-term obligations as they come due.

While the firm should not use short-term finance to acquire long-term assets (rather, it should use long-term sources), the firm may use either short- or long-term sources to acquire short-term assets. Short-term sources may be used to finance inventory and accounts receivable because as these assets are converted into cash, the funds may be used to repay the short-term loans. Long-term sources may be used to finance current assets, since these sources do not have the problem of frequent refunding.

Since long-term sources may be used to finance both short-term and long-term assets, why does the financial manager use short-term sources? The answer revolves around the cost and the risks associated with each source. The choice of long- versus short-term sources of funds is ultimately a question of the funds' impact on earnings and the risk associated with management's choices of finance. Generally, short-term sources are riskier because these obligations have to be refinanced. Long-term sources do not require frequent refinancing and are not as risky as short-term sources.

If the use of short-term sources increases risk, the question again arises, "Why do firms use this source?" There are both specific and general answers to that question. The specific answers will be developed in the next chapter, which covers short-term sources of finance. The general answer is that short-term sources are often less expensive than long-term sources. (This relationship between the yield or cost and the term of a debt instrument was illustrated in Figure 2.1 in Chapter 2.) Short-term lenders accept lower interest rates for rapid repayment of principal. They trade some return for increased liquidity. This lower interest cost results in increased earnings for the firm using short-term rather than long-term debt financing.

The possible impact on the firm's earnings may be shown by the following illustration. Firm A's balance sheet is:

Balance Sheet as of 12/31/X0			
Assets		**Liabilities and Equity**	
Assets	$10,000	Debt	$6,000
		Equity	$4,000

The balance sheet does not specify the term of the debt. For illustrative purposes, we shall assume three cases: (1) one year at 8 percent, (2) five years at 10 percent, and (3) 15 years at 12 percent. If sales are $4,000 and other expenses are $2,500, the profits earned by the firm in each case are

	1	2	3
Sales	$4,000	$4,000	$4,000
Expenses	2,500	2,500	2,500
Earnings before interest expense	1,500	1,500	1,500
Interest expense	480	600	720
Earnings after interest expense	$1,020	$ 900	$ 780

The higher interest cost associated with the long-term debt produces the lowest earnings. The lower interest cost associated with the short-term debt produces the highest earnings.

Now consider what happens to the firm's earnings if after a year the short-term interest rate rises to 13 percent. The income statements now become

	1	2	3
Sales	$4,000	$4,000	$4,000
Expenses	2,500	2,500	2,500
Earnings before interest expense	1,500	1,500	1,500
Interest expense	780	600	720
Earnings after interest expense	$ 720	$ 900	$ 780

If the firm initially uses short-term debt, its earnings are reduced because short-term debt is more expensive. The earnings that resulted from the use of intermediate-term and long-term debt (for instance, five and 15 years, respectively) are not changed. Even if the cost of long-term debt is currently higher (for example, 15 percent), the earnings of the firm are unaffected. Why? Because the firm borrowed in the past at 12 percent, and this rate is fixed for the term of the debt. The current cost of long-term debt matters only if the firm is issuing long-term debt.

Large and rapid changes in the cost of short-term credit imply that the choice of short-term finance can affect both the earnings and the risk exposure of the firm by increasing the variability of the earnings. Managements of companies in cyclical industries, such as construction, may follow a conservative working capital policy and use more long-term sources of finance. Managements of firms with stable revenues, such as electric utilities, may have a less conservative working capital policy. They can afford the risk associated with having a larger proportion of current assets financed by current liabilities.

Differences in working capital policy are illustrated in Exhibit 17.2, which gives the current assets, current liabilities, current ratio, and net working capital for Coca-Cola and Texas Instruments. A high current ratio and large

Firm	Industry	Current Assets*	Current Liabilities*	Current Ratio	Net Working Capital*
Coca-Cola	Beverages	$17,551	$13,721	1.28	$3,830
Texas Instruments	Semiconductors	6,114	1,587	3.85	4,527

*Current assets, current liabilities, and net working capital in millions.

Source: 2009 10-K reports.

amount of net working capital suggest a conservative working capital policy. As may be seen in this exhibit, Texas Instruments has a current ratio that exceeds 3:1 and net working capital of $4,527 billion, which suggests a conservative use of short-term financing. Coca-Cola, however, has a current ratio of only 1.28 to 1. Coke appears to have an aggressive working capital policy. Coke, however, has over $9 billion in marketable securities. These securities may be sold so there is no question of Coke's ability to meet its current obligations as they come due.

The Importance of Cash to Working Capital Management

The previous sections explained the importance of a firm's operating cycle on the management of working capital and the impact of the choice of short-term versus long-term debt to finance current assets on earnings and risk. This section highlights the importance of cash and differentiates cash from earnings.

Firms operate in the present. Even if management has correctly employed the long-term capital budgeting techniques explained in Chapter 14, the mismanagement of working capital may be disastrous. Failure to meet current obligations is often *the* source of business failure. The ability to generate cash is crucial to the firm's survival, and you must realize that operating profitably is not synonymous with generating cash. Firms pay their current obligations with cash and not with earnings. A firm can operate profitably and still run out of cash.

Consider the following firm. As of January 1, its balance sheet is as follows:

Assets		Liabilities and Equity	
Cash	$2,750	Liabilities	$ 0
		Equity	2,750
		Retained earnings	0
	$2,750		$2,750

Anticipated monthly unit sales are

January	February	March	April	May
1,000	1,500	2,000	2,500	3,000

The cost of a unit is $0.75, and units will be sold for $1.00 (a $0.25 profit on each sale). Management must have one month's supply at the beginning of each month. Suppliers require payment on delivery. The firm sells on credit of net 30 days, but there are no defaults.

To meet January's anticipated sales, management buys and pays for 1,000 units. The firm's balance sheet becomes

Assets		Liabilities and Equity	
Cash	$2,000	Liabilities	$ 0
Inventory	750	Equity	2,750
		Retained earnings	0
	$2,750		$ 2,750

Inventory rises by $750 and the purchase is paid for with cash. Expected sales are achieved, so the firm's earnings during January are

Revenues	$1,000
Cost of goods sold	750
Earnings	250

(To simplify the illustration, assume there are no other expenses and no income tax on earnings.) To finance future growth, earnings are retained, so the balance sheet at the end of January is

Assets		Liabilities and Equity	
Cash	$2,000	Liabilities	$ 0
Accounts receivable	1,000		
Inventory	0	Equity	2,750
		Retained earnings	250
	$3,000		$3,000

The inventory was sold and the firm has accounts receivable of $1,000; $250 is added to retained earnings.

To meet anticipated February sales, management buys 1,500 units at a cost of $1,125 and pays for the units with cash. The balance sheet becomes

Assets		Liabilities and Equity	
Cash	$ 875	Liabilities	$ 0
Accounts receivable	1,000		
Inventory	1,125	Equity	2,750
		Retained earnings	250
	$3,000		$3,000

February's anticipated sales are achieved. The income generated is $1,500 − $1,125 = $375, so the new balance sheet at the end of February is

Assets		Liabilities and Equity	
Cash	$1,875	Liabilities	$ 0
Accounts receivable	1,500		
Inventory	0	Equity	2,750
		Retained earnings	625
	$3,375		$3,375

January's accounts receivable are collected, which increases cash, but February's sales are for credit, which increases accounts receivable. Since the firm operated profitably, retained earnings increase.

The process is once again repeated, and management buys inventory (2,000 × $0.75 = $1,500) for the anticipated March sales and the balance sheet becomes

Assets		Liabilities and Equity	
Cash	$ 375	Liabilities	$ 0
Accounts receivable	1,500		
Inventory	1,500	Equity	2,750
		Retained earnings	625
	$3,375		$3,375

By now you should have noticed that even though the firm is operating profitably, it cash position is deteriorating.

Let's proceed on to March. The $1,500 units are sold for $2,000 and a $500 profit is earned. The $1,500 in receivables is collected but the credit sales generate $2,000 of new receivables. In addition, management buys the 2,500 units (costing $1,875) for anticipated sales in April. What is the balance sheet at the end of March (beginning of April)? The answer is

Assets		Liabilities and Equity	
Cash	$ 0	Liabilities	$ 0
Accounts receivable	2,000		
Inventory	1,875	Equity	2,750
		Retained earnings	1,125
	$3,875		$3,875

The firm is now out of cash! All of its assets are either accounts receivable or inventory. If the current process continues, the firm will not be able to buy the required inventory for May. How could this happen? Inventory is being sold, sales are profitable, and receivables are being collected. What is the problem and what are possible solutions?

The problem is that in order to meet the increasing sales, management has to acquire increasing amounts of inventory and that disbursements are preceding collections. Several possible solutions to this problem exist. For example, management may find another source of funds, collect the receivables faster, or convince its suppliers to defer immediate payment. In any event, the current situation is not sustainable.

The remainder of this chapter considers the management of specific current assets: inventory, accounts receivable, and cash. Initially the optimal size of an inventory order is determined. After this inventory is sold, the firm receives either accounts receivable or cash. Once the receivables are collected, the firm has cash, which may be used to pay current obligations or invested. Since cash generates no income, the last section is devoted to short-term cash equivalents (money market instruments) and the calculation of the yield these substitutes for cash may generate.

The Inventory Cycle

A firm produces output to sell, or it buys items wholesale and retails the product. In either case the firm acquires inventory. This inventory must be paid for; it must be financed by either borrowed funds or equity. The more rapidly the firm turns over the inventory, the less finance is necessary to carry the inventory. (In Chapter 9, one of the ratios used to analyze a firm was inventory turnover.) Rapid turnover indicates that the firm sells the inventory quickly and ties up less of its funds. Rapid turnover, however, is not in itself desirable, for such turnover may result in the firm's not having inventory available when there are buyers. Being out of stock may result in the loss of sales. While rapid inventory turnover decreases the firm's financial needs, it may also result in lower earnings.

The inventory cycle is illustrated by Figure 17.1. The firm initially purchases inventory (AB). As time passes, some inventory is sold, and the stock of inventory

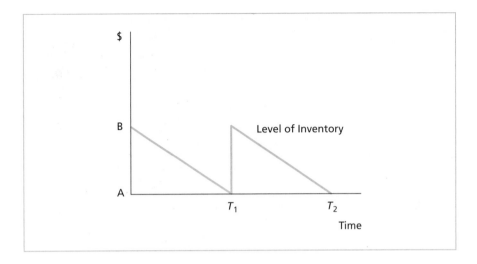

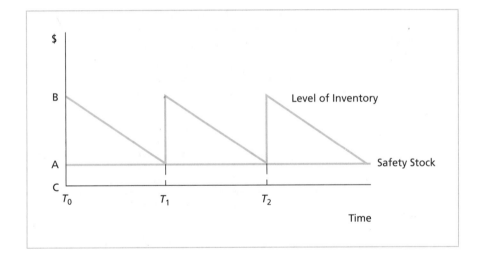

is drawn down, and at T_1 the inventory is sold and the stock is depleted. The firm then purchases new inventory (AB), and the cycle is repeated (T_1 to T_2).

In reality management would not let inventory fall to zero before it restocked the shelves. Instead, it would maintain a minimum level of inventory (a safety stock) to assure that some stock is always available for sale. Such a safety stock is illustrated in Figure 17.2. The minimum level of inventory (the safety stock) is CA. The inventory order is added to the safety stock, so that the firm has a maximum inventory of CB, which consists of the safety stock CA and the order AB. This total inventory is drawn down as sales are made. As the level of inventory approaches the safety stock, the firm reorders.

Safety stock

Desired minimum level of inventory designed to protect against loss of sales due to being out of stock

Management could avoid reordering the inventory by increasing the initial purchase. By doubling the initial purchase, management can double the time before it has to reorder. Of course, the firm could avoid all inventory cycles if it had sufficient inventory. However, it costs to carry inventory; hence, management determines the best level of inventory to purchase to reduce the carrying costs. One possible model that determines this level is the economic order quantity (EOQ) covered in the next section.

The Economic Order Quantity

Economic order quantity (EOQ)

Optimal size of an order of inventory

The optimal size of an order of inventory, the economic order quantity (EOQ), is the order size that minimizes the total cost of carrying and processing inventory. This cost has several components, and minimizing one component increases another component. What are these components? First, there is the cost of placing the order, which includes shipping, brokerage, and processing costs. These costs decline (are lower per unit) as inventory increases.

A second set of costs consists of those associated with carrying the inventory. These costs include insurance, storage, and the cost of financing the inventory. Carrying costs increase as the size of the inventory increases and offset the lower per-unit costs of larger orders. The job of management, then, is to balance the savings from larger orders with the increased carrying costs.

The total annual cost associated with inventory is the sum of ordering costs and carrying costs. Ordering cost (OC) is the product of (1) the number of orders and (2) the cost per order (F). The number of orders depends on the number of units sold (S) and the size of each order (Q). The number of orders equals units sold divided by the size of each order. Thus, total ordering costs are

$$OC = \left(\frac{S}{Q}\right)F. \qquad (17.1)$$

If annual sales are 10,000 units and the size of each inventory order is 1,000 units, the firm places 10 orders a year. If the cost of placing an order is $50,[1] then total ordering costs are $500.

$$OC = \left(\frac{10,000}{1,000}\right)\$50 = \$500.$$

---

[1]In this illustration, the shipping and ordering costs are fixed at $50. The cost of each order is independent of the size of the order, and as the number of orders is reduced, total costs decline. It is possible, however, that the cost of ordering may increase with the size of the order but per-unit costs still decline. For example, suppose it costs $2 to ship one book but $3 to ship two books. Even though the ordering cost of a larger shipment rises, the per-unit cost of shipping each book is lower, and fewer but larger shipments reduce total ordering costs.

Annual carrying costs (CC) are the product of average inventory ($Q/2$) and per-unit carrying costs (C). Total carrying costs are

$$CC = \left(\frac{Q}{2}\right)C. \qquad (17.2)$$

If the firm orders 1,000 units of inventory and sells them evenly over the year, its average inventory is 500 units (1,000/2). If the per-unit carrying cost is $10, the annual carrying cost is $5,000.

$$CC = \left(\frac{1,000}{2}\right)\$10 = \$5,000.$$

Total inventory costs (TC) are the sum of the two components:

$$TC = OC + CC = \left(\frac{S}{Q}\right)F + \left(\frac{Q}{2}\right)C. \qquad (17.3)$$

In this example, total inventory costs are

$$TC = \left(\frac{10,000}{1,000}\right)(\$50) + \left(\frac{1,000}{2}\right)(\$10) = \$5,500.$$

The relationships between inventory and ordering costs and between inventory and carrying costs are presented in Exhibit 17.3. The first column presents the given level of sales, while the second and third columns give various possible order sizes and the number of inventory orders for the given level of sales. As the size of each order is increased, the number of orders is reduced. The fourth column specifies the cost of placing an order. Column 5, which is the product of the number of orders and the cost per order (the product of columns 3 and 4), presents the total order costs associated with various levels of inventory. Notice how the total ordering costs decline with larger orders (higher levels of inventory) because the firm is placing fewer orders and thus is incurring fewer ordering costs.

The second part of Exhibit 17.3 presents in column 6 the average level of inventory (column 2 divided by 2) and the per-unit carrying costs (column 7). The total carrying costs (column 8) are the product of columns 6 and 7. Notice how total carrying costs rise with the level of inventory. Higher levels of inventory inflict more costs on the firm to carry the inventory.

The sum of the total ordering costs (column 5) and the carrying costs (column 8) is the total cost associated with each level of inventory. That cost is presented in column 9. As may be seen in this column, total costs initially decline as the level of inventory is increased. However, the decline moderates, reaches a minimum point at 316 units, and then starts to increase. The level of

EXHIBIT 17.3 Relationships between Inventory and Ordering Costs and between Inventory and Carrying Costs

Total Sales (S = 10,000 units)	Size of Inventory Order	Number of Orders	Cost per Order (F = $50)	Total Order Costs	Average Inventory	Per Unit Carrying Cost (C = $10)	Total Carrying Costs	Total Costs
10,000	50	200	$50	$10,000	25	$10	$250	$10,250
10,000	100	100	50	5,000	50	10	500	5,500
10,000	200	50	50	2,500	100	10	1,000	3,500
10,000	300	34	50	1,700	150	10	1,500	3,200
10,000	316	32	50	1,600	158	10	1,580	3,180
10,000	400	25	50	1,250	200	10	2,000	3,250
10,000	500	20	50	1,000	250	10	2,500	3,500
10,000	600	17	50	850	300	10	3,000	3,850
10,000	800	13	50	650	400	10	4,000	4,650
10,000	1,000	10	50	500	500	10	5,000	5,500

FIGURE 17.3
Determination of EOQ

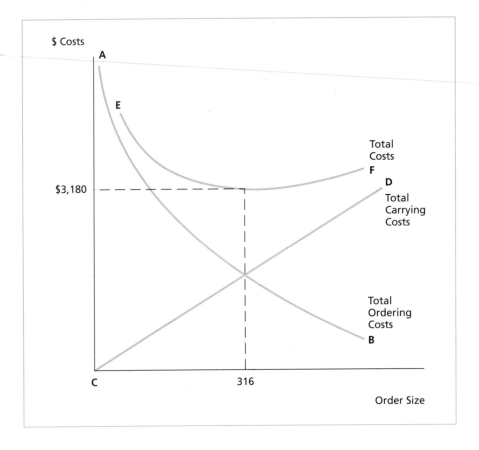

inventory that minimizes the total cost of the inventory is the best quantity for the firm to order. That quantity is the "economic order quantity" or EOQ.

The trade-off between ordering costs and carrying costs demonstrated in Exhibit 17.3 is illustrated in Figure 17.3. The horizontal axis measures the size of the inventory order while the vertical axis shows the total costs associated with those orders. Line AB shows total ordering costs, which decline as the size of each order increases. This decline occurs because the total number of orders is reduced. Line CD shows total carrying costs, which rise with increased order size. These increased costs are the result of the firm having more inventory. Line EF combines these two costs and illustrates the total costs associated with each level of inventory. It clearly demonstrates the initial decline in total costs, their minimum value ($3,180 at 316 units), and their subsequent increase as the size of the inventory order increases beyond 316 units.

Mathematical models have been developed to help determine this economic order quantity. One simple model starts with Equation 17.3:

$$TC = OC + CC = \left(\frac{S}{Q}\right)F + \left(\frac{Q}{2}\right)C.$$

and then determines the order size that minimizes total costs. The resulting solution is referred to as the economic order quantity (EOQ) and is given in Equation 17.4.[2]

$$EOQ = \sqrt{\frac{2SF}{C}}. \tag{17.4}$$

The example in Exhibit 17.3 may be used to illustrate how the formula works. A firm uses 10,000 units of an item each year, and it costs the firm $10 to carry each unit. (The cost to carry may also be expressed as the percentage of carrying costs times the cost of a unit of inventory. If inventory costs $100 per unit, and the percent cost of carry is 10 percent, then the cost of carrying is $100 \times 0.10 = $10.) The cost of an order is $50. When these values are substituted into Equation 17.4, the economic order quantity is

$$EOQ = \sqrt{\frac{2(10{,}000)(\$50)}{(\$10)}} = 316.$$

Thus, the most economical order size for this item is 316 units.

How this information is related to the inventory cycle is illustrated in Figure 17.4. In this illustration a safety stock of 50 units is added. The initial order is 366 units, which is the sum of the safety stock (50) and the economic order quantity (316). Since annual sales are 10,000 units, sales per day are

$$\text{Sales per day} = 10{,}000/365 = 27.4.$$

If sales per day are approximately 28 units, the economic order quantity is sold in approximately 11 days.

$$\text{Duration of the EOQ} = \text{EOQ/Daily sales}$$

$$316/28 = 11.3.$$

---

[2]Calculus is used to determine the EOQ. The calculation is as follows:

$$TC = (S)(F)(Q)^{-1} + (Q)(C)/2.$$

Take the first derivative with respect to Q:

$$\frac{d(TC)}{d(Q)} = -(S)(F)(Q^{-2}) + C/2.$$

Set the first derivative equal to zero and solve for Q:

$$(S)(F)(Q^{-2}) = C/2$$

$$C = \frac{2(S)(F)}{Q^2}$$

$$Q^2 = \frac{2(S)(F)}{C}$$

$$Q = \sqrt{\frac{2(S)(F)}{C}}.$$

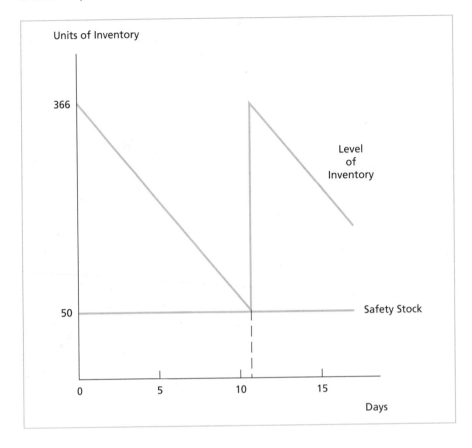

This passage of time is shown in Figure 17.4 from day 0 to day 11, at which time the level of inventory has declined to the safety stock and must be replenished. Then the cycle is repeated. The amount of inventory the firm should reorder is the EOQ, which remains 316 units unless the carrying costs or the ordering costs have changed.

When will management place an order for the 316 units? The answer depends on how long it takes to receive delivery. For example, if shipment takes 5 days and the EOQ lasts 11 days, then management must place an order 6 days after receiving the inventory to be certain to receive the next order on time. If the order is late, the firm will start to use its safety stock, so the possibility of late shipments is one reason for carrying a safety stock. If delivery is slow, the reorder point may be several weeks before the inventory is needed. For example, if delivery requires 14 days, the firm will have to place a second order before the first order is received, since the duration of the EOQ is 11 days. If delivery is rapid, however, the reorder may occur close to when shipment is needed. If the firm could receive shipment within a day, the reorder point would be only one day before the inventory is needed.

A change in any of the variables used to calculate the EOQ will, of course, affect the desired amount of each order. For example, if the cost of placing an order increases from $50 to $100, the economic order quantity becomes:

$$EOQ = \sqrt{\frac{2(10,000)(\$100)}{\$10}} = 447.$$

The increase in the cost of processing the order raises the best reorder size from 316 to 447 units. If the carrying costs were to rise from $10 to $20, the EOQ would decline from 316 to 224:

$$EOQ = \sqrt{\frac{2(10,000)(\$50)}{\$20}} = 224.$$

These changes in costs do not produce proportionate changes in the economic order quantity. The doubling of the order cost does not double the economic order quantity and a doubling of the carrying cost does not result in halving the optimal order. There is more than one variable affecting the optimal order quantity. If one variable changes and the others are unaffected, there is no reason to assume that there will be a proportionate change in the economic order quantity. Hence, there is no simple proportionate relationship between one component of the costs and the EOQ.

Weaknesses in the EOQ

The EOQ model is a simple model for the determination of the optimal order quantity. It is based on simplifying assumptions that rarely apply to all firms at all times. Of course, this criticism may apply to other models explained in this text. Each model has a set of assumptions. However, of all the models presented in this text, the simple EOQ may have the least realistic assumptions.

A major assumption is that sales occur smoothly during the time period. This assumption permits the line representing the level of inventory in Figure 17.4 to decline at the same rate of 27.4 units a day. Sales, however, generally do vary over a period of time. Some sales are seasonal, and even nonseasonal sales may occur at different rates throughout the year. There are periods when sales are sluggish, and inventory is drawn down at a slower rate. Even stable sales do not imply that the same amount is sold daily as suggested by the simple EOQ model.

In addition, the simple EOQ model does not consider quantity discounts and delays in processing orders. Of course, discounts for large purchases and delays in shipping can affect the level of inventory carried by the firm. There is also a problem applying the model if the firm carries many products. A retailer like Home Depot carries thousands of items, and applying the EOQ model may be impossible. For example, how would you allocate the shipping costs for the various items received in one shipment? The ordering costs of each item cannot be known, so the model could not be applied to each item but to batches.

Even if the model could be expanded and made more sophisticated, the basic concept that it illustrates remains unaltered. The EOQ seeks to determine the size of the order that minimizes the total costs of carrying and processing inventory. It brings to the foreground the *trade-off between carrying and ordering costs*. These costs move in opposite directions, so decreasing one tends to increase the other. If management underestimates ordering costs (or overestimates carrying costs), the firm may lose sales from lack of inventory. In the opposite situation in which management overestimates the cost of ordering (or underestimates carrying costs), the effect will be to order too much inventory. *Carrying excess inventory is costly.* One of the quickest means to place a firm in financial difficulty is to have excess inventory, especially during a period of rising short-term interest rates or declining sales. Under that scenario, unsold inventory is being financed with increasingly expensive short-term credit.

A firm could reduce these problems if it could better coordinate the receiving of inventory with its sale. Raw materials would arrive "just in time" for the production process, and the production process would be completed "just in time" for delivery. Inventory would consist only of work-in-process for a manufacturer and would be virtually nonexistent for a retailer.

A "just-in-time" inventory system is designed to achieve that result. Raw materials arrive only as needed and finished goods are immediately shipped. Just-in-time inventory management requires (1) accurate sales forecasts that are updated often, (2) a flexible production schedule with tight deadlines, (3) reliable equipment and preventive maintenance programs (a breakdown in part of the process throws the tight schedules off), and (4) frequent communication with and cooperation from suppliers.

When successful, just-in-time inventory management erases the need for determining the economic order quantity. Just-in-time reduces the need for safety stocks and excess capacity, since facilities and labor are used more intensely, and increases the firm's ability to respond to changes in customers' demands. The system manufactures exactly what customers need when they need it, permitting customers to also institute just-in-time inventory management. Shipping costs tend to increase because the firm must make more (and smaller) shipments; however, increased supplier and buyer loyalty, the savings in inventory carrying costs, and the reduced need for plant and equipment result in increased earnings when just-in-time inventory management is successfully employed.

One advantage of e-commerce is the ability to better control inventory and practice "just-in-time" inventory management. A firm such as Amazon.com does not rent retail stores and carry large quantities of inventory. Instead it leases inexpensive centralized warehouse space. While Amazon.com carries inventory, it avoids display expense and reduces carrying costs by ordering replacement inventory as shipments are made and in some cases even avoids shipping expenses by charging customers for the service.

Maximum, Minimum, and Average Inventory

The EOQ gives the optimal order quantity for inventory; that, however, is not the same as the maximum inventory to be carried by a firm. Consider the firm in Figure 17.4 at the beginning of day 1. Its maximum inventory is the EOQ (316) plus the safety stock (50). The minimum inventory at the end of day 11 is the safety stock, if sales occur as anticipated. Of course, the minimum possible inventory is 0 if the entire safety stock is sold before new inventory is received.

The average inventory depends on the EOQ and the safety stock. If sales occur evenly throughout the time period (approximately 28 units per day), the average inventory associated with the EOQ has to be the EOQ/2. The inventory at the beginning of day 1 is 316 units and at the end of day 11 is 0. The average of these two numbers is 158 ([316 + 0]/2). At the beginning of the second day, inventory is 288 units because 28 were sold during the first day. At the end of the tenth day, inventory is 28 units. The average of these two numbers is 158 ([288 + 28]/2). By similar reasoning, it may be shown that the average inventory associated with the EOQ is always the EOQ/2, as long as sales occur evenly throughout the period.

The average inventory associated with the safety stock is the amount of safety stock. Consider the safety stock in Figure 17.4. At the beginning of day 1, the safety stock is 50 units. At the end of day 11, the safety stock is still 50 units. The average of these two numbers is obviously 50. As long as the safety stock is not drawn down, the average safety stock is 50 units.

Of course, the firm's average inventory is the sum of the two averages. Thus,

$$\text{Average inventory} = \text{EOQ}/2 + \text{Safety stock.}$$

The average inventory for the firm in Figure 17.4 is 208 units ([316/2] + 50), while the maximum and minimum levels of inventory are 366 and 50 units, respectively.

Management of Accounts Receivable

As was discussed in the previous section, management must balance the costs of carrying inventory with the costs associated with being out of stock and ordering/shipping. The problem facing management concerning accounts receivable is similar. The expenses associated with offering credit and collecting receivables must be offset by the costs associated with lost sales and revenues from not offering credit.

Accounts receivable arise from credit sales, in which the firm accepts a promise of future payment instead of immediate cash. Many consumers use credit extensively, and many firms (e.g., retailers) also buy on credit. But credit involves costs. There are the obvious processing fees, for the firm must bill its credit customers and maintain records. These processing costs have encouraged many retail firms to accept such credit cards as MasterCard or VISA.

The retailer accepts the card and lets the issuing agent process and collect the accounts receivable. The retailer, however, collects only a percentage of the credit sales, such as $0.98 on every $1.00, with the $0.02 going to the collecting agent. While this arrangement reduces the proceeds of the sale, it virtually eliminates the processing costs of credit.

Offering credit also involves the possibility of loss; not all credit sales are collected. Some purchasers will default. Of course, many accounts are of excellent quality, as is illustrated by the accounts receivable of utilities. These accounts are generally of high quality because the company can force payment by threatening to discontinue service. One method of increasing the safety of accounts receivable is to require the buyer to pledge an asset against the loan. In case of default the seller repossesses the asset, which may then be resold. The seller, however, may be unable to obtain the full value of the account receivable. In such a case the seller still has a claim on the original buyer for the balance but may never be able to collect that claim.

Credit Policy

Credit policy has three components: the selection of those customers who will be granted credit, the terms of credit, and the collection policy. While all three components are important, the firm faces legal constraints with regard to the granting of credit and the terms. For example, the firm may not discriminate in granting credit; it must be given to all who meet the standards. Furthermore, the firm may not discriminate in terms offered. Once the firm establishes the terms, they apply to all.

To determine who will be granted credit, the firm establishes credit standards. These standards consider such factors as the capacity of the borrower to pay, the collateral the borrower may have to secure the loan, and the borrower's record of payment. The capacity to pay primarily depends on the borrower's earnings or other sources of cash. Individuals with higher levels of income have more capacity to meet credit payments and are better credit risks. However, income or earnings are not the only consideration because an individual or firm may have other debt obligations. Thus, the lender also considers the amount of debt the borrower already has outstanding.

Collateral refers to specific assets that may be pledged to secure a loan and reduce the risk of loss to the lender. Not all assets make good collateral. For an asset to be good collateral, it must be saleable. For this reason, marketable securities, such as stocks and bonds, make excellent collateral, for they may be readily sold. Real estate may also serve as collateral. However, it may take an extended period to sell real estate, during which time the lender's funds are tied up in the bad loan. Since the marketability of assets differs, their usefulness as collateral varies. The variation in marketability and quality explains why creditors lend varying amounts against specific assets. The more readily the asset may be sold near its assessed value, the more it can be used to secure the loan.

It is important to realize that lenders do not want the collateral that is used to secure the loan. For example, a bank makes its profits through lending; it is not in the business of selling assets seized for the nonpayment of debt. Thus, part of the role of collateral is psychological. The purpose is to encourage the borrower to meet the required payments because failure to meet the payments may result in the borrower losing the pledged asset. Since the pledged asset is worth more than the amount of the loan, the borrower may suffer a loss if the asset is sold to meet the loan payments. This threat of loss gives the use of collateral teeth and increases the likelihood that the borrower will meet the required payments.

In addition to the borrower's capacity to meet its debt obligations and the assets that are available to secure the loans, the lender considers the borrower's past credit history. Does the borrower have a history of slow payment? Has the borrower ever declared bankruptcy? A good track record implies that the borrower is a safer risk. This information may be obtained through credit-rating agencies and credit bureaus that maintain credit histories. While such past histories do not assure the debtor will continue to be a good risk, they do differentiate borrowers with a good credit history from those who have been slow payers or who have defaulted in the past.

After establishing who will be granted credit, the firm must establish the terms. The terms of the loan include the time period for the loan, the discount (if any) for early payment, and the penalty for late payment. In the next chapter, the terms of trade credit are illustrated by phrases like 2/10, n30. In that case, the term is 30 days with a 2 percent discount for payment by the 10th day. (These terms do not specify any penalty for failure to pay by the 30th day.) Often terms are n30 (or n60) with interest on the unpaid balance at 1.5 percent monthly (18 percent annually) after the initial 30 days have elapsed. Such terms let the borrower have the "free" use of credit for 30 days (60 days if the terms are n60). The lender is carrying the loan for the specified term and has built this cost of credit into the price of the goods sold to the borrower. Since the credit is already paid for, such terms encourage the borrower not to pay until the term of the loan has elapsed.

Actually, the lender may have little flexibility in the terms that are offered, since competition forces firms to offer similar terms. (If a major retailer in the mall accepts VISA, virtually all other retailers are forced to accept VISA.) However, while competition may determine the terms and legal constraints that restrict the selection of potential borrowers, the firm has more flexibility with regard to its collection policy. Such policy can range from sending a second billing or an overdue statement, to harsher measures such as threats of legal action. Failure to collect forces the lender to (1) write off the loan as uncollectible, (2) take more drastic action, such as legal action designed to force payment, or (3) sell the account to a collection agency.

The Decision to Grant Credit

Like all assets, accounts receivable require financing. All accounts receivable must offer an implied return or benefit (for example, increased profitable sales) to justify their use of funds. If credit sales do not yield this return, they decrease the profitability of the firm. Credit policy, then, is ultimately designed to assure that the extension of credit increases the firm's profitability.

The decision to grant credit compares the benefits from an increase is sales (an increase in cash inflows) with the additional costs (cash outflows) associated with granting credit. These outflows include (1) the cost of the additional goods sold, (2) the cost of credit checks, (3) collection and bad debt expenses, and (4) the cost of carrying the accounts receivable. Suppose a firm has sales of $100,000 without offering credit, but management believes that it can increase sales by 50 percent (from $100,000 to $150,000) if the firm offers customers 30 days to pay (n30). Should the firm make the offer?

The answer depends on the costs associated with the additional sales. To ease the illustration, make the following assumptions:

1. The cost of the additional goods sold is 60 percent of sales.

2. Credit checks and collection costs are $7,000.

3. Five percent of the new sales will be uncollectible.

4. In addition to new customers, all existing customers will take 30 days to pay, while previously they paid immediately.

5. The cost of borrowing the funds to carry the receivables is 10 percent.

Consider the following projected income statement that will result from offering customers credit for 30 days:

Additional sales		$50,000
Costs		
Cost of additional goods sold ($50,000 × 0.6)	$30,000	
Credit/collection costs	7,000	
Bad debt expense ($50,000 × 0.05)	2,500	
Carrying costs (interest)	1,250	
Total costs		40,750
Net increase in earnings		$ 9,250

The carrying costs are figured as follows. Annual credit sales will be $150,000; all sales will now be on credit. All accounts receivable will be collected at the end of 30 days, so accounts receivable will be $150,000/12 = $12,500. Since the cost of carrying the receivables is 10 percent, the interest expense is $1,250.

The analysis indicates a net increase in earnings of $9,250, which argues for granting the credit. However, several crucial assumptions were made. First, and most important, offering the credit increases sales. If the firm's competitors offer similar credit terms, the projected sales increase may not materialize. Second, the costs were known. However, an increase in any of the costs—increased collection expense, an increase in defaults (bad debt), or an increase in the rate of interest—will reduce earnings. Third, the analysis assumed that payments are made on the 30th day. If customers pay late, the accounts receivable will remain outstanding for a longer period of time and increase the carrying costs even if the rate of interest remains unchanged.

In summary, a firm's credit policy, like all economic decisions, involves a balancing of offsetting variables. By offering credit, a firm may increase sales, but with these increased sales come increased costs, including the cost of processing collections, the cost of financing the accounts, and the risk of loss. Like any investment decision, a firm's credit policy considers the potential benefits of offering credit (increased cash inflows) versus the increased expenses (increased cash outflows). If these benefits exceed their present costs, the firm extends credit, for such a credit policy enhances the value of the firm.

Analyzing Accounts Receivable

Having granted credit, management needs to supervise and analyze the firm's accounts receivable. One technique for monitoring accounts receivable is to analyze their turnover. Turnover ratios, such as annual sales/accounts receivable or the average collection period (days that sales are outstanding), were discussed in Chapter 9. The faster the accounts receivable turn over, the faster they are collected and converted into cash. This cash may then be used to acquire other income-earning assets or to retire debt.

Receivables Turnover

The potential for savings from increasing turnover of accounts receivable may be seen in the following example. The industry average turnover ratio is 6 (that is, every two months). This particular firm has credit sales of $100,000,000 and accounts receivable of $25,000,000. Thus, its accounts receivable turn over four times a year (Credit sales/Accounts receivable = $100,000,000/$25,000,000 = 4). If this firm were able to match the industry average, what would be the amount of its accounts receivable? The answer is

$$\frac{\text{Credit sales}}{\text{Accounts receivable}} = 6$$

$$6 = \frac{\$100,000,000}{X}$$

$$X = \$100,000,000/6 = \$16,666,667.$$

If the firm achieved a receivables turnover that was comparable to the industry average, its accounts receivable would decline from $25,000,000 to $16,666,667. That is a net reduction of $8,333,333 in accounts receivable. If funds cost 10 percent annually, the reduction in the accounts receivable would save the firm $833,333 a year in finance charges ($8,333,333 × 0.10 = $833,333).

Aging Schedules

Another tool used to analyze credit sales is to age the accounts. This technique constructs a table showing the length of time each account has been outstanding (unpaid). How this technique works is illustrated by the following example. A firm has total accounts receivable of $1,100, which are composed of five customers. The amount of each account and the number of days outstanding are as follows:

Customer	Amount of the Account	Number of Days Outstanding
A	$300	45
B	100	70
C	200	20
D	200	35
E	300	15

From this information, the following table can be constructed:

	Aging Schedule (in Days)			
Accounts	0–30	31–60	61–90	More Than 90
A	—	$300	—	—
B	—	—	$100	—
C	$200	—	—	—
D	—	200	—	—
E	300	—	—	—
	$500	$500	$100	$0
Percentage of total accounts receivable	45.5%	45.5%	9.1%	0%

This table shows that $600 (or 54.6 percent) of the accounts receivable has been outstanding for more than a month and that one account has not been paid for more than two months.

By aging the receivables, a pattern, or norm, is established. Then, if the percentage of slow accounts increases, the financial manager has identified a problem and can take action either to force collection or to acknowledge the accounts to be bad and discontinue carrying them at the stated value on the firm's books. However, slow accounts are not necessarily bad and may eventually be collected. In many cases a firm's best or most important customers may be slow payers. This may be especially true if the buyer is larger than the seller and accounts for a major portion of the smaller firm's sales. Such a buyer has the power to ride the credit, and the small supplier may not press for payment because it fears loss of future sales.

Cash Management

After inventory flows through the firm into sales and after accounts receivable have been collected, the financial manager must decide what to do with the cash. Cash management is important, because the firm must have sufficient liquidity to meet its obligations as they come due. However, liquidity reduces profitability because cash itself earns nothing. The cash must be used to purchase an income-earning asset in order to increase profitability.

Cash Management Policies

Cash management policies revolve around (1) hastening collections and retarding disbursements and (2) investing excess short-term funds into income-earning assets, especially money market securities that offer yield plus safety of principal. Increasing the speed of collections is not to be confused with increased turnover of inventory or accounts receivable. The turnover of these assets depends on inventory control and credit policy. Cash management is concerned with the speed with which cash is processed, especially the speed with which checks clear.

The more rapidly checks payable to the firm clear, the sooner the firm has the use of the funds. Correspondingly, the slower the checks that the firm has distributed clear, the longer the firm has the use of the funds. If the firm can increase the time that it has the use of the funds, it increases its profitability. An extension of just one day can generate thousands of dollars in earned interest. For example, suppose a firm were to increase its cash holdings by $1 million a day. At 5 percent, such a holding generates $136.98 in interest daily ($1,000,000 × 0.05/365) and $50,000 annually.

Lockbox

System of collections designed to increase the speed of collecting checks to obtain the use of the funds more quickly

To generate this additional cash, the firm may establish a lockbox system of collections. When a firm bills a customer, the customer sends a check for payment, but the firm does not have the use of the funds until the check clears. Instead of having a central billing location to which all payments are sent, the firm establishes several collection points (the lockbox). A local bank removes the checks and immediately processes them for payment. At the end of each day the bank sends by wire (electronically) the funds that have cleared and are available for use to a central location, which is usually another bank in a financial center (or the firm's corporate headquarters). The funds are now available for the firm to use either to reduce its outstanding short-term debt (and thus reduce interest expense) or to invest in short-term securities.

For such a lockbox system to be profitable, the firm must have a sufficient volume of business. The banks that operate the lockboxes, process the checks, and wire the funds charge for this service. The firm obviously must earn a sufficient return on the additional funds generated by the system to justify the expenses associated with the lockboxes.

Cash receipts may also be collected faster by the use of electronic funds transfers. Under such a system, funds are transferred electronically from one account to another through the use of computer terminals instead of checks. For example, you make a purchase and use a debit card. This produces an immediate transfer of funds from your account to the seller's account. (The bank charges the seller a fee for providing the service.)

Management of disbursements is, of course, the exact opposite of collections. Except in those cases in which immediate payment reduces interest charges (for example, a commercial bank loan in which interest owed is determined daily), the intent is to retard payment so the firm may have the use of the money for a longer period of time. This may be achieved by making payments on Friday so the checks cannot clear until the next week or by remitting funds drawn on banks in another geographic location. The recipients of the checks will consider the funds received, even though the checks may take several days to clear. In such cases, the firm disbursing the funds drawn on a distant bank is increasing its use of the cash at the expense of the recipient of the check.

The financial manager's capacity to execute such a strategy is enhanced by two facts. First, since firms obtain lines of credit from commercial banks, these lines may be used to meet the checks should they clear more rapidly than anticipated. Second, the market for short-term investments is so sophisticated that the financial manager may invest excess funds for as short a period as one day. If the financial manager can determine that the cash will be available for an additional day, it may be invested for that short a time and need not lie idle.

Money Market Securities and Yields

Excess short-term cash may be invested in a variety of money market securities including corporate commercial paper, negotiable certificates of deposit issued by banks, and U.S. Treasury bills. (In Chapter 2, various money market instruments were described in the section on money market mutual funds.) These short-term, liquid securities are bought and sold is what is called the *money market*. This name differentiates short-term securities from long-term securities, such as stocks and bonds, which trade in what is sometimes referred to as the *capital market*.

While many money market instruments exist, they have common characteristics. All money market securities offer investors short-term yields, liquidity, and safety of principal. They may be readily converted into cash with little risk of loss. Thus, these instruments are a safe haven for funds that would otherwise sit idle. Individual investors and financial managers of firms (and governments and nonprofit organizations) may invest in these securities and earn interest for brief periods of time.

Yields on money market instruments are similar but do vary with the term and small differences in risk. For example, in July 2010, the yield on a 6-month negotiable CD was 0.15 percent while the 12-month negotiable CD paid 0.60 percent. Since Treasury bills are considered the safest of the money market instruments, they offer the lowest yields. The 12-month bill paid 0.52 percent.

Money market instruments are illustrations of discounted securities. They pay no set rate of interest; instead the securities are sold at a discount. Although the denomination for many market instruments is $1,000,000, Treasury bills are sold in units as small as $10,000. Thus Treasury bills are one of the few short-term securities available to the individual investor. (Small investors participate in the market for money market instruments indirectly by acquiring shares in money market mutual funds, which invest in commercial paper, negotiable CDs, and other money market securities.)

The Calculation of Yields

Because most short-term money market instruments are discounted securities, the difference between the discounted price and the face value (or subsequent sales price) is the source of the return the investor earns. For example, if a $10,000 security such as a U.S. Treasury bill is purchased for $9,791, the $209 difference between the sale price and the amount received when the bill is redeemed is the interest earned. (It is also the interest the issuer pays.) The amount of interest plus the time period determine the yield.

Unfortunately the word "yield" is ambiguous; it can have more than one meaning. You may compute the discount yield, the simple yield, and the compound annualized yield.

The "discount" yield (y_d) is calculated as follows:

$$y_d = \frac{\text{Par value} - \text{Price}}{\text{Par value}} \times \frac{360}{\text{Number of days to maturity}}. \qquad (17.5)$$

In the preceding example, the "discount yield" is

$$y_d = \frac{\$10,000 - \$9,791}{\$10,000} \times \frac{360}{180} = 4.18\%.$$

The discount yield understates the true yield because it uses (1) the par value and not the amount the individual must invest and (2) a 360-day year.

An alternative method corrects these two problems. The calculation for the "simple" yield (y_s) is

$$y_d = \frac{\text{Interest earned}}{\text{Amount invested}} \times \frac{365}{\text{Number of days to maturity}}. \qquad (17.6)$$

In this illustration, the simple yield is

$$\frac{\$209}{\$9,791} \times \frac{365}{180} = 4.33\%.$$

This rate is higher than the discount rate because it uses the amount invested ($9,791) instead of the principal amount ($10,000) in the denominator and 365 days instead of 360 days.

The simple yield, however, is not the true annualized rate when compounding is considered. In the previous example, the term of the investment is

180 days, so the investor can repeat the process twice a year. The annualized "compound" yield (i) is determined by the following equation:

$$\$9,791(1 + i)^n = \$10,000,$$

in which n is 180/365 or 0.49315. Rephrased, the question is: At what rate does $9,791 grow to $10,000 in 0.49315 of a year? The solution for the compound interest rate the borrower is paying and the investor is earning is

$$\$9,791(1 + i)^{0.49315} = \$10,000$$

$$(1 + i)^{0.49315} = \$10,000/\$9,791 = 1.02135$$

$$i = (1.02135)^{2.0278} - 1 = 4.38\%.$$

Thus, the true, annualized compound yield is 4.38 percent. ($[1.02135]^{2.0278}$ may be determined by using an electronic calculator with a y^x key. Enter 1.02135; press the y^x key; enter 2.0278, and press =.)

In this illustration, the difference between the true annualized rate and the simple rate is small (4.38 percent versus 4.33 percent). However, as the time period shortens (so the frequency of compounding increases) and the amount of the discount increases (so more interest is earned), the difference between the two calculations increases. Suppose you purchase a Treasury bill for $9,560 and sell it for $9,630 after 30 days. The simple rate is

$$\frac{\$70}{\$9,560} \times \frac{365}{30} = 8.91\%.$$

The true, annualized compounded interest rate is

$$\$9,560(1 + i)^{30/365} = \$9,630$$

$$\$9,560(1 + i)^{0.08219} = \$9,630$$

$$(1 + i)^{0.08219} = \$9,630/\$9,560 = 1.007322$$

$$i = 1.007322^{12.1669} - 1 = 9.28\%.$$

The difference between the simple rate and the true compounded rate is greater than in the previous example.

The discount rate and the simple rate give a less accurate indication of the true annual yield being earned. Selecting among the various money market instruments with differences in prices, interest earned, and time horizons (and hence differences in compounding) requires that the cash manager determine the true yield on each security. Reliance on the discount rate or the simple rate may lead to the selection of a security with a lower yield. The financial manager may select an alternative with a lower yield for a valid reason, such as selecting a Treasury bill over commercial paper because it is the less risky of the two alternatives. But that is different than selecting one security over another based on inaccurate estimates of their respective yields.

Summary

This chapter is devoted to a firm's current assets. How these assets are managed and financed is a firm's working capital policy. In general, the cost of short-term funds is less than the cost of long-term funds. Thus, the use of short-term credit tends to increase a firm's profitability. However, sources of short-term finance are riskier because they must be retired or renewed within a year. The terms may become more onerous or the costs may increase when the firm refinances these short-term obligations.

Inventory is acquired and sold, generating accounts receivable or cash. To facilitate the flow of current assets through the firm, the financial manager analyzes the speed with which inventory and accounts receivable turn over and determines how much inventory to order and carry through use of the economic order quantity (EOQ) model.

Inventory is sold either for cash or on credit. Increased sales may be generated by a more lenient credit policy. However, more credit sales will require that the firm carry more accounts receivable, which must be financed. The firm's credit policy is a crucial component of working capital management, as the credit policy determines who will be granted credit, the terms of the credit, and the enforcement of the terms. The financial manager faces a typical economic trade-off: additional sales through easier credit versus the increased cost of carrying the receivables. Once the credit policy has been established, the financial manager monitors the collection of accounts receivable through turnover ratios and aging schedules, which identify slow-paying accounts.

Increasing the turnover of inventory or accounts receivable will generate more cash, which may be used to acquire other income-earning assets or to retire debt. If there is a temporary lag between the receipt of the cash and its subsequent disbursement, the funds may be invested in money market securities, including U.S. Treasury bills, corporate commercial paper, and negotiable certificates of deposit. Money market securities are safe havens for funds that are invested for short periods of time. These securities offer the financial manager a means to increase profitability by earning money market rates of interest instead of holding non-interest-bearing cash.

Review Objectives

Now that you have completed this chapter, you should be able to

1. Define working capital, net working capital, working capital policy (p. 380).
2. Isolate the risk and advantages of an aggressive working capital policy that emphasizes short-term over long-term debt financing (pp. 383–386).
3. Explain how the operating cycle leads to fluctuations in the need for current assets (pp. 381–383).
4. Differentiate earnings from cash (p. 386).
5. Calculate the economic order quantity (EOQ) (pp. 391–397).
6. Determine the maximum inventory, the average, and the minimum inventory using the EOQ model (p. 399).
7. Enumerate the components of credit policy (pp. 400–401).

8. Determine if a change in credit policy will generate increased earnings (pp. 401–403).

9. Calculate the different annual yields on a discounted, money market security (pp. 406–408).

Problems

1. A firm needs $1 million in additional funds. These can be borrowed from a commercial bank with a loan at 6 percent for one year or from an insurance company at 9 percent for five years. The tax rate is 30 percent.

   a. What will be the firm's earnings under each alternative if earnings before interest and taxes (EBIT) are $430,000?

   b. If EBIT will remain $430,000 next year, what will be the firm's earnings under each alternative if short-term interest rates are 4 percent? If short-term interest rates are 14 percent?

   c. Why do earnings tend to fluctuate more with the use of short-term debt than with long-term debt? If long-term debt had a variable interest rate that fluctuated with changes in interest rates, would the use of short-term debt still be riskier than long-term debt?

2. The following structure of interest rates is given:

Term of Loan	Interest Rate
1 year	3%
2 years	4%
5 years	6%
10 years	8%

Your firm needs $2,000 to finance its assets. Three possible combinations of sources of finance are listed below:

(1)

Assets	$2,000	Liabilities	$ 0
		Equity	2,000

(2)

Assets	$2,000	Liabilities	$ 800 (a one-year loan)
		Equity	1,200

(3)

Assets	$2,000	Liabilities	$ 800 (a 10-year loan)
		Equity	1,200

   a. The firm expects to generate revenues of $2,400 and have operating expenses of $2,080. If the firm's tax rate is 40 percent, what is the return on equity under each choice?

b. During the second year, sales decline to $2,100 while operating expenses decline to $1,900. The structure of interest rates becomes:

Term of Loan	Interest Rate
1 year	6%
2 years	7%
5 years	8%
10 years	10%

c. Given the three choices in the previous year, what is the return on equity for the firm during the second year?

d. What is the implication of using short-term instead of long-term debt during the two years?

3. a. What is the EOQ for a firm that sells 5,000 units when the cost of placing an order is $5 and the carrying costs are $3.50 per unit?

b. How long will the EOQ last? How many orders are placed annually?

c. As a result of lower interest rates, the financial manager determines the carrying costs are now $1.80 per unit. What are the new EOQ and annual number of objects?

4. Given the following information:

Annual sales in units	30,000
Cost of placing an order	$60.00
Per-unit carrying costs	$ 1.50
Existing units of safety stock	300

a. What is the EOQ?

b. What is the average inventory based on the EOQ and the existing safety stock?

c. What is the maximum level of inventory?

d. How many orders are placed each year?

5. Taylor Glass has annual sales of $1,750,000. Although it extends credit for 30 days (n30), the receivables are 20 days overdue. What is the average accounts receivable outstanding, and how much could the company save in interest expense if customers paid on time and if it costs Taylor Glass 10 percent to carry its receivables?

6. To increase sales, management is considering reducing its credit standards. This action is expected to increase sales by $125,000. Unfortunately, it is anticipated that 7 percent of the sales will be uncollectible. Accounts receivable turnover is expected to be six times a year, and it costs the firm 10 percent to carry its receivables. Collection costs will be 4 percent of sales, and the cost of the additional goods sold is $64,000. Will earnings increase?

7. If a firm's sales are $1,500,000 and it costs 9 percent to carry current assets, what is the potential savings if management can increase inventory turnover from 3 to 4 times a year and increase receivables turnover from 4.5 to 6 times a year?

8. As of January 1, Paul's Car Repair has the following accounts receivable:

Receivable	Amount Due	Days Outstanding
A	$1,000	35
B	2,500	42
C	1,500	57
D	3,500	29
E	1,200	48
F	3,100	52
G	1,700	39

As of March 1, the firm's receivables are

Receivable	Amount Due	Days Outstanding
A	$2,000	28
B	1,500	51
C	1,800	47
D	2,500	63
E	3,500	42
F	1,200	40
G	2,700	56

Paul's offers credit terms of net 30 days. Construct aging schedules that show the amount and percentage of total accounts receivable that are 0, 10, 20, and 30 days overdue. Has there been any change in the firm's collections?

9. ELLA T., Inc. has annual sales of 5,000 units; management decides to establish the EOQ model. The firm has two possible suppliers:

Supplier A	Shipping costs $1,000
	Per-unit carrying costs $74
Supplier B	Shipping costs $800
	Per-unit carrying costs $80

a. What is the EOQ for each supplier?

b. If the firm establishes a safety stock of 100 units, what is the firm's average inventory for both suppliers?

   c. What will be the firm's expected maximum and minimum inventory with each supplier?

   d. If delivery takes eight days, what should be the firm's level of inventory when it places an order with supplier A?

10. Big Toy, Inc. annually sells 100,000 units of Big Blobs. Currently, inventory is financed through the use of commercial bank loans. Big Toy pays $12.20 per Big Blob. The cost of carrying this inventory is $3.20 per unit while the cost of placing an order involves expenses of $400 per order. Since Big Blobs are imported, delivery is generally 20 days but may be as long as 30 days. In order to manage inventory more efficiently, the management of Big Toy, Inc. has decided to use the EOQ model plus a safety stock to determine inventory levels.

   a. What is the economic order quantity?

   b. Today is January 1 and the current level of inventory is 10,000 units; when should the first order be placed based on the economic order quantity?

   c. Management always wants sufficient Big Blobs so that they never are out of stock. If management considers late deliveries to be the prime reason for being out of stock, what should be the safety stock?

   d. According to the above analysis, what are the maximum inventory, the minimum inventory, and the average inventory?

   e. If sales of Big Blobs double, will the average inventory also double?

11. Firm X has sales of $5,000,000; $3,000,000 are for cash, but two customers who generate sales of $2,000,000 pay after 30 days. Management believes that sales will increase by 20 percent if all customers have 30 days to pay. Should the firm change its credit policy given the following information?

   a. The cost of the additional goods sold is 70 percent of sales.

   b. Credit checks and collection costs will be $5,000.

   c. Three percent of the new sales will be uncollectible.

   d. The cost of borrowing the funds to carry the receivables is 12 percent.

12. If you purchase a $10,000 short-term (90-day) negotiable certificate of deposit for $9,814, what is the discount yield, the simple yield, and the true compound yield?

13. What is the compound yield on a Treasury bill that costs $98,760 and will be redeemed for $100,000 after 90 days? How much additional return would you have to earn if you had bought $100,000 worth of 90-day commercial paper for $98,478?

14. What is the effective, compound rate of interest you earn if you enter into a repurchase agreement in which you buy a Treasury bill for $76,789 and agree to sell it after a month (30 days) for $77,345? What is the compound rate of interest you pay if you sell a Treasury bill for $76,789 and repurchase it after 30 days for $77,345?

1. What is the total inventory cost if annual sales in units are 100,000; the number of orders is 50 (that is, 2,000 units per order); the cost per order is $5, and the per unit carrying costs are $1?

2. What is the economic order quantity if annual sales are 10,000 units, the cost of placing an order is $1,000, and the per unit carrying costs are $100?

3. If you purchase a $10,000 short-term (90 day) security for $9,814, what is the discount yield, the simple yield, and the compound yield?

4. Stella Corp. (ticker symbol: STAR) has the following accounts receivable:

Receivable	Amount Due	Days Outstanding
A	$11,000	10
B	13,456	35
C	23,110	42
D	13,222	9
E	9,776	28

The firm sells on credit (2/10, n30). What proportion of its receivables are not overdue?

5. A firm with sales of $10,000,000 has inventory of $1,000,000. The firm has no cash sales; all sales are on credit and are collected within 40 days. You are willing to sell inventory to the firm on credit provided that you will be paid within 60 days. Should you sell to this firm on credit? Explain how you derived your answer.

6. Firm A expects sales of $120,000 under its current credit terms of n30. All customers pay on the 30th day. The head of finance suggests a new strategy designed to increase sales and receive cash quicker: offer a discount of 3 percent for immediate cash or full invoice price after 60 days (3/0, n60). The new policy may increase sales by $20,000, and the cost of production will increase by $12,000. It is anticipated that 60 percent of the customers ($84,000) will take the discount and $56,000 will pay the 60th day. Collection expense will decline from $2,000 to $1,000, but bad debt expense will be unchanged. The cost of carrying accounts receivable is 10 percent. If you are the firm's management, can you support the change in terms?

To help you come to a conclusion, answer the questions and fill in the following chart.

a. What are the firm's receivables at the end of the fiscal year under the old and new policies? (Use a 360-day year.)

b. What is the cost of carrying the receivables under the old and new policies?

c. Change resulting from the new terms:

Sales	$20,000
Less	
Discounts	
Production costs	12,000
Cost of carry	
Collection expense	
Bad debt expense	
Net change in earnings	

d. What is the implication of change in net income?

Answers

1. Total inventory costs = order costs + carry costs = (sales/size of each order)(cost per order) + (size of each order/2)(per unit carrying cost)

$$TC = (S/Q)F + (Q/2)C.$$

Definitions of symbols:
TC total costs
S sales in units
Q quantity of inventory order
F fixed cost per order
C per-unit carrying costs
Total costs = $(100,000/2,000)($5) + (2,000/2)($1) = $1,250.$

2. Economic Order Quantity (EOQ):

$$EOQ = (2SO/C)^{.5}$$

Definitions of the symbols:
S number of units sold during the year
O cost of placing an order
C per-unit cost of carrying the inventory

$$EOQ = [(2)(10,000)(1,000)/100]^{.5} = 447$$

3. a. Discount yield (y_d) :

$$y_d = \frac{\text{Par value} - \text{Price}}{\text{Par value}} \times \frac{360}{\text{Number of days to maturity}}$$

$$y_d = \frac{\$10,000 - \$9,814}{\$10,000} \times \frac{360}{90} = 7.44\%.$$

b. Simple (noncompound) yield (y_s) :

$$y_s = \frac{\text{Interest earned}}{\text{Amount invested}} \times \frac{365}{\text{Number of days to maturity}}$$

$$y_s = \$186/\$9,814 \times 365/.90 = 7.69\%.$$

c. The compound yield:

$$(\$10,000/\$9,814)^{365/90} - 1 = 7.91\%.$$

4. This problem does not ask you to construct an aging schedule but rather to interpret one. If the terms are 2/10, n30, only those receivables that have been outstanding for more than 30 are overdue (B and C). A, D, and E are not overdue. Since the question asks what percentage are not overdue, the answer is 48.2 percent ($11,000 + $13,222 + $9,776)/$70,564 = 48.2%).

5. This problem is more subtle than it first appears. To be paid, the firm has to sell the inventory and collect the receivables. Inventory turnover is 10 times a year ($10,000,000/$1,000,000), which is 36 days. However, it takes an additional 40 days to collect the receivables. The total time from when the inventory arrives to when the receivables are collected is 76 days. Since you want to be paid in 60 days, you should not lend to this firm.

6. a. The receivables at the end of the fiscal year under the old and new policies:

$$\text{Old: } \$120,000/12 = \$10,000$$

$$\text{New: } \$56,000/60 = \$9,333$$

b. Cost of carrying the receivables under the old and new policies:

$$\text{Old: } \$10,000 \times 0.10 = \$1,000$$

$$\text{New: } \$9,333 \times 0.10 = \$933$$

c. Change in net income resulting from the new terms:

Sales	$ 20,000
Discounts (0.03 × $84,000)	−2,500
Production costs	−12,000
Cost of carry ($933 − 1,000)	+67
Collection expense	+1,000
Bad debt expense	0
Net change in earnings	$ 6,567

d. Implication of change in net income: the change is positive, which argues for changing the terms. Notice that the discounts and production costs reduce the income but the lower carrying costs and collection expense increase the net income.

Relationships

1. An increase in delivery time _____ the economic order quantity.

2. A decrease in the safety stock _____ the economic order quantity.

3. An increase in sales _____ the EOQ, and an increase in the interest rate (carrying costs) _____ the EOQ.

4. An increase in depreciation _____ the EOQ.

5. A reduction in credit standards _____ accounts receivable.

6. An increase in accounts receivable _____ turnover of receivables.

7. An increase in accounts receivable turnover implies _____ in days sales outstanding.

8. If a Treasury bill sells for a larger discount, interest rates have _____.

9. If short-term interest rates increase, the cost (price) of Treasury bills _____.

10. An increase in the frequency of compounding _____ returns.

Answers

1. increases

2. does not affect (no change)

3. increases; decreases

4. does not affect (no change)

5. increases

6. decreases

7. decrease

8. increased

9. declines

10. increases

CHAPTER 18

Management of Short-Term Liabilities

R alph Waldo Emerson wrote, "Pay every debt, as if God wrote the bill."
While short-term creditors are not God, they do possess substantial
power. When a firm has financial difficulties, the problem generally
arises from its inability to pay its short-term creditors. Even firms with quality
long-term assets can be forced into bankruptcy if they fail to meet current obligations. Such failure is not limited to firms. Governments and charitable organizations can also be forced into bankruptcy if they cannot meet their current
liabilities as they come due.

Few firms can exist without short-term funds. Washington Real Estate Trust,
a firm that owns properties and leases them to others, has a few short-term obligations. (In 2009, about $170 million of its $1,296 million in liabilities was short-
term.) For other firms, a large proportion of their debt obligations are short-term.
Goldman Sachs, a large investment banker and securities dealer, reported assets
of $848.9 billion, of which 67.3 percent was financed by a variety of short-term
debt obligations. That amounts to $571.3 billion in short-term debt.

Commercial banks are a major source of short-term financing for large
and small firms, especially manufacturers, wholesalers, and retailers. Unless the
firm is exceptionally risky, commercial banks may individually be the most important source of short-term funds. The first section of this chapter is devoted
to the short-term loans made by commercial banks.

Many firms use their suppliers as a source of funds. Such trade credit
is spontaneous and a major source of short-term finance for small firms, especially retailers. Large, creditworthy firms have alternative sources of trade
credit, such as commercial paper, which is an unsecured promissory note issued

by a corporation with an excellent credit rating. Since commercial paper is unsecured, its use is limited primarily to large firms. Although bank loans, trade credit, and commercial paper are the primary sources of short-term finance, other sources include secured loans, warehouse financing, and factoring.

Chapter 22 covers the variety of corporate bonds, which are sources of long-term funds. This chapter considers short-term sources. (Intermediate-term sources and leases are covered in the next chapter.) The general terms of each source are described and the determination of the true, effective rate the borrower pays is illustrated. Since the terminology used for each source varies, it is hard to compare them. The determination of the effective interest rate puts each source on a common ground. Without the common ground, there would be no basis for selecting among commercial bank loans, commercial paper, or trade credit.

Accruals

In Chapter 17, the operating cycle illustrated how the normal course of business generates accruals. Wages, taxes, and other short-term obligations accrue with the passage of time. The accruals then are paid as of a particular date.

Because the amount paid to employees (or accrued taxes owed the government or any other accrual) is not affected by when payments are made, accruals are often thought of as free sources of funds. If management can convince employees to accept payment every month instead of every two weeks, accruals increase. The increase is a source of finance because the firm has the use of the funds longer. In effect, the firm receives an interest-free loan from the employees, who are not compensated for waiting longer to receive payment.

Although firms (and governments and nonprofit organizations) have free use of the funds, there are limits to expanding accruals as a source of funds. While employees realize that payments will not be made daily, they will not wait several months for payment. Thus, increases in accruals as a source of additional short-term finance are unrealistic. The firm in need of additional short-term finance will have to use the short-term sources that compose the body of this chapter.

Commercial Bank Loans

Commercial banks are concerned with liquidity and safety of principal. They prefer to make loans that are of short duration and, hence, are a primary source of short-term financing. Although bank loans are obtained by virtually all types of firms, the primary borrowers are retailers and wholesalers. Firms that have large investments in fixed assets do not use short-term bank financing to purchase the fixed assets, for such financing is inappropriate. Such long-term assets should be financed by long-term financing, such as bonds or equity. Retailers and wholesalers, however, are concerned with short-term assets, and bank loans are an appropriate means to finance these assets.

A loan from a commercial bank is a package that is individually negotiated between the borrower and the bank. The negotiated package includes the size of the loan, the maturity date, the amount of the interest, any security requirements (that is, the pledging of specific assets), the subordination of other debt, and other limitations on the financial activity of the firm. Since the bank is lending its funds, it is generally in a position to demand financial constraints. For example, the bank may demand that the firm maintain a minimum current ratio (such as 2:1), or the bank may place limitations on dividend payments.

The firm may borrow a specific amount of money or it may arrange for the right to borrow up to a specified amount. The former creates a promissory note while the latter is called a line of credit. A promissory note is an agreement between the borrower and the commercial bank for a specific amount of money for a specified time period. When the note is signed ("executed"), the bank credits the funds to the borrower's account with the bank. The note specifies the rate of interest, collateral requirements (if any), and the repayment schedule. Repayment either may be made in one lump payment or may be spread over time through a series of payments.

A line of credit is an informal (noncontractual) agreement that grants the firm an option to borrow up to a specified amount whenever the firm needs the funds. For example, the financial manager may arrange a line of credit for $500,000. If the firm requires $100,000 to finance inventory, the financial manager draws $100,000 from the line of credit. The firm now has a $100,000 loan outstanding but still can borrow an additional $400,000 if the funds are needed. The credit line offers the borrower the flexibility to use the credit only when it is needed. Under this type of agreement, the firm has a source of short-term financing but does not have to use the funds. Interest is paid only on the funds the firm actually borrows.

An alternative to the credit line is the revolving credit agreement. Revolving credit is similar to the line of credit in that the bank agrees to extend the firm credit up to a specified limit whenever the firm needs the funds. However, while the line of credit is an informal agreement, revolving credit is a formal, contractual obligation of the bank. The agreement has a time limit (generally a year to 15 months), after which the terms are renegotiated. The bank charges a commitment fee ("origination" fee) for establishing revolving credit, which tends to be 1/4 of a percent of the amount of credit granted by the bank. Thus, a revolving credit agreement for $10 million requires a payment of $25,000.

Fees charged by commercial banks for establishing revolving lines of credit may be paid either at the beginning or at the end of the loan period. If the fee is solely for establishing the credit, it is paid up front. If the fee is on the unused balance, the bank will not know the amount of the fee until after the

Promissory note

Document specifying the amount owed, the interest rate, the maturity date, and other features of a loan

Line of credit

Informal agreement in which a bank extends the right to borrow (at the option of the borrower) up to a specified amount

Revolving credit agreement

Formal agreement in which the bank extends the right to borrow up to a specified amount within a specified time period

period of the loan has elapsed. These differences may be seen by the following illustration of terms:

Bank A: $1,000,000 revolving credit for one year at 10 percent with a fee of 1/2 percent of the amount of the loan

Bank B: $1,000,000 revolving credit for one year at 10 percent with a fee of 1/2 percent on the unused balance of the loan

Bank C: $1,000,000 revolving credit for one year at 10 percent with a fee of 1/4 percent of the amount of the loan and 1/4 percent on the unused balance of the loan

Bank A requires a payment of $5,000 when the credit is granted, whether the revolving credit is or is not used. If the borrower lacks the $5,000, the borrower may have to use the credit to cover this fee. Bank B requires a payment of $5,000 only if the credit is not used. Obviously, this payment cannot be made when the loan is granted. (The bank often collects this fee monthly instead of waiting until the end of the year.) Bank C initially charges $2,500, with the balance dependent upon the use of the revolving credit.

Revolving credit agreements are used primarily by large firms, and the amount of the loans can be substantial. VF Corporation, the manufacturer of Wrangler jeans, Healthtex clothes, and Riders reported in its 2009 10-K report that it had an unsecured revolving credit loan of up to $1 billion. Because revolving credit loans can be substantial, the bank usually parcels out some of the loans so that a group of banks participate in the revolving credit agreement.

Revolving credit, like the line of credit, is used to finance short-term assets. However, the firm may also use revolving credit to finance the development of long-term assets. For example, the firm may draw on its revolving credit to pay for the construction of plant and equipment. After the plant is completed, the revolving credit is converted into an intermediate-term loan, or the firm may retire the outstanding balance on the revolving credit loan. This can be done through an issue of long-term bonds, new equity, or any other source of funds available to the borrower.

Cost of Commercial Bank Credit

The costs of the line of credit and revolving credit and their effective interest rates depend on the commitment fees charged, the interest paid, the amount borrowed, and how long the firm has the use of the funds. For example, a firm obtains revolving credit for $1,000,000 at 6 percent annually (0.5 percent monthly) plus a commitment fee of 3/4 percent on the *unused* balance. If the firm borrows the entire $1,000,000, the annual interest is $60,000. If the firm uses only $600,000 for the year, the interest cost will be $36,000 ($600,000 × 0.06) *plus* 3/4 percent of the unused balance of $400,000 ($400,000 × 0.0075 = $3,000). The total amount paid is $39,000 ($36,000 + 3,000) for the use of $600,000. If the firm does not use the credit, it must pay the $7,500 commitment fee, which is the cost of obtaining, but not using, the credit.

Prime rate

Interest rate charged
by commercial banks
on loans to their best
customers

In addition to the terms, the cost of a bank loan varies with the quality of the borrower. The bank's best credit risks are charged the prime rate. Other customers may be charged the prime plus a percentage, such as 2 percent. Thus, if the prime rate is 6.5 percent, the rate to other customers might be 8.5 percent. If the prime rate rises, the cost of other loans also rise, so any interest rate that is tied to the prime will vary as the prime rate varies.

During periods of tight money, the prime rate can rise very rapidly. For example, the prime rate was 11.5 percent in July 1979, 15.5 percent in December 1979, and 20 percent in April 1980. The increase from 11.5 percent to 20 percent occurred in *less than a year.* While the period July 1979 to April 1980 is unique, it does illustrate the potential volatility in short-term interest rates.

While commercial banks often quote a prime rate, some large corporate borrowers are able to negotiate loans at interest rates below the prime. Many commercial business loans made by the nation's largest banks are at a discount from the prime. This means that in effect there are two prime rates: the announced rate and the discounted rate, which is available to large corporate borrowers.

Since the effective cost of a commercial bank loan (or any loan) may not be the stated rate of interest, it is important to be able to determine the true, effective rate. This cost is related to the interest paid, the amount of funds that the borrower can use, and the term of the loan. The commercial bank can increase the cost of the loan by altering the amount that the borrower can use or by altering the length of time the loan is outstanding.

Equation 18.1 may be used to calculate the simple interest rate of a loan (i_{CB}) that is paid off *with interest at maturity.*

$$i_{CB} = \frac{\text{Interest paid}}{\substack{\text{Proceeds of the} \\ \text{loan that the borrower} \\ \text{may use}}} \times \frac{12}{\substack{\text{Number of months} \\ \text{that the firm has} \\ \text{use of the proceeds}}} \tag{18.1}$$

This equation is appropriate only if interest and any applicable fees are paid at the end of the period and the loan is not renewed, so there is no compounding (that is, it is simple and not compound interest).

How this equation may be used can be illustrated by a simple example in which a borrower obtains a $1,000 loan for a year and pays $60 in interest when the loan is repaid. In that case the rate of interest is

$$\frac{\$60}{\$1,000} \times \frac{12}{12} = 6\%.$$

Since the borrower has use of the $1,000 for the entire year and pays $60 for the use of the proceeds, the true rate of interest is 6 percent.

An alternative approach to determine the rate of interest expresses the problem in terms of the time value of money. This example has a single cash outflow and a single cash inflow. To calculate the rate of interest for the loan, rephrase the question as "What is the interest rate if I borrow $1,000 and re-pay $1,060 at the end of the year?" In this form, the calculation is

$$P_0(1 + i)^n = P_n$$

$$\$1,000(1 + i)^1 = \$1,060$$

$$1 + i = 1.06$$

$$i = 1.06 - 1 = 0.06 = 6\%.$$

The 6 percent is the same answer derived above, but this approach yields compound rates that are more accurate if the loan is renewed and compound interest, instead of simple interest, applies.

How commercial banks (or any lender) may increase the effective interest rate on a loan may be illustrated by using the previous simple example of a $1,000 loan with a $60 interest payment. For example, suppose the borrower must pay the interest up front (that is, the loan is discounted in advance). The borrower does not get to use $1,000 but receives $940 ($1,000 − 60). In effect the borrower is paying $60 for the use of $940, which increases the cost of the loan to

$$\frac{\$60}{\$940} \times \frac{12}{12} = 6.38\%.$$

The alternative calculation is

$$\$940(1 + i)^1 = \$1,000$$

$$1 + i = 1.0638$$

$$i = 1.06 - 1 = 0.0638 = 6.38\%.$$

The 6.38 percent is the same answer derived above. Notice that since the interest has already been paid, the cash outflow is the principal owed, $1,000, and not $1,060.

If the firm needs the entire $1,000, it will have to borrow more than $1,000 to have $1,000 to use. The amount of the loan necessary to cover the needed funds and the interest paid in advance is

$$\text{The amount of the loan} = \frac{\text{Funds needed}}{1.0 - \text{The stated rate of interest}} \qquad (18.2)$$
$$\text{(as a decimal)}$$

Thus the amount of the loan is $1,000/(1.0 − 0.06) = $1,063.83. The financial manager will have to borrow $1,063.83 to have the use of

CALCULATOR SOLUTION

Function Key	Data Input
PV =	−1000
FV =	1060
PMT =	0
N =	1
I =	?
Function Key	Answer
I =	6

CALCULATOR SOLUTION

Function Key	Data Input
PV =	−940
FV =	1000
PMT =	0
N =	1
I =	?
Function Key	Answer
I =	6.38

$1,000 and pay the interest in advance. This amount may be confirmed as follows:

Amount borrowed	$1,063.83
Interest paid in advance ($1,063.83 × 0.06)	63.83
Amount available	$1,000.00

Since the interest is $63.83 paid for the use of the $1,000 for the year, the effective interest rate is

$$\frac{\$63.83}{\$1,000} \times \frac{12}{12} = 6.38\%$$

or

$$\$100(1 + i)^1 = \$1,063.83$$

$$i = 6.38\%.$$

Notice that the interest paid is figured on the total amount borrowed but the effective rate of interest is based on the amount the borrower actually gets to use.

Another means for the bank to affect the cost of the loan is to require the borrower to pay an origination fee. For example, the bank may charge 1 percent to process the application and originate the loan. The $1,000 loan will require an immediate payment of $10, which, like discounting the loan in advance, reduces the amount the borrower may use.

If the firm needs the entire $1,000, it will have to borrow more than $1,000 to have $1,000 to use. The amount of the loan necessary to cover the needed funds and the interest paid in advance is

$$\text{The amount of the loan} = \frac{\text{Funds needed}}{1.0 - \text{The origination fee (as a decimal)}}.$$

Thus the amount of the loan is $1,000/(1.0 − 0.01) = $1,010.10. The financial manager will have to borrow $1,010.10 to have the use of $1,000 and pay interest of $60.60. The amount of the loan may be confirmed as follows:

Amount borrowed	$1,010.10
Origination fee ($1,010.10 × 0.01)	10.10
Amount available	$1,000.00

In addition to origination fees, commercial banks may charge a fee on the unused balance of a loan. For example, the borrower may arrange for a revolving line of credit for $1,000 at 6 percent with a fee on the unused balance. If the borrower uses only $600, the bank charges a fee on the unused balance of $400. In effect, the borrower has the option to borrow the money but does not exercise it. The bank is compensated by the interest charged on the amount borrowed and the fee on the unused balance. Thus, in this example if the fee is 2 percent of the unused balance and borrower uses $600 for the entire year, the total paid for the use of the $600 is $44 ($600 × 0.06 + $400 × 0.02). The interest rate is

$$\frac{\$44}{\$600} \times \frac{12}{12} = 7.33\%$$

or

$$\$600(1 + i)^1 = \$644$$

$$1 + i = 1.0733$$

$$i = 1.0733 - 1 = 0.0733 = 7.33\%.$$

Notice that the effective cost depends on (1) the interest paid plus the fee, (2) the amount borrowed, and (3) time, or how long the funds were borrowed. Notice also that the fee on the unused balance can be assessed only at the end of the time period. While origination fees are paid up front and subtracted from the amount the borrower may use, the fee on the unused balance is added to the interest paid to determine the effective cost of the loan.

In the previous example, the borrower used the $600 for the entire time period. That is rarely the case, because the amount borrowed (and the resulting unused balance) varies during the term of the loan. Suppose the borrower used the above loan as follows:

Months	Amount Borrowed	Unused Balance
1–3	$1,000	$ 0
4–9	300	700
10–12	0	1,000

The interest and fees for each period would be as follows:

Months	Amount Borrowed	Unused Balance
1–3	(0.25)(0.06)($1,000)	(0.25)(0.01)($0)
4–9	(0.50)(0.06)($300)	(0.50)(0.01)($700)
10–12	(0.00)(0.06)($0)	(0.25)(0.01)($1,000)

The total interest is $15 + 9 + 0 = $24, and the total fee is $0 + 3.50 + 2.5 = $6.00, so the total cost of the loan is $30. What is the interest rate? That depends on the amount borrowed, which is a weighted average:

$$(0.25)(\$1,000) + (0.5)(\$300) + (0.25)(\$0) = \$400$$

so the interest rate is $30/$400 = 7.5%. Once again the stated rate is less than the effective rate paid on the amount borrowed.

Trade Credit

Trade credit

Credit extended by suppliers to their customers

Trade credit is credit granted by a firm's suppliers and is the most important source of short-term finance for small firms. Trade credit arises when a supplier sells goods but does not demand immediate payment. Instead, the purchaser is permitted to choose between immediate payment and payment in the future. For immediate payment, or for payment within a short time period such as 10 days, the buyer may receive a discount, such as 2 percent off the purchase price. If the buyer does not remit during the first 10 days, payment in full must be made within a specified time period, such as 30 days. These terms are written 2/10, net 30, which means a 2 percent discount for payment within the first 10 days or the net (full) price within 30 days.

The impact of trade credit on the supplier's and the retailer's balance sheets is as follows:

Supplier		Retailer	
Assets	**Liabilities**	**Assets**	**Liabilities**
Accounts receivable ↑		Inventory ↑	Accounts payable ↑
Inventory ↓			

The supplier trades an account receivable for its inventory. The retailer's inventory is increased, which is a use of funds. This use must be balanced by a source. This source is the increase in accounts payable. The increase in liabilities finances the increase in inventory.

Trade credit may be very beneficial to a firm that must carry a large amount of inventory. As the firm expands its inventory, its suppliers expand their credit. The expansion of trade credit, then, is a *spontaneous* response to the expansion in inventory and comes automatically without the need for the firm to seek credit elsewhere. If the firm is able to turn over the inventory rapidly, it may obtain cash quickly enough to pay the suppliers without having to use other sources of credit. For example, if the terms of trade credit are net 30 (n30), the firm has the use of the goods for a month before payment is due. If the inventory turns over once a month, trade credit may be sufficient to cover the entire inventory. If the firm turns over the inventory only six times a year (every two months), trade credit will carry only one-half of the firm's inventory. Management must find other sources of financing to cover the inventory for the second month.

The important question that the financial manager must consider is whether trade credit is the best source of finance for carrying the inventory. This is the question of the cost of trade credit versus the cost and availability of other sources of finance. The cost of trade credit depends on the terms of the credit. If the terms are net 30 days (n30), the cost of the credit is nil. The supplier has built the cost of offering the credit into the price of the goods. Unless the financial manager can negotiate a discount for prompt payment, the firm should use the credit as extensively as possible, for there is no advantage to paying before the 30th day.

Cost of Trade Credit

If the terms are 2/10, net 30, trade credit is not free. It may appear that trade credit is free, for the supplier is permitting the buyer to use the goods for no explicit interest charge. That, however, is a misconception of what constitutes the *price* of the goods and the *interest charge*. In finance, the price of the product is the discounted price, since that is the price the buyer pays if cash is available. The full price, then, includes the discounted price plus a penalty for not paying the bill promptly. This penalty should be treated as the interest charge for the use of the goods. If an item costs $100 and is supplied under the terms 2/10, net 30, the price of the goods is $98, and the firm has 10 days in which to pay. If the firm does not pay within 10 days, there is a finance charge of $2 for the use of the goods for the next 20 days. When expressed in those terms, the interest charge becomes evident.

How expensive trade credit really is may be seen when the interest rate (i_{TC}) is expressed in annual terms. This calculation of the *simple interest rate* is given by Equation 18.3.

$$i_{TC} = \left(\frac{\text{Percentage discount}}{\substack{100\% \text{ minus} \\ \text{percentage discount}}} \right) \times \left(\frac{360}{\substack{\text{Payment period minus} \\ \text{discount period}}} \right) \quad (18.3)$$

The component parts of the equation are the percentage discount, the number of days for which the credit is extended (that is, the payment period minus the discount period), and 360, which is the term that converts the cost to an annualized basis. (The use of 360 is a common convenience that has the effect of understating the interest rate.) When the terms are substituted into this equation, the cost of credit is determined. For 2/10, n30, the cost of trade credit (i_{TC}) is

$$i_{TC} = \left(\frac{0.02}{1 - 0.02} \right) \left(\frac{360}{30 - 10} \right) = 36.7\%.$$

On an annual basis 2/10, n30 costs 36.7 percent, which is expensive compared with other sources of credit. Since 36.7 percent is a simple rate, the compound rate is even higher. (The computation of the compound rate will be illustrated subsequently.)

Equation 18.3 may be used to illustrate the factors that affect the cost of trade credit. As may be seen from the equation, the interest rate for trade credit is related to (1) the amount of the discount and (2) the length of time for which the buyer has the use of the goods. An increase in the amount of the discount increases the cost of trade credit. An increase in the payment period reduces the cost of trade credit.

An increase in the discount in effect reduces the price of the goods and increases the interest cost of carrying the goods on credit. If the discount were 3 percent instead of 2 percent (3/10, net 30) then the firm would pay $97 for the goods during the first 10 days and a $3 penalty for the use of the goods after the discount period. Using Equation 18.3, the interest rate is

$$i_{TC} = \left(\frac{0.03}{1 - 0.03}\right)\left(\frac{360}{30 - 10}\right) = 55.7\%.$$

The cost of trade credit is now 55.7 percent. The increase in the discount then increases the cost of trade credit, for the lost discount is larger (the interest charge is greater). Thus, if a supplier wants to induce prompt payment, one method is to increase the discount. This tells the buyer that credit is more expensive and should encourage the buyer to find credit elsewhere and pay the supplier promptly.

An increase in the payment period means that the buyer has the use of the goods longer, and thus the cost of trade credit is less. If the payment period is increased from 30 days to 60 days (2/10, net 30 to 2/10, net 60), the interest rate becomes

$$i_{TC} = \left(\frac{0.02}{1 - 0.02}\right)\left(\frac{360}{60 - 10}\right) = 14.7\%.$$

By lengthening the payment period from 30 to 60 days, the supplier has reduced the interest rate from 36.7 percent to 14.7 percent. The cause of this reduction in cost is, of course, the fact that the buyer has the use of the goods for 30 additional days. If a supplier wishes buyers to use trade credit, increasing the length of the payment period reduces the cost and encourages the increased use of trade credit.

The previous calculations understate the true annualized rates of interest, because they fail to consider the impact of compounding. If a supplier grants credit such as 2/10, n30 and collects the receivable after 20 days, the process may be repeated every 20 days. The supplier compounds the interest more than 18 times annually.

To determine the compound interest rate, treat the credit as a discounted note and rephrase 2/10, n30 into the following question: $98 at the beginning of the period (P_0) grows to $100 at the end of the time period (P_n) of 20 days *at what rate* (i)? That is,

$$P_0(1 + i)^n = P_n$$

in which n is the number of days in the credit period divided by 365. If the terms of credit are 2/10, n30, then n is 20/365, and the equation to be solved is

$$98(1 + i)^{20/365} = \$100.$$

The solution is

$$(1 + i)^{0.05479} = \$100/\$98 = 1.0204$$

$$i = (1.0204)^{18.25} - 1 = 1.4456 - 1 = 44.56\%.$$

The effective rate of interest is 44.56 percent when the interest is compounded 18.25 times a year.[1]

You may better perceive the process for determining the rate of interest if you rearrange the terms as follows:

$$i = (P_n/P_0)^{365/n} - 1. \qquad (18.4)$$

Notice that this calculation has several steps. First, divide the future amount by the present amount ($100/$98); second, raise that result by 365 divided by the number of days (365/20); and third, subtract 1.0. That is,

$$i = (\$100/\$98)^{365/20} - 1 = 44.56\%.$$

This general calculation may be used to determine the compound rate of interest for any terms of trade credit.

If a firm uses trade credit, when should it make payments? If a firm intends to pay the discount price, the payment should be made as late as possible during the discount period. The price that the seller is charging includes the cost of supplying the goods during the discount period. Thus, the purchaser should take advantage of this "free" use of the goods during the entire discount period. If the buyer is unable to make the payment by the end of the discount period, payment should be made at the end of the payment period. Once the discount period has passed, the buyer pays the cost of the trade credit. Nothing is gained by paying early. If early payment is made, the cost of trade credit is increased, for the buyer does not have the use of the credit for the entire period.

While the terms of trade credit set the cost of the credit, what affects these terms? Trade credit is competitive, and suppliers are aware that the terms they offer affect the sale of their products. By offering more generous terms, the supplier may increase sales. The terms of credit then become a means to differentiate one supplier from another. As each supplier tries to encourage sales by offering trade credit, the terms of the various offers should be similar, for competition will force the suppliers to offer comparable terms.

If trade credit tends to be expensive, why is it used? There are several explanations. First, it is convenient. By deferring payment until the end of the payment period, the buyer automatically receives the trade credit. Second, trade credit avoids sources of financial interrogation. A public offering of

---

[1] $(1.0204)^{18.25}$ may be determined by using an electronic calculator with a y^x key. Enter 1.0204; press the y^x key; enter 18.25; press =, and 1.4456 is derived. Then subtract: $1.4456 - 1 = 44.56\%$.

securities is subject to the securities laws, and a bank scrutinizes the financial condition of the borrower before a bank loan is granted. Trade credit, however, may come from suppliers who do not require the buyer to be subjected to this financial analysis. Third, the buyer may lack an alternative source of credit. While bank credit is almost inevitably cheaper, it may not be available. Suppliers, however, need outlets for their goods, and offering trade credit may be a way to assure buyers for their goods. These suppliers are usually larger firms with established sources of credit. They are able to borrow at cheaper rates from their sources and in turn pass on the credit to small retail firms by offering trade credit.

This section has covered the mechanics and cost of trade credit. In reality, trade credit may work differently. Buyers may stretch the terms of credit by either (1) remitting the discounted price after the payment period instead of the net price, or (2) "riding the credit" and paying after the payment period. This latter situation often occurs if the buyer has not sold the inventory and does not have the funds to pay the supplier. Such practices, of course, reduce the cost of credit because the firm has the use of the funds for a longer period of time. When such practices occur, the suppliers must decide whether to enforce the terms of the credit or be lenient and let the credit ride. In many cases the suppliers may not enforce the terms, for they need the retailers to purchase their goods. Such extensions of credit, however, cannot be indefinite. Eventually the supplier must decide how rapidly it wants to collect its accounts receivable. While suppliers may initially be lenient and not enforce the terms of trade, their cost of carrying the receivable eventually forces them to seek payment.

Commercial Paper

Commercial paper is an unsecured short-term promissory note issued by a corporation. The debt is issued in denominations of $100,000 or greater and usually matures in two to six months. It may have a maturity date as short as one day and rarely has a maturity date beyond nine months (270 days).

Since no specific assets back commercial paper, only companies with good credit ratings are able to issue this type of debt. Even though the paper is issued by large corporations with excellent credit ratings, an occasional default does occur. Perhaps the most celebrated example was Lehman in 2008. When the firm went bankrupt, it defaulted on its commercial paper. This failure inflicted large losses upon the buyers of the paper. And these losses then made it more difficult for other firms to sell their commercial paper.

Evidence of the quality of a firm's credit rating may be obtained through one of the credit rating services. These services and their respective ratings for commercial paper are

Moody's Investor Service: Prime 1 (P-1), Prime 2 (P-2), and Prime 3 (P-3);

Standard & Poor's Corporation: A1, A2, and A3;

Fitch Investors Service: F-1, F-2, and F-3.

P-1, A-1, and F-1 are the highest ratings, and these are obtained only by the best and most creditworthy firms.

While commercial paper is issued by a variety of firms, the primary users are finance companies and large bank holding companies, which account for about three-fourths of all commercial paper sold. The rest is issued by manufacturers and utilities. Manufacturers may use it as a source of funds to meet seasonal needs, and utilities may issue commercial paper to help finance construction of plant and equipment. After the construction is completed, the firm sells new debt or equity, and the proceeds of the sale are used to retire the commercial paper. In this case the commercial paper is being used as a temporary source of funds prior to the firm's obtaining more permanent financing.

Firms may issue commercial paper and sell it directly to buyers (*direct paper*). Direct sales require a sales staff or the service of an investment banker to place the paper. Such direct sales require sufficient volume of commercial paper to justify the sales expense and constitute the bulk of commercial paper issued. The remaining sales are made through dealers (*dealer paper*). These dealers charge for selling the paper (for example, $1,250 for $1 million principal amount).

Commercial paper is purchased by banks, insurance companies, financial institutions, pension funds, trust departments, and companies that have excess liquidity and need a safe short-term investment. Individual investors rarely have a sufficient amount of money to participate in the market for commercial paper, since it is issued in large denominations, such as $100,000 or $1,000,000. Of course, individuals indirectly participate by purchasing shares of money market mutual funds, which in turn buy commercial paper.

For large corporations, commercial paper is a substitute for other types of short-term debt and is usually cheaper than bank loans. The interest cost is generally about 0.5 percent less than the prime rate. Unlike bank loans, commercial paper does not have restrictive convenants. This is particularly true for paper with the highest credit ratings. However, the investment community frequently requires that the issuing firm have unused credit lines at a bank to support the paper. To get these credit lines, the firm may have to pay a commitment fee. Thus, to sell commercial paper the firm must still bear the cost of obtaining a credit line, but other restrictions often required by banks are not placed on the firm.

Commercial paper does not pay a stated amount of interest and is another example of a discounted note. A $1 million 180-day note may be sold for $970,000. When the paper matures, the firm retires $1 million of debt and thus pays $30,000 for the use of $970,000 for six months (180 days). To figure the interest rate, Equation 18.1, which was used earlier to calculate the cost of a bank loan, may be rephrased and used to calculate the cost of commercial paper. In this example, the *simple, annual interest rate* on commercial paper (i_{CP}) is

$$i_{CP} = \frac{\text{Interest}}{\text{Proceeds used}} \times \frac{12}{\text{Number of months paper is outstanding}}$$

$$= \frac{\$30,000}{\$970,000} \times \frac{12}{6} = 6.19\%.$$

If the paper is sold for $940,000, the simple interest rate rises to

$$i_{CP} = \frac{\$60,000}{\$940,000} \times \frac{12}{6} = 12.77\%,$$

because the firm now pays $60,000 for the use of $940,000, while in the previous example it paid $30,000 for the use of $970,000.

As with the cost of trade credit, this calculation is an oversimplification, because it does not consider the impact of compounding. This omission is corrected by rephrasing the problem as follows: $970,000 grows to $1,000,000 in 180 days at what rate? The answer is

$$\$970,000(1 + i)^{180/365} = \$1,000,000,$$

so, the *compound interest rate* is

$$(1 + i)^{180/365} = \$1,000,000/\$970,000 = 1.03093$$

$$i = (1.03093)^{2.0278} - 1 = 1.0637 - 1 = 6.37\%.$$

If the 180-day paper were sold for $940,000, the rate would be

$$(1 + i)^{180/365} = \$1,000,000/\$940,000 = 1.0638$$

$$i = (1.0638)^{2.0278} - 1 = 1.1336 - 1 = 13.36\%.$$

In these illustrations, the compound rates of interest are only slightly higher than the simple rates (6.37 percent versus 6.19 percent and 13.36 percent versus 12.77 percent). Compounding makes a difference, but the difference is small since commercial paper with a term of 180 days compounds only twice a year. Obviously, commercial paper with a shorter maturity (30 days or less) compounds more frequently, and the impact of such compounding increases the difference between the simple and compound rates.

Even after adjusting for compounding, the rate may still understate the true cost of the paper. If the firm pays a dealer a fee to sell the paper, the proceeds of the sale are reduced, which raises the cost. If the issuer must maintain a credit line with a commercial bank in order to sell the paper, the costs associated with the credit line also reduce the amount of cash the issuer can use from the sale of the paper. Once again, these expenses raise the cost of borrowing through the issuance of commercial paper.

Secured Loans

An alternative to trade credit and unsecured commercial paper is the secured loan. Inventory, accounts receivable, or any other sound short-term asset (for example, a government security) may be used to secure a short-term loan. This collateral serves to protect the lender who has a lien against the asset. This security should increase the availability of credit and reduce the interest cost of the loan to the borrower.

Secured loans are made by commercial banks and insurance companies. These lenders make their profits through the lending process; they do not want to take title to the pledged assets. If they are forced to take the pledged asset, they can choose either to hold the asset or to liquidate it. Liquidation may not bring the face value of the asset; thus, the lender will not grant a loan for the entire value of the pledged asset. Instead, the bank or finance company may lend some proportion, such as 70 percent of the asset's stated value. The borrower must have some equity in the asset that will be lost in case of default and seizure of the asset.

The amount that the creditor will lend against the pledged asset depends on the quality of the pledged asset, the ease with which the asset can be liquidated should the debtor default, the anticipated sale value, and the transaction costs of liquidation. A firm's short-term assets are not equally desirable for pledging against short-term loans. Inventory is less liquid than accounts receivable (especially raw materials and work-in-process). Hence, creditors may be less willing to accept inventory than accounts receivable as collateral to secure short-term loans.

Inventory Loans

When inventory is pledged to secure a loan, one of three general types of agreement is used. In the first type of agreement, the lender receives a lien against all of the borrower's inventory. Such an agreement is a *blanket inventory loan* because it covers all of the inventory. The second type of inventory loan is a *trust receipt*. The borrower holds specified inventory in trust for the lender. As these goods are sold, the borrower remits the proceeds to the lender to retire the loan.

The third type of loan secured by inventory involves a third party (in addition to the borrower and the lender). The pledged inventory is placed in a warehouse controlled by the third party. When purchase orders for the merchandise are received, the borrower informs the lender of the pending sales. The lender instructs the warehouse to deliver the goods, and the proceeds of the sale are then used to repay the loan. Such *warehouse financing* obviously reduces the risk of loss to the creditor, because the creditor has effective control over the goods. The warehouse will release the inventory only on the instructions of the lender.

Just as warehouse financing is advantageous to lenders, it can also have advantages for borrowers. Manufacturers know that finished goods may not be sold as soon as they are available for sale. (If finished goods were sold that quickly, the need to finance them would be limited to the time required to convert the raw materials into finished goods.) Obviously, the goods have to be stored until they are sold and delivered. Unless the firm uses its own facilities, it will store the inventory at a warehouse and pay for the space. Thus, the warehouse may offer the manufacturer both space and the custodial service that facilitate financing the inventory.

Accounts Receivable Loans

When accounts receivable are used to help obtain short-term financing, the firm may either pledge the accounts to secure the loan or sell them outright for cash. When the accounts are pledged, the borrower retains them and, of course, must collect them. If an account cannot be collected, the firm still owes the bank or finance company the amount of the loan that was secured by the account.

The lender is aware that not all accounts receivable may be collected. If an account does not meet the lender's standards, it is not accepted as collateral for a loan. The lender realizes that if a buyer were to default on the receivable, the seller (the borrower and owner of the account receivable) might not be able to pay off the loans. By refusing to accept riskier accounts receivable as collateral, lenders protect themselves from the risk of loss.

Pledging short-term assets offers the firm a cost advantage over other sources of finance. The security for the loan reduces the cost of obtaining short-term financing from finance companies, and secured loans are cheaper than trade credit. Secured credit from finance companies is generally more expensive than credit from commercial banks, but it has the advantage of avoiding the restrictions placed on the firm by commercial banks. While these restrictions may not have stated costs, the management may believe that there are implicit costs in the restrictions and avoid bank credit when other sources of short-term financing exist. Bank credit can then be used in addition to secured credit should the need arise.

Factoring

Each of the preceding sources created liabilities. Notes payable to the bank, accounts payable to suppliers, and commercial paper are liabilities that the firm must repay. Sources of funds, however, are not limited to increases in liabilities. A decrease in an asset is also a cash inflow. Selling an asset is also a source of funds, and those funds may be used to meet the firm's obligations as they come due.

Factoring

Selling accounts receivable

Factoring is selling accounts receivable. The cash received is an inflow just as borrowing funds from a commercial bank is a cash inflow. The firm sells its receivable to a "factor" at a discount, so the factor's source of return on the investment in the receivables is the discount.

As in the case of trade credit, the firm selling the receivables should view the amount received as the loan and lost discount as the interest. Suppose a firm sells goods for $100 with n30 as the terms of credit. The $100 will not be collected for 30 days, so management sells the receivables to a factor for $95. In this illustration, the loan is $95 and the interest paid is $5. When expressed in this manner, factoring is an expensive cost of short-term financing. The simple interest rate is

$$\frac{\$5}{\$95} \times \frac{360}{30} = 63.2\%$$

and the compound rate is

$$\$95(1 + i)^{36/365} = \$100$$

$$i = (\$100/\$95)^{365/30} - 1 = 1.0526^{12.1667} - 1 = 86.6\%.$$

If the receivables had been sold for a higher price (smaller discount) the interest cost would have been lower, but the interest rate would have been even higher if the sale price were lower.

Unfortunately, determining the true interest cost is not as easy as the previous illustration suggests because the amount of the discount is not the only consideration. When the receivables are sold, the factor becomes responsible for collecting them. The selling firm saves the collection costs, which reduces the interest rate. The factor, however, may not be willing to accept the risk associated with collecting the receivables and demands recourse in case of default. As long as the receivables are collected, recourse is not a problem for either the selling firm or the factor. But, in the case of default, the factor has passed the risk and collection costs back to the seller.

Other considerations also affect the cost of factoring. The factor may not remit the entire sale price if the factor anticipates default. Part of the funds may be held in reserve against default and remitted only after the receivable is collected. The factor may charge a commission for executing the transaction to cover the costs of credit checks and collections. Holding a reserve and charging a commission increase the effective cost of factoring. These considerations also increase the difficulty of comparing the cost of factoring with the cost of other sources of short-term funds.

Factoring may also be considered a type of treadmill; once you are on, it is difficult to get off. Suppose a firm normally uses the collection of its receivables to pay its bills. In January the firm sells goods on credit (n30) and uses the collections to pay February's bills. February's credit sales are used to cover March's bills, and the process is repeated. For some reason, management needs short credit in January and sells the receivables. What happens in February? The receivables that would normally be collected during February have been sold and February's credit sales will not be collected until March. Management then factors February's receivables to meet current obligations. The problem occurs again in March. Once the receivables have been factored, the process becomes selfsustaining. Unless management can find another source of funds, the factoring treadmill continues indefinitely into the future.

Summary The management of a firm's current assets and liabilities is one of the most important facets of the financial manager's job. The firm must meet its current obligations as they come due or face bankruptcy. Short-term debt (current liabilities) is a major source of finance for current operations, but it is also a potential problem since it must be frequently retired or rolled over.

The major sources of short-term funds are loans from commercial banks, trade credit, commercial paper, secured loans, and factoring. Commercial banks grant short-term loans (promissory notes), lines of credit, and revolving term credit agreements. These short-term loans may be converted into intermediate-term or mortgage loans upon maturity. Banks increase the interest cost to the borrower by discounting loans in advance and by charging origination fees and fees on a credit line's unused balance.

Many firms use trade credit, which is spontaneously generated through purchases of inventory. The seller grants the credit (an account receivable to the seller and an account payable for the borrower) to encourage the sale. Trade credit is a particularly important source of credit for small retailers who lack other sources of short-term finance. The terms of credit (such as 2/10, net 30) establish the cost of this credit, but many firms attempt to ride their accounts payable, which reduces the cost of trade credit.

Large, creditworthy firms are able to issue commercial paper, which consists of unsecured promissory notes sold in large denominations through dealers or directly placed with buyers. Commercial paper is sold for a discount. At maturity the issuing firms pay the principal, so the cost of the paper to the issuing firm depends upon how long the security is outstanding and the difference between the discounted price and the principal amount.

Firms may also factor (sell) accounts receivable to raise cash, and they may pledge current assets, such as inventory or accounts receivable, as collateral for loans. These secured loans are for less than the value of the collateral, because the creditors do not want to take title to the collateral, and liquidation will rarely bring the face value of the asset. Without this reduction in risk, it is doubtful that the lenders would be willing to grant the short-term credit.

Factoring is selling accounts receivable. The sale is a cash inflow, and these funds may be used to meet financial obligations. The cost of factoring primarily depends on the amount of the discount necessary to sell the receivables. Other determinants of the cost include savings in collection expenses, commissions charged by the factor, and any reserve held to cover receivables that are not collected. The total cost associated with factoring suggests that it is an expensive source of short-term funds.

Review Objectives

Now that you have completed this chapter, you should be able to

1. Distinguish among commercial bank loans, trade credit, and commercial paper as a source of funds (pp. 420, 426, and 430).

2. List common features of a commercial bank loan (pp. 419–421).

3. Explain why trade credit is a spontaneous source of funds (p. 426).

4. Estimate the interest rate paid on a commercial bank loan, trade credit, and commercial paper (422–425, 427–429, and 431–432).

5. Explain why trade credit is a source of credit for many firms while commercial paper is a source for larger, creditworthy companies (pp. 430–432).

6. Illustrate how pledging an asset may be used as a source of short-term financing (pp. 432–434).

7. Identify why factoring may be an expensive source of funds (pp. 434–435).

Problems

1. Firm A borrows $1 million from a commercial bank. The bank charges an annual rate of 10 percent and requires a 3 percent origination fee. How much does the firm have to borrow to have $1 million? Confirm your answer and determine the effective rate of interest. (Assume the loan is outstanding for one year.)

2. Tinker, Inc. finances its seasonal working capital need with short-term bank loans. Management plans to borrow $65,000 for a year. The bank has offered the company a 3.5 percent discounted loan with a 1.5 percent origination fee. What are the interest payment and the origination fee required by the loan? What is the rate of interest charged by the bank?

3. You can borrow $5,000 for 60 days with an interest payment of $125. What is the simple rate of interest? What is the compound rate of interest?

4. Stella & Chloe, Inc. needs to borrow $2,000,000 for six months. It can sell 180-day commercial paper with a face value of $2,000,000 for $1,900,000 or borrow the money from a commercial bank at 10 percent. In both cases the interest is $100,000. Which loan is more expensive and why?

5. An individual wishes to borrow $10,000 for a year and is offered the following alternatives:

   a. A 10 percent loan discounted in advance

   b. An 11 percent straight loan (i.e., interest paid at maturity)

   Which loan is more expensive?

6. Which of the following terms of trade credit is the more expensive?

   a. A 3 percent cash discount if paid on the 15th day with bill due on the 45th day 3/15, net 45)

   b. A 2 percent cash discount if paid on the 10th day with the bill due on the 30th day 2/10, net 30)

7. Trade credit may be stated as n60 plus 18 percent on the balance outstanding after two months. What is the cost of this credit?

8. Dash Construction needs to borrow $200,000 for 45 days in order to take advantage of the cash discount of 3/10, n55 offered by a supplier. Dash Construction can borrow the funds from a bank with an interest payment of $5,000 at the maturity of the loan. Should management borrow the funds from the bank to take advantage of the discount?

9. If $1 million face amount of commercial paper (270-day paper) is sold for $982,500, what is the simple rate of interest being paid? What is the compound annual rate?

10. A financial manager may sell $1 million of six-month commercial paper for $950,000 or borrow $1 million for six months from a commercial bank for 10 percent annually and a 2 percent origination fee. Which set of terms is more expensive?

11. Bank A offers the following terms for a $10 million loan:
    - interest rate: 8 percent for one year on funds borrowed
    - fees: 0.5 percent of the unused balance for the unused term of the loan

    Bank B offers the following terms for a $10 million loan:
    - interest rate: 6.6 percent for one year on funds borrowed
    - fees: 2 percent origination fee

    a. Which terms are better if the firm intends to borrow the $10 million for the entire year?
    b. If the firm plans to use the funds for only three months, which terms are better?

12. A commercial bank offers you a $200,000 annual line of credit with the following terms:
    - origination fee: $2,000 paid when the line is accepted
    - fees: 1 percent on unused balance, paid at the end of the year
    - interest rate: 9 percent

    What is the effective cost of the loan
    a. if you expect to borrow the entire $200,000 for the year?
    b. if you expect to borrow the $200,000 for only three months?

13. Little Store buys inventory using trade credit. The terms are stated as 2/10, n30, but Little Store *rides the credit* and generally *pays on the 40th day*. Occasionally, payment is made as late as the 50th day. What is the approximate cost of the credit
    a. if paid on time?
    b. if paid on the 40th day?
    c. if paid on the 50th day?

    What is the compound cost of credit in each case? Why does the cost change?

14. High Time's suppliers tend to offer generous terms of trade credit (2/30, n90), but High Time can also issue commercial paper, receive $0.978, and repay $1.00 at the end of 60 days. What are the compound interest rates offered by the two alternatives? What would be the impact if High Time's suppliers changed the terms to n30?

1. What is the simple interest rate on a $1,000 loan for six months if the borrower pays $55 in interest at the maturity of the loan?

2. How much must a firm borrow if it needs $2,300,000 and the originating fee is 2 percent?

3. What is the cost of 3/20, n60?

4. What is the effective rate of interest if $96,382 is borrowed and the borrower pays $100,000 after 95 days?

5. What is the approximate, simple interest rate on $1,000,000 three-month (i.e., 90-day) commercial paper that is sold for $987,654? What is the compound, annual rate of interest?

6. What is the effective, compound rate of interest you pay if you sell (factor) $100,000 worth of accounts receivable for $97,400, and terms of the credit sales are n60?

7. What is the effective, compound rate of interest you earn if you buy $100,000 worth of accounts receivable for $97,400, and terms of the credit sales are n60?

Answers

1. The simple interest rate:

$$i_{CB} = (\$55/\$1,000) \times (12/6) = 11\%.$$

2. The amount of a loan necessary to cover the desired funds plus any originating fee is

Funds needed/(1.0 − originating fee as a decimal)

$$\$2,300,000/(1.0 − .02) = \$2,346,938.78.$$

If the firm borrows $2,346,938.78, it will cover the origination fee (1.02 × $2,346,938.78 = $46,938.78) and have $2,300,000 to use.

3. Cost of trade credit (i_{TC}):

$$i_{TC} = \text{percentage discount}/(100\% − \text{discount})$$
$$\times 360/(\text{payment minus the discount period})$$
$$= .03/(1 − .03) \times 360/(60 − 20) = 27.8\%.$$

4. The effective, compound rate of interest on a discounted note:

$$i = (P_n/P_0)^{365/n} - 1$$

$$i = (\$100,000/\$96,382)^{365/95} - 1 = 15.2\%.$$

5. The simple rate of interest (i_{CP}):

$$i_{CP} = \frac{\text{interest}}{\text{proceeds used}} \times \frac{12}{\text{number of months paper is outstanding}}$$

$$i_{CP} = (\$12,346)/(\$987,654) \times (\$12/3) = 5\%.$$

The effective, compound rate of interest:

$$i = (\$100,000/\$987,654)^{365/90} - 1 = 5.17\%.$$

6. and 7. These problems are identical except that 6 illustrates the cost of selling the receivables and 7 illustrates the return the buyer earns. It is important to remember that the cost to one of the parties (the borrower) is the source of the return to the other party (the lender).

Effective, compound rate of interest:

$$i = (\$100,000/\$97,4006)^6 - 1 = 17.12\%.$$

Relationships

1. An increase in a commitment fee _____ the cost of a loan.

2. An increase in a compensating balance _____ the cost of a loan.

3. A change in the terms of credit from 2/10, n30 to 3/10, n30 _____ the cost of a loan.

4. A change in the terms of credit from n30 to n60 _____ the cost of a loan.

5. An increase in the discount _____ the cost of carrying inventory.

6. If commercial paper sells for a smaller discount, the return _____.

7. If accounts receivable are sold to a factor for a larger discount, the implied interest cost _____.

8. An increase in inventory _____ total asset turnover.

9. An increase in accruals _____ the firm's need for external finance.

Answers

1. increases
2. increases
3. increases
4. does not affect (no change) There is no lost discount.
5. increases
6. decreases
7. increases
8. decreases
9. decreases

CHAPTER

19

Intermediate-Term Debt and Leasing

The previous chapter covered various short-term sources of finance, commercial bank loans, trade credit, commercial paper, secured loans, and factoring. Chapters 22 through 25 will cover a variety of long-term, fixed-income securities ranging from straight bonds to convertible bonds and preferred stock. Between these extremes are intermediate-term bonds and leasing. Intermediate-term debt ranges from 5 to 10 years and is obtained through commercial banks and insurance companies. Term notes may also be sold to the general public.

Some firms own properties in order to lease the properties to others. Washington Real Estate Trust owns office buildings, industrial centers, apartments, and shopping centers in the Washington, D.C., area and rents the space to stores such as Williams-Sonoma, Laura Ashley, and Giant Food. These retail establishments want the use of the asset but not ownership. They prefer to lease the space instead of buying and operating the buildings.

The term of a lease may range from a short period such as a year or two to many years. Since leases create legal obligations (the lease payments), they are an alternative to short-, intermediate-, and long-term debt as a source of funds. This chapter describes the terms of a lease and illustrates the basic analysis of leasing versus borrowing and buying the asset. Since leases are an alternative to debt financing, this section also covers when lease obligations must be capitalized and placed on the firm's balance sheet as a debt obligation.

Intermediate-Term Debt

Intermediate-term debt

Debt instrument with 5 to 10 years to maturity

While accountants classify all liabilities as either short-term (due in less than one year) or long-term (due in more than one year), debt can also be classified as short-term, intermediate-term, or long-term. Intermediate-term debt is outstanding for more than a year (and hence appears as long-term debt on the firm's balance sheet), but it matures quicker than long-term debt. While long-term bonds may mature 20, 25, or 30 years after being issued, most intermediate-term debt will mature in 5 to 10 years.

Intermediate-term debt issued by corporations and sold to the general public may be referred to as "notes" to differentiate it from the bonds of the corporation, which are long-term debt. For example, in July 2008, H. J. Heinz issued $500 million of 5.35 percent notes due in 2013 (5 years to maturity). Different terminology may be used when intermediate-term debt is obtained from a commercial bank or an insurance company. Such debt is often referred to as a term loan.

Term loan

Loan obtained from a bank or insurance company for a period of 5 to 10 years

Term loans are usually secured by equipment or real estate. Commercial banks, which make term loans of 1 to 5 years' duration, generally require that the loan be secured by equipment. Insurance companies, which tend to make term loans of from 5 to 15 years, generally use real estate as collateral for the loan.

In addition to the collateral, term loans have restrictive covenants that are negotiated between the debtor and the creditor. Common restrictions include a minimum current ratio such as 2.0:1, or a minimum amount of net working capital (that is, the difference between current assets and current liabilities must exceed some specified dollar amount). The creditors also require periodic financial statements from the borrower and may require prior approval before the debtor can issue additional debt. While these restrictive covenants are common in term loan agreements, they do not exhaust all the possibilities, as each loan is individually negotiated. Conditions in the credit markets and the relative strengths of the parties also affect the terms.

Term loans are generally retired in periodic payments and hence are like mortgage loans. The repayment schedules call for the payment of interest and the retirement of the principal. For example, a firm buys equipment that costs $12,000 and has an expected life of 5 years. The firm arranges a term loan with a commercial bank. The following conditions apply:

1. a down payment of 20 percent of the cost of the equipment
2. five equal annual payments to pay the interest and retire the loan
3. a 9 percent interest rate on the declining balance
4. the loan to be secured by the equipment

The first condition establishes the amount that the bank is willing to loan. Notice that the bank does not lend the entire amount; the borrower must put up $2,400 ($0.20 \times \$12,000$) and the bank finances the balance, $9,600. Terms 2 and 3 establish the rate of interest and the payment schedule. The fourth term designates the equipment as collateral against the loan and gives the bank the right to take the equipment and sell it should the debtor default.

The repayment schedule is determined as follows. The borrower must make equal payments so that the bank earns 9 percent annually and the loan is retired in 5 years. This is another illustration of the time value of money. The equation necessary to solve this problem (that is, to determine the annual payments) is

$$\$9,600 = \frac{PMT}{(1 + 0.09)^1} + \frac{PMT}{(1 + 0.09)^2} + \frac{PMT}{(1 + 0.09)^3} + \frac{PMT}{(1 + 0.09)^4}$$
$$+ \frac{PMT}{(1 + 0.09)^5}.$$

This is an example of an annuity, so the problem collapses to:

$$PMT(PVAIF\ 9I,\ 5N) = \$9,600$$
$$PMT(3.890) = \$9,600$$
$$PMT = \$9,600/3.890 = \$2,467.87.$$

Thus, $2,467.87 is the annual payment that retires this loan and pays 9 percent of the declining balance.

The actual payment schedule and the division of the payment into interest payment and principal reduction are given in Exhibit 19.1. This table is essentially the same as the mortgage loan amortization schedule illustrated in Exhibit 7.2 (page 124) in Chapter 7. In both examples, the amount of the interest declines with each payment as the outstanding balance on the loan is reduced. Conversely, the amount of the principal repayment rises with each payment as the interest payment is reduced.

Generally, the depreciation of the equipment and the resulting cash flow cover the required loan payments. In this case, the annual straight-line depreciation expense would be $2,400 ($12,000/5). The cash flow generated by this $2,400 noncash depreciation expense is approximately equal to the

EXHIBIT 19.1
Repayment Schedule for a $9,600 Term Loan at 9 Percent for Five Years

Year	Payment	Interest	Principal Retirement	Balance Owed on Loan
1	$2,467.87	$864.00	$1,603.87	$7,996.13
2	2,467.87	719.65	1,748.22	6,247.91
3	2,467.87	562.31	1,905.56	4,342.35
4	2,467.87	390.81	2,077.06	2,265.29
5	2,467.87	203.87	2,264.00	1.29*

*The $1.29 results from rounding off in using the interest tables. The $2,468.09 payment determined by the financial calculator avoids this error.

EXHIBIT 19.2
Repayment Schedule for a
$9,600 Term Loan at
9 Percent with Equal
Principal Repayments

Year	Principal Repayment	Interest	Balance of Loan	Total Payment
1	$1,920	$864.00	$7,680	$2,784.00
2	1,920	691.20	5,760	2,611.20
3	1,920	518.40	3,840	2,438.40
4	1,920	345.60	1,920	2,265.60
5	1,920	172.80	0	2,092.80

$2,467.87 payment required by the loan. (In many cases accelerated depreciation is used so that the initial depreciation expense is increased.) By matching the repayment schedule with the cash flow, the firm enhances its capacity to service the debt.

Since each loan is individually negotiated between the borrower and the lender, a variety of possible terms exist. One possibility is for the lender to require equal principal repayments with interest being computed on the remaining balance for each period. The repayment schedule under these terms for the $9,600 term loan is presented in Exhibit 19.2. In this case, the principal is retired in five equal installments of $1,920 ($9,600/5 = $1,920 in the second column). The amount of interest (column 3) depends on the balance owed (column 4). Thus, the payment in the second year is the sum of the principal repayment ($1,920) plus the interest on the balance owed at the end of the first year ($691.20), for a total payment of $2,611.20 (column 5).

Other possible terms include no principal repayment until the loan is due at the end of the fifth year. In this case, the firm would annually remit the $864 interest payment, and at the end of the fifth year make the last interest payment plus the principal repayment ($864 + $9,600 = $10,464). The lender could combine the two previous illustrations and annually require a partial principal repayment (for example, $1,000 annually) with the balance of $4,600 ($9,600 − $5,000) paid at the end of the term of the loan. Such a lump repayment at the end of a loan is referred to as a balloon payment.

Balloon payment

Large, single payment to retire a debt obligation at maturity

Although firms obtain intermediate-term credit from banks and insurance companies, intermediate-term securities may be sold to the general public. Notes sold to the general public are not collateralized, while term loans usually are, and generally the notes do not have a compulsory repayment schedule. Such notes are really more similar to long-term bonds than to term loans. However, these notes may have specific features that make them attractive to investors. The intermediate term (for example, 7 years) may make these notes attractive to investors who do not want to make investments for a longer term (such as 20 years). In addition, intermediate-term notes frequently cannot be called and refunded before maturity. Since the notes lack a call feature, the investor knows that the firm cannot force the buyer to give up the security should interest rates fall. Many long-term bonds are called and refunded when long-term interest rates fall, so this noncallability of intermediate-term notes assures investors of their interest income (if no default) for the term of the notes.

Leasing

Lessee

Firm that rents (leases) property or equipment for its own use

Lessor

Firm that owns property or equipment and rents it (leases the equipment) to other firms or individuals (the lessees)

Lease

Renting (as opposed to owning) property or equipment; the contract between the lessee and the lessor

Operating lease

Lease for the use and maintenance of equipment in which the term is less than the expected life of the asset

Financial (capital) lease

Lease in which the term is equal to the expected life of the asset

Direct lease

Lease agreement in which the owner (the lessor) directly leases the asset to the user (the lessee)

Sale and leaseback

Financial agreement in which a firm sells an asset such as a building for cash and subsequently rents (leases) that asset

Leasing is essentially renting, and the two terms are often interchanged. Since lease contracts may cover any time period, lease financing may be an alternative to short- or long-term debt.

A lease contract is for the use of an asset such as plant or equipment. Firms want the use of the asset. They use the capital budgeting techniques (net present value and internal rate of return) to determine which investments are profitable. After deciding which investments to make, they must decide how to finance the asset. Notice that it is the use of the asset that the firm desires and not necessarily title to the asset. Leasing permits the firm (lessee) to *use the asset without acquiring title*, which is retained by the owner (the lessor). In return, the lessee enters into a contract (the lease) to make specified payments for the use of the asset.

Leases take one of two forms. An operating lease provides the lessee with the use of the asset and may include a maintenance contract. The cost of servicing the equipment is built into the lease. The contract may be canceled after proper notice if the lessee wants to change equipment. This type of lease is primarily used for renting equipment, cars, and trucks. The length of the lease is less than the expected life of the asset but the lease may be renewed. Since the lease is not for the life of the asset, the lessor anticipates either having the lease renewed or selling the asset at the lease's expiration.

A financial lease, which may also be referred to as a capital lease, differs from an operating lease in several significant ways. These contracts are not cancelable and do not include a service clause. The duration of a financial lease is the expected life of the asset. The lease payments cover the cost of the asset and earn a set return for the lessor. Thus, a financial lease is similar to debt financing. If the firm had issued bonds to obtain the funds to acquire the asset, the payments to the bondholders would cover the cost of the equipment plus their return (the rate of interest). Of course, if debt had been used, the firm would own the asset, while with leasing it does not acquire title. This difference is important if at the end of the asset's life there is residual value that accrues to the asset's owner.

While there are two classes of leases, there are three types of lease agreements. From the viewpoint of the lessee, the type of lease agreement is immaterial; the firm still acquires the use of the asset. The type of lease has an impact only on the lessor. The first type of lease agreement is the direct lease. The lessor owns the asset and directly leases it to the lessee. Direct leases are offered by manufacturers who build the asset, such as IBM, as well as by finance companies and leasing companies that acquire assets with the intent to lease them to prospective users.

The second type of lease is a sale and leaseback. Under this type of agreement, the firm that owns the asset sells it to the lessor and then leases it back. The selling firm receives cash from the sale to the lessor that can be put to other uses but still retains the use of the asset. The lessee, however, relinquishes title to the asset and thus loses any residual value that the asset might have. And, of course, the firm must now make the lease payments.

Leveraged lease

Lease agreement in which the lessor acquires an asset (which it subsequently leases) through the use of debt financing

The third type of lease is a leveraged lease. Since the lessor owns the asset, that firm must have the funds to acquire it. In a leveraged lease the lessor borrows part of the funds necessary to acquire the asset. For example, a finance company may borrow from a commercial bank so that it may acquire an asset that it in turn leases to the ultimate users. If financial leverage is favorable, the lessor will increase the return on its funds invested in the asset.

Lease or Purchase

The question of whether it is better to buy or to lease depends on several crucial variables. These include the firm's tax bracket, the terms of the lease, the asset's anticipated residual value, and the cost of obtaining funds to buy the asset. While this introductory text cannot develop this topic, the following example will provide some of the essential information necessary to make the choice.

A firm decides to acquire equipment that costs $5,000. The equipment has an expected life of five years, after which the equipment will be sold for an expected salvage value of $500. Depreciation will be straight-line. (The firm would use accelerated depreciation if possible, and the depreciation expense would start after six months have elapsed. These normal conditions are ignored to simplify the illustration.) Maintenance is expected to be $200 annually, and the firm's tax rate is 40 percent. The purchase is financed entirely with a $5,000 loan that is retired through an annual $1,285 payment covering interest and principal (that is, the payments are a mortgage schedule). The annual cash outflows and inflows are shown in Exhibit 19.3.

Initially, there is an immediate cash $5,000 outflow to pay for the equipment but that is covered by the loan, so there is no immediate cash outflow. At the end of the first year, there is a $200 cash outflow for maintenance, $450 for interest, and $835 for principal repayment, for a total of $1,485. Notice that the $1,000 depreciation is not a cash outflow because it is a noncash expense.

EXHIBIT 19.3
Determination of Cash Outflows from Owning

Year	0	1	2	3	4	5
Purchase price	$5,000					
Amount of the loan	$5,000					
Maintenance		$ 200	200	200	200	200
Depreciation		$1,000	1,000	1,000	1,000	1,000
Interest payment		$450	375	293	204	106
Principal repayment		$835	911	993	1,082	1,179
Tax-deductible expenses		$1,650	1,575	1,493	1,404	1,306
Tax savings		$660	630	597	562	522
Sale of asset after tax						300
Cash outflows before tax	$0	1,485	1,486	1,486	1,486	1,485
Cash outflows after tax	$0	825	856	889	924	663

The outflows are partially offset by the tax savings that result from tax-deductible expenses. These expenses are the $200 maintenance, the $450 interest, and the $1,000 depreciation. Notice the principal repayment is not tax deductible. The sum of the tax deductible expense is $1,650, and since the tax rate is 40 percent, these expenses reduce income taxes by $660 so the net cash outflow is $825 ($1,485 − 660). Notice that the net cash outflow grows each year because the principal repayment increases and it is not a tax-deductible expense.

At the end of the fifth year, the equipment is sold for $500. The sale is a cash inflow, but if an asset is sold for more than its book value, the cash inflow is reduced by the taxes generated by the sale. (If the asset were sold for less than its book value, the sale would reduce taxes.) In this illustration, the asset is completely depreciated, so its book value is $0. All of the sale is taxable income, so the firm nets only $300 after paying taxes of $200 on the $500 sale.

Alternatively, the firm could lease the equipment from a lessor who wants a 10 percent return. To determine the annual lease payments, the lessor answers the following question: How much must I charge each year so that my $5,000 invested in the equipment yields 10 percent? (There is no reason to assume the interest rate lessee pays to borrow is the same rate the lessor wants to earn on the lease.) That is,

Function Key	Data Input
PV =	−5,000
FV =	0
I =	10
N =	5
PMT =	?
Function Key	**Answer**
PMT =	1,318.99

$$\frac{PMT}{(1 + 0.1)^1} + \cdots + \frac{PMT}{(1 + 0.09)^5} = \$5,000$$

$$PMT(PVAIF\ 10I,\ 5N) = \$5,000.$$

The interest factor is 3.791, so the equation becomes

$$PMT(3.791) = \$1,319$$

$$PMT = \$5,000/3.791 = \$1,319.$$

For the lessor to earn 10 percent, the annual lease payment should be $1,319. If the lessor charges $1,319 annually, the lessee's annual cash outflows are

Year	1	2	3	4	5
Lease payment	$1,319.00	1,319.00	1,319.00	1,319.00	1,319.00
Tax savings	($527.60)	(527.60)	(527.60)	(527.60)	(527.60)
Cash outflow	$791.40	791.40	791.40	791.40	791.40

As may be seen by comparing the two projections, the cash flows differ under leasing and owning. Leasing produces a constant $791.40 outflow each year, while owning results in varying cash inflows and outflows.

Which alternative is better? That depends on the time value of money. Which alternative produces the *lower* present value of the *cash outflows*? If the financial manager can borrow the funds for 9 percent, the two cash outflows are discounted back at 9 percent. The present value of the cost of owning (that is, the present value of the cash outflows associated with owning) is

$$\text{Present value of cost of owning} = \frac{\$825}{(1+0.09)} + \frac{856}{(1+0.09)^2} + \frac{889}{(1+0.09)^3}$$

$$+ \frac{924}{(1+0.09)^4} + \frac{663}{(1+0.09)^5} = \$3{,}249.$$

The present value of the cost of leasing (that is, the present value of the cash outflows associated with leasing) is

$$\text{Present value of cost of leasing} = \frac{\$791.40}{(1+0.09)^1} + \cdots + \frac{\$791.40}{(1+0.09)^5}$$

$$= \$791.40(3.890)$$

$$= \$3{,}078.55.$$

Since the present value of the cash outflows associated with leasing is less than the present value of the cash outflows associated with borrowing and owning, leasing is preferred.

While this illustration argues for leasing, there are several critical variables in the illustration. The first is the expected residual or salvage value. If the anticipated residual value were higher, that would argue against leasing. The owner of the equipment receives the residual, and this present value is lost if the firm leases. The smaller the expected residual, the stronger is the argument for leasing. Second, the owner pays the maintenance and the lessee does not. However, if the lease contract does not include maintenance, the lessee will also have to pay that expense, and maintenance is a cash outflow.

The present value of the cash outflows also depends on their timing. In this illustration all the cash outflows occur at the end of each year. Lease payments, however, may be made at the beginning of the time period. (You make rent payments at the beginning of the month and not at the end.) If the lease payments were made at the beginning, the present value of the cash outflows would be $3,355.31. Now borrowing and buying would be preferred, since the present value of the cost of leasing is greater than the present value of the cost of borrowing and buying.

Accounting for Leases

Prior to changes in accounting standards, one reason for using leasing was that the lease would not appear on the firm's balance sheet. While the lease would be mentioned in the footnotes, the fact that it did not appear on the balance sheet understated the firm's use of financial leverage. This important distinction between the use of debt, which must appear on the balance sheet, and leasing, which would not appear on the balance sheet, is illustrated by the following example. Both firms initially have the same assets, liabilities, and equity:

Firm A Balance Sheet As Of 12/31/X0				Firm B Balance Sheet As Of 12/31/X0		
Assets	$10,000	Debt	$5,000	Assets	$10,000	Debt	$5,000
		Equity	5,000			Equity	5,000

Both firms acquire equipment worth $5,000. Firm A purchases the equipment and sells bonds to acquire the funds to pay for it. Firm B leases the equipment. After these transactions, their respective balance sheets become:

Firm A Balance Sheet As Of 12/31/X1				Firm B Balance Sheet As Of 12/31/X1		
Assets	$10,000	Debt	$5,000	Assets	$10,000	Debt	$5,000
Equipment	5,000	Bends	5,000			Equity	5,000
		Equity	5,000				

Both firms have use of equipment, but firm A has more debt outstanding. Firm A appears to be riskier because its debt ratio is now higher. In reality, however, it is no riskier than firm B, which also has a contractual obligation: the lease payment. Since the lease does not appear on the balance sheet, firm B appears to be less risky.

The use of leases to obtain such "off the balance sheet" financing may no longer be possible. The Financial Accounting Standards Board ruled that if the lease gives the lessee substantially all the benefits and risks of ownership, the lease must be "capitalized" and included on the firm's balance sheet. This means that the present value of the asset is listed as an asset, and the present value of the lease payments is listed as a liability. The value of the asset then diminishes over time as it is depreciated, and the liability is reduced as the lease payments are made.

The lease must be included on the balance sheet if it meets any of the following four conditions:

1. The lease transfers ownership of the asset at the end of the lease.
2. The lease permits the lessee to buy the asset below its value at the expiration of the lease.
3. The length of the lease is more than 75 percent of the asset's estimated life.
4. The present value of the lease payments exceeds 90 percent of the fair market value of the property to the lessor.

The first two conditions obviously give the lessee the benefits and risks of ownership. In the first condition, ownership is transferred, and in the second condition, the lessee has the option to buy the asset at a bargain price. While the lessee does not have to exercise the option and buy the asset, the important consideration is the existence of the option.

The third and fourth conditions require some explanation. Consider the illustration presented earlier in which the financial manager had to choose between either the lease or borrowing and buying. In the illustration, the analysis indicated that leasing is the better alternative. Will the lease have to be capitalized? The answer is "yes" because it meets the third condition. The life of the asset is five years and the lease is for five years, so the length of the lease exceeds 75 percent of the estimated life of the asset.

The fourth condition requires calculating the present value of the lease payments. In the illustration, that is the present value of the $1,319 lease payments. Of course, the present value of the lease payments depends upon the discount rate. This rate has to be the lower of (1) the rate used by the lessor to establish the lease payments or (2) the interest rate the lessee would pay to borrow the funds to purchase the assets. In the illustration, the lessor used 10 percent and the lessee used 9 percent, so 9 percent must be the discount rate. When the lease payments are discounted at 9 percent, the present value is

$$\$1,319(3.890) = \$5,131.$$

The present value of the lease payment is greater than 90 percent of the cost of the investment; hence, the lease must be capitalized.

Many leases do not meet any of the preceding criteria for capitalizing a lease. If an employee rents a car for a week, that is certainly an operating lease, and it will not be capitalized. But if the car is rented for several years, the terms of the lease may meet one of the criteria and hence must be capitalized. If management wants to avoid having to capitalize the lease, then the terms must be structured in such a way as to avoid all the criteria.

The inclusion of the lease would have the following impact on the balance sheet of firm B if the lease were capitalized:

Firm B Balance Sheet As Of 1/31/X1			
Assets	$10,000	Debt	$5,000
Assets under capital lease	5,000	Capital lease	5,000
		Equity	5,000

This revised balance sheet for firm B brings to the foreground the fact that *a financial lease is an alternative to debt financing*. Both firms A and B have $15,000 in assets and $5,000 in equity. The remaining sources of funds are either debt or the capitalized lease. The debt ratio for both firms then is $10,000/$15,000 = 67 percent. Now the balance sheets indicate that firm A and firm B are equally leveraged financially.

While financial leases must be capitalized, leases often avoid being capitalized. For example, many firms lease equipment and rent space. These agreements are usually operating leases that are not capitalized and do not appear on the balance sheet. The firm, however, must report future lease payments. Payments for the next four years and for all subsequent years are provided in a footnote to the balance sheet, so the information is not hidden. In some cases, these lease payments are substantial. For example, Limited Brands leases space in malls and shopping centers but has no capitalized leases on its balance sheet. Limited Brands stated in its 2009 10-K report that the company had the following minimum rent commitments under noncancelable leases:

2010	$478,000,000
2011	444,000,000
2012	396,000,000
2013	362,000,000
Thereafter	1,452,000,000

These rental payments are obviously a sizable commitment!

Summary

Intermediate-term debt and leasing are alternatives to short- and long-term debt financing. Intermediate-term debt is generally outstanding for 5 to 10 years. While the features are similar to other debt instruments, the shorter maturity and the use of collateral differentiate intermediate-term debt from long-term bonds. The repayment schedule for intermediate-term debt is generally paired with the asset's anticipated cash inflows.

Leasing is essentially renting. The firm (the lessee) acquires the use of the asset but not the title. The lessee makes periodic lease payments to the owner (the lessor) for the use of the asset. Leases may be classified as operating leases or financial leases. The latter type is similar to purchasing the asset with debt financing. The present value of the lease payments must be capitalized and included on the lessee's balance sheet as a liability.

The cash inflows and outflows generated by leasing may differ from the cash flows generated through borrowing and purchasing. The financial manager needs to determine the present value of the cost of leasing and the present value of the cost of owning to determine which is cheaper. Depreciation, taxation, the timing of lease payments, the timing of interest and principal repayments, and the residual or salvage value of the asset affect the present value of the cash outflows and thus affect the decision to lease or to borrow and purchase.

Review Objectives

Now that you have completed this chapter, you should be able to

1. List the features of intermediate-term debt (pp. 443–444).
2. Construct a repayment schedule (pp. 444–445).
3. Define a balloon payment and explain when it applies (p. 445).
4. Contrast operating and financial leases (p. 446).
5. Determine if a firm should lease or buy equipment (pp. 447–448).
6. Isolate the importance of an asset's residual value to the lease-versus-buy decision (p. 449).
7. Describe the impact of capitalizing a lease on a firm's balance sheet, its financial ratios, and the use of financial leverage (pp. 449–452).

Problems

1. A five-year $100,000 term loan has an interest rate of 7 percent on the declining balance. What are the equal annual payments required to pay interest and principal on the loan? Construct a table showing the declining balance owed after each payment.

2. What are the repayment schedules for each of the following five-year, 10 percent $10,000 term loans?
   a. equal annual payments that amortize (retire) the principal and pay the interest owed on the declining balance
   b. equal annual principal repayment, with interest calculated on the remaining balance owned
   c. no principal repayment until after five years, with interest paid annually on the balance owned
   d. $1,000 annual principal repayment, with the balance paid at the end of five years and annual interest paid on the balance owed

3. Corgi, Inc. plans to update its equipment at a total cost of $90,000. Management anticipates making a $15,000 down payment and borrowing the remainder from a local commercial bank at 12 percent interest. The first option provides for five equal, annual payments to be made at the end of the year. The second option requires five equal, annual payments plus a balloon payment of $15,000 at the end of the fifth year. What are the annual payments required by each option?

4. Northwest Bank has been asked to purchase and lease to Fafner Construction equipment that costs $1,200,000. The lease will run for six years. If Northwest seeks a minimum return of 12 percent, what will be the required lease payment?

5. A lessor acquired equipment for $83,250 and plans to lease it for a period of five years. If the equipment has no estimated residual value, what must be the annual lease charge for the lessor to earn 12 percent on the investment? What would be the annual lease charge if the lessor sought to earn 8 percent? If the equipment will have a residual value of $10,000, what lease payment will earn the lessor 12 percent?

6. A firm wants the use of a machine that costs $100,000. If the firm purchases the equipment, it will depreciate the equipment at the rate of $20,000 a year for four years, at which time the equipment will have a residual value of $20,000. Maintenance will be $2,500 a year. The firm could lease the equipment for four years for an annual lease payment of $26,342. Currently, the firm is in the 40 percent income tax bracket.

   a. Determine the firm's cash inflows and outflows from purchasing the equipment and from leasing.

   b. If the firm uses a 14 percent cost of funds to analyze decisions that involve payments over more than a year, should management lease the equipment or purchase it?

   c. Would your answer differ if the cost of funds were 8 percent?

Additional
Problem
with Answer

Management has decided to acquire a new asset that costs $200,000. The estimated economic life of the asset is five years, but the firm wants the use of the asset only for three years. If the firm purchases the asset, it anticipates selling it at the end of three years for $50,000.

   The firm may lease the asset for $55,000 a year paid at the end of each year. The lease does not include maintenance. It is estimated that annual maintenance initially will be $5,000 (paid at the end of the year), but that cost will increase by $1,000 each year as the asset ages.

   The firm could purchase the asset with a five-year loan of $200,000. The loan will be retired in five payments of $40,000 unless the equipment is sold, in which case the loan must be paid off at closing of the sale. The interest rate is 10 percent and is paid at the end of each year on the balance owed. The annual interest payment is provided below.

   If the firm does purchase the asset, it will enter into a maintenance agreement with the manufacturer that costs $5,000 a year. The annual depreciation expense is provided below. The firm's tax bracket is 40 percent.

   Based on the above information, should the firm borrow and purchase or should the firm lease?

   To help answer the question, fill in the following tables. (It is not necessary to have an entry in every blank.)

Cash Outflows/Inflows Associated with Leasing					
Year	1	2	3	4	5
Lease payments					
Maintenance					
Total tax-deductible expenses					
Tax savings					
After-tax net cash outflow from leasing					

Cash Outflows/Inflows Associated with Owning					
Year	1	2	3	4	5
Maintenance					
Depreciation	40,000	60,000	40,000	30,000	20,000
Interest	20,000	16,000	12,000	8,000	4,000
Principal Repayment					
Total tax-deductible expences					
Tax savings					
Sale of equipment					
After-tax inflow from sale of equipment					
After-tax net cash outflow from owning					

Answer

Since the present value of the cash outflows from owning exceed the present value of the cash outflows from leasing, leasing is preferred.

Cash Outflows/Inflows Associated with Leasing			
Year	1	2	3
Lease payments	$55,000	55,000	55,000
Maintenance	5,000	6,000	7,000
Total tax-deductible expenses	60,000	61,000	62,000
Tax savings	24,000	24,400	24,800
After-tax net cash outflow from leasing	36,000	36,600	37,200

Present value of the cost of leasing (using the 10 percent interest rate):

$36,000(0.909) + $36,600(0.826) + $37,200(0.751) = $90,892

Cash Outflows/Inflows Associated with Owning					
Year	1	2	3	4	5
Maintenance	$ 5,000	5,000	5,000		
Depreciation	40,000	60,000	40,000	Not applicable	
Interest	20,000	16,000	12,000	Not applicable	
Principal Repayment	40,000	40,000	40,000 + 80,000 balance repaid = 120,000		
Total tax-deductible expenses	65,000	81,000	67,000		
Tax savings	26,000	32,400	26,800		
Sale of equipment			50,000		
After-tax inflow from sale of equipment			54,000		
After-tax net cash outflow from owning	39,000	28,600	56,200		

Present value of the cost of leasing (using the 10 percent interest rate):

$$\$39,000(0.909) + 28,600(0.826) + 56,200(0.751) = \$101,281$$

Since the asset is sold at the end of the third year, there are no entries for years 4 and 5 even though the expected life of the asset is five years.

The $80,000 balance of the loan must be repaid when the asset is sold.

The asset is sold for $50,000 but its book value is $60,000. The book value is the $200,000 cost minus the sum of the amount of depreciation during the first three years ($40,000 + $60,000 + $40,000). Since the asset is sold for $50,000, the firm has a $10,000 loss ($50,000 − $60,000). The $10,000 loss produces a $4,000 tax savings ($10,000 × 0.4). The net cash inflow from the sale is $50,000 + $4,000 = $54,000.

The cash outflow at the end of the third year is maintenance ($5,000) plus interest ($12,000) plus principal repayment ($120,000) minus the tax savings ($26,800) plus the after-tax proceeds from the sale ($54,000). That is $5,000 + $12,000 + $120,000 − $26,800 − $54,000 = $56,200.

Relationships

1. An increase in interest rates _____ the value of an intermediate-term loan.

2. Intermediate-term loans and traditional mortgage loans are constructed so that principal repayments _____ with time.

3. An increase in depreciation expense _____ the cost of a lease.

4. An increase in the residual value of the property _____ the attractiveness of leasing.

5. An increase in lease payments _____ cash outflows.

6. If a lease is capitalized, the firm's assets _____ and the firm's equity _____.

7. Leasing _____ the firm's use of financial leverage.

Answers

1. decreases

2. increase

3. does not affect (no change) The owner and not the lessee gets the benefit of the depreciation expense.

4. decreases

5. increases

6. increase; is not affected (no change)

7. increases

Investments

Virtually everyone makes investment decisions. My youngest daughter had a savings account before she was a year old. My late father owned stock in Ford at the age of 90. In between these extremes, every member of my family has made an investment in some type of asset.

The same is true for many families. Individuals purchase homes, make contributions to tax-deferred pension plans, acquire shares in mutual funds, and purchase precious metals, such as gold. Some individuals actively manage their portfolios and make their own investment decisions, such as which specific stocks or bonds to buy and sell. Other individuals delegate this decision making. They may purchase the shares in an investment company or participate in a pension plan and let the plan's management decide which specific assets to acquire.

Part 4 is concerned with the financial assets the individual or portfolio manager may acquire. These assets range from relatively safe debt obligations, such as the bonds issued by the federal government, to risky investments, such as common stock. Of course, a person should first decide why he or she is investing (in other words, what are the financial objectives of the portfolio?) before making investment decisions. Not all assets are appropriate to meet every financial goal, so portfolio constructing should begin with specifying the investor's objectives. Then the assets considered in the following chapters can be allocated to meet the financial goals.

The Features of Stock

The 17th-century English poet George Herbert wrote, "By no means run in debt; take thine own measure." Few firms are able to achieve that advice and completely avoid debt, but they all need to take their own measure. Equity is a necessary source of funds. The single proprietor invests money, assets, and time in the business and has equity in the firm. Partners invest funds and have an equity claim on the business.

Corporations raise funds by selling preferred and common stock to individuals and other investors who are owners (shareholders) in the firm. While the features of preferred stock are more similar to debt than common stock, it remains a class of equity. (Since it is similar to debt, the discussion of preferred stock is deferred to Chapter 24 after the coverage of debt financing in Chapters 22 and 23.) Many corporations do not issue preferred stock, but all issue common stock. These stockholders are the ultimate owners and bear the risk and reap the rewards associated with owning stock. It is, of course, the anticipation of the return through dividends and price appreciation that induces investors to purchase the stock.

This chapter covers the features of common stock, the firm's dividend policy and the distribution or retention of earnings, stock dividends, and stock splits. If you know this material, you may read the chapter as a refresher and move on to stock valuation in the next chapter.

Equity

A firm's sources of finance are either debt or equity. As will be discussed in Chapter 22, a corporation may issue a variety of debt instruments to tap the funds of investors who purchase debt securities. Equity represents ownership in a firm. Since the firm's debt obligations have a prior claim, equity represents a residual claim. Interest on debt must be paid before there are any earnings available to the owners. If the firm is dissolved, debts must be paid first, and any remaining assets are distributed to the owners.

Being the residual claim is one of the reasons why equity is riskier than debt. If the firm performs poorly, there may be little or nothing available to the owners. However, a profitable firm can generate a large return for its owners, since after the debt obligations are met, the residual accrues solely to the equity. Higher earnings, thus, accrue solely to the owners.

Stock represents equity in a corporation. While there may be many different types of debt instruments, there are only two types of stock: preferred stock and common stock. (Some companies have two [or more] classes of common stock. For example, Oshkosh B'Gosh has two classes of common stock. Class A shares have limited voting rights and receive 15 percent higher dividends than the class B shares. Having different classes of common stock facilitates controlling the corporation by a few stockholders.) As the name implies, preferred stock has a preferred or superior position. Common stock thus represents the final claim on a corporation's earnings and assets. While equity (ownership) represents the residual claim on a firm's earnings and assets, it still is a claim. The managers and employees work for and are responsible to the owners.

For the vast majority of firms, the owners, managers, and employees are one and the same. The owner of a small store must perform all the roles required to operate and manage the business. While the owner may employ individuals with special skills (for example, an accountant or a lawyer) to perform specific tasks, management, marketing, and financing decisions all fall on the owner/manager. Since the owner and manager are one and the same, it seems reasonable to assume that management decisions are made with the welfare of the owner as a primary consideration.

In large corporations, the owners, managers, and employees differ. As is explained later in this chapter, the owners are represented by an elected board of directors. The board employs management that, in turn, hires the various individuals who staff the operation. You could assume that the goals of management are consistent with the owners' goals, since the managers have a fiduciary responsibility to the corporate owners (that is, they are the "agents" of the owners). However, such an assumption may be at odds with reality. For example, higher salaries may be a goal of individual managers, but higher salaries will reduce earnings and come at the expense of the owners.

Owners, therefore, must monitor managerial decisions and take steps to reduce the potential conflict between managers and owners. These actions may include (1) developing a structure in which the chain of command and responsibility starts with the owners and flows to the employees, (2) forming a system for the removal of employees who act in a way that is harmful to owners, or (3) instituting a system of rewards that is tied to performance so that the welfare of the owners, managers, and employees is interrelated. Many companies have an employee stock option award that grants most of its employees the right to purchase stock at a set price. If the company is profitable, the value of the stock and the options will increase and reward employees as well as stockholders.

Linking the welfare of owners, managers, and employees involves expenses. These expenditures are sometimes referred to as the "agency costs" that owners must bear to ensure that management acts in the best interests of the owners and not solely on its own behalf. Creditors also have similar costs, since owners and managers can take actions that reduce the safety of debt instruments. For example, the paying of bonuses and stock options may reward management, but such payments reduce the money available to pay interest and repay principal.

Common Stock

Common stock

Security representing ownership in a corporation; common stock owners have a final claim on the firm's assets and earnings after the firm has met its obligations to creditors and preferred stockholders

Board of directors

Body elected by and responsible to stockholders to set policy and hire management to run a corporation

Although preferred stock legally is equity and hence represents ownership, in financial reality it is similar to debt, while common stock represents the bottom line. Common stock represents the residual claim on the assets and earnings of a corporation. In case of liquidation, the holder of common stock receives whatever is left after all other claims have been satisfied; he or she receives earnings that have accrued after expenses, interest, and preferred stock dividends are paid. These investors bear the risk and reap the rewards associated with the ownership of a corporation.

The investors who purchase common stock receive all the rights of ownership. These rights include the option to vote the shares. The stockholders elect a board of directors that selects the firm's management. Management is then responsible to the board of directors, which, in turn, is responsible to the firm's stockholders. If the stockholders do not think that the board is doing a competent job, they may elect another board to represent them.

For publicly held corporations, stockholder democracy may not work. Stockholders are usually widely dispersed, while the firm's management and board of directors generally form a cohesive unit in which the board supports management. However, the recent explosive growth in institutional investors (that is, mutual funds and pension plans with common stock investments) may be changing the relationship between stockholders and management. Professional money managers often press corporate executives to achieve higher earnings and returns for stockholders. If management is unable to achieve these goals, the money managers may seek the replacement of management or the acquisition of the corporation by another firm whose goal is higher stock returns. The threat of a change in management or a takeover often encourages a corporation's board of directors and current executives to pursue strategies that increase the value of the firm's stock.

A stockholder generally has one vote for each share owned, but there are two ways to distribute this vote. The difference between these two methods is best explained by an example. Suppose a firm has 1,000 shares outstanding and a board of directors composed of five members. With the traditional method of voting, each share gives the stockholder the right to vote for one individual for each seat on the board. Under this system, if a majority group voted as a block, a minority group could not select a representative. For example, a majority group of 70 percent of the stockholders could give each of its candidates 70 percent of the vote, thus denying representation to a minority group of 30 percent of the stockholders.

Cumulative voting

Voting system that encourages minority representation by permitting stockholders to cast all their shares (votes) for one candidate for the firm's board of directors

Another system, called cumulative voting, gives minority stockholders a means to obtain representation, but not a majority, on the firm's board of directors. Under cumulative voting, the stockholder in the previous example who owns one share has a total of five votes (one vote for each seat on the board of directors). That stockholder may cast up to five votes for one candidate. (Of course, then the stockholder could not vote for anyone else running for the remaining seats.) The 70 percent majority would have a total of 3,500 votes (700 shares $\times$ 5). The 30 percent minority would have 1,500 votes (300 shares $\times$ 5), and by voting as a block for specific candidates could assure itself of representation on the board of directors.

For example, if the 30 percent minority ran two candidates against the five candidates of the majority, the following voting could occur:

Majority Candidates	Votes
A	700
B	700
C	700
D	700
E	700
Minority Candidates	Votes
F	750
G	750

The majority has cast its 3,500 votes evenly among its candidates, and the minority has also cast its 1,500 votes evenly between its two candidates. In this election the minority wins two seats. Even if the majority were to cast more votes for candidates A through D, these votes would be at the expense of candidate E. For example, if the majority cast 800 votes for each of candidates A through D, it would have only 300 votes available for candidate E. These

300 votes are not enough to gain election, and the minority would still win one seat on the board of directors.[1]

Although cumulative voting can help a minority group obtain representation, it cannot assure representation if the minority is too small. If the minority in this example had been 15 percent, it would have had 750 votes and the 85 percent majority would have had 4,250 votes. Each of the five majority candidates would have received 850 votes (4,250/5) and would have beaten any single minority candidate with 750 votes. For the minority to win representation, the total of its combined votes must be large enough to exceed the majority's per-seat voting capacity.

Preemptive Rights

Preemptive rights

Right of current stockholders to maintain their proportionate ownership in the firm

Rights offering

Sale of new securities to stockholders by offering them the option (right) to purchase new shares

Some stockholders have preemptive rights, which is the right to maintain their proportionate ownership in the firm. If the firm wants to sell additional shares to the general public, these new shares must be offered initially to the existing stockholders in a sale called a rights offering. If the stockholders wish to maintain their proportionate ownership in the firm, they can exercise their rights by purchasing the new shares. However, if they do not want to take advantage of this offering, they may sell their privilege to whoever wants to purchase the new shares.

Preemptive rights may be illustrated by a simple example. If a firm has 1,000 shares outstanding and an individual has 100 shares, that individual owns 10 percent of the firm's stock. If the firm wants to sell 400 new shares and the stockholders have preemptive rights, these new shares must be offered to the existing stockholders before they are sold to the general public. The individual who owns 100 shares would have the right to purchase 40, or 10 percent, of the new shares. If the purchase is made, then the stockholder's relative position is maintained, for the stockholder owns 10 percent of the firm both before and after the sale of the new stock.

Although preemptive rights are required in some states for incorporation, their importance has diminished. (Rights offerings are more common in foreign countries, such as the United Kingdom.) Some firms have changed their bylaws to eliminate preemptive rights. For example, AT&T asked its

---

[1]The number of shares (S) required to elect a specific number of seats can be determined by the following equation:

$$S = \frac{V \times P}{D + 1} + 1$$

The definition of each symbol is
    V: number of voting shares,
    P: number of positions desired on the board of directors,
    D: total number of directors to be elected.
Thus, in the above example, if the minority wanted to elect two seats, it would have to control 334 shares. That is,

$$S = \frac{1,000 \times 2}{5 + 1} + 1 = 334.33$$

Since it controls only 300 shares, the minority can be assured of electing only one director.

stockholders to relinquish these rights. The rationale was that issuing new shares through rights offerings was more expensive than selling the shares to the general public through an underwriting. Investors who desired to maintain their relative position could still purchase the new shares, and all stockholders would benefit through the cost savings and the flexibility given to the firm's management. Most stockholders accepted the management's request and voted to relinquish their preemptive rights.

Dividend Policy

Cash dividends

Distribution from earnings paid in the form of cash

After a corporation has earned profits, management must decide what to do with these earnings: retain them and increase each stockholder's investment in the firm, or distribute them in cash dividends. If the earnings are distributed, the cash flows out of the firm. If the earnings are retained, management will put the funds to work by purchasing income-earning assets or retiring outstanding debt.

To see the impact of distributing or not distributing cash dividends, consider the equity section of a firm's balance sheet. On most balance sheets, stockholders' equity is listed after the liabilities and deferred taxes (if any). In its simplest form, equity consists of three entries: the stock outstanding, additional paid-in capital (which may also be referred to as "paid-in capital"), and retained earnings. A fourth entry, treasury stock, may appear if the firm has repurchased some of its outstanding stock. The stock outstanding shows the various types of stock the firm has issued. A typical entry is as follows:

Common stock ($1.00 par, 50,000 shares authorized, 35,000 shares issued)	$35,000

Additional paid-in capital represents the funds paid in excess of the stock's par value when the shares are initially sold. If the par value is $1.00 and the shares are sold for $5.00, $1.00 is credited to common stock and the $4.00 balance is considered paid-in capital. If all the 35,000 shares in the example were sold for $5.00, the paid-in capital entry is

Additional paid-in capital	$140,000

The third entry under common stock is retained earnings, which represents the accumulated earnings of the firm that have not been distributed. (The entry could be negative if the firm has operated at a loss, in which case it is called "cumulative deficit" or similar wording that connotes that the firm has operated at a loss.) The retained earnings represent the firm's undistributed earnings since its inception and, like the common stock and paid-in capital, represent an investment in the firm by common stockholders. Because these stockholders would receive the earnings if they were distributed, retained earnings are part of the stockholders' contribution to the firm.

If this firm has retained earnings of $234,000, the balance sheet entry is

Retained earnings	$234,000

The complete equity section for this firm is as follows:

Common stock ($1.00 par, 50,000 shares authorized, 35,000 shares issued)	$ 35,000
Additional paid-in capital	140,000
Retained earnings	234,000
Total equity	$409,000

The total equity is the sum of the three individual entries and represents the stockholders' total contribution to the firm. Notice that neither the total equity nor the retained earnings are assets. Equity and retained earnings are not cash! While the firm may hold cash or short-term securities, which may be referred to as "cash equivalents," *retained earnings are not synonymous with cash*.

The distribution of dividends does not affect paid-in capital, so the following simple example excludes paid-in capital. Initially the firm's balance sheet is as follows:

Assets		Liabilities and Equity	
Assets	$10,000	Debt	$ 3,000
		Common stock	4,000
		Retained earnings	3,000
	$10,000		$10,000

During the year the firm earns $1,000. The impact of the dividend policy on the firm's balance sheet depends on whether it (1) distributes the earnings, (2) retains the earnings and acquires more assets, or (3) retains the earnings and retires debt. The impact on the balance sheet of these alternatives is as follows:

The firm's balance sheet after earning $1,000 and

1. distributing the earnings:

Assets		Liabilities and Equity	
Assets	$10,000	Debt	$ 3,000
		Equity	4,000
		Retained earnings	3,000
	$10,000		$10,000

2. retaining the earnings and investing the funds in income-earning assets:

Assets		Liabilities and Equity		
Assets	Increase in —$11,000 assets by $1,000	Debt	$ 3,000	Increase in retained earnings by $1,000
		Equity	4,000	
		Retained earnings	4,000	
	$11,000		$11,000	

3. retaining the earnings and using the funds to retire outstanding debt:

Assets		Liabilities and Equity		
Assets	$10,000	Debt	Reduction—$ 2,000 in debt by $1,000	Increase in retained earnings by $1,000
		Equity	4,000	
		Retained earnings	4,000	
	$10,000		$10,000	

As the first case illustrates, if earnings are distributed as cash dividends, the firm's equity is not increased. If management wants to invest in additional assets, it will have to use an alternative source of funds. This money may be borrowed, which may increase the financial risk of the firm. Or the funds may be obtained by issuing additional stock, but it may not make sense to distribute earnings and then issue new shares to raise equity. The retention of the earnings would achieve the same effect and not involve the costs associated with selling new stock.

In the second and third cases, the firm retained all of the earnings, so retained earnings increased by $1,000. In case 2, the additional retained earnings are used to acquire additional assets, and in the third case, the additional retained earnings are used to retire debt.

Few firms distribute all of their earnings and many distribute no earnings. Since the stockholders are the owners of the firm and are entitled to the earnings, the question becomes: What do the stockholders want? What is best for them, additional investment in the firm or cash dividends? This would seem to be an easy question to answer but, in reality, is not. Usually, many different stockholders own shares, and some may seek income through dividends while others may seek capital gains.

The decision concerning the distribution of earnings is sometimes viewed as that of management serving various clients. The intent is to identify what the clients (the stockholders) want and to satisfy that want. Retirees, individuals seeking supplementary income, managers of pension plans and trust funds, and corporate stockholders may prefer dividends to capital gains. Other investors with current income may prefer capital gains that may be realized in the future when the funds are needed. If management can identify which of these groups are the primary stockholders, then dividend policy may be designed to meet the needs of those stockholders.

Actually, the decision to retain versus distribute may be irrelevant. Suppose that at the beginning of the year a stock is selling for $100 and an individual buys 100 shares ($10,000). During the year, the firm earns $10 per share. As a result of the earnings growth, the value of a share rises to $110, and the stockholder's shares are now worth $11,000.

If the firm distributes the earnings, the stockholder receives $1,000 ($10 × 100 shares). However, the value of the share will fall by the amount of the dividend, so the price returns to the original $100. (That the price of a stock declines by the amount of the dividend is explained in the section on cash dividends.) The investor experiences neither a capital gain nor a loss and will have earned 10 percent on the investment (the $1,000 in dividends divided by the $10,000 cost of the investment).

Suppose the firm does not distribute the earnings, and the investor needs the cash. The individual could sell 9 shares to obtain $990 (9 shares × $110 a share). Of course, the investor retains 91 shares worth $10,010. Except for the $10 difference resulting from the inability to sell fractional shares, the investor's position is the same as before when earnings were distributed. In either case, the investor has $1,000 in cash and $10,000 worth of stock.

This discussion suggests that the stockholder's position is unaffected by the dividend policy of the firm. Transaction costs, such as commissions on the purchase and sale of securities or investment banking fees from the sale of new securities, taxation, and the firm's cash needs affect the dividend policy of the individual firm.

Impact of Transaction Costs

If an investor must sell part of his or her holdings in order to generate cash, that argues for cash distributions of earnings. It is not cost-effective to sell 9 shares of stock. Commissions would consume a large proportion of the proceeds of the sale. This expense is avoided by the receipt of dividends. However, if management paid dividends and then had to sell additional shares to raise funds, the firm would incur investment banking fees that would have been avoided if earnings had been retained.

These transaction costs do not conclusively argue for or against the distribution of dividends. If the corporation's primary stockholders desire dividends, then there may be a net cost saving from the distribution of earnings and flotation of new shares. Those stockholders who want the additional shares could purchase them, in which case they bear the expense. If the corporation's primary stockholders seek capital gains, then there may be a net cost saving from retaining the earnings. Those stockholders who want cash could sell part of their holdings, in which case they bear the expense.

Impact of Taxation

Taxes have a major impact on financial decisions, and dividend policy is no exception. Consider the earlier example in which the stockholder received either a cash dividend or sold some of the stock. Dividends are subject to federal income taxes, while profits from security sales are subject to federal capital gains taxes. If these taxes are the same, then taxation does not matter. However, they may not be the same. As of 2011, the maximum federal income tax rate on most dividend payments was 15 percent. The federal tax rate on capital gains depended on whether the gains were long-term (more than a year) or short-term (a year or less). While long-term gains were taxed up to 15 percent, short-term rates were higher.

Even if dividends and capital gains were taxed at the same rate, there remains an argument in favor of capital gains. Dividends are taxed when they are received; the tax on capital gains is deferred until the shares are sold. If a corporation retains earnings and grows, the value of the shares should rise in response to the growth. You will not pay any tax on that growth unless you sell the shares. (The possibility always exists that tax rates may change. If you follow an investment strategy based solely on avoiding taxes, you may be unpleasantly surprised if the tax code is altered.)

The Firm's Need for Funding

The previous discussion suggested that transaction costs and taxation may affect a firm's dividend policy. The firm's need for cash may also have an impact. For example, in Chapter 16, a cash budget illustrates a case in which the firm's needs for funding fluctuate during the year. Such variations in cash requirements affect the firm's capacity to pay dividends. If management must pay dividends during a period when the firm has insufficient cash, such payments will require the firm to borrow money. Management may be reluctant to borrow funds just to pay the dividend, since such borrowings will require interest payments and principal repayment. Thus, the fluctuation in the firm's cash needs can have an impact on the desirability of distributing cash dividends as well as the firm's capacity to pay the dividend.

Firms in cyclical industries have a similar problem except that it is spread over a longer period. These firms are primarily in industries that produce capital goods (manufacturers of machinery and machine tools) or durable goods (automobiles and housing). Firms in cyclical industries experience fluctuations in earnings that affect both their capacity to pay dividends and their need to retain earnings. During periods of economic prosperity their earnings tend to expand, which would permit higher dividends. However, management may prefer to retain the earnings to help finance the firm's operations during periods of economic slowdown and stagnation. During recessions the firm's earnings may decline severely, or the firm may even operate at a loss. If the firm had previously retained earnings, its capacity to endure economic stagnation would be increased.

Inflation also has an impact on dividend policy. Since the cost of plant and equipment rises during a period of inflation, the firm will need more sources of funds to finance the replacement of worn-out assets. Notice that this replacement of plant and equipment is not the same as expansion of the firm's operations; inflation means that the firm will have to spend more to maintain its current operations. Such expenditures require financing, and the retention of earnings is a source of those funds. Of course, if the firm distributes its earnings, it will have to find other sources of funds to replace the obsolete plant and equipment.

The preceding discussion has indicated that there is no unique dividend policy that all firms follow. Such reasons as saving brokerage commission explain why the individual investor may prefer cash to capital gains. Other reasons, such as deferring capital gains taxes, explain why the individual investor may prefer the retention of earnings. There are also reasons, such as the availability of investment opportunities or the need for cash, that explain why management may prefer to retain earnings.

If management seeks to maximize the wealth of the stockholders, the dividend decision basically depends on who has the better use for the money—the stockholders or the firm. Management, however, may not know the stockholders' alternative uses for the money, or may choose to ignore the stockholders' alleged uses, and decide to retain the earnings. Stockholders who do not like the firm's dividend policy may then sell their shares. If stockholders like the dividend policy, they may purchase more shares. If the sellers exceed the buyers, the value of the shares will fall, and management will become aware of the stockholders' preference for the cash dividends instead of the retention of earnings.

Cash Dividends

Payout ratio

Ratio of cash dividends to earnings

Dividend policy is a question of how much of a firm's earnings should be distributed. Companies that do pay cash dividends usually have a policy that is either stated or implicitly known by the investment community. If an American company pays a cash dividend, the dollar amount is often stable and well known. The proportion of the earnings distributed is measured by the payout ratio, which is the cash dividend divided by earnings per share. If the dollar amount of the dividend is stable, the payout ratio will fluctuate with fluctuations in earnings. The stability of dividends coupled with fluctuations in earnings means that the amount of earnings retained varies each year and that management has decided to maintain a stable dividend at the expense of stable increases in retained earnings.

American companies that pay cash dividends distribute a regular cash dividend on a quarterly basis. A few companies make monthly distributions, and some pay semiannually or annually. Foreign firms typically pay cash dividends semiannually. For example, Canon, Inc. paid $0.412 in June 2007 and $0.447 in December 2007. Even if the amount of the dividend is stable, fluctuations in exchange rates imply that the amount of the dividend received varies with each payment.

While most companies with cash dividend policies pay regular quarterly dividends, there are other types of dividend policies. Some companies pay quarterly dividends plus extras. Redwood Trust pays a quarterly dividend but may distribute an extra dividend at year end if the company has a good year. In 2004, the firm paid an additional $5.50 extra dividend. Such a policy is appropriate for a firm in a cyclical industry because earnings fluctuate, and the firm may be hard pressed to maintain a higher level of regular quarterly dividends. By having a set cash payment supplemented with extras in good years, the firm maintains a fixed payment and supplements the dividend when appropriate.

As earnings grow, the firm can increase its cash dividends. There is, however, a reluctance to increase the cash dividend immediately with an increase in earnings. This lag occurs because of management's reluctance to reduce cash dividends if earnings decline. The unwillingness to cut dividends has resulted in a tendency for management to raise dividends only when it is certain that the higher level of earnings can be maintained.

Date of record

Day on which an investor must own stock in order to receive the dividend payment

Distributing dividends takes time. The first step is the dividend meeting of the firm's directors. If they decide to distribute a cash dividend, two important dates are established. The first date determines who is to receive the dividend. On a particular day the ownership books of the corporation are closed, and everyone owning stock in the company at the end of that day receives the dividend. This is called the date of record. If investors buy the stock after the date of record, they do not receive the dividend. The stock is purchased excluding the dividend; this is referred to as ex dividend, for the price of the stock does not include the dividend payment. The ex dividend day is two working days before the date of record, because the settlement date is three working days after the transaction.

Ex dividend

Stock purchases exclusive of any dividend payment

Pay date or distribution date

Day on which a dividend is paid to stockholders

The second important date is the day that the dividend is distributed, or the pay date or distribution date. The distribution date may be several weeks after the record date, as the company must determine the owners on the record date and process the checks. The company may not perform this task itself; instead it uses its commercial bank, for which service the bank charges a fee. The day that the dividend is received by the stockholder is thus likely to be many weeks after the board of directors announced the dividend payment.

The time frame for the declaration and payment of a dividend is illustrated by the following time line:

Declaration Date (July 1)	Ex Div Date (July 30)	Date of Record (August 1)	Distribution Date (September 1)

On July 1, the board of directors declares a dividend to be paid September 1 to all stockholders of record August 1. To receive the dividend, the individual must own the stock at the close of trading on August 1. To own the stock

August 1, the stock must have been purchased on or before July 29. If the stock is bought July 29, settlement will occur after three days on August 1 (assuming three workdays), so the investor owns the stock at the close of August 1. If the investor buys the stock on July 30, that individual does not own the stock on August 1 (the seller owns the stock) and cannot be the owner of record on August 1. On July 30, the stock trades ex dividend, or "ex div," and the buyer does not receive the dividend.

When a stock goes ex div, its price is adjusted downward for the dividend. This price change makes logical sense. If a stock were selling for $50 and paid a $2 dividend, the stock could not be worth $50 on the ex div date. If the price were not adjusted, you could buy the stock for $50 the day before it went ex div, sell it for $50 on the ex div date, collect the $2 dividend, and net $2. If you could make the $2, everyone could make the $2, but such easy profits do not happen. Instead the price of the stock becomes $48 on the ex div date. Your total position remains $50, consisting of the $48 stock plus the $2 dividend.

If the stock closed at $49, the net change for the day is +1 and not −1 because the change is figured from the adjusted price ($48) and not from the previous day's closing price ($50). If the stock closed at $47.88, the net change would be −.12 and not −2.12. Once again the change in the stock's price from the previous day's trading is figured from the adjusted price ($50 minus the $2 dividend).

Stock Dividends

Stock dividends

Distribution from earnings paid in additional shares of stock

Some firms distribute stock dividends in addition to (or instead of) cash dividends. For example, Tootsie Roll distributed a 3 percent stock dividend in addition to its cash dividend for every year during 2000–2009. (According to Tootsie Roll's *2010 Annual Report*, the company has distributed a stock dividend for 45 consecutive years.) Stock dividends alter the entries on the firm's equity section of its balance sheet, but they have no impact on the firm's assets and liabilities. Since assets are neither increased nor decreased, stock dividends do not affect the company's earning capacity.

The following equity section of a balance sheet is used to illustrate a stock dividend:

Equity: $1 par common stock (2,000,000 shares authorized; 1,000,000 outstanding)	$1,000,000
Additional paid-in capital	500,000
Retained earnings	5,000,000
	$6,500,000

A stock dividend does not affect a firm's assets and liabilities. Only the entries in the equity section of the balance sheet are affected by a stock dividend. The stock dividend transfers amounts from retained earnings to common stock and additional paid-in capital. The amount transferred depends on (1) the number of new shares issued through the stock dividend and (2) the market price of the stock. If the above company issued a 10 percent stock dividend when the market price of the common stock was $20 a share, this would cause the issuing of 100,000 shares with a value of $2,000,000. This amount is subtracted from the retained earnings and transferred to the common stock and additional paid-in capital. The amount transferred to common stock will be 100,000 times the par value of the stock ($1 × 100,000 = $100,000). The remaining amount ($1,900,000) is transferred to additional paid-in capital. The equity section then becomes:

Equity: $1 par common stock (2,000,000 shares authorized; 1,100,000 outstanding)	$1,100,000
Additional paid-in capital	2,400,000
Retained earnings	3,000,000
	$6,500,000

Although there has been an increase in the number of shares outstanding, there has been no increase in cash and no increase in assets that may be used to earn profits. All that has happened is a recapitalization: the equity entries have been altered.

The stock dividend does not increase your wealth but does increase the number of shares you own. In the above example, if you owned 100 shares before the stock dividend, you had stock worth $2,000. After the stock dividend, you own 110 shares, and the 110 shares are also worth $2,000, for the price per share falls from $20 to $18.18 ($2,000/110 = $18.18). Why does the price of the stock fall? The answer is that there are 10 percent more shares outstanding, but there has been no increase in the firm's assets and earning power. The old shares have been *diluted* and hence the price of the stock must decline to indicate this dilution. If the price of the stock did not fall, all companies could make their stockholders wealthier by declaring stock dividends. But investors would soon realize that the stock dividend does not increase the assets and earning power of the firm, and they would not be willing to pay the old price for a larger number of shares. The market price would fall to adjust for the dilution of the old shares, and that is what happens.

The major misconception concerning the stock dividend is that it increases the ability of the firm to grow. If the stock dividend were a substitute for a cash dividend, the statement would be partially true, because the firm still has the asset cash that would have been paid to stockholders if a cash dividend had been declared. The firm, however, would still have the cash if it did not pay the stock dividend, for a firm may retain its cash and not pay a stock dividend. Hence, the decision to pay the stock dividend does not increase the firm's cash; it is the decision *not to pay the cash dividend* that conserves the cash.

Dilution

Reduction in earnings per share as the result of issuing additional shares

Stock Splits

After the price of a stock has risen substantially, management may choose to split the stock. This stock split lowers the price of the stock and makes it more accessible to investors. Implicit in this statement is the belief that investors prefer lower-priced shares and that reducing the price of the stock benefits the current stockholders by widening the market for their stock.

Like the stock dividend, the stock split alters the equity section on the balance sheet. It does not affect the assets or liabilities of the firm. It does not increase the earning power of the firm, and the wealth of the stockholder is not increased unless other investors prefer lower-priced stocks and increase the demand for this stock.

The equity section of a balance sheet used previously for illustrating the stock dividend will now be employed to demonstrate a two-for-one stock split. In a two-for-one stock split, one old share becomes two new shares, and the par value of the stock is halved from $1.00 to $0.50. There are no changes in the additional paid-in capital, retained earnings, or total equity. All that has happened is that there are now twice as many shares outstanding, and each share is worth half as much as an old share.

Equity: $0.50 par common stock (2,000,000 shares authorized; 2,000,000 outstanding)	$1,000,000
Additional paid-in capital	500,000
Retained earnings	5,000,000
	$6,500,000

Stock splits may be in any combination of terms, such as four for one or seven for four, but the most common splits are two for one or three for two. There are also reverse splits, which reduce the number of shares and raise the price of the stock. For example, AIG split its stock one for 20 in 2009. Thus, 100 shares became 5 shares after the split.

All stock splits affect the price of the stock. With a two-for-one split, the stock's price is cut in half. A one-for-10 split raises the price by a factor of 10. An easy method for finding the price of the stock after the split is to multiply the stock's price before the split by the reciprocal of the terms of the split. For example, if a stock is selling for $54 a share and is split 3 for 2, then the price of the stock after the split will be $54 \times 2/3 = 36.

Stock splits, like stock dividends, do not by themselves increase your wealth, because the stock split does not increase the assets and earning power of the firm. All that changes is the number of shares and their price. (In a scene in that wonderful movie *Rainman*, Raymond [the Rainman, played by Dustin Hoffman] receives four fish sticks. Raymond says that he always gets eight fish sticks, so his brother, played by Tom Cruise, cuts them in half and says, "You now have eight." That's a two-for-one stock split. Four fish sticks become eight fish sticks. It's like cutting a pizza into eight slices instead of four. The size of the pizza remains the same; you just get more slices.)

The usual rationale given by management for splitting a stock is that a lower selling price increases the marketability of the shares. That is, the split produces a wider distribution of ownership and increases investor interest in the company. This increased interest and marketability may ultimately cause the value of the stock to appreciate. For example, if Ford splits its stock (as it did in 1988), the wider distribution may lead to an increase in sales. Larger sales then produce higher earnings and an increase in the price of the shares. If such a scenario were to occur (and there is no evidence that it will), the current stockholders would benefit; however, the source of a subsequent price increase in the stock's value would still be the increase in the earnings and not the stock split.

A stock split may even lead the individual to reason that the lower-priced stock will rise more than the higher-priced stock. If a $50 stock is split two for one, 100 shares become 200 shares and the price becomes $25. If the stock rises by $5, the gain is $1,000 instead of $500. This line of reasoning assumes that a $25 stock will rise by 20 percent but the $50 stock will increase by only 10 percent. Of course, if a $25 stock rises by 20 percent, there is no reason why the same stock priced at $50 wouldn't also increase by 20 percent to $60. The increase in value is $1,000 in either case.

There is even a reason to prefer the higher-priced stock. Full-service brokerage firms tend to charge commissions based on the number of shares as well as the price. The full-service brokerage commission on 200 shares at $25 is greater than the commission on 100 shares at $50 even though the value of both transactions is $5,000. (The author once heard two full-service brokers discussing the difference in their commissions before and after Disney split four for one. The difference exceeded $100. That will cover your cost of admission to Disneyland.)

Dividend Reinvestment Plans

Dividend reinvestment plans (DRIPs)

Plans that permit stockholders to have cash dividends reinvested in additional shares instead of receiving the cash

Many corporations that pay cash dividends also have dividend reinvestment plans (sometimes referred to as DRIPs). These permit stockholders to have cash dividends used to purchase additional shares of stock. In most plans a bank acts on behalf of the corporation and its stockholders. The bank collects the cash dividends and, in some plans, offers the stockholders the option of making additional cash contributions. The bank pools all the funds and purchases the stock in the secondary market. Since the bank purchases a large block of shares, it receives a substantial reduction in the per-share commission cost of the purchase. This reduced brokerage fee is spread over all the shares, so even the smallest investor receives the advantage of the reduced brokerage fees. The bank does charge a fee for its service, but this fee is usually modest and does not offset the potential savings in brokerage fees.

In the second type of reinvestment plan, the company issues new shares of stock, and the money goes directly to the company. The investor may also have the option of making additional cash contributions. This type of plan offers the investor a further advantage in that the brokerage fees are entirely circumvented. The entire amount of the cash dividend is used to purchase shares, with the issuing cost paid by the company.

Perhaps the most important advantage to investors of dividend reinvestment plans is the "forced savings." Such forced saving may be desirable if you wish to save but have a tendency to spend money once you receive it. The plans also offer advantages to the firm. They create goodwill and may result in some cost savings (for instance, lower costs of preparing and mailing dividend checks). The reinvestment plans that result in the new issue of stock also increase the company's equity base.

Repurchase of Stock

A firm with cash may choose to repurchase some of its stock. Stock repurchases decrease the number of shares outstanding. Since the earnings will be spread over fewer shares, the earnings per share should increase. The higher per share earnings then may lead to a higher stock price in the future.

Repurchasing shares may be viewed as an alternative to paying cash dividends. Instead of distributing the money as cash dividends, the firm offers to purchase the shares from the stockholders. This offers the stockholders a major advantage. They have the option to sell or retain their shares. If the stockholders believe that the firm's potential is sufficient to warrant retention of the shares, they do not have to sell them. The decision to sell the shares rests with the stockholder.

One particularly noteworthy repurchase occurred when Teledyne bought 8.7 million of its shares at $200 each for a total outlay of $1.74 billion. Teledyne initially offered to repurchase 5 million shares at $200. At that time the stock was selling for $156, so the offer represented a 28 percent premium over the current price. The large premium probably caused more shares to be tendered than 5 million. While Teledyne could have prorated its purchases, it instead chose to accept all the shares. The result was to reduce the amount of outstanding stock by 40 percent. The reduction in the number of shares outstanding increased Teledyne's earnings per share by more than $7. After the repurchase had been completed, the stock's price continued to increase and sold for *more than $240 a share within a few weeks.* Obviously the securities market believed that the repurchase was in the best interests of the remaining stockholders!

Summary

Stock represents ownership (equity) in a corporation. Common stockholders are the residual owners and have the final claim on the corporation's earnings and assets after the firm's obligations to creditors and preferred stockholders have been met. Common stockholders have the right to vote their shares and elect the firm's board of directors. Once a corporation has generated earnings, the earnings are either distributed or retained. The retention of earnings is an important source of funds for corporations and increases the stockholders' investment in the firm. Retained earnings may be used to finance future growth or to retire existing debt.

Many corporations distribute a part of their earnings as cash dividends. Some corporations pay stock dividends, which increase the number of shares but do not decrease the firm's assets. Stock splits alter the number of outstanding shares and, like stock dividends, do not affect the firm's assets, liabilities, or earning capacity. Stock splits and stock dividends affect the price of the stock in proportion to the number of shares issued.

Many firms offer dividend reinvestment plans as a convenience to stockholders. These plans permit the stockholders to accumulate shares with little or no costs. Occasionally a corporation will elect to repurchase shares. Such repurchases may be an alternative to distributing cash dividends. If current stockholders want to retain their ownership in the company, they may choose not to sell their stock.

Review Objectives

Now that you have completed this chapter, you should be able to

1. Identify the features of common stock (pp. 462–463).

2. Explain why cumulative voting may give minority stockholders representation on a firm's board of directors (pp. 463–464).

3. Contrast the impact of retaining earnings versus paying cash dividends on a corporation's balance sheet (pp. 465–468).

4. Explain why brokerage commissions and capital gains taxation may affect an investor's preference for the distribution or the retention of earnings (pp. 468–469).

5. Identify the important dates for the distribution of a cash dividend (pp. 471–472).

6. Compare the impact of a cash dividend, stock dividend, and stock split on a firm's balance sheet (pp. 472–474).

7. List the advantages associated with dividend reinvestment plans and stock repurchases (pp. 475–476).

Internet Assignments

1. You may obtain information on dividend reinvestment plans from DRIP Investor (**http://www.dripinvestor.com**), DRIP Central (**http://dripcentral.com**), and ShareBuilder (**http://www.sharebuilder.com**). What are the features of the IBM and ExxonMobil dividend reinvestment plans? Do these plans permit investors to purchase additional shares? If

they do, may the stockholder buy the shares at a discount? You may also find information on specific plans through the company's home page.

2. While stock splits may not increase the wealth of stockholders, many companies do split their stock. You may obtain a calendar of stock splits through Google by searching for "stock splits." Identify a company whose stock is being split and trace the stock's price prior to and after the split. Did the stock price adjust for the split?

Problems

1. West Wind, Inc. has 5,000,000 shares of common stock outstanding with a market value of $60 per share. Net income for the coming year is expected to be $6,900,000. What impact will a three-for-one stock split have on the earnings per share and on the price of the stock?

2. Sharon Bohnette owns 1,000 shares of Northern Chime Company. There are four seats on the board of directors up for election and Ms. Bohnette is one of the nominees. Under the traditional method of voting, how many votes may she cast for herself? How many votes may she cast for herself under the cumulative method of voting?

3. Jersey Mining earns $9.50 a share, sells for $90, and pays a $6 per share dividend. The stock is split two for one and a $3 per share cash dividend is declared.

   a. What will be the new price of the stock?

   b. If the firm's total earnings do not change, what is the payout ratio before and after the stock split?

4. Firm A had the following selected items on its balance sheet:

Cash	$ 28,000,000
Common stock ($50 par; 2,000,000 shares outstanding)	100,000,000
Additional paid-in capital	10,000,000
Retained earnings	62,000,000

   How would each of these accounts appear after:

   a. a cash dividend of $1 per share?

   b. a 5 percent stock dividend (fair market value is $100 per share)?

   c. a one-for-two reverse split?

5. Jackson Enterprises has the following capital (equity) accounts:

Common stock ($1 par; 100,000 shares outstanding)	$100,000
Additional paid-in capital	200,000
Retained earnings	225,000

The board of directors has declared a 20 percent stock dividend on January 1 and a $0.25 cash dividend on March 1. What changes occur in the capital accounts after each transaction if the price of the stock is $4?

6. A firm's balance sheet has the following entries:

Cash	$10,000,000
Total liabilities	30,000,000
Common stock ($5 par; 2,000,000 shares outstanding)	10,000,000
Additional paid-in capital	3,000,000
Retained earnings	42,000,000

What will be each of these balance sheet entries after:

a. a three-for-one stock split?

b. a $1.25 per share cash dividend?

c. a 10 percent stock dividend (current price of the stock is $15 per share)?

7. What effect will a two-for-one stock split have on the following items found on a firm's financial statements?

a. earnings per share $4.20

b. total equity $10,000,000

c. long-term debt $4,300,000

d. additional paid-in capital $1,534,000

e. number of shares outstanding 1,000,000

f. earnings $4,200,000

8. A firm has the following balance sheet:

Assets		Liabilities and Equity	
Cash	$ 20,000	Accounts payable	$ 20,000
Accounts receivable	110,000	Long-term debt	100,000
Inventory	120,000	Common stock ($8 par; 4,000 shares outstanding)	32,000
Plant and equipment	250,000	Additional paid-in capital	148,000
		Retained earnings	200,000
	$500,000		$500,000

a. Construct a new balance sheet showing the impact of a three-for-one split. If the current market price of the stock is $54, what is the price after the split?

Assets		Liabilities and Equity	
Cash	$_____	Accounts payable	$_____
Accounts receivable	_____	Long-term debt	_____
Inventory	_____	Common stock	
		($_____ par;	
		shares outstanding)	_____
Plant and equipment	_____		
		Additional paid-in capital	_____
		Retained earnings	_____
	$══════		$══════

b. Construct a new balance sheet showing the impact of a 10 percent stock dividend. After the stock dividend, what is the new price of the common stock?

Assets		Liabilities and Equity	
Cash	$_____	Accounts payable	$_____
Accounts receivable	_____	Long-term debt	_____
Inventory	_____	Common stock	
		($_____ par;	
		shares outstanding)	_____
Plant and equipment	_____		
		Additional paid-in capital	_____
		Retained earnings	_____
	$══════		$══════

Additional Problems with Answers

1. A stock is currently selling for $100. What will be the impact on the stock's price if the company (a) pays a $2.35 cash dividend, (b) splits the stock four for one, (c) splits the stock one for two, and (d) distributes a 10 percent stock dividend?

2. A corporation has the following items on its balance sheet:

Cash	$ 1,000,000
Accounts receivable	10,000,000
Total assets	50,000,000
Long-term debt	25,000,000
Equity	10,000,000

The number of shares outstanding is 50,000, and the earnings per share is $3.00.

a. A $2.00 cash dividend has what effect on each of the above items?

b. A two-for-one stock split has what effect on each of the above items?

3. A corporation has the following balance sheet:

Assets		Liabilities and Equity	
Cash	$ 48,000	Accruals	$ 14,000
Accounts receivable	145,000	Accounts payable	98,000
Inventory	142,000	Bank loans	100,000
Plant	259,000	Bonds	89,000
		Common stock ($10 par; 10,000 shares outstanding)	100,000
		Additional paid-in capital	20,000
		Retained earnings	173,000
	$594,000		$594,000
Earnings	$ 89,000		
Earnings per share	$ 8.90		
Price of stock	$ 98.00		

a. Construct a new balance sheet if the firm splits the stock three for two. What are the adjusted earnings per share and the price of the stock after the split?

b. Construct a new balance sheet if the firm pays a $1 per share cash dividend. What are the earnings per share and the price of the stock after the stock trades ex dividend?

c. Construct a new balance sheet if the firm distributes a 10 percent stock dividend. What are the earnings per share and the price of the stock after the stock dividend?

Answers

1. In each case the price of the stock adjusts for the dividend or split. The new prices are

a. $100 − $2.35 = $97.65

b. $100/4 = $25

c. $100/.5 = $200

d. $100/1.1 = $90.91

The implication of the price adjustments is that the investor's total wealth is unchanged.

2. a. The effect of the $2 cash dividend:

Cash	$ 900,000
Accounts receivable	10,000,000
Total assets	49,000,000
Long-term debt	25,000,000
Equity	9,900,000

b. The effect of the two-for-one stock split:

Cash	$ 1,000,000	None
Accounts receivable	10,000,000	None
Total assets	50,000,000	None
Long-term debt	25,000,000	None
Equity	10,000,000	None

The number of shares outstanding doubles to $50,000 \times 2 = 100,000$. The earnings per share is cut in half: $3.00/2 = $1.50.

3. a. The balance sheet after the three-for-two stock split:

Assets		Liabilities and Equity	
Cash	$ 48,000	Accruals	$ 14,000
Accounts receivable	145,000	Accounts payable	98,000
Inventory	142,000	Bank loans	100,000
Plant	259,000	Bonds	89,000
		Common stock	100,000
		($6.67 par; 15,000 shares outstanding)	
		Additional paid-in capital	20,000
		Retained earnings	173,000
	$594,000		$594,000
Earnings	$ 89,000		
Earnings per share	$ 5.93		
Price of stock	$ 59.33		

The stock split only affects the number of shares, the earnings per share, and the price of the stock.

b. The balance sheet after the $1 per share cash dividend:

Assets		Liabilities and Equity	
Cash	$ 38,000	Accruals	$ 14,000
Accounts receivable	145,000	Accounts payable	98,000
Inventory	142,000	Bank loans	100,000
Plant	259,000	Bonds	89,000
		Common stock ($10 par; 10,000 shares outstanding)	100,000
		Additional paid-in capital	20,000
		Retained earnings	163,000
	$584,000		$584,000
Earnings	$ 89,000		
Earnings per share	$ 8.90		
Price of stock	$ 97.00		

The cash dividend reduces cash and assets by $10,000 ($1 × 10,000). It also reduces retained earnings by an equal amount. Since the dividend is paid from earnings, earnings per share is unaffected but the price of the stock declines by the amount of the dividend from $98 to $97.

c. The balance sheet after the 10 percent stock dividend:

Assets		Liabilities and Equity	
Cash	$ 38,000	Accruals	$ 14,000
Accounts receivable	145,000	Accounts payable	98,000
Inventory	142,000	Bank loans	100,000
Plant	259,000	Bonds	89,000
		Common stock ($10 par; 11,000 shares outstanding)	110,000
		Additional paid-in capital	108,000
		Retained earnings	75,000
	$594,000		$594,000
Earnings	$ 89,000		
Earnings per share	$ 8.09		
Price of stock	$ 89.09		

The 10 percent stock dividend has no impact on assets, liabilities, equity, and earnings. Common shares outstanding increases by 10 percent to 11,000 shares. Since the value of the new shares is $98,000 (1,000 × $98), that amount is subtracted from the retained earnings. The new retained earnings is $75,000 ($173,000 − 98,000). Since only $10,000 is added to common stock, the difference ($88,000) between the increase in stock and the decrease in retained earnings is added to the additional paid-in capital. The new shares cause the dilution of the original shares by 10 percent, so earnings per share and the price of the stock adjust for the dilution.

Notice that the stock split and the stock dividend had no effect on total assets, total liabilities, and total equity. They only affected the number of shares outstanding and their price. The cash dividend reduced the firm's assets, equity, and the price of its stock.

Relationships

1. Increasing a firm's dividend payment _____ retained earnings.
2. Retaining earnings and using the funds to retire debt _____ total assets.
3. For a given amount of earnings, increasing the dividend _____ the payout ratio.
4. When a stock trades ex div, the market price of the stock _____.
5. The distribution of a stock dividend _____ the firm's total assets.
6. A stock dividend _____ the number of shares outstanding, and a cash dividend _____ the number of shares outstanding.
7. A one-for-10 stock split _____ the number of shares outstanding.
8. A two-for-one stock split _____ the price of the stock.
9. A four-for-one stock split _____ the firm's equity
10. The repurchase of stock _____ the firm's assets, _____ the firm's liabilities, and _____ the firm's equity.

Answers

1. decreases
2. does not affect (no change)
3. increases
4. decreases
5. does not affect (no change)
6. increases; does not affect (no change)
7. decreases
8. decreases
9. does not affect (no change)
10. decreases; does not affect (no change); decreases

CHAPTER

21

Stock Valuation

I f I offered to pay you $3,345 after 10 years, what is that worth to you today? If I offered you $268 every year for the next 10 years, what is that annuity worth today? Which is the better offer? How would you answer those questions?

You should immediately realize that these questions are illustrations of the time value of money covered in Chapter 7. To find the present values, you would discount the $3,345 lump sum and discount the $268 annuity at some rate to determine their present values. If that rate is 9 percent, the present values of the lump sum and the annuity are $1,413 and $1,720, respectively. If you have to choose, the $268 annuity is better, because its present value is higher.

This process of discounting future cash inflows is the essence of valuation and it appears throughout this text. The present value of a bond is the present value of the interest payments and principal repayment. The present value of equipment or plant is the present value of future inflows generated by these assets. And the same concept applies to the value of stock. What you think a stock is worth depends on the future cash inflows the stock will generate.

This chapter applies the concept of discounting future cash flows to stock valuation. Identifying and estimating these future cash flows is not easy. Initially, the chapter explains a dividend growth model that is an example of discounted cash flows. Future dividends are discounted back to the present to determine the value of the stock. Unfortunately, the amount of future dividends cannot be known with certainty, and many companies do not currently pay dividends. As an alternative to discounted cash flows valuation models, various ratios such as price to earnings are used to compare stocks. This chapter ends with a discussion of these pragmatic tools for valuing common stock.

Valuation of Common Stock: The Present Value and the Growth of Dividends

The valuation of common stock involves bringing future payments back to the present at the appropriate discount factor. The discount factor is the required rate of return. Thus, the valuation involves discounting future cash flows (dividends) back to the present at the investor's required rate of return. The present value is then compared with the current price to determine if the stock is a good purchase.

Constant Dividends

The process of valuation and security selection is readily illustrated by the simple case in which the common stock pays a fixed dividend of $1 that is not expected to change. That is, anticipated flow of cash dividend payments is

Year	1	2	3	4	. . .
	$1	$1	$1	$1	. . .

The current value of this indefinite flow of payments depends on the discount rate (the investor's required rate of return). If this rate is 10 percent, the stock's value (V) is

$$V = \frac{\$1}{(1 + 0.1)^1} + \frac{\$1}{(1 + 0.1)^2} + \frac{\$1}{(1 + 0.1)^3} + \frac{\$1}{(1 + 0.1)^4} + \cdots$$

$$V = \$10.00.$$

This process is expressed in the following equation in which the variables are the dividend (D) and the required rate of return (k):

$$V = \frac{D}{(1 + k)^1} + \frac{D}{(1 + k)^2} + \frac{D}{(1 + k)^n},$$

which simplifies to

$$V = \frac{D}{k}. \tag{21.1}$$

If a stock pays a dividend of $1 and your required rate of return is 10 percent, the valuation is

$$V = \frac{D}{k} = \frac{\$1}{0.1} = \$10.00.$$

If you buy this stock for $10.00, your return (before considering any price change) is 10 percent. If you pay more, the return will be less, and if you buy the stock for less than $10.00, your return will be higher.

Growth in the Dividend

There is, however, no reason to anticipate that common stock dividends will be fixed indefinitely into the future. Common stocks offer the potential for growth, both in value and in dividends. For example, if the investor expects the current $1 dividend to grow annually at 6 percent, the anticipated dividend payments are

Year	1	2	3	. . .
	$1.06	$1.124	$1.191	. . .

The current value of this flow of growing dividend payments also depends on the discount rate (the investor's required rate of return). If this rate is 10 percent, the stock's value is

$$V = \frac{\$1.06}{(1 + 0.1)^1} + \frac{\$1.124}{(1 + 0.1)^2} + \frac{\$1.191}{(1 + 0.1)^3} + \cdots$$

Dividend-growth model

Valuation model for common stock that discounts future dividends

In this form, the value cannot be determined. If, however, you assume that the dividend will grow (g) indefinitely at the same rate, the dividend-growth model is

$$V = \frac{D(1 + g)^1}{(1 + k)^1} + \frac{D(1 + g)^2}{(1 + k)^2} + \frac{D(1 + g)^3}{(1 + k)^3} + \cdots + \frac{D(1 + g)^n}{(1 + k)^n},$$

which simplifies to

$$V = \frac{D_0(1 + g)}{k - g}. \tag{21.2}$$

The stock's intrinsic value depends on (1) the current dividend, (2) the growth in that dividend, and (3) the required rate of return. The application of this model may be illustrated by a simple example. If your required return is 10 percent and the stock is currently paying a $1 per share dividend that is growing indefinitely into the future at 6 percent annually, its value is

$$V = \frac{\$1(1 + 0.6)}{0.1 - 0.06} = \$26.50.$$

Any price greater than $26.50 will result in a total yield of less than 10 percent. Conversely, a price less than $26.50 will produce a return in excess of 10 percent.

This return can be determined by rearranging the equation and substituting the current price for the value of the stock. Thus the return (r) on an investment in stock is

$$r = \frac{D_0(1 + g)}{P} + g. \tag{21.3}$$

The $D_0(1 + g)/P$ is the dividend yield, and g is the expected rate of growth in the dividend. If the price were $30, the anticipated return would be

$$r = \frac{\$1(1 + 0.06)}{\$30} + 0.06$$

$$= 9.5\%.$$

Since 9.5 percent is less than the required 10 percent, you will not purchase the stock. If the price is $15, the anticipated return is

$$r = \frac{\$1(1 + 0.06)}{\$15} + 0.06$$

$$= 13.1\%.$$

This return is greater than the 10 percent you required. Since the stock offers a superior return, it is undervalued, and you would buy it. (You should notice that valuation compares dollar amounts. That is, the dollar value of the stock is compared with its price. Returns compare percentages. That is, the expected percentage return is compared with the required return. In either case, the decision will be the same. If the valuation exceeds the price, the expected return exceeds the required return.)

Only at a price of $26.50 does the stock offer a return of 10 percent. At that price the stock's anticipated return equals the required return, which is the return available on alternative investments of the same risk (that is, $r = k$). The investment will yield 10 percent because the dividend yield during the year is 4 percent and dividends are growing annually at the rate of 6 percent (that is, the anticipated capital gain is 6 percent). These relationships are illustrated in Figure 21.1, which shows the growth in dividends and the price of the stock that will produce a constant return of 10 percent. After 12 years the dividend will have grown to $2.01, and the price of the stock will be $53.32. The annual return on this investment remains 10 percent. During the year the dividend grows to $2.13, giving a 4 percent dividend yield, and the price appreciates annually at the 6 percent growth rate in dividends.

Notice that the lines in Figure 21.1 representing the dividend and the price of the stock are curved. The dividends and the price of the stock are growing at the same rate, but they are not growing by the same amount each year. This is another illustration of compounding, as the dividends (and presumably earnings) and the price of the stock are compounded annually at 6 percent.

FIGURE 21.1
Dividends and Price of
Stock over Time Yielding
10 Percent Annually

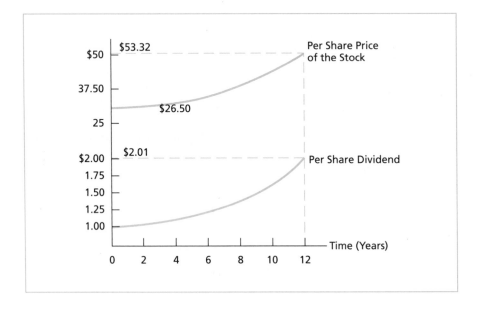

A firm's earnings and dividends need not grow steadily at this rate. Figure 21.2 illustrates a case in which the firm's earnings grow annually at an average of 6 percent, but the year-to-year changes stray from 6 percent. These fluctuations are not in themselves necessarily reason for concern. The firm exists within the economic environment, which fluctuates over time. Factors such as a recession or increase in gas prices may affect earnings during a particular year. If these factors continue to plague the firm, they will obviously play an important role in the valuation of the shares. However, the emphasis in the dividend valuation model is on the growth of dividends

FIGURE 21.2
Earnings Growth Averaging 6 Percent Annually

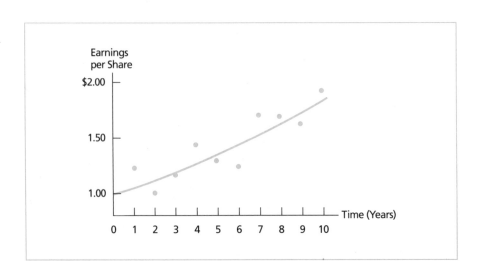

and the growth in earnings to pay the dividend over a period of years. This longer time dimension smooths out temporary fluctuations in earnings and dividends.

The dividend-growth stock valuation model assumes that (1) the firm's dividends will grow indefinitely at a certain rate and (2) the firm's earnings increase so the dividend may also grow. These assumptions need not apply, so the model may have to be modified so that different growth patterns can be built into the valuation.

Uneven Dividend Growth

Dividends can increase (or decrease), and these increments need not be at a constant rate. For example, a small, emerging firm may not pay any dividends but retain all earnings to finance expansion. After achieving a certain level of growth, management may start to pay cash dividends. The initial rate of growth in the dividend may be very large, if for no other reason than that an increment from $0.02 to $0.04 is a 100 percent increase. As the firm matures and the rate of growth in earnings declines, the rate of growth in the dividend will also decline. The firm's dividend may then increase at a stable rate. This pattern of dividends is illustrated in the following table, which represents the cash dividend and the percentage change from the preceding year:

Year	Cash Dividend	Percentage Change in the Dividend
1	—	—
2	—	—
3	$0.10	—
4	0.20	100.0%
5	0.35	75.0
6	0.50	42.9
7	0.60	20.0
8	0.66	10.0
9	0.726	10.0
10	0.799	10.0
.	.	.
.	.	.

Initially (years 1 and 2), the firm did not distribute a cash dividend. Years 3 through 7 represent a period during which the dividend rose rapidly. From year 8 into the indefinite future, the dividend grows at a constant rate of 10 percent.

The dividend-growth model may still be used to value this stock. Each of the individual dividend payments for years 1 through 7 are discounted back to the present at the required rate (for example, 12 percent) and are summed:

$$V = \frac{\$0.00}{(1.12)^1} + \frac{0.00}{(1.12)^2} + \frac{0.10}{(1.12)^3} + \frac{0.20}{(1.12)^4} + \frac{0.35}{(1.12)^5} + \frac{0.50}{(1.12)^6} + \frac{0.60}{(1.12)^7}$$

$$= \$0.00 + 0.00 + 0.10(0.712) + 0.20(0.636) + 0.35(0.567)$$

$$+ \ 0.50(0.507) + 0.60(0.452)$$

$$= \$0.92.$$

Thus the flow of dividends during years 1 through 7 is currently worth $0.92.

For year 8 and all subsequent years, the dividend grows annually at 10 percent, so the constant dividend-growth model may be applied. The value of future dividends is

$$V = \frac{\$0.06(1 + 0.1)}{0.12 - 0.10} = \$33.$$

This value, however, is as of the end of year 7, so the $33 must be discounted back to the present at 12 percent to determine its current value:

$$\frac{\$33}{(1.12)^7} = \$33(0.452) = \$14.92.$$

(The 0.452 is the interest factor for the present value of $1 at 12 percent for seven years.)

The value of the stock is the sum of the two pieces: the present value of the dividends during the period of variable growth ($0.92) plus the present value of the dividends during the period of stable growth ($14.92). Thus the value of the stock is

$$V = \$0.92 + \$14.92 = \$15.84.$$

Although the preceding illustration appears complicated, the valuation process is not. Valuation remains the present value of future cash flows (that is, the dividend payments). Each anticipated future payment is discounted back to the present at the required rate of return, and the present value of each payment is summed to determine the current value of the stock. Thus, the valuation of a common stock and the valuations of preferred stocks, bonds, and plant and equipment all involve the same basic process. Each asset is worth the present value of the expected cash inflows that the asset will generate.

Risk and Stock Valuation

The previous discussion presented a model for the valuation of stock based on discounted cash flows. However, no statement was made concerning the risk associated with an individual stock. Not all firms are equally risky, and you would require a higher return for riskier stocks.

Such a risk adjustment can be part of the valuation process, for the investor's required return (k) may be adjusted for risk. In the capital asset pricing model (Chapter 8), the required return was divided into two components: (1) the risk-free return that you can earn on a risk-free security such as a Treasury bill and (2) a risk premium. The risk premium is also composed of two components: (1) the additional return that investing in securities offers above the risk-free rate and (2) the volatility of the particular stock relative to the market as a whole. The volatility of the individual stock is measured by beta (b), and the additional return is measured by the difference between the expected return on the market (r_m) and the risk-free rate (r_f). This differential ($r_m - r_f$) is the risk premium that is required to induce individuals to purchase stocks.

To induce the investor to purchase a particular security, the risk premium associated with the market must be adjusted by the risk associated with the individual security. This adjustment is achieved by using the stock's beta, so the required return for investing in a particular stock, as specified in Equation 21.4, is

$$k = r_f + (r_m - r_f)\beta. \tag{21.4}$$

Security market line

Line specifying the required return for different levels of risk

The relationship between the required return and beta is illustrated in Figure 21.3. This security market line (AB) represents all the required returns associated with each level of market risk. In this figure, the risk-free rate is 5 percent and the expected return on the market is 11 percent. Thus for a beta of 0.8, the required return is 9.8 percent [$0.05 + (0.11 - 0.05)0.8 = 9.8$ percent], and for a beta of 1.8, the required return is 15.8 percent [$0.05 + (0.11 - 0.05)1.8 = 15.8$ percent].

Line AB crosses the vertical axis at the current risk-free rate (5 percent). The slope of the line is the difference between the market return and the risk-free rate ($0.11 - 0.05$). Movements along the line represent changes in risk as measured by beta (that is, the increase in beta from 0.8 to 1.8 and the corresponding increase in the required return from 9.8 percent to 15.8 percent). The line shifts if either the risk-free rate or the expected return on the market changes. Such a shift is illustrated in Figure 21.4, in which the risk-free rate rises from 5 percent to 6 percent and the expected return on the market rises from 11 percent to 12 percent. The security market line shifts from AB to A' B'. Thus, the required return at each level of risk (at each beta) correspondingly increases. The required return for a stock with a beta of 0.8 now becomes 10.8 percent, while the required return for a stock with a beta of 1.8 rises to 16.8 percent.

How this risk-adjusted discount may be applied to the valuation of a specific stock is illustrated by the following example. Suppose a company pays a $1.10 dividend that has risen at an annual compound growth rate

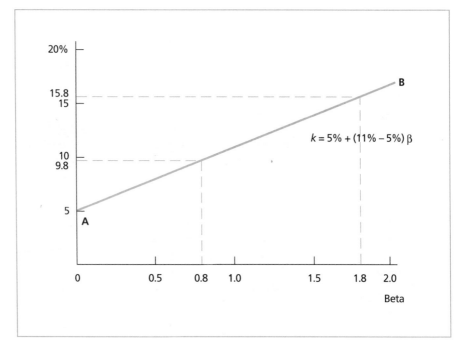

of 5.4 percent, and the stock has a beta of 0.8. If (1) U.S. Treasury bills of 6-month duration offered a risk-free return of 3.5 percent, (2) you anticipate that the market will rise annually at a compound rate of 9.5 percent (about 6 percentage points more than the risk-free rate), and (3) the dividend growth will continue indefinitely at 5.4 percent, what would be the maximum price you should pay for the stock?

The first step in answering the question is to determine the risk-adjusted required return:

$$k = r_f + (r_m - r_f)\beta$$
$$= 0.035 + (0.095 - 0.035)0.8$$
$$= 0.083 = 8.3\%.$$

Next, this risk-adjusted required return is used in the dividend-growth model presented earlier:

$$V = \frac{D_0(1 + g)}{k - g}$$
$$= \frac{1.10(1 + .054)}{0.083 - 0.054}$$
$$= \$39.98.$$

F I G U R E   21.4
Relation between Beta and
Required Return After a
Change in Interest Rates

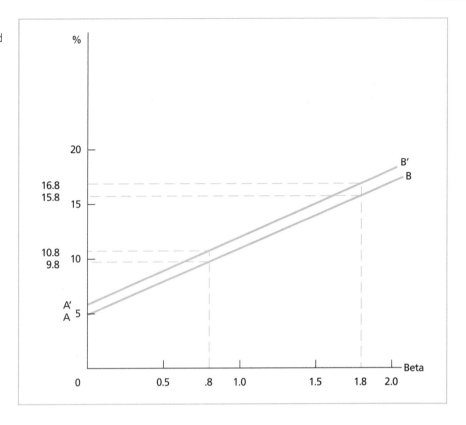

If the price of the stock is less than $39.98, the stock is underpriced and should be bought. Conversely, if the price exceeds $39.98, the stock is overpriced and should be sold.

Although this procedure does bring a risk adjustment into the valuation model, remember that the results or conclusions can be only as good as the data employed. The application of this model and others presented in this text (for example, the net present value of an investment presented in Chapter 14) depends on the data used. Any of the estimates—the growth rate, the expected return on the market, the beta coefficient—may be incorrect, in which case the resulting valuation is incorrect. For example, if the expected growth rate were increased from 5.4 percent to 6.4 percent, the effect would be to increase the valuation from $39.98 to $61.60. As may be seen in this illustration, the modest change in the growth rate produces a large change in the stock valuation.

The problem of inaccurate data does not mean that the use of models in financial decision making is undesirable. Without such models there would be no means to value an asset. Hunches, intuition, or just plain guessing would then be used to value and select assets. Theoretical models force investors and financial managers to identify real economic forces (such as earnings and growth rates) and alternatives (for example, the risk-free rate and the return earned by the market as a whole). Stock valuation based on discounted cash flows is fundamentally sound and is the theoretical basis for value investing.

Alternative Valuation Techniques: Multiplier Models

Even if the dividend-growth model is theoretically sound, it is difficult to make operational. There are problems associated with estimating future growth rates and determining the appropriate required return. In addition, many common stocks do not pay a cash dividend. In fact, the vast majority of stocks traded through the Nasdaq stock market do not pay dividends and cannot be expected to distribute dividends for the foreseeable future. Without a dividend payment, the numerator in the dividend-growth model is $0.00, which makes the value equal to $0.00.

The Price-to-Earnings Ratio

P/E ratio

The ratio of a stock's price to earnings per share

An alternative method uses a variety of multiplier models. That is, the value of the stock is related to a variable such as earnings, sales, or book value times a multiplier. The most common of these approaches is the price-to-earnings or P/E ratio.

The P/E technique is essentially very easy. The value of a stock is a specified multiple of earnings. That is,

Value of the stock = Earnings × Earnings multiple.

To use this technique, the investor needs only earnings and the appropriate earnings multiple. For example, if the earnings are $2.45 and the appropriate multiple is 13 (that is, the appropriate P/E ratio is 13), then the value of the stock is

$$\$2.45 \times 13 = \$31.85.$$

This value is then compared to the current price of the stock. If the price is less than $31.85, the stock is undervalued and should be purchased. If the price of the stock is greater than $31.85, the stock is overvalued and should not be purchased.

The use of P/E ratios, however, is not without problems. First, what earnings should be used in the calculation? You could select either historical earnings or forecasted earnings. If historical earnings, do you use earnings before nonrecurring earnings or net earnings? If forecasted earnings, which forecast? Forecasted earnings may be available from investment advisory services, such as the *Value Line Investment Survey*, or through the Internet. Estimates, however, will differ, so the question remains which estimate to use.

The next problem is to determine the appropriate multiple. One possible solution is to use the historic P/E ratios. Most firms tend to trade within a range of P/E values. For example, for 10 years the historic low P/E ratio for Bristol-Myers Squibb has averaged 18.8 while the historic high P/E ratio has averaged 27.8. Thus, if the estimated earnings are $2.00, the price of the stock should tend to trade between $37.60 ($2.00 × 18.8) and $55.60 ($2.00 × 27.8). If the stock is trading outside this range, that would suggest it may be currently undervalued or overvalued.

This use of P/E ratios provides a range of values but not a unique value. To obtain a unique value, the individual would have to determine a unique earnings multiple. If the average P/E ratio of all firms in an industry is 13.2, then that earnings multiple may be applied to a specific firm within the industry. For example, if the average P/E ratio for household products, toiletries, and drugs is 13.2 and Bristol-Myers Squibb is expected to earn $2.00, then the value of the stock is $26.40 (13.2 × $2.00).

Such application of P/E ratios for valuation suggests that there is a unique P/E ratio for all firms within an industry. This is, of course, an oversimplification since there are differences among firms within an industry, such as size, product lines, sources of finance, and domestic versus foreign operations. These factors can affect the risk associated with a particular firm, so using a unique average P/E ratio to value all firms may be inappropriate.

The Price-to-Sales Ratio

An alternative valuation ratio that has achieved some prominence is the ratio of the stock price to per share sales (P/S). This ratio offers one particular advantage over the P/E ratio. If a firm has no earnings (and many firms, especially small firms, operate at a loss), the P/E ratio has no meaning. The P/S ratio, however, can be computed even if the firm is operating at a loss, thus permitting comparisons of all firms, including those that are not profitable.

Even if the firm has earnings and has a positive P/E ratio, the price-to-sales ratio remains a useful analytical tool. Earnings are ultimately related to sales. A low P/S ratio indicates a low valuation; the stock market is not placing a large value on the firm's sales. Even if the firm is operating at a loss, a low P/S ratio may indicate an undervalued investment. A small increase in profitability may translate these sales into a large increase in the stock's price. When the firm returns to profitability, the market may respond to the earnings, and both the P/E and P/S ratios increase. Thus, a current low price-to-sales ratio may suggest that there is considerable potential for the stock's price to increase. Such potential would not exist if the stock were selling for a high price-to-sales ratio.

The essential weakness that applies to P/E ratios also applies to price-to-sales ratios. Essentially there is no appropriate or correct ratio to use for the valuation of a stock. While one investor may believe that a low P/E ratio is indicative of financial weakness, another investor may draw the opposite conclusion. The same applies to price-to-sales ratios. While some investors and financial analysts isolate firms with low ratios, other analysts would argue the opposite. Low price-to-sales ratios are characteristic of firms that are performing poorly and not worth a higher price. The low ratio then does not indicate undervaluation but is a mirror of financial weakness.

The Price-to-Book Ratio

An alternative to P/E and P/S ratios for the selection of stocks is the ratio of the price of the stock to the per share book value. (*Book value* is another term for the firm's equity found on a firm's balance sheet.) Essentially, the application is the same as with the other two ratios. The investor or securities analyst compares the price of the stock with its per share book value. A low ratio suggests that the stock is undervalued while a high ratio suggests the opposite. Once again, determining what constitutes a low or a high value is left to the discretion of the analyst, but the ratio (like all ratios) does facilitate comparisons of firms.

Stock Valuation and a Word of Caution

The valuation methods described in this chapter may give you the impression that stock valuation is mechanical. Nothing could be further from the truth. Stock valuation is often subjective, and analytical techniques may be manipulated to achieve any preconceived results. For example, if you want to buy a stock, increasing your valuation makes it easier to rationalize the purchase. Increased growth rates, lower beta coefficients, or higher estimates of earnings make a stock look better and may justify its purchase. The converse would be true if you want to convince yourself to sell.

You need to realize that stock valuation and security selection are not mechanical. Neither are they scientific. Personal judgment and expectations play a large role in the valuation of assets. And few investors and securities analysts will be consistently correct. That, of course, is the basic idea of the efficient market hypothesis discussed in Chapter 4. Securities markets are exceedingly competitive. Prices tend to mirror expectations and changes in information affect securities prices rapidly, so that few investors consistently outperform the market on a risk-adjusted basis.

Summary   Conceptually, valuation is the process of discounting future cash flows. This process is important because you need an estimate of an asset's worth, its value, prior to purchasing the asset.

One possible discounted cash flow model for valuing common stock is the dividend-growth model. In its simplest form, the model assumes the current dividend will grow indefinitely into the future at a constant rate. This growing dividend is discounted back to the present using the investor's required return. The required return is specified by the capital asset pricing model in which the return depends on the risk-free rate plus a risk premium. The risk premium depends on the return on the market and the systematic risk associated with the stock as measured by its beta coefficient.

Alternative methods to the dividend-growth model use ratios to determine the value of a stock. These techniques include the price-to-earnings (P/E) ratio, the price-to-sales (P/S) ratio, and the price-to-book (P/B) ratio. In each case, the firm's earnings, sales, or book value are multiplied by an appropriate factor to value the stock. This value is then compared to the price of the stock to determine if the stock should be bought or sold.

The valuation of stock can be subjective, since the dividend-growth model uses estimates of future dividends, the firm's growth rate, the expected return on the market, and an estimate of the firm's systematic risk. The P/E, P/S, and P/B ratios all use estimates of the appropriate multiplier. By manipulating the data, it is possible to justify virtually any stock valuation and hence rationalize any course of action.

Review Objectives

Now that you have completed this chapter, you should be able to

1. Calculate the value of a common stock using the dividend-growth model to determine if the stock is over- or undervalued (pp. 488–491).

2. Specify the components of the security market line (p. 493).

3. Adjust the required return for risk (pp. 493–495).

4. Illustrate the impact of changes in the dividend, the growth rate, the expected return on the market, and the beta on the value of a stock (pp. 493–495).

5. Use multiplier models such as the price/earnings (P/E) ratio to value common stock (pp. 496–498).

Internet Assignments

1. Go to a site that provides price-to-earnings, price-to-sales, and price-to-book ratios and compare four firms in the same industry, such as telecommunications, retailing, or pharmaceuticals. Compare each firm's valuation ratios. Which stock appears to be the best to buy? Possible sites include MarketWatch (**http://marketwatch.com**), CNBC/Microsoft (**http://moneycentral.msn.com**), Motley Fool (**http://www.fool.com**), Smart Money (**http://smartmoney.com**), The Street.com (**http://www.thestreet.com**), and Yahoo! Finance (**http://finance.yahoo.com**).

   (If you have a brokerage account, the same information may be available through your account.)

2. Using the previous sites, locate each stock's growth rate and beta coefficient. Apply the dividend-growth model to the firms you have selected. (In order to make the model applicable, you will have to select companies that pay a cash dividend.) Since you will also need a risk-free rate and a return on the market, obtain the rate on a 12-month Treasury bill and arbitrarily add 6 percent. The rationale for the additional 6 percent is that historical yields on stock have tended to average 6 percent above the Treasury bill rate. Treasury bill rates are available through the Federal Reserve (**http://www.federalreserve.gov**) or the federal government's public debt Web site (**http://www.publicdebt.treas.gov**).

3. If you went to more than one site, did each site provide the same information? Were the numerical values of the data equal? If they were different, are there any obvious explanations for the discrepancies?

Problems

1. The dividend-growth model may be used to value a stock:

$$V = \frac{D_0(1 + g)}{k - g}$$

a. What is the value of a stock if:

$$D_0 = \$2$$
$$k = 10\%$$
$$g = 6\%$$

b. What is the value of this stock if the dividend is increased to $3 and the other variables remain constant?

c. What is the value of this stock if the required return declines to 7.5 percent and the other variables remain constant?

d. What is the value of this stock if the growth rate declines to 4 percent and the other variables remain constant?

e. What is the value of this stock if the dividend is increased to $2.30, the growth rate declines to 4 percent, and the required return remains 10 percent?

2. Last year Artworks, Inc. paid a dividend of $3.50. You anticipate that the company's growth rate is 10 percent and have a required rate of return of 15 percent for this type of equity investment. What is the maximum price you would be willing to pay for the stock?

3. An investor with a required return of 14 percent for very risky investments in common stock has analyzed three firms and must decide which, if any, to purchase. The information is as follows:

Firm	A	B	C
Current earnings	$2.00	$3.20	$7.00
Current dividend	$1.00	$3.00	$7.50
Expected annual growth rate in dividends and earnings	7%	2%	−1%
Current market price	$23	$47	$60

a. What is the maximum price that the investor should pay for each stock based on the dividend-growth model?

b. If the investor does buy stock A, what is the implied percentage return?

    c. If the appropriate P/E ratio is 12, what is the maximum price the investor should pay for each stock? Would your answers be different if the appropriate P/E were 7?

    d. What does stock C's negative growth rate imply?

4. TSC, Inc. sells for $26 and pays an annual per share dividend of $1.30, which you expect to grow at 12 percent. What is your expected return on this stock? What would be the expected return if the price were $40 a share?

5. Jersey Jewel Mining has a beta coefficient of 1.2. Currently the risk-free rate is 5 percent and the anticipated return on the market is 11 percent. JJM pays a $4.50 dividend that is growing at 6 percent annually.

    a. What is the required return for JJM?

    b. Given the required return, what is the value of the stock?

    c. If the stock is selling for $80, what should you do?

    d. If the beta coefficient declines to 1.0, what is the new value of the stock?

    e. If the price remains $80, what course of action should you take given the valuation in d?

6. The risk-free rate of return is 3 percent, and the expected return on the market is 8.7 percent. Stock A has a beta coefficient of 1.4, an earnings and dividend growth rate of 5 percent, and a current dividend of $2.60 a share.

    a. What should be the market price of the stock?

    b. If the current market price of the stock is $27, what should you do?

    c. If the expected return on the market rises to 10 percent and the other variables remain constant, what will be the value of the stock?

    d. If the risk-free return rises to 4.5 percent and the return on the market rises to 10.2 percent, what will be the value of the stock?

    e. If the beta coefficient falls to 1.1 and the other variables remain constant, what will be the value of the stock?

    f. Explain why the stock's value changes in c through e.

7. The security market line is estimated to be

$$k = 5\% + (10.4\% - 5\%)b.$$

You are considering two stocks. The beta of A is 1.4. The firm offers a dividend yield during the year of 4 percent and a growth rate of 7 percent. The beta of B is 0.8. The firm offers a dividend yield during the year of 5 percent and a growth rate of 3.8 percent.

    a. What is the required return for each security?

    b. Why are the required rates of return different?

    c. Since A offers higher potential growth, should it be purchased?

    d. Since B offers higher dividend yield, should it be purchased?

    e. Which stock(s) should be purchased?

8. Two stocks each currently pay a dividend of $1.75 per share. It is anticipated that both firms' dividends will grow annually at the rate of 8 percent. Firm A has a beta coefficient of 0.88 while the beta coefficient of firm B is 1.35.

   a. If U.S. Treasury bills currently yield 6.4 percent and you expect the market to increase at an annual rate of 12.1 percent, what are the valuations of these two stocks using the dividend-growth model?

   b. Why are your valuations different?

   c. If stock A's price were $51 and stock B's price were $42, what would you do?

9. The dividend-growth model,

$$V = \frac{D_0(1 + g)}{k - g},$$

suggests that an increase in the dividend growth rate will increase the value of a stock. However, an increase in the growth may require an increase in retained earnings and a reduction in the current dividend. Thus, management may be faced with a dilemma: current dividends versus future growth. As of now, investors' required return is 13 percent. The current dividend is $1 a share and is expected to grow annually by 7 percent, so the current market price of the stock is $17.80. Management may make an investment that will increase the firm's growth rate to 10 percent, but the investment will require an increase in retained earnings, so the firm's dividend must be cut to $0.60 a share. Should management make the investment and reduce the dividend?

Additional Problems with Answers

1. What is the value of a stock currently paying a dividend of $1.50 that is growing annually at 8 percent when investors require a rate of return of 12 percent?

2. What is the return on the stock in Problem 1 if it is purchased for $38 (i.e., for less than its valuation)?

3. If the risk-free rate of interest is 6.84 percent, and an investor anticipates that the market will rise by 12.5 percent, what is the required return on a stock with a beta of 1.34?

4. Use the risk-adjusted required return from Problem 3 in the dividend-growth valuation model: What is the value of the stock in Problem 1 if the risk-free rate is 8 percent, the return on the market is 12 percent, and this stock's beta is 1.4?

5. What is the value of a stock if it is earning $2.47 a share and the appropriate earnings multiple or P/E is 12? (The same technique applies to price-to-book and price-to-sales ratios.)

Answers

1. The dividend-growth model for the determination of the value of a common stock is

$$V = \frac{D_0(1 + g)}{k - g}$$

Definitions of the symbols:

V valuation of the stock

D_0 the current dividend

g the annual rate of growth in dividends

k investors' required rate of return

The model assumes that the dividend will grow at the same rate indefinitely into the future. The application to this problem is

$$V = \frac{\$1.50(1 + .08)}{.12 - .08}$$

$$= \$40.50.$$

2. Using the dividend-growth model, the return on an investment is

$$r = [D_0 (1 + g)]/P + g$$

The new symbols are r, the rate of return, and P, the price of the stock. In this example, the answer is

$$r = \frac{\$1.50(1 + .08)}{\$38} + .08 = 12.26\%.$$

Notice that the return of 12.26 percent exceeds the 12 percent required return because the stock is undervalued, that is, it is selling for a price that is less than the valuation.

3. The risk-adjusted required rate of return (i.e., the required return in the capital asset pricing model) is

$$k = r_f + (r_m + r_f)\text{beta}$$

Definition of symbols:

r_f risk-free rate of return

r_m return on the market

In this illustration the required return is

$$k = r_f + (r_m + r_f) \text{ beta} = .0684 + (.125 - .0684)1.34 = 14.42\%$$

4. $k = .08 + (.12 - .08)1.4 = .136$

$$V = \frac{\$1.50(1 + .08)}{.136 - .08} = \$28.93$$

5. Earnings multiple (P/E ratio):

Value of the stock = Earnings × earnings multiple

$\$2.47 \times 12 = \$29.64$

Relationships

1. For a given discount rate, an increase in dividends _____ the value of a stock.
2. In the dividend-growth model, an increase in the required return _____ the value of the stock.
3. If a stock is overvalued, the price of the stock should _____.
4. An increase in a stock's beta coefficient _____ the required return.
5. A decrease in a stock's beta coefficient implies that systematic risk _____.
6. If the price of a stock rises, the P/E ratio _____.
7. If the book value of a corporation increases, the P/B ratio _____.
8. Lower growth rates and higher beta coefficients suggest that the price of a stock should _____.

Answers

1. increases
2. decreases
3. decrease
4. increases
5. decreases
6. increases
7. decreases
8. decrease

CHAPTER
22
The Features of Long-Term Debt—Bonds

I n *The Merchant of Venice*, Antonio sealed his debt to Shylock with a "pound of flesh." Today, the terms of a bond are not so severe, but the terms can still kill a firm. When Eastern Airlines filed for bankruptcy, the secured creditors with liens on the airline's planes had the right to take possession of the aircraft. Without its planes, Eastern was dead; it would never fly again.

Many corporations and governments issue long-term debt (bonds) to finance expansion of plant and equipment or to carry inventory and other assets. For example, as of 2010, Alcoa had over $8 billion in bonds outstanding. Southern Company, a large utility, had over $19 billion in long-term debt. Financing fixed assets such as power plants with bonds offers the company the advantage of financial leverage, and the debt may be retired by the cash flow generated by the assets.

The markets for bonds are essentially no different from the markets for corporate stock. Bonds are initially sold through investment bankers to the public and are privately placed with specific investors such as a pension plan. Once issued, secondary markets develop in which you may buy and sell bonds. You probably do not think about investing in bonds, since stocks receive more publicity. This is unfortunate because bonds offer you interest income, safety of principal, and potential diversification. While there is no requirement that bonds be part of your portfolio, you certainly should consider including them.

This chapter covers the features of bonds such as the interest they pay and the retirement of the principal. The next chapter is concerned with bond pricing and how bond yields are calculated. The initial emphasis will be on the variety of corporate debt, but the general features of bonds also apply to government securities, which are covered later in this chapter.

Characteristics of All Debt Instruments

Bond

Long-term debt instrument that specifies (1) the **principal** (amount owed), (2) the **interest** (payment for the use of the principal), and (3) the **maturity date** (the day on which the debt must be repaid)

Yield

Return on a bond expressed as (1) a **current yield** (interest divided by the current price of the bond) or (2) the **yield to maturity** (return earned from holding the bond until it matures)

Indenture

Document specifying the terms of a debt issue

Default

Failure to meet the terms specified in the indenture of a debt issue

Trustee

Representative of the rights of bondholders who enforces the terms of the indenture

All bonds (that is, long-term debt instruments) share a number of characteristics. They are liabilities of their issuers for a specified amount, called the principal. Virtually all debt has a maturity date; it must be paid off by a specified date. If maturity occurs after a year, it is long-term debt. When this debt is issued, the length of time to maturity can range from a few years to 20 or 30 years. (Coca-Cola has a bond outstanding that matures in 2093!) The owners of debt instruments receive payments (interest). The payments are usually fixed and are often referred to as the "coupon." Interest should not be confused with other forms of income, such as cash dividends paid by common and preferred stock. Dividends come from the firm's earnings, while interest is an expense. Sometimes interest is called yield and may be expressed as current yield or yield to maturity. The difference between the two is discussed in the next chapter on yields.

Each debt agreement has terms that the debtor must meet, and these are stated in a legal document called the indenture. One of the most frequent requirements is the pledging of collateral that the borrower must put up to secure the loan. For example, the collateral for a mortgage loan is the building and land. Other assets, such as securities or inventory owned by the borrower, may also be pledged to secure the loan. If the borrower defaults on the loan (in other words, if the borrower fails to pay the interest or fails to meet other terms of the indenture), the creditor may seize the collateral and sell it to recoup the principal.

Other examples of common loan restrictions are (1) limits on dividend payments, (2) limits on the issue of additional debt, and (3) the requirement to periodically retire a proportion of the debt. These examples do not exhaust all the possible conditions of a given loan. Since each loan is separately negotiated, there is ample opportunity for subtle differences among loan agreements. The important point, however, is that if any part of the loan agreement is violated, the creditor may declare that the debt is in default and the entire loan is due. Default is not just the failure to pay the interest. Failure to meet *any* of the indenture provisions places the loan in default, even though the interest is still being paid.

Many debt instruments are purchased by investors who may be unaware of the terms of the indenture. Even if they are aware of the terms, the investors may be too geographically dispersed to take concerted action in case of default. To protect their interests, a trustee is appointed for each publicly held bond issue. It is the trustee's job to see that the terms of the indenture are upheld and to take remedial action if the company should default on the terms of the indenture. If the firm should default on the interest payments or other terms of the indenture, the trustee may take the firm to court on behalf of all the bondholders in order to protect their principal.

Another characteristic of all debt is risk—risk that the interest will not be paid, risk that the principal will not be repaid, risk that the price of the debt instrument may decline, and risk that inflation will erode the purchasing power of the interest payments and principal repayment. The risk of default is firm specific, so the impact of a bond's failure to pay interest or be retired is reduced through the construction of a diversified bond portfolio. The other sources of risk, however, apply to all bonds and cannot be reduced through the construction of a diversified portfolio.

Risk of default on interest and principal payments varies with different types of debt. The debt of the federal government has no risk of default on its interest payments and principal repayments. The reason for this absolute safety is that the government has the power to print money. The government can always issue the money necessary to pay the interest and repay the principal. (There is, however, no guarantee what the money will buy.)

Credit ratings

Classification schemes designed to indicate the risks associated with a particular debt instrument

The debt of firms and individuals is not so riskless, for both may default on their obligations. To aid potential buyers of debt instruments, credit rating services have developed (Mergent's, Dun & Bradstreet, and Standard & Poor's). These services rate the degree of risk of a debt instrument. Exhibit 22.1 illustrates the risk classifications offered by Mergent's and Standard & Poor's. High-quality debt receives a rating of triple A, while poorer-quality debt receives progressively lower ratings. Although not all debt instruments are rated, the services do cover a significant number of debt obligations.

Ratings play an important role in the marketing of debt obligations. Since the risk of default may be substantial for poor-quality debt, some financial institutions and investors will not purchase debt with a low credit rating. If a firm's or municipality's debt rating falls, the entity may have difficulty selling its debt. Corporations and municipal governments thus seek to maintain good credit, for good credit ratings reduce the cost of borrowing and increase the marketability of the debt.

Debt is also subject to the risk of price fluctuations. Once it has been issued, the market price of the debt will rise or fall depending on market conditions. If interest rates rise, the price of debt must fall so that its fixed interest payment is competitive. The opposite is true if interest rates decline. The price of debt will rise, for the fixed interest payment makes it more attractive, and buyers bid up the debt's price. Why these fluctuations in the price of debt instruments occur is explained in more detail in the next chapter on the pricing of debt instruments.

There is, however, one feature of debt that partially compensates for the risk of price fluctuations. The holder knows that the debt ultimately matures; the principal must be repaid. Thus, if the price falls and the debt instrument sells for a discount (less than the face value), the price of the bond must appreciate as it approaches maturity. For on the day it matures, the full amount of the principal must be repaid.

The final risk that all creditors must endure is inflation, which reduces the purchasing power of the interest and principal. If the lenders anticipate inflation, they will demand a higher rate of interest to help protect their purchasing power. For example, if the rate of inflation is 4 percent, the creditors may demand 6 percent, which nets them 2 percent in real terms. While the inflation causes the real value of the capital to deteriorate, the interest rate partially offsets the effects of inflation. Thus creditors must demand a rate of interest at least equal to the rate of inflation to maintain their purchasing power.

EXHIBIT 22.1
Bond Ratings

Mergent's Bond Ratings

Aaa	Bonds of highest quality	Ba	Bonds of speculative quality whose features cannot be considered well assured
Aa	Bonds of high quality		
A	Bonds whose security of principal and interest is considered adequate but may be impaired in the future	B	Bonds that lack characteristics of a desirable investment
		Caa	Bonds in poor standing that may be defaulted
Baa	Bonds of medium grade that are neither highly protected nor poorly secured	Ca	Speculative bonds that are often in default
		C	Bonds with little probability of any investment value (lowest rating)

For ratings Aa through B, 1, 2, and 3 represent the high, middle, and low ratings within the class.

Standard & Poor's Ratings

AAA	Bonds of highest quality	BB	Bonds of lower medium grade with few desirable investment characteristics
AA	High-quality debt obligations		
A	Bonds that have a strong capacity to pay interest and principal but may be susceptible to adverse effects	B and CCC	Primarily speculative bonds with great uncertainties and major risk if exposed to adverse conditions
BBB	Bonds that have an adequate capacity to pay interest and principal but are more vulnerable to adverse economic conditions or changing circumstances	C	Income bonds on which no interest is being paid
		D	Bonds in default

Plus (+) and minus (–) are used to show relative strength within a rating category.

Source: Adapted from *Mergent's Bond Record*, January 2005, and *Standard & Poor's Bond Guide*, January 2005.

Types of Corporate Bonds

Corporations issue a variety of bonds. These include

- mortgage bonds
- equipment trust certificates
- debentures
- subordinated debentures
- income bonds
- convertible bonds
- variable interest rate bonds
- zero coupon bonds

Each type of bond has characteristics that differentiate it from the others. You need to be aware of the differences, for some types of bonds are decidedly more risky.

Mortgage Bonds

Mortgage bonds

Bonds secured by a claim on real estate

Collateral

Assets used to secure a loan or debt instrument

Mortgage bonds are issued to purchase specified real estate assets, and the acquired assets serve as collateral. That means the assets are pledged to secure the debt. If the firm should default on the interest or principal repayment, the creditors may take title to the pledged property. They may then choose to operate the fixed asset or to sell it. While the pledging of property may decrease the risk of loss, lenders are rarely interested in taking possession and operating the property. Lenders earn their income through interest payments, not by the operation of the fixed assets. Creditors are rarely qualified to operate the assets if they were to take possession of them. If the creditors were forced to sell the assets, they might find few buyers and have to sell at distress prices. For example, if a school defaults on interest on the mortgage payments for its dormitories, what can the creditors do with the buildings if they take possession of them? While the pledging of the assets increases the safety of the principal, the lenders prefer the prompt payment of interest and principal.

Equipment Trust Certificates

Equipment trust certificates

Serial bonds issued by transportation companies that are secured by the equipment purchased with the proceeds of the loan

Equipment trust certificates are issued to finance specified equipment, and the assets are pledged as collateral. These certificates are primarily issued by railroads (for example, Southern Pacific) and airlines (for example, Delta Airlines) to finance rolling stock and airplanes, and this equipment is the collateral. This collateral is considered to be of excellent quality, for unlike fixed assets, this equipment can be readily *moved* and sold to other railroads and airlines should the firm default on the certificates.

A typical illustration of this type of bond is the 8.41 percent equipment trust certificates issued by CSX to acquire railroad gondola cars. CSX is required to retire annually a specified amount of the certificates, which started with $3,289,427 in 1993 and rose to $10,647,655 in 2006. The revenues generated by the railroad cars secured the interest and principal repayment. In case of default, the trustee could sell the equipment to recoup funds due that were owed the owners of the certificates.

Debentures

Debentures

Unsecured bonds

Subordinated debentures

Bonds with a lower (subordinate) claim on the firm's assets than the claims of other debt instruments

Debentures are *unsecured* bonds supported by the general credit of the firm. This type of debt is more risky, for in case of default or bankruptcy, the secured debt is redeemed before the debentures. Some debentures are subordinated debentures, and these are even riskier because they are subordinate to other debts of the firm. Even unsecured debt has a superior position to the subordinated debenture. These bonds are among the riskiest types of debt issued and usually have higher interest rates or other features, such as convertibility into the stock of the company, to compensate the lenders for the increased risk.

Financial institutions often prefer a firm to sell debentures to the general public. Since the debentures are general obligations of the company, they do not tie up its assets. If the firm needs additional money, it can use these assets as collateral. The financial institutions will be more willing to lend the firm the additional funds because of the collateral. If the assets had been previously pledged, the firm would lack this flexibility in its financing.

While the use of debentures may not decrease the ability of the firm to issue additional debt, default on the debentures usually means that all superior debt is in default. A frequent indenture clause stipulates that *if any of the firm's debt is in default*, all debt issues are in default, in which case the creditor may declare the entire debt to be due. Thus, a firm should not overextend itself through excessive use of unsecured debt any more than it should use excessive amounts of secured debt.

Income Bonds

Income bonds

Bonds whose interest is paid only if it is earned by the firm

Income bonds require that the interest be paid only if the firm earns it. If the firm is unable to cover its other expenses, it is not legally obligated to pay the interest on these bonds. These are among the riskiest of all types of corporate bonds and are rarely issued. There is, however, a type of bond frequently issued by state and local governments that is similar to corporate income bonds. These are revenue bonds, which pay the interest only if the revenue is earned. Examples of this type are the bonds issued to finance toll roads, such as the New Jersey Turnpike. The interest on the debt is paid if the tolls generate sufficient revenue (after operating expenses) to cover the interest payments.

Revenue bonds

Bonds supported by the assets the bonds financed; income bonds issued by state and local governments

Convertible Bonds

Convertible bonds

Bonds that may be converted into (exchanged for) stock at the option of the bondholder

Convertible bonds are a hybrid type of security. Technically they are debt: The bonds pay interest that is a fixed obligation of the firm, and the bonds have a maturity date. But these bonds have a special feature—they may be converted into a specified number of shares of common stock. For example, a Textron $1,000 convertible bond may be exchanged for 76.1905 shares of Textron's common stock. The value or market price of these bonds depends on both the value of the stock and the interest that the bonds pay.

This type of bond offers the investor the advantages of both debt and equity. If the price of the common stock rises, the value of the bond must rise. The investor has the opportunity for capital gain should the price of the common stock rise. If, however, the price of the common stock does not appreciate, the investor still owns a debt obligation of the company. The company must pay interest on this debt and must retire it at maturity. Thus, the investor has the safety of an investment in a debt instrument.

The convertible bond also offers the firm several advantages. First, if the firm gives investors the conversion feature, it is able to issue the bond with a lower rate of interest. Second, the conversion price is set above the market price of the stock when the bond is issued. If the bond is converted, the firm issues fewer shares than would have been issued if the firm had sold common stock. Therefore, the current stockholders' position is diluted less by the issuing of convertible bonds. Third, when the convertible bond is issued, the management of the firm does not anticipate having to retire the bond. Instead, management anticipates that the bond will be converted into stock, and this conversion ends the necessity to retire the debt. Fourth, when the bond is converted, the transfer of debt to common stock increases the equity base of the firm. Since the firm will then be less financially leveraged, it may be able to issue additional debt.

Convertible bonds appear to offer advantages to both investors and firms. They have been a popular financing vehicle for firms ranging from large established firms like IBM to small firms. However, since convertible bonds are a hybrid security that mixes elements of debt and equity, they are difficult to analyze. For this reason, a detailed discussion is deferred to Chapter 25.

Variable Interest Rate Bonds

Variable interest rate bonds

Long-term debt instruments whose interest payments vary with changes in short-term interest rates or the Consumer Price Index

Most bonds make periodic *equal payments*, but bonds with variable coupons have become a popular alternative to the traditional bond with a fixed coupon. These variable interest rate bonds make payments that vary with changes in the rate of inflation or changes in interest rates. For example, SLM Corporation, which is the nation's leading source of private funds for higher education loans, issued variable rate bonds during 2005. Interest payments will be made *monthly* and consist of a fixed amount plus an amount adjusted each month for changes in the Consumer Price Index. Initially the bond paid an annual rate of 4.95 percent, consisting of a fixed 1.8 percent plus 3.15 percent, which was the adjustment for the change in the CPI.

Zero Coupon Bonds

Zero coupon bonds

Bonds that are initially sold at a discount and on which interest accrues and is paid at maturity

While the majority of bonds periodically pay interest, bonds exist that pay no interest. These zero coupon bonds sell for a discount from face value, and the interest accrues. At maturity the investor receives the bond's face value. The pathbreaking issue was a JC Penney bond that was sold in 1981 for $330 and paid $1,000 at maturity in 1989. If you bought the bond when it was issued for $330 and held it to maturity, you earned a return of 14.86 percent.[1]

---

[1]This yield is calculated as follows:

$$\$330(1 + i)^8 = \$1,000$$
$$(1 + i)^8 = \$1,000/\$300 = 3.0303$$
$$i = (3.0303)^{125} - 1 = 14.86$$

If a financial calculator is used, the yield is determined as follows: $PV = -330$; $N = 8$; $PMT = 0$; $FV = 1,000$, and $I = ?$ When these data are entered into the calculator, $I = 14.86$ percent.

After the initial success of this issue, other firms, including IBM Credit Corporation (the financing arm of IBM), issued similar bonds. In each case the firm makes no cash interest payments. The bond sells for a discount, and the investor's return accrues from the appreciation of the bond's value as it approaches maturity.

One tax feature, however, reduces the attractiveness of zero coupon bonds. The IRS taxes the accrued interest as if it were received. You must pay federal income tax on the earned interest even though you receive the funds only when the bond matures. Thus, zero coupon bonds are of little interest to investors except as part of tax-deferred pension plans, because the tax on the accrued interest in the account is deferred until the funds are withdrawn. Therefore, the primary reason for acquiring a zero coupon bond is to use it in conjunction with a tax-deferred pension plan.

High-Yield Securities—Junk Bonds

High-yield (junk) bonds

Poor-quality debt with high yields and high probability of default

High-yield securities (junk bonds) are not a particular type of bond but a name given to debt of low quality (that is, bonds rated below triple B). Junk bonds are usually debentures and may be subordinated to the firm's other debt obligations. The poor quality of this debt requires that junk bonds offer high yields, which may be three to four percentage points greater than the yield available on high-quality bonds. Junk bonds are bought by financial institutions and individuals who are accustomed to investing in poor-quality bonds and who are willing to accept the larger risk in order to earn the higher yields.

Foreign Bonds

U.S. firms may also issue bonds in foreign countries to raise funds for foreign investments, such as plant and equipment. For example, Merck reported in its 2009 10K report that it had long-term debt of $16.07 billion, of which $2.99 billion (18.6 percent) was payable in foreign countries. These bonds fall into two basic types, depending on the currency in which they are denominated. U.S. companies can sell bonds denominated in the local currency (for example, British pounds), or the firm can sell abroad bonds denominated in U.S. dollars. Correspondingly, non–U.S. firms can sell bonds denominated in their local currency or a foreign currency. If these bonds are issued in the United States by a foreign company and denominated in U.S. dollars, they are referred to as "Yankee bonds."

Firms that sell bonds denominated in another currency have the risk associated with changes in exchange rates. Thus, issuers of Yankee bonds bear the risk associated with fluctuations in the value of the dollar. If the value of the dollar were to rise, more domestic currency would be required to retire the debt. Of course, the converse also applies. If the value of the dollar were to fall, the firm would profit because less domestic currency would be needed to pay off the bonds.

Eurobond

Bond sold in a foreign country but denominated in the currency of the issuing firm

Eurobonds are sold outside of the country of issue but denominated in the currency of the issuing company. Such bonds can be denominated in pounds or yen, so the term is not limited to European currencies. If IBM sells Eurobonds in Europe, it promises to make payments in dollars and avoids the risk associated with changes in exchange rates. U.S. investors who purchase these bonds also do not have to convert the payments from the local currency into dollars and thereby also avoid currency risk. Foreign investors, however, do have to convert the dollar payments into their currency, and do not avoid exchange rate risk. This is an essential reality: When investments and currencies cross international borders, someone must bear the risk associated with fluctuations in exchange rates.

Although Eurobonds are debt instruments, they are different from bonds issued in the United States. First, they pay interest annually instead of semiannually so their yields are not comparable to yields on U.S. bonds unless adjusted for the differences in compounding. Second, Eurobonds are not registered with the SEC for sale in the United States, so American investors must purchase them in another country.

Registered and Book Entry Bonds

In the past, bonds were issued in bearer form with physical coupons attached. Possession of the bond was evidence of ownership, and the owner would detach the interest coupons and send them to the paying agent for collection. Individuals who owned these bonds and lived on the fixed interest payments were referred to as "coupon clippers." Under current law, new issues of coupon bonds are no longer permitted. (They are an easy means to evade income and estate taxes. Coupon bonds are issued in foreign countries.) Even though coupon bonds are no longer being issued, the word *coupon* continues to be used to mean the periodic interest payment made by a bond. Today bonds are issued in either registered or book entry form.

Even registered bonds are ceasing to exist because the current trend is to issue bonds as book entries. All U.S. Treasury bonds are now issued in book entry form, and the same applies to many corporate and municipal bonds. No actual physical bonds are issued; instead a record of owners is maintained by the issuer (or the bank that acts as the transfer and paying agent). Such a system is obviously more cost efficient than issuing actual physical certificates.

Retiring Debt

Debt must ultimately be repaid. This often occurs before the maturity date. When the bond is issued, a method for periodic retirement is usually specified, for very few debt issues are retired in one lump payment at the final maturity date. Instead, part of the issue is systematically retired each year. This systematic retirement may be achieved by issuing the bond in series or by having a sinking fund. In addition, dramatic changes in interest rates may cause a corporation to retire bonds before maturity by repurchasing or by calling the debt.

Serial Bonds

Serial bonds

Debt issued in a series so that some of the bonds periodically mature

In an issue of serial bonds, some bonds mature each year. This type of bond is usually issued by a corporation to finance specific equipment (for example, the CSX railroad cars), and the equipment is pledged as collateral. As the equipment is depreciated, the cash flow generated by the profits and depreciation expense is used to retire the bonds in each series as they mature.

Exhibit 22.2 presents the repayment schedule for a typical issue of serial bonds. The entire issue of Norfolk Redevelopment and Housing Authority Educational Facility Revenue Bonds is for $9,115,000. Most the bonds are retired in a series over a period of 14 years. The amount of debt redeemed each year started at $280,000 in 2000 and rises to $515,000 in 2013. (Notice that

EXHIBIT 22.2
Example of a Serial Bond

$9,115,000 Norfolk Redevelopment and Housing Authority Educational Facility Revenue Bonds Tidewater Community College Series of 1999		
Maturity	Date Amounts	Interest Rates
2000	$280,000	3.65%
2001	290,000	4.15
2002	305,000	4.30
2003	315,000	4.40
2004	330,000	4.50
2005	345,000	4.65
2006	365,000	4.75
2007	380,000	4.85
2008	400,000	4.95
2009	420,000	5.05
2010	440,000	5.15
2011	465,000	5.25
2012	490,000	5.35
2013	515,000	5.40
2019	3,775,000	5.65

the interest rate paid by each bond in the series rises as the time to maturity increases. This positive relationship between time and the interest rate depicts a positive yield curve.) This particular issue also includes $3,775,000 of term bonds, which mature in 2019.

While a few corporate bonds are issued in series such as the CSX equipment trust certificates, most serial bonds are issued by state and local governments. The funds raised by issuing the bonds are used for capital improvements such as new school buildings. The serial bonds are then retired over a number of years by the tax revenues or fees charged by the governmental unit. (Municipal bonds are covered later in the section on government securities.)

Sinking Funds

Sinking fund

Series of periodic payments to retire a bond issue

Sinking funds are generally employed to ease the retirement of corporate bonds. A sinking fund is a periodic payment for the purpose of retiring the debt issue. The payment may be made to a trustee, who invests the money to earn interest. The periodic payments plus the accumulated interest retire the debt when it matures.

In another type of sinking fund, the firm is required to retire a specified amount of the principal each year. The firm may randomly identify the bonds to be retired. Once the sinking fund has selected the individual bonds, the holders must surrender the bonds to receive the principal. There is no reason for the bondholders to continue to hold the bonds, for interest payments cease.

A variation on this type of sinking fund permits the firm to buy back the bonds on the open market instead of randomly selecting and retiring them at par. If the bonds are currently selling at a discount, the firm does not have to expend $1,000 to retire the bonds. For example, if the current price of a bond is $800, the firm can retire a $1,000 bond with an outlay of only $800. Such a repurchase meets the sinking fund requirement and obviously is advantageous for the firm.

Repurchasing Debt

If interest rates have risen and bond prices have declined, a firm may retire debt by repurchasing it. The purchases may be made from time to time, and sellers of the bonds need not know that the company is purchasing and retiring the bonds. The company may also announce the intention to purchase and retire the bonds at a specified price. The bondholders then may sell their bonds at the specified price.

The advantage to the firm of retiring debt that is selling at a discount is the immediate savings. If $1,000 bonds are currently selling for $600, the firm reduces its debt by $1,000 with only a $600 outlay in cash. There is a $400 saving (in other words, extraordinary gain) from purchasing and retiring the debt at a discount.

This gain generates income for the firm's stockholders. For example, in 2001 RCN earned over $409 million from repurchasing $816 million of its long-term debt at a discount.

On the surface, this method may appear to be a desirable means to retire debt, but such appearances may be deceiving. Using money to repurchase debt is an investment decision just like buying plant and equipment. If the firm repurchases the debt, it cannot use the money for other purposes. The question is, which is the better use of the money: purchasing other income-earning assets, or retiring the debt? Unlike a sinking fund requirement (which management must meet), repurchasing the debt is a voluntary act. The lower the price of the debt, the greater the potential benefit from the purchase, but the firm's management must determine if it is the best use of the firm's scarce resource—cash.

Calling the Debt

Call feature

Right of a debtor to retire (call) a bond prior to maturity

Some bonds have a call feature, which permits the issuer to redeem the bond prior to maturity. If interest rates fall after a bond has been issued, it may be advantageous for the company to issue a new bond at the lower interest rates. The proceeds then can be used to retire the older bond with the higher interest rates. The company "calls" the older bond and retires it.

Of course, such a refunding hurts the bondholders, who lose the higher-yielding instruments. To protect these creditors, a call feature usually has a *call penalty*, such as a year's interest. If the initial issue had a 9 percent interest rate, the company would have to pay $1,090 to retire $1,000 worth of debt. While such a call penalty does protect bondholders, a company can still refinance if interest rates decline enough to justify paying the call penalty.

Government Securities

In addition to corporations, federal, state, and local governments issue a variety of debt instruments to tap the funds of individuals, firms, and other governments with funds to invest. The general features of these securities are essentially the same as corporate debt; they pay interest and must be retired at some specified time in the future. The bonds may be callable, and while many do not have sinking funds, the debt is often issued in series, so that a specified series periodically matures.

Federal Government Debt

The federal government issues securities that range from short-term Treasury bills to long-term Treasury bonds with denominations ranging from $50 to $1,000,000. The variety of this debt is illustrated in Exhibit 22.3, which gives the type of debt, the term, the amount outstanding, and the percentage of the total debt composed by each issue. The emphasis is on short- to intermediate-term financing, primarily because interest rates on short-term debt are usually less than on long-term debt. Thus, the use of short-term debt instead of long-term debt reduces the Treasury's interest expense.

Perhaps the most widely held federal government debt is the Series EE savings bond, which is issued in denominations as small as $50 and sold at

E X H I B I T 22.3
The Variety and Amount of
Federal Government Debt
as of January 2009

	Length of Time to Maturity	Value (in Billions of Dollars)	Percentage of Total Debt
Treasury bills	Up to 1 year	$ 1,867	17.4%
Intermediate-term bonds	1 to 10 years	2,792	25.9
Long-term bonds	10 or more years	594	5.5
Inflation-protected bonds	various maturities	530	4.9
Savings bonds	various maturities	194	1.8
Other*	various maturities	4,784	44.5
		$10,761	100.0%

*Primarily debt held by U.S. government agencies, trust funds, and state and local governments

Source: Bureau of Public Debt.

a discount, so the earned interest accrues but is not paid until the bond is redeemed or matures.[2] EE bonds are designed to attract the funds of modest investors and compete directly with other savings vehicles, such as savings accounts or certificates of deposit issued by banks. EE bonds have one significant feature that differentiates them from traditional savings vehicles: The earned interest may be tax deferred until you redeem the bond or it matures (whichever comes first). While you can choose to pay the tax as the interest accrues, most individuals take advantage of the tax deferral.

Series EE bonds are an illustration of a bond with no secondary market. The majority of federal government Treasury bills and bonds may be bought and sold in the secondary markets. Treasury bills are short-term securities issued by the federal government that compete against other money market instruments.

Intermediate-term federal government debt consists of Treasury notes, which are issued in denominations of $1,000 to more than $100,000 and mature in one to 10 years. Treasury bonds are issued in denominations of $1,000 to $1,000,000 and mature in more than 10 years from date of issue. New issues of Treasury bonds may be purchased through banks and brokerage firms. These firms charge commissions, but the investor may avoid such fees by purchasing the bonds directly through any of the Federal Reserve banks.

---

[2]Effective May 1, 1995, the term of the new EE bond was set at 17 years. If the bonds are not redeemed at maturity, they will continue to earn interest for an additional 13 years, for a total of 30 years. The rate of interest was divided into a short-term rate that applies for the first 5 years and a long-term rate that applies to the last 12 years. The interest rates are announced every May 1 and November 1 and apply for the following six months. For years 1 through 5, the rate will be 85 percent of an average of the rate paid by six-month Treasury securities for the preceding three months. For years 6 through 17, the rate will be 85 percent of an average of the rate paid by five-year Treasury securities for the preceding three months. Interest is added to the value of the bonds every six months after they are purchased.

Once you purchase a Treasury bond or bill, it may be readily sold, because there is an active market in these securities. Quotes, however, differ from the bid and ask prices for stocks. While the stock of IBM may be quoted 90.24–90.25, the quotes for Treasury securities are given in 32nds. A price of 90:26 means $90 26/32 per $100 face amount and 101:24 means $101 24/32 per $100 face amount. If a bond is quoted 101:23–101:24, the bond has a bid price of $101 23/32 ($1,017.19) and an ask price of $101 24/32 ($1,017.50) for a $1,000 bond.

Treasury bills are quoted in *terms of yields*. A typical quote may be

Bid	Ask
2.66	2.65

which means the bill is priced so that the selling price yields 2.66 percent but the asking price you pay yields 2.65 percent. (The calculation of these yields is illustrated in the next chapter on bond pricing.) These yields appear to be backwards. Since the ask price is higher, the yield you earn is lower (2.65). However, the market maker pays you less when you sell the bill. Remember market makers profit from the spread. They buy from you at the lower price (higher yield) and sell to you at the higher price (lower yield).

While Treasury securities are among the safest investments, there are ways in which you can lose when investing in these securities. As is explained in the next chapter, changes in the current rate of interest cause bond prices to fluctuate, so you could purchase a Treasury bond and its market price could decline. Second, when you reinvest the interest or the principal, interest rates could be lower, so you must bear this reinvestment rate risk. Third, if inflation increases, the purchasing power of the payments is diminished. There is also the risk associated with exchange rates. While that risk may not apply to you, it does apply to everyone who must convert dollars into their currency. Certainly the decline in the dollar during 2004 inflicted losses on foreign investors who held Treasury securities. Of course, if the dollar were to strengthen as it did in 2010, these investors would experience higher returns as the interest payments would buy more units of their currency.

Municipal Bonds

State and local governments also issue a variety of debt instruments to finance capital expenditures, such as schools or roads. The government then retires the debt as the facilities are utilized and funds are raised through taxes, such as property taxes, or through revenues generated by the facilities, such as the tolls collected by the New Jersey Turnpike.

The primary factor that differentiates state and local government securities from other forms of debt is the tax advantage they offer investors. The interest earned on state and municipal debt is exempt from federal income taxation. Although state and local governments may tax the interest, the federal government may not. Hence, these bonds are frequently referred to as

Tax-exempt bonds

Bonds issued by a state
or municipal government
whose interest is exempt
from federal income
taxation

tax-exempt bonds. (Conversely, the interest earned on federal government debt is exempt from state and local government income taxation.) Since the interest paid by all other debt, including federal government and corporate bonds, is subject to federal income taxation, this exemption is advantageous to state and local governments. They are able to issue debt with substantially lower interest costs.

Investors are willing to accept a lower interest rate on state and local government debt because the after-tax return is equivalent to higher yields on other debt. For example, if the individual is in the 28 percent federal income tax bracket, the return after taxes is the same for a corporate bond paying 7.0 percent and a municipal bond that pays 5.04 percent. The after-tax return is 5.04 percent in either case.

The individual investor may determine the equivalent yields on tax-exempt bonds and nonexempt bonds by using the following equation:

$$i_c(1 - t) = i_m \qquad (22.1)$$

in which i_c is the interest rate paid on the corporate debt, i_m is the interest rate paid by the municipal bond, and t is the individual's tax bracket. Thus, if the corporate bond pays 7.0 percent and the individual's tax bracket is 28 percent, the equivalent yield on a municipal bond is $0.07(1 - 0.28) = 0.0504 = 5.04\%$.

Although state and municipal bonds offer an important tax advantage, they do subject the investor to risk. Inflation erodes the purchasing power of the interest and the principal, and fluctuations in interest rates cause the prices of municipal bonds to fluctuate. Lower interest rates reduce the investor's ability to reinvest at the previous, higher rates, and there is the possibility of default.

There is little you can do to reduce the risks associated with inflation and fluctuations in interest rates, but you may reduce the impact of the risk of default. First, acquire a well-diversified portfolio of tax-exempt bonds that spreads the risk over many state and local governments. Second, limit purchases to bonds with high credit ratings, such as triple or double A. Third, acquire bonds that are insured. Several insurance companies guarantee municipal bonds with regard to the payment of interest and repayment of principal. By purchasing insured bonds, you have a claim on both the government that issued the bonds and the insurance company that guaranteed them.

Summary   This chapter has discussed the general features of long-term debt (bonds). While a corporation may issue a variety of bonds, ranging from secured mortgage bonds to unsecured subordinated debentures and income bonds, the general terms of each issue include the coupon rate of interest and the maturity date. A trustee is appointed for each bond issue to protect the rights of the individual investors. The risks associated with investing in bonds include default on interest and principal repayment, increased interest rates that decrease the current market value of the bond, and loss of purchasing power through inflation.

Bonds may be retired through the use of a sinking fund, which requires the issuer to retire a specified amount of the bonds each year or make a periodic payment to retire the debt issue. Some bonds are issued in series; each year one of the series within the issue is retired. Bonds may also be callable, which permits the issuer to pay off the entire issue prior to maturity. A bond will be called only if interest rates have fallen. If interest rates rise and cause a bond's price to fall, it would be more advantageous for the issuer to repurchase the bonds than to call and retire them at par.

Governments as well as corporations issue bonds. The general features and risks associated with investing in government bonds are the same as with corporate bonds. The big difference between government bonds and corporate bonds is the taxation of the interest income. The interest on state and local government bonds is exempt from federal income taxation, while the interest on federal government debt is exempt from state taxation. The interest earned on an investment in corporate debt may be taxed by the federal, state, or local government. The tax exemption of interest earned on state and local government debt increases the appeal of municipal bonds, as investors seek to reduce their tax obligations.

Review Objectives

Now that you have completed this chapter, you should be able to

1. Identify the general characteristics of bonds (pp. 506–507).
2. Explain the roles of the trustee and credit ratings (p. 507).
3. Differentiate the types of corporate bonds (pp. 508–513).
4. Contrast the means for retiring bonds (pp. 513–516).
5. Differentiate the types of federal government debt (pp. 516–519).
6. Isolate the tax feature associated with municipal bonds (pp. 518–519).

N ow that you know the features of bonds, we shall proceed to their pricing and the calculation of the yields that you earn. You certainly need to know the cost of the bond and the potential return before purchasing it! The value or price of a bond depends on future cash flows: the interest (the coupon) and the repayment of principal. As is subsequently explained, this value fluctuates with change in interest rates.

The yield also depends on the future cash flows. Instead of asking what is the present value of future interest payments and the principal repayment, determining the yield reverses the process. That is, if a bond costs a specified amount, pays interest each year, and repays the principal after a number of years, what return (yield) will you earn?

This chapter is devoted solely to these two topics. It is, however, an important chapter because it explains and illustrates the factors that affect bond prices and yields. The first section covers pricing and the second covers yields. At the end of the chapter, a variety of problems are provided. I heartily recommend that you work through these problems to test your ability to calculate bond prices and bond yields.

Bond Pricing

You buy bonds in the same way that you buy stocks; however, only a few bond prices are given in the financial press such as the *Wall Street Journal*. Prices are quoted in 100s so that 98 represents $980 for a $1,000 bond and 56.7 represents $567 for a $1,000 bond.

Bond prices certainly do differ. In July 2010, one federal government bond was selling for 132.9 ($1,329) while another was selling for 44.6 ($446). While both bonds had a face value of $1,000, one was selling for a considerable premium over its face value and the other was selling for a large discount from the face value. Why would one sell for a premium and the other for a discount? The explanation revolves around the amount of the interest paid by each bond and the timing of the payments and principal repayment.

The price of a bond (in a given risk class) depends on (1) the interest paid by the bond, (2) the interest rate you may earn on competitive bonds, and (3) the maturity date. Part of the bond's value is the present value of the interest payments. The remainder of the bond's value is the present value of the principal repayment. Thus, the price of a bond is the sum of the present value of both the interest payments and the principal repayment.

This value is expressed algebraically in Equation 23.1. (Later this value will be presented in terms of the present value formulas discussed in Chapter 7.) A bond's value is

$$P_B = \frac{PMT}{(1 + i)^1} + \frac{PMT}{(1 + i)^2} + \cdots + \frac{PMT}{(1 + i)^n} + \frac{FV}{(1 + i)^n} \qquad (23.1)$$

in which P_B indicates the current price of the bond; PMT, the periodic interest payment; n, the number of years (payments) to maturity; FV, the principal amount to be received in the future; and i, the current interest rate.

The calculation of a bond's price using Equation 23.1 may be illustrated by a simple example. A firm has a $1,000 bond outstanding that matures in three years with a 6 percent coupon rate ($60 annually). All that is needed to determine the price of the bond is the current interest rate, which is the interest rate that is being paid by newly issued, competitive bonds with the same length of time to maturity and the same degree of risk. If comparable bonds yield 6 percent, then the price of this bond will be par ($1,000), for:

$$P_B = \frac{\$60}{(1 + 0.06)^1} + \frac{\$60}{(1 + 0.06)^2} + \frac{\$60}{(1 + 0.06)^3} + \frac{\$1,000}{(1 + 0.06)^3}$$

$$= \$56.60 + \$53.40 + \$50.38 + \$839.62$$

$$= \$1,000.00$$

If comparable bonds are selling to yield 8 percent, this bond will be unattractive to investors. They will not be willing to pay $1,000 for a bond yielding 6 percent when they could buy competing bonds at the same price that yield 8 percent. In order for this bond to compete with the others, its price must decline sufficiently to yield 8 percent. In terms of Equation 23.1, the price must be

$$P_B = \frac{\$60}{(1 + 0.08)^1} + \frac{\$60}{(1 + 0.08)^2} + \frac{\$60}{(1 + 0.08)^3} + \frac{\$1,000}{(1 + 0.08)^3}$$

$$= \$60(0.926) + \$60(0.857) + \$60(0.794) + \$1,000(0.794)$$

$$= \$55.56 + \$51.42 + \$47.64 + \$794$$

$$= \$948.62.$$

The price of the bond must decline to approximately $949. The bond must sell for a *discount* (a price less than the stated principal) to be competitive with comparable bonds. At that price, you will earn $60 per year in interest and $51 in capital gains over the three years, for a total annual return of 8 percent on the investment. The capital gain occurs because the bond is purchased for $948.62, but when it matures, you will receive $1,000.

If comparable debt were to yield 4 percent, the price of the bond in the previous example would rise. In this case the price of the bond would be

$$P_B = \frac{\$60}{(1 + 0.04)^1} + \frac{\$60}{(1 + 0.04)^2} + \frac{\$60}{(1 + 0.04)^3} + \frac{\$60}{(1 + 0.04)^3}$$

$$= \$60(0.962) + \$60(0.925) + \$60(0.889) + \$1,000(0.889)$$

$$= \$1,055.56.$$

The bond, therefore, would sell at a *premium* (over its face value). Although it may seem implausible for the bond to sell at a premium, this would occur if the market interest rate were to fall below the bond's coupon rate.

Using Interest Tables to Determine a Bond's Price

These calculations are lengthy and would be considerably worse if the bond matured after 20 years. The number of computations, however, can be reduced when you realize that the valuation of a bond has two components: a flow of interest payments and a final repayment of principal. Since interest payments are fixed and are paid every year, they may be treated as an annuity. The principal repayment may be treated as a simple lump-sum payment. Thus the price of a bond is

Price of bond = coupon × interest factor for the present value of an annuity of $1.00 + principal × interest factor for the present value of $1.00

= coupon × *PVAIF* + principal × *PVIF*.

If a $1,000 bond pays $60 per year in interest and matures after three years, its current value is the present value of the $60 annuity for three years and the present value of the $1,000 that will be received after three years. If the interest rate is 8 percent, the current value of the bond is

$$P_B = \$60(PVAIF\ 8I,\ 3N) + \$1,000(PVIF\ 8I,\ 3N)$$

$$P_B = \$60(2.577) + \$1,000(0.794) = \$948.62.$$

Here 2.577 is the interest factor for the present value of a $1 annuity at 8 percent for three years and 0.794 is the interest factor for the present value of $1 at 8 percent after three years. This is the same answer that was derived earlier, but the amount of arithmetic has been reduced.

Since most bonds pay interest semiannually, the above illustration should be adjusted for semiannual interest payments. First, divide the coupon by 2 to determine the six-month payment ($60/2 = $30); second, divide the rate of interest by 2 to determine the semiannual interest rate (8%/2 = 4%); and third, multiply the number of years by 2 to determine the number of time periods, denoted by the letter n when other than one year (3 × 2 = 6). After these adjustments, the value of the bond is

$$P_B = \$30(PVAIF\ 4I,\ 6N) + \$1,000(PVIF\ 4I,\ 6N)$$

$$= \$30(5.242) + \$1,000(0.790) = \$947.26.$$

This valuation is marginally smaller than when annual compounding was used, since the bond's price must decline slightly more to compensate for the more frequent compounding. If interest rates rise and bond prices fall, the decline will be greater when the price is calculated using semiannual payments, because the investor forgoes more lost interest from the higher rates when interest is paid semiannually. The lower price compensates the buyer for the lost interest.

Using a Financial Calculator to Determine a Bond's Price

In many cases, interest tables are impractical for determining a bond's price. The tables are constructed with discrete units such as 20 years or 5 percent. The price of a bond that matures in 19.4 years cannot be determined. The same applies if the current interest rate is 5.42 percent. While you could interpolate, that only increases the number of calculations.

If you use a financial calculator (or a computer program), these problems disappear. In addition, a bond's price is easy to compute using a financial calculator. Consider the 6 percent coupon bond that matures in three years that was used in the previous illustrations. If the current interest rate is 8 percent, enter the payment (PMT = 60), the amount of the principal (FV = 1000), the number of years (N = 3), and the current rate (I = 8). Instruct the calculator is solve for the present value ($PV = ? = -948.50$). This is essentially the same answer derived using the interest tables with the small difference resulting from rounding off. Also notice that the calculator's present value is a negative number. You have to pay $948.50 (an outflow) to receive the interest payments and the principal repayment, both of which are inflows. (If you need to determine the value of the bond using semiannual interest payments, enter $N = 6$, $PMT = 30$, $FV = 1000$, and $I = 4$. The calculator derives an answer of $947.60.)

The Inverse Relationship between Changes in Interest Rates and Bond Prices

The preceding examples illustrate an important general conclusion: *Bond prices and changes in market interest rates are inversely related.* When interest rates rise, bond prices decline. When interest rates fall, bond prices rise. Higher interest rates depress the bond's current value. You are discounting the future payments at a higher rate, which decreases their current value. Lower interest rates increase a bond's current value. You are discounting the future payments at a lower rate, which increases their current value.

You may see this inverse relationship in the following example, which uses a 10-year bond with an 8 percent annual coupon. The first column gives various interest rates and the second column gives the corresponding price of the bond:

Current Interest Rate	Bond Price
12%	$ 774
11	823
10	877
9	936
8	1,000
7	1,070
6	1,147
5	1,232

This negative relationship between the price of a bond and changes in interest rates is, of course, the interest rate risk discussed in Chapter 8.

Although all bonds exhibit this price volatility, the price fluctuations of bonds with longer terms to maturity tend to have greater price fluctuations than the bonds with shorter terms to maturity. You may see this relationship by comparing the impact of changes in interest rates on the prices of two bonds with different terms to maturity. The following illustration repeats the previous one but adds the price of an 8 percent coupon bond that matures after 20 years.

Current Interest Rate	Price of the 10-year Bond	Price of the 20-year Bond
12%	$ 774	$ 701
11	823	761
10	877	830
9	936	909
8	1,000	1,000
7	1,070	1,106
6	1,147	1,229
5	1,232	1,374

In both cases, higher interest rates cause the bond to sell for a discount, but the price decline is greater for the bond that matures after 20 years. And lower interest rates cause the price of the 20-year bond to sell for a greater premium.

If you anticipate that interest rates will decline, you are also expecting bond prices to rise. The converse is also true. If you anticipate that interest rates will rise, you are expecting that bond prices will fall. If you can anticipate correctly the direction of changes in interest rates, you will also correctly anticipate the direction of change in bond prices.

You, however, may incorrectly anticipate the change in interest rates and suffer losses in the bond market. If you buy bonds in anticipation of declining interest rates and interest rates rise, you will sustain a loss. The market value of your bonds will fall and buying longer-term bonds will generate larger losses. There is, however, one thing in your favor. The bond must ultimately be retired. Since the principal must be redeemed, an investment error may be corrected when the bond's price rises as it approaches maturity. The loss will eventually be erased (assuming the issuer does not default). The correction, however, may take years, during which time you have lost the higher yields that were available after you made the initial purchases.

Yields

The word *yield* is frequently used with regard to investing in bonds. Two important uses of the word are the current yield and the yield to maturity. This section differentiates between these two yields.

The Current Yield

The current yield (CY) is the percentage that you earn annually. It is simply

$$CY = \frac{\text{Annual interest payment}}{\text{Price of the bond}}. \tag{23.2}$$

If a bond has a coupon rate of 6 percent and sells for $948.62, the current yield is

$$\frac{\$60}{\$948.62} = 6.3\%.$$

The current yield is important because it gives you an indication of the current return that will be earned on the investment. Investors who seek high current income prefer bonds that offer a high current yield.

The current yield, however, can be misleading, for it fails to consider any change in the price of the bond that may occur if the bond is held to maturity. Obviously, if a bond is bought at a discount, its value must rise as it approaches maturity. The opposite occurs if the bond is purchased for a premium, for its price will decline as maturity approaches. For this reason it is desirable to know the bond's yield to maturity.

The Yield to Maturity

The yield to maturity considers both the current interest and any change in the bond's value when it is held to maturity. If a bond is purchased for $948.62 and held to maturity after three years, you will receive a return of 8 percent. This is the yield to maturity, because this return considers not only the current interest return of 6.3 percent but also the price appreciation of the bond from $948.62 at the time of purchase to $1,000 at maturity. Since the yield to maturity considers both the flow of interest income and the price change, it is a more accurate measure of the return offered investors by the bond over its life.

The yield to maturity may be determined by using Equation 23.1. That equation is:

$$P_B = \frac{PMT}{(1 + i)^1} + \frac{PMT}{(1 + i)^2} + \cdots + \frac{PMT}{(1 + i)^n} + \frac{FV}{(1 + i)^n}.$$

Previously you used that equation to determine the price of the bond. Given the interest payment (the coupon or *PMT*), the principal repayment (*FV*), maturity date (*n*), and the current rate on comparable debt (*i*), you determined the price of the bond. You also use the equation to determine the yield to maturity by substituting the current price of the bond. The yield (the *i*) is now the unknown and is the yield to maturity. If you buy the bond for the given price and hold the bond until maturity, the *i* is the return (the yield to maturity) you earn on the investment.

Using interest tables to determine the yield to maturity can be a tedious task. For example, if a $1,000 bond that matures in three years and pays $100 annually were selling for $952 and the investor wanted to know the yield to maturity, the calculation would be

$$\$952 = \frac{\$100}{(1 + i)^1} + \frac{\$100}{(1 + i)^2} + \frac{\$100}{(1 + i)^3} + \frac{\$1,000}{(1 + i)^3}.$$

PART 4 Investments

Solving this equation can be a formidable task because there is no simple arithmetical computation to determine the value of i. Instead, you select a value for i and plug it into the equation. If this value equates the left-hand and right-hand sides of the equation, then that value of i is the yield to maturity.

If the value does not equate the two sides of the equation, another value must be selected. This process is repeated until a value for i is found that equates both sides of the equation. Obviously, that can be a tedious process. For example, suppose you select 14 percent and substitute it into the right-hand side of the equation:

$$P_B = \frac{\$100}{(1 + 0.14)^1} + \frac{\$100}{(1 + 0.14)^2} + \frac{\$100}{(1 + 0.14)^3} + \frac{\$1,000}{(1 + 0.14)^3}.$$

Since you have both an interest rate (0.14) and the number of years (3), the interest factors for the present value of an annuity and of a dollar may be obtained from the appropriate interest tables and used to determine the value of the bond at that rate for that term to maturity. That is,

$$P_B = \$100(PVAIF\ 14I, 3N) + \$1,000(PVIF\ 14I, 3N)$$

$$= \$100(2.322) + \$1,000(0.675)$$

$$= \$907.20.$$

If the yield to maturity were 14 percent, the bond would sell for \$907.20; however, the bond is selling for \$952, so 14 percent cannot be its yield to maturity. The yield you selected was too high, which caused the present value (the price of the bond) to be too low. You must select another, lower rate and repeat the process. (If you had obtained a value greater than the current price, the selected rate would be too low, and you would select a higher rate.) If you had selected 12 percent, then

$$P_B = \$100(PVAIF\ 12I, 3N) + \$1,000(PVIF\ 12I, 3N)$$

$$= \$100(2.402) + \$1,000(0.712)$$

$$= \$952.20.$$

Thus, the yield to maturity, compounded annually, is 12 percent.

The preceding process argues for your using a financial calculator (or computer program) to compute the yield to maturity. In addition, since interest tables have only discrete rates and numbers of periods, the resulting yield to maturity is often only approximate. However, the use of interest tables to solve the equation is important from an instructional perspective. The yield to maturity is the unique rate that equates both sides of the bond valuation equation. If you just plug numbers into a calculator or computer, you may not perceive what the yield to maturity accomplishes. Once you understand the process and what the yield to maturity tells you, then using a more convenient method is acceptable. (The calculation of returns covered in Chapter 26 uses the same process, so learning to use a financial calculator or computer program will also facilitate making those calculations.)

To use a financial calculator, enter the price of the bond as the present value ($PV = -952$), the interest payments ($PMT = 100$), the maturity value ($FV = 1000$), the number of periods ($N = 3$), and instruct the calculator to determine the rate ($I = ? = 12$), which is the yield to maturity. Notice that the price of the bond is entered as a negative number. You make that payment (a cash outflow) and receive the interest and principal repayments (the cash inflows).

A Comparison of the Current Yield and the Yield to Maturity

The current yield and the yield to maturity are equal only if the bond sells for its principal amount or par. *If the bond sells at a discount, the yield to maturity exceeds the current yield.* This may be illustrated by the bond in the previous example. When it sells at a discount (such as $952), the current yield is only 10.5 percent. However, the yield to maturity is 12 percent. The appreciation on the value of the bond increases the return, so the yield to maturity exceeds the current yield.

If the bond sells at a premium, the current yield exceeds the yield to maturity. For example, if the bond sells for $1,052, the current yield is 9.5 percent ($100/$1,052) and the yield to maturity is 8 percent. The yield to maturity is less because the loss that occurs when the price of the bond declines from $1,052 to $1,000 at maturity has been incorporated into the calculation of the yield.

Exhibit 23.1 presents the current yield and the yield to maturity at different prices for a bond with an 8 percent coupon that matures in 10 years. As may be seen in the table, the larger the discount (or the smaller the premium), the greater are both the current yield and the yield to maturity. For example, when the bond sells for $882, the yield to maturity is 9.9 percent, but it rises to 11.5 percent when the price declines to $798.

EXHIBIT 23.1
Current Yields and Yields to Maturity for a 10-Year Bond with an 8 Percent Annual Coupon

Price of Bond	Coupon	Current Yield	Yield to Maturity
$1,107	8.0%	7.2%	6.5%
1,048	8.0	7.6	7.3
1,000	8.0	8.0	8.0
967	8.0	8.3	8.5
911	8.0	8.8	9.4
882	8.0	9.1	9.9
883	8.0	9.6	10.8
798	8.0	10.0	11.5

The Yield to Maturity and Returns

You should realize that the yield to maturity and the return that you earn on a bond investment need not be the same. To earn the yield to maturity, you have to hold the bond until it matures. If the issuer calls the bond, you will not earn the yield to maturity. If you sell the bond, there is no reason to assume that your return will be same as the yield to maturity. Also, the yield to maturity is a compound rate. If you spend the interest payments, there will be no compounding. While you will earn a simple rate of interest, it will not be the yield to maturity. To achieve a compound rate, you must reinvest the interest payments. When you reinvest these payments, you may earn more if interest rates have risen, but you will earn less if interest rates have declined. To earn the yield to maturity, you must reinvest all the interest payments at that rate. For these reasons, it is highly unlikely that you will earn the yield to maturity.

Summary

The current price of a bond depends on the bond's interest payments (the coupon) and the repayment of the principal, both discounted back to the present at the current rate of interest on comparable debt. When interest rates rise, the prices of existing bonds fall, but declining interest rates cause the prices of existing bonds to rise. These price fluctuations result because bonds pay a fixed amount of interest each year.

Since a bond's price fluctuates with changes in interest rates, it may sell for a discount below its face value or for a premium over the face value. The current yield expresses the bond's annual interest payment relative to the price of the bond. The yield to maturity equates the bond's price with the present value of the interest and principal repayments. If a bond sells for a discount, its yield to maturity exceeds the current yield. If the bond sells for a premium, the yield to maturity is less than the current yield. Since the yield to maturity factors in any premium or discount in the calculation of the yield, it is a better indicator of the return an investor actually earns from the date of purchase to the bond's maturity.

Review Objectives

Now that you have completed this chapter, you should be able to

1. Determine the price of a bond (pp. 522–525).
2. Explain the relationship between changes in interest rates and bond prices (pp. 525–526).
3. Calculate the yield to maturity (pp. 527–529).
4. Differentiate the current yield from the yield to maturity (p. 529).
5. Demonstrate when the current yield exceeds (or is less than) the yield to maturity (p. 529).
6. Explain why the realized return on an investment in a bond may not equal the yield to maturity (pp. 529–530).

Problems Before doing these problems, here are two comments. First, the majority of bonds pay interest semiannually, but the points illustrated by these problems apply to annual payments as well as semiannual interest payments. Ask your instructor which you should use, annual or semiannual payments, to solve the problems. Second, several of the problems have questions that are not explicitly covered in this chapter, such as sinking funds and call features. If necessary, review the material in the previous chapter.

1. A $1,000 bond has a coupon of 6 percent and matures after 10 years.
   a. What would be the bond's price if comparable debt yields 8 percent?
   b. What would be the price if comparable debt yields 8 percent and the bond matures after five years?
   c. Why are the prices different in a and b?
   d. What are the current yields and the yields to maturity in a and b?

2. a. A $1,000 bond has a 7.5 percent coupon and matures after 10 years. If current interest rates are 10 percent, what should be the price of the bond?
   b. If after six years interest rates are still 10 percent, what should be the price of the bond?
   c. Even though interest rates did not change in a and b, why did the price of the bond change?
   d. Change the interest rate in a and b to 6 percent and rework your answers. Even though the interest rate is 6 percent in both calculations, why are the bond prices different?

3. A bond with 15 years to maturity has a semiannual interest payment of $40. If the bond sells for its par value, what are the bond's current yield and yield to maturity?

4. Carrie's Clothes, Inc. has a five-year bond outstanding that pays $60 annually. The face value of each bond is $1,000, and the bond sells for $890.
   a. What is the bond's coupon rate?
   b. What is the current yield?
   c. What is the yield to maturity?

5. Charlotte's Clothing issued a 5 percent bond with a maturity date of 15 years. Five Years have passed and the bond is selling for $690.
   a. What is the current yield?
   b. What is the yield to maturity?
   c. If five years later the yield to maturity is 10 percent, what will be the price of the bond?

6. Your broker offers to sell for $1,200 a AAA-rated bond with a coupon rate of 10 percent and a maturity of eight years. Given that the interest rate on comparable debt is 8 percent, is your broker fairly pricing the bond?

7. Ten years ago your grandfather purchased for you a 25-year $1,000 bond with a coupon rate of 10 percent. You now wish to sell the bond and read that yields are 8 percent. What price should you receive for the bond?

8. Bond A has the following terms:
   - Coupon rate of interest: 10 percent
   - Principal: $1,000
   - Term to maturity: 8 years

   Bond B has the following terms:
   - Coupon rate of interest: 5 percent
   - Principal: $1,000
   - Term to maturity: 8 years

   a. What should be the price of each bond if interest rates are 10 percent?

   b. What will be the price of each bond if, after five years have elapsed, interest rates are 10 percent?

   c. What will be the price of each bond if, after eight years have elapsed, interest rates are 8 percent?

9. A bond has the following features:
   - Coupon rate of interest: 5 percent
   - Principal: $1,000
   - Term to maturity: 10 years

   a. What will the holder receive when the bond matures?

   b. If the current rate of interest on comparable debt is 8 percent, what should be the price of this bond? Would you expect the firm to call this bond? Why?

   c. If the bond has a sinking fund that requires the firm to set aside annually with a trustee sufficient funds to retire the entire issue at maturity, how much must the firm remit each year for 10 years if the funds earn 8 percent annually and there is $100 million outstanding?

10. You are given the following information concerning a noncallable, sinking fund debenture:
   - Principal: $1,000
   - Coupon rate of interest: 7 percent
   - Term to maturity: 15 years
   - Sinking fund: 5 percent of outstanding bonds retired annually; the balance at maturity

   a. If you buy the bond today at its face amount and interest rates rise to 12 percent after three years have passed, what is your capital gain (loss)?

b. If you hold the bond 15 years, what do you receive at maturity?

c. What is the bond's current yield as of right now?

d. Given your price in *a*, what is the yield of maturity?

e. Is there any reason to believe that the bond will be called after three years have elapsed if interest rates decline?

f. What proportion of the total debt issue is retired by the sinking fund?

g. What assets secure this bond?

h. If the final payment to retire this bond is $1,000,000, how much must the firm invest annually to accumulate this sum if the firm is able to earn 7 percent on the invested funds?

Additional Problems with Answers

1. A bond has a maturity date of 10 years and the following features:
   - Principal $1,000
   - Annual interest $50

   Currently the yield on comparable bonds is 9 percent. What should be the price of this bond?

2. A bond has a maturity date of 10 years and the following features:
   - Principal $1,000
   - Annual interest $50

   Currently the bond is selling for its face value ($1,000). How much will you gain or lose if, after two years, the yield on comparable preferred stock is 9 percent?

3. A bond pays annual interest of $50 and currently sells for $743.30. If you buy the bond and hold it until it matures and is redeemed after 10 years, what is your annual yield over the 10 years?

4. What is the price of a zero coupon bond that matures after six years if the bond is priced to yield 7 percent?

5. What is the yield to maturity if you buy a zero coupon bond for $666 and it is redeemed after six years for $1,000?

6. The table on page 526 is used to illustrate the price fluctuations of two bonds with the same coupon but different terms to maturity. The price of the bond with the longer term is more volatile. Construct a similar table comparing the price volatility of two bonds with the same term to maturity but different coupons. Use a term to maturity of 10 years and coupon rates of 4 and 10 percent. Which bond's price is more volatile?

In all three problems, the bonds pay $50 in interest and will be redeemed after 10 years.

1. The current price is

$$\$50(6.418) + 1{,}000(0.422) = \$742.90.$$

$$PMT = 50;\ FV = 1000;\ N = 10;\ I = 9;\ P = 743.29$$

2. With eight years to maturity, the price is

$$\$50(5.535) + 1{,}000(0.502) = \$778.75.$$

$$PMT = 50;\ FV = 1000;\ N = 8;\ I = 9;\ P = 778.60$$

If you bought the bond for $1,000, the loss is $221.40 ($1,000 − 778.60). The potential loss is reduced as the bond approaches maturity.

3. The annual return equates the current cost $743.30 with the present value of the cash flows. Using a financial calculator shows that the return is 9 percent.

$$PMT = 50;\ FV = 1000;\ N = 10;\ P = 743.29,\ I = ? = 9$$

Solving this problem is more difficult using interest tables. Select a rate such as 9 percent, substitute in the equation and continue the process until both sides of the equation are equal (or approximately equal).

$$\$743 = 50(PVAIF) + 1{,}000(PVIF)$$

$$\$743 = 50(6.418) + 1{,}000(0.422)$$

4. Zero coupon bonds pay no interest. You purchase the bond for a discount and receive the principal amount ($1,000) at maturity. The price of the bond is

$$\$0(4.766) + 1{,}000(0.666) = \$666.$$

$$PMT = 0;\ FV = 1000;\ N = 6;\ 1 = 7;\ P = ? = 666$$

5. You purchase the bond for a discount (e.g., $666) and receive the principal amount ($1,000) at maturity. The yield to maturity is

$$\$666 = \$(1{,}000)(PVIF)$$

$$PVIF = 666/1{,}000 = 0.666$$

The present value of a $1 interest factor for six years determines that the yield is 7 percent.

$$PMT = 0; FV = 100; N = 6; P = 666, I = ? = 7$$

Problems 4 and 5 use the same zero coupon bond. In Problem 4 you are asked to determine its price given the yield to maturity. In Problem 5 you are asked to determine the yield to maturity given the bond's price.

6.

Current Interest Rate	Price of the 4 percent coupon bond	Price of the 10 percent coupon bond
12%	$ 548	$ 887
11	588	941
10	631	1,000
9	679	1,064
8	732	1,134
7	789	1,211
6	853	1,294
5	923	1,386
4	1,000	1,487

While the absolute price changes are larger for the 10 percent coupon bond, the percentage changes are larger for the 4 percent coupon bond. For example, the price movement from $548 to $588 is 7.3 percent while the price movement from $887 to $941 is 6.1 percent.

Relationships

1. If interest rates increase, bond prices _____.

2. The premium paid for a bond with a 5 percent coupon _____ when interest rates decline from 4 to 3 percent.

3. If a bond's price declines, the yield to maturity _____.

4. If a bond's price increases, the current yield _____.

5. If the yield to maturity diminishes, that suggests interest rates have _____.

6. A bond's sinking fund should _____ the investor's risk.

7. An increase in the price of a firm's stock should _____ the price of its bonds.

8. If a bond sells for a discount, that discount _____ as the bond approaches maturity.

9. If a bond sells for its face value (principal amount), that suggests interest rates have _____ since the bond was issued.

10. Lower bond prices are associated with _____ yields.

Answers

1. decrease

2. increases

3. increases

4. decreases

5. decreased

6. decrease

7. have no impact on (no change)

8. decreases

9. not been affected (no change)

10. increased

24

Preferred Stock

P referred stock is like a mixed-breed dog. It's legally equity, but its features are more like debt than common stock. Many companies, especially financial institutions such as Bank of America, Citicorp, and Merrill Lynch have issued a variety of preferred stocks that may appeal to specific types of investors or that may be appropriate for specific types of investment accounts.

This is a relatively brief chapter. It describes the basic features of preferred stock, how it may be valued, and tools used to analyze it. Most of this material you have seen earlier in the chapters on common stock and bonds. What is new is the application to preferred stock.

The Features of Preferred Stock

Preferred stock

Class of stock (equity) that has a claim prior to common stock on the firm's earnings and assets

Preferred stock is an equity instrument that usually pays a fixed dividend. While most firms have only one issue of common stock, they may have several issues of preferred stock. Virginia Electric and Power (a subsidiary of Dominion Resources) has eight issues of preferred stock. In seven cases the dividend rate is fixed. Thus for the series $5.00 preferred, the annual dividend is $5.00, which is distributed at the rate of $1.25 per share quarterly. For the remaining issue, the dividend is tied to the yields on short-term money market securities and changes quarterly.

The dividend is paid from the firm's earnings. If the firm does not have the earnings, it may not declare and pay the preferred stock dividends. If the firm should omit the preferred stock's dividend, the dividend is said to be in

Arrears

Dividends on a cumulative preferred stock that have not been paid and have accumulated

Cumulative preferred stock

Preferred stock whose dividends accumulate (accrue) if not paid

Noncumulative preferred stock

Preferred stock whose dividends do not accumulate if the firm misses a dividend payment

arrears. The firm does not have to remove this arrearage. In most cases, however, any omitted dividends have to be paid in the future before any dividends may be paid to the holders of the common stock. Such cases, in which the preferred stock's dividends accumulate, are called cumulative preferred stocks. Most preferred stock is cumulative, but there are examples of noncumulative preferred stocks, whose dividends do not have to be made up if not paid. For example, Aegon, a life and health insurance company, issued a perpetual noncumulative preferred stock. The annual dividend is 6.35 percent, but payment is not a legal obligation of the company and Aegon is not required to make up any missed payments.

For investors holding preferred stock in firms having financial difficulty, the difference between cumulative and noncumulative preferred may be immaterial. Forcing the firm to pay dividends to erase the arrearage may further weaken the company and hurt the owner of the preferred stock more than forgoing the dividends. Once the firm has regained its profitability, erasing the arrearage may become important to both the holders of the stock and the company, especially if the firm needs to raise external funds. For example, both Unisys and Chrysler paid the arrearages on their preferred stock when the firms regained profitability.

Once a preferred stock is issued, the corporation may never have to retire it, because preferred stock may be perpetual. This can be both an advantage and a disadvantage. If the firm does not have to retire the preferred stock, it does not have to generate the money to retire it. The firm may instead use its funds elsewhere (for example, to purchase equipment). However, should the firm ever want to change its capital structure and substitute debt financing for the preferred stock, the firm may have difficulty in retiring the preferred stock. The firm may have to purchase the preferred stock on the open market, and, in order to induce the holders to sell the preferred shares, the firm will probably have to bid up the price of the preferred stock.

To maintain some control over the preferred stock, the firm often adds a call feature, which gives the firm the option to call and redeem the issue. Although the actual terms of a call feature will vary with each preferred stock issue, the general features are similar. First, the call is at the option of the firm. Second, the call price is specified. Third, the firm may pay a call penalty (for example, a year's dividends). Fourth, after the preferred stock is called, future dividend payments cease, which forces holders to surrender their securities.

The call feature works to the issuer's benefit, since it gives management the option to retire the stock. Many issues of preferred stock also have a mandatory sinking fund and maturity dates. For example, the Virginia Electric and Power $7.30 preferred stock requires the company to redeem 15,000 shares annually at $100 a share. Such a mandatory sinking fund favors investors, as the firm must generate the funds to systematically retire the stock. Such issues of preferred stock are similar to bonds, which are not perpetual and must be retired through sinking funds or eventually reach a final maturity date.

Preferred Stock and Bonds Contrasted

Because preferred stock pays a fixed dividend, it is purchased primarily by investors seeking a fixed flow of income. Since preferred stock pays a fixed dividend, it is analyzed and valued like a bond. But preferred stock differs from long-term debt, as the subsequent discussion will demonstrate, and these differences are significant.

First, for investors, preferred stock is riskier than debt. The terms of a bond are legal obligations of the firm. If the corporation fails to pay the interest or meet any of the terms of the indenture, the bondholders may take the firm to court to force payment of the interest or to seek liquidation of the firm in order to protect the bondholders' principal. Preferred stockholders do not have that power, for the firm is not legally obligated to pay the preferred stock dividends.

In addition, debt must be retired, while preferred stock may be perpetual. If the security is perpetual, the only means to recoup the amount invested is to sell the preferred stock in the secondary market. You cannot expect the issuer to redeem a perpetual security, and the price of a perpetual preferred stock will fluctuate more than the price of a long-term bond with a finite life.

Second, the yield differential between preferred stock and bonds is smaller than would be expected on the basis of risk differentials. This small differential may be explained by the corporate income tax laws. Dividends paid by one corporation to another receive favorable tax treatment. Only 30 percent of the dividends are taxed as income of the corporation receiving the dividends. Thus for a firm such as an insurance company in the 34 percent corporate income tax bracket, this shelter is important. If the company receives $100 in interest, it nets only $66 as $34 is taxed away. However, if this company were to receive $100 in preferred stock dividends, only $30 would be subject to federal income tax. Thus the firm pays only $10.20 ($30 × 0.34) in taxes and gets to keep the remaining $89.80 of the dividends.

For this reason, a corporate investor may choose to purchase preferred stocks instead of long-term bonds. The impact of this preference is to drive up the prices of preferred stocks, which reduces their yields. Since individual investors do not enjoy this tax break, they may prefer bonds that offer yields comparable to preferred stock but are less risky. To induce these investors to purchase preferred stock, the firm often offers other features, such as the convertibility of the preferred stock into the firm's common stock.

A third important difference (from the viewpoint of the issuing corporation) between debt and preferred stock is that the interest on debt is a tax-deductible expense while the dividend on preferred stock is not. Preferred dividends are paid out of earnings. This difference in the tax treatment of interest expense and preferred stock dividends affects the firm's earnings available to its common stockholders. The use of debt instead of preferred stock as a source of funds will result in higher earnings per common share.

Consider a firm with operating income of $1,000,000 (that is, earnings before interest and taxes). The firm has 100,000 common shares outstanding and is in the 40 percent corporate income tax bracket. If the firm issues

$2,000,000 of *debt* with a 10 percent rate of interest its *earnings per common share* are

Earnings before interest and taxes	$1,000,000
Interest	200,000
Earnings before taxes	800,000
Taxes	320,000
Net income	$ 480,000

Earnings per common share: $480,000/100,000 = $4.80

If the firm had issued $2,000,000 in *preferred stock* that also paid 10 percent, the earnings per common share would be

Earnings before interest and taxes	$1,000,000
Interest	00
Earnings before taxes	1,000,000
Taxes	400,000
Earnings before preferred stock dividends	600,000
Preferred stock dividends	200,000
Earnings available to common stock	$ 400,000

Earnings per common share: $400,000/100,000 = $4.00

The use of preferred stock has resulted in lower earnings per common share. This reduction in earnings is the result of the different tax treatment of interest, which is a tax-deductible expense, and the preferred stock dividends, which are not deductible.

Valuation (Pricing) of Preferred Stock

The process of valuing (pricing) preferred stock discounts future cash inflows (dividends) back to the present at the appropriate discount rate. If the preferred stock is perpetual, the fixed dividend (D_p) will continue indefinitely. These dividends are discounted by the yield being earned on newly issued preferred stock (k_p). The present value of a preferred stock (P_p) is

$$P_p = \frac{D_p}{(1 + k_p)^1} + \frac{D_p}{(1 + k_p)^2} + \frac{D_p}{(1 + k_p)^3} + \cdots$$

which reduces to

$$P_p = \frac{D_p}{K_p}. \tag{24.1}$$

Thus, if a preferred stock pays an annual dividend of $4 and the appropriate discount rate is 8 percent, the present value of the stock is

$$P_p = \frac{\$4}{(1 + 0.08)^1} + \frac{\$4}{(1 + 0.08)^2} + \frac{\$4}{(1 + 0.08)^3} + \cdots$$

$$P_p = \frac{\$4}{0.08} = \$50.$$

If you buy this preferred stock for $50, you can expect to earn 8 percent ($50 × 0.08 = $4) on the investment. Of course, your realized return on the investment will not be known until you sell the stock and adjust this 8 percent return for any capital gain or loss. However, at the current price, the preferred stock is selling for an 8 percent dividend yield.

If the preferred stock has a finite life, this fact must be considered in determining its value. The amount to be repaid when the preferred stock is retired must be discounted back to the present value. Thus, when preferred stock has a finite life, the valuation equation becomes

$$P_p = \frac{D_p}{(1 + k_p)^1} + \frac{D_p}{(1 + k_p)^2} + \cdots + \frac{D_p}{(1 + k_p)^n} + \frac{S}{(1 + k_p)^n}. \quad (24.2)$$

S represents the amount that is repaid when the preferred stock is retired after n number of years. If the preferred stock in the previous example is retired after 30 years for $100 per share, its current value would be

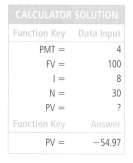

$$P_p = \frac{\$4}{(1 + 0.08)^1} + \cdots + \frac{\$4}{(1 + 0.08)^{30}} + \frac{\$100}{(1 + 0.08)^{30}}$$

$$= \$4(PVAIF\ 8I,\ 30N) + \$100(PVAIF\ 8I,\ 30N)$$

$$= \$4(11.258) + \$100(0.099)$$

$$= \$54.93.$$

Note that 11.258 is the interest factor for the present value of an annuity of $1 for 30 years at 8 percent (Appendix D), and 0.099 is the interest factor for the present value of $1 to be received after 30 years when yields are 8 percent (Appendix B). Instead of being valued at $50, the preferred stock would be valued at $54.93. This yield is still 8 percent, but the return in this case consists of a current dividend yield of 7.28 percent ($4 + $54.93) and a capital gain as the price of the stock rises from $54.93 to $100 over the 30 years.

Since preferred stock pays a fixed dividend, its price rises and declines with changes in interest rates. If rates rise, future cash inflows are discounted at a higher rate, which causes the price of the preferred stock to decline. When interest rates fall, the discount rate also falls, causing the preferred stock's price to rise. Just as the prices of bonds move inversely with changes in interest rates, the prices of preferred stock also move inversely with changes in interest rates.

Analysis of Preferred Stock

Because preferred stock is an income-producing investment, the analysis is primarily concerned with the capacity of the firm to meet the dividend payments. Although dividends must ultimately be related to current earnings and the firm's future earning capacity, preferred dividends are paid from cash. Even if the firm is operating at a loss, it may still be able to pay dividends to the preferred stockholders if it has sufficient cash. In fact, cash dividends might be paid despite the earnings deficit to indicate that the losses are expected to be temporary and that the firm is financially strong.

An analysis of the firm's financial statements (such as the ratios used to analyze a firm's financial condition in Chapter 9) may reveal the liquidity position and profitability of the firm. The more liquid and profitable the firm, the safer should be the dividend payment. The investor may also analyze how well the firm covers its preferred dividend by computing the times-preferred-dividend-earned ratio:

Times-preferred-dividend-earned

Ratio of earnings divided by preferred dividend requirements

$$\frac{\text{Earning after taxes}}{\text{Divided on preferred stock}}.$$

The larger this ratio, the safer should be the preferred stock's dividend. Notice that the numerator uses *total* earnings. Although the preferred stock dividends are subtracted from the total earnings to derive earnings available to the common stockholders, all of the firm's earnings are available to pay the preferred stock dividend.

A variation on this ratio is earnings per preferred share. This ratio is

Earnings per preferred share

Total earnings divided by the number of preferred shares outstanding

$$\frac{\text{Earnings after taxes}}{\text{Number of preferred shares outstanding}}.$$

The larger the earnings per preferred share, the safer should be the dividend payment. However, neither of these ratios indicates whether the firm has *sufficient cash* to pay the dividends. They can indicate only the extent to which earnings cover the dividend requirements of the preferred stock.

How each ratio is computed can be illustrated by the following simple example. A firm has earnings of $6,000,000 and is in the 40 percent tax bracket. It has 100,000 shares of preferred stock outstanding, and each share pays a dividend of $5. The times-preferred-dividend-earned ratio is

$$\frac{\$6,000,000 - \$2,400,000}{\$500,000} = 7.2,$$

and the earnings per preferred share are

$$\frac{\$6,000,000 - \$2,400,000}{\$100,000} = \$36.$$

Both ratios, in effect, show the same thing. In the first, the preferred dividend is covered by a multiple of 7.2:1. The second ratio shows an earnings per preferred share of $36, which is 7.2 times the $5 dividend paid for each share.

Disadvantages of Preferred Stock from an Investor's Perspective

Although most preferred stock does offer you the advantage of a fixed flow of income, this advantage may be more than offset by several disadvantages. Like any fixed income security, preferred stock offers no protection from inflation. If the rate of inflation increases, the real purchasing power of the dividend is diminished. In addition, increased inflation will probably lead to higher interest rates, which will drive down the market value of all fixed income securities, including preferred stock. Thus, higher rates of inflation doubly curse preferred stock as the purchasing power of the dividend and the market value of the stock will both be diminished. (This disadvantage, of course, applies to all fixed income, long-term securities.)

Preferred stock may be less marketable than other securities. Marketability of a particular preferred stock depends on the size of the issue. If the preferred stock is bought by insurance companies and pension plans, the market for the remaining shares may be small, so the spread between the bid and ask prices can be substantial. While this may not be a disadvantage if you intend to hold the security indefinitely, it will reduce the attractiveness of the preferred stock.

The impact of inflation and reduced marketability are not the only disadvantages associated with preferred stock. Other disadvantages were alluded to earlier in the chapter but were not explicitly stated as disadvantages. The first of these is the inferior position of preferred stock to debt obligations. The investor must realize that preferred stock is perceptibly riskier than bonds. For example, Zapata Corporation omitted dividends on its two issues of preferred stock but continued to make the interest payments on its bonds. One of these preferred stocks was noncumulative, so those dividend payments were lost forever.

The second disadvantage that was previously alluded to is that the yields offered by preferred stock are probably insufficient to justify the additional risk. The yields on preferred stock are not necessarily higher than those available on bonds because of the tax advantages that preferred stock offers corporate investors. Only 30 percent of the dividends paid by one corporation and received by a second corporation are subject to corporate income tax. This tax advantage artificially drives up the price of preferred stock and drives down the yield. Since you cannot take advantage of the tax break, you may earn an inferior yield after adjusting for the additional risk associated with investing in a security that is subordinated to the firm's bonds.

Summary   Preferred stock is legally equity, but its features are more similar to those of bonds than of common stock. Preferred stock pays a fixed dividend that may accumulate if it is not paid. Some preferred stock is perpetual, in which case the company never has to retire it. Other issues, however, have mandatory repayment of the principal at a specified date. Preferred stock may also have mandatory sinking funds and be callable.

The dividends paid to preferred stockholders are distributions from earnings. Unlike interest payments to bondholders, preferred dividends are not tax deductible expenses. The lack of tax deductibility reduces the attractiveness of preferred stock to issuers.

Since preferred stock pays a fixed dividend, its valuation is the same as a bond. The fixed dividend is discounted back to the present at the appropriate rate. If applicable, the repayment of the principal value is also discounted back to the present. Higher interest rates cause the prices of preferred stocks to fall, but lower interest rates cause their prices to rise. Analysis of a preferred stock is based upon the company's ability to cover (i.e., pay) the dividend. Higher numerical values for times-preferred-dividend-earned and earnings per preferred share suggest that the firm will be able to make the dividend payments.

Review Objectives   Now that you have completed this chapter, you should be able to

1. List the features of preferred stock (pp. 537–538).

2. Contrast preferred stock and bonds (pp. 539–540).

3. Calculate earnings per share, earnings per preferred share, and times-preferred-dividend-earned (pp. 540–543).

4. Determine the value of a preferred stock (pp. 540–542).

5. Isolate the relationship between changes in interest rates and the price of a preferred stock (p. 543).

Problems   1. Big Oil Inc. has a preferred stock outstanding that pays a $9 annual dividend. If investors' required rate of return is 13 percent, what is the market value of the shares? If the required return declines to 11 percent, what is the change in the price of the stock?

2. What should be the prices of the following preferred stocks if comparable securities yield 7 percent? Why are the valuations different?

   a. MN Inc., $8 preferred ($100 par)

   b. CH Inc., $8 preferred ($100 par) with mandatory retirement after 20 years

3. Repeat the previous problem but assume that comparable yields are 10 percent.

4. You are considering purchasing the preferred stock of a firm but are concerned about its capacity to pay the dividend. To help allay that

fear, you compute the times-preferred-dividend-earned ratio for the past three years from the following data taken from the firm's financial statements:

Year	20X1	20X2	20X3
Operating income	$12,000,000	$15,000,000	$17,000,000
Interest	3,000,000	5,900,000	11,000,000
Taxes	4,000,000	5,400,000	4,000,000
Preferred dividends	1,000,000	1,000,000	1,500,000
Common dividends	3,000,000	2,000,000	—

What does your analysis indicate about the firm's capacity to pay preferred stock dividends?

Additional Problems with Answers

1. A $100 perpetual preferred stock pays an annual dividend of $5. Currently the yield on comparable preferred stock is 9 percent. What should be the price of this stock?

2. A $100 perpetual preferred stock pays an annual dividend of $5. Currently the stock is selling for its face value ($100). How much will you gain or lose if, after two years, the yield on comparable preferred stock is 9 percent?

3. A preferred stock with a maturity date of 10 years has the following features:

Face value	$100
Annual dividend	$ 5

Currently the yield on comparable preferred stock is 9 percent. What should be the price of this stock?

4. A preferred stock with a maturity date of 10 years has the following features:

Face value	$100
Annual dividend	$ 5

Currently the bond is selling for its face value ($100). How much will you gain or lose if, after two years, the yield on comparable preferred stock is 9 percent?

5. A preferred stock pays an annual dividend of $5 and currently sells for $74.33. If you buy the preferred stock and hold it until it is redeemed after 10 years, what is your annual yield over the 10 years?

Compare your answer to Problems 3 through 5 with your answers to additional Problems 1 through 3 in the preceding chapter on bond pricing.

In all five problems, the stock pays a $5 dividend. In Problems 1 and 2, the stock is perpetual. In Problems 3 through 5, the stock will be redeemed after 10 years.

1. Price: $5/0.09 = $55.56

2. The price after two years have lapsed is $5/0.09 = $55.56. If you bought the stock for $100, the loss is $44.44 ($100 − 55.56). Notice that in Problems 1 and 2, the price is the same because the preferred stock is perpetual.

3. In Problems 3 and 4, the preferred stock is to be redeemed after 10 years. The current price is

$$\$5(6.418) + 100(0.422) = \$74.29$$

$$\text{PMT} = 5, \text{FV} = 100; \text{N} = 10; \text{I} = 9; \text{P} = 74.33$$

4. With eight years to redemption, the price is

$$\$5(5.535) + 100(0.502) = \$78.88$$

$$\text{PMT} = 5; \text{FV} = 100; \text{N} = 8; \text{I} = 9; \text{P} = 77.86$$

If you bought the stock for $100, the loss is $22.12 ($100 − 78.88). The fact that this preferred stock has only eight years to redemption reduces the potential for loss compared to the perpetual preferred stock.

5. The annual return equates the current cost of $74.33 with the present value of the cash flows. Using a financial calculator, the return is 9 percent.

$$\text{PMT} = 5; \text{FV} = 100; \text{N} = 10; \text{P} = 74.33, \text{I} = ? = 9.$$

Solving this problem is more difficult using interest tables. Select a rate such as 9 percent, substitute in the equation and continue the process until both sides of the equation are equal (or approximately equal).

$$\$74.33 = 5(PVAIF) + 100(PVIF)$$

$$\$74.29 = \$5(6.418) + 100(0.422)$$

Relationships

1. If interest rates increase, preferred stock prices _____.

2. If a preferred stock's price declines, the yield _____.

3. If a preferred stock's price increases, its current yield _____.

4. An increase in the price of a firm's stock should _____ the price of its preferred stock.

5. An increase in earnings _____ times-dividend-earned.

6. Increased earnings implies _____ risk for owners of preferred stock.

Answers

1. decrease

2. increases

3. decreases

4. have no impact on (no change)

5. increases

6. decreased

Convertible Securities

The preceding chapters have considered the features of bonds, preferred stock, and their valuation. This one adds another variation—bonds and preferred stocks that may be converted into common stock. Thus the value of a convertible security is related to its value as debt and its value as common stock. This can be both a plus and a minus. If interest rates decline, the value of a convertible bond (or preferred stock) must rise. However, when interest rates rise and stock prices decline, a convertible security is doubly cursed. The security's value as both stock and debt falls, so the price of the convertible bond and convertible preferred stock must decline.

This is another relatively short chapter devoted solely to convertibles. The emphasis is on convertible bonds, but the features of convertible preferred stock are essentially the same. The chapter starts by explaining the conversion features, followed by a convertible bond's value as stock and as debt and the premiums you pay for a convertible. The chapter ends with a discussion of the return you may earn from an investment in a convertible.

Features of Convertible Bonds

Convertible bonds

Bonds that may be converted into (exchanged for) stock at the option of the bondholder

Convertible bonds are debentures (that is, unsecured debt instruments) that may be converted at the *holder's option* into the stock of the issuing company. Since the firm has granted the holder the right to convert the bonds, these bonds are often subordinated to the firm's other debt. They also tend to offer a lower rate of interest (coupon rate) than is available on nonconvertible debt. Thus, the conversion feature means that the firm can issue lower-quality debt at a lower interest cost. Investors are willing to accept this reduced quality and interest income because the market value of the bond will appreciate *if* the price of the stock rises. These investors are thus trading quality and interest for possible capital gains.

Since convertible bonds are long-term debt instruments, they have features that are common to all bonds. They are usually issued in $1,000 denominations, pay interest semiannually, and have a fixed maturity date. However, if you convert the bond into stock, the maturity date is irrelevant because the bonds are retired when they are converted. Convertible bonds frequently have a sinking fund requirement, which, like the maturity date, is meaningless once the bonds are converted.

Convertible bonds are *always callable*. The firm uses the call to force you to convert the bonds. Once the bond is called, you must convert, or any appreciation in price that has resulted from an increase in the stock's value will be lost. Such forced conversion is extremely important to the issuing firm, because it no longer has to repay the debt.

Convertible bonds are attractive to some investors because they offer the safety features of debt. The firm must meet the terms of the indenture, and the bonds must be retired if they are not converted. The flow of interest income usually exceeds the dividend yield that may be earned on the firm's stock. In addition, since the bonds may be converted into stock, you will share in the growth of the company. If the price of the stock rises in response to the firm's growth, the value of the convertible bond must also rise. It is this combination of the safety of debt and the potential for capital gain that makes convertible bonds an attractive investment, particularly to investors who desire income and some capital appreciation.

Like all investments, convertible bonds subject you to risk. If the company fails, you will lose the funds invested in the debt. This is particularly true with regard to convertible bonds, because they are usually subordinated to the firm's other debt. Thus, convertible bonds are less safe than senior debt or debt that is secured by specific collateral. In case of a default or bankruptcy, holders of convertible bonds may at best realize only a fraction of the principal amount invested. However, your position is still superior to that of the stockholders.

Default is not the only potential source of risk to investors. Convertible bonds are actively traded, and their prices can and do fluctuate. As is explained in the next section, their price is partially derived from the value of the stock into which they may be converted. Fluctuations in the value of the stock produce fluctuations in the price of the bond. These price changes are *in addition* to price movements caused by changes in interest rates. Thus, during periods of higher interest rates and lower stock prices, convertible bonds are doubly cursed. Their lower coupon rates of interest cause their prices to decline more than those of nonconvertible debt. This, in addition to the decline in the value of the stock into which they may be converted, results in considerable price declines for convertible bonds.

The Valuation of Convertible Bonds

The value of a convertible bond is derived from (1) the value of the stock into which it may be converted and (2) the value of the bond as a debt instrument. Although each of these factors affects the market price of the bond, the importance of each element varies with changing conditions in the securities markets. In the final analysis, the valuation of a convertible bond is difficult, because it is a hybrid security that combines debt and equity.

This section has three subdivisions. The first considers the value of the bond solely as stock. The second covers the bond's value only as a debt instrument, and the last section combines these values to show the hybrid nature of convertible bonds. In order to differentiate the value of the bond as stock from its value as debt, subscripts are added to the symbols used. S will represent stock, and D will represent debt.

The Convertible Bond as Stock

The value of a convertible bond in terms of the stock into which it may be converted (C_S) depends upon (1) the principal amount of the bond or face value (FV) of the bond, (2) the conversion (or exercise) price per share of the bond (P_e), and (3) the market price of the common stock (P_S). The principal divided by the conversion price of the bond gives the number of shares into which the bond may be converted. For example, if a $1,000 bond may be converted at $20 per share, the bond may be converted into 50 shares ($1,000/$20). The number of shares times the market price of a share gives the value of the bond in terms of stock. If the bond is convertible into 50 shares and the stock sells for $15 per share, the bond is worth $750 in terms of stock.

This conversion value of the bond as stock is expressed in Equation 25.1:

$$C_S = \frac{FV}{P_e} \times P_S \qquad (25.1)$$

and is illustrated in Exhibit 25.1. In this example a $1,000 bond is convertible into 50 shares (a conversion price of $20 per share). The first column gives

Price of the Stock	Number of Shares into Which the Bond Is Convertible	Value of the Bond in Terms of Stock
$ 0	50	$ 0
5	50	250
10	50	500
15	50	750
20	50	1,000
25	50	1,250
30	50	1,500

FIGURE 25.1
Relationship between
the Price of a Stock and
the Conversion Value
of the Bond

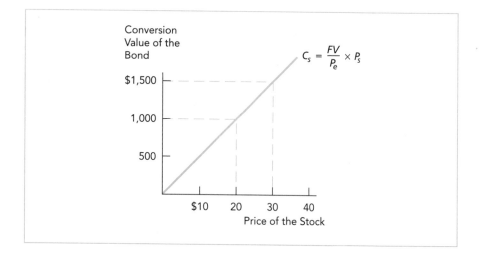

various prices of the stock. The second column presents the number of shares into which the bond is convertible (in this case, 50 shares). The third column gives the value of the bond in terms of stock (the product of the values in the first two columns). Thus, if the price of the stock is $15, the conversion value of the bond is $1,000/$20 × $15 = $750. As may be seen in the exhibit, the value of the bond in terms of stock rises as the price of the stock increases.

This relationship between the price of the stock and the conversion value of the bond is illustrated in Figure 25.1. The price of the stock (P_S) is given on the horizontal axis, and the conversion value of the bond (C_S) is shown on the vertical axis. As the price of the stock rises, the conversion value of the bond increases. This is shown in the graph by line C_S, which represents the value of the bond in terms of stock. Line C_S, is a straight line running through the origin. If the stock has no value, the value of the bond in terms of stock is also worthless. If the exercise price of the bond and the market price of the stock are equal (that is, $P_S = P_e$, which in this case is $20), the bond's value as stock is equal to the principal amount. As the price of the stock rises above the exercise price of the bond, the value of the bond in terms of stock increases to more than the principal amount of the debt.

The market price of a convertible bond cannot be less than the bond's conversion value as stock. If the price of the bond were less than its value as stock, an opportunity for profit would exist. You would purchase the convertible bond, exercise the conversion feature, and simultaneously sell the shares acquired through the conversion. You would then make a profit equal to the difference between the price of the convertible bond and the conversion value of the bond. For example, if in the preceding example the bond were selling for $800 when the stock sold for $20, the bond would be worth $1,000 in terms of the stock ($20 × 50). You would buy the bond for $800, convert it, sell the 50 shares for $1,000, and earn $200 profit (before commissions).

As you and other investors sought to purchase the bonds, the price of the bonds would increase. The price increase would continue until there was no opportunity for profit, which would occur when the price of the bond was equal to or greater than the bond's value as stock. Thus the value of the bond in terms of stock sets the minimum price of the bond. The market price of a convertible bond will be at least equal to its conversion value.

However, the market price of the convertible bond is rarely equal to the conversion value of the bond. The bond frequently sells for a premium over its conversion value, because the convertible bond may also have value as a debt instrument. As a pure (nonconvertible) bond, it competes with other nonconvertible debt. Like the conversion feature, this element of debt may affect the bond's price. Its impact is important, for it has the effect of putting a minimum price on the convertible bond, giving investors in convertible bonds an element of safety that stock lacks.

The Convertible Bond as Debt

The value of a convertible bond as debt (C_D) is related to (1) the annual interest or coupon rate that the bond pays (PMT), (2) the current interest rate being paid on comparable nonconvertible debt (i), and (3) the requirement that the principal or face value (FV) be retired at maturity (after n years) if the bond is not converted. In terms of present value calculations, the value of a convertible bond as nonconvertible debt is

$$C_D = \frac{PMT}{(1 + i)^1} + \frac{PMT}{(1 + i)^2} + \cdots + \frac{PMT}{(1 + i)^n} + \frac{FV}{(1 + i)^n}.$$

This equation is, of course, Equation 13.1 used to value any nonconvertible bond. If a convertible bond matures in 10 years, pays a 5 percent annual interest payment, and the yield on comparable nonconvertible debt is 8 percent, the value of this bond as a straight debt instrument is $798.50:

$$C_D = \frac{\$50}{(1 + 0.08)^1} + \frac{\$50}{(1 + 0.08)^2} + \cdots + \frac{\$50}{(1 + 0.08)^9}$$

$$+ \frac{\$50}{(1 + 0.08)^{10}} + \frac{\$1,000}{(1 + 0.08)^{10}}$$

$$= \$50(PVAIF\ 8I,\ 10N) + \$1,000(PVIF\ 8I,\ 10N)$$

$$= \$50(6.710) + \$1,000(0.463) = \$798.50.$$

The relationship between the price of the common stock and the value of this bond as nonconvertible debt is illustrated in Figure 25.2. This figure consists of a horizontal line (C_D) that shows what the price ($798.50) of the bond would be if it were not convertible into stock, in which case the price

FIGURE 25.2
Relationship between the
Price of a Stock and the
Value of the Bond as
Nonconvertible Debt

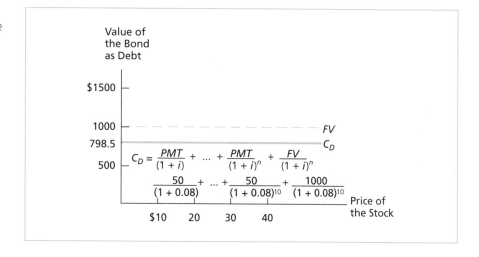

FIGURE 25.2
Relationship between the
Price of a Stock and the
Value of the Bond as
Nonconvertible Debt

is independent of the value of the stock. The principal amount of the bond is also shown in Figure 25.2 by the broken line *FV*, which is above the line C_D. The principal amount exceeds the value of the bond as pure debt because this bond must sell at a discount to be competitive with nonconvertible debt.

The value of the convertible bond as debt varies with market interest rates. Since the interest paid by the bond is fixed, the value of the bond as debt varies inversely with interest rates. An increase in interest rates causes this value to fall; a decline in interest rates causes the value to rise.

The relationship between the value of the preceding convertible bond as debt and various interest rates is presented in Exhibit 25.2. The first column gives various interest rates; the second column gives the nominal (coupon) rate of interest; and the last column gives the value of the bond as nonconvertible debt (as determined using a financial calculator). The inverse relationship is readily apparent, for as the interest rate rises from 3 percent to 12 percent, the value of the bond declines from $1,170.60 to $604.48.

EXHIBIT 25.2
Relationship between
Interest Rates and the
Value of a Bond

Interest Rate	Coupon Rate	Value of a 10-Year Bond
3%	5%	$1,170.60
4	5	1,081.11
5	5	1,000.00
6	5	926.40
7	5	859.53
8	5	798.70
10	5	692.77
12	5	604.48

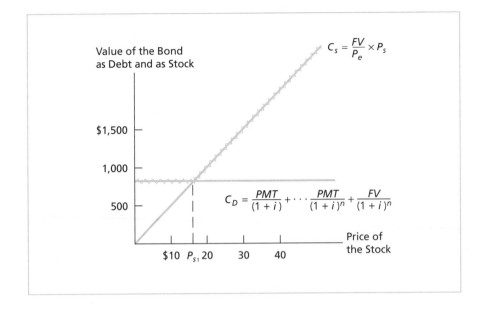

The value of the bond as nonconvertible debt is important because it sets another minimum value that the bond will command in the market. At that price the convertible bond is competitive with nonconvertible debt of the same maturity and degree of risk. If the bond were to sell below this price, it would offer a yield that is higher than that of nonconvertible debt. Investors would buy the convertible bond to attain this higher yield and bid up the bond's price until its yield was comparable to that of nonconvertible debt. Thus, the bond's value as nonconvertible debt becomes a floor on the price of the convertible bond. Even if the value of the stock into which the bond may be converted were to fall, this floor would halt the decline in the price of the convertible bond.

The actual minimum price of a convertible bond combines its value as stock and its value as debt. This is illustrated in Figure 25.3, which combines the preceding figures for the value of the bond in terms of stock and the value of the bond as nonconvertible debt. The bond's price is always equal to or greater than the higher of the two valuations. If the price of the convertible bond were below its value as common stock, investors would bid up its price. If the bond sold for a price below its value as debt, investors in debt instruments would bid up the price.

While the minimum price of the convertible bond is either its value in terms of stock or its value as nonconvertible debt, the importance of these determinants varies. For low stock prices (stock prices less than P_{S_1} in Figure 25.3), the minimum price is set by the bond's value as debt. However, for stock prices greater than P_{S_1}, it is the bond's value as stock that determines the minimum price.

F I G U R E 25.4

Determining the Market
Price of a Convertible Bond

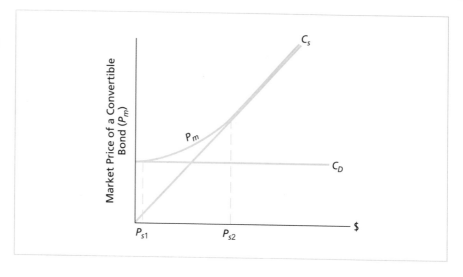

F I G U R E 25.4

Determining the Market
Price of a Convertible Bond

The Bond's Value as a Hybrid Security

The market price (P_m) of the convertible bond combines both the conversion value of the bond and its value as nonconvertible debt. If the price of the stock were to decline below the exercise price of the bond, the market price of the convertible bond would be influenced primarily by the bond's value as non-convertible debt. In effect, the bond would be priced as if it were a pure debt instrument. As the price of the stock rises, the conversion value of the bond rises and plays an increasingly important role in the determination of the market price of the convertible bond. At sufficiently high stock prices, the market price of the bond is identical with its conversion value.

These relationships are illustrated in Figure 25.4, which reproduces Figure 25.3 and adds to it the market price of the convertible bond (P_m). For prices of the common stock below P_{S1}, the market price is identical to the bond's value as nonconvertible debt. For prices of the common stock above P_{S2}, the price of the bond is identical to its value as common stock. At these extreme stock prices, the bond may be analyzed as if it were either pure debt or stock. For all prices between these two extremes, the market price of the convertible bond is influenced by the bond's value both as non-convertible debt and as stock.

Premiums Paid for Convertible Debt

One way to analyze a convertible bond is to measure the premium over the bond's value as debt or as stock. For example, if a particular convertible bond is commanding a higher premium than is paid for similar convertible securities, perhaps this bond should be sold. Conversely, if the premium is low, the bond may be a good investment. Of course, the lower premium may indicate financial

E X H I B I T　25.3　Premiums Paid for Convertible Debt

Price of the Stock	Shares into Which the Bond May Be Converted	Value of the Bond in Terms of Stock	Value of the Bond as Nonconvertible Debt	Hypothetical Price of the Convertible Bond	Premium in Terms of Stock*	Premium in Terms of Nonconvertible Debt†
$ 0	50	$ 0	$798.50	$ 798.50	$798.50	$ 0.00
5	50	250	798.50	798.50	548.50	0.00
10	50	500	798.50	798.50	298.50	0.00
15	50	750	798.50	900.00	150.00	101.50
20	50	1,000	798.50	1,100.00	100.00	301.50
25	50	1,250	798.50	1,300.00	50.00	501.50
30	50	1,500	798.50	1,500.00	0.00	701.50

*The premium in terms of stock is equal to the hypothetical price of the convertible bond minus the value of the bond in terms of stock.
†The premium in terms of nonconvertible debt is equal to the hypothetical price of the convertible bond minus the value of the bond as nonconvertible debt.

weakness, in which case the bond would not be a good investment. Thus, a lower premium is not a sufficient reason to acquire a convertible bond, but it may suggest that the bond be considered for purchase after further analysis.

The premiums paid for a convertible bond are illustrated in Exhibit 25.3, which reproduces Exhibit 25.1 and adds the value of the bond as nonconvertible debt (column 4) along with hypothetical market prices for the bond (column 5). The premium that an investor pays for a convertible bond may be viewed in either of two ways: the premium over the bond's value as stock or the premium over the bond's value as debt. Column 6 gives the premium in terms of stock. This is the difference between the bond's market price and its value as stock (the value in column 5 minus the value in column 3). This premium declines as the price of the stock rises and plays a more important role in the determination of the bond's price. Column 7 gives the premium in terms of nonconvertible debt. This is the difference between the bond's market price and its value as debt (the value in column 5 minus the value in column 4). This premium rises as the price of the stock rises, because the debt element of the bond is less important.

The inverse relationship between the two premiums is also illustrated in Figure 25.5. The premiums are shown by the differences between the line representing the market price (P_m) and the lines representing the value of the bond in terms of stock (C_S), and the value of the bond as nonconvertible debt (C_D).

When the price of the stock is low and the bond is selling close to its value as debt, the premium above the bond's value as stock is substantial, but the premium above the bond's value as debt is small. For example, at P_{S1} the price of the stock is $10, the bond's value in terms of stock is $500 (line AB in Figure 25.5), and the premium is $298.50 (line BC). However, the bond is selling for its value as nonconvertible debt ($798.50), and there is no premium over its value as debt. When the price of the stock is $25 and the bond is selling

FIGURE 25.5
Premiums Paid for a
Convertible Bond

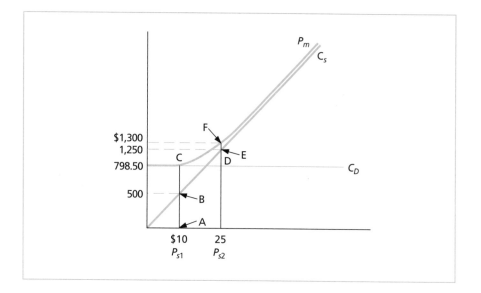

for $1,300, the premium in terms of stock is only $50 (line EF). However, the bond's premium over its value as nonconvertible debt is $501.50 (line DF).

As these examples illustrate, the premium paid for the bond over its value as stock declines as the price of the stock rises. This decline in the premium is the result of the increasing importance of the conversion value on the bond's market price and the decreasing importance of the debt element on the bond's price.

As the price of the stock rises, the safety feature of the debt diminishes. If the price of the common stock ceased to rise and started to fall, then the price of the convertible bond could decline considerably before it reached the floor price set by the nonconvertible debt. For example, if the price of the stock declined from $30 to $15 (a 50 percent decline), the price of the convertible bond could fall from $1,500 to $798.50 (a 46.8 percent decline). Such a price decline would indicate that the floor value of $798.50 had little impact on the decline in the price of the bond.

In addition, as the price of the stock (and hence the price of the convertible bond) rises, the probability that the bond will be called rises. When the bond is called, it can be worth only its value as stock. The call forces the holder to convert the bond into stock. For example, when the price of the stock is $30, the bond is worth $1,500 in terms of stock. Should the company call the bond and offer to retire it for its face value ($1,000), no one would accept the offer. Instead the bondholders would convert the bond into $1,500 worth of stock. If the investor paid a premium over this conversion value (such as $1,600) and the bond were called, the investor would suffer a loss. Thus, as the probability of a call increases, the willingness to pay a premium over the bond's value as stock declines, and the price of the convertible bond ultimately converges with its value as stock.

This decline in the premium also means that the price of the stock will rise more rapidly than the price of the bond. As may be seen in both Exhibit 25.3

and Figure 25.5, the market price of the convertible bond rises and falls with the price of the stock, because the conversion value of the bond rises and falls. However, the market price of the convertible bond does not rise as rapidly as the conversion value of the bond. For example, when the stock's price increased from $20 to $25 (a 25 percent increase), the convertible bond's price rose from $1,100 to $1,300 (an 18.2 percent increase). The reason for this difference in the rate of increase is the declining premium paid for the convertible bond. Since the premium declines as the price of the stock rises, the rate of increase in the price of the stock must exceed the rate of increase in the price of the bond. In summary, convertible bonds offer investors the opportunity for some capital growth with less risk.

Convertible Preferred Stock

Convertible preferred stock

Preferred stock that may be converted into common stock at the option of the holder

In addition to convertible bonds, firms may issue convertible preferred stock. As its name implies, this stock is convertible into the common stock of the issuing corporation. Although convertible preferred stock is similar to convertible debt, there are important differences. The differences are primarily the same as those between nonconvertible preferred stock and nonconvertible debt. Preferred stock is an equity instrument. Thus, the firm may not pay the dividend. In addition, the preferred stock may be a perpetual security and may not have to be retired. However, convertible preferred stocks are always callable, so the firm can force investors to convert the preferred stock into common stock.

The value of convertible preferred stock (like convertible bonds) is derived from the price of the stock into which it may be converted and the value of comparable nonconvertible preferred stock. As with convertible bonds, these values set floors on the price of the convertible preferred stock. It cannot sell for any length of time below its value as stock. If it did, investors would buy the preferred stock, which would increase its price. Thus, the minimum value of the convertible preferred stock (like the minimum value of the convertible bond) must be equal to the conversion value of the stock (P_e). In equation form that is

$$P_e = P_S \times N, \tag{25.2}$$

in which P_S is the market price of the stock into which the convertible preferred stock may be converted, and N is the number of shares an investor obtains through conversion. Equation 25.2 is similar to Equation 25.1, which gave the value of the convertible bond as stock.

The convertible preferred stock's value as nonconvertible preferred stock (P) is related to the dividend it pays (D) and to the appropriate discount factor (k), which is the yield earned on competitive nonconvertible preferred stock. In equation form that is

$$P = \frac{D}{k}, \tag{25.3}$$

which is the same as the convertible bond's value as debt, if the preferred stock has no definite maturity date. This value sets a floor on the price of a convertible preferred stock because at that price it is competitive with nonconvertible preferred stock.

As with convertible bonds, the convertible preferred stock is a hybrid security whose value combines its worth both as stock and as nonconvertible preferred stock. Convertible preferred stock tends to sell for a premium over both its value as stock and its value as straight preferred stock. Figures 25.4 and 25.5, which illustrated the value of the convertible bond at various prices of the stock into which it may be converted, also apply to convertible preferred stock. The primary difference is the premium that the preferred stock commands over the value as common stock. This premium tends to be smaller. This reduced premium occurs because the preferred stock does not have the safety associated with debt. Thus, its price usually commands less of a premium over its value as stock.

Calling Convertibles and Investment Returns

When a company issues a convertible bond, the expectation is that the bond will never be redeemed. Management does not plan to retire the bond; instead management expects to force conversion. Once the bond is converted, it ceases to exist.

To force conversion, the value of the stock must rise. How much of an increase is impossible to determine, but you can draw some commonsense conclusions. First, if the $1,000 bond is convertible into 50 shares ($20 per share), the price of the stock must exceed $20. No one will convert the bond into stock if the conversion value is less than $1,000 face amount. If the bond were called, you would take the $1,000 and not convert. Second, the price of the stock must rise sufficiently to also cover any call penalty. You will not convert unless the value of the stock exceeds the principal value plus the call penalty. If the bond has a $50 call penalty, the price of the stock must rise to $21 to cover both the $1,000 principal and the penalty ($21 × 50 shares = $1,050).

Even if the price of the stock has risen sufficiently to cover the principal and the call penalty, management may not immediately call the bond. Suppose the stock is selling for $22, so the conversion value is $1,100 ($22 × 50). Management calls the bond and the price of the stock immediately declines to $20. What will you do? The obvious answer is that you will not convert and accept $1,000 worth of stock when you would receive $1,050, the principal plus the penalty. The price of the stock must rise sufficiently to allow for the possibility that the price of the stock may decline so that conversion does not occur. You cannot know in advance how much the stock must rise to erase this risk, but it is reasonable to assume that as the price of the stock rises above the conversion price, the probability of the bond being called increases. Certainly, if the price of the stock is less than the conversion price, there is virtually no chance that management will call the bond.

The return that you ultimately earn on a convertible depends on what happens to the stock. If the stock goes nowhere, the return on the convertible depends solely on the interest and your cost of the bond. If you purchase a 5 percent convertible bond for $1,000 and hold it to maturity, you earn a return of 5 percent. If you purchase the bond for a discount ($895) or premium ($1,076) and hold the bond to maturity, you earn the yield to maturity. That yield was illustrated in Chapter 23. (See the application of Equation 23.1 in the section "The Yield to Maturity" to illustrate the calculation.)

If all you earn is the yield to maturity, you will certainly be disappointed. In that case, you would have been better off buying a nonconvertible bond that would have paid more interest and generated a higher return. A primary reason for buying a convertible bond is to participate in any increase in the price of the stock. If that price increase does not occur, one source of your expected return is not realized.

Thus, the return that you do earn depends on the interest and any appreciation generated by an increase in the price of the stock. Suppose you were to purchase the bond for $1,000 and collect the $50 each year in interest payments. The price of the stock rises to $30, so the value of the bond in terms of stock is $1,500 (50 shares × $30). If the bond is converted or if you sell the bond for its conversion value, you will earn the $50 a year in interest plus the $500 capital gain. (The amount of the capital gain would be more if you purchased the bond at a discount and less if you paid a premium.)

The actual calculation of the return is covered in the next chapter. This calculation includes the interest, the price appreciation, and how long you held the bond. This calculation is another illustration of the time value of money and is important because it applies to investments in plant and equipment as well as stocks and bonds. The anticipated return on an investment in plant and equipment is necessary for management to determine if the assets should be acquired. Refer back to Chapter 14 on capital budgeting, where this decision-making process is covered.

Summary

A convertible bond is a debt instrument that may be converted at the owner's option into stock. The value of the bond depends on the value of the stock into which the bond may be converted and on the value of the bond as a debt instrument. As the price of the stock rises, so does the value of the convertible bonds. Since a convertible bond's price rises with the price of the stock, the bond offers you an opportunity for capital gains.

The bond pays interest income and its value as a debt instrument sets a floor on the bond's price. This floor reduces your risk of loss. If the price of the stock declines, the value of the bond will also fall. But the price of the stock will decline faster, because the bond's value as debt will halt the decline in the bond's price.

Convertible preferred stock is similar to convertible debt, except that it lacks the safety implied by a debt instrument. The price of a convertible preferred is related to its conversion value, the flow of dividend income, and the return that investors may earn on nonconvertible preferred stock.

The return that you earn primarily depends on the value of the underlying stock. If the price of the stock does not rise, you earn a return as if the bond were nonconvertible (i.e., the yield to maturity). If the price of the stock rises, the return is related to the interest paid, the value of the bond in terms of stock, and how long you hold the bond.

Review Objectives

Now that you have completed this chapter, you should be able to

1. Enumerate the features of convertible securities (pp. 548–549).
2. Calculate the value of a convertible security as stock (pp. 550–552).
3. Calculate the value of a convertible security as debt (pp. 552–554).
4. Describe the premiums paid for a convertible bond (pp. 555–558).
5. Explain why a convertible security is always callable and when a company may call the security (pp. 559–560).
6. Determine what affects the return on an investment in a convertible (pp. 559–560).

Problems

1. Given the following information concerning a convertible bond:
   - Principal: $1,000
   - Coupon: 5 percent
   - Maturity: 15 years
   - Call price: $1,050
   - Conversion price: $37 (i.e., 27 shares)
   - Market price of the common stock: $32
   - Market price of the bond: $1,040
   a. What is the current yield of this bond?
   b. What is the value of the bond based on the market price of the common stock?
   c. What is the value of the common stock based on the market price of the bond?
   d. What is the premium in terms of stock that the investor pays when he or she purchases the convertible bond instead of the stock?
   e. Nonconvertible bonds are selling with a yield to maturity of 7 percent. If this bond lacked the conversion feature, what would the approximate price of the bond be?

f. What is the premium in terms of debt that the investor pays when he or she purchases the convertible bond instead of a nonconvertible bond?

g. What is the probability that the corporation will call this bond?

h. Why are investors willing to pay the premiums mentioned in questions *d* and *f*?

2. Given the following information concerning a convertible bond:

- Coupon: 6 percent ($60 per $1,000 bond)
- Exercise price: $25
- Maturity date: 20 years
- Call price: $1,040
- Price of the common stock: $30

a. If this bond were nonconvertible, what would be its approximate value if comparable interest rates were 9 percent?

b. How many shares can the bond be converted into?

c. What is the value of the bond in terms of stock?

d. What is the current minimum price that the bond will command?

e. Is there any reason to anticipate that the firm will call the bond?

f. What do investors receive if they do not convert the bond when it is called?

g. If the bond were called, would it be advantageous to convert?

Additional Problems with Answers

1. A $1,000 convertible bond may be converted into 25 shares of stock (i.e., an exercise price of $40 per share). If the price of the stock is $44, what is the value of the bond in terms of stock?

2. What is the value of the above convertible bond as debt if it pays interest of $70 (7 percent coupon) and matures after 12 years if the current rate of interest is 10 percent?

3. What is the value as common stock of a convertible preferred if it may be converted into 2.6 shares and the current price of a share of common stock is $57? What is the value of this preferred stock if it pays an annual dividend of $6.60 and investors require a return of 11 percent?

4. Given the following information concerning a convertible bond:

- Principal $1,000
- Maturity date   20 years
- Interest $40 (4 percent coupon)
- Call price $1,040
- Exercise price $25 a share

a. The bond may be converted into how many shares?

b. If comparable nonconvertible debt offered an annual yield of 9 percent, what would be the value of this bond as debt?

c. If the stock were selling for $32, what is the value of the bond in terms of stock?

d. Would you expect the bond to sell for its value as debt (i.e., the value determined in *b*) if the price of the stock were $32?

e. If the price of the bond were $1,300, what are the premiums paid over the bond's value as stock and its value as debt?

f. If the price of the stock were $29, what would be the minimum price of the bond?

g. If the price of the stock were $10, what would be the minimum price of the bond?

h. If the price of the stock were $10, would investors convert the bond if it were called?

i. What is the probability that the bond will be called when the price of the stock exceeds $50?

j. If the price of the stock were $50, what would the investor receive if the bond were called? What would the investor receive if the bond were called and the investor did not convert?

k. What will the investor receive when the bond matures?

Answers   1. The value of a convertible bond as stock:

$$C_S = \frac{P}{P_e} \times P_S.$$

Definitions of the symbols:

C_S value of the bond as stock

P_e exercise price of the bond

P_S price of the stock into which the bond may be converted

P principal or face amount of the bond

If a $1,000 convertible bond may be converted into 25 shares of stock (i.e., an exercise price of $40 per share), and the price of the stock is $44, the value of the bond in terms of stock is

$$C_S = \$1,000/\$40 \times \$44 = \$1,100.$$

2. Value of the bond as debt:

$$C_D = \frac{I}{(1 + i)} + \cdots + \frac{I}{(1 + i)^n} + \frac{P}{(1 + i)^n}.$$

Definitions of the symbols:

C_D value of the convertible bond as debt
I interest paid by the bond
n maturity date
P principal (or face amount) of the bond
i current interest on comparable nonconvertible bonds

If the convertible bond pays interest of $70 (7 percent coupon), matures after 12 years, and the current rate of interest is 10 percent, the value of the bond as debt is

$$C_D = \frac{\$70}{(1 + .1)} + \cdots + \frac{\$70}{(1 + .1)^n} + \frac{\$1,000}{(1 + .1)^n}$$

$$= \$70(6.814) + \$1,000(0.319) = \$795.99.$$

3. The value of a convertible preferred as common stock, if it may be converted into 2.6 shares and the current price of a share of common stock is $57, is

$$P_e = P_S \times \text{number of shares}$$

$$= \$57 \times 2.6 = \$148.20.$$

Value of the convertible preferred stock as a nonconvertible preferred stock is

$$P = D/k = \$6.60/.11 = \$60.$$

(This valuation assumes the preferred stock is perpetual. If the stock is not perpetual, that is, has a finite maturity date, the bond valuation equation is used to value the convertible preferred stock as a nonconvertible preferred stock.)

4. a. Number of shares: $1,000/$25 = 40 shares

   b. Value of the bond as debt:

   $$\$40(9.128) + \$1,000(.178) = \$543.$$

   $$PV = ?; N = 20; I = 9; PMT = 40; \text{ and } FV = 1000.$$

   $$PV = -543.$$

   c. Value of the bond as stock: $40 \times \$32 = \$1,280.$

   d. The bond would not sell for $543 but for at least $1,280, its value as stock.

e. Premium over its value as stock: $1,300 − $1,280 = $20.

Premium over its value as debt: $1,300 − $543 = $757.

f. If the price of the stock were $29, the value of the bond as stock would be $29 × 40 = $1,160. The bond would sell for at least its value as stock ($1,160).

g. If the price of the stock were $10, the value of the bond as stock would be $10 × 40 = $400. The bond would sell for at least its value as debt ($543).

h. The value of the bond as stock is $400. No one would convert the bond if it were called; everyone would accept the call price instead ($1,040). Thus, there is no reason to expect the firm to call the bond.

i. The value of the bond as stock would be

$$\$50 \times 40 = \$2,000.$$

Since the bond's value as stock perceptibly exceeds the face amount and the call price ($1,040), there is a high probability that the firm will call the bond.

j. Since the bond is worth $2,000 in terms of stock, the holders would convert the bond. If they did not convert the bond, they would receive only the call price ($1,040).

k. The face value: $1,000.

Relationships

1. An increase in interest rates and lower stock prices _____ the price of a convertible bond.

2. The intrinsic value of a convertible bond as stock _____ as the price of the stock increases.

3. If the intrinsic value of a convertible bond as stock decreased, that implies the price of the stock _____.

4. The value of a convertible bond as debt _____ as the price of the stock increases.

5. The value of a convertible bond as debt _____ as interest rates increase.

6. The premium over a convertible bond's value as debt _____ as the price of the underlying stock rises.

7. The premium over a convertible bond's value as stock _____ as the price of the underlying stock rises.

8. The value of a convertible preferred stock _____ as the price of the underlying stock declines.

9. An increase in interest rates and declining stock prices suggests that a convertible bond's coupon _____.

10. The return on an investment in a convertible security _____ as interest rates rise.

Answers

1. decrease
2. increases
3. decreased
4. is not affected (no change)
5. decreases
6. increases
7. decreases
8. decreases
9. is not affected (no change)
10. declines

CHAPTER
26

Investment Returns

I f you buy stocks and bonds, what returns can you expect? One means to answer that question is to determine historical returns and assume that, over an extended period of time, historical returns forecast future returns. That is, if the historical return on investments in common stock is 10 percent, then over time investments in common stock will continue to generate returns of 10 percent.

This assumption certainly will *not* hold for all periods of time. Securities prices fluctuate daily. There have been periods (1998–1999) when stock prices rose dramatically, but there certainly have been periods (2000–2002 and 2007–2008) when stock prices fell. If you bought stock during 2002 and sold at the end of 2006, you probably did very well. During that period, selecting a stock whose price subsequently rose was similar to shooting fish in a barrel. It was hard to miss.

If, however, you came to the party late and started buying stocks in 2007, you probably ended 2008 with a hangover! In March 2009, the S&P 500 stock index was less than half of its all-time high in 2007. Unless you sold the index short, you sustained a loss.

This chapter covers only two topics: the computation of returns and the historical returns that classes of securities have earned. Since the historical returns are aggregates, it is possible that particular investors did better than the averages. If some investors did better, some also did worse. It is doubtful, however, that you read about these investors in financial publications or heard them being interviewed on TV. Winners are the subjects of articles, and money tends to follow them. Funds flow to portfolio managers who do well, so outperforming the averages is obviously important from their perspective. But there are thousands of portfolio managers, and the vast majority of them will earn returns that only mirror the market.

The Computation of Returns

Holding period return (HPR)

Total return (income plus price appreciation during a specified time period) divided by the cost of the investment

To answer the question of what returns have been earned, it is necessary to determine how returns are computed. The simplest calculation is the holding period return (HPR). This return is derived by dividing the gain (or loss) plus any income (dividends or interest) by the purchase price. That is,

$$HPR = \frac{P_1 + D - P_0}{P_0}, \qquad (26.1)$$

in which P_1 is the sale price, D is the income, and P_0 is the purchase price. If you buy a stock for $40, collect dividends of $2, and sell the stock for $50, the holding period return is

$$HPR = \frac{\$50 + \$2 - \$40}{\$40} = 30\%.$$

The holding period return has a major weakness because it fails to consider how long it took to earn the return. This problem is immediately apparent if the information in the previous example had been a stock that cost $40, paid annual dividends of $1, and was sold at the end of the *second* year for $50. Given this information, what is the return? While the holding period return remains the same, 30 percent is obviously higher than the true annual return. If the time period is greater than a year, the holding period return *overstates* the true annual return. (Conversely, for a period that is less than a year, the holding period return understates the true annual return.)

Because the holding period return is easy to compute, it is frequently used, producing misleading results. Consider the following example. You buy a stock for $10 per share and sell it after 10 years for $20. What is the holding period return on the investment? This simple question can produce several misleading answers. You may respond by answering, "I doubled my money!" or "I made 100 percent!" That certainly sounds impressive, but it completely disregards the *length of time* needed to double your money. You may compute the arithmetic average and assert that you made 10 percent annually (100% ÷ 10 years). This figure is less impressive than the claim that the return is 100 percent, but it is also misleading because it fails to consider compounding. Some of the return earned during the first year in turn earned a return in subsequent years, which was not taken into consideration when you averaged the return over the 10 years.

The correct way to determine an annualized return that was earned is to phrase the question as follows: "At what rate does $10 grow to $20 after 10 years?" You should recognize this as another example of the time value of money. The equation used to answer this question is

$$P_0(1 + r)^n = P_n.$$

P_0 is the cost of the security, r is the rate of return per period, n is the number of periods (e.g., years), and P_n is the price at which the security is sold. When the proper values are substituted, the equation becomes

$$\$10(1 + r)^{10} = \$20,$$

solving for r yields

$$\$10(1 + r)^{10} = \$20.00,$$

$$(1 + r)^{10} = 2,$$

$$r = \sqrt[10]{2} - 1 = 1.0718 - 1 = 7.18\%,$$

so the annual rate of return is 7.18 percent. The correct rate of return on the investment (excluding any dividend income) is considerably less impressive than "I doubled my money!" or "I made 10 percent each year."

In the previous illustration, you know the beginning and the ending values. Suppose you computed each year's percentage return and averaged them. Is this approach acceptable? For example, suppose you bought a stock for $20 and its price rose to $25. The return is 25 percent ($5/$20). The next year the price declined back to $20, for a 20 percent loss (−$5/$25). You obviously earned nothing over the time period and the return should indicate this fact.

If, however, you average the annual returns, the investment will have generated a positive return:

$$\frac{25\% - 20\%}{2} = 2.5\%.$$

Owing to the magic of numbers, you have earned a 2.5 percent positive return, even though the investment produced neither a gain nor a loss. Unless you want to overstate your return, *do not average positive and negative percentage changes.*

The correct method to determine the annualized return is to compute a geometric average. In the first year, the stock rose from $20 to $25 (or $25 ÷ $20 = 1.25). In the second year, the stock declined from $25 to $20 (or $20 ÷ $25 = 0.8). The geometric average is

$$\sqrt[2]{(1.25)(0.80)} = 1.00,$$

so the return is $1.00 - 1.00 = 0.0\%$. (Notice that you subtract 1.0 to get the net change. Look back at the earlier illustration of the return earned on the $10 stock that you sold after 10 years for $20. You subtracted 1.0 from the 1.0718 to determine the return of 7.18 percent. The 1.0 that you subtract represents the amount initially invested.)

Geometric averages are often used to obtain rates of return over a period of years. Suppose the annual returns are as follows:

Year	Annualized Return
1	25%
2	3
3	−18
4	−10
5	15

The geometric average return is

$$\sqrt[5]{1.25(1.03)(0.82)(0.90)(1.15)} - 1 = 0.0179 = 1.79\%.$$

This annual return is lower than the arithmetic return of 3 percent that would be obtained by adding each of the returns and dividing by 5. As in the previous example, the averaging of positive and negative annual returns (i.e., the computation of an arithmetic average) overstates the true return.

The inclusion of income makes the calculation of the return more difficult. Consider the example that started this section in which you bought a stock for $40, collected $2 in dividends for two years, and then sold the stock for $50. What is the rate of return? The holding period return is overstated because it fails to consider the time value of money. If you compute the rate of growth and consider only the original cost and the terminal value, the return is understated because the dividend payments are excluded.

Internal rate of return

Percentage return that equates the present value of an investment's cash inflows with its cost

These problems are avoided by computing an investment's internal rate of return, which is the rate that equates the present value of all cash inflows with the present cost of the investment. An example of an internal rate of return is the yield to maturity on a bond in Chapter 23. (Internal rates of return also apply to investments in plant and equipment. See Chapter 14.) Since the yield to maturity equates the present value of the interest and principal repayment with the cost of the bond, it is the internal rate of return on the investment.

The general equation for the internal rate of return (r) for a stock is

$$P_0 = \frac{D_1}{(1 + r)} + \cdots + \frac{D_n}{(1 + r)^n} + \frac{P_n}{(1 + r)^n}. \qquad (26.2)$$

D is the annual dividend received in n years, and P_n is the price received for the stock in the nth year.

If the internal rate of return were computed for the previous illustration of a stock that cost $40, paid an annual dividend of $1, and was sold at the end of the second year for $50, the equation to be solved is

$$\$40 = \frac{\$1}{(1 + r)} + \frac{\$1}{(1 + r)^2} + \frac{\$50}{(1 + r)^2}.$$

Notice that there are three cash inflows: the dividend received each year and the sale price. The internal rate of return equates *all* cash inflows to the investor with the cost of the investment. These cash inflows include periodic payments as well as the sale price. (The calculation for the holding period return combined the dividend plus the capital gain on the investment and treated them as occurring at the end as a single cash inflow.)

As with the yield to maturity, there is no easy, manual solution to this equation. Even if you try to solve by trial and error using an interest table, the answer will be only an approximation. However, a financial calculator or program such as Excel can readily and accurately solve the problem. When the data are entered into a financial calculator, the internal rate of return on the investment, 14.17 percent, is readily determined. This 14.17 percent is the true, annualized rate of return on the investment. (The use of a financial calculator facilitates the computation of the internal rate of return, but calculators do have weaknesses. In this illustration, the yearly payments are equal and are entered into the calculator as an annuity. If the yearly payments were unequal, each payment would have to be individually entered. Because calculators limit the number of individual entries, they may not be used to determine the internal rate of return for problems with large numbers of cash inflows.)

The internal rate of return has a major weakness: it assumes that cash inflows are *reinvested at the investment's internal rate*. In the preceding illustration that means the $1 received in the first year is reinvested at 14.17 percent. If the dividend annualized payment is reinvested at a lower rate or not reinvested (e.g., it is spent), the true annualized return on the investment will be less than the rate determined by the equation. Conversely, if you earn more than 14.17 percent when the $1 is reinvested, the true return on the investment will exceed the internal rate of return determined by the equation. This weakness, however, is small compared to the weaknesses associated with the holding period return.

CALCULATOR SOLUTION	
Function Key	Data Input
PV =	−40
FV =	50
PMT =	1
N =	2
I =	?
Function Key	Answer
I =	14.17

Historical Investment Returns

Several studies have been conducted by academicians on the returns earned by investments in common stocks. (Brokerage firms, investment advisory services, and other financial institutions have also computed returns, but you should be skeptical of the results.) Initial studies found the annual returns on investment in common stocks to be 9–10 percent. There were, of course, periods during which stocks declined and periods when returns exceeded 10 percent, but over an extended period, the annual return approximated 10 percent.

These initial annual returns were confirmed and extended by Ibbotson and Sinquefield. Since 1981, returns have been updated annually by Ibbotson Associates and reported in *The Stocks, Bonds, Bills, & Inflations (SBBI) Yearbook*. This comprehensive publication subdivides equities into large-company and small-company stocks. As would be expected, the smaller, riskier stocks generated higher returns, 12 versus 10 percent.

The SBBI data also include returns on corporate bonds, U.S. Treasury bonds, U.S Treasury bills, and the rate of inflation. The returns on stocks exceed the returns on bonds, and riskier corporate bonds generate higher returns than the federal government securities. Over time the Treasury bills earned a return that slightly exceeded the rate of inflation. Standard deviations of the returns are also reported so an investor can readily obtain a measure of the variability of the returns.

If you are interested in historical returns, the *SBBI Yearbook* should be your source for that information. Be forewarned that the period you select is important. For example, in 1965–1974 the return for stocks was only 1.4 percent. The return was positive but considerably less than the 10 percent reported for the period 1926–2000. And the decade 2000–2009 generated losses. The S&P 500 stock index closed 2009 at 1,115, which is 24 percent less than the 1,469 opening value on January 2000. Even if dividend income were added back to the index, most investors sustained losses during that decade.

Historical returns are often used to value stocks and to provide forecasts of future returns. For example, historical returns may be used in the Capital Asset Pricing Model as the measure of the return on the market. This approach to stock valuation assumes historical returns will be repeated in the future. Anyone who made that assumption in 2000 was certainly disappointed with the results achieved during 2000–2009.

In addition, studies of historical return make an important assumption that you may not be able to fulfill. These studies compute internal rates of return that assume cash inflows are reinvested at that rate. While it is obvious that the assumption does not apply if you spend the cash flows, the assumption might still not apply even if the income were reinvested. Because you have to pay income tax on the dividend and interest income, the funds available for reinvestment are reduced. Even if all the funds were reinvested, you would have to pay the taxes from other sources. In either case, the comparability of historical returns with the return you earn is diminished. (This problem reappears in Chapter 27. In that discussion, a mutual fund's return is stated before tax while the individual has to pay tax on any distributions.)

Summary

The return an investor earns depends on the flow of income (dividends or interest), the price paid for the security, and the sale price. The holding period return is the percentage earned on an investment without considering how long the investor held the security. Since the holding period return disregards time, it does not include the impact of compounding. The holding period return often overstates an investment's true, compounded return for securities held for more than a year.

The true annualized return, which is also referred to as the internal rate of return, determines the rate that equates the present value of an investment's cash inflows and its cash outflows. This return encompasses the initial cost of an investment, any dividends or interest received, the sale price, and the time period. The computation produces a true, compounded rate of return.

Studies of returns from investments in common stock have found that investors earned, over extended periods of time, returns in excess of 10 percent. This annualized return varies with the time period selected and varies from year to year. The annualized returns were higher for smaller stocks, but their returns are also more variable. Bonds and Treasury bills generated lower returns than stocks but their returns were less variable, indicating that these investments were less risky.

Review Objectives

Now that you have completed this chapter, you should be able to

1. Compute rates of return (pp. 568–571).

2. Differentiate the holding period and the annualized rate of return (pp. 568–570).

3. Compare aggregate returns on different classes of assets (pp. 571–572).

4. Distinguish between an investor's return and historical returns (p. 572).

Problems

1. What are the holding period and the annualized compounded returns if you buy a stock for $30 and sell it for $90 after 10 years?

2. You sold a stock for $50 that you purchased five years earlier for $24. What was the holding period return? Prove that this return overstates the annualized, compound return.

3. A stock costs $90 and pays a $4 annual dividend. If you expect to sell the stock after five years for $100, what is your anticipated return on the investment?

4. A $1,000 bond has a 4 percent coupon and currently sells for $900. The bond matures after five years. What is the bond's anticipated yield? Compare this return with the answer to the previous problem.

5. You purchased 100 shares in a real estate investment trust for $30 a share. The trust paid the following annual dividends:

Year	Dividend
1	$2.00
2	1.50
3	2.34
4	2.76

What was your annualized return on the investment if you sell the stock for (a) $30 and (b) $50?

6. You invest $1,000 in a stock and $1,000 in a corporate bond. If you earn 10 percent on the stock and 6 percent on the bond and hold each security for 20 years, what are the terminal values for each investment? If you continue to hold each security and earn the same returns for 30 years,

how much more will the stock generate than the bond over the entire time period? (When you invest for retirement, you should think about the answer to this problem.)

7. Assume that the rate of inflation is 3 percent and continues indefinitely and that the cost of a car is currently $25,000. How much will that car cost 25 years from today?

Additional Problems with Answers

1. You buy a stock for $40 and sell it for $60 after five years. What are the (1) holding period return, (2) the average percentage return, and (3) the annualized, compound rate of return?

2. A stock costs $900 and pays an annual $46.50 cash dividend. If you expect to sell the stock for $1,000 after 10 years, what is your anticipated return on the investment?

3. A $1,000 bond has a 4.65 percent coupon and currently sells for $900. The bond matures after 10 years. What is the bond's anticipated return? Compare this return with the answer to the preceding problem.

Answers

1. Problem 1 compares return calculations. The holding period and average return overstate the true annual return.

The holding period return: $(\$60 - 40)/\$40 = 50\%$

The average annual return: $50\%/5 = 10\%$

The annualized compound return:

$$\$40(1 + r)^5 = \$60$$

$$(1 + r)^5 = 60/40 = 1.5$$

$$R = \sqrt[5]{1.5} - 1 = 8.45\%$$

$$\text{PMT} = 0; \text{FV} = 60; \text{N} = 5; \text{PV} = -40; \text{I} = ? = 8.45$$

2. and 3. Problems 2 and 3 are identical except the first applies to a stock and the second to a bond. They illustrate that the calculation of returns is the same for all assets: rate equates the present cost (outflow) of the investment and the future cash inflows. In both examples you buy the security for $900, collect $46.50 income, and sell (redeem) the security for $1,000. The return is

$$\$46.50(7.360) + 1,000(0.558) = \$900.$$

$$\text{PMT} = 46.50; \text{FV} = 1000; \text{N} = 10; \text{P} = -900 \text{ I} = ? = 6.0$$

Relationships

1. The holding period return increases as dividend payments _____.

2. The holding period return _____ as the time period increases.

3. As the time period increases, the difference between the holding period return and the compound return _____.

4. The internal rate of return _____ as the cost of an investment increases.

5. If the internal rate of return on an investment in a bond increases, the yield to maturity _____.

Answers

1. increase

2. is not affected (no change)

3. increases

4. decreases

5. increases

Investment Companies

D
o you change the oil in your car, or do you have someone else change it? What about the cartridge in your printer? Do you hang wallpaper and paint your home, or do you use a painter? What about a broken window or a clogged toilet? These are but a few of many possible questions with the same basic idea: Do you do it yourself or do you use a professional? We all do some things for ourselves, but we often use the services of others. You may use a plunger to open a clogged toilet but for more serious problems you call the plumber. The reasons are obvious, such as your lack of skills, tools, or time to complete the task.

The same applies to your portfolio: Do you select individual stocks or let someone else make those decisions? Many people do not choose to manage their own portfolios and delegate that authority to a portfolio manager. The reasons are obvious, such as their lack of skills, tools, or time to complete the task.

Mutual funds would not exist if everyone managed his or her own portfolio. In some cases, even if you want to select individual stocks and bonds, you cannot. Employee retirement plans often offer choices of investment options but not the selection of individual assets. Your choices may include an intermediate-term bond fund, a long-term bond fund, a growth mutual fund, a global fund, and a real estate trust. But you will not select the specific assets owned by each alternative. Instead, the fund's portfolio managers invest your contributions, and it is these portfolio managers who select the individual assets that compose the fund.

This chapter covers investment companies, especially mutual funds. Even if you manage your own portfolio, you may purchase shares in an investment company to meet a specific portfolio need such as diversification through foreign investments. This chapter covers the mechanics of buying and selling the shares, their taxation, and the costs and potential returns associated with investment companies. The chapter includes a discussion of factors to consider when selecting among the thousands of investment companies available to you. These factors include your allocation of assets among investment alternatives, the fees associated with each fund, and a fund's prior performance. The chapter ends with coverage of specialized investment companies such as index funds and the exchange-traded funds. These funds offer you an alternative that you should consider even if you manage your own portfolio and select individual stocks and bonds.

Investment Companies: Origins and Terminology

Closed-end investment company

Investment company with a fixed number of outstanding shares that are bought and sold through secondary markets

Open-end investment company

Mutual fund that issues new shares and agrees to redeem the shares on the demand of the shareholder

Mutual fund

Open-end investment company that stands to issue and redeem its shares on demand

Investment companies are not a recent development but were established in Britain during the 1860s. Initially, these investment companies were referred to as *trusts* because the securities were held in trust for the firm's stockholders. These firms sold a specified number of shares and used the proceeds to acquire shares of other firms. Today the descendants of these companies are referred to as closed-end investment companies because the number of shares is fixed (that is, closed).

The first trusts offered a specified number of shares. Today, however, the most common type of investment company does not. Instead, the number of shares varies as investors purchase more shares or sell them back. This open-end investment company is commonly called a mutual fund. Such funds started in 1924 when Massachusetts Investor Trust offered new shares and redeemed (bought) existing shares on demand by stockholders.

The rationale for investment companies is both simple and appealing. The firms receive the funds from many investors, pool them, and purchase securities. The individual investors receive (1) the advantage of professional management of their money, (2) the benefit of ownership in a diversified portfolio, (3) the potential savings in commissions, as the investment company buys and sells in large blocks, and (4) custodial services, such as the collecting and disbursing of funds.

The advantages offered by funds and the general increase in security prices help explain why both the number of mutual funds and the dollar value of their shares have grown since the 1940s. This trend dramatically increased during the 1990s. From 1990 through 1999, equity and bond mutual fund assets grew from $571 billion to $5,233 billion.

PART 4 Investments

Unfortunately, stock prices subsequently fell, and mutual funds' assets also declined to $4,109 billion at the end of 2002. During 2003 and 2004, a rise in stock prices plus additional contributions by investors increased mutual fund assets to $6,194 billion. A similar pattern occurred during 2008–2009. When the market declined during 2008, mutual fund assets fell from $8,914 billion to $5,771 billion. However, as the market started to recoup its losses, mutual fund assets rebounded to $7,805 billion at the end of 2009, but this amount remained below the high of $8,914 billion at the end of 2007. (Information and data of mutual funds may be found at the Investment Company Institute's Web site, http://www.ici.org.)

Investment companies receive special tax treatment. Their dividend and interest income and realized capital gains are exempt from taxation at the corporate level. Instead, these profits are taxed through their stockholders' income tax returns.

For this reason, income that is received by investment companies and realized capital gains are distributed. Investment companies, however, offer their stockholders the option of having the fund reinvest these distributions. While such reinvestments do not erase the stockholders' tax liabilities, they are a convenient means to accumulate shares. The advantages offered by the dividend reinvestment plans of individual firms (discussed in Chapter 20) also apply to the dividend reinvestment plans offered by investment companies. Certainly the most important of these advantages is the element of forced savings. Since you do not receive the money, there is no temptation to spend it. Rather, the funds are immediately channeled back into additional income-earning assets.

One term frequently encountered concerning an investment company is its per share net asset value (NAV). The per share net asset value of an investment company is the total value of its stocks, bonds, cash, and other assets minus any liabilities (for example, accrued expenses) divided by the number of shares outstanding. Thus, net asset value may be obtained as follows:

Net asset value (NAV)

Asset value of a share in an investment company; investment company's assets minus liabilities divided by the number of shares outstanding

Value of stock owned	$1,000,000
Value of debt owned	+1,500,000
Value of total assets	$2,500,000
Liabilities	−100,000
Net worth	$2,400,000
Number of shares outstanding	1,000,000
Net asset value per share	$ 2.40

The net asset value is important because changes in the net asset value alter the value of the investment company's shares. If the value of the firm's assets appreciates, the net asset value will increase, which should cause the price of the investment company's stock to rise.

Based on the number of mutual funds and their total assets, open-end investment companies are more important than closed-end investment companies. This discussion, however, begins with closed-end investment companies, which developed before mutual funds. Closed-end investment companies also have characteristics that are similar to the trading in stocks discussed in Chapter 4.

Closed-End Investment Companies

As was explained in the previous section, the difference between open-end and closed-end investment companies is the nature of their capital structure. The closed-end investment company has a set capital structure that may be composed of all stock or a combination of stock and debt. The number of shares and the dollar amount of debts that the company may issue are specified. In an open-end investment company (a mutual fund), the number of shares outstanding varies as investors purchase and redeem them. Since the closed-end investment company has a specified number of shares, if you want to invest in a particular company, you must purchase existing shares from current stockholders. Conversely, if you own shares and wish to liquidate the position, you must sell the shares. Thus, the shares in closed-end investment companies are bought and sold just as the stock of IBM is traded. Shares of these companies are traded on the New York and American stock exchanges and through the Nasdaq Stock Market.

The market price of stock in a closed-end company need not be the net asset value per share: it may be above or below this value, depending on the demand and the supply of stock in the secondary market. If the market price is below the net asset value of the shares, the shares are selling for a discount. If the market price is above the net asset value, the shares are selling for a premium.

These differences between the investment company's net asset value per share and the stock price are illustrated in Exhibit 27.1, which gives the price, the net asset value, and the discount or the premium as of July 9, 2010, for selected investment companies. As may be seen in the exhibit, most closed-end investment companies sell for a discount (that is, below their net asset values).

While most closed-end investment companies sell for a discount, some do sell for a premium. For example, during 2009, the India Fund commanded a premium of 17.5 percent above the net asset value. Often, closed-end investment companies that sell for a premium have a specialized portfolio that

Discount

Extent to which the price of a closed-end investment company's stock is less than the share's net asset value

Premium

Extent to which the price of a closed-end investment company's stock exceeds the share's net asset value

EXHIBIT 27.1
Net Asset Value and Market Prices of Selected Closed-End Investment Companies as of July 2010

Company	Net Asset Value	Price	Discount as a Percentage of Net Asset Value
Adams Express (ADX)	$11.31	$9.43	16.6%
Gabelli Trust (GAB)	4.85	4.60	5.2
General American Investors (GAM)	26.31	22.22	15.5

Source: Company reports available on the Internet at the funds' home pages.

appeals to some investors. For example, some countries, such as India, place restrictions on foreign investments. If an individual wants to acquire shares in firms in these countries (perhaps for potential growth or for diversification purposes), a closed-end investment company may be one of the few means to make the investments. The effect is to bid up the price of the shares so that the closed-end investment company sells for a premium over its net asset value.

Since the shares may sell for a discount or a premium relative to their net asset value, it is possible for the market price of a closed-end investment company to fluctuate more or less than the net asset value. Since the market price can change relative to the net asset value, you are subject to an additional source of risk. The value of the investment may decline because the net asset value decreases and because the shares sell for a larger discount from their net asset value.

Some investors view the market price relative to the net asset value as a guide to buying and selling the shares of a closed-end investment company. If the shares are selling for a sufficient discount, they are considered for purchase. If the shares are selling for a small discount or at a premium, they are considered for sale. Of course, determining the premium that will justify the sale or the discount that will justify the purchase is not simple (and may be arbitrary).

Sources of Return from Investing in Closed-End Investment Companies

Profits are the difference between revenues and costs. Investing in closed-end investment companies involves several costs. First, since the shares are purchased on the secondary market, you pay the brokerage commission for the purchase and for any subsequent sale. Second, the investment company charges a fee to manage the assets. This management fee is subtracted from any income that the fund's assets earn and ranges from 0.5 percent to 2 percent of the net asset value. Third, when the investment company purchases or sells securities, it also has to pay brokerage fees, which are passed on to you.

The purchase of shares in closed-end investment companies thus involves three costs that you must bear. Some alternative investments, such as savings accounts in commercial banks, do not involve these expenses. Although commission fees are incurred when you buy a stock such as IBM, the other expenses associated with a closed-end investment company are avoided.

Investors in closed-end investment companies may earn returns in a variety of ways. If the investment company collects dividends and interest on its portfolio of assets, this income is distributed to the stockholders in the form of dividends. Second, if the value of the firm's assets increases, the company may sell the assets and realize profits. These profits are then distributed as capital gains to the stockholders. Third, the net asset value of the portfolio may increase, which should cause the market price of the fund's stock to rise. In this case you may sell the shares and realize a capital gain. Fourth, the market price of the shares may rise relative to the net asset value (that is, the premium may

EXHIBIT 27.2 Annual Returns on an Investment in Salomon Brothers Fund, a Closed-End Investment Company

Distributions and Price Changes	2003	2002	2001	2000	1999	1998	1997
Per-share income distributions	$ 0.13	0.11	0.11	0.14	0.18	0.27	$ 0.27
Per-share capital gains distributions	—	$ 0.07	0.33	2.41	3.63	3.19	$ 2.63
Year-end net asset value	$14.04	10.75	14.07	16.27	19.24	18.76	$18.51
Year-end market price	$12.03	9.12	12.42	16.25	20.375	18.19	$17.625
Annual return based on prior year's market price			Annual percentage loss		Annual percentage gain		
a. Dividend yield	1.4%	0.8	0.7	0.7	1.0	1.5	1.7%
b. Capital gains yield	—	0.5	1.8	11.8	20.2	18.1	16.4%
c. Change in price	31.9%	−35.2	−13.4	−20.2	12.0	3.2	10.2%
Total return	33.3%	−33.9	−10.9	−7.7	33.2	22.8	28.3%

Source: Salomon Brothers Fund annual reports.

increase or the discount may decrease); you may then earn a profit through the sale of the shares.

These sources of return are illustrated in Exhibit 27.2, which presents the distributions and price changes for Salomon Brothers Fund from December 31, 1997, through December 31, 2003. As may be seen in the exhibit, the investment company distributed cash dividends of $0.27 and capital gains $3.19 in 1998. The net asset value rose from $18.51 to $18.76, and the price of the stock likewise rose (from $17.625 to $18.19). An investor who bought the shares on December 31, 1997, earned a total return of 22.8 percent (before commissions):

$$\frac{\$18.19 + \$0.27 + \$3.19 - \$17.625}{\$17.625} = 22.8\%.$$

The potential for loss is also illustrated in the exhibit. If an investor bought the shares on December 31, 1999, he or she suffered a loss during 2000. While Salomon Brothers distributed $0.14 per share in income and $2.41 in capital gains, the price of the stock declined sufficiently to more than offset the income and capital gains distributions.

Mutual Funds

Open-end investment companies, commonly called mutual funds, are similar to closed-end investment companies with some important differences. The first concerns how their shares are bought and sold. Shares in mutual funds are not traded like other stocks and bonds. Instead, you purchase shares directly from the company. After receiving the money, the mutual fund issues new shares and purchases assets with these newly acquired funds. If you own shares in the fund and want to liquidate the position, you sell the shares back to the fund. The shares are redeemed, and the fund pays from its cash holdings. If the fund lacks sufficient cash, it must sell some of the securities it owns to obtain the money to redeem the shares. The fund cannot suspend this redemption feature except in an emergency, and then it can be done only with the permission of the Securities and Exchange Commission (SEC).

A second important difference between open-end and closed-end investment companies pertains to the cost of investing. Mutual funds continuously offer to sell new shares at their net asset value plus a sale fee, which is commonly called a *loading charge*. The loading fee may range from zero for no-load mutual funds to between 3 and 6 percent for load funds. When you sell your position back to the fund, the shares are redeemed at their net asset value. Most funds do not charge for the redemption, but some do assess a back-end load if you redeem the shares soon after they were purchased (such as six months later). Such exit fees are designed to discourage quick redemption of the shares.

In addition to loading charges, investors in mutual funds have to pay management fees, which are deducted from the income earned by the fund's portfolio. The fund also pays brokerage commissions when it buys and sells securities. The total cost of investing in mutual funds may be substantial when all the costs (the loading charge and management and brokerage fees) are considered. Of course, the cost of investing is substantially reduced when the individual buys shares in no-load funds. The investor, however, must still pay the management fees and commission costs.

Some no-load funds (and even some load funds) have adopted an SEC rule that permits management to use the fund's assets to pay for marketing expenses. These are referred to as 12b-1 fees (or 12b-1 plan) and are named for the SEC rules that enable funds to charge this expense. The fee covers a variety of expenses such as advertising, the distribution of fund literature, and even sale commissions to brokers. Unlike the load fee, which is a one-time, up-front expense that is paid when the shares are purchased, the 12b-1 fees can be a *continuous annual expense*. Over a number of years, this fee can and often does exceed the load fee.

The third difference between closed-end and open-end investment companies is the source of returns to the investor. Any income is distributed as dividends and realized gains are distributed. If the net asset value of the shares appreciates, the investor may redeem them at the appreciated price. Thus, in general, the open-end mutual fund offers investors the same sources of return that the closed-end investment company does, with one exception. In the case of closed-end investment companies, the price of the stock may rise relative to the net asset value of the shares. The possibility of a decreased discount or an increased premium is a potential source of return that is available only through closed-end investment companies. It does not exist for mutual funds because you can *never buy the shares for a discount*. Mutual funds are sold at

No-load fund

Mutual fund that does not charge a sales commission when individuals purchase shares from the fund

Load fund

Mutual fund that charges commissions when individuals purchase shares from the fund their net asset value or for a premium (the load fee) and are redeemed at their net asset value minus any applicable fees.

Mutual fund data are reported in the following general form:

	NAV	NET CHG	YTD %RET
First Fund	11.12	+0.03	−12.4

The information covers the fund's name (First Fund), its net asset value (11.12), the change in the net asset value from the previous day (+0.03), and the percentage return on the fund since the beginning of the calendar year (year to date, YTD, which for First Fund was −12.4). The reporting may also include the return for a longer time period such as three years. *The returns do not reflect any load charges and redemption fees*, so the percentages are not necessarily indicative of the return you would have earned during the comparable time period.

While purchases of shares in investment companies may generate a return, they also subject the investor to risk. Because many investment companies construct diversified portfolios, the impact of a particular investment on the outcome of the portfolio as a whole is reduced. Thus, the unsystematic risk associated with an individual firm's securities may be small. The investor, however, must still bear the unsystematic risk associated with the individual investment company's strategy and management. (This source of risk may be reduced by acquiring the shares in several investment companies with different strategies and different portfolio managers.)

Other sources of risk cannot be eliminated through purchasing the shares of mutual funds and closed-end investment companies. If securities prices in general fall, the value of the investment company will probably also fall. A fund's management cannot consistently predict changes in the market and adjust the portfolio accordingly. The value of the portfolio tends to move with the market. Thus, the risk associated with movements in the market is not eliminated through the purchase of shares in investment companies. And this general conclusion applies to all the sources of nondiversifiable risk. Changes in interest rates, the impact of inflation, and exchange rate risk are not reduced through the acquisition of a well-diversified portfolio, and that conclusion also applies to the purchase of the shares of a well-diversified investment company.

The Portfolios of Mutual Funds

Mutual funds may be classified by *investment objective*, such as income or growth, or by *investment style*. Income funds stress assets that produce income: they buy stocks and bonds that pay dividends or interest income. The Value Line Income Fund is an example of a fund whose objective is income. Virtually all of its assets are income stocks, such as those of utilities, which pay dividends and periodically increase them as their earnings grow.

Growth funds stress appreciation in the value of the assets, and little emphasis is given to current income. The portfolio of the Value Line Fund is an example of a growth fund. The majority of the assets are the common stocks of companies with potential for growth. These growth stocks include the shares of well-known firms as well as those of smaller firms that may offer superior growth potential. A balanced fund (for example, Fidelity Balanced Fund) combines income and growth. Such funds own a variety of stocks, some of which offer potential growth while others are primarily income producers. A balanced portfolio may also include short-term and long-term debt and preferred stock. Such a portfolio seeks a balance of income from dividends and interest and capital appreciation.

Mutual funds may also be classified according to *investment style*. Investment style refers to a portfolio manager's investment philosophy or investment strategy. Possible styles include the size of firms acquired by the fund or the approach (growth or value) used to select the firms.

Firm size refers to *large cap*, *midsize cap*, or *small cap*. The word *cap* is short for *capitalization*, which refers to the market value of the company. The market value is the number of shares outstanding times the market price. Large-cap stocks are the largest companies, with market value exceeding $10 billion. A small-cap stock is a much smaller firm, with, perhaps, a total value between $2 billion and $300 million. Mid-cap is, of course, between the two extremes. (The difference among a small-cap, a mid-cap, and a large-cap stock is arbitrary. A small-cap stock could be defined as less than $1 billion or less than $500 million or less than $300 million total market value. The definition used by the fund is generally specified in the fund's prospectus.)

Two stocks illustrate this difference in firm size. Pier 1 Imports has 117,160,000 shares outstanding; at a price of $6.50, the total value of the stock is $761,540,000. This is a modest-sized firm, so Pier 1 Imports could be classified as a mid-cap stock. Coca-Cola has over 2.3 billion shares and, at a price of $52, the total value exceeds $119.6 billion. Coca-Cola is a large-cap stock. It is obvious that Pier 1 Imports is small compared to Coca-Cola and would not be an acceptable investment for a large-cap portfolio.

A fund can have more than one strategy, such as "small cap–value," which suggests that the portfolio manager acquires shares in small companies that appear to be undervalued. A "small cap–growth" fund would stress small companies offering potential growth but not necessarily operating at a profit. Without earnings, a firm's P/E cannot be computed, and comparisons with other firms become more difficult.

The Portfolios of Specialized Mutual Funds

Investment companies initially sought to pool the funds of many savers and to invest these funds in a diversified portfolio of assets. Such diversification spreads the risk of investing and reduces the risk of loss to the individual investor. While a particular investment company has a specified goal, such as growth or income, the portfolio is still sufficiently diversified so that the element of unsystematic risk is reduced.

Today, however, a variety of investment companies have developed that have moved away from this concept of diversification and the reduction of risk. Instead of offering investors a cross section of American business, many funds have been created to offer investors specialized investments. For example, an investment company may be limited to investments in the securities of a particular sector of the economy or particular industry, such as ASA, Limited (a gold fund). There are also funds that specialize in a particular type of security, such as the American General Bond Fund.

In addition to these specialized funds, several investment companies have been established that offer real alternatives to traditional types of mutual funds. For example, money market mutual funds provide you with a means to invest indirectly in money market instruments, such as Treasury bills and negotiable certificates of deposit. Funds that acquire foreign securities offer a means to invest in stocks of companies located in Europe and Asia. From an American perspective, there are basically three types of mutual funds with international investments. Global funds invest in foreign and American securities. Many American mutual funds are global, as they maintain some part of their portfolios in foreign investments. While these funds do not specialize in foreign securities, they do offer you the advantages associated with foreign investments: returns through global economic growth, diversification from assets whose returns are not positively correlated, and possible excess returns from inefficient foreign financial markets.

In addition to global funds, there are international funds, which invest solely in foreign securities and hold no American securities, and regional funds, which specialize in a particular geographical area, such as Asia. While the regional funds obviously specialize, the international funds may also specialize in specific countries during particular time periods.

The purpose of an index fund is almost diametrically opposed to the traditional purpose of a mutual fund. Instead of identifying specific securities for purchase, the managements of these funds seek to duplicate the composition of an index, such as the Standard & Poor's 500 Index. Such funds should then perform in tandem with the market as a whole. Although they cannot generally outperform the market, neither should they underperform the market. Part of the popularity of such funds has been attributed to the poor performance of mutual funds in general in the past. (The returns earned by mutual funds are discussed in the next section.) While these funds cannot overcome any risk associated with price fluctuations in the market as a whole, they do eliminate the risk associated with the selection of specific securities (that is, unsystematic risk).

In addition to erasing asset-specific risk, index funds help you manage systematic risk. Index funds permit investors to tailor their portfolios in accordance with the level of systematic risk they are willing to accept. By altering the proportion of risk-free assets in a diversified portfolio, you may establish different levels of risk and return. Thus, conservative investors may invest a large proportion of their wealth in risk-free assets (such as federally insured savings accounts, shares in money market mutual funds, and U.S. Treasury bills) and a small proportion in an index fund. Such portfolios would have a modest expected return but would involve nominal risk. More aggressive investors may commit a larger proportion of their wealth to the index fund. These individuals would expect a higher return because they are bearing more risk.

Global fund

Mutual fund whose portfolio includes foreign and U.S. firms, especially those with international operations

International fund

Mutual fund whose portfolio is limited to non–U.S. securities

Regional fund

Mutual fund that specializes in the firms in a particular geographical area

Index fund

Mutual fund whose portfolio seeks to duplicate an index of stock prices

The Returns Earned on Investments in Mutual Funds

As was previously explained, the securities of investment companies offer individuals several advantages. First, you receive the advantages of a diversified portfolio, which reduces risk. Some investors may lack the resources to construct a diversified portfolio, and the purchase of shares in an investment company permits these investors to own a portion of a diversified portfolio. Second, the portfolio is professionally managed and under continuous supervision. You may not have the time and expertise to manage your own portfolio and, except in the case of large portfolios, may lack the funds to obtain professional management. By purchasing shares in an investment company, you buy the services of professional management. Third, the administrative detail and custodial aspects of the portfolio (for example, the physical handling of securities) are taken care of by the management of the company.

Although investment companies offer advantages, there are also disadvantages. The services offered by an investment company are not unique but may be obtained elsewhere. In addition, the investor may acquire a diversified portfolio with only a modest amount of capital. Diversification does not require 100 different stocks. If you have $20,000, a reasonable diversified portfolio may be produced by investing $2,000 in the stock of eight to 10 companies in different industries. You do not have to purchase shares in an investment company to obtain the advantage of diversification.

Studies of Returns

Investment companies do offer the advantage of professional management, but this management cannot guarantee to outperform the market. A particular fund may do well in any given year, but it may do poorly in subsequent years. Several studies have been undertaken to determine if professional management results in superior performance for mutual funds.

The first study, conducted for the SEC, found that the performance of mutual funds was not significantly different from that of an unmanaged portfolio of similar assets. About half the funds outperformed Standard & Poor's indexes, but the other half underperformed these aggregate measures of the market. In addition, there was no evidence of superior performance by a particular fund over a number of years. These initial results were confirmed by later studies. When the loading charges are included in the analysis, the return earned by investors tends to be less than that which would be achieved through a random selection of securities.

Support for these conclusions is given in Exhibit 27.3, which provides annualized returns and their standard deviations for several classes of funds for different time periods. The data in Exhibit 27.3 were reported by the American Association of Individual Investors (AAII), a nonprofit corporation whose purpose is to "assist individuals in becoming effective managers of their own assets through programs of education, information, and research." AAII is

E X H I B I T 27.3
Annualized Returns for
Different Time Periods
for Various Types of
Mutual Funds

	Return	Standard Deviation of Return
1985–1994		
Growth funds	13.1%	12.2%
Aggressive growth funds	14.4	16.7
Growth and income funds	11.8	10.9
Balanced funds	11.7	10.9
International funds	16.7	21.2
S&P 500	14.3	12.2
1993–1997		
Growth funds	17.4%	11.3%
Aggressive growth funds	17.0	15.5
Growth and income funds	17.3	9.9
Balanced funds	13.4	7.1
International funds	10.8	11.9
S&P 500	20.2	11.0
1996–2000		
Growth funds	16.1%	19.5%
Aggressive growth funds	14.5	32.5
Growth and income funds	14.3	17.4
Balanced funds	11.4	11.0
International funds	8.3	22.7
S&P 500	18.3	17.7
1999–2003		
Growth funds	0.9%	21.7%
Aggressive growth funds	NA	NA
Growth and income funds	NA	NA
Balanced funds	3.7	10.4
International funds	3.2	18.9
S&P 500	−0.5	18.3
2004–2009		
Growth funds	−2.8	20.0
Aggressive growth funds	NA	NA
Growth and income funds	NA	NA
Balanced funds	0.9	11.0
International funds	1.6	22.0
S&P 500	−2.2	15.3

Source: Adapted from *The Individual Investor's Guide to the Top Mutual Funds*, various issues
(Chicago: American Association of Individual Investors). Information on AAII is available at its
Web site **http://www.aaii.org**.

not a trade organization that supports the mutual fund industry. With the exception of international funds during 1985–1994, none of the fund groups achieved higher returns than the S&P 500 for 1985–2000 time periods. In addition, the funds' standard deviations were often higher than the standard deviation of the S&P 500 returns. These results suggest that investors experienced lower returns coupled with increased risk! Additional risk does not appear to have been rewarded. Investors would have been better off by simply buying an index fund such as those discussed later in this chapter.

The periods 1999–2003 and 2004–2009 provide different results. The S&P 500 generated negative returns and the other groups achieved at best marginally positive returns. You should also note the change in fund emphasis. Returns on aggressive growth funds and growth and income funds are no longer reported (not available—NA). Instead AAII started reporting returns earned by large-cap, mid-cap, and small-cap funds and by sector funds.

Consistency of Returns

The preceding discussion suggests that mutual funds in the aggregate have not consistently outperformed the market. Is it possible that selected funds may outperform the market or at least consistently outperform other funds? If a type of fund consistently outperforms other funds, the implication for investors is obvious: Purchase shares in a fund that has done well on the premise that the best-performing funds will continue to do well (that is, go with the "Hot Hands").

Certainly the popular financial media's coverage of funds that do well during a particular period encourages individuals to invest in those funds. Money flows into funds that have a superior track record, and because fees increase as the funds under management grow, you should not be surprised to learn that mutual funds tout any evidence of superior performance.

Consistency of mutual fund performance is intuitively appealing. Such consistency seems to apply to many areas of life, especially professional sports. The New York Yankees and the Atlanta Braves make the play-offs virtually every year. However, the principle of efficient markets suggests the opposite may apply to mutual funds. Essentially, the question is: If past stock performance has no predictive power, why should historical mutual fund performance have predictive power? The answer, of course, may lie in the superior skills of the funds' managers. If fund managers have superior skills, then the portfolios they manage should consistently outperform the portfolios of less-skilled managers.

Studies have been conducted to determine the consistency of fund returns. Nonacademic studies tend to suggest consistency. The results are consistent over different time horizons; for example, 26-week returns forecast the next 26-week returns, and one-year returns predict the next-year returns. Results tend to be best over the longest time horizons. Funds with the highest returns over a period of five years consistently do better during the next two years than the funds with the lowest returns.

The results of academic studies, however, are ambiguous. Although some support consistency, others do not.[1] At least one study explained the observed consistency on the basis of the fund's investment objective or style and not on the basis of the portfolio manager's skill.[2] For example, suppose large-cap stocks do well while small-cap stocks do poorly. Large-cap mutual funds should consistently outperform small-cap funds. Once the returns are standardized for the investment style, the consistency of the returns disappears. The superior performance of the large-cap mutual funds is the result of market movements and *not the result of the skill of the portfolio managers*. The consistently better performing large-cap stocks give the impression that the large-cap mutual funds are the consistently better performing mutual funds. These findings, of course, support the concept of efficient markets. One set of portfolio managers is not superior to another.

Selecting a Mutual Fund

You may choose from over 8,000 funds. You cannot buy all of them. Thus, while investment companies relieve you from having to select individual stocks and bonds, they do not relieve you from having to select the specific fund.

A good starting point is to match your financial goals with the fund's objectives. If your goal is primarily long-term growth, a bond fund or money market fund is not appropriate. Such funds would be appropriate for investors who need an increased current flow of income (the bond fund) or a short-term liquid investment (the money market fund). Your need for custodial services, diversification, and tax management may also affect the decision. Additional factors that you want to consider follow.

Fees and Expenses

As explained earlier in this chapter, mutual fund investors pay a variety of fees. These include the loading charge (the sales fee paid to the broker or financial advisor for buying the shares), management fees, 12b-1 fees, and transaction costs incurred by the fund. Whether the load charge is worth the cost is, of course, open to debate, but there is little evidence that load funds earn a higher return than no-load funds. The load must be justified on the basis of services received. You must find a broker or financial advisor whose advice and assistance is worth the cost.

---

[1]A sampling of this research includes Ronald N. Kahn and Andrew Rudd, "Does Historical Performance Predict Future Performance?" *Financial Analysts Journal* (November–December 1995): 43–51; William N. Goetzmann and Roger G. Ibbotson, "Do Winners Repeat?" *Journal of Portfolio Management* (winter 1994): 9–18; and W. Scott Bauman and Robert E. Miller, "Can Managed Portfolio Performance Be Predicted?" *Journal of Portfolio Management* (summer 1994): 31–39.

[2]See, for instance, F. Larry Detzel and Robert A. Weigand, "Explaining Persistence in Mutual Fund Performance," *Financial Services Review* 7, no. 1 (1998): 45–55; and Gary E. Porter and Jack W. Trifts, "Performance of Experienced Mutual Fund Managers," *Financial Services Review* 7, no. 1 (1998): 56–68.

By acquiring no-load funds, the load expense is avoided. You, however, still pay management fees, operating expenses, and transaction costs, which apply to all funds. While these expenses cannot be avoided, they do differ among the various funds. You should consider these costs, because they obviously decrease returns. Higher than average management and operating expenses and frequent portfolio turnover, which generates higher transaction costs, are possible red flags you should consider when selecting a particular mutual fund.

You may particularly want to analyze 12b-1 fees, which are marketing expenses and are assessed each year by many no-load funds (and even some load funds). Over a period of years, 12b-1 fees can exceed load expenses. A $0.50 annual 12b-1 fee exceeds a $3.00 load fee after six years. If you hold the shares for 10 years and pay the 12b-1 fee each year, you would have been better off buying a load fund without the 12b-1 fee.

The Timing of Distributions and Income Taxation

Taxation is another important consideration when buying the shares of a mutual fund. Tax issues essentially revolve around the timing of distributions from the fund and the fund's ability to minimize your tax obligations. While many U.S. corporations distribute dividends quarterly, most mutual funds make two distributions. The first is a six-month income distribution. A second and year-end distribution consists of both income and capital gains. As a stock's price is adjusted downward for the dividend (see the discussion of the distribution of dividends in Chapter 20), the net asset value of the fund declines by the amount of the dividend. For example, if the NAV is $34 and the fund distributes $2.00 ($0.50 in income and $1.50 in capital gains), the NAV declines to $32.

If you buy the shares at the NAV ($34) just prior to the distribution, you pay the tax. Even though the appreciation may have occurred prior to the purchase of the shares, you must pay the appropriate tax on the distribution. Thus, it may be desirable to defer the purchase until after the fund goes ex-dividend and the NAV declines to $32.

Tax Efficiency

Differences in mutual funds' portfolio strategies can cause differences in tax obligations, so a fund that generates lower taxes may be preferred. The ability of the fund to earn a return without generating large amounts of tax obligations is often referred to as the fund's "tax efficiency." Obviously, if the fund never realizes any capital gains and does not receive any income, there will be no distributions and you have no tax obligations. This, however, is unlikely. (Even a passively managed index fund may receive dividend income from its portfolio. This income is distributed and the investor becomes liable for taxes on the distribution.)

At the other extreme are funds that frequently turn over their portfolios. Since each security sale is a taxable event, frequent turnover implies the fund will *not* generate long-term capital gains. The capital gain distributions will be short-term and subject to tax at the stockholder's marginal federal income tax rate rather than the lower long-term capital gains tax rate.

A "tax efficiency index" permits comparisons based on a fund's ability to reduce stockholder tax obligations. The index expresses after-tax returns as a percentage of before-tax returns. The computation of a tax efficiency index requires assumptions concerning tax rates. In the following example, the income tax rate is 35 percent, and the long-term capital gains tax rate is 15 percent. Fund A's $2.00 distribution is entirely income, so the tax is $0.70 (0.35 × $2.00 = $0.70), and the investor nets, after tax, $1.30. If the before-tax return is 10 percent, the after-tax return is 6.5 percent ($1.30/$2.00). The tax efficiency index is 65 (6.5%/10%). Fund B's $2.00 distribution consists solely of realized long-term capital gains, which generate $0.30 in taxes (0.15 × $2.00). The after-tax return is 8.5 percent ($1.70/$2.00), so the tax efficiency index is 85. Since the tax efficiency index is 65 for A and 85 for B, B is more tax efficient than A.

While this index may seem appealing, it has weaknesses. To construct the tax efficiency index, you need the composition of the returns and the appropriate tax rates in effect when the returns were earned. Tax rates vary with changes in the tax laws, but even without changes in the tax laws, the appropriate income tax rate may differ as you move from one tax bracket to another. The tax efficiency index varies among investors, and published tax efficiency rankings may not be appropriate for an investor whose tax brackets differ from those used to construct the index.[3]

A second weakness is that a high tax efficiency index in a particular year may be achieved when the fund does not realize capital gains. If these gains are subsequently realized, the tax efficiency ratio will decline. For this reason, the index needs to be computed over a period of years so that the impact of differences in the timing of security sales from one year to the next are eliminated.

A third weakness is that high efficiency may not alter performance rankings. Funds with similar objectives and styles (for example, long-term growth through investments in large-cap stocks) may generate similar tax obligations. Suppose one fund's return is 20 percent while another fund generates 16 percent. All gains are distributed and are long-term. The tax efficiency for both funds is the same, so the relative rankings are unchanged. The performance is inferior on both a before- and after-tax basis.

---

[3]*The Individual Investor's Guide to the Top Mutual Funds*, published by the American Association of Individual Investors, provides both actual returns and tax-adjusted returns. In the 2009 edition, the returns for 2008 were adjusted using a 35 percent income tax rate and a 15 percent long-term capital gains tax rate. For example, Fidelity Small Cap Growth Fund reported a return of 16.8 percent but the tax-adjusted return was 15.7 percent. While 35 percent and 15 percent tax would not apply to all investors, they were a worst-case scenario in 2009.

Exchange-Traded Funds (ETFs)

Few funds outperform the market over an extended period of time. This result should not be surprising in an efficient financial market environment. Over time, most returns should mirror the market unless the portfolio is riskier than the market. Since mutual funds have expenses (for example, operating expenses and management fees), the return after these costs should be lower than the market return, which is not reduced by any expenses.

The inability of many mutual funds to outperform the market led to an increase in the popularity of index funds, which mirror the market (or a subsection of the market). Their appeal is obvious. They offer (1) portfolio diversification, (2) a passive portfolio whose minimal turnover and minimal supervision result in lower expenses, and (3) lower taxes because the index fund has few realized capital gains.

Support for acquiring index funds may be found in both the popular press and the professional literature.[4] It is, of course, not surprising to learn that strong believers in efficient markets favor index funds. Even with index funds, you must still choose: About 50 mutual funds track the S&P 500 Index. Index funds are also not limited to funds that mimic the S&P 500. For example, the Dreyfus S&P MidCap Index fund specializes in moderate-sized equities that match the S&P MidCap 400 Index. The Vanguard Balanced Index fund mimics a combination of stocks and bonds. The Schwab International Index fund tracks the 350 largest non–U.S. firms.

An alternative to the index fund is the exchange-traded fund or ETF, which is an outgrowth of the index fund. While index funds permit the investor to take a position in the market as a whole, purchases and redemptions occur only at the end of the day when the fund's net asset value is determined. Standard & Poor's Depositary Receipts or SPDRs (commonly pronounced "spiders") overcome this limitation. The shares may be bought and sold on an exchange; they trade like stocks and bonds.

The first SPDR comprised all the stocks in the S&P 500 stock index. The second SPDR was based on the S&P MidCap stock index and was followed by nine "Select Sector SPDRs" based on subsections of the S&P 500 stock index. These sectors include basic industry, consumer products, utilities, health care, financial, technology, and energy stocks. If you believe that large-cap energy companies will do well, you do not have to select specific companies. You can buy the energy SPDRs. Since each SPDR includes *all* the stocks in the appropriate subsection, there is no selection process for the SPDR. Operating expenses should be minimal, and the performance of the SPDR should mirror the return earned by the subsection (e.g., energy).

Since SPDRs and ETFs trade like the shares of any closed-end investment company, can their shares sell for a discount or premium over net asset value?

---

[4]See, for instance, Burton G. Maikiel, *A Random Walk Down Wall Street*, 10th ed. (New York W. W. Norton, 2011); and John C. Bogle, "Selecting Equity Mutual Funds," *Journal of Portfolio Management* (winter 1992): 94–100. Bogle's arguments however, may be self-serving—he introduced the first index fund, the Vanguard 500, in 1976.

The answer is no. ETFs permit large institutions to exchange shares in the companies for ETF shares and vice versa. Suppose an ETF were to sell for a discount from NAV. The financial institutions could buy the ETF shares and exchange them for shares in the underlying companies. Simultaneously, the financial institution would sell the exchanged shares in the secondary markets and make the difference between the cost of the ETF and the proceeds from the sale of the underlying stock. The process would be reversed if the ETF shares were selling for a premium. The financial institution would buy the underlying shares, exchange them for shares in the ETF, and simultaneously sell the ETF shares. Once again, the financial institution would make the difference between the cost of the underlying stock and the proceeds from the sale of the ETF shares. These actions by the financial institutions would assure that the price of an ETF approximates its net asset value. Any remaining difference would be small, perhaps trivial.

While an ETF will not sell for a significant discount or a premium from its net asset value, its price movement may *not* mirror movement in the underlying index. Suppose an ETF sought to replicate the return on an index that encompassed 100 stocks. To achieve the same percentage change as the benchmark, the ETF would have to *own all 100 stocks in the same proportion as the index*. ETFs rarely do this; instead they own a set of stocks that are highly correlated with the index. For example, iShares US Medical Devices (IHI) tracks the Dow Jones U.S. Medical Equipment index. The fund usually invests 90 percent of its assets in the stocks in the index. The fund, however, does not invest in all the stocks in the index, and over 50 percent of its assets are in just 10 stocks. The fund may also invest in other assets that management believes will track the index. For this reason the change in an ETF's price can deviate from the change in the index. The difference is referred to as the "tracking error." If you acquire an ETF with a large tracking error, you may not earn the return generated by the underlying index.

After the initial success of index funds and SPDRs, the next logical step was to extend the concept to other areas. Barclays Global Investor created "iShares," which extended the concept to foreign stock indexes. Investors can now buy iShares based on a broad overview of international stock markets such as the iShares MSCI Index Fund (EFA) or specific countries such as the iShares Germany Index Fund (EWG). (MSCI stands for Morgan Stanley Capital International and the EAFE index encompasses Europe, Australasia, and the Far East.) ETFs were created for geographical regions such as the iShares S&P Europe 350 Index (IEV) and for emerging markets such as iShares Brazil Index Fund (EWZ).

Quickly other financial firms developed ETFs such as the streetTRACKS ETFs, which are based on various Dow Jones averages and indexes. By 2010 almost 1,000 ETFs had been created. You can invest in virtually any index or subset of an index. Instead of having to select individual securities, you may select among sectors of the economy, foreign or domestic markets, or types of securities. ETFs even exist for currencies and commodities. In a sense, ETFs permit passive investors to actively manage their portfolios. You may alter the composition of your portfolio without ever having to buy individual stocks or bonds. You may take long or short positions in ETFs and include ETFs in your IRA (individual retirement account). It is perhaps no surprise that various ETFs have become popular vehicles for investors. ETFs based on the S&P 500 and the NASDAQ 100 Index (commonly referred to by its symbol QQQQ or the "QQQs") are among the most actively traded securities on the various securities markets.[5]

---

[5]As you might anticipate, a large number of Internet sites provide information on exchange-traded funds. As a starting point you may use Index Funds, Inc., http://www.indexfunds.com, which provides information on index and exchange-traded funds.

Information on specific ETFs include the following:

http://www.sectorspdr.com for the nine sector SPDRs based on the S&P 500 Index

http://www.ishares.com for iShares

http://www.holdrs.com for Holding Company Depositary Receipts or HOLDRs. Bank of New York, which acts as the trustee and transfer agent for the securities, also provides a Web site devoted to depositary receipts (http://www.adrbnymellon.com). Information includes current pricing and a link that provides the composition of each HOLDR portfolio.

http://www.vanguard.com for ETFs created by the Vanguard Group, Inc.

Summary

Instead of directly investing in securities, you may buy shares in investment companies. These firms, in turn, invest the funds in various assets, such as stocks and bonds.

There are two types of investment companies. A closed-end investment company has a specified number of shares that are bought and sold in the same manner as the stock of firms such as IBM. An open-end investment company (a mutual fund) has a variable number of shares sold directly to investors. Investors who desire to liquidate their holdings sell them back to the company.

Investment companies offer several advantages, including professional management, diversification, and custodial services. Dividends and the interest earned on the firm's assets are distributed to stockholders. In addition, if the value of the company's assets rises, the stockholders profit as capital gains are realized and distributed.

Mutual funds may be classified by the types of assets they own. Some stress income-producing assets, such as bonds, preferred stock, and common stock of firms that distribute a large proportion of their income. Other mutual funds stress growth in their net asset values through investments in firms with the potential to grow and generate capital gains. There are also investment companies that specialize in large-cap or small-cap stocks, particular sectors of the economy, and tax-exempt securities. There are even mutual funds that duplicate an index of the stock market.

To select an investment company, you should match your objectives with those of the particular fund. The past performance of the fund may also be used to select funds; however, the historical returns may not indicate future returns. The managements of few mutual funds have outperformed the market over a number of years. Instead, mutual funds tend to achieve about the same results as the market as a whole. This performance is consistent with the efficient market hypothesis, which suggests that few, if any, investors will outperform the market over an extended period of time.

Exchange-traded funds (ETFs) combine features of mutual funds and closed-end investment companies. Their shares trade through the secondary securities markets, so they may be readily bought and sold by investors. The first ETF tracked an aggregate market index, the S&P 500 stock index. Subsequently, ETFs were created to track sectors of the S&P 500, other market indexes, subsets of the market, and even foreign currencies and commodities.

Review Objectives

Now that you have completed this chapter, you should be able to

1. Differentiate closed-end and open-end investment companies (p. 577).

2. Determine a fund's net asset value (p. 578).

3. Contrast a closed-end investment company's discount or premium (pp. 579–580).

4. Enumerate the sources of return from an investment company (pp. 580–581).

5. List several costs associated with investing in a mutual fund (pp. 581–583).

6. Differentiate mutual funds based on their portfolios (pp. 583–585).

7. Explain why mutual fund returns over time tend to track the market as a whole (pp. 586–589).

8. Identify several considerations when selecting an investment company for possible inclusion in your portfolio (pp. 589–591).

9. Identify the features that differentiate exchange-traded funds and other investment companies (pp. 592–594).

Internet Assignments

1. Many mutual funds are part of a family of funds under the umbrella of a fund sponsor. Select four of these fund sponsors and answer the following questions.

American Century: **http://www.americancentury.com**

Columbia Funds: **http://www.columbiamanagement.com**

Dreyfus Funds: **http://www.dreyfus.com**

DWS Investments: **http://www.dws-investments.com**

Fidelity Investments: **http://www.fidelity.com**

T. Rowe Price: **http://www.troweprice.com**

Vanguard: **http://www.vanguard.com**

a. Does the sponsor offer a growth fund or large-cap fund and an income fund?

b. What are the funds' load fees and 12b-1 fees?

c. What were the income and capital gains distributions made by the funds during the last year?

d. What were each fund's annual expenses (expense ratio) and annual return?

e. Do any of the funds offer retirement accounts?

f. What was each fund's portfolio turnover?

g. Would an index fund have outperformed the growth funds during the preceding year?

2. The Internet is a major source of information concerning mutual funds. General sources include:

American Association of Individual Investors: **http://www.aaii.com**

Bloomberg Financial: **http://www.bloomberg.com**

Morningstar: **http://www.morningstar.com**

MSN Money: **http://www.moneycentral.msn.com/investor**

Yahoo! Finance: **http://finance.yahoo.com**

Select three of these sources and answer the following questions.

a. Do the sources offer price quotes and links to specific funds?

b. Will the source let you track a stock, a fund, or a portfolio of stocks and funds?

c. Do the sources recommend specific funds?

d. Do the sources offer on-line brokerage services?

e. Does the source charge for its services or recoup its costs through advertising?

f. Does the source provide nonfinancial information?

Problems

1. What is the net asset value of an investment company with $10,000,000 in assets, $600,000 in current liabilities, and 1,200,000 shares outstanding?

2. If a mutual fund's net asset value is $23.40 and the fund sells its shares for $25, what is the load fee as a percentage of the net asset value?

3. An investor buys shares in a mutual fund for $20. At the end of the year the fund distributes a dividend of $0.58, and after the distribution the net asset value of a share is $24.31. What is the investor's percentage return on the investment?

4. If an investor buys shares in a no-load mutual fund for $30 and after five years the shares appreciate to $50, what is (1) the percentage return and (2) the annual compound rate of return using time value of money?

5. Twelve months ago, you purchased the shares of a no-load mutual fund for $22.50 per share. The fund distributed cash dividends of $0.75 and capital gains of $1.25 per share. If the net asset value of the fund is currently $24.45, what was your annual return on the investment? If the value of the shares had been $21.24, what would have been your annual return?

6. The Global Growth Fund is a load fund with a 6 percent front load fee. It started the year with a net asset value (NAV) of $16.50. During the year the fund distributed $1.05, and at the end of the year its NAV was $17.95. What was the fund's return, and what was an investor's return? Why are they different?

7. A closed-end investment company has a net asset value of $12.75. A year ago the shares sold for a 20 percent discount but that discount has narrowed (i.e., declined) to 10 percent. If the company distributed $1.25 a share, what was the return on an investment in the shares before considering commissions on the purchase?

Additional Problems with Answers

1. You purchase 100 shares of a no-load mutual fund for $100 per share and redeem the shares for $120 per share after a year. What is the percentage return (holding period return) on your investment?

2. You purchase 100 shares of a no-load mutual fund for $100. The fund makes distributions of $6 a share, and you redeem the shares for $120 after a year. What is the percentage return (holding period return) on your investment?

3. You purchase 100 shares of a load mutual fund for $100. The load fee is 5 percent, and you redeem the shares for $120 after a year. What is the percentage return (holding period return) on your investment?

4. You purchase 100 shares of a mutual fund for $100. The fund does not have a load fee but charges an exit fee of 5 percent. You redeem the shares for $120 (before the fee) after a year. What is the percentage return (holding period return) on your investment?

Answers

In each of the problems, the starting point is a net asset value of $100 per share and a redemption value of $120 per share. The problems illustrate the impact of distributions and fees on your return.

1. The gain is $2,000 and the holding period return is 20 percent ($2,000/$10,000).

2. The net gain is $2,600 ($2,000 plus the $600 distribution) and the holding period return is 26 percent ($2,600/$10,000).

3. The gain is $2,000 but the *cost is $10,500* ($10,000 + $10,000 × 0.05). If you invest $10,500, the holding period return is 19.05 percent ($2,000/$10,500).

   If you invest *$10,000 instead of $10,500*, the net amount invested in the shares would be $9,524 (95.24 shares) since the cost of the shares plus the load fee is $10,000 ($9,524 + 0.05($9,524) = $10,000). After the year has passed, 95.24 shares are worth $11,428 (95.24 × $120), and the holding period return is $1,428/$10,000 = 14.28%.

4. The redemption value is $11,400 ($12,000 × 0.95), and the gain is $1,400. The holding period return is 14 percent ($1,400/$10,000). Notice that if you compare the $10,000 invested including the load fee with the case in which you pay the 5 percent exit fee, the returns are essentially the same. The larger return in Problem 3 occurred because *you invested $10,500 and not $10,000*. The increase in the amount invested biases the return on a $10,000 investment. If you want to compare load fees and exit fees, you need to have a comparable initial cash outflow.

Relationships

1. A mutual fund's net asset value (NAV) diminishes when the value of its portfolio _____.

2. A decrease in mutual fund load fees _____ an investor's return.

3. A decrease in redemption fees _____ an investor's return.

4. An increase in the standard deviation of a fund's return _____ the return.

5. A decrease in the variability of a fund's return _____ the standard deviation of the return.

6. The 12b-1 fees _____ a mutual fund's return.

7. Brokerage commissions _____ the return on an investment in an ETF.

8. Brokerage commissions _____ the return on an investment in a mutual fund.

9. If an investor sells an ETF short, higher prices _____ the return on the investment.

Answers

1. decreases
2. increases
3. increases
4. has no impact on (no change)
5. decreases
6. decrease
7. decrease
8. have no impact on (no change)
9. decrease

Derivatives

The last chapters in this text introduce derivatives, those fascinating securities whose value depends upon and is derived from another asset. During my many years of teaching, nothing has interested students more than these speculative securities.

Chapter 28 covers put and call options; Chapter 29 considers futures contracts and swaps. Options and futures are means to speculate on price changes, but they can also be used to help manage risk. Essentially the risk managers (the hedgers) are passing the risk on to the speculators. These speculators are willing to accept the risk in return for the possibility of increasing or leveraging their potential return. Since derivatives serve both the hedgers and the speculators, they are an exceedingly important part of financial markets.

If you continue your study of corporate finance and investments, you will be unable to avoid derivatives. You may never buy or sell derivatives, but information and jargon concerning them permeates finance and investments. The following two chapters can, at best, serve as an elementary introduction to derivatives. If you find them fascinating, you will pursue that fascination with little provocation from other sources. Be forewarned—derivatives can be addictive.

Puts and calls are options to buy and sell stock and other securities. You can find many instances in which one of these options sold for $50 one day and $500 six months later. There are even cases of options selling for $50 one day and $500 the next. In 2005, a Google call option sold for $170 on Thursday and $1,830 on Friday after the company announced a large increase in earnings.

Just think of that. You converted $170 into $1,830 in one day. Of course, it works both ways. You could convert $1,830 into $170 or even $0. The possibility of a large return also implies the possibility of a large loss! Human nature, being what it is, tends to concentrate on the large potential return and not the large potential loss. Please try to overcome that psychological tendency. If you are going to use the material in this chapter, you need a cool, unemotional approach to investing.

Puts and calls are sophisticated securities (as are the futures contracts covered in the next chapter), and you may never buy or sell them. Puts and calls are examples of derivatives. As the name implies, a derivative is an asset whose value depends upon another asset. Entire books are written on puts and calls and other derivatives. This chapter can serve as only a basic introduction to these securities. It describes the features of puts and calls, the mechanics of establishing positions, the role of leverage, and how some positions such as the "covered call" and the "protective put" help you manage risk. This material is not easy. Read it thoroughly, and after you complete the body of the text, please do the problems, which illustrate the material in the chapter.

Options

Warrant

Option (issued by a corporation) to buy stock at a specified price within the specified time period

Call

Option (issued by an individual) to buy stock at a specified price within a specified time period

Put

Option to sell stock at a specified price within a specified time period

Premium

Market price of an option

Strike price/Exercise price

Price at which the option holder may buy the underlying stock

Expiration date

Date by which an option must be exercised

An option is the right to do something. When the term *option* is used with regard to securities, it means the right to buy or sell stock. The word *right* is extremely important: the owner of an option is *not obligated* to do anything. The owner of an option to buy stock does not have to buy the stock, nor does the owner of a right to sell stock have to sell the stock. This makes options different from futures contracts, discussed later in the next chapter. If you enter a futures contract, you must either close the position or meet the obligation.

The rights to buy and sell stock are not the only options in finance. For example, many bonds are callable. Such a call feature is an example of an option because the firm has the right to call the bonds and retire them prior to maturity. Many business transactions involve options. For example, a landowner may sell to a developer an option to buy the land. The developer does not have to buy the land but has the right to purchase it.

Options to buy stock are called warrants if they are issued by firms and calls if they are issued by individuals. A warrant or a call is the right to buy stock at a specified price within a specified time period. Options to sell stock are called puts. A put is the right to sell stock at a specified price within a specified time period. In the jargon of option trading, the market price of the option is the premium. The price at which you may buy or sell the shares is called the strike price or exercise price, and the day on which the option expires is called the expiration date.

A firm may also issue an option called a "right." Rights are issued to current stockholders when the firm is issuing new shares. By exercising the rights and buying new shares, current stockholders maintain their proportionate ownership in the company. Rights have a very short duration, such as four weeks, while a warrant may be outstanding for years.

Since calls constitute the vast majority of options to buy stock, the remainder of this chapter is devoted to calls and the opposite option to sell stock, the put. The chapter is limited to buying and selling these options, their secondary markets, the leverage and risks associated with puts and calls, and how they may be used as tools for risk management.

The Intrinsic Value of a Call Option

Intrinsic value

Value of an option as stock

The intrinsic value of an option is its value as stock. For a call option to buy stock, this intrinsic value is the difference between the price of the stock and the per share exercise price (strike price) of the option. If an option is the right to buy stock at $30 a share and the stock is selling for $40, then the intrinsic value is $10 ($40 − $30 = $10).

If the stock is selling for a price greater than the strike price, the call has positive intrinsic value. This may be referred to as the option's being "in the money." If the common stock is selling for a price that equals the strike price,

EXHIBIT 28.1

The Price of a Stock and the Intrinsic Value of an Option to Buy the Stock at $50 per Share

Price of the Stock	Per Share Strike Price of the Option	Intrinsic Value of the Option
$ 0	$50	$ 0
10	50	0
20	50	0
30	50	0
40	50	0
50	50	0
60	50	10
70	50	20
80	50	30
90	50	40

the call is "at the money." And if the price of the stock is less than the strike price, the call has no intrinsic value. The option is "out of the money." You would not purchase and exercise an option to buy stock for $50 when the stock could be purchased for a price that is less than the strike price of the option (for example, $40).

The relationships among the price of a stock, the strike price (the exercise price of an option), and the call's intrinsic value are illustrated in Exhibit 28.1 and Figure 28.1. In these examples, the option is the right to buy the stock at $50 per share. The first column of the exhibit (the horizontal axis on the graph) gives various prices of the stock. The second column presents the strike price ($50), and the last column gives the intrinsic value of the call (the difference between the values in the first and second columns). The values in this third column are illustrated in the figure by line ABC, which shows the relationship between the price of the stock and the call's intrinsic value. It is evident from both the exhibit and the figure that as the price of the stock rises, the intrinsic value of the option also rises. However, for all stock prices below $50, the intrinsic value is zero, since option prices are never negative. Only after the stock's price has risen above $50 does the option's intrinsic value become positive.

The intrinsic value is important because the market price of a call must approach its intrinsic value as the option approaches its expiration date. On the day that the call is to expire, its market price can be only what the option is worth as stock. It can be worth only the difference between the market price of the stock and the exercise price of the option. You may use the intrinsic value of an option as an indication of the option's future price, for you know that the market price of the call must approach its intrinsic value as the option approaches expiration.

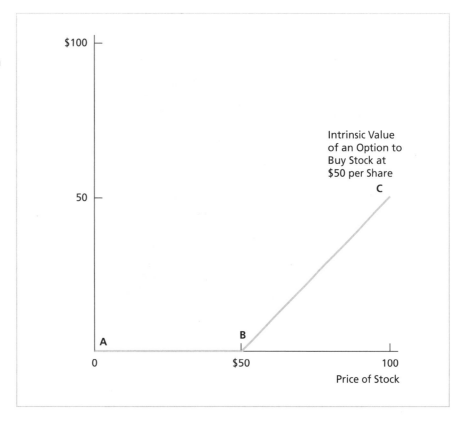

The intrinsic value also sets the minimum price that the option will command.[1] Suppose the price of a stock is $60 and the strike price of the option is $50. The call's intrinsic value is $10 ($60 − $50). If the current market price of the call were $6, you could buy the option and exercise it to acquire stock worth $60. You would then sell the stock and make a $4 profit.

The act of buying the option and selling the stock will increase the price of the call and decrease the price of the stock. As long as the call sells for less than its intrinsic value, investors will buy the call and sell the stock, and the price of the call will rise while the price of the stock declines. Such price changes continue until the option sells for at least its intrinsic value. The intrinsic value thus sets the minimum price that an option will command, for as soon as an option sells for less than its intrinsic value, forces will be set in motion to assure that the option's market price returns to the option's intrinsic value.

---

[1]To be more precise, the minimum value of the option cannot be less than the difference between the price of the stock and the present value of the strike price. Unless the interest rate is zero or the option is at expiration, this difference must exceed the option's intrinsic value.

Leverage

Although an option is a "right," it represents none of the legal rights of ownership. An option does, however, offer you one important advantage: leverage. The potential return on an investment in an option may exceed the potential return on an investment in the underlying stock. Like the use of margin, this magnification of the potential return is an example of financial leverage.

Exhibit 28.1, which illustrates the relationship between the price of a stock and a call's intrinsic value, also demonstrates the potential leverage that options offer. For example, if the price of the stock rose from $60 to $70, the intrinsic value of the call would rise from $10 to $20. The percentage increase in the price of the stock is 16.67 percent ([$70 − $60] ÷ $60), whereas the percentage increase in the intrinsic value is 100 percent ([$20 − $10] ÷ $10). The percentage increase in the intrinsic value exceeds the percentage increase in the price of the stock. If you purchased the option for its intrinsic value and the price of the stock then rose, the return on the investment in the call would exceed the return on the investment in the stock.

Leverage, however, works in both directions. Although it may increase your potential return, it may also increase your potential loss if the price of the stock declines. For example, if the price of the stock in Exhibit 28.1 fell from $70 to $60 for a 14.3 percent decline, the intrinsic value of the call would fall from $20 to $10 for a 50 percent decline. As with any investment, you must decide if the increase in the potential return offered by leverage is worth the increased risk.

If an option offers a greater potential return than does the stock, investors may prefer to buy the option. In an effort to purchase the option, investors bid up its price, so the market price exceeds the option's intrinsic value. Since the market price of an option is referred to as the premium, the extent to which this price exceeds the intrinsic value is referred to as the time premium or time value. Investors are willing to pay this time premium for the potential leverage the call offers. This time premium, however, reduces the potential return and increases the potential loss.

Time premium

Amount by which an option's price exceeds its intrinsic value

The time premium is illustrated in Exhibit 28.2, which adds to Exhibit 28.1 a hypothetical set of call prices in column 4. The hypothetical market prices are greater than the intrinsic values of the option because investors have bid up the prices. To purchase the option, an investor must pay the market price and not the intrinsic value. Thus, in this example when the market price of the stock is $60 and the intrinsic value of the option is $10, the market price of the option is $15. The investor must pay $15 to purchase the option, which is $5 more than the option's intrinsic value.

The relationships in Exhibit 28.2 among the price of the stock, the intrinsic value, and the hypothetical price are illustrated in Figure 28.2. The time premium paid for the call is easily seen in the graph, for it is the shaded area that is the difference between the line representing the market price of the option (line DE) and the line representing its intrinsic value (line ABC). Thus, when the prices of the stock and call are $60 and $15, respectively, the time premium is $5 [the price of the option ($15) minus its intrinsic value ($10)].

EXHIBIT 28.2
Relationships among the
Price of Stock, the Intrinsic
Value of the Call, and the
Hypothetical Market Price

Price of the Common Stock	Option Per Share Strike Price	Intrinsic Value	Hypothetical Market Price
$ 10	$50	$ 0	$ 0.00
20	50	0	0.25
30	50	0	0.50
40	50	0	1.25
50	50	0	6.75
60	50	10	15.00
70	50	20	23.00
80	50	30	32.63
90	50	40	41.25
100	50	50	50.00

FIGURE 28.2
Relationships among
the Price of the Stock, the
Intrinsic Value of the
Option, and the Hypotheti-
cal Price of the Option

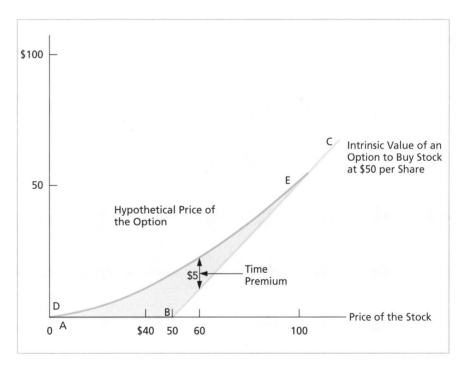

As may be seen in the figure, the amount of the time value varies at the
different price levels of the stock. The time premium declines as the price of the
stock rises above the strike price. Once the price of the stock has risen, the call
may command virtually no time premium. At $100 per share, the call is selling
at approximately its intrinsic value of $50. The primary reason for this decline
in the time premium is that as the price of the stock and the intrinsic value

rise, the potential leverage is reduced. In addition, at higher prices the potential price decline in the option is greater if the price of the stock falls. For these reasons investors are less willing to bid up the price of the call as the price of the stock rises, and, hence, the amount of the time premium diminishes.

The time premium decreases the potential leverage and return from investing in calls. If, for example, this stock's price rose from $60 to $70 for a 16.7 percent gain, the option's price would rise from $15 to $23 for a 53.3 percent gain. The percentage increase in the price of the call still exceeds the percentage increase in the price of the stock; however, the difference between the two percentage increases is smaller. The time premium has reduced the potential leverage that the option offers investors.

Several factors affect an option's time premium. As an option approaches expiration, its market price must approach the intrinsic value. On the expiration date, the option cannot command a price greater than its intrinsic value based on the underlying stock. Thus, as a call nears expiration, it will sell for a lower time premium, and that premium disappears at the option's expiration.

Other determinants of a call's time premium include the payment of cash dividends, the volatility of the underlying stock, and interest rates. Options of companies that pay cash dividends tend to sell for lower time premiums. There may be two possible explanations for this relationship. First, companies that retain (do not distribute) earnings have more funds available for investments. By retaining and reinvesting earnings, a company may grow more rapidly, and the potential gain in the price of the call may be greater if the firm retains its earnings and does not pay a cash dividend. Second, if a company pays a dividend, the owner of the call does not receive the cash payment. Since the owner of the option must forgo the dividend, investors will not be willing to pay as much for the call, and it will sell for a lower time premium.

Another factor that affects the time premium paid for a call is the price volatility of the common stock. Since the price of the option follows the price of the underlying stock, fluctuations in the price of the stock will be reflected in the call's price. The more volatile the price of the stock, the more opportunity the option offers for a price increase. Thus, calls on volatile stocks tend to be more attractive and command a higher time premium than options on stocks whose prices are more stable and less volatile.

Interest rates affect options by their impact on the present value of the funds necessary to exercise the call. Since options are exercised in the future, higher interest rates imply that the investor must set aside a smaller amount of money to exercise the call. Since the intrinsic value is the price of the stock minus the strike price, a lower strike must increase the value of the call. In effect, higher interest rates reduce the present value of the strike price, which makes the call more valuable and increases the time premium.[2]

---

[2]The process of option valuation, such as the Black-Scholes option pricing model, and the use of options in various portfolio strategies are complex topics that are discussed in texts devoted exclusively to derivative securities. See, for example, Don Chance and Robert Brooks, *An Introduction to Derivatives and Risk Management*, 8th ed. (Mason, Ohio: Thomson South-Western, 2009). For a more pragmatic approach to options, consult Lawrence G. McMillan. *Options as a Strategic Investment*, 4th ed. (New York: New York Institute of Finance, 2001).

In summary, calls are primarily purchased if you want to leverage your position in a stock. Should the price of the stock rise, the price of the call will also rise. Since the cost of the call is less than the cost of the stock, the percentage increase in the call may exceed that of the stock, so you earn a greater percentage return on the call option than on the underlying stock. If the price of the stock declines, the value also falls, so you sustain a larger percentage loss on the option than on the stock. However, since the cost of the call is less than the stock, the absolute loss on the investment in the call may be less than the absolute loss on the stock.

The potential profits and losses at expiration on the purchase of the call for $15 when the stock sells for $60 is illustrated in Figure 28.3. As long as the price of the stock is $50 or less, the entire investment in the call ($15) is lost. As the price of the stock rises above $50, the loss is reduced. You break even at $65, because the intrinsic value of the call is $15—the cost of the option. You earn a profit as the price of the stock continues to rise above $65. (Remember that in this illustration the starting price of the stock was $60. The price has to rise only by more than $5 to assure profit on the position in the call.)

Figure 28.4 adds the profits and losses from buying the stock at $60. Both involve purchases and therefore are *long positions* in the securities. If the price of the stock rises above or declines below $60, you earn a profit or sustain a loss. The important difference between the lines indicating the profit and loss on the long positions in the two securities is the possible large dollar loss from buying the stock compared to the limited dollar loss on the call. In the worst case scenario, you could lose $60 on the stock but only $15 on the call.

FIGURE 28.3
Profits and Losses at Expiration for the Buyer of a Call

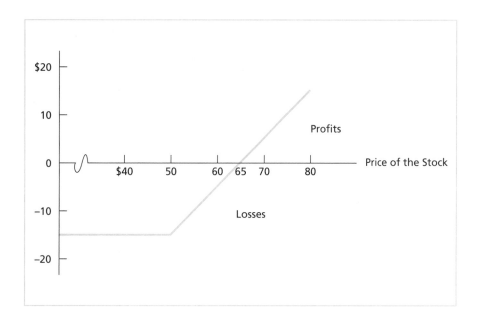

FIGURE 28.4
Profits and Losses from Purchasing the Stock Compared to Purchasing the Call Option

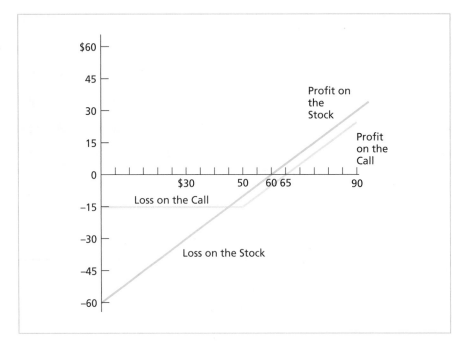

Writing Call Options

The preceding section considered purchasing calls; this section considers writing them. The process of issuing and selling an option is referred to as "writing." While buying calls gives you an opportunity to profit from the leverage that call options offer, issuing calls produces revenue from their sale. You earn a return from the proceeds of the sale.

There are two ways to write options. The first is the less risky strategy, which is called covered option writing. You buy the stock and then sell the call. If the option is exercised, you supply the stock that was previously purchased (in other words, "cover" the option with the stock). The second method is to sell the call without owning the stock. This is referred to as naked option writing, for you are exposed to considerable risk. If the price of the stock rises and the call is exercised, you must buy the stock at the higher market price in order to supply it to the buyer. With naked option writing, the potential for loss is greater than with covered option writing.

Covered option writing

Selling an option by an individual who has a long position in the underlying stock

Naked option writing

Selling an option by an individual who does not have a position in the underlying stock

The Covered Call

The reason for writing options is the income generated by the sale. The potential profit from writing a *covered call option* is shown in Exhibit 28.3. In this example you purchase 100 shares of stock at the current market price of $50 per share and simultaneously sell for $5 a call to buy the shares at the strike price of $50 (i.e., sell the call for $500 ($5 × 100 shares). Possible future prices for the stock at the expiration of the call are given in column 1. Column 2

EXHIBIT 28.3

Profits and Losses on a
Covered Call Consisting of
the Purchase of 100 Shares
and the Sale of One Call
to Buy 100 Shares at $50
a Share

Price of Stock at Expiration of the Call	Net Profit on the Stock	Value of the Call at Expiration	Net Profit on the Sale of the Call	Net Profit on the Position
$40	−$1,000	$ 0	$ 500	−$500
42	−800	0	500	−300
44	−600	0	500	−100
46	−400	0	500	100
48	−200	0	500	300
50	0	0	500	500
52	200	200	300	500
54	400	400	100	500
56	600	600	−100	500
58	800	800	−300	500
60	1,000	1,000	−500	500

presents your net profit from the purchase of the stock. Column 3 gives the value of the call at expiration, and column 4 presents your profit from the sale of the call. As may be seen in column 4, the sale of the call is profitable as long as the price of the common stock remains below $55 per share. The last column gives the net profit on the entire position. As long as the price of the common stock stays *above $45 per share*, the entire position will yield a profit (before commissions). The maximum amount of this profit, however, is limited to $500. Thus, by selling the covered call, you *forgo* the possibility of large gains but keep the premium. For example, if the price of the stock were to rise to $70 per share, the holder of the call would exercise it and purchase the 100 shares at $50 per share. You would then make only the $500 that was received from the sale of the call.

If the price of the stock were to fall below $45, the entire position would result in a loss. For example, if the price of the common stock fell to $40, you would lose $1,000 on the purchase of the stock. However, you received $500 from the sale of the call. Thus, your net loss is only $500. You still own the stock and may now write another call on that stock. As long as you own the stock, the same 100 shares may be used over and over to cover the writing of options. Thus, even if the price of the stock does fall, you may continue to use it to write more options. The more options that can be written, the more profitable the strategy becomes. For individuals who write covered options, the best possible situation would be for the stock's price to remain stable. In that case you would receive the income from writing the options and never suffer a capital loss from a decline in the price of the stock on which you are writing the options.

The relationship between the price of the stock and the profit or loss on writing a covered call is illustrated in Figure 28.5, which plots the first and fifth columns of Exhibit 28.3. As may be seen from the figure, the sale of the covered option produces a profit (before commissions) for all prices of the stock above $45. However, the maximum profit (before commissions) is limited to $500.

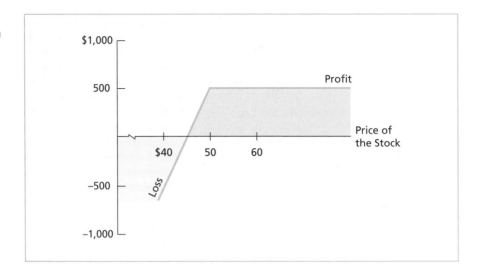

The Naked Call

Option writers do not have to own the common stock on which they write calls. Although such naked or uncovered option writing exposes you to a large amount of risk, the potential return is increased. If the writer of the call option given in Exhibit 28.3 had not owned the stock and had sold the option for $500, the position would have been profitable as long as the price of the common stock remained below $55 per share at the expiration of the call. The potential loss, however, is theoretically infinite, for the naked option loses $100 for every $1 increase in the price of the stock above the call's exercise price. For example, if the price of the stock were to rise to $70 per share, the call would be worth $2,000. The owner of the call would exercise it and purchase the 100 shares for $5,000. The writer of the naked call would have to purchase the shares for $7,000. Since the writer received only $500 when the call was sold and $5,000 when the call was exercised, the loss is $1,500. Therefore, uncovered option writing exposes the writer to considerable risk if the price of the stock rises.

The relationship between the price of the stock and the profit or loss on writing a naked call option is illustrated in Figure 28.6. In this case the option writer earns a profit (before commissions) as long as the price of the stock does not exceed $55 at the expiration of the call. Notice that you earn the entire $500 if the stock's price falls below $50. However, the potential for loss is large if the price of the stock increases.

You should write naked call options only if you anticipate a decline (or at least no increase) in the price of the stock. You may write covered call options if you believe the price of the stock may rise but are not certain of the price increase. And you may purchase the stock (or the option) and not write calls if you believe there is substantial potential for a price increase.

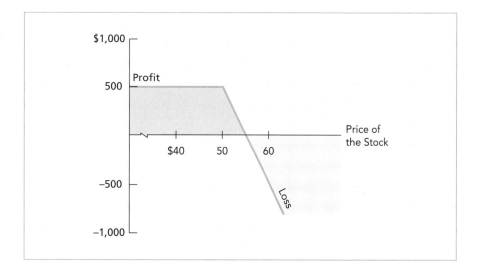

FIGURE 28.6
Profit or Loss on Selling a
Naked Call

Put Options

A put option is an option to sell stock (usually 100 shares) at a specified price within a specified time period. As with calls, the time period is short—three, six, or nine months. Like all options, a put has an intrinsic value. A put's intrinsic value is the *difference between the strike price of the put and the price of the stock* and is illustrated in Exhibit 28.4. Notice that the intrinsic value of a put is the *reverse* of the intrinsic value of an option to buy. (Compare Exhibits 28.1 and 28.4.) This put is an option to sell 100 shares at $30 per share. The first column gives the strike price of the put, the second column presents the price of the stock, and the third column gives the intrinsic value of the put (the strike price minus the price of the stock).

If the price of the stock is less than the strike price, the put has a positive intrinsic value and is "in the money." If the price of the stock is greater than the strike price, the put has no intrinsic value and is "out of the money." If the price of the stock equals the strike price, the put is "at the money." As with call options, the market price of a put is called "the premium."

As may be seen in the exhibit, when the price of the stock declines, the intrinsic value of the put rises. Since the owner of the put may sell the stock at the price specified in the option agreement, the value of the option rises as the price of the stock falls. Thus, if the price of the stock is $15 and the exercise price of the put is $30, the put's intrinsic value as an option must be $1,500 (for 100 shares). You can purchase the 100 shares of stock for $1,500 on the stock market and sell them for $3,000 to the person who issued the put. The put, then, must be worth the $1,500 difference between the purchase and sale prices.

Why should you purchase a put? One reason is the same for puts as it is for other options: The put offers potential leverage. Such leverage may be seen in the example presented in Exhibit 28.4. When the price of the stock declines from $25 to $20 (a 20 percent decrease), the intrinsic value of the put rises from $5 to

Strike Price of the Put	Price of the Stock	Intrinsic Value of the Put	Hypothetical Price of the Put
$30	$15	$15	$15
30	20	10	12
30	25	5	8
30	30	0	6
30	35	0	3
30	40	0	1
30	50	0	—

$10 (a 100 percent increase). In this example, a 20 percent decline in the price of the stock produces a larger percentage increase in the intrinsic value of the put. It is the potential leverage that makes put options attractive to investors.

As with other options, you pay a price that exceeds the put's intrinsic value: The put commands a time premium above its intrinsic value as an option. As with calls, the amount of this time premium depends on such factors as the volatility of the stock's price and the duration of the put.

The relationship between the price of the stock and hypothetical prices of the put are also illustrated in Exhibit 28.4, in which the fourth column presents prices of the put. As may be seen, the price of the put exceeds the intrinsic value, for the put commands a time premium over its intrinsic value as an option.

Figure 28.7 illustrates the relationships among the price of the common stock, the intrinsic value of the put, and the hypothetical market value of the put that were presented in Exhibit 28.4. This figure shows the inverse relationship between the price of the stock and the put's intrinsic value. As the price of the stock declines, the intrinsic value of the put increases (for example, from $5 to $10 when the stock's price declines from $25 to $20). The figure also shows the time premium paid for the option, which is the difference between the price of the put and the option's intrinsic value. If the price of the put is $8 and the intrinsic value is $5, the time premium is $3.

As may be seen in both Exhibit 28.4 and Figure 28.7, the market price of the put converges with the put's intrinsic value as the price of the stock declines. If the price of the stock is sufficiently high (for example, $50), the put will not have any market value because the price of the stock must decline substantially for the put to have any intrinsic value. At the other extreme, when the price of the stock is low (for example, $10), the price of the put is equal to the put's intrinsic value as an option. Once again, there are two reasons for this convergence. First, as the price of the stock declines below the strike price of the put, the potential risk to the investor if the price of the stock should start to rise becomes greater. Thus, put buyers are less willing to pay a time premium above the put's intrinsic value. Second, as the intrinsic value of a put rises when the price of the stock declines, the investor must spend more to buy the put; therefore, the potential return on the investment is less. As the potential return declines, the willingness to pay a time premium diminishes.

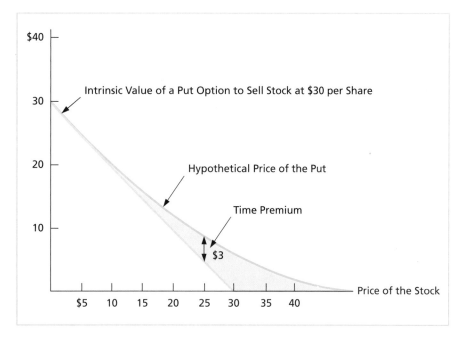

Stock Index Options

Stock index option

Right to buy or sell stock
based on an index of
stock prices

Although put and call options were initially created for individual stocks, stock index options also have developed. These stock index options are similar to options based on individual stocks, but the index option is based on an aggregate measure of the market, such as the Standard & Poor's 500 Index. There are also options based on subsets of the market, such as computer technology stocks or oil stocks. A list of selected options and their ticker symbols is provided in Exhibit 28.5. Stock index options have proved to be particularly popular and account for a substantial proportion of the daily transactions in options.

These options are popular because they permit you to take a position in the market or in a group of companies without having to select specific securities. For example, suppose you anticipate that the stock market will rise. What do you do? You cannot buy every stock but must select individual stocks.[3] Remember from the discussion of risk in Chapter 8 that two sources of risk are associated with the individual stock: nondiversifiable (systematic) risk, and diversifiable (unsystematic) risk. Systematic risk refers to the tendency of a stock's price to move with the market. Unsystematic risk refers to price movements generated by the security that are independent of the market (for example, a takeover announcement, dividend cut, or large increase in earnings).

---

[3]As is explained in Chapter 27, you could buy an index mutual fund or exchange traded fund. Such funds construct portfolios that mirror aggregate measures of the stock market.

EXHIBIT 28.5
Selected Index Options
and and Ticker symbols

Index Options
Dow Jones Industrials (DJX)
S&P 100 (OEX)
S&P 500 (SPX)
Nasdaq 100 (NDX)
NYSE (NYA)
Russell 2000 (RUT)
Value Line (VAY)

Sector Options
MS Consumer (CMR)
MS Cyclical (CYC)
MS Internet (MDX)

Industry options
Bank (BKX)
Biotech (BTK)
Gold/Silver (XAU)
Pharmaceuticals (DRG)
Oil Service (OSX)
Semiconductors (SOX)

If you buy a particular stock on the expectation of a rising market, it does not necessarily follow that the individual stock's price will increase when the market rises. Investors construct diversified portfolios to reduce the unsystematic risk associated with the individual asset. As the portfolio becomes more diversified, unsystematic risk is reduced further and the return on the portfolio mirrors the return on the market.

Index options offer you an alternative to creating diversified portfolios as a means to earn the return associated with movements in the market. For example, if you anticipate that the market will rise in the near future, you may purchase a call option based on an index of the market as a whole. If the market does rise, the value of the call option also increases. You have avoided the unsystematic risk associated with the individual stock.

Stock index options also give you a means to reduce risk. Consider a substantial stock portfolio that has appreciated in value. If you anticipate declining stock prices and sell the shares, this transaction is taxable. Instead of selling the stocks, you may purchase stock index puts. Then if the market declines, the value of the puts increases, so the profits in the position in the puts will help offset the losses on the individual stocks. To see how this "protective put" strategy works, do Problem 6.

There is one major difference between stock index options and call options on specific stocks. With a call option to buy shares of IBM, you may exercise the option and buy the stock. Such purchases are not possible with a stock index option; you cannot exercise it and receive the index. Instead stock index options are settled in cash. For example, suppose you own a call based on the Standard & Poor's 500 Index. At expiration the intrinsic value of the option is determined and that amount is paid by the seller of the option to the owner. Of course, if the option has no intrinsic value at expiration, it is worthless and expires, and the seller of the option then has no further obligation.

In addition to stock index options, there are options on debt instruments (such as Treasury bonds) and foreign currencies. Each of these options permits you to take positions on the underlying assets without actually acquiring them or to reduce the risk of loss from price fluctuations. For example, if you anticipate declining interest rates, you will buy a call option to purchase bonds. If interest rates do fall, the value of bonds will rise, increasing the value of the call option. However, if you were to purchase the call option and interest rates rose, your maximum possible loss would be limited to the cost of the option.

The same concepts apply to options on foreign currencies. If you expect the value of the British pound to rise, you buy a call option on the pound. Of course, if you anticipate a price decline in the pound, you would acquire a put option on the pound. If the anticipated price change were to occur, then you would earn a profit. However, if the price were to move in the opposite direction (rise after the purchase of the put), the maximum you would lose is the cost of the option.

The Volatility Index (The VIX)

Volatility is a source of risk and an important component of the valuation of put and call options. The Chicago Board Options Exchange (CBOE) has developed a volatility index, which is commonly referred to by its ticker symbol: "VIX." The VIX is based on S&P 500 stock index put and call option prices and measures investors' expectation (or "sentiment") of near-term stock market volatility. (The VIX is also referred to as the "investor fear gauge.")

The VIX is expressed in percentages. A numerical value of 20 suggests that market participants expect the S&P 500 to swing by 20 percent over the next 12 months. As market participants become more pessimistic and markets become more volatile and uncertain, the value of the index rises. A value of 50 suggests an expectation of large swings in the S&P 500. Lower values (e.g., 10) suggest that market participants are less pessimistic or even complacent.

No actual securities or ETFs are based on the VIX, but the CBOE has created VIX put and call options. These derivatives permit individuals and portfolio managers to take positions based on expected volatility. For example, anticipation of increased volatility argues for buying calls or selling puts. In addition, a relationship between the level of the VIX and the future direction of stock prices may exist. High values of the VIX and increased volatility suggest that stock prices are at their peak, so investors and portfolio managers sell VIX call options or purchase put options. Low values of the VIX have the opposite implication. Unfortunately, successful trading based on implied volatility is not easy. Signals can be contradictory. For example, the VIX reached 43.7 in 2001 and the market did decline during 2002. However, the exact opposite occurred during 1998–1999. The VIX reached a high of 47.3 in 1998 but the S&P 500 rose 21 percent during 1999.

Summary

A derivative is a financial asset whose value depends upon (is derived from) another asset. This chapter has covered puts and calls, which are options to sell and buy stock. In both cases, the option's value is derived from the underlying stock.

Calls are options to buy stock at a specified price within a specified time period. The intrinsic value of a call option is the difference between the price of the stock and the exercise (strike) price. Puts are options to sell stock at a specified price within a specified time period. The intrinsic value of a put option is the difference between the exercise (strike) price and the price of the stock. Both calls and puts offer buyers potential leverage, but they sell for a time premium, which reduces the potential leverage.

On the expiration date, puts and calls can be worth only their intrinsic values. Any time premium that the options commanded prior to expiration must disappear, since the option can be worth only its intrinsic value. If the option is out of the money, the option has no value and expires.

Puts and calls are created and sold by investors (writers) who are either naked or covered. Covered call writing occurs when the individual owns the underlying stock. If the individual does not own the stock and writes a call (is a naked writer), the individual is exposed to substantial risk if the price of the stock rises.

In addition to options on individual stocks, put and call options exist on indexes of stock prices. Stock index options permit individuals to take long and short positions on the market without having to select individual stocks. These investors avoid the risk associated with individual securities. Options also exist on bonds and foreign exchange, which grant individuals the right to buy and sell these assets instead of actually buying and selling the bonds or currencies.

Review Objectives

Now that you have completed this chapter, you should be able to

1. Describe the features of put and call options (pp. 603–605).
2. Explain how options offer leverage (pp. 606–609).
3. Differentiate an option's market value, intrinsic value, and time premium (pp. 603–605).
4. Explain the relationship between the market price of a stock and the prices of put and call options (pp. 607–608 and 613–615).
5. Compare buying a stock and a call option (pp. 609–610).
6. Contrast naked and covered call option writing (pp. 610–611).
7. Identify the advantages associated with stock index options (pp. 615–617).

Internet Assignment

Go to the CBOE home page (**http://www.cboe.com**) and select an index option based on each of the following stock indexes: (1) the S&P 500, (2) the Russell 1000, and (3) the Dow Jones Industrial Average. Select options with the same expiration dates and strike prices close to the current value of the index (i.e., options near being "in the money"). Track the prices of the options and each index for periods of two and four weeks. What was the percentage change in each option and each index? How highly related (correlated) were the percentage changes in each index and each option?

Problems

1. A six-month call is the right to buy stock at $20. Currently, the stock is selling for $22, and the call is selling for $5. You buy 100 shares ($2,200) and sell one call (in other words, you receive $500).

   a. Does this position illustrate covered or naked call writing?

   b. If, at the expiration date of the call, the price of the stock is $29, what is your profit on the combined position?

   c. If, at the expiration date of the call, the price of the stock is $19, what is your profit on the combined position?

2. A put is the option to sell stock at $50. It expires after three months and currently sells for $3 when the price of the stock is $52.

   a. If an investor buys this put, what will the profit be after three months if the price of the stock is $55? $50? $45?

   b. What will be the profit from selling this put after three months if the price of the stock is $55? $50? $35?

3. The price of a stock is $39, and a six-month call with a strike price of $35 sells for $8.

   a. What is the option's intrinsic value?

   b. What is the option's time premium?

   c. If the price of the stock rises, what happens to the price of the call?

   d. If the price of the stock falls to $36, what is the maximum you could lose from buying the call?

   e. What is the maximum profit you could earn by selling the call uncovered (naked)?

   f. If, at the expiration of the call, the price of the stock is $35, what is the profit (or loss) from buying the call?

   g. If, at the expiration of the call, the price of the stock is $35, what is the profit (or loss) from selling the call naked?

   h. If, at the expiration of the call, the price of the stock is $46, what is the profit (or loss) from buying the call?

   i. If, at the expiration of the call, the price of the stock is $46, what is the profit (or loss) from selling the call naked?

4. The price of a stock is $61, and a six-month call with a strike price of $60 sells for $5.

   a. What is the option's intrinsic value?

   b. What is the option's time premium?

c. If the price of the stock falls, what happens to the price of the call?

d. If the price of the stock falls to $45, what is the maximum you could lose from buying the call?

e. What is the maximum profit you could earn by selling the call covered?

f. If, at the expiration of the call, the price of the stock is $66, what is the profit (or loss) from buying the call?

g. If, at the expiration of the call, the price of the stock is $66, what is the profit (or loss) from selling the call covered?

h. If, at the expiration of the call, the price of the stock is $46, what is the profit (or loss) from buying the call?

i. If, at the expiration of the call, the price of the stock is $46, what is the profit (or loss) from selling the call covered?

5. A Long-term Equity AnticiPation Security (LEAPS) to buy stock at $25 expires after one year and currently sells for $4. The underlying stock is selling for $26.

a. What is the intrinsic value and the time premium paid for the LEAPS?

b. What will be the value of this LEAPS if the price of the stock at the expiration of the LEAPS is $20? $25? $30? $40?

c. If the price of the stock is $45 at the expiration of the LEAPS, what is the percentage return that is earned by an investor in the stock and an investor in the LEAPS? Why does the option in this problem illustrate the successful use of financial leverage?

6. The price of a stock is $29. A put option to sell that stock at $30 is currently selling for $3. You buy the stock and the put. Complete the following table and answer the questions.

Price of the stock	Profit on stock	Profit on put	Net profit
$20			
25			
30			
35			
40			
50			

a. What is the maximum possible profit on the position?

b. What is the maximum possible loss on the position?

c. What is the range of stock prices that generates a profit?

d. What advantage does this position offer?

1. A stock is selling for $48. The three-month call with a strike (exercise) price of $50 is selling for $2, and the put option with a strike price of $50 is selling for $5.

   a. What are the intrinsic values of each option?

   b. What is the time premium commanded by each option?

   c. If the price of the stock is $55 at the options' expiration date, what is the percentage change in the price each option?

   d. If the price of the stock is $44 at the options' expiration date, what is the percentage change in the price of each option?

2. Given the following information,

price of a stock	$102
strike price of a six-month call	$100
market price of the call	$ 6
strike price of a six-month put	$100
market price of the put	$ 3

   finish the following sentences.

   a. The option that is "in the money" is _____.

   b. The time premium paid for the put is _____.

   c. If an investor establishes a naked call position, the amount received is _____.

   d. The most the buyer of the call can lose is _____.

   e. The maximum amount a short seller (of the stock) can lose is _____.

   At the expiration of the options (i.e., after six months have elapsed), the price of the stock is $95.

   f. The profit (loss) from buying the stock is _____.

   g. The profit (loss) from buying the call is _____.

   h. The profit (loss) from writing the call covered is _____.

   i. The profit (loss) from selling the put is _____.

   j. At expiration, the time premium paid for the call is _____.

Answers   1. a. The intrinsic value of the call is zero ($0). The price of the stock ($48) is less than the strike price ($50). The intrinsic value of the put is $2. The price of the stock ($48) is less than the strike price ($50).

b. The time premiums are the difference between the option's price and its intrinsic value. For the call, the time premium is $2 ($2 − $0). For the put, the time premium is $3 ($5 − $2).

c. Each option must sell for its intrinsic value at expiration. If the price of the stock is $55, the call must sell for $5. The percentage increase in the price of the call is 150 percent ($3/$2). The put, however, has no value, so the percentage decrease in its price is 100 percent.

d. If the price of the stock is $44, the call has no value, so the percentage loss is 100 percent. The put is now worth $6, so the percentage increase in the price of the put is 20 percent ($1/$5).

Notice that the answers to *c* and *d* both indicate that the percentage changes in the options exceeded the percentage changes in the price of the underlying stock.

2. a. An "in the money" option has positive intrinsic value. The call option's intrinsic value is $2 ($102 − $100).

b. The time premium is the difference between the option's price and its intrinsic value. For the put option, that value is $3 ($3 − $0).

c. If you sell a naked call, you receive the price of the call: $6.

d. The most you can lose is the cost of the option: $6.

e. If you sell the stock short, there is no limit to the potential loss if the price of the stock were to rise.

f. If you bought the stock for $102 and it is currently selling for $95, you lost $7 ($95 − $102).

g. If you bought the call for $6 and the stock is currently selling for $95, the call is worthless and you lost $6 ($0 − $6). (Notice the difference in the percentage loss for the answers to *f* and *g*. Options offer a means to magnify your percentage gains, but leverage works both ways. You also magnify your percentage loss.)

h. If you write a covered call, you buy the stock ($102) and receive the proceeds from the sale of the call ($6) for a net cash outflow of $96. If the price of the stock is $95, you lost $7 on the stock ($95 − $102) but made $6 on the call that you sold. The call is worthless for any price of the stock $100 or less. The net loss on the covered call is $1 ($6 − $7).

i. If the price of the stock is $95, the put is worth $5 ($100 − $95). Since you sold the put for $3, the net loss is $2 ($5 − $3).

j. At expiration, an option must sell for its intrinsic value, so the time premium for both the put and the call must be $0.

Relationships

1. An increase in the price of a stock _____ a call option's intrinsic value.

2. An increase in the price of a stock _____ a put option's intrinsic value.

3. As a call option approaches expiration, the time premium paid for an option _____.

4. Higher strike prices for call options _____ the options' intrinsic value.

5. As the price of a stock rises, the time premium paid for a call option _____.

6. As the price of a stock rises, a call option's potential leverage _____.

7. If a call option's strike price is $50, the potential leverage from buying the call _____ as the price of the stock rises.

8. As a stock market index declines, the value of an index call option _____ and the value of an index put option _____.

Answers

1. increases
2. decreases
3. decreases
4. decrease
5. decreases
6. decreases
7. decreases
8. decreases; increases

CHAPTER 29

Futures and Swaps

P uts and calls offer you possible large returns on modest investments. Futures contracts do the same, but that virtually ends any similarity to options. Instead the action with futures is faster and the probability of your sustaining large losses is even greater than with puts and calls. Futures contracts are among the riskiest of all possible investments.

There are two participants in the futures markets: the speculators who establish a position in anticipation of a price change and hedgers who employ futures to reduce the risk from price changes. By hedging, the hedgers pass the risk to the speculators. The prices of futures contracts ultimately depend on the interactions of these two participants, the speculators and the hedgers.

This chapter is a brief introduction to futures contracts and swap agreements. It describe the mechanics of buying and selling futures, the role of margin, speculators' long and short positions, and how hedgers use futures contracts to manage risk. While the initial illustrations use physical commodities such as corn, the concepts apply to finance and exchange rate futures. The chapter ends with swap agreements in which two parties agree to exchange payments. While swaps were at the center of the recent financial crises, this discussion explains how they may be used by financial managers to reduce risk.

Futures Contracts

The preceding chapter considered put and call options to sell and buy stock. Such options are used to magnify the investor's return or, in combination with other securities, to reduce the investor's risk exposure. A futures contract performs the same functions. Futures are used by speculators to increase the potential return or by hedgers to reduce the risk of loss.

Futures contract

Agreement for the future delivery or receipt of a commodity or security at a specified price and time

A commodity such as wheat or a financial asset such as a Treasury bond may be purchased for current delivery or for future delivery. A futures contract is a formal agreement executed through a commodity exchange for the delivery of goods or securities in the future. One party agrees to accept a specific commodity that meets a specified quality in a specified month. The other party agrees to deliver the specified commodity during the designated month.

Individuals who enter futures contracts but do not deal in the actual commodities are called speculators. This distinguishes them from the growers, processors, warehousers, and other participants who also enter contracts but who deal in the actual commodity. Such participants are the hedgers, who use the contracts to reduce the risk of loss from fluctuating prices. (Hedging is explained later in the chapter.)

Speculators

Individuals who are willing to accept substantial risk for the possibility of a large return

The appeal of futures contracts to speculators is the potential for a large return on the investment. The large return is the result of the leverage that exists because (1) a futures contract controls a substantial amount of the commodity and (2) the speculator must make only a small payment to enter into a contract to buy or sell a commodity (that is, there is a small margin requirement). These two points are discussed in detail later in this chapter.

Hedgers

Individuals or firms that enter into offsetting contracts

The Mechanics of Trading Futures

Like stocks and bonds, futures contracts are traded in several markets, such as the Chicago Mercantile Exchange (**http://www.cme.com**), which executes contracts in agricultural commodities, such as wheat, soybeans, and livestock. More than 50 commodities are traded on 10 exchanges in the United States and Canada. These markets developed close to the regions in which each commodity is produced. Thus, the markets for wheat are located in Chicago, Kansas City, and Minneapolis.

Futures contracts are entered into through brokers, just as stocks and bonds are bought and sold. Brokerage firms own seats on the commodity exchange. Membership on each exchange is limited, and only members are allowed to execute contracts. If your brokerage firm lacks a seat, that broker must have a correspondent relationship with another firm that does own a seat. As with stocks and bonds, brokers charge a commission fee for executing trades.

The Units of Commodity Contracts

To facilitate trading, contracts must be uniform. For a particular commodity the contracts must be identical. Besides identifying the delivery month, the contract must specify the grade and type of the commodity (for example, a particular type of wheat) and the units of the commodity (such as 5,000 bushels). Thus, when you enter a contract, there can be no doubt as to the nature of the obligation. For example, if you enter into a contract to buy wheat for January delivery, there can be no confusion with a contract for the purchase of wheat for February delivery. These are two different commodities in the same way that Verizon common stock, Verizon preferred stock, and Verizon bonds are all different securities. Without such standardization of contracts, there would be chaos in the futures (or any) markets.

Commodity Positions

Long position

Contract to accept delivery, to buy

Short position

Contract to make delivery, to sell

Futures price

Price for the future delivery of a commodity or financial asset

You may acquire a contract to accept future delivery (to buy). This is the long position, in which you profit if the price of the commodity, and hence the value of the contract, rises. You may also enter into a contract to make future delivery (to sell). This is the short position, in which you agree to make good the contract (that is, to deliver the goods) sometime in the future. You profit if the price of the commodity, and hence the value of the contract, declines.

How each position generates a profit can be seen in a simple example. Assume that the futures price of wheat is $3.50 per bushel. If a contract is made to accept delivery in six months at $3.50 per bushel, you will profit from this long position if the price of wheat rises. If the price increases to $4.00 per bushel, you can exercise the contract by taking delivery and paying $3.50 per bushel. You then sell the wheat for $4 per bushel, which produces a profit of $0.50 per bushel.

The opposite occurs when the price of wheat declines. If the price of wheat falls to $3.00 per bushel, the individual who made the contract to accept delivery at $3.50 suffers a loss. But the speculator who made the contract to deliver wheat (the short position) earns a profit from the price decline. The speculator can then buy wheat at the market price of $3.00, deliver it for the contract price of $3.50, and earn a $0.50 profit per bushel.

If the price rises, the short position produces a loss. If the price increases from $3.50 to $4.00 per bushel, the speculator who made the contract to deliver suffers a loss of $0.50 per bushel, because he or she must pay $4.00 to obtain the wheat that will be delivered for $3.50 per bushel.

Actually, these losses and profits are generated without the goods being delivered. Of course, when you make a contract to accept future delivery, the possibility always exists that you will receive the goods and have to buy them. Conversely, if you enter into a contract to make future delivery, the possibility exists that the goods will have to be supplied. Such deliveries occur infrequently, however, because you can offset the contract before the delivery date.

This process of offsetting existing contracts is illustrated as follows. Suppose you have a contract to buy wheat in January. If you want to close the position, you can enter a contract to sell wheat in January. The two contracts offset each other, as one is a purchase and the other is a sale. If you actually received the wheat by executing the purchase agreement, you could pass on the wheat by executing the sell agreement. However, since the two contracts offset each other, the actual delivery and subsequent sale are not necessary. Instead, the position in wheat is closed, and the actual physical transfers do not occur.

Correspondingly, if you have a contract for the sale of wheat in January, you can offset it by entering a contract for the purchase of wheat in January. If you were called upon to deliver wheat as the result of the contract to sell, you would exercise the contract to purchase wheat. The buy and sell contracts offset each other, and no physical transfers of wheat occur. Once again you have closed the initial position by taking the opposite position (that is, the sales contract is canceled by a purchase contract).

Because these contracts are offset and no actual deliveries take place, it should not be assumed that profits or losses do not occur. The two contracts need not be executed at the same price. For example, you may have entered into a contract for the future sale of wheat at $3.50 per bushel. Any contract for the future purchase of comparable wheat can offset the contract for the sale. But the cost of the wheat for future delivery could be $3.60 or $3.40 (or any conceivable price). If the price of wheat rises (for example, from $3.50 to $3.60 per bushel), the long position earns a profit, but the short position suffers a loss. If the price declines (for example, from $3.50 to $3.40 per bushel), the short seller earns a profit, but the long position sustains a loss.

Reporting of Futures Trading

Commodity futures prices and contracts are reported in the same general form as stock and bond transactions. Typical reporting is as follows:

| | | | | | | LIFETIME | | Open |
	Open	High	Low	Settle	Change	High	Low	Interest
Corn 5,000 bu; cents per bushel								
Jan	231.0	231.5	230.5	230.50	−3.00	243	210.75	36,790
Mar	240.0	241.5	236.5	237.25	. . .	270	205.0	10,900
May	244.5	244.5	241.0	241.75	+0.25	286	221.0	5,444

The unit of trading for corn is 5,000 bushels (bu), and prices are quoted in cents. The opening price for January delivery was 231.0¢ ($2.31) per bushel, while the high, low, and closing (settle) prices were 231.5¢, 230.5¢, and 230.5¢, respectively. This closing price was 3¢ below the closing price on the previous day. The high and low (prior to the reported day of trading) for the lifetime of the contract were 243¢ and 210.75¢, respectively. The open interest, which is the number of contracts in existence, was 36,790.

This open interest varies over the life of the contract. Initially, the open interest rises as buyers and sellers establish positions. Then it declines as the delivery date approaches and the positions are closed. This changing number of contracts is illustrated in Figure 29.1, which plots the spot and futures prices

Open interest

The number of futures contracts in existence for a particular commodity

FIGURE 29.1
Spot and Futures Prices
and Open Interest for a
September Contract for
Kansas City Wheat

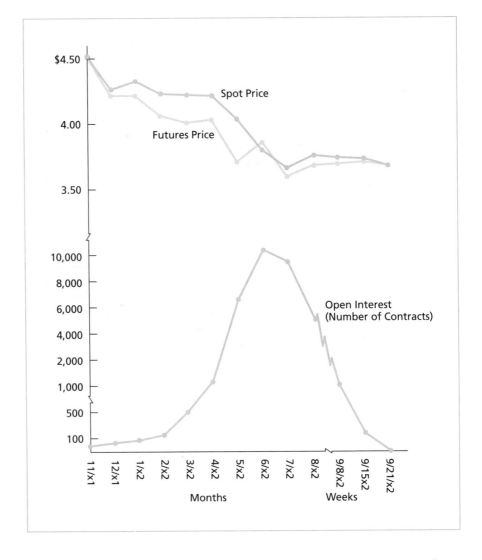

FIGURE 29.1
Spot and Futures Prices and Open Interest for a September Contract for Kansas City Wheat

and the open interest for a September contract to buy Kansas City wheat. When the contracts were initially traded in November X1, there were only a few contracts in existence. By June X2 the open interest had risen to more than 10,000 contracts. As the remaining life of the contracts declined, the number of contracts fell as the various participants closed their positions. By late September only a few contracts were still outstanding.

Figure 29.1 also shows the spot price (the current price) and the futures price for Kansas City wheat. In this case the futures price was generally less than the spot price. This relationship between the two prices occurs when speculators believe that the price of the commodity will decline. These speculators sell contracts now to lock in the higher prices so they may buy back the contracts at a lower price in the future. This selling of the futures drives the futures price down below the spot price.

Spot price

Current price of a commodity

If speculators anticipated higher prices for wheat, they would enter contracts to buy (that is, to accept the future delivery of wheat). This would drive up the futures price relative to the spot price. The value of the futures would then exceed the current price of the commodity.

The value of the futures contract can be worth only the value of the underlying commodity at the expiration date. Hence the spot and futures prices must converge with the approach of the expiration date. This pattern of price behavior is also illustrated in Figure 29.1. In March, April, and May, there was a differential between the two prices. However, in late September the futures and spot prices converged and erased the differential.

Leverage

Margin

Good-faith deposit used to secure a futures contract

Commodities are paid for on delivery. An individual who enters into a contract for future delivery does not pay for the commodity unless actual delivery is made. When the contract is made, the investor provides an amount of money, called margin, to guarantee the contract. This margin applies to *both buyers and sellers* of futures contracts and is not to be confused with the margin that is used in the purchase of stocks and bonds. In the trading of stocks and bonds, margin represents the investor's equity in the position, whereas margin for a commodity contract is a deposit to show the investor's good faith and to protect the broker and the exchange against an adverse change in the price of the commodity.

In the stock market, the amount of margin that is required varies with the price of the security, but in the commodity markets the amount of margin does not vary with the dollar value of the transaction. Instead, each contract has a fixed minimum margin requirement. For example, the investor who makes a contract to buy cocoa must put up $980. These margin requirements are established by the commodity exchanges, but individual brokers may require more.

The margin requirements are only a small percentage of the value of the contract. For example, the $980 margin requirement for cocoa gives the owner of the contract to buy a claim on 10 metric tons of cocoa. If cocoa is selling for $1,400 a metric ton, the total value of the contract is $14,000. The margin requirement as a percentage of the value of the contract is only 7.0 percent ($980/$14,000). This small amount of margin is one reason why a commodity contract offers so much potential leverage.

The potential leverage from speculating in commodity futures may be illustrated in a simple example. Consider a contract to buy wheat at $3.50 per bushel. Such a contract controls 5,000 bushels of wheat worth a total of $17,500 (5,000 × $3.50). If you own this contract to buy and the margin requirement is $1,000, you must remit $1,000. An increase of only $0.20 per bushel in the price of the commodity produces an increase of $1,000 in the value of the contract. This $1,000 is simply the product of the price change ($0.20) and the number of units in the contract (5,000). The profit on the contract is $1,000.

What is the percentage return on the investment? With a margin of $1,000 the return is 100 percent, because you put up $1,000 and then earned an additional $1,000. An increase of less than 6 percent in the price of wheat produced a return of 100 percent. Such a return is the result of leverage that comes from the small margin requirement and the large amount of the commodity controlled by the contract.

Leverage, of course, works both ways. In the previous example, if the price of the commodity declines by $0.10, the contract will be worth $17,000. A decline of only 2.9 percent in the price reduces your margin from $1,000 to $500. To maintain the position, you must deposit additional funds with the broker. The broker's request for additional funds is referred to as a margin call. Failure to meet the margin call will result in the broker's closing the position. Should you default on the contract, the broker becomes responsible for the execution of the contract. The margin call thus protects the broker.

Actually, there are two margin requirements. The first is the minimum initial deposit, and the second is the maintenance margin. The maintenance margin specifies when you must deposit additional funds with the broker to cover a decline in the value of a commodity contract. For example, the margin requirement for wheat is $1,000 and the maintenance margin is $750. If you own a contract for the purchase of wheat and the value of the contract declines by $250 to the level of the maintenance margin ($750), the broker makes a margin call. This requires you to deposit an additional $250 into the account, which restores the initial $1,000 margin. This additional deposit protects the broker, since the value of the contract has declined and you have sustained a loss.

Like the initial margin requirement, the maintenance margin also applies to both buyers and sellers. If, in the previous example, the price of wheat were to rise by $250, the speculators who had entered the contract to deliver wheat would see their margin decline from the initial deposit of $1,000 to $750. The broker would then make a margin call, which would require the short sellers to restore the $1,000 margin. Once again this protects the broker, since the value of the contract has risen and the short seller has sustained the loss.

These margin adjustments occur *daily*. After the market closes, the value of each account is totaled. In the jargon of futures trading, each account is *marked to the market*. If the account does not meet the maintenance margin requirement, the broker issues a margin call that the individual must meet or the broker will close the position.

Margin call

Request by the broker for an investor to place additional funds to restore the good-faith deposit

Maintenance margin

Minimum level of funds in a margin account that triggers a margin call

Hedging

One of the prime reasons for the development of futures markets was the desire of producers to reduce the risk of loss from price fluctuations. The procedure for this reduction in risk is called hedging, which consists of taking opposite positions at the same time. In effect, a hedger simultaneously takes the long and the short positions in a particular commodity.

Hedging is best explained by illustrations. In the first example, a wheat farmer expects to harvest a crop at a specified time. Since the costs of

Hedging

Simultaneous purchase and sale designed to reduce risk of loss from price fluctuations production are determined, the farmer knows the price that is necessary to earn a profit. Although the price that will be paid for wheat at harvest time is unknown, the current price of a contract for the future delivery of wheat is known. The farmer can then enter a contract to sell (to make future delivery). Such a contract is a hedged position, because the farmer has a long position (the wheat in the ground) and a short position (the sale of the contract for future delivery).

Such a position reduces the farmer's risk of loss from a price decline. Suppose the cost to produce the wheat is $3.50 per bushel and September wheat is selling in June for $3.75. If the farmer sells wheat for September delivery, a $0.25 per bushel profit is assured, because the buyer of the contract agrees to pay $3.75 per bushel upon delivery in September. If the price of wheat declines to $3.50, the farmer is still assured $3.75. However, if the price of wheat rises to $4.10 in September, the farmer still receives only $3.75. The additional $0.35 gain goes to the owner of the contract for delivery who buys the wheat for $3.75 but can now sell it for $4.10.

Is this transaction unfair? Remember that the farmer wanted protection against a decline in the price of wheat. If the price had declined to $3.40 and the farmer had not hedged, the farmer would have suffered a loss of $0.10 (the $3.40 price minus the $3.50 cost) per bushel. To obtain protection from this risk of loss, the farmer accepted the profit of $0.25 per bushel and relinquished the possibility of a larger profit. The speculator who entered the contract to buy the wheat bore the risk of loss from a price decline and received the reward from a price increase.

Users of wheat hedge in the opposite direction. A user of wheat (Kellogg) desires to know the future cost of wheat in order to plan production levels and the prices that will be charged to distributors. However, the spot price of wheat need not hold into the future. This company then enters a contract to accept future delivery and thereby hedges the position. This is hedging because Kellogg has a long position (the contract to accept the future delivery of wheat) and a short position (the future production of cereal, which requires the future delivery of wheat).

If Kellogg enters a contract in June for the delivery of wheat in September at $3.75 per bushel, the future cost of the grain becomes known. The company cannot be hurt by a price increase in wheat from $3.75 to $4.10, because the contract is for delivery at $3.75. However, the company has forgone the chance of profit from a decline in the price of wheat from $3.75 to $3.40 per bushel.

Instead, the possibility of profit from a decline in the price of wheat rests with the speculator who entered the contract to deliver wheat. If the price of wheat were to decline, the speculator could buy the wheat in September at the lower price, deliver it, and collect the $3.75 that is specified in the contract. However, this speculator would suffer a loss if the price of September wheat rose over $3.75. Then the cost would exceed the delivery price specified in the contract.

These two examples illustrate why growers and users of a commodity hedge. They often take the opposite side of hedge positions. If all growers and users were to agree on prices for future delivery, there would be no need for speculators; but this is not the case. Speculators enter contracts when there is an excess or an insufficient supply. If the farmer in the preceding example could not find a user to enter into the contract to accept the future delivery of wheat, a speculator would make the contract and accept the risk of a price decline. If the user could not find a farmer to supply a contract for the future delivery of wheat, the speculator would make the contract to sell (to deliver) and accept the risk of a price increase.

Of course, farmers, users, and speculators are simultaneously entering contracts. No one knows who buys and who sells at a specific moment. However, if there is an excess or a shortage of one type of contract, the futures price of the commodity changes, which induces a certain behavior. For example, if September wheat is quoted at $3.75 per bushel, but no one is willing to buy at that price, the price declines. This induces some potential sellers to withdraw from the market and some potential buyers to enter the market. By this process, an imbalance of supply and demand for contracts for a particular delivery date is erased. It is this interaction of the hedgers and the speculators that establishes the futures price of each contract.

Financial and Currency Futures

Financial futures

Contract for the future delivery of a financial asset

Currency futures

Contract for the future delivery of a currency

In the previous discussion, futures contracts meant commodity contracts for the delivery of physical goods. However, there are also financial futures, which are contracts for the future delivery of a security, such as a Treasury bill, and currency futures, which are contracts for the future delivery of currencies (for example, the British pound or the European euro). The market for financial futures, like the market for commodity futures, has two participants: the speculators and the hedgers. It is the interaction of their demands for and supplies of these contracts that determines the price of a given financial futures contract.

While any speculator may participate in any of the financial or currency futures markets, the hedgers differ from the speculators because they also deal in the security or the currency. The hedgers in currency futures are primarily multinational firms that make and receive payments in foreign moneys. Since the value of these currencies can change, the value of payments that the firms must make or receive can change. Firms thus establish hedge positions in order to lock in the price of the currency and thereby avoid the risk associated with fluctuations in the value of one currency relative to another.

Financial futures are used in hedge positions by financial institutions and borrowers to lock in yields. As interest rates and bond prices change, the yields from lending and the cost of borrowing are altered. To reduce the risk of loss from fluctuations in interest rates, borrowers and lenders may establish hedge positions to lock in a particular interest rate.

Speculators, of course, are not seeking to reduce risk but to reap large returns for taking risks. The speculators bear the risk that the hedgers want to avoid. The speculators anticipate changes in the value of currencies and the direction of changes in interest rates and security prices and take positions that will yield profits. The return the speculators earn (if successful) is magnified because of the leverage offered by the small margin requirements necessary to establish the positions.

How financial futures may produce profits for speculators may be illustrated with an example that employs the futures contract for the delivery of U.S. Treasury bonds. Suppose a speculator expects interest rates to fall and bond prices to rise. This individual enters into a contract *to buy* and take delivery of Treasury bonds in the future (the *long* position). If interest rates do fall and bond prices rise, the value of this contract increases, because the speculator has the contract to buy bonds at a lower price (in other words, higher yield). If, however, interest rates rise, bond prices fall, and the value of this contract declines. The decline in the value of the contract inflicts a loss on the speculator who bought the contract when yields were lower.

If speculators expect interest rates to rise, they enter into a contract *to sell* and to make future delivery of Treasury bonds, thus establishing a *short* position. If interest rates do rise and the value of the bond declines, the value of this contract must decline. The speculators earn a profit because the short sellers can buy the bonds at a lower price and deliver them at the higher price specified in the contract. Of course, if the speculators are wrong and interest rates fall, the value of the bonds increases, which inflicts a loss on the speculators who must now pay more to buy the bonds to cover the contract.

While speculators use financial futures as a means to take advantage of fluctuations in interest rates and security prices, financial managers or investors may use futures to reduce the risk of loss from the same price fluctuations. For example, suppose a firm has decided to invest in plant and equipment. Building a new plant and installing new equipment takes time, during which the cost of capital may change as interest rates and security prices fluctuate. If the cost of capital falls, the investment may become even more profitable. However, if interest rates rise and security prices fall (that is, the cost of capital rises), an investment that was previously judged to be profitable may now be unprofitable.

It is the risk associated with fluctuations in interest rates and security prices that the financial manager seeks to reduce. The financial manager then uses financial futures as a means to reduce the risk of loss from an increase in the cost of capital. Of course, hedging reduces the possibility of gain should the cost of capital fall. However, the emphasis is on risk reduction and not on increased profitability through speculating on changes in the cost of funds.

The reduction in risk is achieved by the financial manager entering a contract to make future delivery (taking a short position). The impact of this hedge may be seen in the following illustration. In six months a firm plans to issue $1 million of 20-year bonds. If interest rates increase, the firm will have to pay an additional $10,000 annually for every 1 percent increase in the rate of interest. To hedge against the potential loss if interest rates rise, the financial manager takes a short position in a contract to deliver Treasury bonds. If interest rates do rise, the value of these contracts declines. The financial manager may then close out the position in these contracts at a profit, which will help offset the loss resulting from the increased cost of funds.

The previous illustration considered the borrower's reduction of loss through hedging. Lenders also bear risk associated with fluctuations in interest rates, but the risk is from lower, not higher, interest rates. For example, suppose a financial institution agrees to make a loan in six months at the then current rate of interest. That rate could be higher or lower than the current rate. If interest rates rise, the lender will earn a higher return on the loan; if interest rates fall, the yield will be lower. Lenders can protect themselves from a decline in interest rates by hedging through the use of financial futures.

Unlike borrowers, who enter futures contracts to sell (or deliver) to hedge their positions, lenders enter futures contracts to buy (or accept delivery). If interest rates do fall, the value of the contracts will increase. This increase in the value of the contract will partially offset the interest lost as a result of lower rates. Of course, the lender will have forgone the possibility of earning a higher yield if interest rates were to increase. Higher interest rates would reduce the value of the contract and thus offset the higher rate earned on the loan.

Risk Reduction with Currency Futures Contracts

As with interest rate financial futures, one means to reduce risk of loss from exchange rate fluctuation is to enter a contract, which establishes the future price of the currency. For example, a firm contracts to buy a plant in Germany for 40,000,000 euros in six months (line 1 in Exhibit 29.1). If the current price of the euro is $1.20, the cost of the plant is $48,000,000 ($1.20. × 40,000,000 in line 2). If the price of the euro were to fall to $1.15, the cost of the plant would decline to $46,000,000 and save the firm $2,000,000 (line 4). However, if the price of the euro were to rise to $1.25, the cost would increase to $50,000,000, for a net increase of $2,000,000 (line 6).

Since the payment will be made in the future, the cost of the euro necessary to make the future payment may rise or fall depending on fluctuations in the demand for and supply of euros. To avoid the possibility of loss through an increase in the price, the financial manager enters into a contract for the purchase of euros (in other words, to sell dollars) after six months for a specified price. If the current six-month price of the euro is $1.205, the financial manager can enter a contract to purchase euros for delivery in six months for $1.205. The total cost of the euros necessary to pay for the plant will then be $48,200,000 (line 7). If the firm does enter the contract, it has a hedged position. In effect, the firm has agreed to purchase 40,000,000 euros for $48,200,000; the firm then can use these euros to pay for the plant. The net effect is to increase the cost of the plant by $200,000 (line 8).

By constructing a hedge, the financial manager protects the firm against an increase in the price of the euro, because the firm now has a contract to buy euros for $1.205. If the value of the euro did increase to $1.25, the contract for future delivery at $1.205 would appreciate in value, offsetting the increased cost of the currency. The price of the euro, and thus the price of the plant, cannot exceed $48,200,000. By hedging, the financial manager has locked in the price of the currency. However, while the firm is protected if the price of the euro were

E X H I B I T   29.1

Gains or Losses from
Changes in the Value of
the Euro Relative to the
U.S. Dollar

Current Cost of the Plant

1. Cost of the plant in euros	40,000,000
2. Cost of the plant in dollars (based on a $1.20 price of euros)	$48,000,000

Possible Gain from Decrease in the Cost of the Euro

3. Cost of the plant in dollars (if the price of the euro declines to $1.15)	$46,000,000
4. Decrease in cost from the depreciation in the euro (line 2 minus line 3)	$2,000,000

Possible Loss from Increase in the Cost of the Euro

5. Cost of the plant in dollars (if the price of the euro rises to $1.25	$50,000,000
6. Increase in cost from the appreciation in the euro (line 5 minus line 2)	$2,000,000

Impact of Hedging

7. Cost of the plant in dollars (based on the future contract price of euros)	$48,200,000
8. Cost of hedging (line 7 minus line 2)	$200,000

to increase, the firm would not gain from a decline in the value of the euro. If the price declined to $1.15, the value of the contract to buy in the future would also decline, thus offsetting the firm's gain from the euro's price decline.

A firm expecting to receive payment in the future would use the opposite procedure. For example, if a firm anticipates a payment in British pounds after three months, it would enter a contract to sell pounds. If the current price of the pound is $1.95 and the future price is $1.94, the firm is assured of receiving $1.94 for a pound. Thus, for the cost of 1 cent per pound, the firm is protected from an exchange rate fluctuation. If the pound were to decline to $1.75, the firm would still receive $1.94. Conversely, the possibility of gain is lost. If the pound were to rise to $2.18, the firm would receive only $1.94. Of course, the purpose of entering into the contract is to reduce the risk of loss from changes in exchange rates. To achieve this reduction in risk, the firm must give up the potential for profit from a price increase.

Entering contracts for the future purchase or sale (that is, hedging) reduces the risk of loss from unexpected fluctuations in currency values. If a price change in a currency is widely anticipated, the future price will indicate that expectation. In the preceding example, the current price of the British pound was $1.95, and the future price was $1.94. If there were widespread belief that the pound would decline in value, the future price would be lower. No one would want to enter into a contract to buy the pounds for $1.94 if they expected the value of the pounds to be $1.80 after three months. If a substantial price decline were anticipated, there might be no buyers for future delivery of pounds, or the future price might be so low that sellers would prefer to hold the currency and bear the risk.

Stock Index Futures

The previous section covered financial futures whose value fluctuates with changes in interest rates and exchange rates. This section considers stock index futures whose value is derived from and fluctuates with changes in the stock market. Stock index futures are contracts based on an aggregate measure of the stock market, such as the S&P 500, the New York Stock Exchange stock index, or the Value Line stock index. These stock index futures contracts offer speculators and hedgers opportunities for profit or risk reduction that are not possible through the purchase of individual securities. For example, the NYSE Composite Index futures contracts have a value that is $500 times the value of the NYSE Index. Thus, if the NYSE Index is 1000, the contract is worth $50,000. By entering a contract to buy (establishing a long position), you profit if the market rises. If the NYSE Index rose to 1050, the value of the contract would increase to $52,500. You would then earn a profit of $2,500. Of course, if the NYSE Index declined, you would experience a loss.

The sellers of those contracts also participate in the fluctuations of the market, but their positions are the opposite of the buyers (that is, they have established a short position). If the value of the NYSE Index fell from 1000 to 950, the value of the contract would decline from $50,000 to $47,500, and the short seller would earn a $2,500 profit. Of course, if the market rose, the short seller would suffer a loss. Obviously, if you anticipate a rising market, you should take a long position in a stock index futures contract. Conversely, if you expect the market to fall, you should take a short position.

These contracts may also be used by professional money managers who are not speculating on price movements but who seek to hedge against adverse price movements. For example, suppose a portfolio manager has a well-diversified portfolio of stocks as part of a firm's pension plan. If the market rises, the value of this portfolio appreciates. However, there would be the risk of loss if the market were to decline. The portfolio manager can reduce this risk by entering an NYSE Index futures contract to sell at the specified price (a short position). If the market declines, the losses experienced by the portfolio will at least be partially offset by the appreciation in the value of the short position in the futures contract.

NYSE Index futures contracts are similar to other futures contracts. The buyers and sellers must make good-faith deposits (margin payments). Since the amount of this margin is modest, these contracts offer considerable leverage. If stock prices move against you and your equity in the position declines, you will have to place additional funds in the account to support the contract. Since there is an active market in the contracts, you may close a position at any time by taking the opposite position. Thus if you have a contract to buy, that long position is closed by a contract to sell. If you have a contract to sell (to deliver), that short position is closed by a contract to buy (to accept delivery).

There is one important difference between stock market futures and other futures contracts. Settlement at the expiration or maturity of the contract occurs in cash. There is no physical delivery of securities as could occur with a commodity futures contract to buy or sell wheat or corn. Instead, gains and losses are totaled and are added to or subtracted from the participants' accounts. The long and the short positions are then closed.

Swap

An agreement to exchange payments

In addition to options and futures, another derivative is the "swap." A swap is an agreement between two entities, such as two firms, that agree through a formal contract to exchange (i.e., swap) payments. (The two participants are often referred to as the party and counterparty.) While individuals rarely, if ever, swap payments, firms and financial institutions often participate in the swap market. Firms earn profits from operations and not from speculating on price changes. To reduce the risk of loss from change in prices, management may enter into a swap agreement.

Consider a firm with foreign operations. It may enter into a swap to reduce the risk of loss from changes in exchange rates. A U.S. firm with operations in Britain has to make payments in pounds. The dollar cost of the payments will rise if the value of the pound rises (the dollar declines). Of course, if the cost of the pound were to fall (the dollar rises), the firm would profit. The cost in dollars would be reduced. The emphasis, however, is not on increased profits from a lower British pound but on avoiding the risk of loss if the pound were to increase in value.

Conversely, a British firm has operations in the United States and has to make payments in dollars. If the dollar rises (the pound falls), its costs increase. Of course, if the dollar were to fall (the pound increases), the British firm would profit, but once again the emphasis is on reducing the risk of loss.

One means to reduce this risk of loss is to hedge by using futures contracts (as was covered earlier in this chapter). Another means to reduce the risk of loss is to swap payments. The British firm agrees to make the American firm's payments in pounds, and the American firm agrees to make the British firm's dollar payments. Since both companies are now making the payments in their native currency, neither has the risk associated with changes in the exchange rate. If the dollar rises (pound falls) or if the dollar falls (pound rises), the effect on either firm is immaterial. Of course, for this swap to occur, both parties must perceive a benefit and the amounts of the payments must be comparable.

Swap agreements are not limited to payments involving exchange rates. One firm may have to make variable interest rate payments and want to convert the variable payments to fixed payments. Another party may wish to convert fixed payments into variable payments. Once again, the two parties may enter into a swap agreement in which they agree to swap each other's payments. All that is necessary for the swap to occur is for there to be a benefit to both parties. One party swaps the variable payment to the counterparty in return for the fixed payment.

Perhaps the most famous (or infamous) swap agreement is the "credit default swap." Suppose a portfolio manager of a mutual fund or pension plan owns a variety of bonds. The purpose of the portfolio is to generate interest income, but the issuers of the bonds may default. How can this portfolio manager avoid that risk? The answer is to find a counterparty such as an insurance company or other financial institution that is willing to bear the risk for a price. That is, the portfolio manager agrees to pay the counterparty a specified percentage and the counterparty agrees to compensate the initial party if default were to occur.

For example, suppose fund A owns $10,000,000 of 10 percent bonds and expects to receive $1,000,000 in interest. Fund A enters into a swap with insurance corp A and agrees to pay the insurance company 1 percent ($100,000). That reduces fund A's income to $900,000 but the risk of default has been passed to the insurance company. Notice that fund A has reduced its interest income but swapped away its risk.

Two important observations need to be made. The price paid for the swap should mirror the risk taken by the counterparty. As that risk increases, the price will also increase so the initial party's net income is decreased even more by the swap agreement. For this pricing mechanism to work, you have to assume that the insurance company accurately measures the risk it is assuming. If it underestimates the risk, the price will be too low.

Second, there is also an important assumption that the insurance company will not default. Suppose the issuer of the bonds does default; now the insurance company must make the payment as required by the swap agreement. If the insurance company lacks the funds to make the required payment, it too may default. This is precisely what occurred during the 2008–2009 financial crisis when it appeared that the counterparties would not be able to make their required payments.

While swaps are often used as part of a hedging strategy (all the prior examples are illustrations of hedges), swaps may also be used as speculative tools. If speculators anticipate defaults, they may enter credit default swap agreements even though they do not own the underlying asset on which the swap is based. (Remember: you do not have to own the underlying stock to buy or sell put and call options. That applies to futures as well. You do not have to own the commodity on which the futures contract is based.) Instead the position is a speculation on the default. If the speculator is correct and the issuer defaults, the buyer of the swap receives payment from the seller. If the speculator anticipates that the issuer will *not default*, he or she could sell the swap and receive the payments from the buyer.

Once created, a secondary market can develop in swap agreements. If an investor buys a swap, that party can sell it to another party who assumes the payments and receives the compensation in case of default. The counterparty (seller) may also sell the swap, in which case the new counterparty receives the payment but is responsible for compensating the buyer in case default were to occur. The prices of swaps in these secondary transactions should mirror the perceived risks at the time of the transaction, and that price may not be the price that existed when the credit default swap was initially created.

Summary

Futures are contracts for future delivery of a commodity such as wheat or corn. An individual ("speculator") takes a long position by entering into a contract to buy and accept delivery. The opposite, or short, position occurs when the individual enters into a contract to sell and make future delivery. The long position profits if the price of the commodity rises, since the speculator has a contract to buy at a lower price. The short position profits if the price of the commodity falls, since the speculator has a contract to sell at a higher price.

While speculators seek to profit from changes in prices, growers, fabricators, manufacturers, and other users of commodities want to reduce the risk of loss from price fluctuations. They "hedge" their positions. Growers or miners with long positions in crops and metals sell futures contracts. The sales are short positions that lock in futures prices and reduce the risk of loss from a price decline. Producers who use the crops and the metals do the opposite. They buy futures contracts to lock in prices and reduce the risk of loss from a price increase. This process of buying and selling futures contracts passes the risk associated with price fluctuations from the hedgers to the speculators.

Besides commodity futures there are also financial futures, currency futures, and stock market futures. Financial futures are contracts for the delivery of financial assets such as U.S. Treasury bills and bonds. Currency futures are contracts for the future delivery of foreign moneys such as European euros or British pounds. Stock market futures are based on a broad measure of the market (for example, the New York Stock Exchange Composite Index). Speculators who anticipate movements in interest rates, foreign currencies, or the stock market can speculate on these anticipated price changes by taking appropriate positions in futures contracts. Financial managers may use these contracts as a means to reduce the risk associated with fluctuations in interest rates, security prices, or currency values.

A swap is an agreement in which two parties agree to exchange payments. Possible illustrations include swapping payments in different currencies (foreign exchange swaps) or exchanging fixed for variable payments. These swap agreements are used to reduce the risk of loss from fluctuations in foreign exchange rates or interest rates. Credit default swaps transfer the risk of loss from defaults on debt instruments. One participant pays the counterparty to accept the risk of default. These swaps played an important role in the financial crises of 2008–2009 when the possibility arose that the firms accepting the risk would default on their obligations required by the swap agreement.

Review Objectives

Now that you have completed this chapter, you should be able to

1. List the features of futures contracts (p. 625).

2. Contrast long and short positions in futures contracts (pp. 626–627).

3. Illustrate how speculators earn profits and sustain losses in the futures markets (pp. 626–627).

4. Demonstrate the role of margin requirements in the futures markets, and explain the phrase "marked to the market" (pp. 629–630).

5. Show how the use of margin leverages the potential return in a futures contract (pp. 629–630).

6. Illustrate how hedgers use futures contracts to reduce the risk of loss from fluctuations in prices (pp. 630–632).

7. Explain the roles of financial, currency, and stock index futures (pp. 632–637).

8. Differentiate the roles played by the two parties to a swap agreement (pp. 637–638).

Problems

1. The futures price of gold is $1,000. Futures contracts are for 100 ounces of gold, and the margin requirement is $5,000 a contract. The maintenance market requirement is $1,500. You expect the price of gold to rise and enter into a contract to buy gold.

   a. How much must you initially remit?

   b. If the futures price of gold rises to $1,055, what is the profit and return on your position?

   c. If the futures price of gold declines to $978, what is the loss on the position?

   d. If the futures price declines to $948, what must you do?

   e. If the futures price continues to decline to $932, how much do you have in your account?

2. The futures price of corn is $3.40 a bushel. Futures contracts for corn are based on 10,000 bushels, and the margin requirement is $2,000 a contract. You expect the price of corn to fall and sell the contract short.

   a. What is the value of the contract and how much must you initially remit?

   b. If the futures price of corn rises to $3.51, what is the profit or loss on your position?

   c. If the futures price of gold declines to $3.28, what is the profit or loss on your position?

   d. If the futures price declines to $3.18, what may you do?

   e. How do you close your position?

3. You expect the stock market to increase, but instead of acquiring stock, you decide to acquire a stock index futures contract. That index is currently 1120, and the contract has a value that is $50 times the amount of the index. The margin requirement is $2,500.

   a. When you make the contract, how much must you put up?

   b. What is the value of the contract based on the index?

   c. If the value of the index rises 1 percent to 1131, what is the profit on the investment? What is the percentage earned on the funds you put up?

d. If the value of the index declines 1 percent to 1108, what percentage of your funds will you lose?

e. What is the percentage you earn (or lose) if the index falls to 1108?

4. You expect to receive a payment of 1 million British pounds after six months. The pound is currently worth $1.60 (£1 = $1.60), but the future price is $1.56 (£1 = $1.56). You expect the price of the pound to decline (that is, the value of the dollar to rise). If this expectation is fulfilled, you will suffer a loss when the pounds are converted into dollars when you receive them six months in the future.

a. Given the current exchange rate, what is the expected payment in dollars?

b. Given the future exchange rate, how much would you receive in dollars?

c. If, after six months, the pound is worth $1.40, what is your loss from the decline in the value of the pound?

d. To avoid this potential loss, you enter a contract for the future delivery of pounds at the futures price of $1.56. What is the cost to you of this protection from the possible decline in the value of the pound?

e. If, after entering the contract, the price of the pound falls to $1.40, what is the maximum amount that you lose? (Why is your answer different from your answer to part *c*?)

f. If, after entering the contract, the price of the pound rises to $1.80, how much do you gain from your position?

g. How would your answer to part *f* be different if you had not made the contract and the price of the pound had risen to $1.80?

Additional Problems with Answers

1. The futures price of a commodity such as corn is $1.00. The contracts are for 10,000 bushels, so a contract is worth $10,000. The margin requirement is $1,000 a contract, and the maintenance margin requirement is $600. You expect the price to fall and enter into a contract to sell.

a. How much must you initially remit?

b. If the futures price falls to $0.94, what is the value of the contract?

c. If the futures price rises to $1.04, what is the value of the contract?

d. If the futures price continues to rise to $1.09, what will you have to do?

2. The futures price of gold is $1,200. Futures contracts are for 100 ounces of gold, and the margin requirement is $10,000 a contract.

The maintenance margin requirement is $4,000. You expect the price of gold to rise and enter into a contract to buy gold.

a. How much must you initially remit?

b. If the futures price of gold rises 1 percent to $1,212, what is the profit and percentage return on your position?

c. If the futures price of gold declines 1 percent to $1,188, what is the loss and percentage return on the position?

d. If the futures price falls to $1,175, what must you do?

e. If the futures price continues to decline to $1,134, how much do you have in your account?

f. How do you close your position?

Answers

1. a. The margin requirement: $1,000

   b. $9,400 (10,000 × $0.94)

   c. $10,400 (10,000 × $1.04)

   d. The contract is worth $10,900; you have lost $900. You have $100 left in margin and will have to put up $900 to restore the $1,000 margin requirement.

2. a. $10,000

   b. The contract is now worth $121,200. You gained $1,200 on an investment of $10,000 for a percentage gain of 12 percent ($1,200/ $10,000).

   c. The contract is now worth $118,800. You lost $1,200 on an investment of $10,000 for a percentage loss of 12 percent ($1,200/$10,000). Notice that leverage works both ways.

   d. You have lost $2,500 and your margin has been reduced from $10,000 to $7,500. You remain above the $4,000 maintenance requirement so you are not required to do anything.

   e. You have now lost $6,600 and your margin has been reduced from $10,000 to $3,400. You are below the $4,000 maintenance requirement so you are required to put up $6,600 to meet the $10,000 margin requirement.

   f. You close your position by entering an offsetting contract. Since you have a contract to sell gold, you will have to enter into a contract to buy gold. Once you have done that, you will have closed your position.

Relationships

1. An increase in the price of a commodity futures contract _____ the loss on a short position in the futures.

2. The small margin requirement _____ the potential return and _____ the potential risk from investing in futures contracts.

3. The number of futures contracts _____ as the contracts approach expiration.

4. Investors hedge using futures to _____ the risk of loss.

5. Lower stock prices _____ the return on a long position in a stock index futures.

6. Lower stock prices _____ the return on a short position in a stock index futures.

7. Higher margin requirements _____ the potential leverage offered by futures contracts.

Answers

1. increases

2. increases; increases

3. decreases

4. decrease

5. decrease

6. increase

7. decrease

Interest Factors for the Future Value of One Dollar
$$FVIF = (1 + i)^n$$

Time Period (e.g., year)	1%	2%	3%	4%	5%	6%	7%	8%	9%	10%	12%	14%	15%	16%	18%	20%
1	1.010	1.020	1.030	1.040	1.050	1.060	1.070	1.080	1.090	1.100	1.120	1.140	1.150	1.160	1.180	1.200
2	1.020	1.040	1.061	1.082	1.102	1.124	1.145	1.166	1.188	1.210	1.254	1.300	1.322	1.346	1.392	1.440
3	1.030	1.061	1.093	1.125	1.158	1.191	1.225	1.260	1.295	1.331	1.405	1.482	1.521	1.561	1.643	1.728
4	1.041	1.082	1.126	1.170	1.216	1.262	1.311	1.360	1.412	1.464	1.574	1.689	1.749	1.811	1.939	2.074
5	1.051	1.104	1.159	1.217	1.276	1.338	1.403	1.469	1.539	1.611	1.762	1.925	2.011	2.100	2.288	2.488
6	1.062	1.126	1.194	1.265	1.340	1.419	1.501	1.587	1.677	1.772	1.974	2.195	2.313	2.436	2.697	2.986
7	1.072	1.149	1.230	1.316	1.407	1.504	1.606	1.714	1.828	1.949	2.211	2.502	2.660	2.826	3.186	3.583
8	1.083	1.172	1.267	1.369	1.477	1.594	1.718	1.851	1.993	2.144	2.476	2.853	3.059	3.278	3.759	4.300
9	1.094	1.195	1.305	1.423	1.551	1.689	1.838	1.999	2.172	2.358	2.773	3.252	3.518	3.803	4.436	5.160
10	1.105	1.219	1.344	1.480	1.629	1.791	1.967	2.159	2.367	2.594	3.106	3.707	4.046	4.411	5.234	6.192
11	1.116	1.243	1.384	1.539	1.710	1.898	2.105	2.332	2.580	2.853	3.479	4.226	4.652	5.117	6.176	7.430
12	1.127	1.268	1.426	1.601	1.796	2.012	2.252	2.518	2.813	3.138	3.896	4.818	5.350	5.936	7.287	8.916
13	1.138	1.294	1.469	1.665	1.886	2.133	2.410	2.720	3.066	3.452	4.363	5.492	6.153	6.886	8.599	10.699
14	1.149	1.319	1.513	1.732	1.980	2.261	2.579	2.937	3.342	3.797	4.887	6.261	7.076	7.988	10.147	12.839
15	1.161	1.346	1.558	1.801	2.079	2.397	2.759	3.172	3.642	4.177	5.474	7.138	8.137	9.266	11.973	15.407
16	1.173	1.373	1.605	1.873	2.183	2.540	2.952	3.426	3.970	4.595	6.130	8.137	9.358	10.748	14.129	18.488
17	1.184	1.400	1.653	1.948	2.292	2.693	3.159	3.700	4.328	5.054	6.866	9.276	10.761	12.468	16.672	22.186
18	1.196	1.428	1.702	2.026	2.407	2.854	3.380	3.996	4.717	5.560	7.690	10.575	12.375	14.463	19.673	26.623
19	1.208	1.457	1.754	2.107	2.527	3.026	3.617	4.316	5.142	6.116	8.613	12.056	14.232	16.777	23.214	31.948
20	1.220	1.486	1.806	2.191	2.653	3.207	3.870	4.661	5.604	6.728	9.646	13.743	16.367	19.461	27.393	38.337
25	1.282	1.641	2.094	2.666	3.386	4.292	5.427	6.848	8.623	10.835	17.000	26.462	32.919	40.874	62.688	95.396
30	1.348	1.811	2.427	3.243	4.322	5.743	7.612	10.063	13.268	17.449	29.960	50.950	66.212	85.850	143.370	237.370

Interest Factors for the Present Value of One Dollar
$PVIF = 1/(1 + i)^n$

Time Period (e.g., year)	1%	2%	3%	4%	5%	6%	7%	8%	9%	10%	12%	14%	15%	16%	18%	20%	24%	28%
1	.990	.980	.971	.962	.952	.943	.935	.926	.917	.909	.893	.877	.870	.862	.847	.833	.806	.781
2	.980	.961	.943	.925	.907	.890	.873	.857	.842	.826	.797	.769	.756	.743	.718	.694	.650	.610
3	.971	.942	.915	.889	.864	.840	.816	.794	.772	.751	.712	.675	.658	.641	.609	.579	.524	.477
4	.961	.924	.889	.855	.823	.792	.763	.735	.708	.683	.636	.592	.572	.552	.516	.482	.423	.373
5	.951	.906	.863	.822	.784	.747	.713	.681	.650	.621	.567	.519	.497	.476	.437	.402	.341	.291
6	.942	.888	.838	.790	.746	.705	.666	.630	.596	.564	.507	.456	.432	.410	.370	.335	.275	.227
7	.933	.871	.813	.760	.711	.665	.623	.583	.547	.513	.452	.400	.376	.354	.314	.279	.222	.178
8	.923	.853	.789	.731	.677	.627	.582	.540	.502	.467	.404	.351	.327	.305	.266	.233	.179	.139
9	.914	.837	.766	.703	.645	.592	.544	.500	.460	.424	.361	.308	.284	.263	.226	.194	.144	.108
10	.905	.820	.744	.676	.614	.558	.508	.463	.422	.386	.322	.270	.247	.227	.191	.162	.116	.085
11	.896	.804	.722	.650	.585	.527	.475	.429	.388	.350	.287	.237	.215	.195	.162	.135	.094	.066
12	.887	.788	.701	.625	.557	.497	.444	.397	.356	.319	.257	.208	.187	.168	.137	.112	.076	.052
13	.879	.773	.681	.601	.530	.469	.415	.368	.326	.290	.229	.182	.163	.145	.116	.093	.061	.040
14	.870	.758	.661	.577	.505	.442	.388	.340	.299	.263	.205	.160	.141	.125	.099	.078	.049	.032
15	.861	.743	.642	.555	.481	.417	.362	.315	.275	.239	.183	.140	.123	.108	.084	.065	.040	.025
16	.853	.728	.623	.534	.458	.394	.339	.292	.252	.218	.163	.123	.107	.093	.071	.054	.032	.019
17	.844	.714	.605	.513	.436	.371	.317	.270	.231	.198	.146	.108	.093	.080	.060	.045	.026	.015
18	.836	.700	.587	.494	.416	.350	.296	.250	.212	.180	.130	.095	.081	.069	.051	.038	.021	.012
19	.828	.686	.570	.475	.396	.331	.276	.232	.194	.164	.116	.083	.070	.060	.043	.031	.017	.009
20	.820	.673	.554	.456	.377	.312	.258	.215	.178	.149	.104	.073	.061	.051	.037	.026	.014	.007
25	.780	.610	.478	.375	.295	.233	.184	.146	.116	.092	.059	.038	.030	.024	.016	.010	.005	.002
30	.742	.552	.412	.308	.231	.174	.131	.099	.075	.057	.033	.020	.015	.012	.007	.004	.002	.001

Interest Factors for the Future Value of an Annuity of One Dollar

$$FVAIF = \frac{(1 + i)^{n-1}}{i}$$

Time Period (e.g., year)	1%	2%	3%	4%	5%	6%	7%	8%	9%	10%	12%	14%	16%	20%
1	1.000	1.000	1.000	1.000	1.000	1.000	1.000	1.000	1.000	1.000	1.000	1.000	1.000	1.000
2	2.010	2.020	2.030	2.040	2.050	2.060	2.070	2.080	2.090	2.100	2.120	2.140	2.160	2.200
3	3.030	3.060	3.091	3.122	3.152	3.184	3.215	3.246	3.278	3.310	3.374	3.440	3.506	3.640
4	4.060	4.122	4.184	4.246	4.310	4.375	4.440	4.506	4.573	4.641	4.770	4.921	5.067	5.368
5	5.101	5.204	5.309	5.416	5.526	5.637	5.751	5.867	5.985	6.105	6.353	6.610	6.877	7.442
6	6.152	6.308	6.468	6.633	6.802	6.975	7.153	7.336	7.523	7.716	8.115	8.536	8.978	9.930
7	7.214	7.434	7.662	7.898	8.142	8.394	8.654	8.923	9.200	9.487	10.089	10.730	11.413	12.915
8	8.286	8.583	8.892	9.214	9.549	9.897	10.260	10.637	11.028	11.436	12.300	13.233	14.240	16.499
9	9.369	9.755	10.159	10.583	11.027	11.491	11.978	12.488	13.021	13.579	14.776	16.085	17.518	20.798
10	10.462	10.950	11.464	12.006	12.578	13.181	13.816	14.487	15.193	15.937	17.549	19.337	21.321	25.958
11	11.567	12.169	12.808	13.486	14.207	14.972	15.784	16.645	17.560	18.531	20.655	23.044	25.732	32.150
12	12.683	13.412	14.192	15.026	15.917	16.870	17.888	18.977	20.141	21.384	24.138	27.271	30.850	39.580
13	13.809	14.680	15.618	16.627	17.713	18.882	20.141	21.495	22.953	24.523	28.029	32.089	36.786	48.496
14	14.947	15.974	17.086	18.292	19.599	21.051	22.550	24.215	26.019	27.975	32.393	37.581	43.672	59.195
15	16.097	17.293	18.599	20.024	21.579	23.276	25.129	27.152	29.361	31.772	37.280	43.842	51.659	72.035
16	17.258	18.639	20.157	21.825	23.657	25.673	27.888	30.324	33.003	35.950	42.753	50.980	60.925	87.442
17	18.430	20.012	21.762	23.698	25.840	28.213	30.840	33.750	36.974	40.545	48.884	59.118	71.673	105.93
18	19.615	21.412	23.414	25.645	28.132	30.906	33.999	37.450	41.301	45.599	55.750	68.934	84.140	128.11
19	20.811	22.841	25.117	27.671	30.539	33.760	37.379	41.446	46.018	51.159	63.440	78.969	98.603	154.74
20	22.019	24.297	26.870	29.778	33.066	36.786	40.995	45.762	51.160	57.275	72.052	91.025	115.37	186.68
25	28.243	32.030	36.459	41.646	47.727	54.865	63.249	73.106	84.701	98.347	133.33	181.87	249.21	471.98
30	34.785	40.568	47.575	56.085	66.439	79.058	94.461	113.283	136.308	164.494	241.333	356.878	530.310	1181.8

Interest Factors for the Present Value of an Annuity of One Dollar

$$PVAIF = \frac{1 - \dfrac{1}{(1 + i)^n}}{i}$$

$$= \frac{1 - (1 + i)^{-n}}{i}$$

Time Period (e.g., year)	1%	2%	3%	4%	5%	6%	7%	8%	9%	10%	12%	14%	16%	18%	20%	24%	28%	32%	36%
1	0.990	0.980	0.971	0.962	0.952	0.943	0.935	0.926	0.917	0.909	0.893	0.877	0.862	0.847	0.833	0.806	0.781	0.758	0.735
2	1.970	1.942	1.913	1.886	1.859	1.833	1.808	1.783	1.759	1.736	1.690	1.647	1.605	1.566	1.528	1.457	1.392	1.332	1.276
3	2.941	2.884	2.829	2.775	2.723	2.673	2.624	2.577	2.531	2.487	2.402	2.322	2.246	2.174	2.106	1.981	1.868	1.766	1.674
4	3.902	3.808	3.717	3.630	3.546	3.465	3.387	3.312	3.240	3.170	3.037	2.914	2.798	2.690	2.589	2.404	2.241	2.096	1.966
5	4.853	4.713	4.580	4.452	4.329	4.212	4.100	3.993	3.890	3.791	3.605	3.433	3.274	3.127	2.991	2.745	2.532	2.345	2.181
6	5.795	5.601	5.417	5.242	5.076	4.917	4.766	4.623	4.486	4.355	4.111	3.889	3.685	3.498	3.326	3.020	2.759	2.534	2.399
7	6.728	6.472	6.230	6.002	5.786	5.582	5.389	5.206	5.033	4.868	4.574	4.288	4.039	3.812	3.605	3.242	2.937	2.678	2.455
8	7.652	7.325	7.020	6.733	6.463	6.210	5.971	5.747	5.535	5.335	4.968	4.639	4.344	4.078	3.837	3.421	3.076	2.786	2.540
9	8.566	8.162	7.786	7.435	7.108	6.802	6.515	6.247	5.985	5.759	5.328	4.946	4.607	4.303	4.031	3.566	3.184	2.868	2.603
10	9.471	8.983	8.530	8.111	7.722	7.360	7.024	6.710	6.418	6.145	5.650	5.216	4.833	4.494	4.193	3.682	3.269	2.930	2.650
11	10.368	9.787	9.253	8.760	8.306	7.887	7.499	7.139	6.805	6.495	5.988	5.453	5.029	4.656	4.327	3.776	3.335	2.978	2.683
12	11.255	10.575	9.954	9.385	8.863	8.384	7.943	7.536	7.161	6.814	6.194	5.660	5.197	4.793	4.439	3.851	3.387	3.013	2.708
13	12.134	11.348	10.635	9.986	9.394	8.853	8.358	7.904	7.487	7.103	6.424	5.842	5.342	4.910	4.533	3.912	3.427	3.040	2.727
14	13.004	12.106	11.296	10.563	9.899	9.295	8.745	8.244	7.786	7.367	6.628	6.002	5.468	5.008	4.611	3.962	3.459	3.061	2.740
15	13.865	12.849	11.938	11.118	10.380	9.712	9.108	8.559	8.060	7.606	6.811	6.142	5.575	5.092	4.675	4.001	3.483	3.076	2.750
16	14.718	13.578	12.561	11.652	10.838	10.106	9.447	8.851	8.312	7.824	6.974	6.265	5.669	5.162	4.730	4.003	3.503	3.088	2.758
17	15.562	14.292	13.166	12.166	11.274	10.477	9.763	9.122	8.544	8.002	7.120	6.373	5.749	5.222	4.775	4.059	3.518	3.097	2.763
18	16.398	14.992	13.754	12.659	11.690	10.828	10.059	9.372	8.756	8.201	7.250	6.467	5.818	5.273	4.812	4.080	3.529	3.104	2.767
19	17.226	15.678	14.324	13.134	12.085	11.158	10.336	9.604	8.950	8.365	7.366	6.550	5.877	5.316	4.844	4.097	3.539	3.109	2.770
20	18.046	16.351	14.877	13.590	12.462	11.470	10.594	9.818	9.128	8.514	7.469	6.623	5.929	5.353	4.870	4.110	3.546	3.113	2.772
25	22.023	19.523	17.413	15.622	14.094	12.783	11.654	10.675	9.823	9.077	7.843	6.873	6.097	5.467	4.948	4.147	3.564	3.122	2.776
30	25.808	22.937	19.600	17.292	15.373	13.765	12.409	11.258	10.274	9.427	8.055	7.003	6.177	5.517	4.979	4.160	3.569	3.124	2.778

Using Excel to Solve Financial Problems

E xcel may be used to solve many of the numerical problems in this text. In some cases such as the time value of money, you simply enter the known data and Excel determines the unknown. In other cases such as the cash budget, you set up a spreadsheet to perform the calculations. In either case, you have to determine what data to enter and be able to identify what is known and needs to be determined. And, of course, you have to be able to interpret the results, since solving the numerical problem is not an end in itself. Instead, the solutions provide information to facilitate your making financial decisions.

SOLVING TIME VALUE PROBLEMS USING EXCEL

Future and Present Value of a Dollar

The format in Excel for solving time problems is similar to that employed by a financial calculator. Amounts are entered as cash inflows or cash outflows, with outflows being negative numbers. Excel, however, does follow a specific order. For the determination of the future value of a dollar, the order of the known values is

I interest per period
N number of periods
PMT (payment)
PV (present value)
Type

For the determination of the present value of a dollar, the order of the known values is

I interest per period
N number of periods
PMT (payment)
FV (future value)
Type

The only difference between the two layouts is the substitution of FV for PV, since the future value is known and present value is being determined. "Type" applies only to annuities and does not apply to the future or present value of a dollar. When "type" does not apply, enter a zero.

After entering the data, you enter a formula that solves for the unknown (that is, solves for the future value or the present value). For example, in Chapter 7 on pages 107–108 the illustration asked you to determine the future value of $100 at 5 percent for 20 years. In Excel the entries would be

I	5%
N	20
PMT	0
PV	−100
Type	0

Since FV is the unknown, there is no entry for the future value. The entries are submitted in a grid in the following general form:

	A	B
1	Future Value	
2	I	5%
3	N	20
4	PMT	0
5	PV	−100
6	Type	0
7	FV	= FV (b2, b3, b4, b5, b6)

For convenience (and ease of remembering), the labels have been placed in the first column with the data in the second column and a title (Future Value) is given in column A, row 1. Since the FV is the unknown, you must tell Excel to compute it. This is done by the following formula in cell B7: =FV (b2, b3, b4, b5, b6), and Excel determines the FV to be $265.33.

The impact of changing any of the inputs can be immediately determined using Excel. If the interest rate were 6 percent, replace 5% with 6% in cell B2 and the new future value ($320.71) is immediately determined. If the number of years were 10, replace the 20 in cell B3 and the new future value (at 5 percent) is $162.89. If the initial amount invested were $234.45, enter that amount with a minus sign in cell B5 and the future value becomes $622.07 at 5 percent for 20 years. You may change any combination you like and determine the impact on the future value.

The determination of the present value is essentially the same. The illustration on pages 110–111 asks you to determine the present value of $100 to be received after five years if the rate of interest is 6 percent. Using the above format, the entries would be

I	6%
N	5
PMT	0
FV	100
Type	0

Since PV is the unknown, there is no entry for the present value. The entries are submitted in a grid in the following general form:

	A	B
1	Present Value	
2	I	6%
3	N	5
4	PMT	0
5	FV	100
6	Type	0
7	PV	= PV (b2, b3, b4, b5, b6)

Once again for convenience (and ease of remembering), labels have been placed in the first column with the data in the second column and a title (Present Value) is given in column A, row 1. Since the PV is the unknown, you must tell Excel to compute it by entering the following formula in cell B7: =PV(b2,b3,b4,b5,b6). Excel determines the PV to be −$74.73.

The $74.73 has a negative sign or is in ( ). Since you are receiving $100 at the end of the five years, that is a cash inflow. The $74.73 is the amount you would have to invest today to receive the $100 after five years. Hence, the $74.73 is viewed as a cash outflow. You could have entered the $100 as an outflow (i.e., −100), in which case the $74.73 would be a positive number. Either is acceptable if you interpret the results correctly, and that interpretation is that $100 after five years is worth $74.73 today if the interest rate (or discount rate) is 6 percent.

Future Value of an Annuity Problems Using Excel

The format for solving future value of an annuity is essentially the same as used for future value of a dollar. Amounts are entered as cash inflows or cash outflows with outflows being negative numbers, and the order is

I interest per period

N number of periods

PMT (payment)

PV (present value)

Type

Unlike the cases of future and present value of a dollar, "Type" is used in the determination of the future value of an annuity to differentiate an ordinary annuity from an annuity due. When the problem concerns an ordinary annuity, enter a zero. When the problem concerns an annuity due, enter a 1. The example on page 113 asks you to determine the future value of an ordinary annuity of $100 for three years at 5 percent and the entries would be

I	5%
N	3
PMT	−100
PV	0
Type	0

Since FV is the unknown, you instruct Excel to compute the future value. The entries are submitted in a grid in the following general form:

	A	B
1	Future Value	
2	I	5%
3	N	3
4	PMT	−100
5	PV	0
6	Type	0
7	FV	= FV (b2, b3, b4, b5, b6)

The entries in cell B7: =FV(b2,b3,b4,b5,b6) inform Excel that you want to determine the future value of an ordinary annuity and Excel determines FV to be $315.25.

If the problem had been an annuity due, the entries would be

I	5%
N	3
PMT	−100
PV	0
Type	1

The spreadsheet entries are

	A	B
1	Future Value	
2	I	5%
3	N	3
4	PMT	−100
5	PV	0
6	Type	1
7	FV	= FV (b2, b3, b4, b5, b6)

Notice that since the illustration is an annuity due, Type = 1. Since the FV is the unknown, you instruct Excel to compute it in cell B7: =FV(b2,b3,b4,b5,b6). Since Type = 1, Excel treats the payments as an annuity due and determines the FV to be $331.01.

The impact of changing any of the inputs can be immediately determined using Excel. If the interest rate were 10 percent, replace 5 with 10 in cell B2 and the new future value of an ordinary annuity ($331.01) is immediately determined. If the number of years were 20, replace the 3 in cell B3 and new future value is $3,306.60. You may change any combination you like and determine the impact on the future value of an ordinary annuity and an annuity due.

Present Value of an Annuity

The format for solving present value of an annuity is essentially the same as used for future value of an annuity. Amounts are entered as cash inflows or outflows and in the same order:

I interest per period

N number of periods

PMT (payment)

FV (future value)

Type

When the problem concerns an ordinary annuity, enter a zero. When the problem concerns an annuity due, enter a 1. For example, on page 117 the illustration asks you to determine the present value of an ordinary annuity of $100 for three years at 6 percent. The entries in Excel are

	A	B
1	Present Value	
2	I	6%
3	N	3
4	PMT	100
5	FV	0
6	Type	0
7	PV	= PV (b2, b3, b4, b5, b6)

The entries in cell B7: =FV(b2,b3,b4,b5,b6) inform Excel that you want to determine the present value of an ordinary annuity and Excel determines that PV to be −267.30.

If the problem had been an annuity due, the entries would be

	A	B
1	Present Value	
2	I	6%
3	N	3
4	PMT	100
5	FV	0
6	Type	1
7	PV	= PV (b2, b3, b4, b5, b6)

Cell B7: =PV(b2,b3,b4,b5,b6) informs Excel to treat the payments as an annuity due, and Excel determines the PV to be −283.34.

Once again notice the negative sign or ( ). To receive an annuity of $100 each year for three years (a cash inflow), you must pay $267.30 for an ordinary annuity and $283.34 for an annuity due if the interest rate or discount factor is 6 percent. These initial payments are cash outflows and that is indicated by the negative signs or ( ).

Determination of the Interest Rate, Number of Periods, or the Payment

In each of the previous illustrations, the interest rate, number of periods, or payment (in the case of an annuity) were given. Excel can be used to determine these values. That is, Excel can determine the interest rate for a given present value, future value (or future payments), and number of periods. Or it may also be used to determine the number of years given the present value, the future value (or future payments), and the number of periods. Consider Example 5 on page 121 in which $10 grows to $23.67 in 10 years and you are asked to determine the rate of return.

To use Excel, enter the data in the following order:

N number of periods

PMT (payment)

PV (present value)

FV (future payment)

Type

Since this example is not an annuity, type does not apply and its numerical value is 0. The entries in Excel are

N	10
PMT	0
PV	−10
FV	23.67
Type	0

Since I is the unknown, you instruct Excel to compute the interest rate (or rate of return). The data would be entered as follows:

	A	B
1	Rate of Return	
2	N	10
3	PMT	0
4	PV	−10
5	FV	23.67
6	Type	0
7	Rate	= RATE (b2, b3, b4, b5, b6)

The title Rate of Return is given in column A, row 1. Since the RATE is the unknown, you enter =RATE(b2,b3,b4,b5,b6) in cell B7, and Excel determines the rate of return to be 8.998 ≅ 9 percent.

Determining the number of years is just as easy. Consider Example 8 on page 123 in which you needed to know how long Auntie Bea's funds would last. If the problem illustrates an ordinary annuity, the entries are

I	8%
PMT	−24000
PV	115000
FV	0
Type	0

The entries would be submitted in a grid in the following general form:

	A	B
1	Number of Periods	
2	I	8%
3	PMT	−24000
4	PV	115000
5	FV	0
6	Type	0
7	NPER	= NPER (b2, b3, b4, b5, b6)

The entries in cell B7: =NPER(b2,b3,b4,b5,b6) informs Excel to calculate the number of periods, and Excel determines the number to be 6.3.

If Example 8 is an annuity due and the payments start immediately, the entries are

I	8%
PMT	−24000
PV	115000
FV	0
TYPE	1

The entries would be submitted in a grid in the following general form:

	A	B
1	Number of Periods	
2	I	8%
3	PMT	−24000
4	PV	115000
5	FV	0
6	Type	1
7	NPER	= NPER (b2, b3, b4, b5, b6)

The entries in cell B7: =NPER(b2, b3, b4,b5,b6) informs Excel to calculate the number of periods for an annuity due, and Excel determines the number to be 5.7 years.

The example of the mortgage (Example 7 on pages 122–123) illustrates the determination of the payment. You know the amount borrowed, the interest rate, and the length of the mortgage. You also know that at the end of the time period, the mortgage is completely repaid so the future value is zero. To use Excel to determine the amount of the payment, enter:

I	8%
N	25
PV	80000
FV	0
Type	0

Since PMT is the unknown, you instruct Excel to compute the payment. The entries are submitted in the following general form:

	A	B
1	Payment	
2	I	8%
3	N	25
4	PV	80000
5	FV	0
6	Type	0
7	PMT	= PMT (b2, b3, b4, b5, b6)

The entries in cell B7: =PMT(b2,b3,b4,b5,b6) instruct Excel to determine the payment and Excel determines that PMT to be −7,494.30, the same amount determined by using a financial calculator.

Using Excel to Compute Standard Deviations and Regression Equations

The computation of standard deviation and regression equations is reasonably easy using Excel. Consider the illustration of the computation of stock A's and stock B's return and standard deviation presented in Chapter 8, pages 142–146. Enter the data in an Excel spreadsheet as follows:

1	A Year	B Return Stock A	C Return Stock B
2	1	13.5	11
3	2	14	11.5
4	3	14.25	12
5	4	14.50	12.5
6	5	15	15
7	6	15.5	17.5
8	7	15.75	18
9	8	16	18.5
10	9	16.5	19
	Average	?	?
	Standard Deviation	?	?

The first row gives the titles, and the data are in rows 2 through 10. To calculate the average, enter =AVERAGE(B2:B10) in cell B11 and =AVERAGE(C2:C10) in cell C11. To calculate the standard deviation, enter =STDEV(B2:B10) in B12 and =STDEV(C2:C10) in C12. Excel immediately indicates that the averages are 15 and the standard deviations are 1.01 and 3.30.

Calculating the regression equation for the estimation of a stock's beta coefficient is essentially the same as the calculation of the standard deviation. To calculate the regression equation relating the return on the market (the independent or X variable) and the return on the stock (the dependent or Y variable), locate the regression program in Excel under Tools. (The regression

program is located under "data analysis" and you may have to "add it in.")
Enter the data from page 155:

1	A Year	B Stock A Return	C Market Return
2	1	0.13	0.14
3	2	0.13	0.12
4	3	0.12	0.10
5	4	0.09	0.10
6	5	0.04	0.05
7	6	−0.01	0.02
8	7	0.02	−0.01
9	8	−0.07	−0.05
10	9	−0.08	−0.07
11	10	−0.10	−0.12

Column A gives the years and columns B and C are used for the returns on
the market and stock A. The data for the market return are in cells B2 through
B11, and the data for the stock A return are in cells C2 through C11. The regression program initially asks for the Y variable; type in C2:C11. The next request is for the X variable; type in B2:B11. Have the output placed somewhere

SUMMARY OUTPUT					
Regression Statistics					
Multiple R	0.975707292				
R Square	0.95200472				
Adjusted R Square	0.94600531				
Standard Error	2.084267923				
Observations	10				

ANOVA					
	df	SS	MS	F	Significance F
Regression	1	689.3466178	689.3466178	158.68306	1.47967E-06
Residual	8	34.75338219	4.344172773		
Total	9	724.1			

	Coefficients	Standard Error	t-Stat	P-value	Lower 95%	Upper 95%
Intercept	−0.05975197	0.69456013	−0.08602851	0.9335579	−1.661410504	1.541906559
X Variable 1	0.985625705	0.078243225	12.59694635	1.48E-06	0.805196505	1.166054904

other than over the data, such as A13. Excel quickly provides the following summary output:

Since the purpose of this analysis is to obtain the regression equation, look in the column for coefficients for the Intercept (0.00192) and the X Variable (0.9659). (If this were a multiple regression with more than one independent variable, you would get X Variable 1, Variable 2, etc.). In this example, the regression equation is

$$Y = -0.05975 + 0.9856$$

which is essentially the same as the manual illustration in Exhibit 8.2. The small differences are the result of rounding off in the exhibit.

Excel also provides additional information such as the coefficient of determination (the R Square) and tests of significance. A low R Square and insignificant results would suggest the equation has little value for predicting or for explaining relationships. While the various entries will not be covered in this appendix, you may learn what the various summary output data mean from a statistics textbook such as David R. Anderson, Dennis J. Sweeney, and Thomas A. Williams, *Statistics for Business and Economics*, 9th ed. (Mason, Ohio: South-Western/Thomson Learning, 2005).

BOND PRICING AND YIELDS USING EXCEL

Excel may be readily used to determine the price of a bond and the yield to maturity. Consider the illustration in Chapter 23 on page 522 in which a $1,000 bond annually pays $60 a year and matures after three years. If the comparable interest rate is 6 percent, the entries for Excel are

I	6%
N	3
PMT	60
FV	1000
Type	0

Since price is the unknown, you instruct Excel compute the present value (PV):

	A	B
1	Price of the Bond	
2	I	6%
3	N	3
4	PMT	60
5	FV	1000
6	Type	0
7	PV	= PV (b2, b3, b4, b5, b6)

The entries in cell B7: = PV(b2, b3, b4, b5, b6) inform Excel to determine the present value of the annuity payments and the future amount, and Excel determines PV to be −1000.00.

If the comparable interest rate were 8 percent, the entries are

I	8%
N	3
PMT	60
PV	1000
Type	0

	A	B
1	Price of the Bond	
2	I	8%
3	N	3
4	PMT	60
5	FV	1000
6	Type	0
7	PV	= PV (b2, b3, b4, b5, b6)

and Excel determines the PV to be −948.46. Once again notice the negative sign. To receive an annuity (cash inflow) of $60 each year for three years plus $1,000 after three years (cash inflow), you must pay $948.46 if the comparable interest rate is 8 percent.

The determination of the yield to maturity is essentially the same, except you know the cash inflows and initial outflow and must determine the interest rate that equates the inflows and outflows. The Excel format for the data is

N number of periods
PMT (coupon payment)
PV (price of the bond)
FV (principal amount)
Type

For the illustration on pages 527–529, the entries are

N	3
PMT	100
PV	−952
FV	1000
Type	0

The data are entered in a spreadsheet as:

	A	B
1	Yield to Maturity	
2	N	3
3	PMT	100
4	PV	−952
5	FV	1000
6	Type	0
7	Rate	=RATE (b2, b3, b4, b5, b6)

Since the yield to maturity is the unknown, enter =RATE(b2,b3,b4,b5,b6), and Excel determines that the yield to maturity is 12 percent. If you want to compute the current yield, divide the coupon payment by the bond's price (B3/B4). Since B4 is a negative number, the resulting answer will be negative, but disregard the negative sign.

Calculating Investment Returns Using Excel

The calculation of the yield to maturity in the previous section may also be used to compute the return on an investment in stock. (The process also reappears in Chapter 16 as the internal rate of return on an investment in plant and equipment.) Equation 26.2 on page 570 for the return on an investment in stock is the same calculation as the yield to maturity. Both determine the rate that equates future cash inflows with the initial cash outflow.

Consider the illustration on page 570 in which you buy a stock for $40, collect a $1 dividend for two years, and sell the stock after two years for $50. To solve for the return using Excel, enter the data in the following order:

N number of periods

PMT (payment)

PV (present value)

FV (future value)

Type

That is

N	2
PMT	1
PV	−40
FV	50
Type	0

and instruct Excel to solve for the return: =RATE(b2,b3,b4,b5,b6). (This example is an annuity, since the $1 payment is the same for each year. You can also use the procedure if the annual dollar cash inflows differ. See, for instance, the illustration on pages 672–673 of unequal cash inflows in the next section on the internal rate of return.)

Capital Budgeting and Excel

Since the net present value and internal rate of return use compounding and discounting, Excel's time value programs may be used to determine NPVs and IRRs. In the case of net present value, you determine the present value of an investment's cash flows and subtract the present cost to determine the NPV. For the internal rate of return, use the same approach employed to determine the yield to maturity in the previous section.

To determine an investment's net present value, the future cash flows are entered as inflows. The order of the entries is

I interest per period (the firm's cost of capital)

N number of periods

PMT (future cash inflows)

FV (future value—any residual value for the asset)

Type

In Chapter 14 on pages 294–297 the calculation for the net present value for an investment was illustrated. The data entries for Excel are

I Interest per period

N number of periods

PMT (future cash inflow – an annuity)

FV (future cash inflow – single payment)

Type

In the example, a $400 annuity for four years cost $1,000, and the firm's cost of capital was 8 percent. Since the cash inflows are received at the end of each time period (that is, the illustration is an ordinary annuity), enter 0 for type. The data entries are

I	8
N	4
PMT	400
FV	0
Type	0

Since present value of the cash inflows is the unknown, you instruct Excel to compute the present value:

	A	B
1	Present Value	
2	I	8
3	N	4
4	PMT	400
5	FV	0
6	Type	0
7	PV	= PV (b2, b3, b4, b5, b6)

Notice that Excel presents the present value as a negative number, because Excel is telling you that if you invest $1,324.85 (a cash outflow), you will receive $400 annually for four years if you earn 8 percent. Since you are not spending $1,324.85 to obtain the cash inflows, you must be careful to ignore the negative sign when determining the net present value, which is the difference between the present value and the cost of the investment (that is, $1,324.85 – $1,000). Also, if you instruct Excel to subtract the $1,000 in B7 (that is, you enter =PV(b2,b3,b4,b5,b6)-1000), Excel gives you –$1,324.85. If you are going to combine the determination of the present value and net present value in a cell, enter =PV(b2,b3,b4,b5,b6)+1000, which determines the net present value to be $324.85.

If the cash inflow is a single payment of $1,700 after four years, the data entries are

	A	B
1	Present Value	
2	I	8
3	N	4
4	PMT	0
5	FV	1700
6	Type	0
7	PV	= PV (b2, b3, b4, b5, b6)

The entries in cell B7: =PV (b2, b3, b4, b5, b6) instruct Excel to determine the present value of the single cash inflow. Excel determines PV to be –1,249.55, which tells you that if you invest $1,249.55 (a cash outflow), you will receive $1,700 after four years if you earn 8 percent. Once again, you must be careful to ignore the negative sign when you determine the net present value, which in this illustration is $249.55, the difference between the $1,249.55 present value and the $1,000 cost of the investment.

The determination of the internal rate of return is essentially the same except that you know the cash inflows and the initial outflow and must determine the rate that equates the inflows and outflows. The Excel format for the data is

N number of periods

PMT (the future cash inflows for an annuity)

PV (the initial cash outflow or cost of the investment)

FV (the future cash inflow for a single payment)

Type

For the annuity illustration, the entries are

	A	B
1	Internal rate of return	
2	N	4
3	PMT	400
4	PV	−1000
5	FV	0
6	Type	0
7	Rate	= RATE (b2, b3, b4, b5, b6)

The internal rate of return is the unknown, and Excel determines that rate to be 21.86 percent.

In the previous illustrations the cash inflows were either a single payment or an annuity. Excel can also determine the NPV and IRR for investments with unequal cash inflows. For example, consider investment C on page 295. Its cash inflows were

Year	Cash Inflow
1	$250
2	150
3	330
4	450

Excel can determine this investment's net present value and internal rate of return.

To determine the net present value, set up the data as follows:

	A	B
1	Year	
2	CF0	−1000
3	CF1	250
4	CF2	150
5	CF3	330
6	CF4	450
7	I	8%
8	NPV	= NPV (b7, b2, b3, b4, b5, b6)

The cash flow labels and cash flow for each year are given in columns A and B. Rows 2 through 6 are used for the cash inflows, and the cost of capital is given in row 7. In row 8 column B, type in the instruction =NPV (b7, b2, b3, b4, b5, b6) or =NPV (b7, b2:b6), and Excel determines the net present value to be ($43.69). Since this is a negative number, the investment should not be made.

To determine the internal rate of return for the uneven cash inflow, enter the data as follows:

	A	B
1	Year	
2	CF0	−1000
3	CF1	250
4	CF2	150
5	CF3	330
6	CF4	450
7	Rate	= IRR (b2:b6)

Once again, the initial cash outflow ($−1000) is placed in b2 and the cash inflows are in b3 through b6. The instruction to compute the internal rate of return is placed in b7. Type in =IRR (b2:b6), and Excel determines the internal rate of return to be 6.11 percent. Since 6.11 percent is less than the firm's cost of capital (8 percent), the investment should not be made.

The Cash Budget and Excel

As was illustrated in Chapter 16, a cash budget is a table of receipts and disbursements. The construction of a cash budget can involve a large number of repetitive calculations. Since a spreadsheet facilitates performing a large number of repetitive arithmetical calculations, the cash budget is tailor-made for a spreadsheet application. In addition to performing the initial calculations, the spreadsheet facilitates determining the impact of changing individual numbers within the cash budget without manually recalculating the cash budget.

To illustrate the use of an Excel spreadsheet, consider the cash budget in Exhibit 16.1 on pages 368–369. The data are reproduced below with columns and rows as would be used in a spreadsheet. Column A gives the descriptions of the various entries and columns B through I give the data for the months. Row 1 gives titles and row 2 has the anticipated sales. Row 3 has been left blank to help differentiate anticipated sales from the cash receipts. Correspondingly row 10 has been left blank to differentiate receipts from disbursements and row 20 has been left blank to differentiate disbursements from the determination of the cash budget's bottom line: the cumulative excess or shortage of cash.

	A	B	C	D	E	F	G	H	I
1	Month	May	June	July	Aug	Sept	Oct	Nov	Dec
2	Anticipated sales	15000	20000	30000	50000	40000	20000	10000	
3									
4	Receipts								
5	Cash sales	4500	6000	9000	15000	12000	6000	3000	0
6	Accounts collected (one-month lag)		9450	12600	18900	31500	25200	12600	6300
7	Accounts collected (two-month lag)			1050	1400	2100	3500	2800	1400
8	Other cash receipts		10000						
9	Total cash receipts	4500	25450	22650	35300	45600	34700	18400	7700
10									
11	Disbursements								
12	Variable cash disbursements	3000	25000	38000	30000	10000	5000	3000	
13	Fixed cash disbursements								
14	Interest and rent expenses	1000	1000	1000	1000	1000	1000	1000	
15	Administrative expenses	2000	2000	2000	2000	2000	2000	2000	
16	Other cash disbursements								
17	Estimated taxes					1000			
18	Debt repayment						2500		
19	Total disbursements	6000	28000	41000	34000	15500	8000	6000	
20									
21	Cash gain (loss) during the month	−1500	−2550	−18350	1300	30100	26700	12400	
22	Cash position: beginning of the month	12000	10500	7950	−10400	−9100	21000	47700	
23	Cash position: end of the month	10500	7950	−10400	−9100	21000	47700	60100	
24	Desired minimum cash	10000	10000	10000	10000	10000	10000	10000	
25	Cumulative excess (shortage) of cash	500	−2050	−20400	−19100	11000	37700	50100	

The formulas that instruct Excel to make the calculations are as follows. For example, total cash receipts for June (B9) is the sum of the data in B5+B6+B7+B8, and the cash position at the end of June (B23) is the sum of B21+B22.

By changing any of the amounts, such as the desired minimum level of cash or increasing collections of receivables faster, you can perceive the impact of the change on the firm's need for short-term funds. If, for example, the desired level of cash were reduced from $10,000 to $3,000, the impact would be to decrease the amount of funds borrowed in July and August. The spreadsheet, however, will tell you the exact amount of the impact without having to tediously redo all the calculations. The spreadsheet thus becomes a valuable tool that permits you to work through many possible scenarios and answer a variety of "what if?" questions.

A	B	C	D	E	F	G	H
1 Month	May	June	July	August	September	October	November
2 Anticipated sales	15000	20000	30000	50000	40000	20000	10000
3							
4 Receipts							
5 Cash sales	=0.3*B2	=0.3*C2	=0.3*D2	=0.3*E2	=0.3*F2	=0.3*G2	=0.3*H2
6 Accounts collected (one month lag)		=0.7*0*.9*B2	=0.7*0*.9*C2	=0.7*0*.9*D2	=0.7*0*.9*E2	=0.7*0*.9*F2	=0.7*0*.9*G2
7 Accounts collected (two months lag)			=0.7*0.1*B2	=0.7*0.1*C2	=0.7*0.1*D2	=0.7*0.1*E2	=0.7*0.1*F2
8 Other cash receipts		10000					
9 Total cash receipts	=B5+B6+B7+B8	=C5+C6+C7+C8	=D5+D6+D7+D8	=E5+E6+E7+E8	=F5+F6+F7+F8	=G5+G6+G7+G8	=H5+H6+H7+H8
10							
11 Disbursements							
12 Variable cash disbursements	3000	25000	38000	30000	10000	5000	3000
13 Fixed cash disbursements							
14 Interest and rent expenses	1000	1000	1000	1000	1000	1000	1000
15 Administrative expenses	2000	2000	2000	2000	2000	2000	2000
16 Other cash disbursements							
17 Estimated taxes				1000			
18 Debt repayment					2500		
19 Total disbursements	=B12+B14+B15+B17+B18	=C12+C14+C15+C17+C18	=D12+D14+D15+D17+D18	=E12+E14+E15+E17+E18	=F12+F14+F15+F17+F18	=G12+G14+G15+G17+G18	=H12+H14+H15+H17+H18
20							
21 Cash gain (loss) during the month	=B9-B19	=C9-C19	=D9-D19	=E9-E19	=F9-F19	=G9-G19	=H9-H19
22 Beginning cash position	12000	=B23	=C23	=D23	=E23	=F23	=G23
23 Cash position at the end of the month	=B21+B22	=C21+C22	=D21+D22	=E21+E22	=F21+F22	=G21+G22	=H21+H22
24 Desired minimum cash	10000	10000	10000	10000	10000	10000	10000
25 Cumulative excess (shortage) of cash	=B23-B24	=C23-C24	=D23-D24	=E23-E24	=F23-F24	=G23-G24	=H23-H24

The EOQ and Excel

You may set up a spreadsheet using Excel to perform the calculation of the EOQ. While you should use any format with which you feel comfortable, the following gives an indication of the process using Excel. The following table reproduces the data from Exhibit 17.3 (page 393) with letters representing the columns and numbers representing the rows. (Spacing is used for presentation purposes and is not necessary to complete the spreadsheet. If all you want to calculate is the EOQ, it is not necessary to set up the whole table. The presentation of the table is designed to illustrate how you might construct the table if you have need for it.)

	A	B	C	D	E	F	G	H	I
1	Economic	Order							
2	Total Sales	Size of	Quantity:				Per-unit		
3	(in units)	Inven- tory Order	Number of Orders	Cost per Order ($50)	Total Order Costs	Average Inventory	Carry- ing Costs ($10)	Total Carry- ing Costs	Total Costs
4	10000	50	200	$50	$10,000	25	$10	$ 250	$10,250
5	10000	100	100	$50	$ 5,000	50	$10	$ 500	$ 5,500
6	10000	200	50	$50	$ 2,500	100	$10	$1,000	$ 3,500
7	10000	300	33	$50	$ 1,667	150	$10	$1,500	$ 3,167
8	10000	316	32	$50	$ 1,582	158	$10	$1,580	$ 3,162
9	10000	400	25	$50	$ 1,250	200	$10	$2,000	$ 3,250
10	10000	500	20	$50	$ 1,000	250	$10	$2,500	$ 3,500
11	10000	600	17	$50	$ 833	300	$10	$3,000	$ 3,833
12	10000	800	13	$50	$ 625	400	$10	$4,000	$ 4,625
13	10000	1000	10	$50	$ 500	500	$10	$5,000	$ 5,500
14									
15									
16									
17	EOQ =		316.23	(316 units)					
18									
19	Duration of EOQ	11.54	12 Days						
20									
21									
22	Safety Stock	50.00							
23									
24									
25	Inventory								
26	Maximum	366							
27	Minimum	316							
28	Average	208							

	A	B	C	D	E	F	G	H	I
1	EOQ:								
2	Total Sales	Size of Inven-tory Order	Number of Orders	Cost per Order ($50)	Total Order Costs	Average Inventory	Per-unit Carrying Costs ($10)	Total Carry-ing Costs	Total Costs
3	(in units)								
4	10000	50	=+A5/B5	$50	=+C5*D5	=+B5/2	$10	=+F5*G5	=+E5+H5
5	10000	100	=+A6/B6	$50	=+C6*D6	=+B6/2	$10	=+F6*G6	=+E6+H6
6	10000	200	=+A7/B7	$50	=+C7*D7	=+B7/2	$10	=+F7*G7	=+E7+H7
7	10000	300	=+A8/B8	$50	=+C8*D8	=+B8/2	$10	=+F8*G8	=+E8+H8
8	10000	316	=+A9/B9	$50	=+C9*D9	=+B9/2	$10	=+F9*G9	=+E9+H9
9	10000	400	=+A10/B10	$50	=+C10*D10	=+B10/2	$10	=+F10*G10	=+E10+H10
10	10000	500	=+A11/B11	$50	=+C11*D11	=+B11/2	$10	=+F11*G11	=+E11+H11
11	10000	600	=+A12/B12	$50	=+C12*D12	=+B12/2	$10	=+F12*G12	=+E12+H12
12	10000	800	=+A13/B13	$50	=+C13*D13	=+B13/2	$10	=+F13*G13	=+E13+H13
13	10000	1000	=+A13/B13	$50	=+C14*D14	=+B14/2	$10	=+F14*G14	=+E14+H14
14									
15									
16									
17	EOQ =	=+((2)*(A5)*(D5)/G5)^0.5							
18									
19	Duration	=+B17/(A5/365)							
20	of EOQ								
21									
22	Safety Stock	50.00							
23									
24									
25	Inventory								
26	Maximum	=+B17+B22							
27	Minimum	=+B17							
28	Average	=+B17/2+B22							

Columns A, B, D, and G are given. The number of orders (column C) is column A divided by B. The total order costs (column E) is column C times column D. The average inventory (column F) is column B divided by 2. Column H (total carrying costs) is column F times column G, and total costs (column I) is the sum of columns E and H. The table also has the EOQ, its duration, the given safety stock, and the maximum, minimum, and average inventory. To have Excel perform the various tasks, set up the spreadsheet with the formulas given as follows in the table. Once the formulas are in place, Excel quickly completes the table and calculates the EOQ, its duration, and the maximum, minimum, and average inventory.

Computing Simple and Compound Rates with Excel

Chapter 18 illustrated the computation of the simple and compound rates of interest for credit terms such as 2/10, net 30. You may set up a spreadsheet to perform the calculations. Consider the following spreadsheet. Rows 1 through 7 illustrate the calculation of the simple rate of interest and rows 9 through 16 illustrate the calculation of the compound rate. Labels are given in column A and data entries are in column B. The Excel formulas for the calculations in B6 and B15 are provided in cells A7 and A16.

	A	B
1	Annual simple rate using Excel:	
2	Discount percentage	2%
3	Discount period	10
4	Payment period	30
5		
6	Simple rate of interest	36.73%
7	Cell B6: =+B2/(1−B2)*(360/(B4−B3))	
8		
9	Annualized compound rate using Excel:	
10	N: Cell B10: (B4-B3)/365	0.0548
11	PMT	0
12	PV	$ 98
13	FV	$ (100)
14	Type	0
15	Annualized compound rate	44.59%
16	Cell B15: =+RATE(B10,B11,B12,B13,B14)	

The answers are the same as calculated in the chapter; however, the spreadsheet will readily show you the impact of changing the terms.

Answers to Selected Problems

Chapter 4

1. $2 loss

2. initial investment: $3,600
   necessary increase: $2.25 a share

3. interest expense: $275.40
   return: 69.8%

4. a. required investment: $11,500 × .55 = $6,325
   b. interest paid: $517.50

5. a. loss: $3.50
   b. gain: $3.50

6. at $49 a share, loss = 500 × $7 = $3,500

7. margin = 25%: amount invested: $1,250; return: 80%

8. margin = 75%: amount invested: $3,750; return: (26.7%)

Chapter 6

1. balance on the current account ($1.7)
   balance on the capital account ($16.5)

2. 0.5495

3. in dollars: $50,000
   in euros: $0

Chapter 7

Answers to time value of money problems may be derived using interest tables, financial calculators, or computer software. Since interest tables are rounded off, answers derived using the tables may differ from answers derived by using calculators or computers. Use common sense. If the answer is $13,467 using the tables and $13,487 using a financial calculator, the difference is probably the result of rounding, and either answer may be considered "correct."

1. overvalued ($90,770)

2. PVA: $4,262; Yes
   PVB: $3,936; No

3. $74,000 ($74.012 using a financial calculator)

4. between 5 and 6% (5.5%)

5. a. $29.38
   b. $42.00

6. 9%

7. a. interest: $629
   b. interest: $500

8. a. $219,318
   b. $120,531
   c. $17,671

9. total accumulated: $102,320; annual withdrawal: $11,210

10. your account: $157,751

11. $2,421

12. no; she can withdraw $14,491.

13. approximately 17 years (16.6 years)

14. approximately 12% (12.25%)

15. 15%

16. $27,174

17. at 6%, select the $900; at 14%, select the $150 for 5 years

18. $10,000

19. $45,695 (using interest tables)

20. annual payment: $13,648

21. your withdrawals: $60,792 your twin's with-drawals: $51,984

22. 6.4% (between 6% and 7%)

23. total value: $42,935

24. annuity payments are preferred

25. $1,045,120; approximately 5% (5.2%)

26. select A

27. mortgage payment: $10,180 principal repayment (first year): $1,180

28. exceeds 16% (16.5%)

29. return: 10% (9.84%)

30. approximately 7% (6.9%)

Chapter 8

1. return stock A: 14%
   standard deviation stock B: 3.13

2. 13.1%

3. 4.4%

4. realized return: 3.25%

5. 1.5

6. Stock A: 4%

7. 12.87%

8. a. average return investment Y: 18%
   b. standard deviation investment Y: 2.55

9. a. 12.5%

10. 12.3%

Chapter 9

1. operating profit margin A: 15%
   net profit margin A: 8%
   return on assets A: 8%
   return on equity A: 13.3%

3. inventory turnover: 10 times a year

4. $63,750

5. Accounts receivable before
   allowance: $1,340,000
   Total current assets: $2,980,000

Accumulated depreciation: $690,000
Long-term debt: $1,000,000
Retained earnings: $1,440,000

6. a. receivables turnover: 7
   c. overdue by 22 days

9. Income statement:

Sales	$1,000,000
Cost of goods sold	600,000
Other expenses	100,000
EBIT	300,000
Interest	80,000
EBT	220,000
Taxes	100,000
Net earnings	$ 120,000
Earnings per share	$ 1.20

Balance Sheet:

Assets	
cash	$ 50,000
accounts receivable	250,000
inventory	300,000
plant and equipment	400,000
Total assets	$1,000,000

Liabilities	
accounts payable	$ 200,000
other current liabilities	50,000
Long-term debt	300,000
Equity	450,000
Liabilities & equity	$1,000,000

11. year 2: $9,500 and $9,800

12. return on total equity: 11.7%
    return on common equity: 12.2%

13. $3,167,137

14. current ratio: 1.8:1.0
    quick ratio: 0.9:1.0

15. reduction in inventory:
    $75,000

16. $48,333 saved

Chapter 10

1. income of $2,000: $300
   income of $1,600,000: $340,000

2. a. year 3: $1,075
   b. year 6: $2,400 refund

Chapter 11

1. A: 2.5 years
   C: 3 years and 2.5 months

2. a. earnings: $50,000
   b. 100,000 units
   c. 62,500 units
   e. 14,286 units

3. a. profit at 2,000: $4,600
   b. 1,132 units
   c. 1,887 units

4. a. 2,500 and 3,125
   b. $3,000

5. a. 8,000 units
      $500 earnings

Chapter 12

2. a. $3,000
   b. Firm A: $3,000
      Firm B: $2,500
   c. Firm A: 50%
      Firm B: 60%

3. Case C
   stockholders' equity: $1,000
   interest expense: $120
   return on equity: 10.8%

Chapter 13

1. a. cost of capital at 40% debt: 12.0%
   b. debt $20; equity $80

2. d. break point for debt: $8,000,000
      break point for retained earnings: $8,571,429

3. a. 30% debt; 70% equity
   b. excessive
   d. stockholders earn 12.86%

4. cost of retained earnings: 12.55%
   cost of new stock: 13.04%

5. a. 5.95%
   b. 9.9%
   c. 11.3%
   d. 9.3575%

6. cost of capital at 20% debt: 7.2%
   cost of capital at 40% debt: 8.4%

Chapter 14

1. 8%

2. a. NPVA: $33
      NPVB: $17
   b. IRRA: approximately 14% (14.7%)
      IRRB: 12%

3. a. NPVA: ($165)
      NPVB: $333
   c. IRRA: 5% (4.9%)
      IRRB: 20%
   f. at 10%: $4,356
      at 14%: $4,669

4. at 9%: select B
   at 14%: select neither

5. a. NPVA: ($51)
      NPVC: $108
   b. IRRA: 9%
      IRRC: 24%
   c. at 15%: $1,887

6. NPV: ($6,315)

7. when cost of capital = 12%, NPV = ($177)

8. 8%

9. a. IRR: 16%
   b. at 16%: terminal value : $156,101

10. a. debt: 40%
    b. equity: $300
    c. 20% (19.7%)
    d. liabilities: $360
    e. 30%

11. a. select S
    b. select Q
    c. at 20%: $2,072
       at 10%: $1,791

12. a. NPVA: $75
    b. IRRB: 12%
    d. no

13. a. NPV: $24,096
       IRR: 18%
    b. $29,939
    c. $30,306

14. NPV: $5,160

15. cash inflow: years 1 and 2: $60,400
    year 5: $51,650
    cash outflow: $190,000

16. PV: $30,265

17. a. NPVA: $631
    b. NPVA: $631
       NPVB: ($141.50)
       NPVC: $438.80

18. a. NPV: $93,778
    b. NPV: ($4,305)

Chapter 15

1. a. accounts receivable $300
      inventory   600
      trade accounts payable   300
   b. external funds needed: $50
   c. accounts receivable $300
      inventory   600
      plant   800
      total assets   1,700
      trade accounts   300
      long-term debt   650
      equity   750
      total liabilities and equity 1,700

2. a. accounts receivable $9,000
      inventory   7,625
      accounts payable   6,625
   b. expansion in accounts payable:
      $1,325
   c. increase in retained earnings:
      $3,000

3. a. accounts receivable $12,060
      inventory   9,264
      accounts payable   6,829
   b. increase in accounts payable: $1,529
   c. increase in retained earnings: $3,000
   d. cash: $1,000
      total assets: $26,524

4. cash $30,000
   accounts receivable   60,000
   inventory   90,000
   accounts payable   18,000
   accruals   24,000
   increase in retained earnings 67,500

5. b. external funds needed: $8,027
   c. $1,875 reduction

d. retained earnings increase by $32,813
e. total assets: $253,125
   (answer may be different as result of
   rounding)

6. a. external funds needed 20X1: ($52,000)
      20X2: $1,906,000
   b. maximum increase in retained earnings:
      $1,820,000
   c. current ratio < 2:1
   d. external funds needed 20X1:
      $188,000
      20X2: $1,946,000
   e. current ratio < 2:1

7. b. selected entries
      cash $ 4,200
      accounts receivable   21,420
      inventory   23,980
      plant & equipment   51,000
      retained earnings   19,560

8. a. excess forecasted funds: $7.002

Chapter 16

1. excess cash (shortage):

   January   ($ 120)
   February   ($ 220)
   March   ($ 40)
   April   ($ 240)
   May $ 160
   June $ 100

2. Total receipts
   January: $700,000
   February: $880,000
   Ending cash position
   January: ($88,000)
   February: ($128,000)

3. a. shortage in June: ($3,950)
   b. excess in June: $4,400
   c. excess in June: $10,400

4. cash shortage
   February: ($75,000)
   March: ($105,000)
   ending cash position April: $15,000
   excess cash April: $5,000

Chapter 17

1. a. earnings with bank loan: $259,000 earnings with insurance company loan: $238,000
   b. earnings year 2 with bank loan at 4%: $273,000
   earnings year 2 with insurance company loan: $238,000

2. a. return on equity—alternative a: 9.6%
   return on equity—alternative b: 14.8%
   return on equity—alternative c: 12.8%
   b. return on equity—alternative a: 6.0%
   return on equity—alternative b: 7.6%
   return on equity—alternative c: 6.8%

3. a. 120 units
   b. 9 days (42 orders per year)
   c. 167 units

4. a. 1,549 units
   b. 1,075 units
   c. 1,849 units
   d. 19

5. interest saved: $9,722

6. collection expense: $5,000
   bad debt expense: $8,750
   carrying costs: $2,083

7. $18,720

8. As of January 1: accounts not overdue: 24.1%
   20–30 days overdue: 31.7%

9. a. supplier A: 368 units
   supplier B: 316 units
   b. average inventory supplier A:284
   c. maximum inventory supplier A: 468
   minimum inventory supplier A: 100 (or 0 if safety stock is completely used)
   d. 212 units

10. a. 5,000 units
    b. January 16
    c. maximum safety stock: 2,740 units
    d. maximum inventory: 7,740
    minimum inventory: 2,740
    average inventory: 5,240
    e. EOQ: 7,071 units

11. additional sales: $1,000,000
    total costs: $775,000

12. discount yield: 7.44%
    simple yield: 7.69%
    compound yield: 7.92%

14. 9.17%

Chapter 18

1. 10.3%
   $103,092.80

2. interest payment: $65,000(.1)(4/12) = $2,167
   origination fee: $975
   amount received after the discount: $61,858
   simple interest rate: 15.24%

3. simple interest rate: 15%
   compound rate: 15.96%

4. commercial paper: 10.5%

6. a. 37.1% (compounded: 44.9%)
   b. 36.7% (compounded: 44.6%)

7. 0%

9. 2.37% (compounded: 2.42%)

10. commercial paper: 10.53%
    commercial bank: 10.20%

11. a. Bank A: 8%
    Bank B: 6.73%
    b. Bank A: 9.5%
    Bank B: 6.73%

12. a. 9.09%
    b. 12.12%

13. c. payment on day 50: 18.4%
    (compounded: 20.2%)

Chapter 19

1. annual payment: $24,390.24
   ($24,389.07 using a financial calculator)
   year 1 principal repayment:
   $24,390 – $7,000 = $17,390

2. a. annual payment: $2,637.83
   answers for year 3:
   interest payment: $656.06
   principal repayment: $1,981.77
   balance owed: $4,578.79
   c. answers for year 3:
   interest payment: $1,000
   principal repayment: $0
   balance owed: $10,000

4. $291,890 ($291,871 using a financial calculator)

6. present value of leasing cash outflows: $46,056

Chapter 20

1. EPS: $1.38 before the split
   Price of stock: $20 after the split

2. cumulative voting: 4,000 votes

3. a. new price of the stock: $45
   b. payout ratio: 63.2%

4. a. cash: $26,000,000
      retained earnings: $60,000,000
      additional paid-in capital: no change
      common stock: no change
   b. cash: $28,000,000
      common stock: (2,100,000 shares; $50 par)
      $105,000,000
      additional paid-in capital: $15,000,000
      retained earnings: $52,000,000
   c. cash: $28,000,000
      common stock: (1,000,000 shares; $100 par)
      $100,000,000
      additional paid-in capital: $10,000,000
      retained earnings: $62,000,000

5. The stock dividend reduces retained earnings by
   $80,000 and increases common stock by $20,000
   and additional paid-in capital by $60,000

6. b. cash: $7,750,000
      retained earnings: $39,560,000

7. earnings per share: $2.10
   total equity: no change
   long-term debt: no change
   paid-in capital: no change
   shares outstanding: 2,000,000
   earnings: $4,200,000 (no change)

8. a. new price: $18
      retained earnings: $200,000
   b. new price: $49.09
      retained earnings: $178,400

Chapter 21

1. a. $53
   b. $79.50
   c. $141.33
   d. $34.67
   e. $39.87

2. $77

3. a. stock A: $15.29 < $23
   b. 11.65%
   c. stock A: $14

4. 17.6%

5. a. 12.2%
   c. $80 > $76.94

6. a. $45.65
   c. $35
   e. $63.93

7. a. stock A: 12.56%
   f. neither

8. stock A: $55.26
   stock B: $30.98

9. $22

Chapter 23

1. a. annual interest payment: $866
      semiannual interest payment: $864
   b. annual interest payment: $920
      semiannual interest payment: $921
   d. current yield in (a:) 6.9%

2. a. annual interest payment: $846
      semiannual interest payment: $844
   b. annual interest payment: $921
      semiannual interest payment: $919
   d. annual interest payment: $1,110
      semiannual interest payment: $1,112
      annual interest payment: $1,052
      semiannual interest payment: $1,053

3. current yield: 8%; yield to
   maturity: 8%

4. a. coupon rate: 6%
   b. current yield: 6.7%
   c. yield to maturity: 8.8%

5. a. 7.25%
   b. 10%
   c. annual interest payment: $810
      semiannual interest payment: $807

6. annual interest payment: $1,115
   semiannual interest payment: $1,116
   (The bond is overpriced at an offer price of
   $1,200.)

8. a. Bond A
      annual interest payment: $1,000
      semiannual interest payment: $1,000
      Bond B
      annual interest payment: $733
      semiannual interest payment: $729

b. Bond A
  annual interest payment: $1,000
  semiannual interest payment: $1,000
  Bond B
  annual interest payment: $875
  semiannual interest payment: $873

10. a. $313
  d. 12%
  f. 75%
  h. $39,795

Chapter 24

1. at 13%: $69.23

2. a. $114.29
  b. $110.55

3. b. $83

4. × 1: 5.0
  × 3: 1.3

Chapter 25

1. a. 4.8%
  b. $864
  c. $38.52
  d. $176
  f. $222.60
  g. nil

2. a. 726
  b. 40
  c. $1,200

Chapter 26

1. holding period return: 200%
  annualized return: 11.6%

3. 6.4%

5. sale price of $30: 7.1%
  sale price of $50: 19.5%

6. stock after 20 years: $6,976
  bond after 30 years: $5,583

Chapter 27

1. $7.83

2. 6.8%

3. 24.9%

4. compound return: 10.8%

5. 17.6% and 11.0%

6. individual's return: 8.6% fund's return: 15%

7. 24.8%

Chapter 28

1. b. $3
  c. $2

2. a. at the price of the stock = $45, the buyer makes $2
  b. at the price of the stock = $50, the seller makes $3

3. a. $4
  b. $4
  c. increases
  d. $8
  e. $8
  f. ($8)
  g. $8
  h. $3
  i. $3 loss

4. a. $1
  b. $4
  c. declines
  d. $5
  e. unlimited
  f. $1
  g. ($1)
  h. ($5)
  i. $5

5. a. intrinsic value: $1
    time premium: $3
  b. value if stock = $20: $0
    value if stock = $40: $15
  c. return: 400%

6. a. unlimited
  b. ($2)
  c. $P_s > 32$

Chapter 29

1. a. $5,000
  b. $5,500
    110%
  c. $2,200

2. a. value of the contract: $34,000
  b. loss: $1,100

3. a. $2,500
   b. $29,400
   c. 11.8%
   d. (12%)
   e. (100%)

4. a. $1,600,000
   b. $1,560,000
   c. $250,000
   d. $40,000
   e. $40,000

INDEX

The **bold** entries refer to the page on which the term is defined in the margin notes. While the definition usually occurs the first time the word is used, there are instances in which a term cross-references prior to the marginal definition.